Marketing text in the world?

Answer:
Experience. Leadership. Innovation.

Marketing
The Core

3/e

Roger A. Kerin
Southern Methodist University

Steven W. Hartley
University of Denver

William Rudelius
University of Minnesota

Boston   Burr Ridge, IL   Dubuque, IA   Madison, WI   New York   San Francisco   St. Louis
Bangkok   Bogotá   Caracas   Kuala Lumpur   Lisbon   London   Madrid   Mexico City
Milan   Montreal   New Delhi   Santiago   Seoul   Singapore   Sydney   Taipei   Toronto

McGraw-Hill
Irwin

MARKETING: THE CORE

Published by McGraw-Hill/Irwin, a business unit of The McGraw-Hill Companies, Inc., 1221 Avenue of the Americas, New York, NY, 10020. Copyright © 2009, 2007, 2004 by The McGraw-Hill Companies, Inc. All rights reserved. No part of this publication may be reproduced or distributed in any form or by any means, or stored in a database or retrieval system, without the prior written consent of The McGraw-Hill Companies, Inc., including, but not limited to, in any network or other electronic storage or transmission, or broadcast for distance learning.

Some ancillaries, including electronic and print components, may not be available to customers outside the United States.

This book is printed on acid-free paper.

2 3 4 5 6 7 8 9 0 DOW/DOW 0 9

ISBN   978-0-07-338106-0
MHID   0-07-338106-3

Vice president and editor-in-chief: *Brent Gordon*
Publisher: *Paul Ducham*
Executive editor: *Doug Hughes*
Developmental editor: *Colleen Honan/Gina Huck Siegert*
Editorial coordinator: *Devon Raemisch*
Marketing manager: *Katie Mergen*
Lead project manager: *Christine A. Vaughan*
Lead production supervisor: *Carol A. Bielski*
Lead designer: *Matthew Baldwin*
Senior photo research coordinator: *Jeremy Cheshareck*
Photo researcher: *Mike Hruby*
Senior media project manager : *Susan Lombardi*
Interior design: *Keith J. McPherson*
Cover image: *©Getty Images*
Typeface: *10.5/12 Times Roman*
Compositor: *Aptara, Inc.*
Printer: *R. R. Donnelley*

                    Library of Congress Cataloging-in-Publication Data

Kerin, Roger A.
     Marketing : the core / Roger A. Kerin, Steven W. Hartley, William Rudelius. -- 3/e.
        p. cm.
     Includes index.
     ISBN-13: 978-0-07-338106-0 (alk. paper)
     ISBN-10: 0-07-338106-3 (alk. paper)
     1. Marketing. I. Hartley, Steven William. II. Rudelius, William. III. Title.
HF5415.K452 2009
658.8--dc22
                         2008039064

www.mhhe.com

A MESSAGE FROM THE AUTHORS

It is a dynamic and exciting time for students and instructors, particularly those who are interested in the field of marketing! Each day brings new products, services, technologies, and ideas to the marketplace. You may have observed the growing interest in social networking, environmental sustainability, mobile technologies, the economic growth of China and India, YouTube, iPhones, millennial entrepreneurs, blogs, interactive advertising, social responsibility, and many other new aspects of business. Tomorrow will most certainly add to the list!

As marketing professors we appreciate the opportunity to share our enthusiasm for the field of marketing with you, and to explore the opportunities and challenges it presents to all of us as consumers, managers, and students. This edition of *Marketing: The Core* is designed to (1) build on the **experience** we've developed during the previous editions of the text, (2) continue our **leadership** role in exploring new topics and perspectives, and (3) offer pedagogical **innovation** that matches today's educational demands. We have worked diligently to ensure that the time you invest in *Marketing: The Core* will provide the most up-to-date, comprehensive, engaging, and integrated learning experience available from any text.

This edition of *Marketing: The Core* continues our tradition of using an active-learning approach to bring traditional theories and contemporary concepts to life. You'll find yourself immersed in discussions, examples, and cases based on familiar companies, brands, and products. Feedback from students and instructors both here and abroad has reinforced our commitment to this approach. We are thrilled that *Marketing: The Core* has become a best-selling principles of marketing text in the United States, and, through translations into five other languages around the world. The third edition strives to exceed the standards set by our past success.

We hope you'll enjoy reading and using our text, and that we've sparked your interest in additional learning and career pursuits in marketing!

Roger A. Kerin
Steven W. Hartley
William Rudelius

Preface

Marketing: The Core utilizes a unique, innovative, and effective pedagogical approach developed by the authors through the integration of their combined classroom, college, and university experiences. The elements of this approach have been the foundation for each edition of *Marketing: The Core* and serve as the focus of the text and it supplements as they evolve and adapt to changes in student learning styles, the growth of the marketing discipline, and the development of new instructional technologies. The distinctive features of the approach are illustrated here:

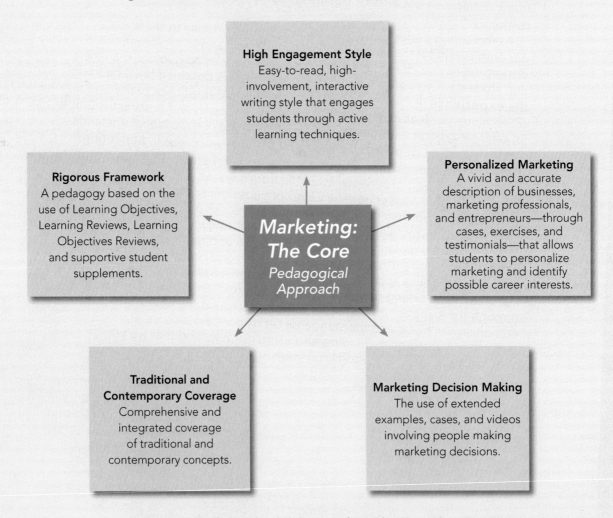

High Engagement Style
Easy-to-read, high-involvement, interactive writing style that engages students through active learning techniques.

Rigorous Framework
A pedagogy based on the use of Learning Objectives, Learning Reviews, Learning Objectives Reviews, and supportive student supplements.

Marketing: The Core
Pedagogical Approach

Personalized Marketing
A vivid and accurate description of businesses, marketing professionals, and entrepreneurs—through cases, exercises, and testimonials—that allows students to personalize marketing and identify possible career interests.

Traditional and Contemporary Coverage
Comprehensive and integrated coverage of traditional and contemporary concepts.

Marketing Decision Making
The use of extended examples, cases, and videos involving people making marketing decisions.

The goal of the third edition of *Marketing: The Core* is to create an exceptional experience for today's students and instructors of marketing. The development of *Marketing: The Core* was based on a rigorous process of assessment and the outcome of the process is a text and package of learning tools that are based on experience, leadership, and innovation in marketing education.

EXPERIENCE

Ten decades combined and more than 50,000 students taught, as instructors.

This is the experience the Kerin author team brings to the newly updated *Marketing: The Core*, 3/e. This experience has shaped the framework for this text and its supplements. How, exactly, do the authors achieve this in the third edition?

- Through the #1 *video case package* in the discipline:

  The Kerin video cases have been praised by users and reviewers as the most customized, engaging, and relevant video cases available. With the third edition, the authors have included eight new video case studies as well as two updated cases to enhance student interest. They present exciting products and companies such as Geek Squad, Starbucks, Best Buy, Rollerblade, Starbury, The Mall of America, Xerox, and General Mills.

He could repair televisions, computers, and a variety of other items, although he decided to focus on computers. His experiences as a consultant led him to realize that most people needed help with technology and that they

FOCUSING ON KEY TERMS

baby boomers p. 62
competition p. 69
consumerism p. 71
culture p. 65
demographics p. 60
economy p. 65
environmental scanning p. 60
Generation X p. 62
Generation Y p. 63
marketspace p. 68
multicultural marketing p. 64
regulation p. 70
self-regulation p. 73
social forces p. 60
technology p. 67

APPLYING MARKETING KNOWLEDGE

1 For many years Gerber has manufactured baby food in small, single-sized containers. In conducting an environmental scan, identify three trends or factors that might significantly affect this company's future business, and then propose how Gerber might respond to these changes.
2 Describe the new features you would add to an automobile designed for consumers in the 55+ age group. In what magazines would you advertise to appeal to this target market?
3 New technologies are continuously improving and replacing existing products. Although technological change is often difficult to predict, suggest how the following companies and products might be affected by

the Internet and digital technologies: (a) Kodak cameras and film, (b) American Airlines, and (c) the Metropolitan Museum of Art.
4 In recent years in the brewing industry, a couple of large firms that have historically had most of the beer sales (Anheuser-Busch and Miller) have faced competition from many small "micro" brands. In terms of the continuum of competition, how would you explain this change?
5 Why would Xerox be concerned about its name becoming generic?
6 Develop a "Code of Business Practices" for a new online vitamin store. Does your code address advertising? Privacy? Use by children? Why is self-regulation important?

building your marketing plan

Your marketing plan will include a situation analysis based on internal and external factors that are likely to affect your marketing program.
1 To summarize information about external factors, create a table similar to Figure 3–2 and identify three trends related to each of the five forces (social, economic, tech-

nological, competitive, and regulatory) that relate to your product or service.
2 When your table is completed, describe how each of the trends represents an opportunity or a threat for your business.

video case 3   Geek Squad: A New Business for a New Environment

 "As long as there's innovation there is going to be new kinds of chaos," explains Robert Stephens, founder of the technology support company Geek Squad. The chaos Stephens is referring to is the difficulty we have all experienced trying to keep up with the many changes in our environment, particularly those related to computers, technology, software, communication, and entertainment. Generally, consumers have found it difficult to install, operate, and use many of the electronic products available today. "It takes time to read

the manuals," continues Stephens. "I'm going to save you that time because I stay home on Saturday nights and read them for you!"

THE COMPANY

The Geek Squad story begins when Stephens, a native of Chicago, passed up an Art Institute scholarship to pursue a degree in computer science. While Stephens was a computer science student he took a job fixing computers for a research laboratory, and he also started consulting.

25 to 35 percent. Geek Squad customer materials now suggest that the service is "Saving the World One Computer at a Time. 24 Hours a Day. Your Place or Ours!"

THE CHANGING ENVIRONMENT

Many changes in the environment occurred to create the need for Geek Squad's services. Future changes are also likely to change the way Geek Squad operates. An environmental scan helps understand the changes.

The most obvious changes may be related to technology. Wireless broadband technology, high-definition televisions, products with Internet interfaces, and a general trend toward computers, phones, entertainment systems, and even appliances being interconnected are just a few examples of new products and applications for consumers to learn about. There are also technology-related problems such as viruses, spyware, lost data, and "crashed" or inoperable computers. New technologies have also created a demand for new types of maintenance such as password management, operating system updates, disk cleanup, and "defragging."

Another environmental change that contributes to the popularity of Geek Squad is the change in social factors such as demographics and culture. In the past many electronics manufacturers and retailers focused primarily on men. Women, however, are becoming increasingly interested in personal computing and home entertainment, and, according to the Consumer Electronics Association, are likely to outspend men in the near future. Best Buy's consumer research indicates that women expect personal service during the purchase and installation after the purchase—exactly the service Geek Squad is designed to provide. Our culture is also embracing the Geek Squad concept. If you follow television programming you may have noticed the series *Chuck* where one of the characters works for the "Nerd Herd" at "Buy More" and drives a car like a Geekmobile on service calls!

Competition, economics, and the regulatory environment have also had a big influence on Geek Squad. As discount stores such as Wal-Mart and PC makers such as Dell began to compete with Best Buy and Circuit City, new services such as in-home installation were needed to

electronics retailer Best Buy for Buy had observed very high re-complex products. Shoppers new products, purchase them get frustrated trying to make then return them to the store fact, Best Buy research re-were beginning to see service the purchase. The partnership Best Buy consumers welcomed Geek Squad's chief inspec-nt and began putting a in every Best Buy store, creat-k Squad Stores, and providing y. There are now more than d States, Canada, the United d return rates have declined by

 Now, just as changes in com-ity for Geek Squad, it is also mpetition as Circuit City has support service called Fire-ll-On-Call, and cable compa-ervices. The economic situa-s to improve as prices decline nited States, particularly for

GEEK SQUAD

sitive environmental factors ary success of Geek Squad. 3,000 PCs a day and gener-evenue. Because Geek Squad margin they contribute to the Buy, and they help generate e store loyalty. To continue uad will need to continue to y new approaches to creating

ch is to find additional loca-onsumers. For example, Geek ed in some FedEx stores and y. Another possible approach are designed for the newest ts. To test this idea Best Buy h home builders to wire new

houses with high-speed cables and networking equipment that Geek Squad agents can use to create ideal computer and entertainment systems. Geek Squad is also using new technology to improve. Agents now use a smart phone to access updated schedules, log in their hours, and run diagnostics tests on client's equipment. Finally, to attract the best possible employees, Geek Squad and Best Buy are trying a "results-only work environment" that has no fixed schedules and no mandatory meetings. By encouraging employees to make their own work-life decisions the Geek Squad hopes to keep morale and productivity high.

Other changes and opportunities are certain to appear soon. Despite the success of the Geek Squad, and the potential for additional growth, however, Robert Stephens is modest and claims, "Geeks may inherit the Earth, but they have no desire to rule it!"

Questions

1 What are the key environmental factors that created an opportunity for Robert Stephens to start the Geek Squad?
2 What changes in the purchasing patterns of (a) all consumers, and (b) women made the acquisition of Geek Squad particularly important for Best Buy?
3 Based on the case information and what you know about consumer electronics, conduct an environmental scan for Geek Squad to identify key trends. For each of the five environmental forces (social, economic, technological, competitive, and regulatory), identify trends likely to influence Geek Squad in the near future.
4 What promotional activities would you recommend to encourage consumers who use independent installers to switch to Geek Squad?

- By integrating assessment tools that allow instructors to meet *AACSB assurance-of-learning requirements:*

  Each chapter begins with learning objectives, includes in-chapter learning reviews, and ends with learning objective summaries. In addition, the *Marketing: The Core,* 3/e Test Bank includes learning objective, AACSB learning outcome, and Bloom's Taxonomy designations for each question. The combination of the objectives, outcomes, and taxonomy designation with the specific questions provides an important tool for meeting AACSB assurance of learning requirements.

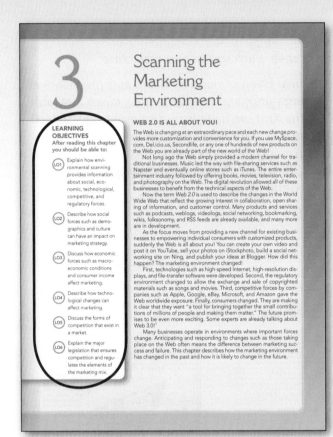

- With the most comprehensive package of *teaching and learning resources:*

  The supplements that accompany *Marketing: The Core,* 3/e are a comprehensive and integrated package of resources designed to ensure the highest level of learning for all students, and assist in making an instructor's life easier in the process. The supplements range from online quizzes, to comprehensive PowerPoint presentation slides, to the one-of-a-kind Instructor's Survival Kit, to an integrated Instructor's Manual, to a world-class test bank.

LEADERSHIP

The first custom-made videos to accompany a marketing text.

The first to integrate new content areas such as ethics, technology, and interactive marketing.

The first to utilize active learning approaches in the text and integrated activities.

These are just a few examples that illustrate how the Kerin author team has played a leadership role in the development and delivery of marketing pedagogy. This book is recognized as a market leader in the United States and Canada, and continues to introduce new, leading-edge principles and practices to students and instructors around the world. How does *Marketing: The Core*, 3/e continue this tradition of leadership?

- With the inclusion of **Customer Experience Management:**

  Customer experience management reflects contemporary thinking about the way marketers view how customers relate to their organizations and offerings. Students will find that marketing efforts to create a favorable customer experience in the interaction with organizations and the acquisition, use, and disposal of offerings result in mutually beneficial exchange relationships.

- With the focus on **Marketplace Diversity:**

  A diverse mix of buyers and sellers populate today's dynamic marketplace. Students will find that successful marketers are not limited to any particular culture, nationality, race, ethnic group, or gender. Rather, like consumers they serve, marketers mirror society, both domestically and globally. This diversity in today's marketplace is reflected in examples throughout the text.

- By creating the new feature, *Using Marketing Dashboards:*

The use of marketing dashboards among marketing professionals is popular today. Marketing dashboards graphically portray the measures that marketers use to track and analyze marketing phenomena and performance. Students will find commonly used measures applied by successful marketers throughout the text and be exposed to their calculation, interpretation, and application.

Using Marketing Dashboards
Are Cracker Jack Prices Above, At, or Below the Market?

How would you determine whether a firm's retail prices are above, at, or below the market? You might visit retail stores and record what prices retailers are charging for products or brands. This laborious activity can be simplified by combining two consumer market share measures to create a "price premium" display on your marketing dashboard.

Your Challenge Frito-Lay is considering whether to buy the Cracker Jack brand of caramel popcorn from Borden Inc. Frito-Lay research shows that Cracker Jack has a strong brand equity. But, Cracker Jack's dollar sales market share and pound volume market share declined recently and trailed the Crunch 'n Munch brand as shown in the table.

Borden's management used an above-market, premium pricing strategy for Cracker Jack. Specifically, Cracker Jack's suggested retail price was set to yield an average price premium per pound of 28 percent relative to Crunch 'n Munch. As a Frito-Lay marketer studying Cracker Jack, your challenge is to calculate and display Cracker Jack's actual price premium relative to Crunch 'n Munch. A price premium is the percentage by which the actual price charged for a specific brand exceeds (or falls short of) a benchmark established for a similar product or basket of products. This premium can be calculated as follows:

$$\text{Price Premium (\%)} = \frac{\text{Dollar Sales Market Share for a Brand}}{\text{Unit Volume Market Share for a Brand}} - 1$$

Brand	Dollar Sales Market Share	Pound Volume Market Share
Crunch 'n Munch	32%	32%
Cracker Jack	26	19
Fiddle Faddle	7	8
Private Brands	4	8
Seasonal, Specialty, and Regional (S,S,R) Brands	31	33
	100%	100%

Your Findings Using caramel popcorn brand market share data, the Cracker Jack price premium is 1.368, or 36.8 percent, calculated as follows: (26 percent ÷ 19 percent) − 1 = 0.368. By comparison, Crunch 'n Munch enjoys no price premium. Its dollar sales market share and unit (pound) market share are equal: (32 percent ÷ 32 percent) − 1 = 0, or zero percent. The price premium, or lack thereof, of other brands can be displayed in a marketing dashboard as shown below.

Your Action Cracker Jack's price premium clearly exceeds the 28 percent Borden benchmark relative to Crunch 'n Munch. Cracker Jack's price premium may have overreached its brand equity. Consideration might be given to assessing Cracker Jack's price premium relative to its market position should Frito-Lay purchase the brand.

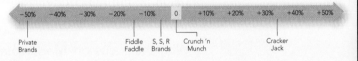

| −50% | −40% | −30% | −20% | −10% | 0 | +10% | +20% | +30% | +40% | +50% |

Private Brands — Fiddle Faddle — S, S, R Brands — Crunch 'n Munch — Cracker Jack

Loss-Leader Pricing For a special promotion retail stores deliberately sell a product below its customary price to attract attention to it. The purpose of this *loss-leader pricing* is not to increase sales but to attract customers in hopes they will buy other products as well, particularly the discretionary items with large markups. For example, Best Buy, Target, and Wal-Mart sell CDs at about half of music companies' suggested retail price to attract customers to their stores.[14]

learning review
1. Value is _____.
2. What are the circumstances in pricing a new product that might support skimming or penetration pricing?

271

x

INNOVATION

What if your research showed that many students in your introductory marketing course don't attempt to read and understand the tables and charts in the textbook? What could you do to increase their interest and involvement? Read on for the answer.

To secure their position in the marketplace, the Kerin author team consistently created innovative pedagogical tools that encourage interaction and match students' learning styles. How did they accomplish this in the third edition?

- With the creation of a **Visually Enhanced Test Bank:**

  The *Marketing: The Core*, 3/e Test Bank has been completely updated to include the latest concepts and ideas from the textbook. When research by the Kerin author team revealed many students were skipping the tables and charts in the chapter, they decided to do something about it: the Visually Enhanced Test Bank! This moves key tables, charts, ads, and photos from the textbook into the test bank to emphasize their importance and reward students who study these key elements.

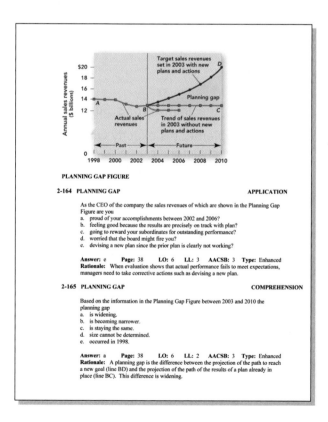

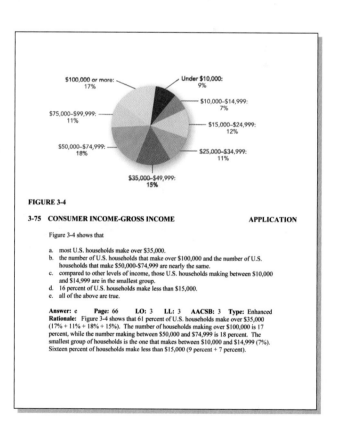

- By including *iPod content* for student use:

  It has become apparent that student study patterns and practices are changing and evolving. With students being more active and on-the-go than ever, we have created study and prep tools that can be as mobile as they are! Specific chapter quizzes, PowerPoint presentations and video cases can now be viewed and manipulated with any MP3 player.

- By including **Core Concept Cards** for students:

  At the end of the book is a new study tool for today's busy students. The perforated pages separate into 90 Core Concept Cards which reinforce key topics, terms, and figures related to each Learning Objective.

- Through the *Instructor's Survival Kit:*

  This supplement is exactly what it says it is: an instructor's guide to surviving in today's classroom. Instructors create interaction by breaking the classroom into teams that analyze marketing problems presented through In-Class Activities. Students who are kinesthetic learners especially appreciate the hands-on product samples that are tied to the activities and are intended to build on the idea of "cooperative learning."

New and Revised Content

Chapter 1: New Innovation Examples and Content. The 3M Post-It Flag Highlighter targeted at college students, opens Chapter 1. This example of new product development and innovation is integrated into the chapter and is featured in the end-of-chapter video case.

Chapter 2: Increased Emphasis on the Importance of Marketing in Organizations. This chapter now includes a discussion of the new title for marketing executives—Chief Marketing Officer (CMO)—and the increasingly important role they play. Chapter 2 also introduces the new Using Marketing Dashboards box.

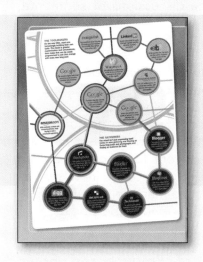

Chapter 3: Introduction of Web 2.0 and New Trends in Marketing. Web logs (blogs), social networking, wikis, RSS feeds, and other elements of Web 2.0 are presented in Chapter 3. Recent trends including the concern about global warming, the growing importance of China and India, and the increase in customer-generated content are also discussed. The chapter also includes discussions of hybrid cars, culture jamming, WiMax, Generation Y entrepreneurs, and a new case on Geek Squad.

Chapter 4: New Detailed Examples of Ethics and Social Responsibility in Marketing. Examples have been expanded to include Anheuser-Busch's new "Responsibility Matters" campaign, Pepsi's reaction to an offer of confidential information, green marketing activities at 3M and Wal-Mart, and cause marketing activities at Avon and P&G.

Chapter 5: Updated Consumer Behavior Coverage. A new chapter-opening example features the importance of and differences in customer experience for men and women when shopping for a new car. It also places increased emphasis on customer experience in the purchase decision process, and includes a new video case on Best Buy.

Chapter 6: New Emphasis on Supplier Development and Diversity. New examples of organization buying, including Lockheed Martin's relationship with NASA, and small business use of business-to-business e-marketplaces have been added to Chapter 6.

Chapter 7: Expanded Coverage of Marketing in Developing Countries. The discussion of marketing in developing countries in Chapter 7 now includes an emphasis on the role of entrepreneurship and innovation to promote a higher standard of living. Marketing opportunities in China are also discussed.

Chapter 8: Updated Marketing Research Examples and Information. Aging actors in movie sequels like those playing Harry Potter and Indiana Jones are just one of the reasons for marketing research for today's movies, as discussed in Chapter 8. It also covers marketing research aspects of Nielsen ratings of TV shows and websites, data mining, and toy testing.

Chapter 9: New Segmentation and Positioning Coverage. New examples of Zappos online shoes, Wendy's innovations, and Apple's new products have been added to the discussions of segmentation and positioning.

Chapter 10: Added Discussion of Sources of New Product Ideas. Where did the idea for Apple's iPhone come from? Chapter 10 opens with Steve Jobs' strategy for developing this revolutionary new product. A new section gives reasons for the huge number of new product failures—ranging from "Groupthink" to not learning lessons from past failures. Given the current focus on enhancing customer experience with products and services, a new discussion and key term on customer experience management has been added to Chapter 10 and integrated throughout the book.

Chapter 11: Expanded Coverage of Product and Brand Management. This chapter has expanded the discussion of the role of a product manager. The new Using Marketing Dashboards box features an application of a category development index (CDI) and a brand development index (BDI). In addition, customer experience is highlighted through Pepsi, Kleenex, and Kraft packaging examples, and brand personality is highlighted through a Harley-Davidson example. The chapter also includes a new section titled "Contemporary Packaging and Labeling Challenges."

Chapter 12: Updated Pricing Coverage. A new discussion of the pricing of athletic shoes and the introduction of Starbury signature sneakers now opens this chapter. Chapter 12 also emphasizes the distinction between a one-price policy and a flexible-price policy given the advances in information technology. In addition a new video case on the Starbury Collection is included.

Chapter 13: New Focus of Channels, Wholesaling, Supply Chain, and Logistics Content. The importance of customer experience management is the focus of Chapter 13 and is discussed in the context of channel management at Apple Stores, in multichannel marketing, and as an element of channel choice.

Chapter 14: Introduction of Social Retailing and Other Retailing Trends. This chapter now opens with a discussion of the growing interest in "social retailing." New discussions of the Macy's mergers, retailer loyalty programs, "site-to-store" services, and multichannel marketing have also been added. The new Using Marketing Dashboards box discusses the sales per square foot and same store growth measures.

Chapter 15: New Integrated Marketing Communications and Direct Marketing Coverage. Integrated marketing communications is discussed as an important tool in the trend toward customer experience management, and as a means of reaching mobile, multitasking audiences. Examples of media use include social media such as blogs, messaging on cell phones, push and pull advertising, sponsorships, logos, and game-movie partnerships. New company examples include Ford and the Beijing Olympics. The chapter also discusses changes in direct marketing such as mandatory opt-in requirement in Europe and the possible "do not mail" registry in the U.S.

Chapter 16: New Forms of Advertising. Discussion of the growth of new forms of advertising have been added. The chapter opening example describes new "virtual" world advertising opportunities such as Second Life. Search engine advertising and interactive advertising are also discussed. Examples of ads from Blackberry, Sony, M&Ms, Diesel, and Samsung are included in the chapter. In addition, the Making Responsible Decisions box discusses the problem of click fraud in online advertising.

Chapter 17: Increased Focus on Delivering Customer Solutions. Xerox and its focus on customer solutions is integrated into the chapter-opening example and the new end-of-chapter video case. An expanded discussion of the use of technology in selling and sales management is also included.

Chapter 18: New Content on Cross-Channel Shoppers and Interactive Marketing. New coverage describes "cross-channel" shoppers—the 51 percent of online consumers who research products online but buy in retail stores. New discussions also add emphasis to privacy and security issues in online buying and the impact of interactive marketing on the customer experience.

Appendix B: New and Updated Career Coverage. This appendix, Planning a Career in Marketing, has been updated to include new salary information, the growing importance of international work experience, and the use of online profiles and networking sites by employers and prospective employees.

Organization

The third edition of *Marketing: The Core* is divided into four parts. Part 1, *Initiating the Marketing Process*, looks first at what marketing is and how it creates customer value and customer relationships (Chapter 1). Then Chapter 2 provides an overview of the strategic marketing process that occurs in an organization—which provides a framework for the text. Appendix A provides a sample marketing plan as a reference for students. Chapter 3 analyzes the five major environmental factors in our changing marketing environment, while Chapter 4 provides a framework for including ethical and social responsibility considerations in marketing decisions.

Part 2, *Understanding Buyers and Markets,* first describes, in Chapter 5, how individual consumers reach buying decisions. Next, Chapter 6 looks at organizational buyers and markets and how they make purchase decisions. And finally, in Chapter 7, the dynamics of world trade and the influence of cultural diversity on global marketing practices are explored.

In Part 3, *Targeting Marketing Opportunities,* the marketing research function and how information about prospective consumers is linked to marketing strategy and decisions is discussed in Chapter 8. The process of segmenting and targeting markets and positioning products appears in Chapter 9.

Part 4, *Satisfying Marketing Opportunities,* covers the marketing mix elements. The product element is divided into the natural chronological sequence of first developing new products and services (Chapter 10) and then managing the existing products, services and brand (Chapter 11). Pricing is covered in terms of the way organizations set prices (Chapter 12). Two chapters address the place (distribution) aspects of marketing: Managing Marketing Channels and Supply Chains (Chapter 13), and Retailing and Wholesaling (Chapter 14). Chapter 15 discusses integrated marketing communications and direct marketing, topics that have grown in importance in the marketing discipline recently. The primary forms of mass market communication—advertising, sales promotion, and public relations—are covered in Chapter 16. Personal selling and sales management are covered in Chapter 17. Chapter 18 describes how interactive and multichannel marketing influences customer value and the customer experience through context, content, community, customization, connectivity, and commerce.

The book closes with several useful supplemental sections. Appendix B, Planning a Career in Marketing, discusses marketing jobs and how to get them. In addition, a detailed Glossary, Learning Review Answers, three indexes (name, company/product, and subject), and 90 new Core Concept Cards complete the book.

Engaging Features

Chapter-opening vignettes introduce students to chapter concepts by using an exciting company as an example. Students are immediately engaged while learning about real-world companies. Chapter 10 discusses Apple, a company recognized by *BusinessWeek* for its innovation.

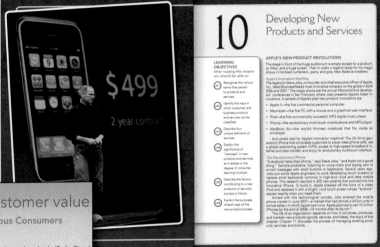

Marketing Matters > > > > > customer value

The Global Teenager—A Market of 500 Million Voracious Consumers with $100 Billion to Spend

The "global teenager" market consists of 500 million 13- to 19-year-olds in Europe, North and South America, and industrialized nations of Asia and the Pacific Rim who have experienced intense exposure to television (MTV broadcasts in 169 countries in 28 languages), movies, travel, the Internet, and global advertising by companies such as Apple, Sony, Nike, and Coca-Cola. The similarities among teens across these countries are greater than their differences. For example, a global study of middle-class teenagers' rooms in 25 industrialized countries indicated it was difficult, if not impossible, to tell whether the rooms were in Los Angeles, Mexico City, Tokyo, Rio de Janeiro, Sidney, or Paris. Why? Teens spend $100 billion annually for a common gallery of products: Sony

Nike athletic shoes, Swatch watches, Apple iPods, Diesel apparel and accessories, and Procter & Gamble Clearasil facial medicine.

Teenagers around the world appreciate fashion and music, and desire novelty and trendier designs and images. They also acknowledge an Americanization of fashion and culture based on another study of 6,500 teens in 26 countries. When asked what country had the most influence on their attitudes and purchase behavior, 54 percent of teens from the United States, 87 percent of those from Latin America, 80 Europeans, of those fr the United States. This phenomenon has no by parents. As one parent in India said, "No

Marketing Matters boxes highlight real-world examples of customer value creation and delivery and entrepreneurship which gives students further insight into the practical world of marketing.

Making Responsible Decisions boxes focus on social responsibility, sustainability, and ethics. These boxes provide exciting, current examples of how companies approach these subjects in their marketing strategy.

Making Responsible Decisions > > > > > > ethics

Corporate Conscience in the Cola War

Suppose you are a senior executive at Pepsi-Cola and that a Coca-Cola employee offers to sell you the marketing plan and sample for a new Coke product at a modest price? Would you buy it knowing Pepsi-Cola could gain a significant competitive edge in the cola war?

When this question was posed in an online survey of marketing and advertising executives, 67 percent said they would buy the plan and product sample if there were no repercussions. What did Pepsi-Cola do when this offer actually occurred? The company immediately contacted Coca-Cola, which contacted the FBI. An undercover FBI ent paid the employee $30,000

dent, a Pepsi-Cola spokesperson said: "We only did what any responsible company would do. Competition must be tough, but must always be fair and legal."

Why did the 33 percent of respondents in the online survey say they would decline the offer? Most said they would prefer competing ethically so they could sleep at night. According to a senior advertising agency executive who would decline the offer: "Repercussions go beyond potential espionage charges. As long as we have a conscience, there are repercussions."

So what happened to the Coca-Cola employee? She was sentenced to eight years in prison and ordered to pay $40,0 in restituti Her

building your marketing plan

To do a consumer analysis for the product—the good, service, or idea—in your marketing plan:

1 Identify the consumers who are most likely to buy your product—the primary target market—in terms of (*a*) their demographic characteristics and (*b*) any other kind of characteristics you believe are important.

2 Describe (*a*) the main points of difference of your product for this group and (*b*) what problem they help

solve for the consumer, in terms of the first stage in the consumer purchase decision process in Figure 5–1.

3 Identify the one or two key influences for each of the four outside boxes in Figure 5–4: (*a*) marketing mix, (*b*) psychological, (*c*) sociocultural, and (*d*) situational influences.

This consumer analysis will provide the foundation for the marketing mix actions you develop later in your plan.

Building Your Marketing Plan is an end-of-chapter feature that requires students to go through the practical application of creating their own marketing plan.

INSTRUCTOR RESOURCES

Element	Online Learning Center www.mhhe.com/kerin	Instructor's Presentation CD (IPCD)	Other
Marketing Walkthrough Video	X	X	
Using Marketing Dashboards Video	X	X	
Instructor's Resource Manual (IRM)	X	X	
New! Visually Enhanced Test Bank	X	X	
PowerPoint Presentations	X (basic)	X (enhanced)	
Video Cases			Video DVD
Instructor's Survival Kit (ISK)			Stand-alone kit
Instructor Newsletter			email

- **Marketing Walkthrough Video:**

  A video description of the text and its supplements is available on the Instructor's Presentation CD and the Online Learning Center. This video provides a description of the many elements of the *Marketing: The Core*, 3/e package including new videos, Visually Enhanced Test Bank, Instructor's Survival Kit, iPod Content, and Marketing Dashboards. It's an easy way to learn about the resources and how they can be used to meet the unique teaching styles of each instructor and the learning styles of their students!

- **Using Marketing Dashboards Video:**

  Marketing dashboards are being used among marketing professionals to graphically portray the measures used to track and analyze marketing performance. The new key feature in *Marketing: The Core*, 3/e, Using Marketing Dashboards, is a way to bring this concept home to your students. Watch this video and even share it with your class for more information on how dashboards are being used today.

- **Instructor's Presentation CD-ROM:**

  The Instructor's Presentation CD-ROM (IPCD) includes a digital version of the Instructor's Resource Manual, PowerPoint slides, and Test Bank. It also contains the EZ Test package.

- **Instructor's Resource Manual:**

  The Instructor's Resource Manual (IRM) to accompany *Marketing: The Core*, 3/e is an all-inclusive resource designed to make an instructor's preparation for teaching much easier. The *Instructor's Resource Manual* includes detailed lectures notes, discussions, and a description of all of the individual multimedia assets from which an instructor can construct a custom presentation. The IRM also includes Supplemental Lecture Notes (SLNs) and In-Class Activities (ICAs) that link to sample products in the Instructor's Survival Kit to make marketing come to life in the classroom.

- ## Visually Enhanced Test Bank:

We offer more than 3,000 test questions categorized by topic and level of learning (knowledge, comprehension, or application) and correlated to both the Learning Objectives and Bloom's Level of Learning to assist instructors in developing their exams. There are also a number of visually enhanced questions in the test bank that include images and figures from the book itself to ensure student learning and preparation.

- ## Test Bank Online:

A comprehensive bank of test questions is provided within a computerized test bank powered by McGraw-Hill's flexible electronic testing software program EZ Test Online (www.eztestonline.com). EZ Test Online allows you to create paper and online tests or quizzes in this easy-to-use program!

Imagine being able to create and access your test or quiz anywhere, at any time without installing the testing software. Now, with EZ Test Online, instructors can select questions from multiple McGraw-Hill test banks or author their own, and then either print the test for paper distribution or give it online.

Test Creation

- Author/edit questions online using the 14 different question type templates
- Create printed tests or deliver online to get instant scoring and feedback
- Create questions pools to offer multiple versions online—great for practice
- Export your tests for use in WebCT, Blackboard, PageOut and Apple's iQuiz
- Compatible with EZ Test Desktop tests you've already created
- Sharing tests with colleagues, adjuncts, TAs is easy

Online Test Management

- Set availability dates and time limits for your quiz or test
- Control how your test will be presented
- Assign points by question or question type with drop-down menu
- Provide immediate feedback to students or delay until all finish the test
- Create practice tests online to enable student mastery
- Your roster can be uploaded to enable student self-registration

Online Scoring and Reporting

- Automated scoring for most of EZ Test's numerous question types
- Allows manual scoring for essay and other open response questions
- Manual re-scoring and feedback is also available
- EZ Test's grade book is designed to easily export to your grade book
- View basic statistical reports

Support and Help

- User's Guide and built-in page specific help
- Flash tutorials for getting started on the support site

- Support Website: www.mhhe.com/eztest
- Product specialist available at 1-800-331-5094
- Online Training: http://auth.mhhe.com/mpss/workshops/

• WebCT/Blackboard/eCollege/TopClass:

You can use *Marketing: The Core*, 3/e online material with any online platform–including Blackboard, WebCT, eCollege, TopClass–to expand the reach of your course and open up distance learning options.

• PowerPoint Presentations:

The PowerPoint presentations feature slides that can be used and personalized by instructors to help present concepts to students efficiently. The Online Learning Center contains a basic version of the media-enhanced PowerPoint presentations that are found on the IPCD. The media-enhanced version has video and commercials embedded in the presentations and makes for an engaging and interested classroom lecture.

• New and Revised Video Cases:

A unique series of 18 contemporary marketing video cases is available on a DVD. Each video case corresponds with chapter-specific topics and the end-of-chapter case in the text. The video cases feature a variety of organizations and provide balanced coverage of services, consumer products, small businesses, *Fortune* 500 firms, and business-to-business examples. The third edition package includes new videos about Xerox, Starbury, Best Buy, Geek Squad, General Mills Warm Delights, 3M Post-it® Flag Highlighters, BP, and Las Vegas.

• Instructor's Survival Kit (ISK):

The Instructor's Survival Kit contains product samples for use in the classroom to illustrate marketing concepts and encourage student involvement and learning, often with teams working on a task for 5 to 15 minutes in class. Today's students are more likely to learn and be motivated by active participative experiences than by classic classroom lecture and discussion. *Marketing: The Core*, 3/e utilizes product samples from both large and small firms that will interest today's students. When appropriate, sample print and TV ads are included among our PowerPoint presentations.

• Instructor Newsletter:

NEW

The Instructor Newsletter has been developed for adopters of *Marketing*. This newsletter is devoted to providing innovative resources to help improve student learning, offer timely marketing examples, and make class preparation easier. The newsletter includes: access to video clips from Fox Business News, links to video clips from *BusinessWeek* and other sources, synopses of articles with in-class discussion and test questions, teaching tips, discussion of pedagogical features of *Marketing,* and feature articles from adopters of *Marketing*. The newsletter will be offered 6 times during the academic year and is available through email and on our website!

STUDENT RESOURCES

Element	Online Learning Center www.mhhe.com/kerin	Other
iPod Content	X	
Chapter Quizzes	X	
Core Concept Cards		X (back of book)

- **iPod Content:**

  This additional student supplement can be purchased on the OLC. The third edition of *Marketing: The Core* is the first to include the multimedia addition of iPod content. With narrated PowerPoint presentation slides, case videos, and quizzes, students can be studying and learning while they are on the go with their MP3 players.

- **Student Online Learning Center (OLC):**

  This rich book-specific Online Learning Center website contains multiple-choice review quizzes, chapter objectives, key term flashcards, and chapters in review. This is also the location for purchasing access to the iPod content.

- **Core Concept Cards:**

  The Core Concept Cards are great mobile study tools for students. At the end of the book are perforated pages that separate into 90 cards. Each card provides a summary of key topics, terms, and figures related to a learning objective. Each learning objective in the text is covered by one of the cards and allows students to study and review material at their convenience in almost any location. The cards provide the chapter number, the learning objective number, and a card number for easy organization.

Acknowledgments

To ensure continuous improvement of our textbook and supplements we have utilized an extensive review and development process for each of our past editions. Building on that history, the *Marketing: The Core*, 3/e development process included several phases of evaluation and a variety of stakeholder audiences (e.g., students, instructors, etc.).

- In the first phase of the review process the authors visited instructors and students at a variety of campuses to discuss the use and effectiveness of the text and supplements.
- The second phase of the review process asked users and nonusers to suggest improvements to the text and supplements through a detailed review of each component while used in the classroom.
- In the third phase, a group of experienced marketing instructors provided feedback through user and nonuser symposia. These sessions provided feedback about the text, supplements, and online resources.
- Finally, a group of instructors provided evaluations of revised materials and tested new technologies related to the third edition supplements.

Reviewers who were vital in the changes that were made to this edition include:

Michele Adams
Erie Community College and Bryant & Stratton Southtowns

Koren Borges
University of North Florida

Ed Cerny
Horry-Georgetown Technical College

Yun Chu
Robert Morris College

Paul W. Clark
Indiana State University

Eloise Coupey
Virginia Tech University

Julie Cross
Chippewa Valley Technical College

Geoffrey Crosslin
Kalamazoo Valley Community College

Andrew J. Czaplewski
University of Colorado at Colorado Springs

Sr. S.J. Garner
Eastern Kentucky University

Kathleen Ghahramani
Johnson County Community College

Jianwei Hou
Minnesota State University, Mankato

Michael A. Jones
Southeastern Louisiana University

William J. Kehoe
University of Virginia

Margaret J. Klemme
Kirkwood Community College

Linda N. LaMarca
Tarleton State University

Rebecca Legleiter
Tulsa Community College

Catherine Lenihan
Delgado Community College

Carolyn Massiah
University of Central Florida

Erika Matulich
The University of Tampa

Michael Mayo
Kent State University

Edward McLaughlin
Cornell University

Robert M. McMillen
James Madison University

Julie M. Pharr
Tennessee Technological University

Stephen Pirog, PhD.
Seton Hall University

Vicki Rostedt
University of Akron

Stacia Wert-Gray
University of Central Oklahoma

Poh-Lin Yeoh
Bentley College

The preceding section demonstrates the amount of feedback and developmental input that went into this project, and we are deeply grateful to the numerous people who have shared their ideas with us. Reviewing a book or supplement takes an incredible amount of energy and attention. We are glad so many of our colleagues took the time to do it. Their comments have inspired us to do our best. Reviewers who contributed to previous editions of this book include:

Donald Auble
Baldwin-Wallace College

Chris Barnes
Lakeland Community College

Sandy Becker
Rutgers University

Pat Bernson
County College of Morris

Mukesh Bhargava
Oakland University

Al Brokaw
Michigan Technological University

Sergio Carvalho
Bernard Baruch College

Solveg Cooper
Cuesta Community College

John Crawford
Lipscomb University

James Cross
University of Las Vegas

Charlene Davis
Trinity University

Dexter Davis
Alfred State College

Richard Davis
California State University, Chico

Kim Donahue
Indiana University

Beth Elam
Western New England College

Vicki Eveland
Mercer University

Medhat Farooque
Central Arizona University

Marty Flynn
Greenville Technical College

P. Renee Foster
Delta State University

Hershey Friedman
Brooklyn College

James Gaubert
Clemson University

Ken Gehrt
San Jose State University

Connie Golden
Lakeland Community College

Stephen Goodwin
Illinois State University

Karen Gore
Ivy Tech State College

Cynthia Gundy
University of Central Florida

Carol Gwin
Baylor University

Randall Hansen
Stetson University

Susan Harmon
Middle Tennessee State University

Dorothy Harpool
Wichita State University

Mary Ann Hocutt
Samford University

Rosemarie Houghton
Northwood University

James Hutton
Fairleigh Dickinson University

Jack Janosik
John Carroll University

Areti Jordan
University of Central Florida

Sungwoo Jung
State University of New York, Oneonta

Dennis Kimble
Northwood University

Anna Kwong
Santa Barbara City College

Russell Lacey
University of New Orleans

Jay Lambe
Virginia Polytechnic Institute and State University

Jane Lang
East Carolina University

Kenneth Lawrence
New Jersey Institute of Technology

Rosa Lemel
Kean University

Kelly Littlefield
Northwestern Michigan College

Lynda Maddox
George Washington University

Donna Mayo
Tennessee State University

Kevin McClean
Grand Canyon University

Kimberley McNeil
North Carolina A&T State University

Rajiv Mehta
New Jersey Institute of Technology

Ronald Michaels
University of Central Florida

Yuko Minowa
Long Island University

Mark Mitchell
University of South Carolina, Spartanburg

James Molinari
State University of New York, Oswego

Lester Niedell
University of Tulsa

Vanessa Gail Perry
George Washington University

Susan Peterson
Scottsdale Community College

Edna Ragins
North Carolina A&T State University

Stephen Ramocki
Rhode Island College

Donald Roy
Tennessee State University

Carl Saxby
University of Southern Indiana

Darrell Scott
Idaho State University

Trina Sego
Boise State University

Marvin Shapiro
South Mountain Community College

Ken Shaw
State University of New York, Oswego

Tom Smith
Texas Wesleyan University

Jerrod Stark
Fort Hays State University

Randy Stuart
Kennesaw State University

Richard Szecsy
Our Lady of the Lake University

Lars Thording
Arizona State University—West

Frank Titlow
St. Petersburg College

Sushila Umashankar
University of Arizona

Denise West
Brevard Community College

Bill Wilkinson
Governor's State University

Thanks are also due to many faculty members who contributed to the text chapters and cases. They include: Linda Rochford of the University of Minnesota–Duluth, Kevin Upton of the University of Minnesota–Twin Cities, Nancy Nentl of Metropolitan State University, David Brennan of St. Thomas University, and Leigh McAlister of the University of Texas at Austin. Michael Vessey provided cases, research assistance, many special images, and led our efforts on the Instructor's Resource Manual, In-Class Activities, Instructor Newsletter, and Instructor's Survival Kit. Kathryn Schifferle of California State University, Nancy Mulder, Thomas Rudelius, and Steven Rudelius assisted with the Instructor Newsletter. Rick Armstrong of Armstrong Photography, Nick Kaufman and Michelle Morgan of NKP Media, Bruce McLean of World Class Communication Technologies, Paul Fagan of Fagan Productions, Dan Hundley and George Heck of Token Media, Martin Walter of White Room Digital, Scott Bolin of Bolin Marketing, and Dan Stephenson of the Philadelphis Phillies produced the videos. William Carner of Columbia College provided the study guide. Carol Johnson of the University of Denver was responsible for the revision of the test bank.

Many businesspeople also provided substantial assistance by making available information that appears in the text, videos, and supplements. Thanks are due to David Ford and Don Rylander of Ford Consulting Group; Mark Rehborg of Tony's Pizza, Ann Hand and Kathy Seegebrecht of BP; Kimberly Mosford and Ryan Schroeder of Business Incentives; Vivian Callaway, Sandy Proctor, and Anna Stoesz of General Mills; David Windorski of 3M; Nicholas Skally, Jeremy Stonier, and Joe Olivas of Rollerblade; Stan Jacot of ConAgra Snack Foods; Sandra Smith of Smith Communications; Erin Patton of the MasterMind Group, LLC; Kim Nagele of JCPenney Inc.; Charles Besio of the Sewell Automotive Group Inc.; and Kate Hodebeck of Cadbury Schweppes America's Beverages Inc.; Beverly Roberts of U.S. Census Bureau; Jennifer Gebert of Ghirardelli Chocolate Company; Michael Kuhl of 3M Sports and Leisure; Stan Jacot of ConAgra Snack Foods; Kerry Barnett of Valassis Communications; and Leslie Herman and Jeff Gerst of Bolin Marketing working with Carma Laboratories (Carmex). We also acknowledge the special help of a team that worked with us on the Fallon Worldwide video case: Fred Senn, Bruce Blister, Kevin Flat, Ginny Grossman, Kim Knutson, Julie Smith, Erin Taut, and Rob White.

Staff support from the Southern Methodist University, the University of Denver, and the University of Minnesota was essential. We gratefully acknowledge the help of Wanda Hanson, Jeanne Milazzo, Gloria Valdez, and Dedre Henderson for their many contributions.

Coordinating activities of authors, designers, editors, compositors, and production specialists is essential in providing an accurate and readable textbook. Christine Vaughan of McGraw-Hill/Irwin's production staff and editorial consultant Gina Huck Siegert of Imaginative Solutions, Inc., provided the necessary oversight and hand-holding for us, while retaining a refreshing sense of humor, often under tight deadlines. Thank you again.

Finally, we acknowledge the professional efforts of the McGraw-Hill/Irwin staff. Completion of our book and its many supplements required the attention and commitment of many editorial, production, marketing, and research personnel. Our Burr Ridge–based team included Paul Ducham, Doug Hughes, Colleen Honan, Kelly Pekelder, Carol Bielski, Matthew Baldwin, Jeremy Cheshareck, Sue Lombardi, Katie Mergen, Nicky Miller, and many others. In addition we relied on Michael Hruby for constant attention regarding photo elements of the text. Handling the countless details of our text, supplement, and support technologies has become an incredibly complex challenge. We thank all these people for their efforts!

Roger A. Kerin
Steven W. Hartley
William Rudelius

BRIEF CONTENTS

DETAILED CONTENTS

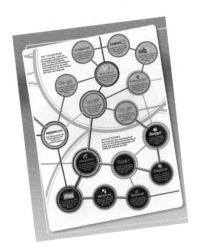

Part 2   Understanding Buyers and Markets

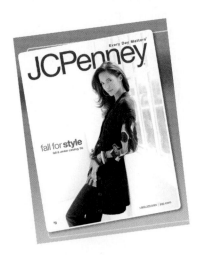

Part 3   Targeting Marketing Opportunities

Part 4   Satisfying Marketing Opportunities

12 PRICING PRODUCTS AND SERVICES   262

18 IMPLEMENTING INTERACTIVE AND MULTICHANNEL MARKETING   404

Marketing
The Core

1

Creating Customer Relationships and Value through Marketing

LEARNING OBJECTIVES

After reading this chapter you should be able to:

LO1 Define marketing and identify the diverse factors influencing marketing activities.

LO2 Explain how marketing discovers and satisfies consumer needs.

LO3 Distinguish between marketing mix factors and environmental forces.

LO4 Explain how organizations build strong customer relationships and customer value through marketing.

LO5 Describe how today's customer relationships era differs from prior eras oriented to production and selling.

HOW DO COLLEGE STUDENTS STUDY? 3M'S RESPONSE TO A NEW-PRODUCT CHALLENGE!

3M inventor David Windorski faced a curious challenge—understanding how college students study! Specifically, how do they read their textbooks, take class notes, and prepare for exams? First, Windorski needed to obtain information on students' study habits. Next, he needed to convert this knowledge into a product that actually helps students improve their studying. Finally, Windorski had to manufacture and market this product using 3M's technology.

Sound simple? Perhaps. But David Windorski invested several years of his life conducting marketing research on students' studying behavior, developing new product ideas, and then creating an actual product students could use.[1] This process of discovering and satisfying consumer needs is the essence of marketing that organizations such as 3M use to generate sales and profits.

In the process of designing a product that satisfies consumer needs, David Windorski's invention got a personal testimonial from host Oprah Winfrey on her TV show in January 2008. More on this later.[2]

Discovering Student Study Needs

As an inventor of Post-it® brand products, David Windorski's main job is to design new products. He had some creative "thinking time" under 3M's "15% Rule" in which inventors can use up to 15 percent of their time to do initially unfunded research that might lead to marketable 3M products. Working with a team of four college students, Windorski and the team observed and questioned dozens of students about how they used their textbooks, took notes, wrote term papers, and reviewed for exams.

Windorski describes what college students told him: "It's natural behavior to highlight a passage and then mark the page with a Post-it® Note or Post-it® Flag of some kind. So it's reasonable to put Post-it® products together with a highlighter to have two functions in one."

Satisfying Student Study Needs

Designing a marketable product for students was not done overnight. It took Windorski a few years of creativity, hard work, and attention to countless details. Windorski went back to his drawing board—or more literally to wood blocks and modeling clay. Some of his early models appear in the photo on the opposite page. These nonworking models showed Windorski how the 2-in-1 product would feel.

  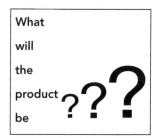

3M's Post-it® Notes or Post-it® Flags

Felt Tip Highlighters

3M product that will combine Post-it® Notes or Post-it® Flags and Highlighters

For the creative way a student project helped lead to a new product for college students using 3M's technology, see the text.

David Windorski's search for the 2-in-1 highlighter plus Post-it® Flags produced working models that students could actually use to give him feedback. Windorski had taken some giant steps in trying not only to discover students' needs for his product but also to satisfy those needs with a practical, useful product. Later in the chapter we'll see what products resulted from his innovative thinking and 3M's initial marketing plan that launched his products.

WHAT IS MARKETING?

For the wild idea these three 20-somethings are hatching, see the Marketing Matters box.

The good news is that you are already a marketing expert! You perform many marketing activities and make marketing-related decisions every day. For example, would you sell more Panasonic Viera 50-inch plasma high-definition TVs at $2,499 or $999 each? You answered $999 right? So your experience in shopping gives you some expertise in marketing. As a consumer, you've been involved in thousands of marketing decisions—but mostly on the buying and not the selling side. But to test your expertise, answer the "marketing expert" questions posed in Figure 1–1. You'll find the answers within the next several pages.

The bad news is, good marketing isn't always easy. That's why every year thousands of new products fail in the marketplace and then quietly slide into oblivion. Examples of new products that vary from spectacular successes to dismal failures appear in the next few pages.

Marketing and Your Career

Marketing affects all individuals, all organizations, all industries, and all countries. This book seeks to teach you marketing concepts, often by having you actually "do

FIGURE 1–1
The see-if-you're-really-a-marketing-expert test

Answer the questions below. The correct answers are given later in the chapter.

1. True or false. You can now buy a robotic floor washer that scrubs your hard-surface floor even when you're not there and better than you can mop it.
2. True or false. The 60-year lifetime value of a loyal Kleenex customer is $994.
3. To be socially responsible, 3M puts what recycled material into its very successful ScotchBrite® Never Rust™ Soap Pads? (a) aluminum cans, (b) steel-belted tires, (c) plastic bottles, (d) computer screens.

Marketing Matters > > > > entrepreneurship

Payoff for the Joys (!) and Sleepless Nights (?) of Starting Your Own Small Business: YouTube!!!!

What happens when you drop Mentos into a bottle of Diet Coke?

Don't know the answer?

Then you're not a serious YouTube viewer! If you need an answer, ask the student sitting next to you in class. But don't try it at home.

In one 12-month period, a single website—YouTube.com—revolutionized the Internet's world of videos and was named *Time* magazine's Invention of the Year for 2006. YouTube's numbers are astounding: In January, 2008, 79 million viewers watched more than three-billion user-posted videos, according to comScore.

The minds behind YouTube are three 20-somethings: Steve Chen, Chad Hurley, and Jawed Karim. Even the three entrepreneurs are astounded at their success. *Time* says the reason for YouTube's success is its rare combination of being both "edgy and easy" for users.

The three men met at PayPal, now the Internet's leading online payment service. The three moved out and worked together on a new concept—a website where anyone could upload content that others could view. That was radical because until then only those who owned the website would provide the content.

Google bought YouTube in October 2006 for $1.65 billion, only 21 months after its founding. Hurley (standing) and Chen (sitting) in the left photo are now Google employees addressing issues such as making YouTube.com profitable through its advertising and avoiding potential lawsuits resulting from uploaded content that is copyrighted. Karim (in the right photo) left the company and is doing graduate work in computer science at Stanford University.

Where will this end? Go to YouTube.com and see for yourself!

marketing"—by putting you in the shoes of a marketing manager facing actual marketing opportunities and problems. The book also shows marketing's many applications and how it affects our lives. This knowledge should make you a better consumer, help you in your career, and enable you to be a more informed citizen.

Perhaps your future may involve doing sales and marketing for a large organization. Working for a well-known company—Apple, General Electric, Target, eBay—can be personally satisfying and financially rewarding, and you may gain special respect from your friends.

Small businesses also offer marketing careers. Small businesses are the source of the majority of new U.S. jobs. So you might become your own boss by being an entrepreneur and starting your own business. The Marketing Matters box describes the revolutionary impact three entrepreneurs in their 20s have had on the Internet—and perhaps on how you spend some of your free time.[3] The three entrepreneurs—Steve Chen, Chad Hurley, and Jawed Karim—founded YouTube, which has achieved tremendous success and is now part of Google. Not every start-up business achieves their spectacular success. In fact, more than half of new businesses fail within five years of their launch.

Marketing: Delivering Benefits to the Organization, Its Stakeholders, and Society

marketing
The activity for creating and delivering offerings that benefit the organization, its stakeholders, and society.

The American Marketing Association represents marketing professionals. Combining its 2004 and 2007 definitions, "**marketing** is the activity for creating, communicating, delivering and exchanging offerings that benefit the organization, its stakeholders and society at large."[4] This definition shows marketing to be a far broader activity than simply advertising or personal selling. It stresses the importance of delivering genuine benefits in the offerings of goods, services, and ideas marketed to customers. Also, note that the organization doing the marketing, the stakeholders affected (such as customers, employees, suppliers, and shareholders), and society should all benefit.

To serve both buyers and sellers, marketing seeks (1) to discover the needs and wants of prospective customers and (2) to satisfy them. These prospective customers include both individuals, buying for themselves and their households, and organizations that buy for their own use (such as manufacturers) or for resale (such as wholesalers and retailers). The key to achieving these two objectives is the idea of **exchange**, which is the trade of things of value between buyer and seller so that each is better off after the trade.[5]

exchange
Trade of things of value between buyer and seller so that each is better off

The Diverse Factors Influencing Marketing Activities

Although an organization's marketing activity focuses on assessing and satisfying consumer needs, countless other people, groups, and forces interact to shape the nature of its activities (Figure 1–2). Foremost is the organization itself, whose mission and objectives determine what business it is in and what goals it seeks. Within the organization, management is responsible for establishing these goals. The marketing department works closely with a network of other departments and employees to help provide the customer-satisfying products required for the organization to survive and prosper.

Figure 1–2 also shows the key people, groups, and forces outside the organization that influence its marketing activities. The marketing department is responsible for facilitating relationships, partnerships, and alliances with the organization's

FIGURE 1–2
A marketing department relates to many people, organizations, and forces. Note that the marketing department both *shapes* and *is shaped by* its relationship with these internal and external groups.

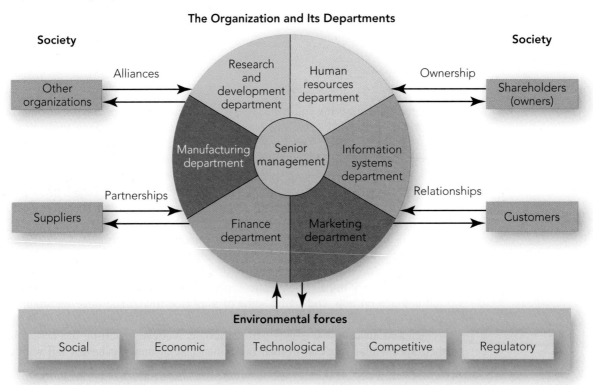

customers, its shareholders (or often representatives of groups served by a nonprofit organization), its suppliers, and other organizations. Environmental forces involving social, economic, technological, competitive, and regulatory considerations also shape an organization's marketing activities. Finally, an organization's marketing decisions are affected by and, in turn, often have an important impact on society as a whole. The organization must also strike a balance among the sometimes differing interests of these individuals and groups.

---

learning review

1. What is marketing?
2. Marketing focuses on _____ and _____ consumer needs.

HOW MARKETING DISCOVERS AND SATISFIES CONSUMER NEEDS

LO2

The importance of discovering and satisfying consumer needs is so critical to understanding marketing that we look at each of these two steps in detail next.

Discovering Consumer Needs

The first objective in marketing is discovering the needs of prospective customers. But these prospective customers may not always know or be able to describe what they need and want. When Apple built its first Apple II personal computer and started a new industry, consumers didn't really know what the benefits would be. So they had to be educated about how to use personal computers. Also, Bell, a U.S. bicycle helmet maker, listened to its customers, collected hundreds of their ideas, and put several into its new products.[6] This is where effective marketing research, the topic of Chapter 8, can help.

The Challenge: Meeting Consumer Needs with New Products
New-product experts generally estimate that up to 94 percent of the more than 33,000 new consumable products (food, beverage, health, beauty, and other household and pet products) introduced in the United States annually "don't succeed in the long run."[7] Robert M. McMath, who has studied more than 100,000 of these new-product launches, has two key suggestions: (1) focus on what the customer benefit is, and (2) learn from the past.[8]

The solution to preventing such product failures seems embarrassingly obvious. First, find out what consumers need and want. Second, produce what they need and want, and don't produce what they don't need and want. The four products shown on the next page illustrate just how difficult it is to achieve new-product success, a topic covered in more detail in Chapter 10.

Without reading further, think about the potential benefits to customers and possible "showstoppers"—factors that might doom the product—for each of the four products pictured. Some of the products may come out of your past, and others may be on your horizon. Here's a quick analysis of the four products, some with comments adapted from McMath:

- *Dr. Care Toothpaste.* As a result of extensive research, Dr. Care family toothpaste in its aerosol container was introduced more than two decades ago. The vanilla-mint-flavored product's benefits were advertised as being easy to use and sanitary. Pretend for a minute that you are five years old and left alone in the bathroom to brush your teeth using your Dr. Care toothpaste. Hmm! Apparently,

For these four products, identify (1) what benefits the product provides buyers and (2) what "showstoppers" might kill the product in the marketplace. Answers are discussed in the text.

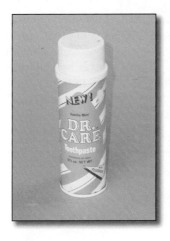

Vanilla-mint-flavored toothpaste in an aerosol container

Meat and cheese microwaveable sandwiches

Robotic floor washer

Reduced-carbohydrate cola with some sugar

surprised parents were not enthusiastic about the bathroom wall paintings by their future Rembrandts—a showstopper that doomed this creative product.[9]

- *Hot Pockets.* Introduced in 1983, these convenient meat and cheese microwaveable sandwiches are a favorite brand among students. More than 20 varieties have been introduced, from Hot Pockets Pizza Snacks to Hot Pockets Subs. A none-too-serious potential showstopper: Excessive ice crystals can form on the product due to variations in freezer temperatures; if this happens and the sandwich is thawed before eaten, it may not taste as good.[10]

- *iRobot's Scooba® robotic floor washer.* The Scooba robotic floor washer washes, scrubs, and dries a hard-surface floor in a single operation (question 1, Figure 1–1). At $299.99 the Scooba does a better job than a mop, which just spreads the dirt around. The thousands of Scoobas sold seem to refute the potential showstopper that it can't get into corners.[11]

- *Coca-Cola's C2.* In summer 2004, Coca-Cola spent $50 million to launch C2, a reduced-carb cola that still contained some sugar to add taste. The company's biggest new-product launch since Diet Coke two decades earlier, C2 was targeted to 20- to 40-year-olds wanting a sweeter cola while also watching the calories.

C2 was sometimes priced 60 percent higher at retail than Coke, a devastating concern to buyers. But the big showstopper: Many cola drinkers were disappointed in C2's taste, complaining it was flat or had an unpleasant aftertaste.[12]

Firms spend billions of dollars annually on marketing and technical research that significantly reduces, but doesn't eliminate, new-product failure. So meeting the changing needs of consumers is a continuing challenge for firms around the world.

Consumer Needs and Consumer Wants Should marketing try to satisfy consumer needs or consumer wants? The answer is both. Heated debates rage over this question, fueled by the definitions of needs and wants and the amount of freedom given to prospective customers to make their own buying decisions.

A *need* occurs when a person feels deprived of basic necessities such as food, clothing, and shelter. A *want* is a need that is shaped by a person's knowledge, culture, and personality. So if you feel hungry, you have developed a basic need and desire to eat something. Let's say you then want to eat an apple or a candy bar because, based on your past experience, you know these will satisfy your hunger need. Effective marketing, in the form of creating an awareness of good products at convenient locations, can clearly shape a person's wants.

Certainly, marketing tries to influence what we buy. A question then arises: At what point do we want government and society to step in to protect consumers? Most consumers would say they want government to protect us from harmful drugs and unsafe cars but not from candy bars and soft drinks. To protect college students, should government restrict their use of credit cards?[13] Such questions have no clear-cut answers, which is why legal and social issues are central to marketing. Because even psychologists and economists still debate the exact meanings of *need* and *want,* we shall use the terms interchangeably throughout the book.

As shown in the left side of Figure 1–3, discovering needs involves looking carefully at prospective customers, whether they are children buying M&Ms candy, college students buying highlighters, or firms buying Xerox photocopying machines. A principal activity of a firm's marketing department is to scrutinize its consumers to understand what they need and want and the forces that shape them.

market

People with desire and ability to buy a specific offering

What a Market Is Potential consumers make up a **market**, which is people with both the desire and the ability to buy a specific offering. All markets ultimately

FIGURE 1–3

Marketing seeks first to discover consumer needs through extensive research. It then seeks to satisfy those needs by successfully implementing a marketing program possessing the right combination of the marketing mix—the four Ps.

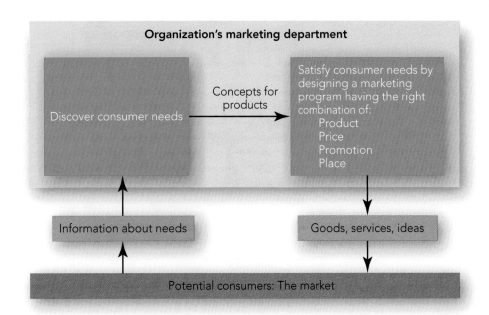

are people. Even when we say a firm bought a Xerox copier, we mean one or several people in the firm decided to buy it. People who are aware of their unmet needs may have the desire to buy the product, but that alone isn't sufficient. People must also have the ability to buy, such as the authority, time, and money. People may even "buy" an idea that results in an action, such as having their blood pressure checked annually or turning down their thermostat to save energy.

Satisfying Consumer Needs

Marketing doesn't stop with the discovery of consumer needs. Because the organization obviously can't satisfy all consumer needs, it must concentrate its efforts on certain needs of a specific group of potential consumers. This is the **target market**—one or more specific groups of potential consumers toward which an organization directs its marketing program.

The Four Ps: Controllable Marketing Mix Factors   Having selected its target market consumers, the firm must take steps to satisfy their needs, as shown in the right side of Figure 1–3. Someone in the organization's marketing department, often the marketing manager, must develop a complete marketing program to reach consumers by using a combination of four tools, often called "the four Ps"—a useful shorthand reference to them first published by Professor E. Jerome McCarthy:[14]

- *Product.* A good, service, or idea to satisfy the consumer's needs.
- *Price.* What is exchanged for the product.
- *Promotion.* A means of communication between the seller and buyer.
- *Place.* A means of getting the product to the consumer.

We'll define each of the four Ps more carefully later in the book, but for now it's important to remember that they are the elements of the **marketing mix**, the marketing manager's controllable factors—product, price, promotion, and place—that can be used to solve a marketing problem. For example, when a company puts a product on sale, it is changing one element of the marketing mix—namely, the price. The marketing mix elements are called controllable factors because they are under the control of the marketing department in an organization.

Costco and Starbucks provide customer value using two very different approaches. For their strategies, see the text.

The Uncontrollable, Environmental Forces   While marketers can generally control their marketing mix factors, other variables are mostly beyond their control (see Figure 1–2). These are the uncontrollable social, economic, technological, competitive, and regulatory forces—the **environmental forces** that affect the results of a marketing decision. Examples are what consumers themselves want and need, changing technology, the state of the economy in terms of whether it is expanding or contracting, actions that competitors take, and government restrictions. These forces may serve as accelerators or brakes on marketing, sometimes expanding an organization's marketing opportunities and other times restricting them.

environmental forces
Uncontrollable social, economic, technological, competitive, and regulatory forces

THE MARKETING PROGRAM: HOW CUSTOMER RELATIONSHIPS ARE BUILT

An organization's marketing program connects it with its customers. To clarify this link, we shall first discuss the critically important concepts of customer value, customer relationships, and relationship marketing, and then illustrate these concepts with 3M's marketing program for its new Post-it®products for students.

Customer Value and Customer Relationships

Intense competition in today's fast-paced domestic and global markets has caused massive restructuring of many American industries and businesses. American managers are seeking ways to achieve success in this new, more intense level of global competition.

This has prompted many successful U.S. firms to focus on "customer value." That firms gain loyal customers by providing unique value is the essence of successful marketing. What is new, however, is a more careful attempt at understanding how a firm's customers perceive value and then actually creating and delivering that value.[15] For our purposes, **customer value** is the unique combination of benefits received by targeted buyers that includes quality, convenience, on-time delivery, and both before-sale and after-sale service at a specific price. Loyal, satisfied customers are likely to repurchase more and therefore be more profitable.[16] Firms now actually try to place a dollar value on the purchases of loyal, satisfied customers during their lifetimes. For example, loyal Kleenex customers average 6.7 boxes a year, about $994 over 60 years in today's dollars (question 2, Figure 1–1).[17]

Research suggests that firms cannot succeed by being all things to all people. Instead, firms must find ways to build long-term customer relationships to provide unique value that they alone can deliver to targeted markets. Many successful firms have chosen to deliver outstanding customer value with one of three value strategies: best price, best product, or best service.

Companies such as Wal-Mart, Southwest Airlines, and Costco have all been successful offering consumers the best price. Other companies such as Starbucks, Nike, and Johnson & Johnson claim to provide the best products on the market. Finally, companies such as Lands' End and Home Depot deliver value by providing exceptional service.

customer value
Buyers' benefits including quality, convenience, on-time delivery, and before- and after-sale service at a specific price

Relationship Marketing and the Marketing Program

A firm achieves meaningful customer relationships by creating connections with its customers through careful coordination of the product, its price, the way it's promoted, and how it's placed.

Relationship Marketing: Easy to Understand, Hard to Do   The hallmark of developing and maintaining effective customer relationships is today called **relationship marketing**. Successful relationship marketing links an organization to its individual customers, employees, suppliers, and other partners for their mutual

relationship marketing
Linking the organization to its individual customers, employees, suppliers, and other partners for their mutual long-term benefit

long-term benefits. In terms of selling a product, relationship marketing involves a personal, ongoing relationship between the organization and its individual customers that begins before and continues after the sale.[18]

Huge manufacturers find this rigorous standard of relationship marketing difficult to achieve. Today's information technology, along with cutting-edge manufacturing and marketing processes, have led to tailoring goods or services to the tastes of individual customers in high volumes at a relatively low cost. So you can place an Internet order for all the components of an Apple computer and have it delivered in four or five days—in a configuration tailored to your unique wants. But with today's Internet purchases, you will probably have difficulty achieving the same personal, tender-loving-care connection that you once had with your own local computer store, bookstore, or other retailer.

The Marketing Program   Effective relationship marketing strategies help marketing managers discover what prospective customers need. As shown earlier in Figure 1–3, they must translate this information into concepts for products the firm might develop to satisfy these needs. These concepts must then be converted into a tangible **marketing program**—a plan that integrates the marketing mix to provide a good, service, or idea to prospective buyers. These consumers then react to the offering favorably (by buying) or unfavorably (by not buying), and the process is repeated. This process is continuous in an effective organization: Consumer needs trigger product concepts that are translated into actual products that stimulate further discovery of consumer needs.

> **marketing program**
> *Plan that integrates the marketing mix to provide a good, service, or idea to prospective buyers*

---

learning review

3. An organization can't satisfy the needs of all consumers, so it must focus on one or more subgroups, which are its _____.

4. What are the four marketing mix elements that make up the organization's marketing program?

5. What are environmental forces?

3M's Strategy and Marketing Program to Help Students Study

To see some specifics of an actual marketing program, let's return to our earlier example of 3M inventor David Windorski and his search for a way to help college students in their studying.

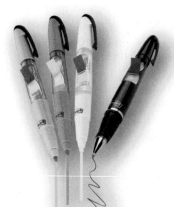

3M's initial product line of Post-it® Flag Highlighters and Post-it® Flag Pens includes variations in color and line widths.

Moving from Ideas to a Marketable Highlighter Product   After working on 15 or 20 wood and clay models, Windorski concluded he had to build a highlighter product that would dispense Post-it® Flags because the Post-it® Notes were simply too large to put inside the barrel of a highlighter.

Hundreds of the initial highlighter prototypes with Post-it® Flags inside were produced and given to students—and also office workers—to get their reactions. This research showed users wanted a convenient, reliable cover to protect the Post-it® Flags in the highlighter. Windorski's rotating cover for the Post-it® Flags was born.

Extending the Product Line   David Windorski also considered other related products. Many people in offices need immediate access to Post-it® Flags while writing with pens. Marketing research among office workers refined the design and showed the existence of a sizable market for a Post-it® Flag Pen.

MARKETING MIX ELEMENT	COLLEGE STUDENT SEGMENT	OFFICE WORKER SEGMENT	RATIONALE FOR MARKETING PROGRAM ACTIVITY
 Product strategy	Offer Post-it® Flag Highlighter to help college students in their studying	Offer Post-it® Flag Pen to help office workers in their day-to-day work activities	Listen carefully to the needs and wants of potential customer segments to use 3M technology to introduce a useful, innovative product
 Price strategy	Seek retail price of about $3.99 to $4.99 for single Post-it® Flag Highlighter or $5.99 to $7.99 for a three-pack	Seek retail price of about $3.99 to $4.99 for a single Post-it® Flag Pen; wholesale prices are less	Set prices that provide genuine value to the customer segment that is targeted
 Promotion strategy	Run limited promotion with a TV ad and some ads in college newspapers and then rely on student word-of-mouth messages	Run limited promotion among distributors to get them to stock the product	Increase awareness of potential users who have never heard of this new, innovative 3M product
Place strategy	Distribute Post-it® Flag Highlighters through college bookstores, office supply stores, and mass merchandisers	Distribute Post-it® Flag Pens through office wholesalers and retailers and mass merchandisers	Make it easy for prospective buyers to buy at convenient retail outlets (both products) or to get at work (Post-it® Flag Pens only)

FIGURE 1–4

Marketing programs for the launch of two Post-it® brand products targeted at two customer market segments.

The second generation of Post-it® Flag Highlighters

A Marketing Program for the Post-it® Flag Highlighter and Pen

After several years of research, development, and production engineering, 3M introduced its new products. Figure 1–4 outlines the strategies for each of the four marketing mix elements in 3M's program to market its Post-it® Flag Highlighters and Post-it® Flag Pens. Although similar, we can compare the marketing program for each of the two products:

- *Post-it® Flag Highlighter.* The target market is mainly college students, so 3M's initial challenge was to build student awareness of a product that they didn't know existed. The company used a mix of print ads in college newspapers and a TV ad, and then relied on word-of-mouth advertising—students telling their friends how great the product is. Gaining distribution in college bookstores and having attractive packaging was also critical. Plus, 3M charged a price to distributors that it hoped would give a reasonable bookstore price to students and an acceptable profit to distributors and 3M.
- *Post-it® Flag Pen.* The primary target market is people working in offices. But some students are potential customers, so 3M gained distribution in some college bookstores of Post-it® Flag Pens, too. But the Post-it® Flag Pens are mainly business products—bought by the purchasing department in an organization and stocked as office supplies for employees to use. So the marketing program in Figure 1–4 reflects the different distribution or "place" strategies for the two products.

How did these new products do for 3M in the marketplace? They have done so well that 3M bestowed a prestigious award on David Windorski and his team. Their success has also led Windorski to design a second generation of Post-it® Flag Highlighters and Pens *without* the rotating cover that makes it easier to insert replacement flags.

The new tapered design is also easier for students to hold and use. Note in the photo (on the previous page) of the new, second-generation Post-it® Flag Highlighters how prominently the "2-in-1" benefit is displayed in the packaging.

In what must be the answer to every almost inventor's dream, Oprah Winfrey flew David Windorski to Chicago to appear on her TV show and thank him in person. She told Windorski and her audience that the Post-it® Flag Highlighter is changing the way she does things at home and at work—especially in going through potential books she might recommend for her book club. "David, I know you never thought this would happen when you were in your 3M lab . . . but I want you to take a bow before America for the invention of this . . . (highlighter). It's the most incredible invention," she said.[19]

HOW MARKETING BECAME SO IMPORTANT

To understand why marketing is a driving force in the modern global economy, let us look at the (1) evolution of the market orientation, (2) ethics and social responsibility in marketing, and (3) breadth and depth of marketing activities.

Evolution of the Market Orientation

Many American manufacturers have experienced four distinct stages in the life of their firms.[20] The first stage, the *production era,* covers the early years of the United States up until the 1920s. Goods were scarce and buyers were willing to accept virtually any goods that were available and make do with them.[21] In the *sales era* from the 1920s to the 1960s, manufacturers found they could produce more goods than buyers could consume. Competition grew. Firms hired more salespeople to find new buyers. This sales era continued into the 1960s for many American firms.

In the 1960s, marketing became the motivating force among many American firms and the *marketing concept era* dawned. The **marketing concept** is the idea that an organization should (1) strive to satisfy the needs of consumers (2) while also trying to achieve the organization's goals. General Electric probably launched the marketing concept and its focus on consumers when its 1952 annual report stated: "The concept introduces . . . marketing . . . at the beginning rather than the end of the production cycle and integrates marketing into each phase of the business."[22]

Firms such as General Electric, Marriott, and Toyota have achieved great success by putting huge effort into implementing the marketing concept, giving their firms what has been called a *market orientation.* An organization that has a **market orientation** focuses its efforts on (1) continuously collecting information about customers' needs, (2) sharing this information across departments, and (3) using it to create customer value.[23] The result is today's *customer relationship era*, in which firms seek continuously to satisfy the high expectations of customers.

This focus on customers has led to *customer relationship management (CRM),* the process of identifying prospective buyers, understanding them intimately, and developing favorable long-term perceptions of the organization and its offerings so that buyers will choose them in the marketplace. This requires the commitment of managers and employees throughout the organization.[24]

Ethics and Social Responsibility: Balancing Interests

Today, the standards of marketing practice have shifted from an emphasis on producers' interests to consumers' interests. Organizations increasingly consider the social and environmental consequences of their actions for all parties.

marketing concept
Idea that an organization should strive to satisfy the needs of consumers while also trying to achieve the organization's goals

market orientation
Focusing organizational efforts to collect and use information about customers' needs to create customer value

Ethics Many marketing issues are not specifically addressed by existing laws and regulations. Should information about a firm's customers be sold to other organizations? Should consumers be on their own to assess the safety of a product? These questions raise difficult ethical issues. Many companies, industries, and professional associations have developed codes of ethics to assist managers.

Social Responsibility While many ethical issues involve only the buyer and seller, others involve society as a whole. A manufacturer dumping toxic wastes into streams has an impact on the environment and society. This example illustrates the issue of social responsibility, the idea that individuals and organizations are accountable to a larger society. The well-being of society at large should be recognized in an organization's marketing decisions. In fact, some marketing experts stress the **societal marketing concept**, the view that an organization should discover and satisfy the needs of its consumers in a way that also provides for society's well-being.[25] For example, Scotchbrite Never Rust Wool Soap Pads from 3M—which are made from recycled plastic bottles—are more expensive than competitors' (SOS and Brillo) but superior because they don't rust or scratch (question 3, Figure 1–1).

The Breadth and Depth of Marketing

Marketing today affects every person and organization. To understand this, let's analyze (1) who markets, (2) what is marketed, (3) who buys and uses what is marketed, (4) who benefits from these marketing activities, and (5) how they benefit.

Who Markets? Every organization markets. It's obvious that business firms involved in manufacturing (Heinz), retailing (Target), and providing services (Marriott) market their offerings. And nonprofit organizations such as your local hospital, your college, places (cities, states, countries), and even special causes (Race for the Cure) also engage in marketing. Finally, individuals such as political candidates often use marketing to gain voter attention and preference.[26]

What Is Marketed? Goods, services, and even ideas are marketed. *Goods* are physical objects such as iron ore, apples, or a computer. *Services* are intangible items such as airline trips, financial advice, or telephone calls. *Ideas* are intangible concepts and thoughts about products, actions, or causes.

In this ad, the Nature Conservancy markets its cause—protecting the environment—by superimposing a 1912 photo on the same location today.

Ideas are most often marketed by nonprofit organizations or the government. For example, your local library may market the idea of developing improved reading skills, and the Nature Conservancy markets the cause of protecting the environment. Charities market the idea that it's worthwhile for you to donate your time or money, and orchestras market fine music. States like Arizona market themselves as attractive places for tourists to visit.

Who Buys and Uses What Is Marketed?   Both individuals and organizations buy and use goods and services that are marketed. **Ultimate consumers** are the people—whether 80 years or eight months old—who use the goods and services purchased for a household. In contrast, **organizational buyers** are those manufacturers, wholesalers, retailers, and government agencies that buy goods and services for their own use or for resale. Although the terms *consumers, buyers,* and *customers* are sometimes used for both ultimate consumers and organizations, there is no consistency on this. In this book you will be able to tell from the example whether the buyers are ultimate consumers, organizations, or both.

ultimate consumers
People who use the goods and services purchased for a household

organizational buyers
Manufacturers, wholesalers, retailers, and government agencies that buy goods and services for their own use or for resale

Who Benefits?   In our free-enterprise society there are three specific groups that benefit from effective marketing: consumers who buy, organizations that sell, and society as a whole. True competition between products and services in the marketplace ensures that consumers can find value from the best products, the lowest prices, or exceptional service. Providing choices leads to the consumer satisfaction and quality of life that we have come to expect from our economic system.

Organizations that provide need-satisfying products with effective marketing programs—for example, Target, IBM, and Avon—have blossomed. But competition creates problems for ineffective competitors, such as eToys and hundreds of other dot-com businesses that failed in the last few years.

Finally, effective marketing benefits society.[27] It enhances competition, which, in turn, both improves the quality of products and services and lowers their prices. This makes countries more competitive in world markets and provides jobs and a higher standard of living for their citizens.

utility
Benefits or customer value received by users of the product

How Do Consumers Benefit?   Marketing creates **utility**, the benefits or customer value received by users of the product. This utility is the result of the marketing exchange process. There are four different utilities: form, place, time, and possession. The production of the good or service constitutes *form utility*. *Place utility* means having the offering available where consumers need it, whereas *time utility* means having it available when needed. *Possession utility* is the value of making an item easy to purchase through the provision of credit cards or financial arrangements. Marketing creates its utilities by bridging space (place utility) and hours (time utility) to provide products (form utility) for consumers to own and use (possession utility).

learning review

6. What are the two key characteristics of the marketing concept?

7. What is the difference between ultimate consumers and organizational buyers?

LEARNING OBJECTIVES REVIEW

LO1   *Define marketing and identify the diverse factors influencing marketing activities.*
Marketing is an organizational function and a set of processes for creating, communicating, and delivering value to customers and for managing customer relationships in ways that benefit the organization and its stakeholders. This definition relates to two primary goals of marketing: (*a*) assessing the needs of prospective customers and (*b*) satisfying them. Achieving these

two goals also involves the four marketing mix factors largely controlled by the organization and the five environmental forces that are generally outside its control.

LO2 *Explain how marketing discovers and satisfies consumer needs.*

The first objective in marketing is discovering the needs and wants of consumers who are prospective buyers and customers. This is not an easy task because consumers may not always know or be able to describe what they need and want. A need occurs when a person feels deprived of basic necessities such as food, clothing, and shelter. A want is a need that is shaped by a person's knowledge, culture, and personality. Effective marketing can clearly shape a person's wants and tries to influence what we buy. The second objective in marketing is satisfying the needs of targeted consumers. Because an organization obviously can't satisfy all consumer needs, it must concentrate its efforts on certain needs of a specific group of potential consumers or target market—one or more specific groups of potential consumers toward which an organization directs its marketing program. Having selected its target market consumers, the organization then takes action to satisfy their needs by developing a unique marketing program to reach them.

LO3 *Distinguish between marketing mix factors and environmental forces.*

Four elements in a marketing program designed to satisfy customer needs are product, price, promotion, and place. These elements are called the marketing mix, the four Ps, or the controllable variables because they are under the general control of the marketing department. Environmental forces, also called

uncontrollable variables, are largely beyond the organization's control. These include social, economic, technological, competitive, and regulatory forces.

LO4 *Explain how organizations build strong customer relationships and customer value through marketing.*

The essence of successful marketing is to provide sufficient value to gain loyal, long-term customers. Customer value is the unique combination of benefits received by targeted buyers that usually includes quality, price, convenience, on-time delivery, and both before-sale and after-sale service. Marketers do this by using one of three value strategies: best price, best product, or best service.

LO5 *Describe how today's customer relationship era differs from prior eras oriented to production and selling.*

U.S. business history is divided into four periods: the production era, the sales era, the marketing concept era, and the current customer relationship era. The production era covers the period to the 1920s when buyers were willing to accept virtually any goods that were available. The central notion was that products would sell themselves. The sales era lasted from the 1920s to the 1960s. Manufacturers found they could produce more goods than buyers could consume, and competition grew, so the solution was to hire more salespeople to find new buyers. In the 1960s, the marketing concept era dawned, when organizations began to integrate marketing into each phase of the business. In today's customer relationship era, organizations focus their efforts on (*a*) continuously collecting information about customers' needs, (*b*) sharing this information across departments, and (*c*) using it to create customer value.

FOCUSING ON KEY TERMS

customer value p. 11
environmental forces p. 11
exchange p. 6
market p. 9
market orientation p. 14

marketing p. 6
marketing concept p. 14
marketing mix p. 10
marketing program p. 12
organizational buyers p. 16

relationship marketing p. 11
societal marketing concept p. 15
target market p. 10
ultimate consumers p. 16
utility p. 16

APPLYING MARKETING KNOWLEDGE

1 What consumer wants (or benefits) are met by the following products or services? (*a*) Carnation Instant Breakfast, (*b*) Adidas running shoes, (*c*) Hertz Rent-A-Car, and (*d*) television home shopping programs.

2 Each of the four products, services, or programs in question 1 has substitutes. Respective examples are (*a*) a ham and egg breakfast, (*b*) regular tennis shoes, (*c*) taking a bus, and (*d*) a department store. What consumer benefits might these substitutes have in each case that some consumers might value more highly than those mentioned in question 1?

3 What are the characteristics (e.g., age, income, education) of the target market customers for the following products or services? (*a*) *National Geographic* magazine, (*b*) *Wired* magazine, (*c*) New York Giants football team, and (*d*) the U.S. Open tennis tournament.

4 A college in a metropolitan area wishes to increase its evening-school offerings of business-related courses such as marketing, accounting, finance, and management. Who are the target market customers (students) for these courses?

5 What actions involving the four marketing mix elements might be used to reach the target market in question 4?

6 What environmental forces (uncontrollable variables) must the college in question 4 consider in designing its marketing program?

7 Does a firm have the right to "create" wants and try to persuade consumers to buy goods and services they didn't know about earlier? What are examples of "good" and "bad" want creation? Who should decide what is good and bad?

If your instructor assigns a marketing plan for your class, don't make a face and complain about the work—for two special reasons. First, you will get insights into trying to actually "do marketing" that often go beyond what you can get by simply reading the textbook. Second, thousands of graduating students every year get their first job by showing prospective employers a "portfolio" of samples of their written work from college—often a marketing plan if they have one. This can work for you.

This "Building Your Marketing Plan" section at the end of each chapter suggests ways to improve and focus your marketing plan. You will use the sample marketing plan in Appendix A (following Chapter 2) as a guide, and this section after each chapter will help you apply those Appendix A ideas to your own marketing plan.

The first step in writing a good marketing plan is to have a business or product that enthuses you and for which you can get detailed information, so you can avoid glittering generalities. We offer these additional bits of advice in selecting a topic:

- *Do* pick a topic that has personal interest for you—a family business, a business or product you or a friend might want to launch, or a student organization needing marketing help.
- *Do not* pick a topic that is so large it can't be covered adequately or so abstract it will lack specifics.

1 Now to get you started on your marketing plan, list four or five possible topics and compare these with the criteria your instructor suggests and those shown above. Think hard, because your decision will be with you all term and may influence the quality of the resulting marketing plan you show to a prospective employer.

2 When you have selected your marketing plan topic, whether the plan is for an actual business, a possible business, or a student organization, write the "company description" in your plan, as shown in Appendix A.

"I didn't go out to students and ask, 'What are your needs, or what are your wants?'" 3M inventor David Windorski explains to a class of college students. "And even if I did ask, they probably wouldn't say, 'Put flags inside a highlighter.'"

So Windorski turned the classic textbook approach to marketing on its head.

That classic approach—as you saw earlier in Chapter 1—says to start with needs and wants of potential customers and then develop the product. But sometimes new-product development runs in the opposite direction: Start with a new product idea—such as personal computers—and then see if there is a market. This is really what Windorski did, using a lot of marketing research along the way after he developed the concept of the Post-it® Flag Highlighter.

EARLY MARKETING RESEARCH

During this new-product development process, Windorski and 3M did a lot of marketing research on students. Some was unconventional, while other research was quite traditional. For example, students were asked to dump the contents of their backpacks on the table and to explain what they carried around and then to react to some early highlighter models. Also, several times six or seven students were interviewed together and observed by 3M researchers from behind a one-way mirror—the focus group technique discussed later in Chapter 8. Other students were interviewed individually. And when early working models of the Post-it® Flag Highlighter finally existed, several hundred were produced and given to students to use for a month. Their reactions were captured on a questionnaire.

THE NEW PRODUCT LAUNCH

After the initial marketing research and dozens of technical tests in 3M laboratories, David Windorski's new 3M highlighter product was ready to be manufactured and marketed.

Here's a snapshot of the pre-launch issues that were solved before the product could be introduced:

- *Technical issues.* Can we generate a computer-aided database for injection molded parts? What tolerances do we need? The 3M highlighter is really a technological marvel. For the parts on the highlighter to work, tolerances must be several thousandths of an inch—less than the thickness of a paper.
- *Manufacturing issues.* Where should the product be manufactured? 3M chose a company outside the U.S., which necessitated precise translations of critical technical specifications. Windorski spent time in the factory working with engineers and manufacturing specialists there to ensure that 3M's precise production standards would be achieved.
- *Product issues.* What should the brand name be for the new highlighter product? Marketing research and many meetings gave the answer: "The Post-it® Flag Highlighter." How many to a package? What color(s)? What should the packaging look like that can (1) display the product well at retail and (2) communicate its points of difference effectively?

- *Price issues.* With many competing highlighters, what should the price be for 3M's premium highlighter that will provide 3M adequate profit? Should the suggested retail price be the same in college bookstores, mass merchandisers (Wal-Mart, Target), and office supply stores (Office Max, Office Depot)?
- *Promotion issues.* How can 3M tell students the product exists? Might office workers want it and use it? Should there be print ads, TV ads, and point-of-sale displays explaining the product?
- *Place (distribution) issues.* With the limited shelf space in college bookstores and other outlets, how can 3M convince retailers to stock its new product?

THE MARKETING PROGRAM TODAY AND TOMORROW

3M has discovered that its highlighter has turned out to be more popular than it expected. 3M often hears from end users how much they like the product.

So what can 3M do for an encore to build on the initial success? This involves taking great care to introduce new product extensions to attract new customers while still retaining its solid foundation of loyal existing customers. Also, 3M's products have to appeal not only to the ultimate consumers but also to retailers who want new items to display in high-traffic areas.

Product and packaging decisions for the Post-it® Flag Highlighter reflect this innovative focus. As to packaging, it's critical that it (1) communicate the 2-products-in-1 idea, (2) be attractive, and (3) achieve both goals with the fewest words.

At 3M, promotion budgets are limited because it relies heavily on its technology for a competitive advantage. This also applies to the Post-it® Flag Highlighter. So you probably have never seen a print or TV ad for it. Yet potential student buyers, the product's main target market, must be made aware that it exists. So 3M searches continually for simple, effective promotions to alert students about this product.

Great technology is meaningless unless the product is available where potential buyers can purchase it. Unlike college bookstores that exist largely to serve students, mass merchandisers and office supply stores track, measure, and seek to maximize the profit of every square foot of selling space. So 3M must convince these retail chains that selling space devoted to its highlighter line will be more profitable than for stocking competing products. The challenge for 3M: Finding ways to make the Post-it® Flag Highlighter prominent on shelves of college bookstores and retail chains.

If the Post-it® Flag Highlighter is doing well in the U.S., why not try to sell it around the world? But even here 3M faces critical questions: Which countries will be the best markets? What highlighter colors and packaging works best in each country? How do we physically get the product to these markets in a timely and cost-efficient basis?

Questions

1 (*a*) How did 3M's David Windorski get ideas from college students to help him in designing the final commercial version of the Post-it® Flag Highlighter? (*b*) How were these ideas important to the success of the product?
2 What (*a*) special advantages and (*b*) potential problems did 3M have in introducing a new highlighter-with-flags product for college students in 2004?
3 Visit your college bookstore before you answer. (*a*) Where would you display the Post-it® Flag Highlighter in a college bookstore, and (*b*) how can the display increase student awareness of the product?
4 In what ways might 3M try to promote its Post-it® Flag Highlighter and make students more aware of the product?
5 What are (*a*) the special opportunities and (*b*) potential challenges for 3M in taking its Post-it® Flag Highlighter into international markets? (*c*) On which countries should 3M focus its marketing efforts?

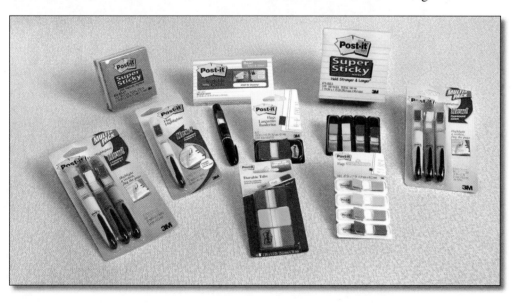

 **Our Company**

▷ About Us

▷ Our Mission

▷ Contact Us

▷ Factory Tours

▷ International

▷ Press Center

▷ Jobs at Ben & Jerry's

▷ FAQ's

▷ Research Library

Our Mission Statement

Ben & Jerry's is founded on and dedicated to a sustainable corporate concept of linked prosperity. Our mission consists of 3 interrelated parts::

Product Mission
To make, distribute & sell the finest quality all natural ice cream & euphoric concoctions with a continued commitment to incorporating wholesome, natural ingredients and promoting business practices that respect the Earth and the Environment.

Economic Mission
To operate the Company on a sustainable financial basis of profitable growth, increasing value for our stakeholders & expanding opportunities for development and career growth for our employees.

Social Mission
To operate the company in a way that actively recognizes the central role that business plays in society by initiating innovative ways to improve the quality of life locally, nationally & internationally.

Learn more! check out our Social Mission News or Our Environment

2

Developing Successful Marketing and Organizational Strategies

LEARNING OBJECTIVES

After reading this chapter you should be able to:

LO1 Describe the core values, mission, organizational culture, business, and goals of an organization.

LO2 Explain why managers use marketing dashboards and marketing metrics to evaluate a marketing program.

LO3 Discuss how an organization assesses where it is now and seeks to be in the future.

LO4 Explain the three steps of the planning phase of the strategic marketing process.

LO5 Describe the four components of the implementation phase of the strategic marketing process.

LO6 Discuss the two aspects of the evaluation phase of the strategic marketing process.

CAN AN "A" IN AN ICE CREAM MAKING COURSE *REALLY* BECOME A BUSINESS?

Here's what the two founding entrepreneurs who aced their $5 college correspondence course in ice cream making and their organization are doing today:

- They buy their milk and cream from one dairy cooperative whose members guarantee the supplies are bovine growth-hormone free.

- They launched several Fair Trade Certified™ flavors to support small-scale family farms and their workers in the developing world through fair prices and eco-friendly farming practices.

- Their PartnerShop, Scoopers Making Change, and Cones 2 Career programs help nonprofit organizations give jobs to and train at-risk youth.

- Their new-product lines include the John Lennon–inspired "Imagine Whirled Peace™" ice cream pint and milk shake flavor in addition to frozen yogurts, sorbets, smoothies, cakes, and waffle cones.

This creative, funky business is Ben & Jerry's Homemade Holdings Inc., which links its mission statement to social causes designed to improve humanity, as shown on the opposite page.

In 1978, long-time friends Ben Cohen and Jerry Greenfield headed north to Vermont to start an ice cream parlor in a renovated gas station. Buoyed with enthusiasm, $12,000 in borrowed and saved money, and ideas from a $5 Penn State correspondence course in ice cream making, Ben and Jerry were off and scooping.[1] Today, Ben & Jerry's is owned by Unilever and is number 2 in market share (16.0 percent) behind Nestlé (17.5 percent) in the $59 billion global ice cream industry—one that is expected to reach $65 billion by 2010.[2] While customers love Cherry Garcia and its other rich premium ice cream flavors, many buy its products to support Ben & Jerry's social mission.

Chapter 2 describes how organizations such as Ben & Jerry's, Medtronic, and Kodak set goals to give an overall direction that is linked to their organizational and marketing strategies. The marketing department of an organization converts these strategies into plans that must be implemented. The results are then evaluated to assess the degree to which they accomplish the organization's goals, consistent with its core values and mission.

TODAY'S ORGANIZATIONS

In today's visionary organizations, it is important to recognize how strategy arises based on their foundations, directions, plans, and structures.

Strategy and Visionary Organizations

An organization develops offerings to accomplish its goals that benefit both it and its customers. An *organization* is a legal entity of people who share a common mission, which motivates it to develop *offerings* (goods, services, or ideas) that create value for both the organization and its customers.[3] Organizations that develop similar offerings, when grouped together, create an *industry,* such as the ice cream industry.[4] An organization must have a clear understanding of the industry within which it competes. Today's organizations can be divided into business firms and nonprofit organizations.

A *business firm* is a privately owned organization that serves its customers in order to earn a profit so that it can survive.[5] **Profit** is the money left after a business firm's total expenses are subtracted from its total revenues or sales and is the reward for the risk it undertakes in marketing its offerings. A *nonprofit organization* is a nongovernmental organization that serves its customers but does not have profit as an organizational goal. Instead, its goals may be operational efficiency or client satisfaction. Examples include the charities and farm cooperatives affiliated with Ben & Jerry's. For simplicity, the terms *firm, company,* and *organization* are used interchangeably to cover both business and nonprofit entities.

A firm has limited human, financial, technological, and other resources to market its offerings—it can't be all things to all people! Therefore, every firm develops strategies to focus and direct its efforts to accomplish its goals. **Strategy** is an organization's long-term course of action designed to deliver a unique customer experience while achieving its goals.[6] Whether explicitly or implicitly, all organizations set a strategic direction.

Successful organizations must be visionary—they must both anticipate future events and respond quickly and effectively to them. This requires a visionary organization to specify its foundation (why), set a direction (what), and formulate strategies (how), as shown in Figure 2–1.[7]

Organizational Foundation

An organization's foundation is its philosophical reason for being—why it exists—and rarely changes. Successful visionary organizations use this foundation to guide and inspire their employees through three elements: core values, mission, and organizational culture.

Core Values An organization's **core values** are the fundamental, passionate, and enduring principles that guide its conduct over time.[8] A firm's founders

profit
Reward to a business firm for the risk it undertakes in marketing its offerings

strategy
An organization's long-term course of action that delivers a unique customer experience while achieving its goals

core values
The fundamental, passionate, and enduring principles that guide an organization

FIGURE 2–1
Today's visionary organizations use key elements to (1) establish a foundation and (2) set a direction using (3) strategies that enable them to develop and market their offerings successfully.

Organizational foundation (why)	Organizational direction (what)	Organizational strategies (how)

• Core values
• Mission (vision)
• Organizational culture
	• Business
	• Goals (objectives)
	  ○ Long-term
	  ○ Short-term
		• By level
		  ○ Corporate
		  ○ SBU
		  ○ Functional
		• By offering
		  ○ Product
		  ○ Service
		  ○ Idea

+ ... =

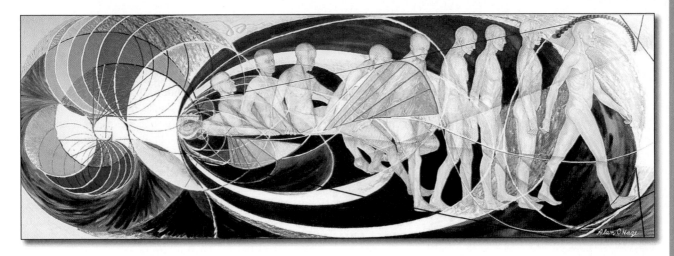

People see this "rising figure" mural in the headquarters of a world-class corporation. What does it signify? What does it say to employees? To others? For some insights and why it is important, see the text.

or senior management develop these core values, which are consistent with their essential beliefs and character.[9] They capture the firm's heart and soul and serve to inspire and motivate its *stakeholders*—employees, shareholders, board of directors, suppliers, distributors, creditors, unions, government, local communities, and customers. Core values also are timeless and should not change due to short-term financial, operational, or strategic concerns. Finally, core values guide the organization's conduct. To be effective, an organization's core values must be communicated to and supported by its top management and employees; if not, they are just hollow words.[10]

mission

A statement or vision of an organization's function in society

Mission By understanding its core values, an organization can define its **mission**, a statement of the organization's function in society, often identifying its customers, markets, products, and technologies. A *mission statement* or *vision* (terms used interchangeably in this textbook) should be clear, concise, meaningful, inspirational, and long-term.[11]

What is the best-known mission statement in America? It's:

> To explore strange new worlds, to seek out new life and new civilizations, to boldly go where no one has gone before.

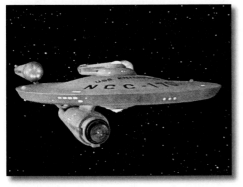

To discover the mission statement in America for this starship, and who it has affected, see the text.

This is the mission statement from the *Star Trek* television series, which has inspired many NASA astronauts and inventors of today's taken-for-granted technologies (personal computers, cellular phones, and so on). Recently, organizations have added a social element to their mission statements to reflect moral ideals.[12] This is what Ben & Jerry's social mission statement is all about, as shown in the chapter-opening example.

organizational culture

Set of values, ideas, attitudes, and behavioral norms that is learned and shared among the members of an organization

Organizational Culture An organization must connect with all of its stakeholders. Thus, an important corporate-level marketing function is communicating its core values and mission to them. Medtronic has a "rising figure" wall mural at its headquarters. The firm also presents every new employee with a medallion depicting this "rising figure" on one side and the company's mission statement on the other. And each December, several patients describe how Medtronic has changed their lives.[13] These activities send clear messages to employees and other stakeholders about Medtronic's **organizational culture**, the set of values, ideas, attitudes, and norms of behavior that is learned and shared among the members of an organization.

Organizational Direction

As shown in Figure 2–1, the organization's foundation enables it to set a direction in terms of (1) the "business" it is in and (2) its specific goals.

business

The underlying industry or market sector of an organization's offering

Business   A **business** describes the clear, broad, underlying industry or market sector of an organization's offering. To help define its business, an organization looks at the set of organizations that sell similar offerings—those that are in direct competition with each other—such as "the ice cream business." The organization can then begin to answer the questions, "What do we do?" or "What business are we in?"

In his famous "Marketing Myopia" article, Theodore Levitt argues that senior managers of 20th century American railroads defined their business too narrowly, proclaiming, "We are in the railroad business!" This myopic focus caused these firms to lose sight of who their customers were and what they needed. Thus, railroads only saw other railroads as direct competitors and failed to develop strategies to compete with airlines, barges, pipelines, and trucks—firms whose offerings carry both goods and people. As a result, many railroads merged or went bankrupt. Railroads would have fared better if they had realized they were in "the transportation business."[14]

In the first half of the 20th century, what "business" did railroads believe they were in? The text reveals their disastrous error.

goals (objectives)

Targets of performance to be achieved, often by a specific time

Goals   **Goals** or **objectives** (terms used interchangeably in the textbook) are statements of an accomplishment of a task to be achieved, often by a specific time. For example, Kodak may have the goal of being the top seller of digital cameras by 2010. Goals convert an organization's mission and business into long- and short-term performance targets to measure how well it is doing (Figure 2–1).

Business firms can pursue several different types of goals:

market share

Ratio of a firm's sales to the total sales of all firms in the industry

- *Profit.* Most firms seek to maximize profits—to get as high a financial return on their investments (ROI) as possible.
- *Sales* (dollars or units). If profits are acceptable, a firm may elect to maintain or increase its sales even though profits may not be maximized.
- *Market share.* **Market share** is the ratio of sales revenue of the firm to the total sales revenue of all firms in the industry, including the firm itself. A firm may choose to maintain or increase its market share, sometimes at the expense of greater profits if industry status or prestige is at stake.
- *Quality.* A firm may offer the highest quality, as Medtronic does with its implantable medical devices.
- *Customer satisfaction.* Customers are the reason the organization exists, so their perceptions and actions are of vital importance. Satisfaction can be measured with surveys or by the number of customer complaints it receives.
- *Employee welfare.* A firm may recognize the critical importance of its employees by stating its goal of providing them with good employment opportunities and working conditions.
- *Social responsibility.* Firms may seek to balance the conflicting goals of its stakeholders to promote their overall welfare, even at the expense of profits.

Nonprofit organizations (such as museums and hospitals) also have goals, such as to serve consumers as efficiently as possible. Similarly, government agencies set goals that seek to serve the public good.

learning review

1. What is the difference between a business firm and a nonprofit organization?

2. What is the meaning of an organization's mission?

3. What are examples of an organization's goals?

FIGURE 2–2
An effective marketing dashboard, like this one of Oracle's, helps managers assess a business situation at a glance.

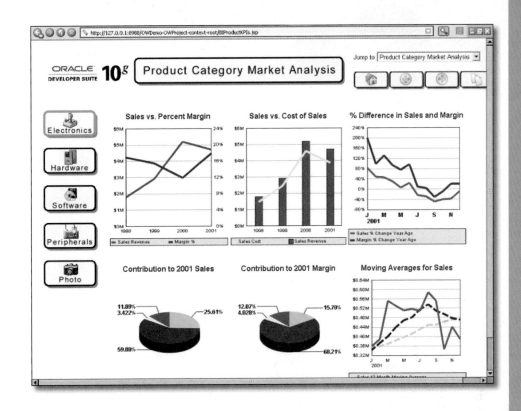

Tracking Strategic Directions with Marketing Dashboards

Although marketing managers can set strategic directions for their organizations, how do they know if they are making progress in getting there? One answer is using marketing dashboards.

marketing dashboard
The visual display of essential marketing information

Car Dashboards and Marketing Dashboards A **marketing dashboard** is the visual display of the essential information related to achieving a marketing objective.[15] Often, it is an Internet-based display with real-time information and active hyperlinks to provide further detail. An example is when a chief marketing officer wants to see daily what the effect of a new TV advertising campaign is on a product's sales.

The idea of a marketing dashboard really comes from that of a car's dashboard. On a car's dashboard we glance at the fuel gauge and take action when our gas is getting low. With a marketing dashboard, a marketing manager glances at a graph or table and makes a decision whether to take action or to analyze the problem further.[16]

marketing metric
A measure of the value or trend of a marketing activity or result

Dashboards, Metrics, and Plans Oracle's marketing dashboard in Figure 2–2 shows graphic displays of key performance measures of a product category such as sales versus cost of sales.[17] Each variable in a marketing dashboard is a **marketing metric**, which is a measure of the quantitative value or trend of a marketing activity or result.[18] The choice of which marketing metrics to display is critical for a busy marketing manager, who can be overwhelmed with too much information.

Dashboard designers take great care to show graphs and tables in easy-to-understand formats to enable clear interpretation at a glance.[19] The Oracle marketing dashboard, with several marketing metrics presented on the screen, and the Using Marketing Dashboards box on the next page are examples. The three-step "challenge-findings-action" format in the Using Marketing Dashboards box for Ben & Jerry's is one used throughout the textbook. This format stresses the importance of using

Using Marketing Dashboards

How Well Is Ben & Jerry's Doing?

As the marketing manager for Ben & Jerry's, you have been asked to provide a snapshot of the firm's total super premium ice cream product line performance for the United States. You choose the following marketing metrics: dollar sales and dollar market share.

Your Challenge Information Resources, Inc. (IRI), provides scanner data from grocery stores and other retailers. It has just sent you a report showing that the total ice cream sales for 2007 were $25 billion. Of that total, 5 percent or $1.25 billion (0.05 × $25 billion) comprises the super premium category—the segment of the market that Ben & Jerry's competes in. Internal company data show you that Ben & Jerry's sold 50 million units at an average price of $5.00 per unit in 2007.

Your Findings Each of the metrics you chose (dollar sales and dollar market share) are goals that firms like Ben & Jerry's use to measure performance. They can be calculated using simple formulas and displayed on the Ben & Jerry's marketing dashboard as follows:

Dollar sales ($) = Average price × Quantity sold

$\qquad$ = $5.00 × 50 million units

$\qquad$ = $250 million

$$\text{Dollar market share (\%)} = \frac{\text{Ben \& Jerry's sales (\$)}}{\text{Total industry sales (\$)}}$$

$$= \frac{\$250 \text{ million}}{\$1.25 \text{ billion}}$$

$$= 0.20 \text{ or } 20\%$$

Your dashboard displays show that from 2006 to 2007 dollar sales increased from $240 million to $250 million and that dollar market share grew from 18.4 to 20.0 percent.

Ben & Jerry's Dollar Sales

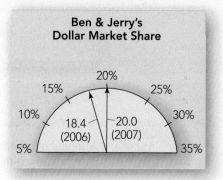

Ben & Jerry's Dollar Market Share

Your Action The results need to be compared with the goals established for these metrics. In addition, they should be compared with previous years' results to see if the trends are increasing, flat, or decreasing. NOTE: Marketers also find it useful to calculate market share based on the number of units sold, if data are available.

marketing dashboards and the metrics contained within them to produce effective marketing strategy and program actions. The Ben & Jerry's dashboard shows that both its dollar sales and dollar market share grew from 2006 to 2007.

Most organizations tie the marketing metrics they track in their marketing dashboards to the quantitative objectives established in their **marketing plan**, which is a road map for the marketing activities of an organization for a specified future time period, such as one year or five years. The planning phase of the strategic marketing process (discussed later in this chapter) usually results in a marketing plan that sets the direction for the marketing activities of an organization.

Appendix A at the end of this chapter provides guidelines for writing a marketing plan and also presents a sample marketing plan for Paradise Kitchens® Inc., a firm that produces and distributes a line of spicy chili under the Howlin' Coyote® brand name. Appendix A also links each section of the marketing plan to the relevant textbook chapter to assist students who are writing marketing plans.

marketing plan

A road map for the marketing activities of an organization for a specified future time period

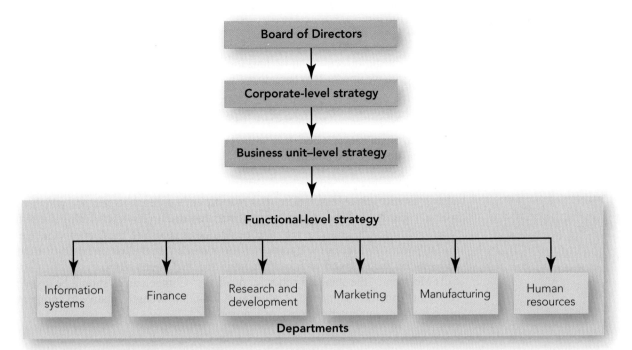

FIGURE 2–3
The board of directors oversees the three levels of strategy in organizations: corporate, business unit, and functional.

Organizational Structure and Strategies

Figure 2–1 shows that goals get converted into organizational strategies at the corporate, business unit, and functional levels. All lower-level goals must contribute to achieving goals at the next, higher level. This is why large firms such as Medtronic and Kodak are extremely complex. As depicted in Figure 2–3, these firms consist of three organizational levels whose strategy is linked to marketing. The *corporate level* is where top management (board of directors, chief executive officer—CEO, and other functional department heads, such as the chief marketing officer—CMO) directs overall strategy for the firm.

Some multimarket, multiproduct firms like General Electric manage a portfolio of businesses called strategic business units.[20] The term *strategic business unit (SBU)* refers to a subsidiary, division, or unit of an organization that markets a set of related offerings to a clearly defined group of customers. At the *business unit level*, managers set a more specific strategic direction for their businesses to exploit value-creating opportunities. For firms with a single business or industry focus like Ben & Jerry's, the corporate and business unit levels may merge.

Each strategic business unit has a *functional level*, where groups of specialists actually create value for the firm. At the functional level, the firm's strategic direction becomes its most specific and focused. The term *department* generally refers to these specialized functions, such as marketing and finance (see Figure 2–3). A key role of the marketing department is to look outward, keeping the organization focused on creating value both for it and for customers.

learning review

4. What is the difference between a marketing dashboard and a marketing metric?

5. Explain what a marketing plan is.

6. Describe the three levels in an organization.

SETTING STRATEGIC DIRECTIONS

To set a strategic direction, an organization needs to answer two difficult questions: (1) Where are we now? (2) Where do we want to go?

A Look Around: Where Are We Now?

Asking an organization where it is at the present time involves identifying its competencies, customers, and competitors.

Competencies   Senior managers must ask the question: What do we do best? The answer involves an assessment of the organization's core *competencies*, which are its special capabilities—the skills, technologies, and resources—that distinguish it from other organizations and provide customer value. Exploiting these competencies can lead to success.[21] Medtronic's competencies include world-class technology, training, and service that respond to life-threatening medical needs. *BusinessWeek* magazine calls Medtronic "the standard setter for quality."[22] Competencies should be distinctive enough to provide a *competitive advantage*, a unique strength relative to competitors, often based on quality, time, cost, or innovation.[23]

Customers   Ben & Jerry's customers are ice cream and frozen yogurt eaters who have different preferences (form, flavor, health, and convenience). Medtronic's customers are cardiologists and heart surgeons who serve patients. Another organization that has a clear customer focus is Lands' End. It communicates a remarkable commitment about its customer experience and product quality with these unconditional words:

Guaranteed. Period.®

The Lands' End website points out that this guarantee has always been an unconditional one. It reads: "If you're not satisfied with any item, simply return it to us at any time for an exchange or refund of its purchase price." But to get the message across more clearly to its customers, it created the two-word guarantee. The point is that Lands' End's strategy must provide genuine value to customers to ensure that they have a satisfying experience.[24]

Lands' End's unconditional guarantee for its products highlights its focus on customers.

Competitors In today's global competition, the distinctions among competitors are increasingly blurred. Lands' End started as a catalog retailer. But today, Lands' End competes with not only other clothing catalog retailers but also traditional department stores, mass merchandisers, and specialty shops. Even well-known clothing brands like Liz Claiborne now have their own chain stores. Although only some of the clothing in any of these stores directly competes with Lands' End offerings, all these retailers have websites to sell their offerings over the Internet. This means there's a lot of competition out there.

Growth Strategies: Where Do We Want to Go?

Knowing where the organization is at the present time enables managers to set a direction for the firm and allocate resources to move in that direction. Two techniques to aid managers with these decisions are (1) business portfolio and (2) diversification analysis strategies.

Business Portfolio Analysis The Boston Consulting Group (BCG), a nationally known management consulting firm, uses *business portfolio analysis* to quantify performance measures and growth targets to analyze its clients' strategic business units (SBUs) as though they were a collection of separate investments.[25] The purpose of the tool is to determine the appeal of each SBU or offering and then determine the amount of cash, if any, each should receive. The BCG analysis can also be applied at the offering, product, or brand level. More than 75 percent of the largest U.S. firms have used this analytical tool.

The BCG business portfolio analysis requires an organization to locate the position of each of its SBUs on a growth-share matrix (see Figure 2–4 on the next page). The vertical axis is the *market growth rate,* which is the annual rate of growth of the SBU's industry. The horizontal axis is the *relative market share,* defined as the sales of the SBU divided by the sales of the largest firm in the industry. A relative market share of $10\times$ (at the left end of the scale) means that the SBU has 10 times the share of its largest competitor, whereas a share of $0.1\times$ (at the right end of the scale) means it has only 10 percent of the share of its largest competitor.

The BCG has given specific names and descriptions to the four resulting quadrants in its growth-share matrix based on the amount of cash they generate for or require from the organization:

- *Cash cows* are SBUs that generate large amounts of cash, far more than they can invest profitably in themselves. They have dominant shares of slow-growth markets and provide cash to cover the organization's overhead and to invest in other SBUs.

Kodak today must make a series of difficult marketing decisions. From what you know about cameras and photos, assess Kodak's sales opportunities for the four products shown here. For some possible answers and a way to show these opportunities graphically, see the text and Figure 2–4.

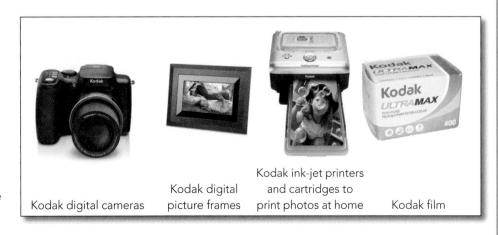

Kodak digital cameras

Kodak digital picture frames

Kodak ink-jet printers and cartridges to print photos at home

Kodak film

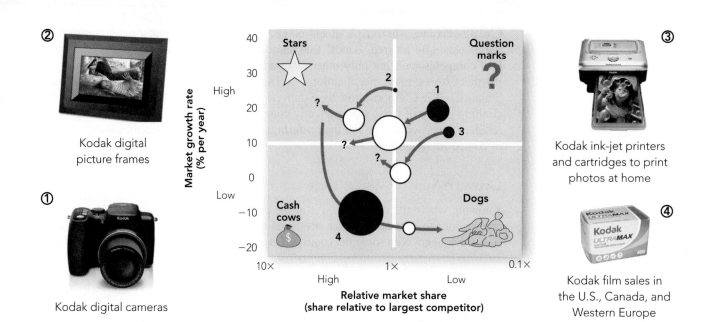

② Kodak digital picture frames

① Kodak digital cameras

③ Kodak ink-jet printers and cartridges to print photos at home

④ Kodak film sales in the U.S., Canada, and Western Europe

FIGURE 2–4

Boston Consulting Group business portfolio analysis for Kodak's consumer-related SBUs as they appeared in 2003 (solid red circle) and might appear in 2011 (white circle).

- *Stars* are SBUs with a high share of high-growth markets that may need extra cash to finance their own rapid future growth. When their growth slows, they are likely to become cash cows.
- *Question marks* are SBUs with a low share of high-growth markets. They require large injections of cash just to maintain their market share, much less increase it. The name implies management's dilemma for these SBUs: choosing the right ones to invest in and phasing out the rest.
- *Dogs* are SBUs with low shares of slow-growth markets. Although they may generate enough cash to sustain themselves, they do not hold the promise of ever becoming real winners for the organization. Dropping SBUs that are dogs may be required, except when relationships with other SBUs, competitive considerations, or potential strategic alliances exist.[26]

An organization's SBUs often start as question marks and go counterclockwise around Figure 2–4 to become stars, then cash cows, and finally dogs. Because an organization has limited influence on the market growth rate, its main alternative is to try to change its relative market share. To accomplish this, management decides what role each SBU should have in the future and either injects or removes cash from it.

Until 2000, Kodak relied on its film for the bulk of its revenues and profits because of the billions of photos taken every year. The company made money on repeat business from traditional film sales and *not* on camera purchases. The appearance of digital cameras radically changed Kodak's business forever as film sales began to evaporate.

Four Kodak SBUs (see the solid red circles in Figure 2–4) are shown as they may have appeared in 2003 and can serve as an example of BCG analysis. The area of each solid red circle in Figure 2–4 is roughly proportional to the SBU's 2003 sales revenue. In a more complete analysis, Kodak's other SBUs would be included. This example also shows the agonizing strategic decisions that executives must make in an industry facing profound change—the situation Kodak was confronted with due to the arrival of digital technology.

The success of Kodak's new digital strategy and its product lines shown in Figure 2–4 depends on how millions of consumers take photos and convert them into printed or online images over the next decade. Here is a snapshot of the sales opportunities Kodak might have envisioned in 2003 in planning toward 2011 (in the white circles) for four consumer product lines:

1. *Kodak film*. An $8 billion *cash cow* in 2003, Kodak film sales were the company's biggest single source of revenue. Now in a free-fall because of digital cameras, Kodak film sales dropped to $500 million in 2008, making it a *dog*. Kodak expects sales to stabilize at this level for the future.[27]

2. *Kodak digital cameras*. Sales of digital cameras grew 24 percent from 2006 to 2007 due to falling prices. But for 2008, sales may slow because 77 percent of U.S. households now have a digital camera. In 2007, Kodak's sales of its digital camera lines were flat, remaining number three in market share behind Canon and Sony. Kodak expects this SBU to continue to be a *star* since it plans to introduce new models. However, it may become a *cash cow* if the market consists of mainly replacement sales at even lower prices.[28]

3. *Kodak ink-jet printers and cartridges to print digital photos at home*. In 2007, about half of digital camera owners actually printed their images at home. In that year, Kodak launched a line of multipurpose machines to print photos, make copies, and send faxes. Kodak's high quality ink cartridges make photos at half the cost of Hewlett-Packard's (HP) printers. Because HP is the entrenched 300-pound gorilla in this market, the future of this *question mark* could evolve into a *star* if Kodak is able to double or triple unit sales by 2010. Or, this SBU may turn into a *dog* because online printing and sharing have taken off and may reach $1 billion by 2011.[29]

4. *Kodak digital picture frames*. In 2007, Kodak introduced a line of digital picture frames that allow consumers to store and view digital images. Some models allow users to upload their images via a wireless connection from their computer and play MP3 audio (songs, narration, and so on). In 2006, global demand was a paltry 2.8 million units but in 2007 it exploded to 8.6 million units. Kodak was the market leader with a 16 percent share—clearly a *star*. By 2011, sales are expected to reach 42 million units![30]

The primary strength of business portfolio analysis lies in forcing a firm to place each of its SBUs in the growth-share matrix, which in turn suggests which SBUs will be cash producers and cash users in the future. Weaknesses of this analysis arise from the difficulty in (1) getting the needed information and (2) incorporating competitive data into business portfolio analysis.[31]

Diversification Analysis   *Diversification analysis* is a tool that helps a firm search for growth opportunities from among current and new markets as well as current and new products.[32] For any market, there is both a current product (what the firm now sells) and a new product (what the firm might sell in the future). And for any product there is both a current market (the firm's existing customers) and a new market (the firm's potential customers). As Ben & Jerry's attempts to increase sales revenues, it must consider all four of the market-product strategies shown in Figure 2–5 on the next page:

- *Market penetration* is a marketing strategy to increase sales of current products in existing markets, such as Ben & Jerry's current ice cream products to U.S. consumers. There is no change in either the basic product line or the markets served. Increased sales are generated by selling either more ice cream (through better promotion or distribution) *or* the same amount of ice cream at a higher price to its existing customers.

- *Market development* is a marketing strategy to sell existing products to new markets. For Ben & Jerry's, Brazil is an attractive new market. There is good news and bad news for this strategy: As household incomes of Brazilians increase, consumers can buy more ice cream; however the Ben & Jerry's brand may be unknown to Brazilian consumers.

How can Ben & Jerry's develop new products and social responsibility programs that contribute to its mission? The text describes how the strategic marketing process and its SWOT analysis can help.

FIGURE 2–5

Four market-product
strategies: alternative ways
to expand sales revenues
for Ben & Jerry's using
diversification analysis.

Markets	PRODUCTS	
	Current	New
Current	**Market penetration** Selling more Ben & Jerry's super premium ice cream to Americans	**Product development** Selling a new product such as children's clothing under the Ben & Jerry's brand to Americans
New	**Market development** Selling Ben & Jerry's super premium ice cream to Brazilians for the first time	**Diversification** Selling a new product such as children's clothing under the Ben & Jerry's brand to Brazilians for the first time

- *Product development* is a marketing strategy of selling new products to existing markets. Ben & Jerry's could leverage its brand by selling children's clothing in the United States. This strategy is risky because Americans may not see a clear connection between the company's expertise in ice cream and children's clothing.
- *Diversification* is a marketing strategy of developing new products and selling them in new markets. This is a potentially high-risk strategy for Ben & Jerry's because the firm has neither previous production nor marketing experience on which to draw to market the offerings to Brazilian consumers.

---

learning review

7. What is business portfolio analysis?

8. Explain the four market-product strategies in diversification analysis.

THE STRATEGIC MARKETING PROCESS

After an organization assesses where it's at and where it wants to go, other questions emerge, such as:

1. How do we allocate our resources to get where we want to go?
2. How do we convert our plans into actions?
3. How do results compare with our plans, and do deviations require new plans?

strategic marketing process

Approach whereby an organization allocates its marketing mix resources to reach its target markets

To answer these questions, an organization uses the **strategic marketing process**, whereby an organization allocates its marketing mix resources to reach its target markets. This process is divided into three phases: planning, implementation, and evaluation (Figure 2–6).

LO4

The Planning Phase of the Strategic Marketing Process

Figure 2–6 shows the three steps in the planning phase of the strategic marketing process: (1) situation (SWOT) analysis, (2) market-product focus and goal setting, and (3) the marketing program.

situation analysis

Taking stock of where a firm or product has been recently, where it is now, and where it is headed

Step 1: Situation (SWOT) Analysis   The essence of **situation analysis** is taking stock of where the firm or product has been recently, where it is now, and where

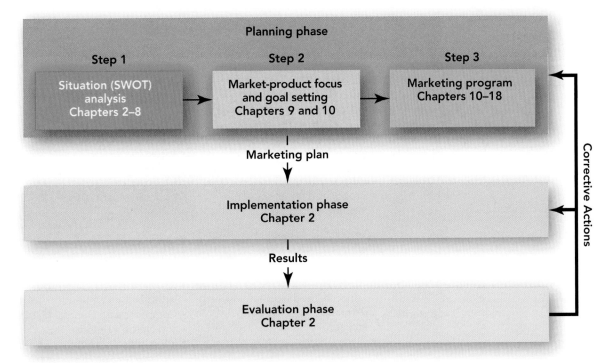

FIGURE 2–6

The strategic marketing process has three vital phases: planning, implementation, and evaluation. The figure also shows where these phases are discussed in the text.

SWOT analysis

Organization's appraisal of its internal strengths and weaknesses and its external opportunities and threats

it is headed in terms of the organization's plans and the external factors and trends affecting it. The situation (SWOT) analysis box in Figure 2–6 is the first of the three steps in the planning phase. An effective summary of a situation analysis is a **SWOT analysis**, an acronym describing an organization's appraisal of its internal **S**trengths and **W**eaknesses and its external **O**pportunities and **T**hreats.

The SWOT analysis is based on an exhaustive study of the four areas shown below. Knowledge of these areas forms the foundation on which the firm builds its marketing program:

- Identify trends in the organization's industry.
- Analyze the organization's competitors.
- Assess the organization itself.
- Research the organization's present and prospective customers.

Assume you are responsible for doing the SWOT analysis for Unilever, Ben & Jerry's parent company shown in Figure 2–7 on the next page. Note that the SWOT table has four cells formed by the combination of internal versus external factors (the rows) and favorable versus unfavorable factors (the columns) that identify Ben & Jerry's strengths, weaknesses, opportunities, and threats.

The task is not simply to conduct a SWOT analysis but to translate its results into specific actions to help the firm grow and succeed. The ultimate goal is to identify the *critical* strategy-related factors that impact the firm and then build on vital strengths, correct glaring weaknesses, exploit significant opportunities, and avoid disaster-laden threats.

The Ben and Jerry's SWOT analysis in Figure 2–7 can be the basis for these kinds of specific actions. An action in each of the four cells might be:

- *Build on a strength.* Find specific efficiencies in distribution with Unilever's existing ice cream brands.
- *Correct a weakness.* Recruit experienced managers from other consumer product firms to help stimulate growth.

FIGURE 2–7

Ben & Jerry's: a SWOT analysis to keep it growing. The picture painted in this SWOT analysis is the basis for management actions.

Location of Factor	TYPE OF FACTOR	
	Favorable	Unfavorable
Internal	**Strengths** • Prestigious, well-known brand name among U.S. consumers • Large share of the U.S. super premium ice cream market • Complements Unilever's other ice cream brands • Recognized for its social mission and actions	**Weaknesses** • B&J's social responsibility actions may add costs, reduce focus on its core business, and alienate some customers • Experienced managers needed to help growth • Modest sales growth and profits in recent years
External	**Opportunities** • Growing demand for quality ice cream in overseas markets • Increasing U.S. demand for "slow churned" low-fat, low-carb ice cream, frozen yogurt, and sorbet • Many U.S. firms successfully use product and brand extensions	**Threats** • Consumer concern with sugary and fatty desserts • B&J customers read nutritional labels • Competes with General Mills' and Nestlé's brands • International downturns increase the risks for B&J in European and Asian markets

- *Exploit an opportunity.* Develop a new line of low-fat, low-carb frozen yogurts and sorbets to respond to consumer health concerns.
- *Avoid a disaster-laden threat.* Focus on less risky international markets, such as Canada and Mexico.

market segmentation

Sorting potential buyers into groups that have common needs and will respond similarly to a marketing action

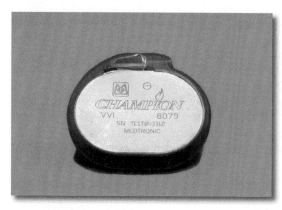

The Champion: Medtronic's high-quality, long-life, low-cost heart pacemaker for Asian market segments.

Step 2: Market-Product Focus and Goal Setting Determining which products will be directed toward which customers (step 2 of the planning phase in Figure 2–6) is essential for developing an effective marketing program (step 3). This decision is often based on **market segmentation**, which involves aggregating prospective buyers into groups, or segments, that (1) have common needs and (2) will respond similarly to a marketing action. This enables an organization to identify the segments on which it will focus its efforts—its target market segments— and develop specific marketing programs to reach them.

As always, understanding the customer is essential. In the case of Medtronic, executives researched a potential new market in Asia by talking extensively with doctors in India and China. They learned that these doctors saw some of the current state-of-the-art features of heart pacemakers as less essential and too expensive. Instead, they wanted an affordable pacemaker that was reliable and easy to implant. This information led Medtronic to develop and market a new product, the Champion heart pacemaker, directed at the needs of these Asian market segments.

Goal setting involves setting measurable marketing objectives to be achieved. For a specific market, the goal may be to introduce a new product, such as Medtronic's Champion pacemaker in Asia or Toyota's launch of its Prius hybrid car in the United States. For a specific brand or product, the goal may be to create a promotional campaign or pricing strategy to get more consumers to purchase.

Let's examine Medtronic's five-year plan to reach the "affordable and reliable" segment of the pacemaker market:[33]

- *Set marketing and product goals.* The chances of new-product success are increased by specifying both market and product goals. Based on their market research showing the need for a reliable yet affordable pacemaker, Medtronic executives set the following as their goal: Design and market such a pacemaker in the next three years that could be manufactured in China for the Asian market.
- *Select target markets.* The Champion pacemaker will be targeted at cardiologists and medical clinics performing heart surgery in India, China, and other Asian countries.
- *Find points of difference.* **Points of difference** are those characteristics of a product that make it superior to competitive substitutes. Just as a competitive advantage is a unique strength of an entire organization compared to its competitors, points of difference are unique characteristics of one of its products that make it superior to competitive products it faces in the marketplace. For the Champion pacemaker, the key points of difference are *not* the state-of-the-art features that drive up production costs and are important to only a minority of patients. Instead, they are high quality, long life, reliability, ease of use, and low cost.
- *Position the product.* The pacemaker will be "positioned" in cardiologists' and patients' minds as a medical device that is high quality and reliable with a long, nine-year life. The name Champion was selected after testing acceptable names among doctors in India, China, Pakistan, Singapore, and Malaysia. So step 2 provides a solid foundation to use in developing the marketing program, step 3 in the planning phase of the strategic marketing process.

points of difference

Those characteristics of a product that make it superior to competitive substitutes

learning review

9. What is market segmentation?

10. What are points of difference and why are they important?

Step 3: Marketing Program   Activities in step 2 tell the marketing manager which customers to target and which customer needs the firm's product offerings can satisfy—the *who* and *what* aspects of the strategic marketing process. The *how* aspect—step 3 in the planning phase—involves developing the program's marketing mix and its budget. Figure 2–8 on the next page shows that each marketing mix element is combined to provide a cohesive marketing program. The five-year marketing plan of Medtronic's Champion pacemaker includes these marketing mix activities:

- *Product strategy.* Offer a Champion brand heart pacemaker with features needed by Asian patients.
- *Price strategy.* Manufacture the Champion to control costs so that it can be priced below $1,000 (in U.S. dollars)—an affordable price for Asian markets.
- *Promotion strategy.* Feature demonstrations at cardiologist and medical conventions across Asia to introduce the Champion and highlight the device's features and application.
- *Place (distribution) strategy.* Search out, utilize, and train reputable medical distributors across Asia to call on cardiologists and medical clinics.

Putting this marketing program into effect requires that the firm commit time and money to it in the form of a sales forecast (see Chapter 8) and budget that must be approved by top management.

FIGURE 2–8
The elements of the
marketing mix must be
blended to produce
a cohesive marketing
program.

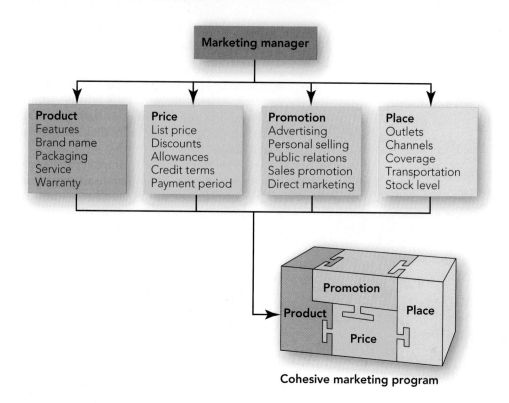

Cohesive marketing program

The Implementation Phase of the Strategic Marketing Process

LO5

As shown in Figure 2–6, the result of the tens or hundreds of hours spent in the planning phase of the strategic marketing process is the firm's marketing plan. Implementation, the second phase of the strategic marketing process, involves carrying out the marketing plan that emerges from the planning phase. If the firm cannot put the marketing plan into effect—in the implementation phase—the planning phase was a waste of time.

There are four components of the implementation phase: (1) obtaining resources, (2) designing the marketing organization, (3) developing planning schedules, and (4) actually executing the marketing program designed in the planning phase. Kodak provides a case example.

Obtaining Resources In 2003, Kodak announced a bold plan to reenergize the film marketer for the new age of digital cameras and prints. Kodak needed money to implement the plan. So, in 2007, Kodak sold its medical imaging unit for $2.4 billion and announced painful employment cuts.[34]

Designing the Marketing Organization A marketing program needs a marketing organization to implement it. Figure 2–9 shows the organization chart of a typical manufacturing firm, giving some details of the marketing department's structure. Four managers of marketing activities are shown to report to the vice president of marketing. Several regional sales managers and an international sales manager may report to the manager of sales. The product or brand managers and their subordinates help plan, implement, and evaluate the marketing plans for their offerings. However, the entire marketing organization is responsible for converting these marketing plans to reality as part of the corporate marketing team.

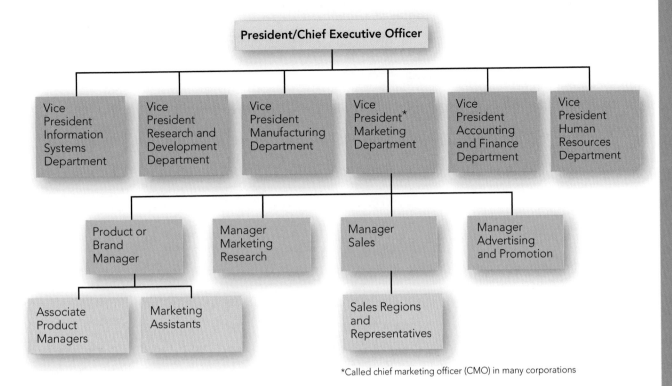

President/Chief Executive Officer

| Vice President Information Systems Department | Vice President Research and Development Department | Vice President Manufacturing Department | Vice President* Marketing Department | Vice President Accounting and Finance Department | Vice President Human Resources Department |

Product or Brand Manager

Manager Marketing Research

Manager Sales

Manager Advertising and Promotion

Associate Product Managers

Marketing Assistants

Sales Regions and Representatives

*Called chief marketing officer (CMO) in many corporations

FIGURE 2–9
Organization of a typical manufacturing firm, showing a breakdown of the marketing department.

Developing Planning Schedules To implement marketing plans, members of the marketing department hold meetings to identify the tasks that need to be done, the time to allocate to each one, the people responsible, and the deadlines for their accomplishment. In most cases, a team works on different parts of the plan.

Executing the Marketing Program Marketing plans are meaningless pieces of paper without effective execution of those plans. This effective execution requires attention to detail for both marketing strategies and marketing tactics. A **marketing strategy** is the means by which a marketing goal is to be achieved, usually characterized by a specified target market and a marketing program to reach it. The term implies both the end sought (target market) and the means to achieve it (marketing program). At this marketing strategy level, Kodak will seek to increase sales of digital cameras and ink-jet printers for consumers and products for commercial printers.

To implement a marketing program successfully, hundreds of detailed decisions are often required. These decisions, called **marketing tactics**, are detailed day-to-day operational decisions essential to the overall success of marketing strategies. At Kodak, writing ads and setting prices for its new lines of digital cameras are examples of marketing tactics.

marketing strategy
Means by which a marketing goal is to be achieved

marketing tactics
Detailed day-to-day operational decisions essential to the overall success of marketing strategies

The Evaluation Phase of the Strategic Marketing Process

LO6

The evaluation phase of the strategic marketing process seeks to keep the marketing program moving in the direction set for it (see Figure 2–6). Accomplishing this requires the marketing manager to (1) compare the results of the marketing program with the goals in the written plans to identify deviations and (2) act on these deviations—correcting negative deviations and exploiting positive ones.

FIGURE 2–10

The evaluation phase of the strategic marketing process requires that the organization compare actual results with goals to identify and act on deviations to fill in its "planning gap." The text describes how Kodak hopes to fill in its planning gap by 2010.

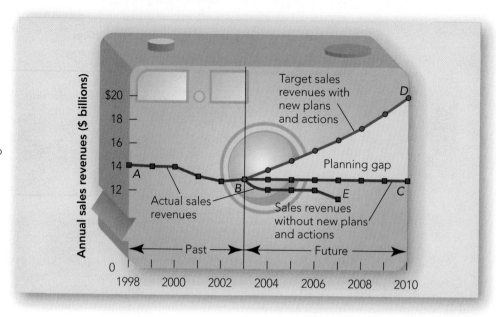

Comparing Results with Plans to Identify Deviations Suppose you are on a Kodak task force in 2003 responsible for making plans through 2010. You observe that Kodak's sales revenues from 1998 through 2003 exhibit a very flat trend, or AB in Figure 2–10. Extending the 1998–2003 trend to 2010 along BC shows declining sales revenues, a totally unacceptable, no-growth strategy.

Kodak's growth target of 5 to 6 percent annually, the line BD in Figure 2–10, would give sales revenues of $16 billion in 2006 and $20 billion in 2010. This reveals a wedge-shaped shaded gap in the figure. Planners call this the *planning gap,* the difference between the projection of the path to reach a new goal (line BD) and the projection of the path of the results of a plan already in place (line BC). The ultimate purpose of the firm's marketing program is to "fill in" this planning gap—in the case of your Kodak task force, to move its future sales revenue line from the no-growth line BC up to the challenging target of line BD. But poor performance can result in actual sales revenues being far less than the targeted levels, the actual situation faced by Kodak in 2008 (line BE). This is the essence of evaluation: comparing actual results with goals set.

Acting on Deviations When evaluation shows that actual performance fails to meet expectations, managers need to take corrective actions. Two possible Kodak midcourse corrections for both positive and negative deviations from targets illustrate these management actions your Kodak task force might take in 2008:

To help fill in its planning gap, Kodak is pursuing opportunities for sales of digital cameras in China.

- *Exploiting a positive deviation.* If Kodak's innovative ink-jet printers sell better than expected, Kodak might try to move quickly to offer these to international customers.
- *Correcting a negative deviation.* However, suppose Samsung is able to surpass Kodak in global market share of digital cameras. Then Kodak might (1) develop more feature-laden digital cameras that use its proprietary sensor technologies that improve image (picture) quality and (2) launch a new aggressive global marketing program to promote integrating its digital cameras with its Kodak Digital Picture Frames.

learning review

11. What is the implementation phase of the strategic marketing process?

12. How do the goals set for a marketing program in the planning phase relate to the evaluation phase of the strategic marketing process?

LEARNING OBJECTIVES REVIEW

LO1 *Describe the core values, mission, organizational culture, business, and goals of an organization.*

Organizations exist to accomplish something for someone. To do this, they must establish a foundation, set a direction, and formulate strategies. To give organizations direction, focus, and inspiration, they continuously assess their core values, mission, organizational culture, business, and goals. Core values are the organization's fundamental, passionate, and enduring principles that guide its conduct over time. The organization's mission is a statement of its function in society, often identifying its customers, markets, products, and technologies. Organizational culture is a set of values, ideas, attitudes, and norms of behavior that is learned and shared among the members of an organization in order to connect with its stakeholders.

To answer the question, "What business are we in?" an organization must define its "business"—the clear, broad, underlying industry or market sector of an organization's offerings. Finally, the organization's goals (or objectives) are statements of an accomplishment of a task to be achieved, often by a specific time. Goals, such as profit, sales, market share, and customer satisfaction, convert an organization's mission and business into long- and short-term performance targets that measure how well it is doing.

LO2 *Explain why managers use marketing dashboards and marketing metrics to evaluate a marketing program.*

Marketing managers use marketing dashboards to visually display on a single computer screen the essential information to make a decision to take an action or further analyze a problem. This information consists of key performance measures of a product category, such as sales or market share, and is known as a marketing metric, which is a measure of the quantitative value or trend of a marketing activity or result. Most organizations tie their marketing metrics to the quantitative objectives established in their marketing plan, which is a road map for the marketing activities of an organization for a specified future time period, such as one year or five years.

LO3 *Discuss how an organization assesses where it is now and seeks to be in the future.*

Managers of an organization ask two key questions to set a strategic direction. The first question, "Where are we now?" requires an organization to (*a*) reevaluate its competencies to ensure that its special capabilities still provide a competitive advantage; (*b*) assess its present and prospective customers to ensure they have a satisfying customer experience—the central goal of marketing today; and (*c*) analyze its current and potential competitors from a global perspective to determine whether it needs to redefine its business.

The second question, "Where do we want to go?" requires an organization to set a specific direction and allocate resources to move it in that direction. Business portfolio and diversification analyses help an organization do this. Managers use business portfolio analysis to assess its strategic business units (SBUs), product lines, or individual products as though they were a collection of separate investments (cash cows, stars, question marks, and dogs) to determine the amount of cash each should receive. Diversification analysis is a tool that helps managers use one or a combination of four strategies to increase revenues: market penetration (selling more of an existing product to existing markets); market development (selling an existing product to new markets); product development (selling a new product to existing markets); and diversification (selling new products to new markets).

LO4 *Explain the three steps of the planning phase of the strategic marketing process.*

An organization uses the strategic marketing process to allocate its marketing mix resources to reach its target markets. This process is divided into three phases: planning, implementation, and evaluation. The planning phase consists of: (*a*) a situation (SWOT) analysis, which involves taking stock of where the firm or product has been recently, where it is now, and where it is headed. This assessment focuses on the organization's internal factors (strengths and weaknesses) and the external factors and trends affecting it (opportunities and threats); (*b*) a market-product focus through market segmentation—grouping buyers into segments with common needs and similar responses to marketing programs—and goal setting, which in part requires creating points of difference—those characteristics of a product that make it superior to competitive substitutes; and (*c*) a marketing program that specifies the budget and activities (marketing strategies and tactics) for each marketing mix element.

LO5 *Describe the four components of the implementation phase of the strategic marketing process.*

The implementation phase of the strategic marketing process carries out the marketing plan that emerges from the planning phase. It has four key elements: (*a*) obtaining resources; (*b*) designing the marketing organization to perform product management, marketing research, sales, and advertising and promotion activities; (*c*) developing schedules to identify the tasks that need to be done, the time that is allocated to each one, the people responsible for each task, and the deadlines for each task's accomplishment; and (*d*) executing the marketing strategies, which are the means by which marketing goals are to be achieved, and their associated marketing tactics, which are the detailed day-to-day operational decisions of a firm's marketing strategies. These are the marketing program actions a firm takes to achieve the goals set forth in its marketing plan.

LO6 *Discuss the two aspects of the evaluation phase of the strategic marketing process.*
The evaluation phase of the strategic marketing process seeks to keep the marketing program moving in the direction that was established in the marketing plan. This requires the marketing manager to compare the results from the marketing program with the marketing plan's goals to (*a*) identify deviations or "planning gaps" and (*b*) take corrective actions to exploit positive deviations or correct negative deviations.

FOCUSING ON KEY TERMS

business p. 24
core values p. 22
goals p. 24
market segmentation p. 34
market share p. 24
marketing dashboard p. 25
marketing metric p. 25

marketing plan p. 26
marketing strategy p. 37
marketing tactics p. 37
mission p. 23
objectives p. 24
organizational culture p. 23
points of difference p. 35

profit p. 22
situation analysis p. 32
strategic marketing process p. 32
strategy p. 22
SWOT analysis p. 33

APPLYING MARKETING KNOWLEDGE

1 (*a*) Using Medtronic as an example, explain how a mission statement gives it a strategic direction. (*b*) Create a mission statement for your own career.

2 What competencies best describe (*a*) your college or university and (*b*) your favorite restaurant?

3 Why does a product often start as a question mark and then move counterclockwise around the BCG's growth-share matrix shown in Figure 2–4?

4 What is the main result of each of the three phases of the strategic marketing process? (*a*) planning, (*b*) implementation, and (*c*) evaluation.

5 Select one strength, one weakness, one opportunity, and one threat from the Ben & Jerry's SWOT analysis shown in Figure 2–7. Suggest an action that a Ben & Jerry's marketing manager might take to address each factor.

6 The goal-setting step in the planning phase of the strategic marketing process sets quantified objectives for use in the evaluation phase. What does a manager do if measured results are below objectives? Above objectives?

building your marketing plan

1 Read Appendix A, "Building an Effective Marketing Plan." Then write a 600-word executive summary for the Paradise Kitchens marketing plan using the numbered headings shown in the plan. When you have completed the draft of your own marketing plan, use what you learned in writing an executive summary for Paradise Kitchens to write a 600-word executive summary to go in the front of your own marketing plan.

2 Using Chapter 2 and Appendix A as guides, give focus to your marketing plan by (*a*) writing your mission statement in 25 words or less, (*b*) listing three nonfinancial goals and three financial goals, (*c*) writing your competitive advantage in 35 words or less, and (*d*) doing a SWOT analysis table.

3 Draw a simple organization chart for your organization.

"We want to get people to drive an extra block or cut across an extra lane of traffic to choose BP over its competitors," claims Ann Hand, senior vice president—Global Brand Marketing and Innovation (photo below). BP, formerly known as British Petroleum, is one of the world's largest producers and marketers of petroleum products. Through innovative marketing and with a focus on the environment, BP has been transforming itself into a consumer-centric provider of energy products and services that are broader than just oil and gas.

KEY ELEMENTS IN BP'S "BEYOND PETROLEUM" TRANSFORMATION

Increased energy demand due to the growing economies of both the developed and developing countries as well as supply constraints have caused oil prices to rise sharply during the past few decades. This, along with the heightened awareness of global climate change in the late 1990s, created an opportunity for BP to transform its mission statement to the following:

> Our business is about finding, producing, and marketing the natural energy resources on which the modern world depends.

BP then reorganized itself primarily into two strategic performance (i.e., business) units to support its mission. These "SPUs" consist of activities related to the (1) discovery and production of oil and natural gas and (2) refining and marketing of petroleum products.

BP also identified and evaluated many opportunities to increase its sales and profits. One strategy was through acquisitions. During the late 1990s, BP invested $120 billion to add competitors Amoco, ARCO, and Castrol to its business portfolio. BP now produces about 3 percent of the planet's oil and gas, operates in over 100 countries around the world, and serves 13 million customers per day at 24,600 retail sites, including 12,300 stations in the United States. The benefits to its stakeholders: BP global sales now exceed $250 billion.

In 2000, BP introduced a new brand identity to reflect the integrated company it had become. The BP shield and Amoco torch were replaced by a new Helios logo that more appropriately reflects BP's corporate and retail brand image as a green, environmentally friendly company. Because a brand image communicates the brand's essence—an emotional tie between the company and its customers—it provides confidence to customers: they know they can get high-quality gas, conveniently purchase food and beverages, and travel onwards refreshed. Thus, BP is not just about gasoline—it goes "beyond petroleum."

Within its refining and marketing SPU, BP sells gasoline at its branded retail gas stations, which include the BP, Amoco Ultimate, Wild Bean Café and BP Connect brands (eastern United States) and the ARCO and *am/pm* brands (western United States). In the near term, BP's retail strategy will focus on high-growth metropolitan areas in the United States through new and franchised service stations. In the long-term, BP plans to transform the retail gasoline landscape with its new Helios House and Helios Power strategies (see below).

BP'S FOUR CORE VALUES

BP specifies four core values to express the way the organization does business and help translate the mission into practical action:

- *Progressive:* BP is always looking for new and better ways to conduct business. It has developed a relationship with Ford to build hydrogen vehicles and fueling stations in California, Michigan, and elsewhere. BP also has reformulated its BP Amoco Ultimate fuel to reduce air pollutants.
- *Innovative:* Through the creative approaches of employees, and the development and application of cutting-edge drilling technology, BP seeks breakthrough solutions for its customers.
- *Green:* BP is committed to environmental leadership— the proactive and responsible treatment of the planet's natural resources and developing lower carbon emission

energy sources. As a result, BP now stores its gasoline in double-skinned tanks to prevent spills and leaks.

- *Performance-driven:* BP sets the global standards of performance on financial and environmental dimensions, as well as safety, growth, and customer and employee satisfaction.

HELIOS HOUSE: TRANSFORMING BP'S GASOLINE RETAILING

Since 1977, the percentage of gasoline stations in the United States that also contain a convenience store has gone from 5 percent to more than 50 percent. To support the demand for convenience store offerings, BP developed a very successful convenience store concept called *am/pm.* This branded offering was created and tested on ARCO sites in the western United States; in the future, *am/pm* will partner with the BP retail brand and penetrate the eastern United States.

Currently, the *am/pm* stores sell both fuel and more than 2,000 convenience items (snacks, beverages, necessities, etc.). Sales from the more than 1,000 *am/pm* stores now exceed $6 billion; both the number and sales revenues are expected to grow significantly during the next several years as BP transforms many of its existing gas stations into *am/pm* stores.

In early 2007, BP launched a two-part strategy to change the way consumers think about its gas stations. One part was Helios House, a new-look gasoline station located in Los Angeles that will serve as a living laboratory to test ideas in a real environment (photo below). Ann Hand, who manages BP's $280 million global marketing programs, was instrumental in the planning and implementation of Helios House. Becoming operational during April 2007, Helios House was designed to be eco-friendly from the top down. The building itself was constructed from recycled, sustainable, and nontoxic materials. Moreover, its canopy has 90 solar panels to generate its own electricity. The roof is covered with grass to reduce the building's heating and cooling needs and has rain collectors to irrigate the surrounding drought-tolerant landscape. The facility also has energy-efficient lighting, using one-fifth less energy than a traditional gas station. As a result of these and other design features, Helios House became the first gas station to be certified as green by the U.S. Green Building Council.

Helios House also offers customers (1) clean, well-maintained restrooms, (2) friendly "green team" employees who will not only greet customers with a smile but also check their cars' tire pressure to ensure proper inflation—which boosts gas mileage, and (3) tips on creating a green lifestyle through its www.thegreencurve.com website. According to Kathy Seegebrecht, BP's U.S. advertising manager, "Helios House will serve as a place where BP can have a conversation with its customers about green ideas and how its gas station can play a part in creating a better environment. It was designed to serve as a beacon to inspire the employees and franchisees through the U.S."

Helios House is *not* a prototype of BP's station of the future. However, it will be an incubator of green ideas that can be implemented among its existing and new stations. It is just too costly to replace 25,000 existing stations throughout the world. Seegebrecht concludes, "Helios House is showing us that in a more brand-conscious world, where we all want the best of everything, people might actually want a better gas station." How successful has the Helios House been? "The site has nearly doubled its fuel volumes."

HELIOS POWER: BP'S PROMOTION OF ITS GASOLINE RETAILING

The second part of BP's strategy was a promotional campaign to transform BP's retail brand image at its locations in the U.S. Buying gasoline is a low involvement purchase and consumers have low expectations regarding their purchase experiences. Armed with that consumer insight, BP created and executed the $45 million Helios Power advertising and brand building campaign, which is an extension of BP's "Beyond Petroleum" corporate campaign that began in the early 2000s. The Helios Power campaign consisted of the following marketing tactics:

- *"A little better" tagline.* BP customers can expect to receive "a little better" experience at its service stations and other retail outlets compared to those of its competitors. Hand elaborates, "In this market, a little better means a lot. People see refueling as a necessary and unpleasant chore. However, BP can be cleaner and friendlier, and that's why people will choose us rather than our competitors." And this choice will be made on an emotional basis because customers "like what we stand for."

- *Animated TV ads.* These feature a family of characters (the Lighthouse family, the Babies, and the Beeps) and a catchy tune designed to reinforce the emotional appeal of the BP brand. The TV ads aired during some of the top U.S. TV shows (*American Idol, Ugly Betty*) and also had exposure on YouTube. The purposes of the ads were to generate awareness of and an emotional connection to the BP brand and its offerings.

- *In-store give-aways.* At the launch in April 2007, environmentally-friendly paper bags, T-shirts with a fun new look from the campaign, kids activity books and trading cards featuring the campaign characters, and sunflower seed packets were handed out to customers throughout the entire network of BP stations.
- *Unique website.* The www.alittlebettergasstation.com website features the "Gas Mania" interactive game, selected animations, ringtones, screensavers, a sweepstakes, and the TV ads.
- *Street teams.* BP and Ford teamed up to promote the use of BP's Ultimate gasoline in Ford's new Edge automobile. Videos featuring groups of college-aged students were created to showcase the BP brand in Florida and the ARCO brand in California.

Questions

1 (*a*) What is BP's "Helios" strategy? (*b*) How does this strategy relate to BP's mission and core values?

2 Conduct a SWOT (strengths, weaknesses, opportunities, and threats) analysis for BP's "Helios" initiative—looking forward globally to the next three years.

3 What are some ways BP could use to effectively communicate its "Helios" strategy to consumers?

4 What are the long-term benefits to (*a*) society and (*b*) BP of its "Helios" initiative?

5 Looking at BP's Helios Power marketing strategy and its "street team" marketing tactic: (*a*) What objectives would you set for this tactic? (*b*) How would you propose BP measure the results?

A BUILDING AN EFFECTIVE MARKETING PLAN

"New ideas are a dime a dozen," observes Arthur R. Kydd, "and so are new products and new technologies." Kydd should know. As chief executive officer of St. Croix Venture Partners, he and his firm have provided the seed money and venture capital to launch more than 60 start-up firms in the last 25 years. Today, those firms have more than 5,000 employees. Kydd explains:

> I get 200 to 300 marketing and business plans a year to look at, and St. Croix provides start-up financing for only two or three. What sets a potentially successful idea, product, or technology apart from all the rest is markets and marketing. If you have a real product with a distinctive point of difference that satisfies the needs of customers, you may have a winner. And you get a real feel for this in a well-written marketing or business plan.[1]

This appendix (1) describes what marketing and business plans are, including the purposes and guidelines in writing effective plans, and (2) provides a sample marketing plan.

MARKETING PLANS AND BUSINESS PLANS

This section first explains the meanings, purposes, and audiences of marketing plans and business plans, and then describes some writing guidelines for them and what external funders often look for in successful plans.

Meanings, Purposes, and Audiences

A marketing plan is a road map for the marketing activities of an organization for a specified future period of time, such as one year or five years.[2] It is important to note that no single "generic" marketing plan applies to all organizations and all situations. Rather, the specific format for a marketing plan for an organization depends on the following:

- *The target audience and purpose.* Elements included in a particular marketing plan depend heavily on (1) who the audience is and (2) what its purpose is. A marketing plan for an internal audience seeks to point the direction for future marketing activities and is sent to all individuals in the organization who must implement the plan or who will be affected by it. If the plan is directed to an external audience, such as friends, banks, venture capitalists, or potential investors, for the purpose of raising capital, it has the additional function of being an important sales document. In this case, it contains elements such as the strategic plan/focus, organization, structure, and biographies of key personnel that would rarely appear in an internal marketing plan. Also, the financial information is far more detailed when the plan is used to raise outside capital. The elements of a marketing plan for each of these two audiences are compared in Figure A–1.

- *The kind and complexity of the organization.* A small neighborhood restaurant has a somewhat different marketing plan than Nestlé, which serves international markets. The restaurant's plan would be relatively simple and directed at serving customers in a local market. In Nestlé's case, because there is a hierarchy of marketing plans, various levels of detail would be used—such as the entire organization, the strategic business unit, or the product/product line.

- *The industry.* Both the restaurant, serving a local market, and Medtronic, selling heart pacemakers globally, analyze competition. Not only are their geographic thrusts far different, but also the complexities of their offerings and, hence, the time periods likely to be covered by their plans differ. A one-year marketing plan may be adequate for the restaurant, but Medtronic may need a five-year planning horizon because product-development cycles for complex, new medical devices may be three or four years.

In contrast to a marketing plan, a **business plan** is a road map for the entire organization for a specified future period of time, such as one year or five years.[3] A key difference between a marketing plan and a business plan is that the business plan contains details on the research and development (R&D)/operations/manufacturing activities of the organization. Even for a manufacturing business, the marketing plan

Element of the plan	Marketing plan		Business plan	
	For internal audience (to direct the firm)	For external audience (to raise capital)	For internal audience (to direct the firm)	For external audience (to raise capital)
1. Executive summary	✓	✓	✓	✓
2. Description of company		✓		✓
3. Strategic plan/focus		✓		✓
4. Situation analysis	✓	✓	✓	✓
5. Market-product focus	✓	✓	✓	✓
6. Marketing program strategy and tactics	✓	✓	✓	✓
7. R&D and operations program			✓	✓
8. Financial projections	✓	✓	✓	✓
9. Organization structure		✓		✓
10. Implementation plan	✓	✓	✓	✓
11. Evaluation and control	✓		✓	
Appendix A: Biographies of key personnel		✓		✓
Appendix B, etc.: Details on other topics	✓	✓	✓	✓

FIGURE A–1

Elements in typical marketing and business plans targeted at different audiences

is probably 60 or 70 percent of the entire business plan. For businesses like a small restaurant or an auto repair shop, their marketing and business plans are virtually identical. The elements of a business plan typically targeted at internal and external audiences appear in the two right-hand columns in Figure A–1.

The Most-Asked Questions by Outside Audiences

Lenders and prospective investors reading a business or marketing plan that is used to seek new capital are probably the toughest audiences to satisfy. Their most-asked questions include the following:

1. Is the business or marketing idea valid?
2. Is there something unique or distinctive about the product or service that separates it from substitutes and competitors?
3. Is there a clear market for the product or service?
4. Are the financial projections realistic and healthy?
5. Are the key management and technical personnel capable, and do they have a track record in the industry in which they must compete?
6. Does the plan clearly describe how those providing capital will get their money back and make a profit?

Rhonda Abrams, author of *The Successful Business Plan,* observes, "Although you may spend five months preparing your plan, the cold, hard fact is that an investor or lender can dismiss it in less than five minutes."[4] While her comments apply to plans seeking to raise capital, the first five questions just listed apply equally well to plans for internal audiences.

Writing and Style Suggestions

There are no magic one-size-fits-all guidelines for writing successful marketing and business plans. Still, the following writing and style guidelines generally apply:[5]

- Use a direct, professional writing style. Use appropriate business terms without jargon. Present and future tenses with active voice ("I will write an effective marketing plan.") are generally better than past tense and passive voice ("An effective marketing plan was written by me.").

- Be positive and specific to convey potential success. At the same time, avoid superlatives ("terrific," "wonderful"). Specifics are better than glittering generalities. Use numbers for impact, justifying projections with reasonable quantitative assumptions, where possible.
- Use bullet points for conciseness and emphasis. As with the list you are reading, bullets enable key points to be highlighted effectively.
- Use A-level (the first level) and B-level (the second level) headings under the numbered section headings to help readers make easy transitions from one topic to another. This also forces the writer to organize the plan more carefully. Use these headings liberally, at least one every 200 to 300 words.
- Use visuals where appropriate. Photos, illustrations, graphs, and charts enable massive amounts of information to be presented succinctly.
- Shoot for a plan 15 to 35 pages in length, not including financial projections and appendixes. An uncomplicated small business may require only 15 pages, while a high-technology start-up may require more than 35 pages.
- Use care in layout, design, and presentation. Laser printers give a more professional look than ink-jet printers do. Use 11- or 12-point type (you are now reading 10.5-point type) in the text. Use a serif type (with "feet," like that you are reading now) in the text because it is easier to read, and sans serif (without "feet") in graphs and charts like Figure A–1. A bound report with a nice cover and clear title page adds professionalism.

These guidelines are used, where possible, in the sample marketing plan that follows.

SAMPLE FIVE-YEAR MARKETING PLAN FOR PARADISE KITCHENS® INC.

To help interpret the marketing plan for Paradise Kitchens Inc., that follows, we will describe the company and suggest some guidelines in interpreting the plan.

Background on Paradise Kitchens, Inc.

With a degree in chemical engineering, Randall F. Peters spent 15 years working for General Foods and Pillsbury with a number of diverse responsibilities: plant operations, R&D, restaurant operations, and new business development. His wife, Leah, with degrees in both molecular cellular biology and food science, held various Pillsbury executive positions in new category development and packaged goods, and restaurant R&D. In the company's start-up years, Paradise Kitchens survived on the savings of Randy and Leah, the cofounders. With their backgrounds, they decided Randy should serve as president and CEO of Paradise Kitchens, and Leah should focus on R&D and corporate strategy.

Interpreting the Marketing Plan

The marketing plan on the next pages, based on an actual Paradise Kitchens plan, is directed at an external audience (see Figure A–1). To protect proprietary information about the company, some details and dates have been altered, but the basic logic of the plan has been kept.

Notes in the margins next to the Paradise Kitchens plan fall into two categories:

1. *Substantive notes* are in blue boxes. These notes elaborate on the significance of an element in the marketing plan and are keyed to chapter references in this textbook.
2. *Writing style, format, and layout notes* are in red boxes and explain the editorial or visual rationale for the element.

A word of encouragement: Writing an effective marketing plan is hard, but challenging and satisfying, work. Dozens of the authors' students have used effective marketing plans they wrote for class in their interviewing portfolio to show prospective employers what they could do and to help them get their first job.

Color-coding Legend

Blue boxes explain significance of marketing plan elements.

Red boxes give writing style, format, and layout guidelines.

The Table of Contents provides quick access to the topics in the plan, usually organized by section and subsection headings.

Seen by many experts as the single most important element in the plan, the two-page Executive Summary "sells" the plan to readers through its clarity and brevity. For space reasons, it is not shown here, but the Building Your Marketing Plan exercise at the end of Chapter 2 asks the reader to write an Executive Summary for this plan.

The Company Description highlights the recent history and recent successes of the organization.

The Strategic Focus and Plan sets the strategic direction for the entire organization, a direction with which proposed actions of the marketing plan must be consistent. This section is not included in all marketing plans. See Chapter 2.

The qualitative Mission statement focuses the activities of Paradise Kitchens for the stakeholder groups to be served. See Chapter 2.

FIVE-YEAR MARKETING PLAN
Paradise Kitchens,® Inc.

Table of Contents

1. Executive Summary

2. Company Description

Paradise Kitchens®, Inc., was started by cofounders Randall F. Peters and Leah E. Peters to develop and market Howlin' Coyote® Chili, a unique line of single serve and microwavable Southwestern/Mexican style frozen chili products. The Howlin' Coyote line of chili was first introduced into the Minneapolis–St. Paul market and expanded to Denver two years later and Phoenix two years after that.

To the Company's knowledge, Howlin' Coyote is the only premium-quality, authentic Southwestern/Mexican style, frozen chili sold in U.S. grocery stores. Its high quality has gained fast, widespread acceptance in these markets. In fact, same-store sales doubled in the last year for which data are available. The Company believes the Howlin' Coyote brand can be extended to other categories of Southwestern/Mexican food products, such as tacos, enchiladas, and burritos.

Paradise Kitchens believes its high-quality, high-price strategy has proven successful. This marketing plan outlines how the Company will extend its geographic coverage from 3 markets to 20 markets by the year 2013.

3. Strategic Focus and Plan

This section covers three aspects of corporate strategy that influence the marketing plan: (1) the mission, (2) goals, and (3) core competence/sustainable competitive advantage of Paradise Kitchens.

<u>Mission</u>
The mission of Paradise Kitchens is to market lines of high-quality Southwestern/Mexican food products at premium prices that satisfy consumers in this fast-growing food segment while providing challenging career opportunities for employees and above-average returns to stockholders.

Goals

For the coming five years Paradise Kitchens seeks to achieve the following goals:

- Nonfinancial goals
  1. To retain its present image as the highest-quality line of Southwestern/ Mexican products in the food categories in which it competes.
  2. To enter 17 new metropolitan markets.
  3. To achieve national distribution in two convenience store or supermarket chains by 2008 and five by 2009.
  4. To add a new product line every third year.
  5. To be among the top five chili lines—regardless of packaging (frozen or canned)—in one-third of the metro markets in which it competes by 2009 and two-thirds by 2011.
- Financial goals
  1. To obtain a real (inflation-adjusted) growth in earnings per share of 8 percent per year over time.
  2. To obtain a return on equity of at least 20 percent.
  3. To have a public stock offering by the year 2009.

Core Competency and Sustainable Competitive Advantage

In terms of core competency, Paradise Kitchens seeks to achieve a unique ability to (1) provide distinctive, high-quality chilies and related products using Southwestern/Mexican recipes that appeal to and excite contemporary tastes for these products and (2) deliver these products to the customer's table using effective manufacturing and distribution systems that maintain the Company's quality standards.

To translate these core competencies into a sustainable competitive advantage, the Company will work closely with key suppliers and distributors to build the relationships and alliances necessary to satisfy the high taste standards of our customers.

To help achieve national distribution through chains, Paradise Kitchens recently introduced this point-of-purchase ad that adheres statically to the glass door of the freezer case.

4. Situation Analysis

This situation analysis starts with a snapshot of the current environment in which Paradise Kitchens finds itself by providing a brief SWOT (strengths, weaknesses, opportunities, threats) analysis. After this overview, the analysis probes ever-finer levels of detail: industry, competitors, company, and consumers.

SWOT Analysis

Figure 1 shows the internal and external factors affecting the market opportunities for Paradise Kitchens. Stated briefly, this SWOT analysis highlights the great strides taken by the company since its products first appeared on grocers' shelves.

Figure 1. SWOT Analysis for Paradise Kitchens

Internal Factors	Strengths	Weaknesses
Management	Experienced and entrepreneurial management and board	Small size can restrict options
Offerings	Unique, high-quality, high-price products	Many lower-quality, lower-price competitors
Marketing	Distribution in three markets with excellent acceptance	No national awareness or distribution; restricted shelf space in the freezer section
Personnel	Good workforce, though small; little turnover	Big gap if key employee leaves
Finance	Excellent growth in sales revenues	Limited resources may restrict growth opportunities when compared to giant competitors
Manufacturing	Sole supplier ensures high quality	Lack economies of scale of huge competitors
R&D	Continuing efforts to ensure quality in delivered products	Lack of canning and microwavable food processing expertise

External Factors	Opportunities	Threats
Consumer/Social	Upscale market, likely to be stable; Southwestern/Mexican food category is fast-growing segment due to growth in Hispanic American population and desire for spicier foods	Premium price may limit access to mass markets; consumers value a strong brand name
Competitive	Distinctive name and packaging in its markets	Not patentable; competitors can attempt to duplicate product; others better able to pay slotting fees
Technological	Technical breakthroughs enable smaller food producers to achieve many economies available to large competitors	Competitors have gained economies in canning and microwavable food processing
Economic	Consumer income is high; convenience important to U.S. households	More households "eating out," and bringing prepared take-out into home
Legal/Regulatory	High U.S. Food & Drug Administration standards eliminate fly-by-night competitors	Mergers among large competitors being approved by government

The text discussion of Figure 1 (the SWOT Analysis table) elaborates on its more important elements. This "walks" the reader through the information from the vantage of the plan's writer.

The Industry Analysis section provides the backdrop for the subsequent, more detailed analysis of competition, the company, and the company's customers. Without an in-depth understanding of the industry, the remaining analysis may be misdirected. See Chapter 2.

Sales of Mexican entrees are significant and provide a variety of future opportunities for Paradise Kitchens.

Even though relatively brief, this in-depth treatment of sales of Mexican foods in the United States demonstrates to the plan's readers the company's understanding of the industry in which it competes.

As with the Industry Analysis, the Competitors Analysis demonstrates that the company has a realistic understanding of its major chili competitors and their marketing strategies. Again, a realistic assessment gives confidence that subsequent marketing actions in the plan rest on a solid foundation. See Chapters 2, 3, 8, and 9.

In the Company's favor internally are its strengths of an experienced management team and board of directors, excellent acceptance of its lines in the three metropolitan markets in which it competes, and a strong manufacturing and distribution system to serve these limited markets. Favorable external factors (opportunities) include the increasing appeal of Southwestern/Mexican foods, the strength of the upscale market for the Company's products, and food-processing technological breakthroughs that make it easier for smaller food producers to compete.

Among unfavorable factors, the main weakness is the limited size of Paradise Kitchens relative to its competitors in terms of the depth of the management team, available financial resources, and national awareness and distribution of product lines. Threats include the danger that the Company's premium prices may limit access to mass markets and competition from the "eating-out" and "take-out" markets.

Industry Analysis: Trends in Frozen and Mexican Foods

Frozen Foods. According to Grocery Headquarters, consumers are flocking to the frozen food section of grocery retailers. The reasons: hectic lifestyles demanding increased convenience and an abundance of new, tastier, and nutritious products.[6] By 2007, total sales of frozen food in supermarkets, drugstores, and mass merchandisers, such as Target and Costco (excluding Wal-Mart) reached $29 billion. Prepared frozen meals, which are defined as meals or entrees that are frozen and require minimal preparation, accounted for $8.1 billion, or 26 percent of the total frozen food market.

Sales of Mexican entrees totaled $506 million.[7] Heavy consumers of frozen meals, those who eat five or more meals every two weeks, tend to be kids, teens, and young adults 35–44 years old.[8]

Mexican Foods. Currently, Mexican foods such as burritos, enchiladas, and tacos are used in two-thirds of American households. These trends reflect a generally more favorable attitude on the part of all Americans toward spicy foods that include red chili peppers. The growing Hispanic population in the U.S., about 44 million and almost $798 billion in purchasing power in 2007, partly explains the increasing demand for Mexican food. This Hispanic purchasing power is projected to be $1.2 trillion in 2011.[9]

Competitors in the Chili Market

The chili market represents over $500 million in annual sales. On average, consumers buy five to six servings annually, according to the NPD Group. The products fall primarily into two groups: canned chili (75 percent of sales) and dry chili (25 percent of sales).

This page uses a "block" style and does *not* indent each paragraph, although an extra space separates each paragraph. Compare this page with page 50, which has indented paragraphs. Most readers find indented paragraphs in marketing plans and long reports are easier to follow.

The Company Analysis provides details of the company's strengths and marketing strategies that will enable it to achieve the mission and goals identified earlier. See Chapters 2 and 8.

The higher-level "A heading" of Customer Analysis has a more dominant typeface and position than the lower-level "B heading" of Customer Characteristics. These headings introduce the reader to the sequence and level of topics covered. The organization of this textbook uses this kind of structure and headings.

Satisfying customers and providing genuine value to them is why organizations exist in a market economy. This section addresses the question of "Who are the customers for Paradise Kitchens' products?" See Chapters 5, 6, 7, 8 and 9.

Bluntly put, the major disadvantage of the segment's dominant product, canned chili, is that it does not taste very good. A taste test described in an issue of *Consumer Reports* magazine ranked 26 canned chili products "poor" to "fair" in overall sensory quality. The study concluded, "Chili doesn't have to be hot to be good. But really good chili, hot or mild, doesn't come out of a can."

Company Analysis

The husband-and-wife team that cofounded Paradise Kitchens, Inc., has 44 years of experience between them in the food-processing business. Both have played key roles in the management of the Pillsbury Company. They are being advised by a highly seasoned group of business professionals, who have extensive understanding of the requirements for new-product development.

The Company now uses a single outside producer with which it works closely to maintain the consistently high quality required in its products. The greater volume has increased production efficiencies, resulting in a steady decrease in the cost of goods sold.

Customer Analysis

In terms of customer analysis, this section describes (1) the characteristics of customers expected to buy Howlin' Coyote products and (2) health and nutrition concerns of Americans today.

Customer Characteristics. Demographically, chili products in general are purchased by consumers representing a broad range of socioeconomic backgrounds. Howlin' Coyote chili is purchased chiefly by consumers who have achieved higher levels of education and whose income is $50,000 and higher. These consumers represent 50 percent of canned and dry mix chili users.

The household buying Howlin' Coyote has one to three people in it. Among married couples, Howlin' Coyote is predominantly bought by households in which both spouses work. While women are a majority of the buyers, single men represent a significant segment.

Because the chili offers a quick way to make a tasty meal, the product's biggest users tend to be those most pressed for time. Howlin' Coyote's premium pricing also means that its purchasers are skewed toward the higher end of the income range. Buyers range in age from 25 to 54 and often live in the western United States, where spicy foods are more readily eaten.

The five Howlin' Coyote entrees offer a quick, tasty meal with high-quality ingredients.

Health and Nutrition Concerns. Coverage of food issues in the U.S. media is often erratic and occasionally alarmist. Because Americans are concerned about their diets, studies from organizations of widely varying credibility frequently receive significant attention from the major news organizations. For instance, a study of fat levels of movie popcorn was reported in all the major media. Similarly, studies on the healthfulness of Mexican food have received prominent play in print and broadcast reports. The high caloric levels of many Mexican and Southwestern-style foods have been widely reported and often exaggerated. Some Mexican frozen-food competitors, such as Don Miguel, Mission Foods, Ruiz Foods, and Jose Ole, plan to offer or have recently offered more "carb-friendly" and "fat-friendly" products in response to this concern.

Howlin' Coyote is already lower in calories, fat, and sodium than its competitors, and those qualities are not currently being stressed in its promotions. Instead, in the space and time available for promotions, Howlin' Coyote's taste, convenience, and flexibility are stressed.

5. Market-Product Focus

This section describes the five-year marketing and product objectives for Paradise Kitchens and the target markets, points of difference, and positioning of its lines of Howlin' Coyote chilies.

Marketing and Product Objectives

Howlin' Coyote's marketing intent is to take full advantage of its brand potential while building a base from which other revenue sources can be mined—both in and out of the retail grocery business. These are detailed in four areas below:

- Current markets. Current markets will be grown by expanding brand and flavor distribution at the retail level. In addition, same-store sales will be grown by increasing consumer awareness and repeat purchases, thereby leading to the more efficient broker/warehouse distribution channel.

- New markets. By the end of Year 5, the chili, salsa, burrito, and enchilada business will be expanded to a total of 20 metropolitan areas. This will represent 70 percent of U.S. food store sales.

- Food service. Food service sales will include chili products and smothering sauces. Sales are expected to reach $693,000 by the end of Year 3 and $1.5 million by the end of Year 5.

- New products. Howlin' Coyote's brand presence will be expanded at the retail level through the addition of new products in the frozen-foods section. This will be accomplished through new-product concept screening in Year 1 to identify new potential products. These products will be brought to market in Years 2 and 3.

Target Markets

The primary target market for Howlin' Coyote products is households with one to three people, where often both adults work, with individual income typically above $50,000 per year. These households contain more experienced, adventurous consumers of Southwestern/Mexican food and want premium quality products.

To help buyers see the many different uses for Howlin' Coyote chili, recipes are even printed on the *inside* of the packages.

Points of Difference

The "points of difference"—characteristics that make Howlin' Coyote chilies unique relative to competitors—fall into three important areas:

- Unique taste and convenience. No known competitor offers a high-quality, "authentic" frozen chili in a range of flavors. And no existing chili has the same combination of quick preparation and home-style taste that Howlin' Coyote does.
- Taste trends. The American palate is increasingly intrigued by hot spices. In response to this trend, Howlin' Coyote brands offer more "kick" than most other prepared chilies.
- Premium packaging. Howlin' Coyote's packaging graphics convey the unique, high-quality product contained inside and the product's nontraditional positioning.

Positioning

In the past chili products have been either convenient or tasty, but not both. Howlin' Coyote pairs these two desirable characteristics to obtain a positioning in consumers' minds as very high-quality "authentic Southwestern/Mexican–tasting" chilies that can be prepared easily and quickly.

Everything that has gone before in the marketing plan sets the stage for the marketing mix actions—the 4 Ps—covered in the marketing program. See Chapters 10 through 18.

The section describes in detail three key elements of the company's product strategy: the product line, its quality and how this is achieved, and its "cutting edge" packaging. See Chapters 10 and 11.

This Price Strategy section makes the company's price point very clear, along with its price position relative to potential substitutes. When appropriate and when space permits, this section might contain a break-even analysis. See Chapter 12.

This "introductory overview" sentence tells the reader the topics covered in the section—in this case in-store demonstrations, recipes, and cents-off coupons. While this sentence may be omitted in short memos or plans, it helps readers see where the text is leading. These sentences are used throughout this plan. This textbook also generally utilizes these introductory overview sentences to aid your comprehension.

6. Marketing Program

The four marketing mix elements of the Howlin' Coyote chili marketing program are detailed below. Note that "chile" is the vegetable and "chili" is the dish.

Product Strategy

This section discusses three key elements of the Howlin' Coyote product strategy: the product line, the approach to product quality, and packaging.

Product Line. Howlin' Coyote chili, retailing for $3.99 for an 11-ounce serving, is available in five flavors. The five are Green Chile Chili, Red Chile Chili, Beef and Black Bean Chili, Chicken Chunk Chili, and Mean Bean Chili.

Unique Product Quality. The flavoring systems of the Howlin' Coyote chilies are proprietary. The products' tastiness is due to extra care lavished upon the ingredients during production. The ingredients used are of unusually high quality. Meats are low-fat cuts and are fresh, not frozen, to preserve cell structure and moistness. Chilies are fire-roasted for fresher taste. Tomatoes and vegetables are select quality. No preservatives or artificial flavors are used.

Packaging. Reflecting the "cutting edge" marketing strategy of its producers, Howlin' Coyote bucks conventional wisdom in packaging. It avoids placing predict-able photographs of the product on its contain-ers. Instead, Howlin' Coyote's package shows a Southwestern motif that communicates the product's out-of-the-ordinary positioning.

Price Strategy

Howlin' Coyote Chili is, at $3.99 for an 11-ounce package, priced comparably to the other frozen offerings and higher than the canned and dried chili varieties. However, the significant taste advantages it has over canned chilies and the convenience advantages over dried chilies justify this pricing strategy.

The Southwestern motif makes Howlin' Coyote's packages stand out in a supermarket's freezer case.

Promotion Strategy

Key promotion programs feature in-store demonstrations, recipes, and cents-off coupons.

In-Store Demonstrations. In-store demonstrations enable consumers to try Howlin' Coyote products and discover their unique qualities. Demos will be conducted regularly in all markets to increase awareness and trial purchases.

Recipes. Because the products' flexibility is a key selling point, recipes are offered to consumers to stimulate use. The recipes are given at all in-store demonstrations, on the back of packages, through a mail-in recipe book offer, and in coupons sent by direct-mail or freestanding inserts.

Cents-Off Coupons. To generate trial and repeat-purchase of Howlin' Coyote products, coupons are distributed in four ways:

- In Sunday newspaper inserts. These inserts are widely read and help generate awareness.

- In-pack coupons. Each box of Howlin' Coyote chili will contain coupons for $1 off two more packages of the chili. These coupons will be included for the first three months the product is shipped to a new market. Doing so encourages repeat purchases by new users.

- Direct-mail chili coupons. Those households that fit the Howlin' Coyote demographics described previously will be mailed coupons.

- In-store demonstrations. Coupons will be passed out at in-store demonstrations to give an additional incentive to purchase.

Sunday newspaper inserts encourage consumer trial and provide recipes to show how Howlin' Coyote chili can be used in summer meals.

Place (Distribution) Strategy

Howlin' Coyote is distributed in its present markets through a food distributor. The distributor buys the product, warehouses it, and then resells and delivers it to grocery retailers on a store-by-store basis. As sales grow, we will shift to a more efficient system using a broker who sells the products to retail chains and grocery wholesalers.

7. Financial Data and Projections

Past Sales Revenues

Historically, Howlin' Coyote has had a steady increase in sales revenues since its introduction in 1999. In 2003, sales jumped spectacularly, due largely to new

The graph shows more clearly the dramatic growth of sales revenue than data in a table would do.

The Five-Year Projections section starts with the judgment forecast of cases sold and the resulting net sales. Gross profit and then operating profit—critical for the company's survival—are projected. An actual plan often contains many pages of computer-generated spreadsheet projections, usually shown in an appendix to the plan.

Because this table is very short, it is woven into the text, rather than given a figure number and title.

Because the plan proposes to enter 17 new metropolitan markets in the coming five years (for a total of 20), it is not possible to simply extrapolate the trend in Figure 2. Instead, management's judgment must be used. Methods of making sales forecasts—including the "lost horse" technique used here—are discussed in Chapter 8.

The Organization of Paradise Kitchens appears here. It reflects the bare-bones organizational structure of successful small businesses. Often a more elaborate marketing plan will show the new positions expected to be added as the firm grows.

promotion strategies. Sales have continued to rise, but at a less dramatic rate. The trend in sales revenues appears in Figure 2.

Five-Year Projections

Five-year financial projections for Paradise Kitchens appear below. These projections reflect the continuing growth in number of cases sold (with eight packages of Howlin' Coyote chili per case) and increasing production and distribution economies.

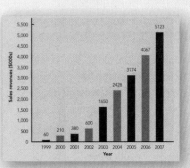

Figure 2.   Sales Revenues for Paradise Kitchens, Inc.

Financial Element	Units	Actual 2007	Projections Year 1 2008	Year 2 2009	Year 3 2010	Year 4 2011	Year 5 2012
Cases sold	1,000	353	684	889	1,249	1,499	1,799
Net sales	$1,000	5,123	9,913	12,884	18,111	21,733	26,080
Gross profit	$1,000	2,545	4,820	6,527	8,831	10,597	12,717
Operating profit (loss)	$1,000	339	985	2,906	2,805	3,366	4,039

8. Organization

Paradise Kitchens' present organization appears in Figure 3. It shows the four people reporting to the President. Below this level are both the full-time and part-time employees of the Company.

Figure 3.   The Paradise Kitchens Organization

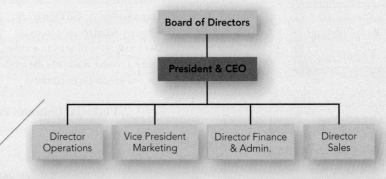

The Implementation Plan shows how the company will turn plans into results. Charts are often used to set deadlines and assign responsibilities for the many tactical marketing decisions needed to enter a new market.

At present Paradise Kitchens operates with full-time employees in only essential positions. It augments its full-time staff with key advisors, consultants, and subcontractors. As the firm grows, people with special expertise will be added to the staff.

9. Implementation Plan

Introducing Howlin' Coyote chilies to 17 new metropolitan areas is a complex task. This requires that creative promotional activities gain consumer awareness and initial trial among the target market households identified earlier. The anticipated rollout schedule to enter these metropolitan markets appears in Figure 4.

Figure 4. Rollout Schedule to Enter New U.S. Markets

New Markets Year	Cumulative Added	Cumulative Percentage of Markets	U.S. Markets
Today (2007)	2	5	16
Year 1 (2008)	3	8	21
Year 2 (2009)	4	12	29
Year 3 (2010)	2	14	37
Year 4 (2011)	3	17	45
Year 5 (2012)	3	20	53

Evaluation involves comparing actual sales with the targeted values set in the plan and taking appropriate actions. Note that the section briefly describes a contingency plan for alternative actions, depending on how successful the entry into a new market turns out to be.

The diverse regional tastes in chili will be monitored carefully to assess whether minor modifications may be required in the chili recipes. As the rollout to new metropolitan areas continues, Paradise Kitchens will assess manufacturing and distribution trade-offs. This is important in determining whether to start new production with selected high-quality regional contract packers.

10. Evaluation

Monthly sales targets in cases have been set for Howlin' Coyote chili for each metropolitan area. Actual case sales will be compared with these targets and marketing programs modified to reflect the unique sets of factors in each metropolitan area. The speed of the roll-out program will increase or decrease, depending on Paradise Kitchens' performance in the successive metropolitan markets it enters.

Appendix A. Biographical Sketches of Key Personnel

Appendix B. Detailed Financial Projections

Various appendixes may appear at the end of the plan, depending on the purpose and audience for them. For example, resumes of key personnel or detailed financial spreadsheets often appear in appendixes. For space reasons these are not shown here.

THE TOOLMAKERS

On the new Web, users are increasingly building their own tools. The result is greater customization and convenience, from maps that can be easily programmed to ads that change with every new blog post

craigslist
The classified-ad service has 23 employees but receives more traffic than all but seven other sites

Linked in
Social networking for suits. It brings together an élite clientele of global executives

ebay

At the auction site, the users are the police: customer ratings weed out the bad eggs

WIKIPEDIA
The ultimate crowdsourcing model, it showed that the masses are as smart as the experts

Google
The search empire built itself around a social function: counting links between websites

myspace.com
a place for friends
With 120 million users, it's a whole new society, with features that maximize individuality

Google AdSense
Provides free ads relevant to your website, then pays you if people click on them

Google Maps
Users can add their own points of interest to create mashups like www.beerhunter.ca

amazon.com
With customer reviews and recommendations, book buying is now a communal experience

THE GATHERERS
The crowd isn't just expressing itself more; it's also gathering and filtering all those blog posts and photographs and finding an audience for them

Blogger
The popular blogging-software service makes every would-be pundit a publisher

iStockphoto
This photo store taps an army of amateurs, who can sell their shots for as little as $1

flickr
The photo-scrapbook site helped popularize tagging as a way to organize information

Bloglines
Lets users subscribe to various sites then receive updates from each one on a single page

digg
The crowd as news editor: readers "digg" stories they like and "bury" ones they don't

del.icio.us
Allows users to share their Web-browser bookmarks, all organized by tags users provide

Technorati
Its search and ranking functions reveal the topics that are burning up the blogosphere

3 Scanning the Marketing Environment

WEB 2.0 IS ALL ABOUT YOU!

The Web is changing at an extraordinary pace and each new change provides more customization and convenience for you. If you use MySpace.com, Del.icio.us, Secondlife, or any one of hundreds of new products on the Web you are already part of the new world of the Web!

Not long ago the Web simply provided a modern channel for traditional businesses. Music led the way with file-sharing services such as Napster and eventually online stores such as iTunes. The entire entertainment industry followed by offering books, movies, television, radio, and photography on the Web. The digital revolution allowed all of these businesses to benefit from the technical aspects of the Web.

Now the term *Web 2.0* is used to describe the changes in the World Wide Web that reflect the growing interest in collaboration, open sharing of information, and customer control. Many products and services such as podcasts, weblogs, videologs, social networking, bookmarking, wikis, folksonomy, and RSS feeds are already available, and many more are in development.

As the focus moves from providing a new channel for existing businesses to empowering individual consumers with customized products, suddenly the Web is all about you! You can create your own video and post it on YouTube, sell your photos on iStockphoto, build a social networking site on Ning, and publish your ideas at Blogger. How did this happen? The marketing environment changed!

First, technologies such as high-speed Internet, high-resolution displays, and file-transfer software were developed. Second, the regulatory environment changed to allow the exchange and sale of copyrighted materials such as songs and movies. Third, competitive forces by companies such as Apple, Google, eBay, Microsoft, and Amazon gave the Web worldwide exposure. Finally, consumers changed. They are making it clear that they want "a tool for bringing together the small contributions of millions of people and making them matter." The future promises to be even more exciting. Some experts are already talking about Web 3.0![1]

Many businesses operate in environments where important forces change. Anticipating and responding to changes such as those taking place on the Web often means the difference between marketing success and failure. This chapter describes how the marketing environment has changed in the past and how it is likely to change in the future.

ENVIRONMENTAL SCANNING

environmental scanning
Process of acquiring information on events outside the organization to identify and interpret potential trends

Changes in the marketing environment are a source of opportunities and threats to be managed. The process of continually acquiring information on events occurring outside the organization to identify and interpret potential trends is called **environmental scanning**. Environmental trends typically arise from five sources: social, economic, technological, competitive, and regulatory forces. As shown in Figure 3–1 and described later in this chapter, these forces affect the marketing activities of a firm in numerous and unexpected ways.

An Environmental Scan of Today's Marketplace

What trends might affect marketing in the future? A firm conducting an environmental scan of the marketplace might uncover key trends such as those listed in Figure 3–2 for each of the five environmental forces.[2] Although the list of trends is far from complete, it reveals the breadth of an environmental scan—from the increasing diversity of the U.S. population, to the growing economic impact of China and India, to the dramatic growth of customer-generated content. These trends affect consumers and the businesses and organizations that serve them. Trends such as these are described in the following discussions of the five environmental forces.

SOCIAL FORCES

The **social forces** of the environment include the demographic characteristics of the population and its values. Changes in these forces can have a dramatic impact on marketing strategy.

Demographics

FIGURE 3–1
Environmental forces affect the organization, as well as its suppliers and customers.

Describing a population according to selected characteristics such as age, gender, ethnicity, income, and occupation is referred to as **demographics**. Several organizations such as the Population Reference Bureau and the United Nations monitor the world

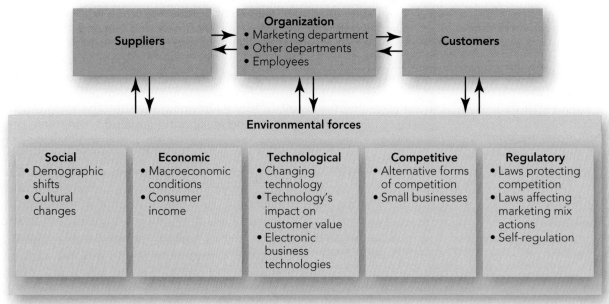

ENVIRONMENTAL FORCE	TREND IDENTIFIED BY AN ENVIRONMENTAL SCAN
Social	• Expanding use of social networks and collaborative web services • Increasing mobility and diversity of the population • Growing concern over global warming and climate change
Economic	• Shift to a global economy and the growing importance of China and India • Baby boomers begin turning sixty and spending retirement funds • Virtual online communities developing their own economies
Technological	• Increasing popularity of mobile TV • Advances in biometrics as a security solution • Growing demand for portable, renewable power sources
Competitive	• Dramatic increase in customer-generated content about competitive options • New metrics for assessment increase performance comparisons • Development and growth of competitive intelligence departments
Regulatory	• Increasing legislation requiring digital storage of corporate records • Greater concern for privacy and personal information collection • New regulations to respond to fear of terrorism

FIGURE 3–2

An environmental scan of today's marketplace shows the many important trends that influence marketing.

social forces

Demographic characteristics of the population and its values

demographics

Description of a population according to characteristics such as age, gender, ethnicity, income, and occupation

population profile, while many other organizations such as the U.S. Census Bureau provide information about the American population.

The World Population at a Glance The most recent estimates indicate there are 6.7 billion people in the world today, and the population is likely to grow to 9.2 billion by 2050. While this growth has led to the term *population explosion,* the increases have not occurred worldwide; they are primarily in the developing countries of Africa, Asia, and Latin America. In fact, India is predicted to have the world's largest population in 2050 with 1.6 billion people, and China will be a close second with 1.4 billion people.

Another important global trend is the shifting age structure of the world population. The number of people older than 60 is expected to more than triple in the coming decades and reach 2 billion by 2050. Again, the magnitude of this trend varies by region, and developed countries such as the United States are expected to face the highest growth rates of the elderly age group. Global income levels and living standards have also been increasing, although the averages across countries are very different. Per capita income, for example, ranges from $43,000 in Luxembourg, to $24,000 in Canada, to $800 in Afghanistan.

For marketers, global trends such as these have many implications. Obviously, the relative size of countries such as India and China will mean they represent huge markets for many product categories. Elderly populations in developed countries are likely to save less and begin spending their funds on health care, travel, and other retirement-related products and services. Economic progress in developing countries will lead to growth in entrepreneurship, new markets for infrastructure related to manufacturing, communication, and distribution, and the growth of exports.[3]

The U.S. Population Studies of the demographic characteristics of the U.S. population suggest several important trends. Generally, the population is becoming larger, older, and more diverse. In 2008, the U.S. population was estimated to be 303 million people. If current trends in life expectancy, birthrates, and immigration continue, by

2030 the U.S. population will exceed 360 million people. This growth suggests that niche markets based on age, life stage, family structure, geographic location, and ethnicity will become increasingly important. The global trend toward an older population is particularly true in the United States. Today, there are approximately 35 million people 65 and older. By 2030, this age group will include more than 70 million people, or 20 percent of the population. You may have noticed companies trying to attract older consumers. Mobile phone manufacturer LG, for example, recently introduced a phone with large easy-to-read buttons for seniors. Finally, the term *minority* as it is currently used is likely to become obsolete as the size of most ethnic groups will double during the next two decades.[4]

Generational Cohorts   A major reason for the graying of America is that the **baby boomers**—the generation of children born between 1946 and 1964—are growing older. As the 78 million boomers have aged, their participation in the workforce and their earnings have increased, making them an important consumer market. This group accounts for an estimated 56 to 58 percent of the purchases in most consumer product and service categories. In the future, boomers' interests will reflect concern for their children and grandchildren, their own health, and their retirement, and companies will need to position products to respond to these interests. Generally, baby boomers are receptive to anything that makes them feel younger. Olay's Total Effects product line, for example, includes anti-aging moisturizers, cleansing cloths, and restoration treatments designed for this age group.

The baby boom cohort is followed by **Generation X**, which includes the 15 percent of the population born between 1965 and 1976. This period is also known as the baby bust, because the number of children born each year was declining. This is a generation of consumers who are self-reliant, supportive of racial and ethnic diversity, and better educated than any previous generation. They are not prone to extravagance and are likely to pursue lifestyles that are a blend of caution, pragmatism, and traditionalism. In terms of net worth, Generation X is the first generation to have less than the previous generation. As baby boomers move toward retirement, however, Generation X is becoming a dominant force in many markets. Generation X, for example, is replacing baby boomers as the largest segment of business travelers. In response, hotel companies are creating new concepts that appeal to the younger market. Surveys of Generation X travelers indicate they want casual, tech-friendly lodging with 24-hour access to food and drinks, so Hyatt Corporation is building

baby boomers
Generation of children born between 1946 and 1964

Generation X
Members of the U.S. population born between 1965 and 1976

Which generational cohorts are these three advertisers trying to reach?

Generation Y Is Becoming a Generation of Entrepreneurs!

Generation Y is known as a savvy and demanding group of consumers who feel personally responsible for making a difference in the world. They also have an extraordinary optimism about their potential for fame and fortune. Rather than pursue traditional "corporate" jobs, however, many millennials are becoming entrepreneurs.

Many Generation Y children grew up in families where their parents found it difficult to create a work–life balance. To avoid that conflict, this generation is attracted to new ventures where they can be their own boss. As management consultant Bruce Tulgan explains, "They want to create a custom life and create the kind of career that fits around the kind of life they want."

Ben Kaufman is a typical example of the Gen Y entrepreneur. As a 20-year-old college student he started a company named Mophie that makes cases, armbands, and belt clips as iPod accessories. The success of the company has attracted $1.5 million in venture capital, but more importantly for Kaufman, it allows him to have a job that he likes. Similarly, Sheena Lindahl used her interest in creating her own career to start a business called Extreme Entrepreneurship Education, a business designed to help and inspire college students.

The Bureau of Labor Statistics predicts that the future will bring many more entrepreneurs like Kaufman. There are currently 370,000 entrepreneurs in the 16 to 24 age category, and the historical growth rate is expected to double through 2014. Are you a future Gen Y entrepreneur?

---

400 new Hyatt Place all-suite hotels featuring control panels for MP3 players and computers, plasma-screen TVs, and coffee and wine bars.[5]

The generational cohort labeled **Generation Y** includes the 72 million Americans born between 1977 and 1994. This was a period of increasing births, which resulted from baby boomers having children, and it is often referred to as the echo-boom or baby boomlet. Generation Y exerts influence on music, sports, computers, video games, and especially cell phones. Generation Y views wireless communication as a lifeline to friends and family and has been the first to use web-enabled mobile phones to stream video, send and receive text messages, play games, and access e-mail. This is also a group that is attracted to purposeful work where they have control. The accompanying Marketing Matters box describes the entrepreneurial spirit of Generation Y.[6] The term *millennials* is also used, with inconsistent definitions, to refer to younger members of Generation Y and sometimes to Americans born since 1994.

Because the members of each generation are distinctive in their attitudes and consumer behavior, marketers have been studying the many groups or cohorts that make up the marketplace and have developed *generational marketing* programs for them. In addition, global marketers have discovered that many of the American generational differences also exist outside of the United States.[7]

Generation Y
The 72 million Americans born between 1977 and 1994

Population Shifts   A major regional shift in the U.S. population toward western and southern states is under way. From 2005 to 2006, Arizona, Nevada, Idaho, Georgia, and Texas grew at the fastest rates. Three states—California, Texas, and Florida—will account for 45 percent of the population change in the United States through 2025, gaining more than 6 million people in each state.[8]

To assist marketers in gathering data on the population, the Census Bureau has developed a classification system to describe the varying locations of the population. The system consists of two types of *statistical areas:*

- A *metropolitan statistical area* has at least one urbanized area of 50,000 or more people and adjacent territory that has a high degree of social and economic integration.
- A *micropolitan statistical area* has at least one urban cluster of at least 10,000 but less than 50,000 people and adjacent territory that has a high degree of social and economic integration.

If a metropolitan statistical area contains a population of 2.5 million or more, it may be subdivided into smaller areas called *metropolitan divisions*. In addition, adjacent metropolitan statistical areas and micropolitan statistical areas may be grouped into *combined statistical areas*.[9]

There are currently 362 metropolitan statistical areas, which include 83 percent of the population, and 573 micropolitan areas, which include 10 percent of the population.

Racial and Ethnic Diversity   A notable trend is the changing racial and ethnic composition of the U.S. population. Approximately one in four U.S. residents is African American, American Indian, Asian, Pacific Islander, or a representative of another racial or ethnic group. Diversity is further evident in the variety of peoples that make up these groups. For example, Asians consist of Asian Indians, Chinese, Filipinos, Japanese, Koreans, and Vietnamese. For the first time, the 2000 Census allowed respondents to choose more than one of the six race options, and more than 6 million reported more than one race. Hispanics, who may be from any race, currently make up 12 percent of the U.S. population and are represented by Mexicans, Puerto Ricans, Cubans, and others of Central and South American ancestry. While the United States is becoming more diverse, Figure 3–3 suggests that the minority racial and ethnic groups tend to be concentrated in geographic regions.[10]

While the growing size of these groups has been identified through new Census data, their economic impact on the marketplace is also very noticeable. By 2010, Hispanics, African Americans, and Asians will spend $1.09 trillion, $1.02 trillion, and $578 billion each year, respectively. To adapt to this new marketplace, many companies are developing **multicultural marketing** programs, which are combinations of the marketing mix that reflect the unique attitudes, ancestry, communication preferences, and lifestyles of different races. Because businesses must now market their products to a consumer base with many racial and ethnic identities, in-depth marketing research that allows an accurate understanding of each culture is essential.[11]

multicultural marketing
Marketing programs that reflect unique aspects of different races

FIGURE 3–3
Racial and ethnic groups (excluding Caucasians) are concentrated in geographic regions of the United States.

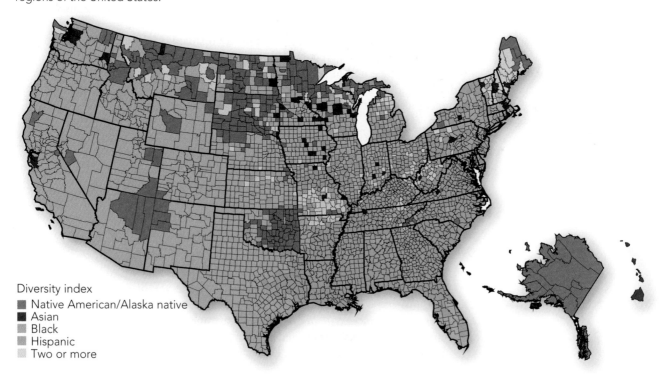

Diversity index
■ Native American/Alaska native
■ Asian
■ Black
■ Hispanic
■ Two or more

Culture

culture
Set of values, ideas, and attitudes that are learned and shared among the members of a group

A second social force, **culture**, incorporates the set of values, ideas, and attitudes that are learned and shared among the members of a group. Because many of the elements of culture influence consumer buying patterns, monitoring national and global cultural trends is important for marketing. Cross-cultural analysis needed for global marketing is discussed in Chapter 7.

Culture also includes values, which vary with age but tend to be very similar for men and women. All age groups, for example, rank "protecting the family" and "honesty" as the most important values. Consumers under 20 years old rank "friendship" third, while the 20-to-29 and 30-to-39 age groups rank "self-esteem" and "health and fitness" as their third most important values, respectively.

Increasingly important values for consumers are preserving the environment and other health issues. These values are reflected in the growth of products that consumers believe are consistent with their values. Dannon Co., for example, has developed probiotic yogurts such as Light & Fit Crave Control yogurt and immunity-boosting DanActive for health-conscious consumers. Concern for the environment is one reason consumers are buying hybrid gas-electric automobiles such as the Toyota Prius and energy-efficient lightbulbs such as General Electric's Energy Smart fluorescent bulbs. Companies are also changing their business practices to respond to trends in consumer values. Wal-Mart has set ambitious goals to cut energy use, switch to renewable power, and reduce packaging on the products it carries.[12]

learning review

1. Describe three generational cohorts.

2. Why are many companies developing multicultural marketing programs?

3. How are important values such as health and fitness reflected in the marketplace today?

ECONOMIC FORCES

LO3

The second component of the environmental scan, the **economy**, pertains to the income, expenditures, and resources that affect the cost of running a business and household. We'll consider two aspects of these economic forces: a macroeconomic view of the marketplace and a microeconomic perspective of consumer income.

Macroeconomic Conditions

economy
Income, expenditures, and resources that affect the cost of running a business or household

Of particular concern at the macroeconomic level is the inflationary or recessionary state of the economy, whether actual or perceived by consumers or businesses. In an inflationary economy, the cost to produce and buy products and services escalates as prices increase. From a marketing standpoint, if prices rise faster than consumer incomes, the number of items consumers can buy decreases. This relationship is evident in the cost of a college education. The price of attending college has increased 29 percent during the past 10 years while median family income rose 3 percent during the same period.[13]

Whereas inflation is a period of price increases, recession is a time of slow economic activity. Businesses decrease production, unemployment rises, and many consumers have less money to spend. The U.S. economy experienced recessions in the early 1970s, early 1980s, and early 1990s. The economy again entered a recessionary period from 2001 through 2003, and then began a period of growth.[14]

FIGURE 3–4
U.S. households have a large
range of gross incomes.
See the text for descriptions
of gross, disposable, and
discretionary incomes.

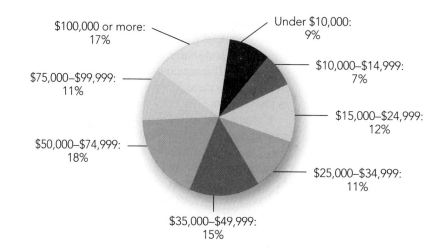

Consumer Income

The microeconomic trends in terms of consumer income are also important issues for marketers. Having a product that meets the needs of consumers may be of little value if they are unable to purchase it. A consumer's ability to buy is related to income, which consists of gross, disposable, and discretionary components.

Gross Income   The total amount of money made in one year by a person, household, or family unit is referred to as *gross income* (or "money income" at the Census Bureau). While the typical U.S. household earned only about $8,700 of income in 1970, it earned about $48,201 in 2006. When gross income is adjusted for inflation, however, income of that typical U.S. household was relatively stable. In fact, inflation-adjusted income has only varied between $40,187 and $49,244 since 1977. Figure 3–4 shows the distribution of annual income among U.S. households.[15] Are you from a typical household?

Disposable Income   The second income component, *disposable income,* is the money a consumer has left after paying taxes to use for food, shelter, clothing, and transportation. Thus, if taxes rise at a faster rate than does income, consumers must economize. In recent years, consumers' allocation of income has shifted. As the marketplace has become more efficient, producing products that are more durable and use less energy, consumers have increased their disposable income. Car maintenance costs, for example, have declined 28 percent since 1985, because automobile quality has improved. Much of the money is being spent on new categories of "necessities" such as vitamins and supplements; antibacterial body washes, lotions, and deodorants; antiwrinkle creams; and children's shampoos, toothpaste, and bath products.[16]

Discretionary Income   The third component of income is *discretionary income,* the money that remains after paying for taxes and necessities. Discretionary income is used for luxury items such as a cruise on the *Queen Mary 2*. An obvious problem in defining discretionary versus disposable income is determining what is a luxury and what is a necessity.

The Department of Labor monitors consumer expenditures through its annual Consumer Expenditure Survey. In 2006, consumers spent approximately 13 percent of their income on food, 34 percent on housing, and 4 percent on clothes. While an additional 35 percent is often spent on transportation, health care, and insurance, the remainder is generally viewed as discretionary. The percentage of income spent on food and housing typically declines as income increases, which can provide an increase in

As consumers' discretionary income increases, so does the opportunity to indulge in the luxurious leisure travel marketed by Cunard.

discretionary income. Discretionary expenditures can also be increased by reducing savings. The Bureau of Labor Statistics has observed that the percentage of income put into savings has been steadily declining and has been negative since 2005.[17]

TECHNOLOGICAL FORCES

LO4

Our society is in a period of dramatic technological change. **Technology**, the third environmental force, refers to inventions or innovations from applied science or engineering research. Each new wave of technological innovation can replace existing products and companies. Do you recognize the items pictured on the next page and what they may replace?

technology
Inventions from applied science or engineering research

Technology of Tomorrow

Technological change is the result of research, so it is difficult to predict. Some of the most dramatic technological changes occurring now, however, include the following:

- Internet TV and mobile TV will become simple and available for most consumers.
- Advances in nanotechnology, the science of unimaginably small electronics, will lead to smaller microprocessors, efficient fuel cells, and cancer-detection sensors.
- Touch-screen and gesture-based navigation technology will change how we interface with computers, phones, and most electronics.
- Companies will begin building software databases so that lines of code can be reused, and open software will allow users to customize products to their specific interests and applications.

These trends in technology are already seen in today's marketplace. Samsung has developed new phones that will utilize the next-generation networks (WiMAX) to allow users to surf the Web and watch TV. Nintendo uses motion-sensing chips in its

Technological change leads to new products. What products might be replaced by these innovations?

Wii game system, and the social networking site, MySpace, allows users to change the software code to customize their profile layout. Other technologies such as high-definition disc players, speech recognition software, and customized music services are likely to replace or substitute for existing products and services such as DVD players, keyboards, and radio.[18]

Technology's Impact on Customer Value

Advances in technology are having important effects on marketing. First, the cost of technology is plummeting, causing the customer value assessment of technology-based products to focus on other dimensions such as quality, service, and relationships. When Plaxo introduced its address book software, it gave the product away at no charge, reasoning that satisfied customers would later buy upgrades and related products. A similar approach is now used by many cellular telephone vendors, who charge little for the telephone if the purchase leads to a telephone service contract.[19]

Technology also provides value through the development of new products. Many automobile manufacturers now offer customers a navigation system that uses satellite signals to help the driver reach any destination. Under development are radarlike collision avoidance systems that disengage cruise control, reduce the engine speed, and even apply the brakes.[20] Other new products likely to be available soon include a "smart ski" with an embedded microprocessor that will adjust the flexibility of the ski to snow conditions; injectable health monitors that will send glucose, oxygen, and other clinical information to a wristwatch-like monitor; and electronic books that will allow you to download any volume and view it on pages coated with electronic "ink" and embedded electrodes.[21]

Electronic Business Technologies

marketspace

Information- and communication-based electronic exchange environment occupied by digitized offerings

The transformative power of technology may be best illustrated by the rapid growth of the **marketspace**, an information- and communication-based electronic exchange environment mostly occupied by computer and telecommunication technologies and digitized offerings. Any activity that uses some form of electronic communication in the inventory, exchange, advertisement, distribution, and payment of goods and services is often called *electronic commerce*. Network technologies are now used for everything from filing expense reports, to monitoring daily sales, to sharing information with employees, to communicating instantly with suppliers.

Many companies have adapted Internet-based technology internally to support their electronic business strategies. An *intranet,* for example, is an Internet-based network used within the boundaries of an organization. It is a private network that may or may not be connected to the public Internet. *Extranets,* which use Internet-based technologies, permit communication between a company and its supplier, distributors, and other partners (such as advertising agencies).

COMPETITIVE FORCES

competition

Alternative firms that could provide a product to satisfy a specific market's needs

The fourth component of the environmental scan, **competition**, refers to the alternative firms that could provide a product to satisfy a specific market's needs. There are various forms of competition, and each company must consider its present and potential competitors in designing its marketing strategy.

Alternative Forms of Competition

LO5

Four basic forms of competition form a continuum from pure competition to monopolistic competition to oligopoly to pure monopoly.

At one end of the continuum is *pure competition,* in which every company has a similar product. Companies that deal in commodities common to agribusiness (for example, wheat, rice, and grain) often are in a pure competition position in which distribution (in the sense of shipping products) is important but other elements of marketing have little impact.

In the second point on the continuum, *monopolistic competition,* the many sellers compete with their products on a substitutable basis. For example, if the price of coffee rises too much, consumers may switch to tea. Coupons or sales are frequently used marketing tactics.

Oligopoly, a common industry structure, occurs when a few companies control the majority of industry sales. For example, AT&T, MCI, Verizon, and Sprint control approximately 80 percent of the $16 billion international long-distance telephone service market. Similarly, the entertainment industry in the United States is dominated by Viacom, Disney, and Time Warner, and the major firms in the U.S. defense contractor industry are Boeing, United Technologies, and Lockheed Martin. Critics of oligopolies suggest that because there are few sellers, price competition among firms is not desirable because it leads to reduced profits for all producers.[22]

The final point on the continuum, *pure monopoly,* occurs when only one firm sells the product. Monopolies are common for producers of goods considered essential to a community: water, electricity, and telephone service. Typically, marketing plays a small role in a monopolistic setting because it is regulated by the state or federal government. Government control usually seeks to ensure price protection for the buyer, although deregulation in recent years has encouraged price competition in the electricity market.[23] Concern that Microsoft's 86 percent share of the PC operating system market is a monopoly has led to lawsuits and consent decrees from the U.S. Justice Department and fines from the European Union.[24]

Small Businesses as Competitors

While large companies provide familiar examples of the forms and components of competition, small businesses make up the majority of the competitive landscape for most businesses. Consider that there are approximately 23 million small businesses in the United States, which employ half of all private sector employees. In addition, small businesses generate 60 to 80 percent of all new jobs annually and 50 percent of the gross domestic product (GDP). Research has shown a strong correlation between national economic growth and the level of new small business activity in the previous years.[25]

REGULATORY FORCES

LO6

regulation
Restrictions state and federal laws place on business

For any organization, the marketing and broader business decisions are constrained, directed, and influenced by regulatory forces. **Regulation** consists of restrictions state and federal laws place on business with regard to the conduct of its activities. Regulation exists to protect companies as well as consumers. Much of the regulation from the federal and state levels is the result of an active political process and has been passed to ensure competition and fair business practices. For consumers, the focus of legislation is to protect them from unfair trade practices and ensure their safety.

Protecting Competition

Major federal legislation has been passed to encourage competition, which is deemed desirable because it permits the consumer to determine which competitor will succeed and which will fail. The first such law was the *Sherman Antitrust Act* (1890). Lobbying by farmers in the Midwest against fixed railroad shipping prices led to the passage of this act, which forbids (1) contracts, combinations, or conspiracies in restraint of trade and (2) actual monopolies or attempts to monopolize any part of trade or commerce. Because of vague wording and government inactivity, however, there was only one successful case against a company in the nine years after the act became law, and the Sherman Act was supplemented with the *Clayton Act* (1914). This act forbids certain actions that are likely to lessen competition, although no actual harm has yet occurred.

In the 1930s, the federal government had to act again to ensure fair competition. During that time, large chain stores appeared, such as the Great Atlantic & Pacific Tea Company (A&P). Small businesses were threatened, and they lobbied for the *Robinson-Patman Act* (1936). This act makes it unlawful to discriminate in prices charged to different purchasers of the same product, where the effect may substantially lessen competition or help to create a monopoly.

Product-Related Legislation

Various federal laws in existence specifically address the product component of the marketing mix. Some are aimed at protecting the company, some at protecting the consumer, and at least one at protecting both.

Company Protection A company can protect its competitive position in new and novel products under the patent law, which gives inventors the right to exclude others from making, using, or selling products that infringe the patented invention. The federal copyright law is another way for a company to protect its competitive position in a product. The copyright law gives the author of a literary, dramatic, musical, or artistic work

These products are identified by protected trademarks. Are any of these trademarks in danger of becoming generic?

the exclusive right to print, perform, or otherwise copy that work. Copyright is secured automatically when the work is created. However, the published work should bear an appropriate copyright notice, including the copyright symbol, the first year of publication, and the name of the copyright owner, and it must be registered under the federal copyright law. Digital technology has necessitated new copyright legislation, called the *Digital Millenium Copyright Act* (1998), to improve protection of copyrighted digital products. In addition, producers of DVD movies, music recordings, and software want protection from devices designed to circumvent antipiracy elements of their products.[26]

Consumer Protection   There are many consumer-oriented federal laws regarding products. The various laws include more than 30 amendments and separate laws relating to food, drugs, and cosmetics, such as the *Infant Formula Act* (1980), the *Nutritional Labeling and Education Act* (1990), new labeling requirements for dietary supplements (1997), and proposed labeling guidelines for trans fats (2006).[27] Various other consumer protection laws have a broader scope, such as the *Fair Packaging and Labeling Act* (1966), the *Child Protection Act* (1966), and the *Consumer Product Safety Act* (1972), which established the Consumer Product Safety Commission to monitor product safety and establish uniform product safety standards. Many of these laws came about because of **consumerism**, a grassroots movement started in the 1960s to increase the influence, power, and rights of consumers in dealing with institutions. This movement continues and is reflected in growing consumer demands for ecologically safe products and ethical and socially responsible business practices. One hotly debated issue concerns liability for environmental abuse.

consumerism

A movement started to increase the influence, rights, and power of consumers

Both Company and Consumer Protection   Trademarks are intended to protect both the firm selling a trademarked product and the consumer buying it. A Senate report states:

> The purposes underlying any trademark statute [are] twofold. One is to protect the public so that it may be confident that, in purchasing a product bearing a particular trademark which it favorably knows, it will get the product which it asks for and wants to get. Secondly, where the owner of a trademark has spent energy, time, and money in presenting to the public the product, he is protected in this investment from misappropriation in pirates and cheats.

This statement was made in connection with another product-related law, the *Lanham Act* (1946), which provides for registration of a company's trademarks. Historically, the first user of a trademark in commerce had the exclusive right to use that particular word,

Are Doppelgangers a First Amendment Right?

Have you seen an ad or a logo that looked like a familiar brand but was slightly different? Some examples you might be familiar with include a commercial for Chevy Tahoe saying "global warming is here," and Starbucks logos that read "Evil Empire" or "Frankenbucks Coffee." These parodies—sometimes called Doppelgangers—are a growing form of citizen protest called culture jamming. The purpose of the parodies is to undermine the integrity of existing brand marketing. Companies currently have different responses to Doppel-

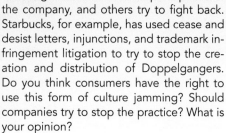

gangers. Some companies ignore them, others try to monitor the parodies for insight about consumer perceptions of the company, and others try to fight back. Starbucks, for example, has used cease and desist letters, injunctions, and trademark infringement litigation to try to stop the creation and distribution of Doppelgangers. Do you think consumers have the right to use this form of culture jamming? Should companies try to stop the practice? What is your opinion?

name, or symbol in its business. Registration under the Lanham Act provides important advantages to a trademark owner that has used the trademark in interstate or foreign commerce, but it does not confer ownership. A company can lose its trademark if it becomes generic, which means that it has primarily come to be merely a common descriptive word for the product. Coca-Cola, Whopper, and Xerox are registered trademarks, and competitors cannot use these names. Aspirin and escalator are former trademarks that are now generic terms in the United States and can be used by anyone.

In 1988, the *Trademark Law Revision Act* resulted in a major change to the Lanham Act, allowing a company to secure rights to a name before actual use by declaring an intent to use the name.[28] In 2003, the United States agreed to participate in the *Madrid Protocol,* which is a treaty that facilitates the protection of U.S. trademark rights throughout the world.[29] See the Making Responsible Decisions box to learn about a use (or misuse) of trademarks called Doppelgangers.[30]

One of the most recent changes in trademark law is the U.S. Supreme Court's ruling that companies may obtain trademarks for colors associated with their products. Over time, consumers may begin to associate a particular color with a specific brand. Examples of products that may benefit from the new law include NutraSweet's sugar substitute in pastel blue packages and Owens-Corning Fiberglas Corporation's pink insulation.[31] Another recent addition to trademark law is the *Federal Dilution Act* (1995), which is used to prevent someone from using a trademark on a noncompeting product (e.g., "Cadillac" brushes).[32]

Pricing-Related Legislation

The pricing component of the marketing mix is the focus of regulation from two perspectives: price fixing and price discounting. Although the Sherman Act did not outlaw price fixing, the courts view this behavior as *per se illegal* (*per se* means "through or of itself"), which means the courts see price fixing itself as illegal.

Certain forms of price discounting are allowed. Quantity discounts are acceptable; that is, buyers can be charged different prices for a product provided there are differences in manufacturing or delivery costs. Promotional allowances or services may be given to buyers on an equal basis proportionate to volume purchased. Also, a firm can meet a competitor's price "in good faith." Legal and ethical aspects of pricing are covered in more detail in Chapter 12.

Distribution-Related Legislation

The government has four concerns with regard to distribution—earlier referred to as "place" actions in the marketing mix—and the maintenance of competition. The first, *exclusive dealing,* is an arrangement a manufacturer makes with a reseller to handle only its products and not those of competitors. This practice is only illegal under the Clayton Act when it substantially lessens competition.

Requirement contracts require a buyer to purchase all or part of its needs for a product from one seller for a period of time. These contracts are not always illegal but depend on the court's interpretation of their impact on distribution.

Exclusive territorial distributorships are a third distribution issue often under regulatory scrutiny. In this situation, a manufacturer grants a distributor the sole rights to sell a product in a specific geographical area. The courts have found few violations with these arrangements.

The fourth distribution strategy is a *tying arrangement,* whereby a seller requires the purchaser of one product to also buy another item in the line. These contracts may be illegal when the seller has such economic power in the tying product that the seller can restrain trade in the tied product.

Advertising- and Promotion-Related Legislation

Promotion and advertising are aspects of marketing closely monitored by the Federal Trade Commission (FTC), which was established by the *FTC Act of 1914.* The FTC has been concerned with deceptive or misleading advertising and unfair business practices and has the power to (1) issue cease and desist orders and (2) order corrective advertising. In issuing a *cease and desist order,* the FTC orders a company to stop practices it considers unfair. With *corrective advertising,* the FTC can require a company to spend money on advertising to correct previous misleading ads. The enforcement powers of the FTC are so significant that often just an indication of concern from the commission can cause companies to revise their promotion.

A landmark legal battle regarding deceptive advertising involved the Federal Trade Commission and Campbell Soup Co. It had been Campbell's practice to insert clear glass marbles into the bottom of soup containers used in print advertisements to bring the soup ingredients (e.g., noodles or chicken) to the surface. The FTC ruled that the advertising was deceptive because it misrepresented the amount of solid ingredients in the soup, and it issued a cease and desist order. Campbell and its advertising agency agreed to discontinue the practice. Future ads used a ladle to show the ingredients.[33]

Other laws have been introduced to regulate promotion practices. The *Deceptive Mail Prevention and Enforcement Act* (1999), for example, provides specifications for direct-mail sweepstakes, such as the requirement that the statement "No purchase is necessary to enter" is displayed in the mailing, in the rules, and on the entry form. Similarly, the *Telephone Consumer Protection Act* (1991) provides requirements for telemarketing promotions, including fax promotions. Telemarketing is also subject to a law that created the *National Do Not Call Registry,* which is a list of consumer phone numbers of people who do not want to receive unsolicited telemarketing calls. Finally, new laws such as the *Children's Online Privacy Protection Act* (1998) and the *Controlling the Assault of Non-Solicited Pornography and Marketing (CAN-SPAM) Act* (2004) are designed to restrict information collection and unsolicited e-mail promotions on the Internet.[34]

Control through Self-Regulation

self-regulation
Alternative to government control where an industry attempts to police itself

The government has provided much legislation to create a competitive business climate and protect the consumer. An alternative to government control is **self-regulation**, where an industry attempts to police itself. The major television networks, for example, have used self-regulation to set their own guidelines for TV ads for children's toys. These

BBB OnLine.

Companies must meet certain requirements before they can display this logo on their websites.

guidelines have generally worked well. There are two problems with self-regulation, however: noncompliance by members and enforcement. In addition, if attempts at self-regulation are too strong, they may violate the Robinson-Patman Act. The best-known self-regulatory group is the Better Business Bureau (BBB). This agency is a voluntary alliance of companies whose goal is to help maintain fair practices. Although the BBB has no legal power, it does try to use "moral suasion" to get members to comply with its ruling. The BBB recently developed a reliability assurance program, called BBB Online, to provide objective consumer protection for Internet shoppers. Before they display the BBB Online logo on their website, participating companies must be members of their local Better Business Bureau, have been in business for at least one year, have agreed to abide by BBB standards of truth in advertising, and have committed to work with the BBB to resolve consumer disputes that arise over goods or services promoted or advertised on their site.[35]

---

learning review

7. The _____ Act forbids monopolies, whereas the _____ Act forbids actions that would lessen competition.

8. Describe some of the recent changes in trademark law.

9. How does the Better Business Bureau encourage companies to follow its standards for commerce?

LEARNING OBJECTIVES REVIEW

LO1 *Explain how environmental scanning provides information about social, economic, technological, competitive, and regulatory forces.*
Many businesses operate in environments where important forces change. Environmental scanning is the process of acquiring information about these changes to allow marketers to identify and interpret trends. There are five environmental forces businesses must monitor: social, economic, technological, competitive, and regulatory. By identifying trends related to each of these forces, businesses can develop and maintain successful marketing programs. Several trends that most businesses are monitoring include the increasing diversity of the U.S. population, the growing economic impact of China and India, and the dramatic growth of customer-generated content.

LO2 *Describe how social forces such as demographics and culture can have an impact on marketing strategy.*
Demographic information describes the world population; the U.S. population; the generational cohorts such as baby boomers, Generation X, and Generation Y; the geographic shifts of the population; and the racial and ethnic diversity of the population that has led to multicultural marketing programs. Cultural factors include the impact of values such as "health and fitness" on consumer preferences.

LO3 *Discuss how economic forces such as macroeconomic conditions and consumer income affect marketing.*
Economic forces include the strong relationship between consumers' expectations about the economy and their spending. Gross income has remained stable for more than 30 years although the rate of saving has been declining.

LO4 *Describe how technological changes can affect marketing.*
Technological innovations can replace existing products and services. Changes in technology can also have an impact on customer value by reducing the cost of products, improving the quality of products, and providing new products that were not previously feasible. Electronic commerce is transforming how companies do business.

LO5 *Discuss the forms of competition that exist in a market.*
There are four forms of competition: pure competition, monopolistic competition, oligopoly, and monopoly. While large companies are often used as examples of marketplace competitors, there are 23 million small businesses in the United States, which have a significant impact on the economy.

LO6 *Explain the major legislation that ensures competition and regulates the elements of the marketing mix.*
Regulation exists to protect companies and consumers. Legislation that ensures a competitive marketplace includes the Sherman Antitrust Act. Product-related legislation includes copyright, patent, and trademark laws that protect companies and packaging and labeling laws that protect consumers. Pricing- and distribution-related laws are designed to create a competitive marketplace with fair prices and availability. Regulation related to promotion and advertising reduces deceptive practices and provides enforcement through the Federal Trade Commission. Self-regulation through organizations such as the Better Business Bureau provides an alternative to federal and state regulation.

FOCUSING ON KEY TERMS

APPLYING MARKETING KNOWLEDGE

1 For many years Gerber has manufactured baby food in small, single-sized containers. In conducting an environmental scan, identify three trends or factors that might significantly affect this company's future business, and then propose how Gerber might respond to these changes.

2 Describe the new features you would add to an automobile designed for consumers in the 55+ age group. In what magazines would you advertise to appeal to this target market?

3 New technologies are continuously improving and replacing existing products. Although technological change is often difficult to predict, suggest how the following companies and products might be affected by the Internet and digital technologies: (*a*) Kodak cameras and film, (*b*) American Airlines, and (*c*) the Metropolitan Museum of Art.

4 In recent years in the brewing industry, a couple of large firms that have historically had most of the beer sales (Anheuser-Busch and Miller) have faced competition from many small "micro" brands. In terms of the continuum of competition, how would you explain this change?

5 Why would Xerox be concerned about its name becoming generic?

6 Develop a "Code of Business Practices" for a new online vitamin store. Does your code address advertising? Privacy? Use by children? Why is self-regulation important?

building your marketing plan

Your marketing plan will include a situation analysis based on internal and external factors that are likely to affect your marketing program.

1 To summarize information about external factors, create a table similar to Figure 3–2 and identify three trends related to each of the five forces (social, economic, technological, competitive, and regulatory) that relate to your product or service.

2 When your table is completed, describe how each of the trends represents an opportunity or a threat for your business.

video case 3   Geek Squad: A New Business for a New Environment

"As long as there's innovation there is going to be new kinds of chaos," explains Robert Stephens, founder of the technology support company Geek Squad. The chaos Stephens is referring to is the difficulty we have all experienced trying to keep up with the many changes in our environment, particularly those related to computers, technology, software, communication, and entertainment. Generally, consumers have found it difficult to install, operate, and use many of the electronic products available today. "It takes time to read the manuals," continues Stephens. "I'm going to save you that time because I stay home on Saturday nights and read them for you!"

THE COMPANY

The Geek Squad story begins when Stephens, a native of Chicago, passed up an Art Institute scholarship to pursue a degree in computer science. While Stephens was a computer science student he took a job fixing computers for a research laboratory, and he also started consulting.

He could repair televisions, computers, and a variety of other items, although he decided to focus on computers. His experiences as a consultant led him to realize that most people needed help with technology and that they saw value in a service whose employees would show up at a specified time, be friendly, use understandable language, and solve the problem. So, with just $200, Stephens formed Geek Squad in 1994.

Geek Squad set out to provide timely and effective help with all computing needs regardless of the make, model, or place of purchase. Geek Squad employees were called "agents" and wore uniforms consisting of black pants or skirts, black shoes, white shirts, black clip-on ties, a badge, and a black jacket with a Geek Squad logo to create a "humble" attitude that was not threatening to customers. Agents drove black-and-white Volkswagen Beetles, or Geekmobiles, with a logo on the door, and charged fixed prices for services, regardless of how much time was required to provide the service. The "house call" services ranged from installing networks, to debugging a computer, to setting up an entertainment system, and cost from $100 to $300. "We're like 'Dragnet;' we show up at people's homes and help," offers Stephens. "We're also like 'Ghostbusters,' and there's a pseudo-government feel to it like 'Men in Black.'"

In 2002, Geek Squad was purchased by leading consumer electronics retailer Best Buy for about $3 million. Best Buy had observed very high return rates for most of its complex products. Shoppers would be excited about new products, purchase them and take them home, get frustrated trying to make them actually work, and then return them to the store demanding a refund. In fact, Best Buy research revealed that consumers were beginning to see service as a critical element of the purchase. The partnership was an excellent match. Best Buy consumers welcomed the help. Stephens became Geek Squad's chief inspector and a Best Buy vice president and began putting a Geek Squad "precinct" in every Best Buy store, creating some stand-alone Geek Squad Stores, and providing 24-hour telephone support. There are now more than 2,000 agents in the United States, Canada, the United Kingdom, and China, and return rates have declined by

25 to 35 percent. Geek Squad customer materials now suggest that the service is "Saving the World One Computer at a Time. 24 Hours a Day. Your Place or Ours!"

THE CHANGING ENVIRONMENT

Many changes in the environment occurred to create the need for Geek Squad's services. Future changes are also likely to change the way Geek Squad operates. An environmental scan helps understand the changes.

The most obvious changes may be related to technology. Wireless broadband technology, high-definition televisions, products with Internet interfaces, and a general trend toward computers, phones, entertainment systems, and even appliances being interconnected are just a few examples of new products and applications for consumers to learn about. There are also technology-related problems such as viruses, spyware, lost data, and "crashed" or inoperable computers. New technologies have also created a demand for new types of maintenance such as password management, operating system updates, disk cleanup, and "defragging."

Another environmental change that contributes to the popularity of Geek Squad is the change in social factors such as demographics and culture. In the past many electronics manufacturers and retailers focused primarily on men. Women, however, are becoming increasingly interested in personal computing and home entertainment, and, according to the Consumer Electronics Association, are likely to outspend men in the near future. Best Buy's consumer research indicates that women expect personal service during the purchase and installation after the purchase—exactly the service Geek Squad is designed to provide. Our culture is also embracing the Geek Squad concept. If you follow television programming you may have noticed the series *Chuck* where one of the characters works for the "Nerd Herd" at "Buy More" and drives a car like a Geekmobile on service calls!

Competition, economics, and the regulatory environment have also had a big influence on Geek Squad. As discount stores such as Wal-Mart and PC makers such as Dell began to compete with Best Buy and Circuit City, new services such as in-home installation were needed to create value for customers. Now, just as changes in competition created an opportunity for Geek Squad, it is also leading to another level of competition as Circuit City has introduced its own computer support service called Firedog, Dell has introduced Dell-On-Call, and cable companies are offering their own services. The economic situation for electronics continues to improve as prices decline and median income in the United States, particularly for women, is increasing. In 2007, consumers purchased 16 million high-definition televisions, but household penetration is still below 40 percent. Finally, the regulatory environment continues to change with respect to electronic transfer of copyrighted materials such as music and movies and software. Geek Squad must monitor the changes to ensure that its services comply with relevant laws.

houses with high-speed cables and networking equipment that Geek Squad agents can use to create ideal computer and entertainment systems. Geek Squad is also using new technology to improve. Agents now use a smart phone to access updated schedules, log in their hours, and run diagnostics tests on client's equipment. Finally, to attract the best possible employees, Geek Squad and Best Buy are trying a "results-only work environment" that has no fixed schedules and no mandatory meetings. By encouraging employees to make their own work-life decisions the Geek Squad hopes to keep morale and productivity high.

Other changes and opportunities are certain to appear soon. Despite the success of the Geek Squad, and the potential for additional growth, however, Robert Stephens is modest and claims, "Geeks may inherit the Earth, but they have no desire to rule it!"

THE FUTURE FOR GEEK SQUAD

The combination of many positive environmental factors helps explain the extraordinary success of Geek Squad. Today, it repairs more than 3,000 PCs a day and generates more than $1 billion in revenue. Because Geek Squad services have a high-profit margin they contribute to the overall performance of Best Buy, and they help generate traffic in the store and create store loyalty. To continue to grow, however, Geek Squad will need to continue to scan the environment and try new approaches to creating customer value.

One possible new approach is to find additional locations that are convenient to consumers. For example, Geek Squad locations are being tested in some FedEx stores and in some Office Depot stores. Another possible approach is to create new houses that are designed for the newest consumer electronics products. To test this idea Best Buy has created partnerships with home builders to wire new

Questions

1 What are the key environmental factors that created an opportunity for Robert Stephens to start the Geek Squad?

2 What changes in the purchasing patterns of (*a*) all consumers, and (*b*) women made the acquisition of Geek Squad particularly important for Best Buy?

3 Based on the case information and what you know about consumer electronics, conduct an environmental scan for Geek Squad to identify key trends. For each of the five environmental forces (social, economic, technological, competitive, and regulatory), identify trends likely to influence Geek Squad in the near future.

4 What promotional activities would you recommend to encourage consumers who use independent installers to switch to Geek Squad?

NATURE AND SIGNIFICANCE OF MARKETING ETHICS

ethics

Moral principles and values that govern the actions and decisions of an individual or a group

laws

Society's standards and values that are enforceable in the courts

Ethics are the moral principles and values that govern the actions and decisions of an individual or a group.[2] They serve as guidelines on how to act rightly and justly when faced with moral dilemmas.

Ethical/Legal Framework in Marketing

A good starting point for understanding the nature and significance of ethics is the distinction between legality and ethicality of marketing decisions. Whereas ethics deal with personal moral principles and values, **laws** are society's values and standards that are enforceable in the courts. This distinction can sometimes lead to the rationalization that if a behavior is within reasonable ethical and legal limits, then it is not really illegal or unethical. When a recent survey asked the question, "Is it OK to get around the law if you don't actually break it?" about 61 percent of businesspeople who took part responded "yes."[3] How would you answer this question?

There are numerous situations in which judgment plays a large role in defining ethical and legal boundaries. Consider the following situations.

1. More than 70 percent of the physicians in the Maricopa County (Arizona) Medical Society agreed to establish a maximum fee schedule for health services to curb rising medical costs. All physicians were required to adhere to this schedule as a condition for membership in the society. The U.S. Supreme Court ruled that this agreement to set prices violated the Sherman Act and represented price fixing, which is illegal. Was the society's action ethical?

2. A company in California sells a computer program to auto dealers showing that car buyers should finance their purchase rather than paying cash. The program omits the effect of income taxes and misstates the interest earned on savings over the loan period. The finance option always provides a net benefit over the cash option. Company employees agree that the program does mislead buyers, but say the company will "provide what [car dealers] want as long as it is not against the law." Is this practice ethical?

3. China is the world's largest tobacco-producing country and has 300 million smokers. Approximately 700,000 Chinese die annually from smoking-related illnesses. This figure is expected to rise to more than 2 million by 2025. China legally restricts tobacco imports. U.S. trade negotiators advocate free trade, thus allowing U.S. tobacco companies to market their products in China. Is the Chinese trade position ethical?

4. A group of college students recorded movies at a local theater and then uploaded the movies to the Internet. Federal statutes state that the unauthorized reproduction, distribution, or exhibition of copyrighted motion pictures is illegal. The students then directed friends and family to a peer-to-peer Internet network that allowed them to download the movies for free. Are the students ethical? Are the students' friends and family ethical?

Would you be able to describe these situations as clearly ethical and legal or unethical and illegal? Probably not. As you read further in this chapter, you will be asked to consider other ethical dilemmas.

Current Perceptions of Ethical Behavior

There has been a public outcry about the ethical practices of businesspeople.[4] Public opinion surveys show that 58 percent of U.S. adults rate the ethical standards of business executives as only "fair" or "poor;" 90 percent think white-collar crime is "very common" or "somewhat common;" 76 percent say the lack of ethics in businesspeople contributes to tumbling societal moral standards; only the U.S. government is viewed as less trustworthy than corporations among institutions in the United States; and advertising practitioners, telemarketers, and car salespeople are thought to be among the least ethical occupations. Surveys of corporate employees generally confirm this public perception. When asked if they were aware of ethical problems in their companies, 56 percent say, "yes."

There are at least four possible reasons the state of perceived ethical business conduct is at its present level. First, there is increased pressure on businesspeople to make decisions in a society characterized by diverse value systems. Second, there is a growing tendency for business decisions to be judged publicly by groups with different values and interests. Third, the public's expectations of ethical business behavior has increased. Finally, and most disturbing, ethical business conduct may have declined.

learning review

1. What are ethics?

2. What are four possible reasons for the present state of ethical conduct in the United States?

UNDERSTANDING ETHICAL MARKETING BEHAVIOR

LO2

Researchers have identified numerous factors that influence ethical marketing behavior.[5] Figure 4–1 presents a framework that shows these factors and their relationships.

Societal Culture and Norms

As described in Chapter 3, *culture* refers to the set of values, ideas, and attitudes that are learned and shared among the members of a group. Culture also serves as a socializing force that dictates what is morally right and just. This means that moral standards are relative to particular societies.[6] These standards often reflect the laws and regulations that affect social and economic behavior, which can create moral dilemmas. For example, Levi Strauss decided to limit its business dealings in China because of what the company called "pervasive human rights abuses." According to its vice president for corporate marketing: "There are wonderful commercial opportunities in China.

FIGURE 4–1

A framework for understanding ethical behavior. Each of these influences will have an effect on ethical marketing behavior.

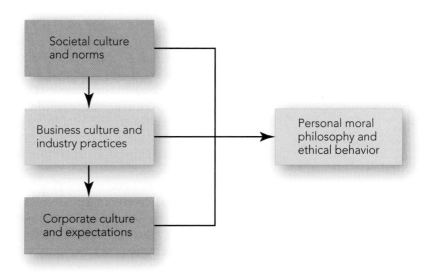

But when ethical issues collide with commercial appeal, we try to ensure ethics as the trump card. For us, ethical issues precede all others."[7]

Societal values and attitudes also affect ethical and legal relationships among individuals, groups, and business institutions and organizations. Consider the copying of another's copyright, trademark, or patent. These are viewed as intellectual property. Unauthorized use, reproduction, or distribution of intellectual property is illegal in the United States and most countries, which can result in fines and prison terms for perpetrators. The owners of intellectual property also lose. For example, annual lost sales from the theft of intellectual property amount to $5 billion in the music industry, $6 billion in the movie industry, and $33 billion in the software industry.[8] Lost sales, in turn, result in lost jobs, royalties, wages, and tax revenue. But what about a person downloading copyrighted music, movies, and software over the Internet or from peer-to-peer file-sharing programs, without paying the owner of this property? Is this an ethical or unethical act? It depends on who you ask. Surveys of the U.S. public indicate that the majority consider these acts unethical. However, only a third of U.S. college students say such practices are unethical.[9]

Business Culture and Industry Practices

Societal culture provides a foundation for understanding moral behavior in business activities. *Business cultures* "comprise the effective rules of the game, the boundaries between competitive and unethical behavior, [and] the codes of conduct in business dealings."[10] Consumers have witnessed numerous instances where business cultures in the brokerage (inside trading), insurance (deceptive sales practices), and defense (bribery) industries went awry. Business culture affects ethical conduct both in the exchange relationship between sellers and buyers and in the competitive behavior among sellers.

Ethics of Exchange   The exchange process is central to the marketing concept. Ethical exchanges between sellers and buyers should result in both parties being better off after a transaction.

Before the 1960s, the legal concept of *caveat emptor*—let the buyer beware—was pervasive in the American business culture. In 1962, President John F. Kennedy outlined a **Consumer Bill of Rights** that codified the ethics of exchange between buyers and sellers. These were the rights (1) to safety, (2) to be informed, (3) to choose, and (4) to be heard. Consumers expect and often demand that these rights be protected, as have American businesses.

The *right to safety* manifests itself in industry and federal safety standards for most products sold in the United States. In fact, the U.S. Consumer Product Safety Commission routinely monitors the safety of 15,000 consumer products. However, even the most vigilant efforts to ensure safe products cannot foresee every possibility. In fact, personal claims and property damage from consumer product safety incidents cost companies more than $700 billion annually. Consider the case of batteries used in laptop and notebook computers. Dell Inc. learned that the lithium-ion batteries in its notebook computers, made by Sony Energy Devices Corporation of Japan, posed a fire hazard to consumers. The company recalled 2.7 million batteries and gave consumers a replacement before any personal injuries resulted.[11]

The *right to be informed* means that marketers have an obligation to give consumers complete and accurate information about products and services, but this is not always the case. For example, three U.S. advertising agencies recently agreed to settle Federal Trade Commission (FTC) claims that they failed to disclose the actual costs of car leases and credit transactions in their advertising for three Japanese carmakers.[12] This right also applies to the solicitation of personal information over the Internet and its subsequent use by marketers.[13] A FTC survey of websites indicated that 92 percent collect personal information such as consumer e-mail addresses, telephone numbers,

Consumer Bill of Rights
Codified the ethics of exchange between buyers and sellers, including rights to safety, to be informed, to choose, and to be heard

The Federal Trade Commission plays an active role in educating consumers and businesses about the importance of personal information privacy on the Internet. FTC initiatives are detailed on its website.

shopping habits, and financial data. Yet, only two-thirds of websites inform consumers of what is done with this information once obtained. The FTC wants more than posted privacy notices that merely inform consumers of a company's data-use policy, which critics say are often vague, confusing, or too legalistic to be understood. This view is shared by two-thirds of consumers who worry about protecting their personal information online. The consumer right to be informed has spawned much federal legislation, such as the *Children's Online Privacy Protection Act* (1998), and self-regulation initiatives restricting disclosure of personal information.

Relating to the *right to choose,* today many supermarket chains demand "slotting allowances" from manufacturers, in the form of cash or free goods, to stock new products.[14] This practice could limit the number of new products available to consumers and interfere with their right to choose. One critic of this practice remarked, "If we had had slotting allowances a few years ago, we might not have had granola, herbal tea, or yogurt."

Finally, the *right to be heard* means that consumers should have access to public-policy makers regarding complaints about products and services. This right is illustrated in limitations put on telemarketing practices. Consumer complaints about late-night and repeated calls resulted in the *Telephone Consumer Protection Act of 1991.* The FTC established the Do Not Call Registry in 2003 for consumers who do not want to receive unsolicited telemarketing calls. Today, 76 percent of U.S. adults have their telephone numbers listed in the registry, which is managed by the FTC. A telemarketer can be fined $11,000 for each call made to a telephone number posted on the registry.

Ethics of Competition Business culture also affects ethical behavior in competition. Two kinds of unethical behavior are most common: (1) economic espionage and (2) bribery.

Economic espionage is the clandestine collection of trade secrets or proprietary information about a company's competitors. This practice is illegal and unethical and carries serious criminal penalties for the offending individual or business. Espionage activities include illegal trespassing, theft, fraud, misrepresentation, wiretapping, the search of a competitor's trash, and violations of written and implicit employment agreements with noncompete clauses. More than half of the largest firms in the United States have uncovered espionage in some form, costing them $300 billion annually in lost sales.[15]

Economic espionage is most prevalent in high-technology industries, such as electronics, specialty chemicals, industrial equipment, aerospace, and pharmaceuticals, where technical know-how and trade secrets separate industry leaders from followers. But espionage can occur anywhere—even in the soft drink industry! Read the Making Responsible Decisions box on the next page to learn how Pepsi-Cola responded to an offer to obtain confidential information in its archrival's marketing plans.[16]

The second form of unethical competitive behavior is giving and receiving bribes and kickbacks. Bribes and kickbacks are often disguised as gifts, consultant fees, and favors. This practice is more common in business-to-business and government marketing than in consumer marketing. For example, two American Honda Motor Company executives were fined and sentenced to prison for extracting $15 million in kickbacks from Honda dealers and advertising agencies, and a series of highly publicized trials uncovered widespread bribery in the U.S. Defense Department's awarding of $160 billion in military contracts.[17]

Making Responsible Decisions > > > > > > > ethics

Corporate Conscience in the Cola War

Suppose you are a senior executive at Pepsi-Cola and that a Coca-Cola employee offers to sell you the marketing plan and sample for a new Coke product at a modest price? Would you buy it knowing Pepsi-Cola could gain a significant competitive edge in the cola war?

When this question was posed in an online survey of marketing and advertising executives, 67 percent said they would buy the plan and product sample if there were no repercussions. What did Pepsi-Cola do when this offer actually occurred? The company immediately contacted Coca-Cola, which contacted the FBI. An undercover FBI agent paid the employee $30,000 in cash stuffed in a Girl Scout cookie box as a down payment and later arrested the employee and accomplices. When asked about the inci-

Pssst!

dent, a Pepsi-Cola spokesperson said: "We only did what any responsible company would do. Competition must be tough, but must always be fair and legal."

Why did the 33 percent of respondents in the online survey say they would decline the offer? Most said they would prefer competing ethically so they could sleep at night. According to a senior advertising agency executive who would decline the offer: "Repercussions go beyond potential espionage charges. As long as we have a conscience, there are repercussions."

So what happened to the Coca-Cola employee? She was sentenced to eight years in prison and ordered to pay $40,000 in restitution. Her accomplices were sentenced to five years in prison.

In general, bribery is most evident in industries experiencing intense competition and in countries in the earlier stages of economic development. According to a recent U.N. study, 15 percent of all companies in industrialized countries have to pay bribes to win or retain business. In Asia, this figure is 40 percent. In Eastern Europe, 60 percent of all companies must pay bribes to do business. A recent poll of senior executives engaged in global marketing revealed that Russia and China were the most likely countries to evidence bribery to win or retain business. Switzerland, Sweden, and Australia were the least likely.[18]

The prevalence of economic espionage and bribery in international marketing has prompted laws to curb these practices. Two significant laws, the *Economic Espionage Act* (1996) and the *Foreign Corrupt Practices Act* (1977), address these practices in the United States. Both are detailed in Chapter 7.

Corporate Culture and Expectations

A third influence on ethical practices is corporate culture. *Corporate culture* reflects the shared values, beliefs, and purpose of employees that affect individual and group behavior. The culture of a company demonstrates itself in the dress (business casual versus business suits), how the working environment is structured (cubicles versus closed offices), and how employees are compensated (stock options versus overtime). Culture is also apparent in the expectations for ethical behavior present in formal codes of ethics and the ethical actions of top management and co-workers.

code of ethics
Formal statement of ethical principles and rules of conduct

Codes of Ethics   A **code of ethics** is a formal statement of ethical principles and rules of conduct. It is estimated that 86 percent of U.S. companies have some sort of ethics code and one of every four large companies has corporate ethics officers.

What does 3M's Scotchgard have to do with ethics, social responsibility, and a $200 million loss in annual sales? Read the text to find out.

At United Technologies, for example, 160 corporate ethics officers distribute the company's ethics code, translated into 24 languages, to employees who work for this defense and engineering giant around the world.[19] Ethics codes and committees typically address contributions to government officials and political parties, relations with customers and suppliers, conflicts of interest, and accurate recordkeeping. For example, General Mills provides guidelines for dealing with suppliers, competitors, and customers, and recruits new employees who share these views.

However, an ethics code is rarely enough to ensure ethical behavior. Coca-Cola has an ethics code and emphasizes that its employees be ethical in their behavior. But that did not stop some Coca-Cola employees from rigging the results of a test market for a frozen soft drink to win Burger King's business. Coca-Cola subsequently agreed to pay Burger King and its operators more than $20 million to settle the matter.[20]

Lack of specificity is a major reason for the violation of ethics codes. Employees must often judge whether a specific behavior is unethical. The American Marketing Association has addressed this issue by providing a detailed statement of ethics, which all members agree to follow. This statement can be found at the American Marketing Association website (www.marketingpower.com).

Ethical Behavior of Top Management and Co-Workers

A second reason for violating ethics codes rests in the perceived behavior of top management and co-workers.[21] Observing peers and top management and gauging responses to unethical behavior play an important role in individual actions. A study of business executives reported that 40 percent had been implicitly or explicitly rewarded for engaging in ethically troubling behavior. Moreover, 31 percent of those who refused to engage in unethical behavior were penalized, either through outright punishment or a diminished status in the company.[22] Clearly, ethical dilemmas often bring personal and professional conflict. For this reason, numerous states have laws protecting *whistle-blowers,* employees who report unethical or illegal actions of their employers. Some firms, such as General Dynamics and Dun & Bradstreet, have appointed ethics officers responsible for safeguarding these individuals from recrimination.

Your Personal Moral Philosophy and Ethical Behavior

Ultimately, ethical choices are based on the personal moral philosophy of the decision maker. Moral philosophy is learned through the process of socialization with friends and family and by formal education. It is also influenced by the societal, business, and corporate culture in which a person finds him- or herself. Two prominent personal moral philosophies have direct bearing on marketing practice: (1) moral idealism and (2) utilitarianism.[23]

moral idealism

Moral philosophy that considers certain individual rights or duties as universal, regardless of the outcome

Moral Idealism

Moral idealism is a personal moral philosophy that considers certain individual rights or duties as universal, regardless of the outcome. This philosophy exists in the Consumer Bill of Rights and is favored by moral philosophers and consumer interest groups. For example, the right to know applies to probable defects in an automobile that relate to safety.

This philosophy also applies to ethical duties. A fundamental ethical duty is to do no harm. Adherence to this duty prompted 3M executives to phase out production of a chemical 3M had manufactured for nearly 40 years. The substance, used in far-ranging products from pet food bags, candy wrappers, carpeting, and 3M's popular Scotchgard fabric protector, had no known harmful health or environmental effect. However, the company discovered that the chemical appeared in minuscule amounts in humans and animals around the world and accumulated in tissue. Believing that the substance could be possibly harmful in large doses, 3M voluntarily stopped its production, resulting in a $200 million loss in annual sales.[24]

utilitarianism

Moral philosophy that focuses on the "greatest good for the greatest number"

Utilitarianism   An alternative perspective on moral philosophy is **utilitarianism**, which is a personal moral philosophy that focuses on "the greatest good for the greatest number" by assessing the costs and benefits of the consequences of ethical behavior. If the benefits exceed the costs, then the behavior is ethical. If not, then the behavior is unethical. This philosophy underlies the economic tenets of capitalism and, not surprisingly, is embraced by many business executives and students.[25]

Utilitarian reasoning was apparent in Nestlé Food Corporation's marketing of Good Start infant formula, sold by Nestlé's Carnation Company. The formula, promoted as hypoallergenic, was designed to prevent or reduce colic caused by an infant's allergic reaction to cow's milk, a condition suffered by 2 percent of babies. However, some severely milk-allergic infants experienced serious side effects after using Good Start, including convulsive vomiting. Physicians and parents charged that the hypoallergenic claim was misleading, and the Food and Drug Administration investigated the matter. A Nestlé vice president defended the claim and product, saying, "I don't understand why our product should work in 100 percent of cases. If we wanted to say it was foolproof, we would have called it allergy-free. We call it hypo-, or less, allergenic."[26] Nestlé officials seemingly believed that most allergic infants would benefit from Good Start—"the greatest good for the greatest number." However, other views prevailed, and the claim was dropped from the product label.

An appreciation for the nature of ethics, coupled with a basic understanding of why unethical behavior arises, alerts a person to when and how ethical issues exist in marketing decisions. Ultimately, ethical behavior rests with the individual, but the consequences affect many.

learning review

3. What rights are included in the Consumer Bill of Rights?

4. Economic espionage includes what kinds of activities?

5. What is meant by moral idealism?

UNDERSTANDING SOCIAL RESPONSIBILITY IN MARKETING

LO3

As we saw in Chapter 1, the societal marketing concept stresses marketing's social responsibility by not only satisfying the needs of consumers but also providing for society's welfare. **Social responsibility** means that organizations are part of a larger society and are accountable to that society for their actions. Like ethics, agreement on the nature and scope of social responsibility is often difficult to come by, given the diversity of values present in different societal, business, and corporate cultures.

social responsibility

Idea that organizations are part of a larger society and are accountable to that society for their actions

Three Concepts of Social Responsibility

Figure 4–2 shows three concepts of social responsibility: (1) profit responsibility, (2) stakeholder responsibility, and (3) societal responsibility.

Profit Responsibility   *Profit responsibility* holds that companies have a simple duty: to maximize profits for their owners or stockholders. This view is expressed by Nobel Laureate Milton Friedman, who said, "There is one and only one social responsibility of business—to use its resources and engage in activities designed to

FIGURE 4–2
Three concepts of social responsibility. Each concept of social responsibility relates to particular constituencies. There is often conflict in satisfying all constituencies at the same time.

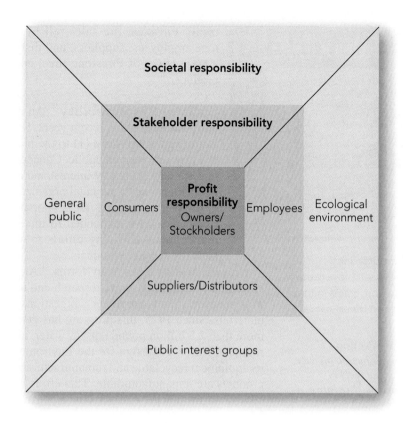

increase its profits so long as it stays within the rules of the game, which is to say, engages in open and free competition without deception or fraud."[27] Genzyme, the maker of Cerezyme, a drug that treats a genetic illness called Gaucher's disease that affects 20,000 people worldwide, has been criticized for apparently adopting this view in its pricing practices. Genzyme charges up to $170,000 for a year's worth of Cerezyme. A Genzyme spokesperson responded saying the company spends about $150 million annually to manufacture Cerezyme and freely gives the drug to patients without insurance. Also, the company invested considerable dollars in research over several years to develop Cerezyme, and the drug's profits are reinvested in ongoing R&D programs. [28]

Stakeholder Responsibility Criticism of the profit view has led to a broader concept of social responsibility. *Stakeholder responsibility* focuses on the obligations an organization has to those who can affect achievement of its objectives. These constituencies include consumers, employees, suppliers, and distributors. Source Perrier S.A., the supplier of Perrier bottled water, exercised this responsibility when it recalled 160 million bottles of water in 120 countries after traces of a toxic chemical were found in 13 bottles. The recall cost the company $35 million, and $40 million more in lost sales. Even though the chemical level was not harmful to humans, Source Perrier's president believed he acted in the best interests of the firm's consumers, distributors, and employees by removing "the least doubt, as minimal as it might be, to weigh on the image of the quality and purity of our product"—which it did.[29]

Failure to consider a company's broader constituencies can have negative consequences. For example, Bridgestone/Firestone Inc. executives were widely criticized for how they responded to complaints about the safety of selected Firestone-brand tires. These tires had been linked to crashes that killed at least 174 people and injured more than 700 in the United States. The company recalled 6.5 million tires under pressure from the National Highway Traffic Safety Administration. After the

Avon Products, Inc., successfully employs cause marketing programs in the fight against breast cancer.

green marketing

Marketing efforts to produce, promote, and reclaim environmentally sensitive products

cause marketing

Tying the charitable contributions of a firm directly to sales produced through the promotion of one of its products

social audit

Systematic assessment of a firm's objectives, strategies, and performance in the domain of social responsibility

recall, Firestone tire sales fell by nearly one-half, which affected Firestone employees, suppliers, and distributors as well. Ford Motor Company, a large buyer of Firestone tires, ended its exclusive contract with the tire producer.[30]

Societal Responsibility   An even broader concept of social responsibility has emerged in recent years. *Societal responsibility* refers to obligations that organizations have (1) to the preservation of the ecological environment and (2) to the general public. Concerns about the environment and public welfare are represented by interest and advocacy groups such as Greenpeace, an international environmental organization.

Chapter 3 detailed the importance of ecological issues in marketing. Companies have responded to this concern through what is termed **green marketing**—marketing efforts to produce, promote, and reclaim environmentally sensitive products.

Green marketing takes many forms.[31] At 3M, product development opportunities emanate both from consumer research and its "Pollution Prevention Pays" program. This program solicits employee suggestions on how to reduce pollution and recycle materials. Since 1975, this program has generated over 6,000 ideas that eliminated more than 2.5 billion pounds of air, water, and solid-waste pollutants from the environment. Xerox's "Design for the Environment" program focuses on ways to make its equipment recyclable and remanufacturable. Today, 90 percent of Xerox-designed products are remanufacturable. This effort has kept more than 1.6 billion pounds of equipment from being discarded in U.S. landfills since 1991. Boise Cascade, a leading North American timber manufacturer, and Lowe's and Home Depot, two home-and-garden center retail chains, have discontinued the sale of wood products from the world's endangered forests. Wal-Mart has instituted buying practices that encourage its suppliers to use containers and packaging made from corn, not oil-based resins. The company expects this initiative will save 800,000 barrels of oil annually. These voluntary responses to environmental issues have been implemented with little or no additional cost to consumers and resulted in cost savings to companies.

Socially responsible efforts on behalf of the general public are becoming more common. A formal practice is **cause marketing**, which occurs when the charitable contributions of a firm are tied directly to the customer revenues produced through the promotion of one of its products.[32] This definition distinguishes cause marketing from a firm's standard charitable contributions, which are outright donations. For example, Procter & Gamble raises funds for the Special Olympics when consumers purchase selected company products, and MasterCard International links usage of its card with fund-raising for institutions that combat cancer, heart disease, child abuse, drug abuse, and muscular dystrophy. Barnes & Noble promotes literacy, and Coca-Cola sponsors local Boys and Girls Clubs. Avon Products, Inc., focuses on different issues in different countries. These include breast cancer, domestic violence, disaster relief among many others. Cause marketing programs incorporate all three concepts of social responsibility by addressing public concerns and satisfying customer needs. They can also enhance corporate sales and profits as described in the Marketing Matters box.[33]

The Social Audit: Doing Well by Doing Good

Converting socially responsible ideas into actions involves careful planning and monitoring of programs. Many companies develop, implement, and evaluate their social responsibility efforts by means of a **social audit**, which is a systematic assessment of a firm's objectives, strategies, and performance in terms of social responsibility. Frequently, marketing and social responsibility programs are integrated, as is the case with McDonald's. The company's concern for the needs of families with children who

Will Consumers Switch Brands for a Cause? Yes, If . . .

American Express Company pioneered cause marketing when it sponsored the renovation of the Statue of Liberty. This effort raised $1.7 million for the renovation, increased card usage among cardholders, and attracted new cardholders. In 2001, U.S. companies raised more than $5 billion for causes they champion. It is estimated that cause marketing will raise over $10 billion in 2010.

Cause marketing benefits companies as well as causes. Research indicates that 92 percent of U.S. consumers say they have a more favorable opinion of companies that support causes. Also, 89 percent of consumers under 25 years old say they will switch to a brand or retailer that supports a good cause if the price and quality of brands or retailers are equal. In short, cause marketing may be a valued point of difference for brands and companies, all other things being equal.

For more information, including news, links, and case studies, visit the Cause Marketing Forum website at www. causemarketingforum.com.

are chronically or terminally ill was converted into more than 265 Ronald McDonald Houses around the world. These facilities, located near treatment centers, enable families to stay together during the child's care. In this case, McDonald's is contributing to the welfare of a portion of its target market.

A social audit consists of five steps:[34]

1. Recognition of a firm's social expectations and the rationale for engaging in social responsibility endeavors.
2. Identification of social responsibility causes or programs consistent with the company's mission.
3. Determination of organizational objectives and priorities for programs and activities it will undertake.
4. Specification of the type and amount of resources necessary to achieve social responsibility objectives.
5. Evaluation of social responsibility programs and activities undertaken and assessment of future involvement.

Corporate attention to social audits will increase as companies seek to achieve sustainable development and improve the quality of life in a global economy. *Sustainable development* involves conducting business in a way that protects the natural environment while making economic progress. Ecologically responsible initiatives such as green marketing represent one such initiative. Recent initiatives related to working conditions at offshore manufacturing sites that produce goods for U.S. companies focus on quality-of-life issues. Public opinion surveys show that 90 percent of U.S. citizens are concerned about working conditions under which products are made in Asia and Latin America. Companies such as Reebok, Nike, Liz Claiborne, Levi Strauss, and Mattel have responded by imposing codes of conduct to reduce harsh or abusive working conditions at offshore manufacturing facilities.[35] Reebok, for example, now

Marketing and social responsibility programs are often integrated, as is the case with McDonald's. Its concern for ill children worldwide is apparent in the opening of another Ronald McDonald House for children and their families, this time in China.

monitors production of its sporting apparel and equipment to ensure that no child labor is used in making its products.

Companies that evidence societal responsibility have been rewarded for their efforts. Research has shown that these companies (1) benefit from favorable word of mouth among consumers and (2) typically outperform less responsible companies on financial performance.[36]

Turning the Table: Consumer Ethics and Social Responsibility

LO4

Consumers also have an obligation to act ethically and responsibly in the exchange process and in the use and disposition of products. Unfortunately, consumer behavior is spotty on both counts.

Unethical practices of consumers are a serious concern to marketers.[37] These practices include: filing warranty claims after the claim period; misredeeming coupons; making fraudulent returns of merchandise; providing inaccurate information on credit applications; tampering with utility meters; tapping cable TV lines; pirating music, movies, and software from the Internet; and submitting phony insurance claims.

Consumers also act unethically toward each other. According to the FBI, consumer complaints about online auction fraud, in which consumers misrepresent their goods to others, outnumbers all reports of online crime. The cost to marketers of such behavior in lost sales and prevention expenses is huge. For example, consumers who redeem coupons for unpurchased products or use coupons for other products cost manufacturers $1 billion each year. Fraudulent automobile insurance claims cost insurance companies more than $10 billion annually. In addition, retailers lose about $30 billion yearly from shoplifting and $9.6 billion annually from fraudulent returns of merchandise.

Research on unethical consumer behavior indicates that these acts are rarely motivated by economic need. This behavior appears to be influenced by (1) a belief that a consumer can get away with the act and it is worth doing and (2) the rationalization that the act is justified or driven by forces outside the individual—"everybody does it." These reasons were vividly expressed by a 24-year-old who pirated a movie, was sentenced to six months of house arrest, three years of probation, and a $7,000 fine. He said, "I didn't like paying for movies," and added, "so many people do it, you never think you're going to get caught."[38]

Reebok has been a leader in improving workplace conditions in Asian factories that produce its sporting apparel and equipment.

Consumer purchase, use, and disposition of environmentally sensitive products relate to consumer social responsibility. Research indicates that consumers are sensitive to ecological issues.[39] However, research also shows that consumers (1) may be unwilling to sacrifice convenience and pay potentially higher prices to protect the environment and (2) lack the knowledge to make informed decisions dealing with the purchase, use, and disposition of products.

Consumer confusion over which products are environmentally safe is also apparent, given marketers' rush to produce "green products." For example, few consumers realize that nonaerosol "pump" hairsprays are the second-largest cause of air pollution, after drying paint. In California alone, 27 tons of noxious hairspray fumes are expelled every day. And "biodegradable" claims on a variety of products, including trash bags, have not proven to be accurate, thus leading to buyer confusion. The FTC has drafted guidelines that describe the circumstances when environmental claims can be made and would not constitute misleading information. For example, an advertisement or product label touting a package as "50 percent more recycled content than before" could be misleading if the recycled content has increased from 2 percent to 3 percent.[40]

Ultimately, marketers and consumers are accountable for ethical and socially responsible behavior. The 21st century will prove to be a testing period for both.

learning review

6. What is meant by social responsibility?

7. Marketing efforts to produce, promote, and reclaim environmentally sensitive products are called _____.

8. What is a social audit?

LEARNING OBJECTIVES REVIEW

LO1 *Explain the differences between legal and ethical behavior in marketing.*

A good starting point for understanding the nature and significance of ethics is the distinction between legality and ethicality of marketing decisions. Whereas ethics deal with personal moral principles and values, laws are society's values and standards that are enforceable in the courts. This distinction can lead to the rationalization that if a behavior is within reasonable ethical and legal limits, then it is not really illegal or unethical. Judgment plays a large role in defining ethical and legal boundaries in marketing. Ethical dilemmas arise when acts or situations are not clearly ethical and legal or unethical and illegal.

LO2 *Identify factors that influence ethical and unethical marketing decisions.*

Four factors influence ethical marketing behavior. First, societal culture and norms serve as socializing forces that dictate what is morally right and just. Second, business culture and industry practices affect ethical conduct both in the exchange relationships between buyers and sellers and the competitive behavior among sellers. Third, corporate culture and expectations are often defined by corporate ethics codes and the ethical behavior of top management and co-workers. Finally, an individual's personal moral philosophy, such as moral idealism or utilitarianism, will dictate ethical choices. Ultimately, ethical behavior rests with the individual, but the consequences affect many.

LO3 *Describe the different concepts of social responsibility.*

Social responsibility means that organizations are part of a larger society and are accountable to that society for their actions. There are three concepts of social responsibility. First, profit responsibility holds that companies have a simple duty: to maximize profits for their owners or stockholders. Second, stakeholder responsibility focuses on the obligations an organization has to those who can affect achievement of its objectives. Those constituencies include consumers, employees, suppliers, and distributors. Finally, societal responsibility focuses on obligations that organizations have to the preservation of the ecological environment and the general public. Companies are placing greater emphasis on societal responsibility today and are reaping the rewards of positive word of mouth from their consumers and favorable financial performance.

LO4 *Recognize unethical and socially irresponsible consumer behavior.*

Consumers, like marketers, have an obligation to act ethically and responsibly in the exchange process and in the use and disposition of products. Unfortunately, consumer behavior is spotty on both counts. Unethical consumer behavior includes filing warranty claims after the claim period, misredeeming coupons, pirating music, movies, and software from the Internet, and submitting phony insurance claims, among other behaviors. Unethical behavior is rarely motivated by economic need. Rather, research indicates that this behavior is influenced by (*a*) a belief that a consumer can get away with the act and it is worth doing and (*b*) the rationalization that such acts are justified or driven by forces outside the individual—"everybody does it." Consumer purchase, use, and disposition of environmentally sensitive products relate to consumer social responsibility. Even though consumers are sensitive to ecological issues they (*a*) may be unwilling to sacrifice convictions and pay potentially higher prices to protect the environment and (*b*) lack the knowledge to make informed decisions dealing with the purchase, use, and disposition of products.

FOCUSING ON KEY TERMS

cause marketing p. 88
code of ethics p. 84
Consumer Bill of Rights p. 82
ethics p. 80

green marketing p. 88
laws p. 80
moral idealism p. 85
social audit p. 88

social responsibility p. 86
utilitarianism p. 86

APPLYING MARKETING KNOWLEDGE

1 What concepts of moral philosophy and social responsibility are applicable to the practices of Anheuser-Busch described in the introduction to this chapter? Why?

2 Compare and contrast moral idealism and utilitarianism as alternative personal moral philosophies.

3 How would you evaluate Milton Friedman's view of the social responsibility of a firm?

4 Cause marketing programs have become popular. Describe two such programs with which you are familiar.

building your marketing plan

Consider these potential stakeholders that may be affected in some way by the marketing plan on which you are working: shareholders (if any), suppliers, employees, customers, and society in general. For each group of stakeholders,

1 Identify what, if any, ethical and social responsibility issues might arise.

2 Describe, in one or two sentences, how your marketing plan addresses each potential issue.

Wake up and smell the coffee—Starbucks is everywhere! As the world's No. 1 specialty coffee retailer, Starbucks serves more than 25 million customers in its stores every week. The concept of Starbucks goes far beyond being a coffeehouse or coffee brand. It represents the dream of its founder, Howard Schultz, who wanted to take the experience of an Italian—specifically, Milan—espresso bar to every corner of every city block in the world. So what is the *Starbucks experience?* According to the company,

> You get more than the finest coffee when you visit Starbucks. You get great people, first-rate music, a comfortable and upbeat meeting place, and sound advice on brewing excellent coffee at home. At home you're part of a family. At work you're part of a company. And somewhere in between there's a place where you can sit back and be yourself. That's what a Starbucks store is to many of its customers—a kind of "third place" where they can escape, reflect, read, chat, or listen.

But there is more. Starbucks has embraced corporate social responsibility like few other companies. A recent Starbucks Corporate Social Responsibility Annual Report described the company's views on social responsibility:

> Starbucks defines corporate social responsibility as conducting our business in ways that produce social, environmental, and economic benefits to the communities in which we operate. In the end, it means being responsible to our stakeholders.
>
> There is a growing recognition of the need for corporate accountability. Consumers are demanding more than "product" from their favorite brands. Employees are choosing to work for companies with strong values. Shareholders are more inclined to invest in businesses with outstanding corporate reputations. Quite simply, being socially responsible is

not only the right thing to do; it can distinguish a company from its industry peers.

Starbucks not only recognizes the central role that social responsibility plays in its business. It also takes constructive action to be socially responsible.

THE COMPANY

Starbucks is the leading retailer, roaster, and brand of specialty coffee in the world with more than 7,500 retail locations in North America, Latin America, Europe, the Middle East, and the Pacific Rim. Beginning in 1971 with a single retail location in Seattle, Washington, Starbucks became a *Fortune* 500 company in 2003 with annual sales exceeding $4 billion. In addition, Starbucks is ranked as one of the "Ten Most Admired Companies in America" and one of the "100 Best Companies to Work For" by *Fortune* magazine. It has been recognized as one of the "Most Trusted Brands" by *Ad Week* magazine. *Business Ethics* magazine placed Starbucks 21st in its list of the "100 Best Citizens" in 2003. Starbucks' performance can be attributed to a passionate pursuit of its mission and adherence to six guiding principles. Both appear in Figure 1.

COMMITMENT TO CORPORATE SOCIAL RESPONSIBILITY

Starbucks continually emphasizes its commitment to corporate social responsibility. Speaking at the annual shareholders meeting in March 2004, Howard Schultz said,

> From the beginning, Starbucks has built a company that balances profitability with a social conscience. Starbucks business practices are even more relevant today as consumers take

FIGURE 1
Starbucks Mission Statement and Guiding Principles

> Establish Starbucks as the premier purveyor of the finest coffee in the world while maintaining our uncompromising principles as we grow.
>
> The following six principles will help us measure the appropriateness of our decisions:
>
> 1. Provide a great work environment and treat each other with respect and dignity.
> 2. Embrace diversity as an essential component in the way we do business.
> 3. Apply the highest standards of excellence to the purchasing, roasting, and fresh delivery of our coffee.
> 4. Develop enthusiastically satisfied customers all the time.
> 5. Contribute positively to our communities and our environment.
> 6. Recognize that profitability is essential to our future success.

a cultural audit of the goods and services they use. Starbucks is known not only for serving the highest quality coffee, but for enriching the daily lives of its people, customers, and coffee farmers. This is the key to Starbucks' ongoing success and we are pleased to report our positive results to shareholders and partners (employees).

Each year, Starbucks makes public a comprehensive report on its corporate social responsibility initiatives. A central feature of this annual report is the alignment of the company's social responsibility decisions and actions with Starbucks Mission Statement and Guiding Principles. The Starbucks 2003 Corporate Social Responsibility Report, titled "Living Our Values," focused on six topical areas: (1) partners, (2) diversity, (3) coffee, (4) customers, (5) community and environment, and (6) profitability.

Partners

Starbucks employs some 74,000 people around the world. The company considers its employees as partners following the creation of Starbucks' stock option plan in 1991, called "Bean Stock." The company believes that giving eligible full- and part-time employees an ownership in the company and sharing the rewards of Starbucks' financial success has made the sense of partnership real. In addition, the company has one of the most competitive employee benefits and compensation packages in the retail industry. Ongoing training, career advancement opportunities, partner recognition programs, and diligent efforts to ensure a healthy and safe work environment have all contributed to the fact that Starbucks has one of the lowest employee turnover rates within the restaurant and fast-food industry.

Diversity

Starbucks strives to mirror the customers and communities it serves. On a quarterly basis, the company monitors the demographics of its workforce to determine whether they reflect the communities in which Starbucks operates. In 2003, Starbucks' U.S. workforce was comprised of 63 percent women and 24 percent people of color. The company also is engaged in a joint venture called Urban Coffee Opportunities (UCO) created to bring Starbucks stores to diverse neighborhoods. There were 52 UCO locations employing almost 1,000 Starbucks partners at the end of 2003.

Supplier diversity is also emphasized. To do business with Starbucks as a diverse supplier, that company must be 51 percent owned, operated, and managed by women, minorities, or socially disadvantaged individuals and meet Starbucks' requirements of quality, service, value, stability, and sound business practice. The company spent $80 million with diverse suppliers in 2003 and expected to spend $95 million with diverse suppliers in 2004.

Coffee

Starbucks' attention to quality coffee extends to its coffee growers located in more than 20 countries. Sustainable development is emphasized. This means that Starbucks pays coffee farmers a fair price for the beans; that the coffee is grown in an ecologically sound manner; and that Starbucks invests in the farming communities where its coffees are produced.

One long-standing initiative is Starbucks' partnership with Conservation International, a nonprofit organization dedicated to protecting soil, water, energy, and biological diversity worldwide. Starbucks is particularly focused on environmental protection and helping local farmers earn more for their crops. In 2003, Starbucks invested more than $1 million in social programs, notably health and education projects, that benefited farming communities in nine countries, from Colombia to Indonesia.

Customers

Starbucks serves customers in 32 countries. The company and its partners are committed to providing each customer the optimal Starbucks experience every time they visit a store. For very loyal Starbucks customers, that translates into 18 visits per month on average.

Making a connection with customers at each store and building the relationship a customer has with Starbucks *baristas,* or coffee brewers, is important in creating the Starbucks experience. Each barista receives 24 hours of training in customer service and basic retail skills, as well as "Coffee Knowledge" and "Brewing the Perfect Cup" classes. Baristas are taught to anticipate the customers' needs and to make eye contact while carefully explaining the various coffee flavors and blends. Starbucks also enhances the customer relationship by soliciting feedback and responding to patrons' experiences and concerns. Starbucks Customer Relations reviews and responds to every inquiry or comment, often within 24 hours for telephone calls and e-mails.

Community and Environment

Efforts to contribute positively to the communities it serves and the environments in which it operates are emphasized in Starbucks' guiding principles. "We aren't in the coffee business, serving people. We are in the people business, serving coffee," says Howard Schultz. Starbucks and its partners have been recognized for volunteer support and financial contributions to a wide variety of local, national, and international social, economic, and environmental initiatives. For example, the "Make Your Mark" program rewards partners' gifts of time for volunteer work with charitable donations from Starbucks. In addition, Starbucks is a supporter of CARE International, a nonprofit organization dedicated to fighting global poverty.

Starbucks is also committed to environmental responsibility. Starbucks has a longtime involvement with Earth Day activities. It has instituted company-wide energy and water conservation programs and waste reduction, recycling, and reuse initiatives proposed by partner *Green Teams.*

Profitability

At Starbucks, profitability is viewed as essential to its future success. When Starbucks' guiding principles were conceived, profitability was included but intentionally placed last on the list. This was done not because profitability was the least important. Instead, it was believed that adherence to the five other principles would ultimately lead to good financial performance. In fact, it has.

Questions

1 How does Starbucks' approach to social responsibility relate to the three concepts of social responsibility described in the text?
2 What role does sustainable development play in Starbucks' approach to social responsibility?

PERFORMED BETTER. After *Car and Driver*, readers put Camry, Accord and the all-wheel-drive Ford Fusion to the test in Washington, D.C., *Road & Track*, invited enthusiasts to do the same in Los Angeles. Once again, for styling, handling and performance, drivers said Fusion kicked the competition. Visit a Ford Dealer or go to fordchallenge.com. Bold Moves.

Ford FUSION

5

Understanding Consumer Behavior

LEARNING OBJECTIVES

After reading this chapter you should be able to:

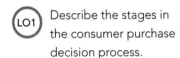

LO1 Describe the stages in the consumer purchase decision process.

LO2 Distinguish among three variations of the consumer purchase decision process: routine, limited, and extended problem solving.

LO3 Identify major psychological influences on consumer behavior.

LO4 Identify the major sociocultural influences on consumer behavior.

WHO'S REALLY BUYING THAT NEW CAR? JUST ASK HER!

Who buys 68 percent of new cars? Who influences 85 percent of new-car-buying decisions? Women. Yes, women.

Women are a driving force in the U.S. automotive industry. Enlightened carmakers have hired women designers, engineers, and marketing executives to better understand and satisfy this valuable car-buying consumer and influencer. What have they learned? Women and men think and feel differently about key elements of the new-car-buying decision process and experience.

- *The sense of styling.* Women and men care about styling. For men, styling is more about a car's exterior lines and accents. Women are more interested in interior design and finishes. Designs that fit their proportions, provide good visibility, offer ample storage space, and make for effortless parking are particularly important.

- *The need for speed.* Both sexes want speed, but for different reasons. Men think about how many seconds it takes to get from zero to 60 miles per hour. Women want to feel secure that the car has enough acceleration to outrun an 18-wheeler trying to pass them on a freeway entrance ramp.

- *The substance of safety.* Safety for men is about features that help avoid an accident, such as antilock brakes and responsive steering. For women, safety is about features that help to survive an accident, including passenger airbags and reinforced side panels.

- *The shopping experience.* The new-car-buying experience differs between men and women. Generally, men decide upfront what car they want and set out alone to find it. By contrast, women approach it as an intelligence-gathering expedition. They actively seek information and postpone a purchase decision until all options have been evaluated. Women frequently visit auto-buying websites, read car-comparison articles, and scan car advertisements. Still, recommendations of friends and relatives matter most. Women typically shop three dealerships before making a purchase decision—one more than men. While only a third of women say that price is the most influential when they shop for a new car, 71 percent say price determines the final decision.

Carmakers have learned that women, more than men, dislike the car-buying experience. In particular, women dread the price negotiations that is often involved in buying a new car. Not surprisingly, 76 percent of women car buyers take a man with them to finalize the terms of sale.[1]

This chapter examines **consumer behavior**, the actions a person takes in purchasing and using products and services, including the mental and social processes that come before and after these actions. This chapter shows how the behavioral sciences help answer questions such as why people choose one product or brand over another, how they make these choices, and how companies use this knowledge to provide value to consumers.

CONSUMER PURCHASE DECISION PROCESS AND EXPERIENCE

LO1

Behind the visible act of making a purchase lies an important decision process and consumer experience that must be investigated. The stages a buyer passes through in making choices about which products and services to buy is the **purchase decision process**. This process has the five stages shown in Figure 5–1: (1) problem recognition, (2) information search, (3) alternative evaluation, (4) purchase decision, and (5) postpurchase behavior.

Problem Recognition: Perceiving a Need

Problem recognition, the initial step in the purchase decision, is perceiving a difference between a person's ideal and actual situations big enough to trigger a decision.[2] This can be as simple as finding an empty milk carton in the refrigerator; noting, as a first-year college student, that your high school clothes are not in the style that other students are wearing; or realizing that your laptop computer may not be working properly.

In marketing, advertisements or salespeople can activate a consumer's decision process by showing the shortcomings of competing (or currently owned) products. For instance, an advertisement for a flash-memory MP3 player could stimulate problem recognition because it emphasizes "maximum music from one device."

Information Search: Seeking Value

After recognizing a problem, a consumer begins to search for information, the next stage in the purchase decision process. First, you may scan your memory for previous experiences with products or brands. This action is called *internal search.* For frequently purchased products such as shampoo and conditioner, this may be enough.

Or a consumer may undertake an *external search* for information.[3] This is needed when past experience or knowledge is insufficient, the risk of making a wrong purchase decision is high, and the cost of gathering information is low. The primary sources of external information are: (1) *personal sources,* such as relatives and friends whom the consumer trusts; (2) *public sources,* including various product-rating organizations such as *Consumer Reports,* government agencies, and TV "consumer programs"; and (3) *marketer-dominated sources,* such as information from sellers including advertising, company websites, salespeople, and point-of-purchase displays in stores.

Suppose you consider buying a flash-memory MP3 player. You will probably tap several of these information sources: friends and relatives, advertisements, brand and company websites, and stores carrying these players (for demonstrations). You might study the comparative evaluation of flash-memory MP3 players appearing in *Consumer Reports,* a portion of which appears in Figure 5–2.[4]

FIGURE 5–1
The purchase decision process consists of five stages.

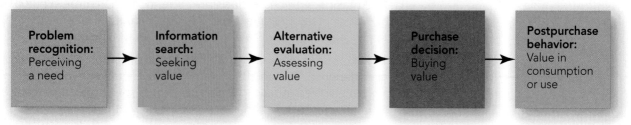

Problem recognition: Perceiving a need	Information search: Seeking value	Alternative evaluation: Assessing value	Purchase decision: Buying value	Postpurchase behavior: Value in consumption or use

Consumer Reports' evaluation of flash-memory MP3 players (abridged):

BRAND	MODEL	RETAIL PRICE	EASE OF USE	HEADPHONE QUALITY	AUDIO QUALITY	PICTURE QUALITY	AUDIO PLAYBACK TIME (HOURS)
Cowon	iAudio U3	$180	Very Good	Very Good	Excellent	Very Good	18
Samsung	YP-T87	175	Very Good	Good	Excellent	Good	17
Apple	iPod Nano	200	Very Good	Very Good	Excellent	Good	15
iRiver	U10	200	Very Good	Very Good	Excellent	Very Good	28
RCA	Lyra RD 2217	125	Good	Good	Excellent	NA	39
Creative	Zen Nano Plus	70	Good	Good	Fair	NA	13
Philips	SA 178	100	Good	Good	Excellent	NA	13
Sony	Network Walkman	95	Good	Good	Excellent	NA	41

Rating: Excellent | Very Good | Good | Fair | Poor

FIGURE 5–2
Consumer Reports' evaluation of flash-memory MP3 players (abridged)

Alternative Evaluation: Assessing Value

The information search stage clarifies the problem for the consumer by (1) suggesting criteria to use for the purchase, (2) yielding brand names that might meet the criteria, and (3) developing consumer value perceptions. Given only the information shown in Figure 5–2, what selection criteria would you use in buying a flash-memory MP3 player? Would you use price, audio quality, ease of use, or some other combination of these and other criteria?

For some of you, the information provided may be inadequate because it does not contain all the factors you might consider when evaluating flash-memory MP3 players. These factors are a consumer's *evaluative criteria,* which represent both the objective attributes of a brand (such as audio playback time) and the subjective ones (such as prestige) you use to compare different products and brands.[5] Firms try to identify and capitalize on both types of criteria to create the best value for the money sought by you and other consumers. These criteria are often displayed in advertisements.

Consumers often have several criteria for evaluating brands. (Didn't you in the preceding exercise?) Knowing this, companies seek to identify the most important evaluative criteria that consumers use when judging brands. For example, among the evaluative criteria shown in the columns of Figure 5–2, suppose you use three in considering flash-memory MP3 players: (1) a list price under $200, (2) audio quality, and (3) audio playback time of at least 15 hours. These criteria establish the brands in your *consideration set*—the group of brands that a consumer would consider acceptable from among all the brands in the product class of which he or she is aware.[6] Your evaluative criteria result in four models and four brands (Cowon, Samsung, RCA, and Sony) in your consideration set. If these alternatives don't satisfy you, you can change your evaluative criteria to create a different consideration set of models and brands. For example, ease of use might join the list of evaluative criteria if this is the first MP3 player you have purchased.

Purchase Decision: Buying Value

Having examined the alternatives in the consideration set, you are almost ready to make a purchase decision. Two choices remain: (1) from whom to buy and (2) when to buy. For a product like a flash-memory MP3 player, the information search process probably involved visiting retail stores, seeing different brands in catalogs, and viewing a flash-memory MP3 player on a seller's website. The choice of which seller to buy from will depend on such considerations as the terms of sale, your past experience buying from the seller, and the return policy. Often a purchase decision involves a simultaneous evaluation of both product attributes and seller characteristics. For example, you might choose the second-most preferred flash-memory MP3 brand at a store or website with a liberal refund and return policy versus the most preferred brand at a store or website with more conservative policies.

Deciding when to buy is determined by a number of factors. For instance, you might buy sooner if one of your preferred brands is on sale or its manufacturer offers a rebate. Other factors such as the store atmosphere, pleasantness or ease of the shopping experience, salesperson assistance, time pressure, and financial circumstances could also affect whether a purchase decision is made or postponed.

Use of the Internet to gather information, evaluate alternatives, and make buying decisions adds a technological dimension to the consumer purchase decision process and buying experience. Consumer benefits and costs associated with this technology and its marketing implications are detailed in Chapter 18.

Postpurchase Behavior: Value in Consumption or Use

A satisfactory or unsatisfactory consumption or use experience is an important factor in postpurchase behavior. Marketer attention to this stage can pay huge dividends as described in the text.

After buying a product, the consumer compares it with his or her expectations and is either satisfied or dissatisfied. A company's sensitivity to a customer's consumption or use experience is extremely important in a consumer's value perception. Studies show that satisfaction or dissatisfaction affects consumer communications and repeat-purchase behavior. Satisfied buyers tell three other people about their experience. Dissatisfied buyers complain to nine people.[7] Satisfied buyers also tend to buy from the same seller each time a purchase occasion arises.

Firms such as General Electric (GE), Johnson & Johnson, Coca-Cola, and British Airways focus attention on postpurchase behavior to maximize customer satisfaction and retention. These firms, among many others, now provide toll-free telephone numbers, offer liberalized return and refund policies, and engage in extensive staff training to handle complaints, answer questions, record suggestions, and solve consumer problems.

Often a consumer is faced with two or more highly attractive alternatives, such as a Cowon or Samsung flash-memory MP3 player. If you choose Cowon, you may think, "Should I have purchased the Samsung?" This feeling of postpurchase psychological tension or anxiety is called *cognitive dissonance*. To alleviate it, consumers often attempt to applaud themselves for making the right choice. So after your purchase, you may seek information to confirm your choice by asking friends questions like, "Don't you like my new MP3 player?" or by reading ads of the brand you chose. You might even look for negative features about the brand you didn't buy and decide that the Samsung headphones didn't feel right. Firms often use ads or follow-up calls from salespeople in this postpurchase stage to comfort buyers that they made the right decision. For many years, Buick ran an advertising campaign with the message, "Aren't you really glad you bought a Buick?"

involvement
Personal, social, and economic significance of a purchase to the consumer

Consumer Involvement Affects the Purchase Process

Sometimes consumers don't engage in the five-stage purchase decision process. Instead, they skip or minimize one or more stages depending on the level of **involvement**, the

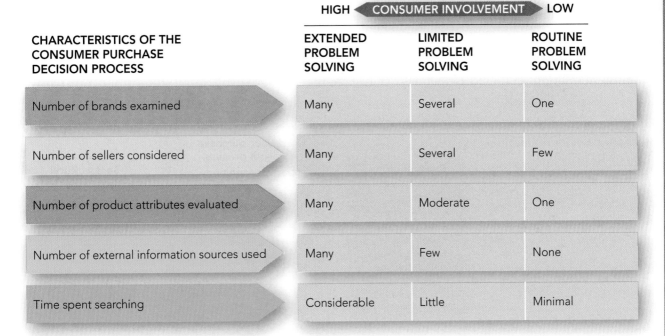

CHARACTERISTICS OF THE CONSUMER PURCHASE DECISION PROCESS	EXTENDED PROBLEM SOLVING	LIMITED PROBLEM SOLVING	ROUTINE PROBLEM SOLVING
Number of brands examined	Many	Several	One
Number of sellers considered	Many	Several	Few
Number of product attributes evaluated	Many	Moderate	One
Number of external information sources used	Many	Few	None
Time spent searching	Considerable	Little	Minimal

FIGURE 5–3

Comparison of problem-solving variations: Extended problem solving, limited problem solving, and routine problem solving

LO2

personal, social, and economic significance of the purchase to the consumer.[8] High-involvement purchase occasions typically have at least one of three characteristics: The item to be purchased (1) is expensive, (2) can have serious personal consequences, or (3) could reflect on one's social image. For these occasions, consumers engage in extensive information search, consider many product attributes and brands, form attitudes, and participate in word-of-mouth communication. Low-involvement purchases, such as toothpaste and soap, barely involve most of us, but audio and video systems and automobiles are very involving.

There are three general variations in the consumer purchase decision process based on consumer involvement and product knowledge. Figure 5–3 shows some important differences between the three problem-solving variations.

Extended Problem Solving In extended problem solving, each of the five stages of the consumer purchase decision process is used, including considerable time and effort on external information search and in identifying and evaluating alternatives. Several brands are in the consideration set, and these are evaluated on many attributes. Extended problem solving exists in high-involvement purchase situations for items such as cars and elaborate audio systems.

Limited Problem Solving In limited problem solving, consumers seek some information or rely on a friend to help them evaluate alternatives. In general, several brands might be evaluated using a moderate number of different attributes. You might use limited problem solving in choosing a toaster, a restaurant for lunch, and other purchase situations in which you have little time or effort to spend.

Routine Problem Solving For products such as table salt and milk, consumers recognize a problem, make a decision, and spend little effort seeking external information and evaluating alternatives. The purchase process for such items is virtually a habit and typifies low-involvement decision making. Routine problem solving is typically the case for low-priced, frequently purchased products.

FIGURE 5–4

Influences on the consumer
purchase decision process
come from both internal and
external sources.

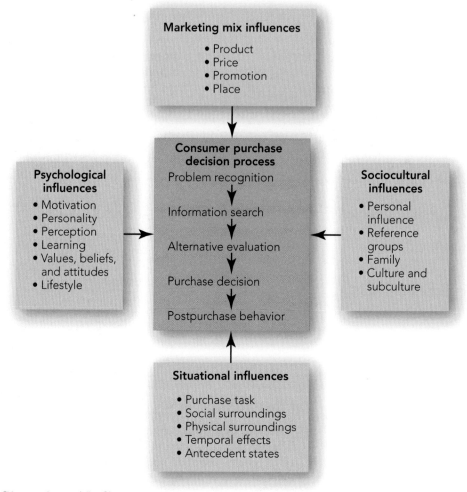

Situational Influences

Often the purchase situation will affect the purchase decision process. Five *situational influences* have an impact on your purchase decision process: (1) the purchase task, (2) social surroundings, (3) physical surroundings, (4) temporal effects, and (5) antecedent states.[9] The purchase task is the reason for engaging in the decision in the first place. Information searching and evaluating alternatives may differ depending on whether the purchase is a gift, which often involves social visibility, or for the buyer's own use. Social surroundings, including the other people present when a purchase decision is made, may also affect what is purchased. Physical surroundings such as decor, music, and crowding in retail stores may alter how purchase decisions are made. Temporal effects such as time of day or the amount of time available will influence where consumers have breakfast and lunch and what is ordered. Finally, antecedent states, which include the consumer's mood or the amount of cash on hand, can influence purchase behavior and choice.

Figure 5–4 shows the many influences that affect the consumer purchase decision process. The decision to buy a product also involves important psychological and sociocultural influences. These two influences are covered in the remainder of this chapter. Marketing mix influences are described later in Part 4 of the book.

---

learning review

1. What is the first stage in the consumer purchase decision process?

2. The brands a consumer considers buying out of the set of brands in a product class of which the consumer is aware is called the _____.

3. What is the term for postpurchase anxiety?

PSYCHOLOGICAL INFLUENCES ON CONSUMER BEHAVIOR

LO3

Psychology helps marketers understand why and how consumers behave as they do. In particular, psychological concepts such as motivation and personality; perception; learning; values, beliefs, and attitudes; and lifestyle are useful for interpreting buying processes and directing marketing efforts.

Motivation and Personality

Motivation and personality are two familiar psychological concepts that have specific meanings and marketing implications. These concepts are closely related and are used to explain why people do some things and not others.

motivation

Energizing force that stimulates behavior to satisfy a need

Motivation   **Motivation** is the energizing force that stimulates behavior to satisfy a need. Because consumer needs are the focus of the marketing concept, marketers try to arouse these needs.

An individual's needs are boundless. People possess physiological needs for basics such as water, shelter, and food. They also have learned needs, including self-esteem, achievement, and affection. Psychologists point out that these needs may be hierarchical; that is, once physiological needs are met, people seek to satisfy their learned needs.

Figure 5–5 shows one need hierarchy and classification scheme that contains five need classes.[10] *Physiological needs* are basic to survival and must be satisfied first. A Red Lobster advertisement featuring a seafood salad attempts to activate the need for food. *Safety needs* involve self-preservation as well as physical and financial well-being. Smoke detector and burglar alarm manufacturers focus on these needs, as do insurance companies and retirement plan advisors. *Social needs* are concerned with love and friendship. Dating services, such as Match.com and eHarmony, and fragrance companies try to arouse these needs. *Personal needs* include the need for achievement, status, prestige, and self-respect. The American Express Platinum Card and Brooks Brothers Clothiers appeal to these needs. Sometimes firms try to arouse multiple needs to stimulate problem recognition. Michelin combined safety with parental love to promote tire replacement for automobiles. *Self-actualization needs* involve personal fulfillment. For example, a long-running U.S. Army recruiting program invited enlistees to "Be all you can be."

FIGURE 5–5

Hierarchy of needs. The hierarchy of needs is based on the idea that motivation comes from a need. If a need is met, it's no longer a motivator, so a higher-level need becomes the motivator. Higher-level needs demand support of lower-level needs.

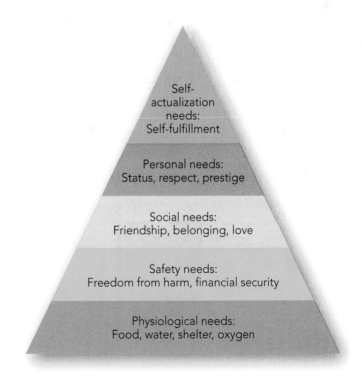

personality
Someone's consistent behaviors or responses to recurring situations

perception
Process by which someone selects, organizes, and interprets information to create a meaningful picture of the world

Why does the Good Housekeeping seal for Clorox's Fresh Step Crystals cat litter appear in the ad? Why does Mary Kay, Inc., offer a free sample of its Velocity brand fragrance through its website? The answers appear in the text.

Personality While motivation is the energizing force that makes consumer behavior purposeful, a consumer's personality guides and directs behavior. **Personality** refers to a person's consistent behaviors or responses to recurring situations.

Although many personality theories exist, most identify key *traits*—enduring characteristics within a person or in his or her relationship with others. Such traits include assertiveness, extroversion, compliance, dominance, and aggression, among others. These traits are inherited or formed at an early age and change little over the years. Research suggests that compliant people prefer known brand names and use more mouthwash and toilet soaps. Aggressive types use razors, not electric shavers, apply more cologne and aftershave lotions, and purchase signature goods such as Gucci, Yves St. Laurent, and Donna Karan as an indicator of status.[11]

These personality characteristics are often revealed in a person's *self-concept,* which is the way people see themselves and the way they believe others see them. Marketers recognize that people have an actual self-concept and an ideal self-concept. The actual self refers to how people actually see themselves. The ideal self describes how people would like to see themselves. These two self-images are reflected in the products and brands a person buys, including automobiles, home appliances and furnishings, magazines, clothing, grooming and leisure products, and frequently, the stores a person shops. The importance of self-concept is summed up by a senior executive at Barnes & Noble: "People buy books for what the purchase says about them—their taste, their cultivation, their trendiness."[12]

Perception

One person sees a Cadillac as a mark of achievement; another sees it as ostentatious. This is the result of **perception**—the process by which an individual selects, organizes, and interprets information to create a meaningful picture of the world.

Selective Perception Because the average consumer operates in a complex environment, the human brain attempts to organize and interpret information with a process called *selective perception,* a filtering of exposure, comprehension, and retention. *Selective exposure* occurs when people pay attention to messages that are

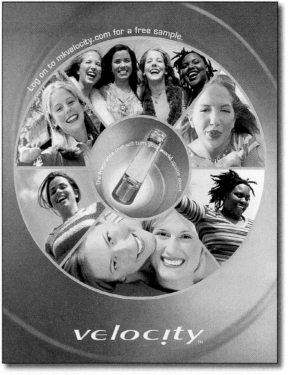

Making Responsible Decisions > > > > > > > > > > ethics

The Ethics of Subliminal Messages

For about 50 years, the topic of subliminal perception and the presence of subliminal messages and images embedded in commercial communications have sparked heated debate.

The Federal Communications Commission has denounced subliminal messages as deceptive. Still, consumers spend $50 million a year for audiotapes with subliminal messages designed to help them raise their self-esteem, quit smoking, or lose weight. Almost two-thirds of U.S. consumers think subliminal messages are present in commercial communications; about half are firmly convinced that this practice can cause them to buy things they don't want.

Subliminal messages are not illegal in the United States, however, and marketers are often criticized for pursuing opportunities to create these messages in both electronic and print media. A book by August Bullock, *The Secret Sales Pitch: An Overview of Subliminal Advertising*, is devoted to this topic. Bullock identifies images and advertisements that he claims contain subliminal messages and describes techniques that can be used for conveying these messages.

Do you believe that a marketer's attempt to implant subliminal messages in electronic and print media is a deceptive practice and unethical, regardless of his or her intent?

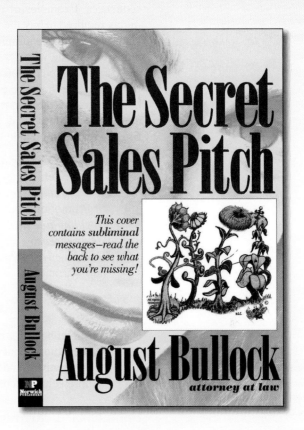

consistent with their attitudes and beliefs and ignore messages that are inconsistent. Selective exposure often occurs in the postpurchase stage of the consumer decision process, when consumers read advertisements for the brand they just bought. It also occurs when a need exists—you are more likely to "see" a McDonald's advertisement when you are hungry rather than after you have eaten a pizza.

Selective comprehension involves interpreting information so that it is consistent with your attitudes and beliefs. A marketer's failure to understand this can have disastrous results. For example, Toro introduced a small, lightweight snowblower called the Snow Pup. Even though the product worked, sales failed to meet expectations. Why? Toro later found out that consumers perceived the name to mean that Snow Pup was a toy or too light to do any serious snow removal. When the product was renamed Snow Master, sales increased sharply.[13]

Selective retention means that consumers do not remember all the information they see, read, or hear, even minutes after exposure to it. This affects the internal and external information search stage of the purchase decision process. This is why furniture and automobile retailers often give consumers product brochures to take home when they leave the showroom.

Because perception plays an important role in consumer behavior, it is not surprising that the topic of subliminal perception is a popular item for discussion. *Subliminal perception* means that you see or hear messages without being aware of them. The presence and effect of subliminal perception on behavior is a hotly debated issue, with more popular appeal than scientific support. Indeed, evidence suggests that such messages have limited effects on behavior.[14] If these messages did influence behavior, would their use be an ethical practice? (See the accompanying Making Responsible Decisions box.)[15]

perceived risk

Anxiety felt when a consumer cannot anticipate possible negative outcomes of a purchase

Perceived Risk   Perception plays a major role in the perceived risk in purchasing a product or service. **Perceived risk** represents the anxiety felt because the consumer cannot anticipate the outcomes of a purchase but believes there may be negative consequences. Examples of possible negative consequences are the size of the financial outlay required to buy the product (Can I afford $500 for those skis?), the risk of physical harm (Is bungee jumping safe?), and the performance of the product (Will the whitening toothpaste work?). A more abstract form is psychosocial (What will my friends say if I get a tattoo?). Perceived risk affects information search, because the greater the perceived risk, the more extensive the external search stage is likely to be.

Recognizing the importance of perceived risk, companies develop strategies to reduce the consumer's risk and encourage purchases. These strategies and examples of firms using them include the following:

* *Obtaining seals of approval:* The Good Housekeeping seal for Fresh Step Crystals cat litter.
* *Securing endorsements from influential people:* The National Fluid Milk Processor Promotion Board "Got Milk" advertising campaign.
* *Providing free trials of the product:* Samples of Mary Kay's Velocity fragrance.
* *Giving extensive usage instructions:* Clairol hair coloring.
* *Providing warranties and guarantees:* Cadillac's 100,000 -mile, five-year power-train warranty.

Learning

learning

Behaviors that result from repeated experience or reasoning

Much consumer behavior is learned. Consumers learn which information sources to consult for information about products and services, which evaluative criteria to use when assessing alternatives, and, more generally, how to make purchase decisions. **Learning** refers to those behaviors that result from (1) repeated experience and (2) reasoning.

Behavioral Learning   *Behavioral learning* is the process of developing automatic responses to a situation built up through repeated exposure to it. Four variables are central to how consumers learn from repeated experience: drive, cue, response, and reinforcement. A *drive* is a need that moves an individual to action. Drives, such as hunger, might be represented by motives. A *cue* is a stimulus or symbol perceived by consumers. A *response* is the action taken by a consumer to satisfy the drive, whereas a *reinforcement* is the reward. Being hungry (drive), a consumer sees a cue (a billboard), takes action (buys a sandwich), and receives a reward (it tastes great!).

Marketers use two concepts from behavioral learning theory. *Stimulus generalization* occurs when a response elicited by one stimulus (cue) is generalized to another stimulus. Using the same brand name for different products is an application of this concept, such as Tylenol Cold & Flu and Tylenol P.M. *Stimulus discrimination* refers to a person's ability to perceive differences in stimuli. Consumers' tendency to perceive all light beers as being alike led to Budweiser Light commercials that distinguished between many types of "lights" and Bud Light.

Cognitive Learning   Consumers also learn through thinking, reasoning, and mental problem solving without direct experience. This type of learning, called *cognitive learning,* involves making connections between two or more ideas or simply observing the outcomes of others' behaviors and adjusting your own accordingly. Firms also influence this type of learning. Through repetition in advertising, messages such as "Advil is a headache remedy" attempt to link a brand (Advil) and an idea (headache remedy) by showing someone using the brand and finding relief.

Brand Loyalty   Learning is also important to marketers because it relates to habit formation—the basis of routine problem solving. Furthermore, there is a close link

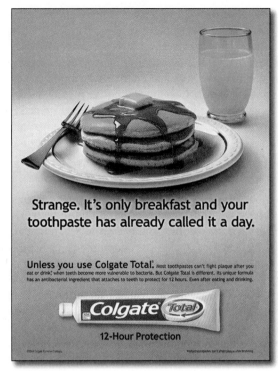

Attitudes toward Colgate Total toothpaste and Extra Strength Bayer aspirin were successfully changed by these ads. How? Read the text to find out how marketers can change consumer attitudes toward products and brands.

brand loyalty
Favorable attitude toward and consistent purchase of a single brand over time

attitude
Tendency to respond to something in a consistently favorable or unfavorable way

beliefs
Consumer's perceptions of how a product or brand performs

between habits and **brand loyalty**, which is a favorable attitude toward and consistent purchase of a single brand over time. Brand loyalty results from the positive reinforcement of previous actions. So a consumer reduces risk and saves time by consistently purchasing the same brand of shampoo and has favorable results—healthy, shining hair.

Values, Beliefs, and Attitudes

Values, beliefs, and attitudes play a central role in consumer decision making.

Attitude Formation An **attitude** is a "learned predisposition to respond to an object or class of objects in a consistently favorable or unfavorable way."[16] Attitudes are shaped by our values and beliefs, which are learned. Values vary by level of specificity. We speak of American core values, including material well-being and humanitarianism. We also have personal values, such as thriftiness and ambition. Marketers are concerned with both but focus mostly on personal values. Personal values affect attitudes by influencing the importance assigned to specific product attributes. Suppose thriftiness is one of your personal values. When you evaluate cars, fuel economy (a product attribute) becomes important. If you believe a specific car brand has this attribute, you are likely to have a favorable attitude toward it.

Beliefs also play a part in attitude formation. **Beliefs** are a consumer's subjective perception of how a product or brand performs on different attributes. Beliefs are based on personal experience, advertising, and discussions with other people. Beliefs about product attributes are important because, along with personal values, they create the favorable or unfavorable attitude the consumer has toward certain products, services, and brands.

Attitude Change Marketers use three approaches to try to change consumer attitudes toward products and brands, as shown in the following examples.[17]

1. *Changing beliefs about the extent to which a brand has certain attributes.* To allay consumer concern that aspirin use causes an upset stomach, Bayer Corporation successfully promoted the gentleness of its Extra Strength Bayer Plus aspirin.

2. *Changing the perceived importance of attributes.* Pepsi-Cola made freshness an important product attribute when it stamped freshness dates on its cans. Before doing so, few consumers considered cola freshness an issue. After Pepsi spent about $25 million on advertising and promotion, a consumer survey found that 61 percent of cola drinkers believed freshness dating was an important attribute.
3. *Adding new attributes to the product.* Colgate-Palmolive included a new antibacterial ingredient, tricloson, in its Colgate Total toothpaste and spent $100 million marketing the brand. The result? Colgate replaced Crest as the market leader for the first time in 25 years.

Consumer Lifestyle

Lifestyle is a mode of living that is identified by how people spend their time and resources, what they consider important in their environment, and what they think of themselves and the world around them. The analysis of consumer lifestyles, called psychographics, provides numerous insights into consumer needs and wants.

Psychographics, the practice of combining psychology, lifestyle, and demographics, is often used to uncover consumer motivations for buying and using products and services. A prominent psychographic system is VALS™ from SRI Consulting Business Intelligence (SRIC-BI).[18] The VALS system identifies eight consumer segments based on (1) their primary motivation for buying and having certain products and services and (2) their resources.

According to SRIC-BI researchers, consumers are motivated to buy products and services and seek experiences that give shape, substance, and satisfaction to their lives. But not all consumers are alike. Consumers are inspired by one of three primary motivations—ideals, achievement, and self-expression—that give meaning to their self or the world and govern their activities. The different levels of resources enhance or constrain a person's expression of his or her primary motivation. A person's resources include psychological, physical, demographic, and material capacities such as income, self-confidence, and risk-taking.

The VALS system seeks to explain why and how consumers make purchase decisions.

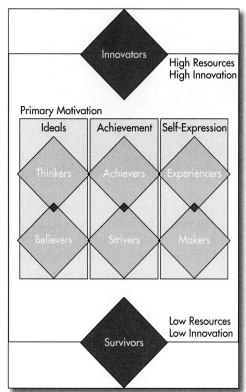

The VALS classification system places consumers with abundant resources—psychological, physical, and material means and capacities—near the top of the chart and those with minimal resources near the bottom. The chart segments consumers by their basis for decision making: ideals, achievement, or self-expression. The boxes intersect to indicate that some categories may be considered together. For instance, a marketer may categorize Thinkers and Believers together.

- *Ideals-motivated groups.* Consumers motivated by ideals are guided by knowledge and principle. These consumers divide into two groups. *Thinkers* are mature, reflective, and well-educated people who value order, knowledge, and responsibility. They are practical consumers, deliberate information-seekers, who value durability and functionality in products over styling and newness. *Believers,* with fewer resources, are conservative, conventional people with concrete beliefs based on traditional, established codes: family, religion, community, and the nation. They choose familiar products and brands, favor American-made products, and are generally brand loyal.
- *Achievement-motivated groups.* Consumers motivated by achievement look for products and services that demonstrate success to their peers or to a peer group they aspire to. These consumers include *Achievers,* who have a busy, goal-directed lifestyle and a deep commitment to career and family. Image is important to them. They favor established, prestige products and services and are interested in time-saving devices given their hectic schedules. *Strivers* are trendy, fun-loving, and less self-confident than Achievers. They also have lower levels of education and household income. Money defines success for them. They favor stylish products and are as impulsive as their financial circumstances permit.
- *Self-expression-motivated groups.* Consumers motivated by self-expression desire social or physical activity, variety, and risk. *Experiencers* are young,

enthusiastic, and impulsive consumers who become excited about new possibilities but are equally quick to cool. They savor the new, the offbeat, and the risky. Their energy finds an outlet in exercise, sports, outdoor recreation, and social activities. Much of their income is spent on fashion items, entertainment, and socializing and particularly on looking good and having the latest things. *Makers,* with fewer resources, express themselves and experience the world by working on it—building a house, raising children, or fixing a car. They are practical people who have constructive skills, value self-sufficiency, and are unimpressed by material possessions except those with a practical or functional purpose.

- *High- and low-resource groups.* Two segments stand apart. *Innovators* are successful, sophisticated, take-charge people with high self-esteem and abundant resources of all kinds. Image is important to them, not as evidence of power or status, but as an expression of cultivated tastes, independence, and character. They are receptive to new ideas and technologies. Their lives are characterized by variety. *Survivors,* with the least resources of any segment, focus on meeting basic needs (safety and security) rather than fulfilling desires. They represent a modest market for most products and services and are loyal to favorite brands, especially if they can be purchased at a discount.

Each of these segments exhibits unique media preferences. Experiencers and Strivers are the most likely to visit Internet chat rooms. Innovators, Thinkers, and Achievers tend to read business and news magazines such as *Fortune* and *Time.* Experiencers read sports and fashion magazines, whereas Makers read hunting and fishing, and automotive magazines. Believers are the heaviest readers of *Reader's Digest.* GeoVALS™ estimates the percentage of each VALS group by zip code.

learning review

4. The problem with the Toro Snow Pup was an example of selective _____.

5. What three attitude-change approaches are most common?

6. What does *lifestyle* mean?

SOCIOCULTURAL INFLUENCES ON CONSUMER BEHAVIOR

LO4

Sociocultural influences, which evolve from a consumer's formal and informal relationships with other people, also exert a significant impact on consumer behavior. These involve personal influence, reference groups, the family, and culture and subculture.

Personal Influence

A consumer's purchases are often influenced by the views, opinions, or behaviors of others. Two aspects of personal influence are very important to marketing: opinion leadership and word-of-mouth activity.

opinion leaders
Individuals who have social influence over others

Opinion Leadership Individuals who have social influence over others are called **opinion leaders**. Opinion leaders are more likely to be important for products and services that provide a form of self-expression. Opinion leadership is widespread in the purchase of cars and trucks, entertainment, clothing and accessories, club membership, consumer electronics, vacation locations, food, and financial investments.

About 10 percent of U.S. adults are opinion leaders.[19] Identifying, reaching, and influencing opinion leaders is a major challenge for companies. Some firms use sports figures or celebrities as spokespersons to represent their products, such as actor Uma Thurman and NASCAR driver Jeff Gordon for TAG Heuer watches. Others promote their products in media believed to reach opinion leaders.

Firms use actors or athletes as spokespersons to represent their products, such as Uma Thurman and Jeff Gordon for TAG Heuer watches, in the hope that they are opinion leaders.

 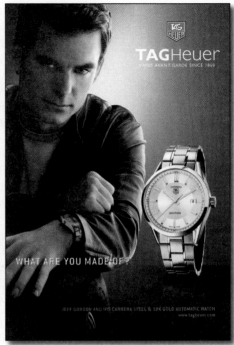

word of mouth

People influencing each other in personal conversations

Word of Mouth The influencing of people during conversations is called **word of mouth**. Word of mouth is the most powerful and authentic information source for consumers because it typically involves friends viewed as trustworthy. According to a recent study, 67 percent of U.S. consumer product sales are directly based on word-of-mouth activity among friends, family, and colleagues.[20]

The power of personal influence has prompted firms to promote positive and retard negative word of mouth. For instance, "teaser" advertising campaigns are run in advance of new-product introductions to stimulate conversations. Other techniques such as advertising slogans, music, and humor also heighten positive word of mouth. Many commercials shown during the Super Bowl are created expressly to initiate conversations about the advertisements and featured product or service the next day. Increasingly, companies recruit and deploy people to produce *buzz*—popularity created by consumer word of mouth. Read the accompanying Marketing Matters box to learn how this is done by BzzAgent.[21]

On the other hand, rumors about McDonald's (worms in hamburgers), Corona Extra beer (contaminated beer), and Snickers candy bars in Russia (a cause of diabetes) have resulted in negative word of mouth, none of which was based on fact. Overcoming or neutalizing negative word of mouth is difficult and costly. Marketers report that supplying factual information, providing toll-free numbers for consumers to call the company, and giving appropriate product demonstrations have proven helpful.

The power of word of mouth has been magnified by the Internet through online forums, chat rooms, blogs, bulletin boards, and websites. In fact, Ford uses special software to monitor online messages and find out what consumers are saying about its vehicles. Chapter 18 describes how marketers track, initiate, and manage word of mouth in an online environment using viral marketing techniques.

reference groups

People to whom an individual looks as a basis for self-appraisal or as a source of personal standards

Reference Groups

Reference groups are people to whom an individual looks as a basis for self-appraisal or as a source of personal standards. Reference groups affect consumer purchases because they influence the information, attitudes, and aspiration levels that help set a consumer's

Marketing Matters > > > > > customer value

BzzAgent—The Buzz Experience

Have you recently heard about a new product, movie, website, book, or restaurant from someone you know... or a complete stranger? If so, you may have had a buzz experience.

Marketers recognize the power of word of mouth. The challenge has been to harness that power. BzzAgent Inc. does just that. Its nationwide volunteer army of more than 425,000 natural-born talkers channel their chatter toward products and services they deem authentically worth talking about. "Our goal is to capture honest word of mouth," says David Balter, BzzAgent's founder, "and to build a network that turns passionate customers into brand evangelists."

BzzAgent's method is simple. Once a client signs on with Bzz-Agent, the company searches its "agent" database for those who match the demographic and psychographic profile of the target market for a client's offering. Agents then can sign up for a buzz campaign and receive a sample product and a training manual for buzz-creating strategies. Each time an agent completes an activity, he or she is expected to file an online report describing the

nature of the buzz and its effectiveness. BzzAgent coaches respond with encouragement and feedback on additional techniques.

Agents keep the products they promote. They also earn points redeemable for books, CDs, and other items by filing detailed reports. Who are the agents? About 65 percent are older than 25, 70 percent are women, and two are *Fortune* 500 CEOs. All are gregarious and genuinely like the product or service, otherwise they wouldn't participate in the buzz campaign.

Estée Lauder, Monster.com, Anheuser-Busch, Penguin Books, Lee jeans, Arby's, Nestlé, Hershey Foods, and Volkswagen have used BzzAgent. But BzzAgent's buzz isn't cheap, and not everything is buzz worthy. Deploying 1,000 agents on a 12-week campaign can cost a company $95,000, exclusive of product samples. BzzAgent researches a product or service before committing to a campaign and rejects about 80 percent of the companies that seek its service. It also refuses campaigns for politicians, religious groups, and certain products, such as firearms. Interested in BzzAgent? Visit its website at www.bzzagent.com.

standards. For example, one of the first questions one asks others when planning to attend a social occasion is, "What are you going to wear?" Reference groups have an important influence on the purchase of luxury products but not of necessities—reference groups exert a strong influence on the brand chosen when its use or consumption is highly visible to others.

Consumers have many reference groups, but three groups have clear marketing implications. A *membership group* is one to which a person actually belongs, including fraternities and sororities, social clubs, and the family. Such groups are easily identifiable and are targeted by firms selling insurance, insignia products, and charter vacations. An *aspiration group* is one that a person wishes to be a member of or wishes to be identified with, such as a professional society. Firms frequently rely on spokespeople or settings associated with their target market's aspiration group in their advertising. A *dissociative group* is one that a person wishes to maintain a distance from because of differences in values or behaviors.

Family Influence

Family influences on consumer behavior result from three sources: consumer socialization, passage through the family life cycle, and decision making within the family or household.

Consumer Socialization The process by which people acquire the skills, knowledge, and attitudes necessary to function as consumers is *consumer socialization*.[22] Children learn how to purchase (1) by interacting with adults in purchase situations and (2) through their own purchasing and product usage experiences. Research shows that children evidence brand preferences at age two, and these preferences often last a lifetime. This knowledge prompted the licensing of the well-known Craftsman brand name to MGA Entertainment for its children's line of My First Craftsman power tools; Time Inc. to launch *Sports Illustrated for Kids;* and Yahoo! and America Online to offer special areas where young audiences can view their children's menu—Yahoo! Kids and Kids Only, respectively.

Family Life Cycle   Consumers act and purchase differently as they go through life. The **family life cycle** concept describes the distinct phases that a family progresses through from formation to retirement, each phase bringing with it identifiable purchasing behaviors.[23] Figure 5–6 illustrates the traditional progression as well as contemporary variations of the family life cycle. Today, the *traditional family—* married couples with children younger than 18 years—constitute just 22 percent of all U.S. households. The remaining 78 percent of U.S. households include single parents, unmarried couples, divorced, never-married, or widowed individuals, and older married couples whose children no longer live at home.

Young singles' buying preferences are for nondurable items, including prepared foods, clothing, personal care products, and entertainment. They represent a target market for recreational travel, automobile, and consumer electronics firms. Young married couples without children are typically more affluent than young singles because usually both spouses are employed. These couples exhibit preferences for furniture, housewares, and gift items for each other. Young marrieds with children are driven by the needs of their children. They make up a sizable market for life insurance, various children's products, and home furnishings. Single parents with children are the least financially secure of households with children. Their buying preferences are often affected by a limited economic status and tend toward convenience foods, child care services, and personal care items.

family life cycle

Family's progression from formation to retirement, each phase bringing with it distinct purchasing behaviors

FIGURE 5–6

Modern family life cycle stages and flows. Can you identify people you know in different stages? Do they follow the purchase patterns described in the text?

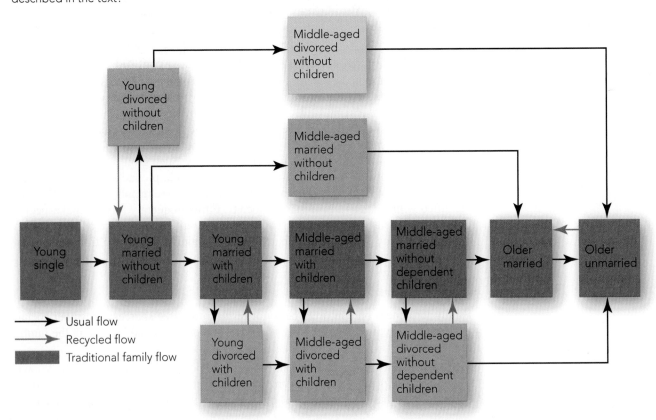

Middle-aged married couples with children are typically better off financially than their younger counterparts. They are a significant market for leisure products and home improvement items. Middle-aged couples without children typically have a large amount of discretionary income. These couples buy better home furnishings, status automobiles, and financial services. Persons in the last two phases—older married and older unmarried—make up a sizable market for prescription drugs, medical services, vacation trips, and gifts for younger relatives.

Family Decision Making   A third influence in the decision-making process occurs within the family.[24] Two decision-making styles exist: spouse-dominant and joint decision making. With a joint decision-making style, most decisions are made by both husband and wife. Spouse-dominant decisions are those for which either the husband or the wife is mostly responsible. Research indicates that wives tend to have more say when purchasing groceries, children's toys, clothing, and medicines. Husbands tend to be more influential in home and car maintenance purchases. Joint decision making is common for cars, vacations, houses, home appliances and electronics, and medical care. As a rule, joint decision making increases with the education of the spouses.

Roles of individual family members in the purchase process are another element of family decision making. Five roles exist: (1) information gatherer, (2) influencer, (3) decision maker, (4) purchaser, and (5) user. Family members assume different roles for different products and services. This knowledge is important to firms. For example, 89 percent of wives either influence or make outright purchases of men's clothing. Knowing this, Haggar Clothing, a menswear marketer, now advertises in women's magazines such as *Vanity Fair* and *Redbook*. Even though women are often the grocery decision maker, they are not necessarily the purchaser. Husbands do about one-half of food shopping alone.

Increasingly, preteens and teenagers are the information gatherers, influencers, decision makers, and purchasers of products and services for the family, given the prevalence of working parents and single-parent households. Children under 12 directly influence more than $325 billion in annual family purchases. Teenagers influence another $600 billion and spend another $190 million of their own money annually. These figures help explain why, for example, Nabisco, Johnson & Johnson, Hewlett-Packard, Apple, Kellogg, Procter & Gamble (P&G), Sony, and Oscar Mayer, among countless

The Haggar Clothing Co. recognizes the important role women play in the choice of men's clothing. The company directs a large portion of its advertising toward women because they influence and purchase men's clothing.

other companies, spend more than $40 billion annually in electronic and print media that reach preteens and teens.

Culture and Subculture

As described in Chapter 3, *culture* refers to the set of values, ideas, and attitudes that are learned and shared among the members of a group. Thus, we often refer to the American culture, the Latin American culture, or the Japanese culture.

Subgroups within the larger, or national, culture with unique values, ideas, and attitudes are referred to as **subcultures**. Various subcultures exist within the American culture. The three largest racial/ethnic subcultures in the United States are Hispanics, African Americans, and Asian Americans. Collectively, they are expected to spend about $3 trillion for goods and services in 2012.[25] Each group exhibits sophisticated social and cultural behaviors that affect buying patterns.

Hispanic Buying Patterns

Hispanics represent the largest racial/ethnic subculture in the United States in terms of population and spending power. About 50 percent of Hispanics in the United States are immigrants, and the majority are under the age of 25. One-third of Hispanics are younger than 18.

Research on Hispanic buying practices has uncovered several consistent patterns:[26]

1. Hispanics are quality and brand conscious. They are willing to pay a premium price for premium quality and are often brand loyal.
2. Hispanics prefer buying American-made products, especially those offered by firms that cater to Hispanic needs.
3. Hispanic buying preferences are strongly influenced by family and peers.
4. Hispanics consider advertising a credible product information source, and U.S. firms spend more than $4 billion annually on advertising to Hispanics.
5. Convenience is not an important product attribute to Hispanic homemakers with respect to food preparation or consumption, nor is low caffeine in coffee and soft drinks, low fat in dairy products, and low cholesterol in packaged foods.

Despite some consistent buying patterns, marketing to Hispanics has proven to be a challenge for two reasons. First, the Hispanic subculture is diverse and composed of Mexicans, Puerto Ricans, Cubans, and others of Central and South American ancestry. Cultural differences among these nationalities often affect product preferences. For example, Campbell Soup Company sells its Casera line of soups, beans, and sauces using different recipes to appeal to Puerto Ricans on the East Coast and Mexicans in the Southwest. Second, a language barrier exists, and commercial messages are frequently misinterpreted when translated into Spanish. Volkswagen learned this lesson when the Spanish translation of its "Driver's Wanted" slogan suggested "chauffeurs wanted." The Spanish slogan was changed to "*Agarra calle*," a slang expression that can be loosely translated as "let's hit the road."

Sensitivity to the unique needs of Hispanics by firms has paid huge dividends. For example, Metropolitan Life Insurance is the largest insurer of Hispanics. Goya Foods dominates the market for ethnic food products sold to Hispanics. Best Foods' Mazola Corn Oil captures two-thirds of the Hispanic market for this product category. Time Inc. has more than 750,000 subscribers to its *People en Espanol*.

African American Buying Patterns

African Americans have the second-largest spending power of the three racial/ethnic subcultures in the United States. Consumer research on African American buying patterns has focused on similarities and differences with Caucasians. When socioeconomic status differences between African Americans and Caucasians are removed, there are more similarities than points of difference. Differences in buying

subcultures

Subgroups within a larger culture that have unique values, ideas, and attitudes

The Hershey Company recently launched a successful line of candy items tailored to Hispanic taste preferences.

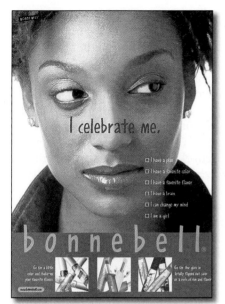

African American women represent a large market for health and beauty products. Cosmetic companies such as Bonne Bell Cosmetics, Inc., actively seek to serve this market.

patterns are greater within the African American subculture, due to levels of socioeconomic status, than between African Americans and Caucasians of similar status.

Even though similarities outweigh differences, there are consumption patterns that do differ between African Americans and Caucasians.[27] For example, African Americans spend far more than Caucasians on boy's clothing, rental goods, and audio equipment. Adult African Americans are twice as likely to own a pager and spend twice as much for online services, on a per capita basis, than Caucasians. African American women spend three times more on health and beauty products than Caucasian women. Furthermore, the typical African American family is five years younger than the typical Caucasian family. This factor alone accounts for some of the observed differences in preferences for clothing, music, shelter, cars, and many other products, services, and activities. Finally, it must be emphasized that, historically, African Americans have been deprived of employment and educational opportunities in the United States. Both factors have resulted in income disparities between African Americans and Caucasians, which influence purchase behavior.

Research indicates that while African Americans are price conscious, they are strongly motivated by quality and choice. They respond more to products such as apparel and cosmetics and advertising that appeal to their African American pride and heritage as well as address their ethnic features and needs regardless of socioeconomic status.

Asian American Buying Patterns   About 70 percent of Asian Americans are immigrants. Most are under the age of 35.

The Asian subculture is composed of Chinese, Japanese, Filipinos, Koreans, Asian Indians, people from Southeast Asia, and Pacific Islanders. The diversity of the Asian subculture is so great that generalizations about buying patterns of this group are difficult to make.[28] Consumer research on Asian Americans suggests that individuals and families divide into two groups. *Assimilated* Asian Americans are

This advertisement featured Chinese basketball star Yao Ming and ran in Asian-language print publications nationwide, focusing on Korean Americans.

conversant in English, highly educated, hold professional and managerial positions, and exhibit buying patterns very much like the typical American consumer. *Non-assimilated* Asian Americans are recent immigrants who still cling to their native languages and customs.

The diversity of Asian Americans evident in language, customs, and tastes requires marketers to be sensitive to different Asian nationalities. For example, Anheuser-Busch's agricultural products division sells eight varieties of California-grown rice, each with a different Asian label to cover a range of nationalities and tastes. The company's advertising also addresses the preferences of Chinese, Japanese, and Koreans for different kinds of rice bowls. McDonald's actively markets to Asian Americans. According to a company executive, "We recognize diversity in this market. We try to make our messages in the language they prefer to see them." Recently McDonald's launched an advertising campaign that emphasized the company's Chicken Select product for Chinese, Vietnamese, and Korean consumers.

Studies show that the Asian American subculture as a whole is characterized by hard work, strong family ties, appreciation for education, and median family incomes exceeding those of any other ethnic group. This subculture is also the most entrepreneurial in the United States, as evidenced by the number of Asian-owned businesses. These qualities led Metropolitan Life Insurance to identify Asian Americans as a target for insurance following the company's success in marketing to Hispanics.

---

learning review	7. What are the two primary forms of personal influence?
	8. Marketers are concerned with which types of reference groups?
	9. What two challenges must marketers overcome when marketing to Hispanics?

LEARNING OBJECTIVES REVIEW

LO1 *Describe the stages in the consumer purchase decision process.*
The consumer purchase decision process consists of five stages. They are problem recognition, information search, alternative evaluation, purchase decision, and postpurchase behavior. Problem recognition is perceiving a difference between a person's ideal and actual situation big enough to trigger a decision. Information search involves remembering previous purchase experiences (internal search) and external search behavior such as seeking information from other sources. Alternative evaluation clarifies the problem for the consumer by (*a*) suggesting the evaluative criteria to use for the purchase, (*b*) yielding brand names that might meet the criteria, and (*c*) developing consumer value perceptions. The purchase decision involves the choice of an alternative, including from whom to buy and when to buy. Postpurchase behavior involves the comparison of the chosen alternative with a consumer's expectations, which leads to satisfaction or dissatisfaction and subsequent purchase behavior.

LO2 *Distinguish among three variations of the consumer purchase decision process: routine, limited, and extended problem solving.*
Consumers don't always engage in the five-stage purchase decision process. Instead, they skip or minimize one or more stages depending on the level of involvement—the personal, social, and economic significance of the purchase. For low-involvement purchase occasions, consumers engage in routine problem solving. They recognize a problem, make a decision, and spend little effort seeking external information and evaluating alternatives. For high-involvement purchase occasions, each of the five stages of the consumer purchase decision process is used, including considerable time and effort on external information search and in identifying and evaluating alternatives. With limited problem solving, consumers typically seek some information or rely on a friend to help them evaluate alternatives.

LO3 *Identify major psychological influences on consumer behavior.*

Psychology helps marketers understand why and how consumers behave as they do. In particular, psychological concepts such as motivation and personality; perception; learning; values, beliefs, and attitudes; and lifestyle are useful for interpreting buying processes. Motivation is the energizing force that stimulates behavior to satisfy a need. Personality refers to a person's consistent behaviors or responses to recurring situations. Perception is the process by which an individual selects, organizes, and interprets information to create a meaningful picture of the world. Consumers filter information through selective exposure, comprehension, and retention.

Much consumer behavior is learned. Learning refers to those behaviors that result from (*a*) repeated experience and (*b*) reasoning. Brand loyalty results from learning. Values, beliefs, and attitudes are also learned and influence how consumers evaluate products, services, and brands. A more general concept is lifestyle. Lifestyle, also called psychographics, combines psychology and demographics and focuses on how people spend their time and resources, what they consider important in their environment, and what they think of themselves and the world around them.

LO4 *Identify the major sociocultural influences on consumer behavior.*

Sociocultural influences, which evolve from a consumer's formal and informal relationships with other people, also affect consumer behavior. These involve personal influence, reference groups, the family, culture, and subculture. Opinion leadership and word-of-mouth behavior are two major sources of personal influence on consumer behavior. Reference groups are people to whom an individual looks as a basis for self-approval or as a source of personal standards. Family influences on consumer behavior result from three sources: consumer socialization; passage through the family life cycle; and decision making within the family or household. A more subtle influence on consumer behavior than direct contact with others is the social class to which people belong. Persons within social classes tend to exhibit common values, attitudes, beliefs, lifestyles, and buying behaviors. Finally, a person's culture and subculture have been shown to influence product preferences and buying patterns.

FOCUSING ON KEY TERMS

attitude p. 107
beliefs p. 107
brand loyalty p. 107
consumer behavior p. 98
family life cycle p. 112
involvement p. 100

learning p. 106
motivation p. 103
opinion leaders p. 109
perceived risk p. 106
perception p. 104
personality p. 104

purchase decision process p. 98
reference groups p. 110
subcultures p. 114
word of mouth p. 110

APPLYING MARKETING KNOWLEDGE

1 Review Figure 5–2 in the text, which shows the flash-memory MP3 player attributes identified by *Consumer Reports*. Which attributes are important to you? What other attributes might you consider? Which brand would you prefer?

2 Suppose research at Panasonic reveals that prospective buyers are anxious about buying high-definition television sets. What strategies might you recommend to the company to reduce consumer anxiety?

3 Assign one or more levels of the hierarchy of needs and the motives described in Figure 5–5 to the following products: (*a*) life insurance, (*b*) cosmetics, (*c*) *The Wall Street Journal,* and (*d*) hamburgers.

4 With which stage in the family life cycle would the purchase of the following products and services be most closely identified: (*a*) bedroom furniture, (*b*) life insurance, (*c*) a Caribbean cruise, (*d*) a house mortgage, and (*e*) children's toys?

building your marketing plan

To do a consumer analysis for the product—the good, service, or idea—in your marketing plan:

1 Identify the consumers who are most likely to buy your product—the primary target market—in terms of (*a*) their demographic characteristics and (*b*) any other kind of characteristics you believe are important.

2 Describe (*a*) the main points of difference of your product for this group and (*b*) what problem they help

solve for the consumer, in terms of the first stage in the consumer purchase decision process in Figure 5–1.

3 Identify the one or two key influences for each of the four outside boxes in Figure 5–4: (*a*) marketing mix, (*b*) psychological, (*c*) sociocultural, and (*d*) situational influences.

This consumer analysis will provide the foundation for the marketing mix actions you develop later in your plan.

"So much of our business success comes down to understanding consumer behavior," explains Joe Brandt, a store service manager at one of Best Buy's newest stores. "What we do is we try to keep our ear to the railroad tracks. In essence, we listen to the customer to be able to change on a dime when a customer wants us to tailor that experience a certain way and provide certain shopping experiences and certain services."

"Consumers look at a lot of different things," Joe added. "They look at brands, shopability of the store, how easy it is to navigate the store, how pleasant the employees are, price, and how we take care of the customer." Overall there are many factors that "customers look at when they're making a purchase decision."

THE COMPANY

Best Buy is the world's largest consumer electronics retailer with 1,172 stores, 140,000 employees, and $35.9 billion in revenue. Its U.S. and Canadian market share is almost 20 percent, far ahead of rivals Circuit City, Wal-Mart, and Costco.

Best Buy operates superstores which provide a limited number of product categories with great depth within the categories. The retailer sells consumer electronics, home office products, appliances, entertainment software, and related services. In addition to its U.S. and Canadian stores, Best Buy has recently opened stores in China and has announced plans to open stores in Puerto Rico, Mexico, and Turkey. Best Buy also offers its products online through bestbuy.com, and design and installation services through Geek Squad and Magnolia Audio and Video.

Best Buy began as The Sound of Music, a small specialty audio retailer, in 1966. A tornado severely damaged one of its stores in 1981. Instead of closing the store for repairs, Dick Schulze, the owner, had a tornado sale in which more goods were brought in from its other stores and prices were slashed. The sale was so successful that it was repeated the following two years. "When the tornado hit, we decided to market to the community as a whole, and get electronics out there to everybody. We geared ourselves up to win by understanding what consumers want in technology," said Joe Brandt. In 1983, The Sound of Music changed its name to Best Buy and opened its first superstore.

The company continued to grow as the consumer electronics category exploded in the 1980s and 1990s. Based on consumer feedback, Best Buy moved away from the traditional sales approach in 1989 by eliminating commissioned sales representatives. This move was embraced by customers, but questioned by some suppliers and Wall Street analysts who thought it would reduce sales and profits. Best Buy's approach was successful at generating growth in stores and revenues. However, company expenses increased and profits declined. When growth of the consumer electronics market slowed and mass marketers like Wal-Mart, Target, Costco, and Sam's Club became competitors, Best Buy considered changes to its approach.

Best Buy began to differentiate itself from the mass marketers by offering more services, delivery, and installation. Instead of selling individual products, it concentrated on selling entire systems. The acquisition of the Geek Squad to provide in-store, home and office computer services and Magnolia Home Theater to provide complete audio and home theater systems reflect these changes. These additions significantly increased profit and insulated the company from discount store competition. Responding to customer needs and competitive changes was an important part of Best Buy's strategy.

ADOPTING "CUSTOMER CENTRICITY" AT BEST BUY

When Dick Schulze stepped down as CEO, his successor, Brad Anderson, began looking for new ideas to continue the company's growth. He invited Larry Seldon of Columbia University to present his theory of "customer centricity." Seldon's theory suggested that some customers account for a disproportionate amount of a firm's sales and profits. Anderson adapted the theory to try to understand the needs and behaviors of specific types of customers, or segments. Initial research identified five segments which included:

- **Barry:** The affluent professional who wants the best technology and entertainment, and who demands excellent service.
- **Jill:** The prototypical "soccer mom" who is a busy suburban mom who wants to enrich her children's lives with technology and entertainment.
- **Carrie and Buzz:** The "early adopter," active, younger customer who wants the latest technology and entertainment.
- **Ray:** The "practical adopter" who is a family man who wants technology that improves his life through technology and entertainment.
- **Small business:** The customer who runs his or her own business and has specific needs relating to growing sales and increasing the profitability of the business.

Best Buy used "lab" stores to test product offerings, store designs, and service offerings targeted at each segment. Successful offerings and designs were then expanded to a larger number of pilot stores which would undergo signifi-

physical changes and require substantial new training of sales associates. The cost of applying customer centricity to a store was often as much as $600,000. Early results were impressive as customer centricity stores reported sales much higher than the chain average. As Best Buy began rapid conversion of hundreds of Best Buy stores to the centricity formats, however, expenses increased and profits declined.

THE ISSUES

The impact of Best Buy's new approach on profitability led the company to continue to adapt its ideas about customers. One consideration, for example, was that the "Jill" segment should be broadened to include all females. Research showed that women spend $68 billion on consumer electronics each year and influence 89 percent of all purchases. Unfortunately, females did not embrace the Best Buy experience, largely because its stores were male-oriented in merchandise, appearance, and staffing. "Men and women shop very differently," observes Brandt. Men "typically love the technology" and they like to "play with it" while women are "looking for a knowledgeable person who can answer their questions in a simple manner." To address this problem Best Buy began to implement many changes that would make Best Buy *the* place for women to shop (and work!).

Today, Best Buy is trying a variety of new approaches. Its stores, for example, are being changed to be more appealing to women. Store layout has been changed to include larger aisles, softer colors, less noise, and reduced visibility of boxes and extra stock. In addition, Best Buy now offers women, and all customers, a personal shopping assistant who will walk a customer through the store, demonstrate how the products function, and arrange for delivery and installation after the sale. Best Buy has also

created rooms that resemble a home in the store to show customers exactly how the products will look when they are installed. According to Brandt, "we try to personalize the experience as much as possible, and we really try to build a relationship. Once we do that we have the opportunity to really listen and answer questions that customers have." Best Buy is undertaking other initiatives as well. It created the Women's Leadership Forum (WOLF) to develop female leaders within the company. Early results have yielded an increase in applications and a decline in turnover. Overall, these changes appear to be working. Best Buy has observed an increase in its female market share in consumer electronics!

In the future Best Buy's customer centricity efforts will continue to focus on understanding consumer behavior and improving the customer experience. Brandt explains: "Customer centricity, in simple terms, is listening to the customer, putting the customer at the forefront of everything we do. That is, whatever shopping experience that they are looking for, we gear our company and our structure to satisfy that need as much as possible."

Questions

1 How has an understanding of consumer behavior helped Best Buy grow from a small specialty audio retailer to the world's largest consumer electronics retailer?

2 What were the advantages and disadvantages of using "customer centricity" to create five segments of Best Buy customers?

3 How are men and women different in their consumer behavior when they are shopping in a Best Buy store?

4 What are two or three (*a*) objective evaluative criteria and (*b*) subjective evaluative criteria female consumers use when shopping for electronics at Best Buy?

5 What challenges does Best Buy face in the future?

Every Day Matters®

JCPenney®

fall for **style**

fall & winter catalog '08

$3

1.800.222.6161 | jcp.com

6

Understanding Organizations as Customers

LEARNING OBJECTIVES

After reading this chapter you should be able to:

LO1 Distinguish among industrial, reseller, and government organizational markets.

LO2 Describe the key characteristics of organizational buying that make it different from consumer buying.

LO3 Explain how buying centers and buying situations influence organizational purchasing.

LO4 Recognize the importance and nature of online buying in industrial, reseller, and government organizational markets.

BUYING PAPER IS A GLOBAL BUSINESS DECISION AT JCPENNEY

Kim Nagele views paper differently than most people do. As the senior procurement agent at JCPMedia, he and a team of purchasing professionals buy more than 260,000 tons of paper annually at a cost of hundreds of millions of dollars.

JCPMedia is the print and paper purchasing arm for JCPenney, the fifth-largest retailer in the United States and the largest catalog merchant of general merchandise in the Western Hemisphere. Paper is serious business at JCPMedia, which buys paper for JCPenney catalogs, newspaper inserts, and direct-mail pieces. Some 10 companies from around the world including International Paper in the United States, Catalyst Paper Inc. in Canada, Stora-Enso in Sweden, and UPM-Kymmene, Inc., in Finland, supply paper to JCPMedia.

The choice of paper and suppliers is also a significant business decision given the sizable revenue and expense consequences. Therefore, JCPMedia paper buyers work closely with JCPenney marketing personnel and within budget constraints to assure that the right quality and quantity of paper is purchased at the right price point for merchandise featured in the millions of catalogs, newspaper inserts, and direct-mail pieces distributed every year.

In addition to paper quality and price, buyers formally evaluate supplier capabilities. These include a supplier's capacity to deliver selected grades of paper from specialty items to magazine papers, the availability of specific types of paper to meet printing deadlines, and ongoing environmental programs. For example, a supplier's forestry management and environmental practices are considered in the JCPMedia buying process.[1]

The next time you thumb through a JCPenney catalog, newspaper insert, or direct-mail piece, take a moment to notice the paper. Considerable effort and attention was given to its selection and purchase by Kim Nagele and JCPMedia paper buyers.

Purchasing paper for JCPMedia is one example of organizational buying. This chapter examines the different types of organizational buyers; key characteristics of organizational buying, including online buying; buying situations; unique aspects of the organizational buying process; and some typical buying procedures and decisions in today's organizational markets.

THE NATURE AND SIZE OF ORGANIZATIONAL MARKETS

business marketing

Marketing to firms, governments, or not-for-profit organizations

organizational buyers

Manufacturers, wholesalers, retailers, and government agencies that buy goods and services for their own use or for resale

Understanding organizational markets and buying behavior is a necessary prerequisite for effective business marketing. **Business marketing** is the marketing of goods and services to companies, governments, or not-for-profit organizations for use in the creation of goods and services that they can produce and market to others. So many firms engage in business marketing that it is important to understand the characteristics of organizational buyers and their buying behavior.

Organizational buyers are those manufacturers, wholesalers, retailers, and government agencies that buy goods and services for their own use or for resale. For example, these organizations buy computers and telephone services for their own use. However, manufacturers buy raw materials and parts that they reprocess into the finished goods they sell. Wholesalers and retailers resell the goods they buy without reprocessing them. Organizational buyers include all buyers in a nation except ultimate consumers. These organizational buyers purchase and lease large volumes of capital equipment, raw materials, manufactured parts, supplies, and business services. In fact, because they often buy raw materials and parts, process them, and sell the upgraded product several times before it is purchased by the final organizational buyer or ultimate consumer, the total annual purchases of organizational buyers are far greater than those of ultimate consumers. IBM alone buys nearly $40 billion in goods and services each year for its own use or resale.[2]

Organizational buyers are divided into three different markets: (1) industrial, (2) reseller, and (3) government markets.[3] Each market is described next.

Industrial Markets

There are about 12 million firms in the industrial, or business, market. These *industrial firms* in some way reprocess a product or service they buy before selling it again to the next buyer. This is certainly true of Corning Inc., which transforms an exotic blend of materials to create optical fiber capable of carrying much of the telephone traffic in the United States on a single strand. It is also true (if you stretch your imagination) of a firm selling services, such as a bank that takes money from its depositors, reprocesses it, and "sells" it as loans to borrowers.

The importance of services in the United States today is emphasized by the composition of industrial markets. Companies that primarily sell physical goods (manufacturers; mining; construction; and farms, timber, and fisheries) represent 26 percent of all the industrial firms. The services market sells diverse services such as legal advice, auto repair, and dry cleaning. Along with finance, insurance, and real estate businesses, and transportation, communication, public utility firms, and not-for-profit organizations (such as the American Red Cross), service companies represent about 74 percent of all industrial firms.

Reseller Markets

Wholesalers and retailers that buy physical products and resell them again without any reprocessing are *resellers*. In the United States there are almost 3 million retailers and 860,000 wholesalers. In this chapter we look at these resellers mainly as organizational buyers in terms of (1) how they make their own buying decisions and (2) which products they choose to carry.

Government Markets

Government units are the federal, state, and local agencies that buy goods and services for the constituents they serve. There are about 88,000 of these government units in the

The Orion lunar spacecraft to be designed, developed, tested, and evaluated by Lockheed Martin Corp. is an example of a purchase by a government unit, namely the National Aeronautics and Space Administration (NASA). Read the text to find out how much NASA will pay for the Orion lunar spacecraft.

United States. These purchases include the $3.9 billion the National Aeronautics and Space Administration (NASA) intends to pay to Lockheed Martin to develop and produce the Orion lunar spacecraft scheduled for launch in 2014 as well as lesser amounts spent by local school and sanitation districts.[4]

MEASURING DOMESTIC AND GLOBAL INDUSTRIAL, RESELLER, AND GOVERNMENT MARKETS

North American Industry Classification System (NAICS)

Provides common industry definitions for Canada, Mexico, and the United States

The measurement of industrial, reseller, and government markets is an important first step for a firm interested in gauging the size of one, two, or all three of these markets in the United States and around the world. This task has been made easier with the **North American Industry Classification System (NAICS)**.[5] The NAICS provides common industry definitions for Canada, Mexico, and the United States, which makes it easier to measure economic activity in the three member countries of the North American Free Trade Agreement (NAFTA). The NAICS replaced the Standard Industrial Classification (SIC) system, a version of which has been in place for more than 50 years in the three NAFTA member countries. The SIC neither permitted comparability across countries nor accurately measured new or emerging industries. Furthermore, the NAICS is consistent with the International Standard Industrial Classification of All Economic Activities, published by the United Nations, to facilitate measurement of global economic activity.

The NAICS groups economic activity to permit studies of market share, demand for goods and services, import competition in domestic markets, and similar studies. It designates industries with a numerical code in a defined structure. A six-digit coding system is used. The first two digits designate a sector of the economy, the third digit designates a subsector, and the fourth digit represents an industry group. The fifth digit designates a specific industry and is the most detailed level at which comparable data is available for Canada, Mexico, and the United States. The sixth digit designates individual country-level national industries. Figure 6–1 on the next page presents an abbreviated breakdown within the information industries sector (code 51) to illustrate the classification scheme.

The NAICS permits a firm to find the NAICS codes of its present customers and then obtain NAICS-coded lists for similar firms. Also, it is possible to

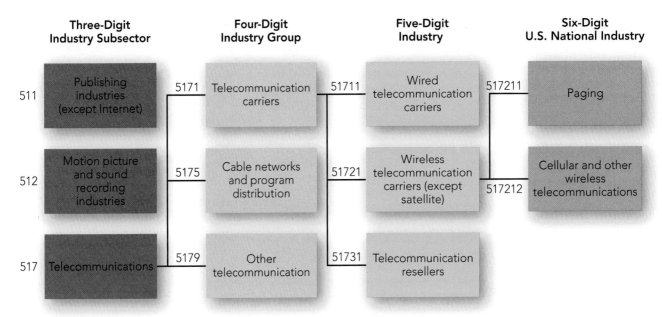

Three-Digit Industry Subsector		Four-Digit Industry Group		Five-Digit Industry		Six-Digit U.S. National Industry
511	Publishing industries (except Internet)	5171	Telecommunication carriers	51711	Wired telecommunication carriers	517211 Paging
512	Motion picture and sound recording industries	5175	Cable networks and program distribution	51721	Wireless telecommunication carriers (except satellite)	517212 Cellular and other wireless telecommunications
517	Telecommunications	5179	Other telecommunication	51731	Telecommunication resellers	

FIGURE 6–1

NAICS breakdown for information industries sector: NAICS code 51 (abbreviated)

monitor NAICS categories to determine the growth in various sectors and industries to identify promising marketing opportunities. However, the NAICS has an important limitation. Five-digit national industry codes are not available for all three countries because the respective governments will not reveal data when too few organizations exist in a category.

---

learning review

1. What are the three main types of organizational buyers?

2. What Is the North American Industry Classification System (NAICS)?

CHARACTERISTICS OF ORGANIZATIONAL BUYING

LO2

Organizations are different from individuals, so buying for an organization is different from buying for yourself or your family. True, in both cases the objective in making the purchase is to solve the buyer's problem—to satisfy a need or want. But unique objectives and policies of an organization put special constraints on how it makes buying decisions. Understanding the characteristics of organizational buying is essential in designing effective marketing programs to reach these buyers. Key characteristics of organizational buying are listed in Figure 6–2 and discussed next.[6]

Demand Characteristics

derived demand

Demand for industrial products and services driven by demand for consumer products and services

Consumer demand for products and services is affected by their price and availability and by consumers' personal tastes and discretionary income. By comparison, industrial demand is derived. **Derived demand** means that the demand for industrial products and services is driven by, or derived from, demand for consumer products and services. For example, the demand for Weyerhaeuser's pulp and paper products is based on consumer demand for newspapers, Domino's "keep warm" pizza-to-go boxes, FedEx packages, and disposable diapers. Derived demand is based on expectations of future

CHARACTERISTICS	DIMENSIONS
Market characteristics	• Demand for industrial products and services is derived. • Few customers typically exist, and their purchase orders are large.
Product or service characteristics	• Products or services are technical in nature and purchased on the basis of specifications. • Many of goods purchased are raw and semifinished. • Heavy emphasis is placed on delivery time, technical assistance, and postsale service.
Buying process characteristics	• Technically qualified and professional buyers follow established purchasing policies and procedures. • Buying objectives and criteria are typically spelled out, as are procedures for evaluating sellers and their products or services. • There are multiple buying influences, and multiple parties participate in purchase decisions. • There are reciprocal arrangements, and negotiation between buyers and sellers is commonplace. • Online buying over the Internet is widespread.
Marketing mix characteristics	• Direct selling to organizational buyers is the rule, and distribution is very important. • Advertising and other forms of promotion are technical in nature. • Price is often negotiated, evaluated as part of broader seller and product or service qualities, and frequently affected by quantity discounts.

FIGURE 6–2

Key characteristics and dimensions of organizational buying behavior

consumer demand. For instance, Whirlpool buys parts for its washers and dryers in anticipation of consumer demand, which is affected by the replacement cycle for these products and by consumer income.

Size of the Order or Purchase

The size of the purchase involved in organizational buying is typically much larger than that in consumer buying. The dollar value of a single purchase made by an organization often runs into thousands or millions of dollars. For example, Siemens Energy & Automation's Airport Logistics Division was recently awarded a $28 million contract to build a baggage handling and security sytem for JetBlue Airways' new terminal at John F. Kennedy International Airport.[7] With so much money at stake, most organizations place constraints on their buyers in the form of purchasing policies or procedures. Buyers often get competitive bids from at least three prospective suppliers when the order is above a specific amount, such as $5,000. When the order is above an even higher amount, such as $50,000, it may require the review and approval of a vice president or even the president of the company. Knowing how the size of the order affects buying practices is important in determining who participates in the purchase decision and makes the final decision, and also the length of time required to arrive at a purchase agreement.

Number of Potential Buyers

Firms selling consumer products or services often try to reach thousands or millions of individuals or households. For example, your local supermarket or bank probably serves thousands of people, and Kellogg tries to reach 80 million North American households with its breakfast cereals and probably succeeds in selling to a third or half of these in any given year. In contrast, firms selling to organizations are often restricted to far fewer buyers. Gulfstream Aerospace Corporation can sell its business jets to a few thousand organizations throughout the world, and B. F. Goodrich sells its original equipment tires to fewer than 10 car manufacturers.

Organizational Buying Objectives

Organizations buy products and services for one main reason: to help them achieve their objectives. For business firms the buying objective is usually to increase profits through reducing costs or increasing revenues. For example, 7-Eleven buys automated inventory systems to increase the number of products that can be sold through its convenience stores and to keep them fresh. Nissan Motor Company switched its advertising agency because it expects the new agency to devise a more effective ad campaign to help it sell more cars and increase revenues. To improve executive decision making, many firms buy advanced computer systems to process data. The objectives of nonprofit firms and government agencies are usually to meet the needs of the groups they serve. Thus, a hospital buys a high-technology diagnostic device to serve its patients.

Many companies today have broadened their buying objectives to include an emphasis on buying from minority- and women-owned suppliers and vendors. Companies such as Pitney Bowes, PepsiCo, Coors, and JCPenney report that sales, profits, and customer satisfaction have increased because of their minority- and women-owned supplier and vendor initiatives.[8] Not surprisingly, "Supplier diversity is no longer an issue of social conscience," says A. G. Lafley, chairman of the board, president, and chief executive officer at Procter & Gamble. "It is a fundamental business strategy."[9]

Other companies include environmental initiatives. For example, Lowe's and Home Depot, two home-and-garden center chains, no longer purchase lumber from companies that harvest timber from the world's endangered forests.[10] Successful business marketers recognize that understanding buying objectives is a necessary first step in marketing to organizations.

Organizational Buying Criteria

In making a purchase, the buying organization must weigh key buying criteria that apply to the potential supplier and what it wants to sell. *Organizational buying criteria* are the objective attributes of the supplier's products and services and the capabilities of the supplier itself. These criteria serve the same purpose as the evaluative criteria used by consumers and described in Chapter 5. Seven of the most commonly used criteria are: (1) price, (2) ability to meet the quality specifications required for the item, (3) ability to meet required delivery schedules, (4) technical capability, (5) warranties and claim policies in the event of poor performance, (6) past performance on previous contracts, and (7) production facilities and capacity.[11] Suppliers that meet or exceed these criteria create customer value.

Many organizational buyers today are transforming their buying criteria into specific requirements that are communicated to prospective suppliers. This practice, called *supplier development,* involves the deliberate effort by organizational buyers to build relationships that shape suppliers' products, services, and capabilities to fit a buyer's needs and those of its customers. For example, consider Deere & Company, the maker of John Deere farm, construction, and lawn-care equipment. Deere employs 94 supplier-development engineers who work full-time with the company's suppliers to improve their efficiency and quality and reduce their costs. According to a Deere

Marketing Matters > > > > > customer value

Harley-Davidson's Supplier Collaboration Creates Customer Value . . . and a Great Ride

It's nice to be admired. Harley-Davidson's well-deserved reputation for innovation, product quality, and talented management and employees has made it a perennial member of *Fortune* magazine's list of "America's Most Admired Companies."

Harley-Davidson is also respected by suppliers for the way it collaborates with them in product design. According to Jeff Bluestein, the company's chairman: "We involve our suppliers as much as possible in future products, new-product development, and get them working with us." Emphasis is placed on quality benchmarks, cost control, delivery schedules, and technological innovation as well as building mutually beneficial, long-term relationships. Face-to-face communication is encouraged, and many suppliers have personnel stationed at Harley-Davidson's Product Development Center.

The relationship between Harley-Davidson and Milsco Manufacturing is a case in point. Milsco has been the sole source of original equipment motorcycle seats and a major supplier of aftermarket parts and accessories, such as saddlebags, for Harley-Davidson since 1934. Milsco engineers and designers work closely with their Harley counterparts in the design of each year's new products.

The notion of a mutually beneficial relationship is expressed by Milsco's manager of industrial design: "Harley-Davidson refers to us as stakeholders, someone who can win or lose from a successful or failed program. We all share responsibility toward one another." He also notes that Harley-Davidson is not Milsco's only customer. It is simply the customer that he most respects.

senior executive, "Their quality, delivery, and costs are, after all, our quality, delivery, and costs."[12] Read the accompanying Marketing Matters box to learn how Harley-Davidson emphasizes supplier collaboration in its product design.[13]

Buyer–Seller Relationships and Supply Partnerships

Another distinction between organizational and consumer buying behavior lies in the nature of the relationship between organizational buyers and suppliers. Specifically, organizational buying is more likely to involve complex negotiations concerning delivery schedules, price, technical specifications, warranties, and claim policies. These negotiations also can last for an extended period of time. This was the case when the Lawrence Livermore National Laboratory acquired two IBM supercomputers—each with capacity to perform 360 trillion mathematical operations per second—at a cost of $290 million.[14]

Reciprocal arrangements also exist in organizational buying. *Reciprocity* is an industrial buying practice in which two organizations agree to purchase each other's products and services. The U.S. Justice Department disapproves of reciprocal buying because it restricts the normal operation of the free market. However, the practice exists and can limit the flexibility of organizational buyers in choosing alternative suppliers. Regardless of the legality of reciprocal buying, do you believe this practice is ethical? See the Making Responsible Decisions box on the next page.[15]

Long-term contracts are also prevalent.[16] As an example, Kraft Foods Inc. recently announced it intends to spend $1.7 billion over seven years for global information

Scratching Each Other's Back—The Ethics of Reciprocity in Organizational Buying

Reciprocity, the buying practice in which two organizations agree to purchase each other's products and services, is frowned upon by the U.S. Justice Department because it restricts the normal operation of the free market. Reciprocal buying practices do exist, however, in a variety of forms, including certain types of trade arrangements in international marketing. Furthermore, the extent to which reciprocity is viewed as an ethical issue varies across cultures. In many Asian countries, for instance, reciprocity is often a positive and widespread practice.

Reciprocity is occasionally addressed in the ethics codes of companies or their purchasing policies. For instance, IBM describes its reciprocity policy in the company's Global Procurement Principles and Practices Statement:

> IBM's goal is to buy goods and services which have the best prices, quality, delivery, and technology. IBM has a policy against reciprocal buying arrangements because those arrangements can interfere with this goal.

Do you think reciprocal buying is unethical?

technology services provided by Electronic Data Systems. Hewlett-Packard is engaged in a 10-year, $3 billion contract to manage Procter & Gamble's information technology in 160 countries.

In some cases, buyer–seller relationships evolve into supply partnerships.[17] A *supply partnership* exists when a buyer and its supplier adopt mutually beneficial objectives, policies, and procedures for the purpose of lowering the cost or increasing the value of products and services delivered to the ultimate consumer. Intel, the world's largest manufacturer of microprocessors and the "computer inside" most personal computers, is a case in point. Intel supports its suppliers by offering them quality management programs and by investing in supplier equipment that produces fewer product defects and boosts supplier productivity. Suppliers, in turn, provide Intel with consistent high-quality products at a lower cost for its customers, the makers of personal computers, and finally you, the ultimate customer. Retailers, too, have forged partnerships with their suppliers. Wal-Mart has such a relationship with Procter & Gamble for ordering and replenishing P&G's products in its stores. By using computerized cash register scanning equipment and direct electronic linkages to P&G, Wal-Mart can tell P&G what merchandise is needed, along with how much, when, and to which store to deliver it on a daily basis.

THE ORGANIZATIONAL BUYING PROCESS AND THE BUYING CENTER

organizational buying behavior

Process by which organizations determine the need for goods and then choose among alternative suppliers

Organizational buyers, like consumers, engage in a decision process when selecting products and services. **Organizational buying behavior** is the decision-making process that organizations use to establish the need for products and services and identify, evaluate, and choose among alternative brands and suppliers. There are important similarities and differences between the two decision-making processes. To better understand the nature of organizational buying behavior, we first compare it with consumer buying behavior. We then describe a unique feature of organizational buying—the buying center.

STAGE IN THE BUYING DECISION PROCESS	CONSUMER PURCHASE: FLASH-MEMORY MP3 PLAYER FOR A STUDENT	ORGANIZATIONAL PURCHASE: EARPHONES FOR A FLASH-MEMORY MP3 PLAYER
Problem recognition	Student doesn't like the features of the MP3 player now owned and desires a new one.	Marketing research and sales departments observe that competitors are improving the earphones on their MP3 players. The firm decides to improve the earphones on its own new models, which will be purchased from an outside supplier.
Information search	Student uses past experience, that of friends, ads, the Internet, and *Consumer Reports* to collect information and uncover alternatives.	Design and production engineers draft specifications for earphones. The purchasing department identifies suppliers of MP3 player earphones.
Alternative evaluation	Alternative flash-memory MP3 players are evaluated on the basis of important attributes desired in a player, and several stores are visited.	Purchasing and engineering personnel visit with suppliers and assess (1) facilities, (2) capacity, (3) quality control, and (4) financial status. They drop any suppliers not satisfactory on these factors.
Purchase decision	A specific brand of flash-memory MP3 player is selected, the price is paid, and the student leaves the store.	They use (1) quality, (2) price, (3) delivery, and (4) technical capability as key buying criteria to select a supplier. Then they negotiate terms and award a contract.
Postpurchase behavior	Student reevaluates the purchase decision, may return the player to the store if it is unsatisfactory.	They evaluate suppliers using a formal vendor rating system and notify a supplier if earphones do not meet their quality standard. If the problem is not corrected, they drop the firm as a future supplier.

FIGURE 6–3
Comparing the stages in a consumer and organizational purchase decision process reveals subtle differences.

Stages in the Organizational Buying Process

As shown in Figure 6–3, the five stages a student might use in buying a flash-memory MP3 player also apply to organizational purchases. However, comparing the two right-hand columns in Figure 6–3 reveals some key differences. For example, when a flash-memory MP3 player manufacturer buys earphones for its units from a supplier, more individuals are involved, supplier capability becomes more important, and the post-purchase evaluation behavior is more formal. The earphone-buying decision process is typical of the steps made by organizational buyers.

The Buying Center: A Cross-Functional Group

LO3

buying center
Group of people in an organization who participate in the buying process

For routine purchases with a small dollar value, a single buyer or purchasing manager often makes the purchase decision alone. In many instances, however, several people in the organization participate in the buying process. The individuals in this group, called a **buying center**, share common goals, risks, and knowledge important to purchase decisions. For most large multistore chain resellers, such as Sears, 7-Eleven convenience stores, Target, or Safeway, the buying center is highly formalized and is called a *buying committee*. However, most industrial firms or government units use informal groups of people or call meetings to arrive at buying decisions.

The importance of the buying center requires that a firm marketing to many industrial firms and government units understands the structure, technical and business

Effective marketing to organizations requires an understanding of buying centers and their role in purchase decisions.

functions represented, and behavior of these groups.[18] Four questions provide guidance in understanding the buying center in these organizations: Which individuals are in the buying center for the product or service? What is the relative influence of each member of the group? What are the buying criteria of each member? How does each member of the group perceive our firm, our products and services, and our salespeople?

People in the Buying Center The compostion of the buying center in a given organization depends on the specific item being bought. Although a buyer or purchasing manager is almost always a member of the buying center, individuals from other functional areas are included, depending on what is to be purchased. In buying a million-dollar machine tool, the president (because of the size of the purchase) and the production vice president or manager would probably be members. For key components to be included in a final manufactured product, a cross-functional group of individuals from research and development (R&D), engineering, and quality control are likely to be added. For new word-processing equipment, experienced secretaries who will use the equipment would be members. Still, a major question in penetrating the buying center is finding and reaching the people who will initiate, influence, and actually make the buying decision.

Roles in the Buying Center Researchers have identified five specific roles that an individual in a buying center can play.[19] In some purchases the same person may perform two or more of these roles.

- *Users* are the people in the organization who actually use the product or service, such as a secretary who will use a new word processor.
- *Influencers* affect the buying decision, usually by helping define the specifications for what is bought. The information systems manager would be a key influencer in the purchase of a new mainframe computer.
- *Buyers* have formal authority and responsibility to select the supplier and negotiate the terms of the contract. Kim Nagele performs this role as senior procurement agent at JCPMedia as described in the chapter opening example.
- *Deciders* have the formal or informal power to select or approve the supplier that receives the contract. Whereas in routine orders the decider is usually the buyer or purchasing manager, in important technical purchases it is more likely to be someone from R&D, engineering, or quality control. The decider for a key component being incorporated in a final manufactured product might be any of these three people.
- *Gatekeepers* control the flow of information in the buying center. Purchasing personnel, technical experts, and secretaries can all keep salespeople or information from reaching people performing the other four roles.

Buying Situations and the Buying Center The number of people in the buying center largely depends on the specific buying situation. Researchers who have studied organizational buying identify three types of buying situations, called **buy classes**. These buy classes vary from the routine reorder, or *straight rebuy,* to the completely new purchase, termed *new buy*. In between these extremes is the *modified rebuy*. Some examples will clarify the differences.[20]

- *Straight rebuy.* Here the buyer or purchasing manager reorders an existing product or service from the list of acceptable suppliers, probably without even checking with users or influencers from the engineering, production, or quality control departments. Office supplies and maintenance services are usually obtained as straight rebuys.

buy classes

Three types of organizational buying situations: new buy, straight rebuy, or modified rebuy

	BUY-CLASS SITUATION		
BUYING CENTER DIMENSION	**NEW BUY**	**STRAIGHT REBUY**	**MODIFIED REBUY**
People involved	Many	One	Two to three
Decision time	Long	Short	Moderate
Problem definition	Uncertain	Well-defined	Minor modifications
Buying objective	Good solution	Low-priced supplier	Low-priced supplier
Suppliers considered	New/present	Present	Present
Buying influence	Technical/operating personnel	Purchasing agent	Purchasing agent and others

FIGURE 6–4

The buying situation affects buying center behavior in different ways. Understanding these differences can pay huge dividends.

- *Modified rebuy.* In this buying situation the users, influencers, or deciders in the buying center want to change the product specifications, price, delivery schedule, or supplier. Although the item purchased is largely the same as with the straight rebuy, the changes usually necessitate enlarging the buying center to include people outside the purchasing department.
- *New buy.* Here the organization is a first-time buyer of the product or service. This involves greater potential risks in the purchase, so the buying center is enlarged to include all those who have a stake in the new buy. Procter & Gamble's purchase of a multimillion-dollar fiber-optic network from Corning Inc. for its corporate offices in Cincinnati, represented a new buy.[21]

Figure 6–4 summarizes how buy classes affect buying center tendencies in different ways.[22]

---

learning review

3. What one department is almost always represented by a person in the buying center?

4. What are the three types of buying situations or buy classes?

ONLINE BUYING IN ORGANIZATIONAL MARKETS

Organizational buying behavior and business marketing continues to evolve with the application of Internet technology. Organizations dwarf consumers in terms of online transactions made, average transaction size, and overall purchase volume. In fact, organizational buyers account for about 80 percent of the global dollar value of all online transactions.[23] Online organizational buyers around the world will purchase between $8 trillion and $10 trillion worth of products and services by 2010. Organizational buyers in the United States will account for about 60 percent of these purchases.

Prominence of Online Buying in Organizational Markets

Online buying in organizational markets is prominent for three major reasons.[24] First, organizational buyers depend heavily on timely supplier information that describes product availability, technical specifications, application uses, price, and delivery schedules. This information can be conveyed quickly via Internet technology. Second, this technology has been shown to substantially reduce buyer order processing costs. At General Electric, online buying has cut the cost of a transaction from $50 to $100 per purchase to about $5. Third, business marketers have found that Internet technology can reduce marketing costs, particularly sales and advertising expense, and broaden their potential customer base for many types of products and services.

For these reasons, online buying is popular in all three kinds of organizational markets. For example, airlines electronically order over $400 million in spare parts from the Boeing Company each year. Customers of W. W. Grainger, a large U.S. wholesaler of maintenance, repair, and operating supplies, buy more than $425 million worth of these products annually online. Supply and service purchases totaling $650 million each year are made online by the Los Angeles County government.

E-Marketplaces: Virtual Organizational Markets

e-marketplaces

Online trading communities that bring together buyers and supplier organizations

A significant development in organizational buying has been the creation of online trading communities, called **e-marketplaces**, that bring together buyers and supplier organizations. These online communities go by a variety of names, including business-to-business (B2B) exchanges and e-hubs, and make possible the real-time exchange of information, money, products, and services.

E-marketplaces can be independent trading communities or private exchanges.[25] Independent e-marketplaces act as a neutral third party and provide an Internet technology trading platform and a centralized market that enable exchanges between buyers and sellers. They charge a fee for their service and exist in settings that have one or more of the following features: (1) thousands of geographically dispersed buyers and sellers, (2) volatile prices caused by demand and supply fluctuations, (3) time sensitivity due to perishable offerings and changing technologies, and (4) easily comparable offerings between a variety of sellers.

Examples of independent e-marketplaces include PlasticsNet (plastics), Hospital Network.com (health care supplies and equipment), and Textile Web (garment and apparel products). Small business buyers and sellers, in particular, benefit from independent e-marketplaces. These e-marketplaces offer them an economical way to expand their customer base and reduce the cost of products and services. To serve entrepreneurs and the small business market in the United States, eBay launched eBay-Business. Read the accompanying Marketing Matters box to learn more about this independent trading community.[26]

Large companies tend to favor private exchanges that link them with their network of qualified suppliers and customers. Private exchanges focus on streamlining a company's purchase transactions with its suppliers and customers. Like independent e-marketplaces, they provide a technology trading platform and central market for buyer–seller interactions. They are not a neutral third party, however, but represent the interests of their owners. For example, Agentrics is an international business-to-business exchange that serves the e-marketplace. It connects more than 250 retail customers with 80,000 suppliers. Its members include Best Buy, Campbell Soup, Costco, Radio Shack, Safeway, Target, Tesco, and Walgreens.[27] The Global Healthcare Exchange engages in the buying and selling of health care products for some 1,400 hospitals and more than 100 health care suppliers, such as Abbott Laboratories, GE Medical Systems, Johnson & Johnson, Medtronic USA, and McKesson Corporation. Each of these private exchanges has saved their members over $2 billion since 2000 due to efficiencies in purchase transactions.[28]

eBay Means Business for Entrepreneurs

San Jose, California–based eBay Inc. is a true Internet phenomenon. By any measure, it is the predominant person-to-person trading community in the world. But there is more.

eBayBusiness offers a trading platform for 23 million small businesses in the United States and even greater numbers around the world. Transactions on eBayBusiness exceed sales of $20 billion annually.

The eBayBusiness platform has proven to be a boon for small businesses. According to an eBay-commissioned survey conducted by ACNielsen, 82 percent of small businesses using eBayBusiness report that it helped their business grow and expand, 78 percent say it helped to reduce their costs, and 79 percent say their business had become more profitable. Additionally, eBayBusiness promotes entrepreneurship. According to the general manager of eBayBusiness, "Many of our sellers started their businesses specifically as a result of the ability to use eBay as their e-commerce platform."

Today, more than 724,000 Americans report that eBay is their primary or secondary source of income—up 68 percent from 2003 when 430,000 Americans were making some or all of their income selling on eBay. According to a spokesperson from the American Enterprise Institute for Public Policy Research, "The potential for entrepreneurs to realize success through eBay is significant."

Online Auctions in Organizational Markets

Online auctions have grown in popularity among organizational buyers and business marketers. Many e-marketplaces offer this service. Two general types of auctions are common: (1) a traditional auction and (2) a reverse auction.[29] Figure 6–5 on the next page shows how buyer and seller participants and price behavior differ by type of auction. Let's look at each auction type more closely to understand the implications of each for buyers and sellers.

In a **traditional auction** a seller puts an item up for sale and would-be buyers are invited to bid in competition with each other. As more would-be buyers become involved, there is an upward pressure on bid prices. Why? Bidding is sequential. Prospective buyers observe the bids of others and decide whether or not to increase the bid price. The auction ends when a single bidder remains and "wins" the item with its highest price. Traditional auctions are often used to dispose of excess merchandise. For example, Dell Inc. sells surplus, refurbished, or closeout computer merchandise at its dellauction.com website.

A reverse auction works in the opposite direction from a traditional auction. In a **reverse auction**, a buyer communicates a need for a product or service and would-be suppliers are invited to bid in competition with each other. As more would-be suppliers become involved, there is a downward pressure on bid prices for the buyer's business. Why? Like traditional auctions, bidding is sequential and prospective suppliers observe the bids of others and decide whether or not to decrease the bid price. The auction ends when a single bidder remains and "wins" the business with its lowest price. Reverse auctions benefit organizational buyers by reducing the cost of their purchases. As an example, United Technologies Corp., estimates that it has saved $600 million on the purchase of $6 billion in supplies using online reverse auctions.[30]

traditional auction

Occurs when a seller puts an item up for sale and would-be buyers bid in competition with each other

reverse auction

Occurs when a buyer communicates a need for something and would-be suppliers bid in competition with each other

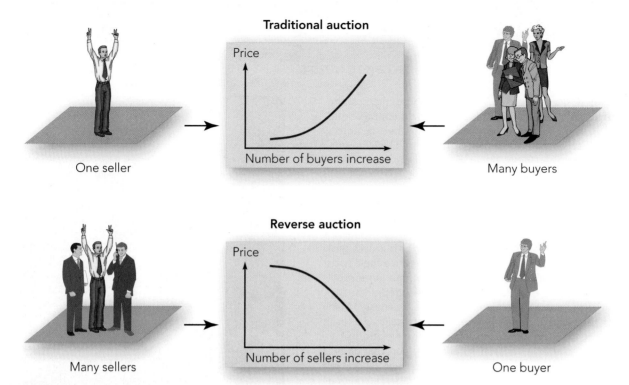

FIGURE 6–5

How buyer and seller participants and price behavior differ by type of online auction. As an organizational buyer, would you prefer to participate in a traditional auction or a reverse auction?

Clearly, buyers welcome the lower prices generated by reverse auctions. Suppliers often favor reverse auctions because they give them a chance to capture business that they might not have otherwise had because of a long-standing purchase relationship between the buyer and another supplier. On the other hand, suppliers say that reverse auctions put too much emphasis on prices, discourage consideration of other important buying criteria, and may threaten supply partnership opportunities.[31]

learning review

5. What are e-marketplaces?

6. In general, which type of online auction creates upward pressure on bid prices and which type creates downward pressure on bid prices?

LEARNING OBJECTIVES REVIEW

LO1 *Distinguish among industrial, reseller, and government organizational markets.*

There are three different organizational markets: industrial, reseller, and government. Industrial firms in some way reprocess a product or service they buy before selling it to the next buyer. Resellers—wholesalers and retailers—buy physical products and resell them again without any reprocessing. Government agencies, at the federal, state, and local levels, buy goods and services for the constituents they serve. The North American Industry Classification System (NAICS) provides common industry definitions for Canada, Mexico, and the United States, which facilitates the measurement of economic activity for these three organizational markets.

LO2 *Describe the key characteristics of organizational buying that make it different from consumer buying.*

Seven major characteristics of organizational buying make it different from consumer buying. These include demand characteristics, size of the order or purchase, number of potential buyers, buying objectives, buying criteria, buyer–seller relationships and supply partnerships, and multiple buying influences within organizations. The organizational buying process itself is more formalized, more individuals are involved, supplier capability is more important, and the postpurchase evaluation behavior often includes performance of the supplier and the item purchased. Figure 6–3 details how the purchase of an MP3 player differs between a consumer and organizational purchase. The case example describing the purchase of machine vision systems by an industrial firm illustrates this process in greater depth.

LO3 *Explain how buying centers and buying situations influence organizational purchasing.*

Buying centers and buying situations have an important influence on organizational purchasing. A buying center consists of a group of individuals who share common goals, risks, and knowledge important to a purchase decision. A buyer or purchasing manager is almost always a member of a buying center. However, other individuals may affect organizational purchasing due to their unique roles in a purchase decision. Five specific roles that a person may play in a buying center include users, influencers, buyers, deciders, and gatekeepers. The specific buying situation will influence the number of people in and the different roles played in a buying center. For a routine reorder of an item—a straight rebuy situation—a purchasing manager or buyer will typically act alone in making a purchasing decision. When an organization is a first-time purchaser of a product or service—a new buy situation—a buying center is enlarged and all five roles in a buying center often emerge. A modified rebuy buying situation lies between these two extremes. Figure 6–4 offers additional insights into how buying centers and buying situations influence organization purchasing.

LO4 *Recognize the importance and nature of online buying in industrial, reseller, and government organizational markets.*

Organizations dwarf consumers in terms of online transactions made and purchase volume. Online buying in organizational markets is popular for three reasons. First, organizational buyers depend on timely supplier information that describes product availability, technical specifications, application uses, price, and delivery schedules. This information can be conveyed quickly via Internet technology. Second, this technology substantially reduces buyer order processing costs. Third, business marketers have found that Internet technology can reduce marketing costs, particularly sales and advertising expense, and broaden their customer base. Two developments in online buying have been the creation of e-marketplaces and online auctions. E-marketplaces provide a technology trading platform and a centralized market for buyer–seller transactions and make possible the real-time exchange of information, money, products, and services. These e-marketplaces can be independent trading communities or private exchanges. Online traditional and reverse auctions represent a second major development. With traditional auctions, the highest-priced bidder "wins." Conversely, the lowest-priced bidder "wins" with reverse auctions.

FOCUSING ON KEY TERMS

business marketing p. 122
buy classes p. 130
buying center p. 129
derived demand p. 124

e-marketplaces p. 132
North American Industry Classification System (NAICS) p. 123
organizational buyers p. 122

organizational buying behavior p. 128
reverse auction p. 133
traditional auction p. 133

APPLYING MARKETING KNOWLEDGE

1 Describe the major differences among industrial firms, resellers, and government units in the United States.

2 List and discuss the key characteristics of organizational buying that make it different from consumer buying.

3 What is a buying center? Describe the roles assumed by people in a buying center and what useful questions should be raised to guide any analysis of the structure and behavior of a buying center.

4 A firm that is marketing multimillion-dollar wastewater treatment systems to cities has been unable to sell a new type of system. This setback has occurred even though the firm's systems are cheaper than competitive systems and meet U.S. Environmental Protection Agency (EPA) specifications. To date, the firm's marketing efforts have been directed to city purchasing departments and the various state EPAs to get on approved bidder's lists. Talks with city-employed personnel have indicated that the new system is very different from current systems and therefore city sanitary and sewer department engineers, directors of these two departments, and city council members are unfamiliar with the workings of the system. Consulting engineers, hired by cities to work on the engineering and design features of these systems and paid on a percentage of system cost, are also reluctant to favor the new system. (*a*) What roles do the various individuals play in the purchase process for a wastewater treatment system? (*b*) How could the firm improve the marketing effort behind the new system?

building your marketing plan

Your marketing plan may need an estimate of the size of the market potential or industry potential (see Chapter 8) for a particular product-market in which you compete. Use these steps:

1 Define the product-market precisely, such as ice cream.
2 Visit the NAICS website at www.census.gov.

3 Click "NAICS" and enter a keyword that describes your product-market (e.g., ice cream).
4 Follow the instructions to the specific NAICS code and economic census data that details the dollar sales and provides the estimate of market or industry potential.

Organizational buying is a part of the marketing effort that influences every aspect of business at Lands' End. As senior vice president of operations Phil Schaecher explains, "When we talk about purchasing at Lands' End, most people think of the purchase of merchandise for resale, but we buy many other things aside from merchandise, everything from the simplest office supply to the most sophisticated piece of material-handling equipment." As a result, Lands' End has developed a sophisticated approach to organizational buying, which is one of the keys to its incredible success.

THE COMPANY

The company started by selling sailboat equipment, duffle bags, rainsuits, and sweaters from a basement location in Chicago's old tannery district. In its first catalog, the company name was printed with a typing error—the apostrophe in the wrong place—but the fledgling company couldn't afford to correct and reprint it. So ever since, the company name has been Lands' End—with the misplaced apostrophe.

When the company outgrew its Chicago location, founder Gary Comer relocated it to Dodgeville, Wisconsin, where he had fallen in love with the rolling hills and changing seasons. The original business ideas were simple: "Sell only things we believe in, ship every order the day it arrives, and unconditionally guarantee everything." Over time, the company developed eight principles of doing business:

- Never reduce the quality of a product to make it cheaper.
- Price products fairly and honestly.
- Accept any return for any reason.
- Ship items in stock the day after the order is received.
- What is best for the customer is best for Lands' End.
- Place contracts with manufacturers who are cost-conscious and efficient.
- Operate efficiently.
- Encourage customers to shop in whatever way they find most convenient.

These principles became the guidelines for the company's dedicated local employees and helped create extraordinary expectations from Lands' End customers.

Today, Lands' End is one of the world's largest direct merchants of traditionally styled clothing for the family, soft luggage, and products for the home. The products are offered through catalogs, on the Internet, and in retail stores. Last year, Lands' End distributed more than 200 million catalogs designed for specific segments, including *The Lands' End Catalog, Lands' End Men, Lands' End Plus Size Collection, Lands' End Kids, Lands' End for School Uniforms, Lands' End Home,* and *Lands' End Business Outfitters.* In a typical day, catalog shoppers place more than 40,000 telephone calls to the company. The Lands' End website (www.landsend.com) also offers every Lands' End product and a wide variety of Internet shopping innovations such as a 3-D model customized to each customer (called My Virtual Model™); individually tailored clothes (called Lands' End Custom™); and a feature that allows customers to "chat" online directly with a customer service representative (called Lands' End Live™). Lands' End also operates stores in the United States, the United Kingdom, Germany, and Japan. Selected Lands' End merchandise is also sold in Sears stores, following the purchase of Lands' End by Sears in 2002.

The company's goal is to please customers with the highest levels of quality and service in the industry. Lands' End maintains the high quality of its products through several important activities. For example, the company works directly with mills and manufacturers to retain control of quality and design. "The biggest difference between Lands' End and some other retailers or catalog businesses is that we actually design all the product here and we do all the specifications. Therefore, the manufacturer is building that product directly to our specs, we are not buying off of somebody else's line," explains Joan Mudget, vice president of quality assurance. In addition, Lands' End tests its products for comfort and fit by paying real people (local residents and children) to "wear-test" and "fit-test" all types of garments.

Service has also become an important part of the Lands' End reputation. Customers expect prompt, professional service at every step—initiating the order, making selections, shipping, and follow-up (if necessary). Some of the ways Lands' End meets these expectations include offering the simplest guarantee in the industry—"Guaranteed. Period."—toll-free telephone lines open 24 hours a day, 364 days a year, continuous product training for telephone representatives, and two-day shipping. Lands' End operators even send personal responses to all e-mail messages, approximately 230,000 per year.

ORGANIZATIONAL BUYING AT LANDS' END

The sixth Lands' End business principle (described earlier) is accomplished through the company's organizational buying process. First, its buyers specify fabric quality, construction, and sizing standards, which typically exceed industry standards, for current and potential Lands' End products. Then the buyers literally search around the world for the best possible source of fabrics and products. Once a potential supplier is identified, one of the company's 150 quality assurance personnel makes an information-gathering visit. The purpose of the visit is to understand the supplier's values, to assess four criteria (economic, quality, service, and vendor), and to determine if the Lands' End standards can be achieved.

Lands' End evaluations of potential suppliers lead to the selection of what the company hopes will become long-term partners. As Mudget explains, "When we're looking for new manufacturers we are looking for the long term. I think one of the most interesting things is we're not out there looking for new vendors every year to fill the same products." In fact, Lands' End believes that the term *supplier* does not adequately describe the importance the company places on the relationships. Lands' End suppliers are viewed as allies, supporters, associates, colleagues, and stakeholders in the future of the company. Once an alliance is formed the product specifications and the performance on those specifications are regularly evaluated.

Lands' End buyers face a variety of buying situations. Straight rebuys involve reordering an existing product—such as shipping boxes—without evaluating or changing specifications. Modified rebuys involve changing some aspect of a previously ordered product—such as the collar of a knit shirt—based on input from consumers, retailers, or other people involved in the purchase decision. Finally, new buys involve first-time purchases—such as Lands' End addition of men's suits to its product line. The complexity of the process can vary with the type of purchase. Schaecher explains, "As you get more complicated in the purchase there are more things you look at to decide on a vendor."

FUTURE CHALLENGES FOR LANDS' END

Lands' End faces several challenges as it pursues improvements in its organizational buying process. First, new technologies offer opportunities for fast, efficient, and accurate communication with suppliers. Ed Smidebush, general inventory manager, describes a new system at Lands' End: "Our quick response system is a computerized system where we transmit electronically to our vendors each Sunday night, forecast information as well as stock positions and purchase order information so that on Monday morning this information will be incorporated directly into their manufacturing reports so that they can prioritize their production." Occasionally Lands' End must work with its suppliers to improve their technology and information system capabilities.

Another challenge for Lands' End is to anticipate changes in consumer interests. While it has many years of

experience with retail consumers, preferences for colors, fabrics, and styles change frequently, requiring buyers to constantly monitor the marketplace. In addition, Lands' End's more recent offerings to corporate customers require constant attention "because business customers' wants and incentives, and the environment in which they're shopping, are very different from consumers at home," explains marketing manager Hilary Kleese.

Finally, Lands' End must anticipate the quantities of each of its products consumers are likely to order. To do this, historical information is used to develop forecasts. One of the best tests of their forecast accuracy is the holiday season, when Lands' End receives more than 100,000 calls each day. Having the right products available is important because, as every employee knows from Principle 4, every order must be shipped the day after it is received.

Questions

1 (*a*) Who is likely to comprise the buying center in the decision to select a new supplier for Lands' End? (*b*) Which of the buying center members are likely to play the roles of users, influencers, buyers, deciders, and gatekeepers?
2 (*a*) Which stages of the organizational buying decision process does Lands' End follow when it selects a new supplier? (*b*) What selection criteria does the company utilize in the process?
3 Describe purchases Lands' End buyers typically face in each of the three buying situations: straight rebuy, modified rebuy, and new buy.

7

Understanding and Reaching Global Consumers and Markets

LEARNING OBJECTIVES

After reading this chapter you should be able to:

LO1 Identify the major trends that have influenced world trade and global marketing.

LO2 Identify the environmental forces that shape global marketing efforts.

LO3 Name and describe the alternative approaches companies use to enter global markets.

LO4 Explain the distinction between standardization and customization when companies craft worldwide marketing programs.

PROCTER & GAMBLE IS CHANGING THE FACE OF CHINA

The face of China is changing thanks to Procter & Gamble. P&G is the largest consumer products company in China due in large measure to the popularity of its skin care and cosmetic brands among Chinese women, including Olay whitening skin creams, SK-11 skin care products, and Cover Girl and Max Factor cosmetics. P&G's success in China results from a passionate effort to meet the beauty needs of Chinese women since 1988.

P&G cosmetics have been adapted to Chinese skin tones and fashion trends. So too, the company's marketing practices have been changed. Consider the Cover Girl brand—the best-selling mass market cosmetic brand in the United States. Only after two years of painstaking R&D and market analysis did P&G launch the Cover Girl brand in China in 2005.

Why didn't P&G simply export Cover Girl products from the United States to China? "You can't just import cosmetics here," says Daisy Ching, the regional account director at Cover Girl's advertising agency in China, Grey Global Group. "Companies have to understand what beauty means to Chinese women and what they look for, and product offerings and communications have to be adjusted accordingly."

For Cover Girl, that meant starting from scratch. "We needed to tailor-make everything for this market—the products, the brand proposition, the packaging. Everything is different. You can say the only thing that didn't change is the Cover Girl brand name," recalled Tasai Hsin-Hsin, P&G's associate marketing director for cosmetics in Greater China.[1]

This chapter describes today's complex and dynamic global marketing environment. It begins with an overview of world trade and the emergence of a borderless economic world. Attention is then focused on prominent cultural, economic, and political-regulatory forces that present both an opportunity and challenge for global marketers. Four major global market entry strategies are then detailed. Finally, the task of designing, implementing, and evaluating worldwide marketing programs for companies and products, such as Procter & Gamble and Cover Girl cosmetics, is described.

DYNAMICS OF WORLD TRADE

The dollar value of world trade has more than doubled in the past decade. Manufactured goods and commodities account for 74 percent of world trade. Service industries, including telecommunications, transportation, insurance, education, banking, and tourism, represent the other 26 percent of world trade.

Four trends have significantly affected world trade and global marketing:

Trend 1: Gradual decline of economic protectionism by individual countries.

Trend 2: Formal economic integration and free trade among nations.

Trend 3: Global competition among global companies for global customers.

Trend 4: Development of networked global marketspace.

Decline of Economic Protectionism

protectionism
Practice of shielding one or more industries of a country's economy from foreign competition through the use of tariffs or quotas

tariff
Government tax on goods or services entering a country, primarily serving to raise prices on imports

quota
Restriction placed on the amount of a product allowed to enter or leave a country

World Trade Organization
Institution that sets rules governing trade between its members through a panel of trade experts

Protectionism is the practice of shielding one or more industries within a country's economy from foreign competition, usually through the use of tariffs or quotas. The economic argument for protectionism is that it preserves jobs, protects a nation's political security, discourages economic dependency on other countries, and encourages the development of domestic industries.

A **tariff** is a tax on goods or services entering a country. Because a tariff raises the price of an imported product, tariffs give a price advantage to domestic products competing in the same market. The effect of tariffs on world trade and consumer prices is substantial.[2] Consider U.S. rice exports to Japan. The U.S. Rice Millers' Association claims that if the Japanese rice market were opened to imports by lowering tariffs, lower prices would save Japanese consumers $6 billion annually, and the United States would gain a large share of the Japanese rice market. Similarly, tariffs imposed on bananas by Western European countries cost consumers $2 billion a year.

A **quota** is a restriction placed on the amount of a product allowed to enter or leave a country. By limiting supply of foreign products, an import quota helps domestic industries retain a certain percentage of the domestic market. For consumers, however, the limited supply may mean higher prices for domestic products. The best-known quota concerns the limits of foreign automobile sales in many countries. Less visible quotas apply to the importation of mushrooms, heavy motorcycles, textiles, color TVs, and sugar. For example, U.S. sugar import quotas have existed for over 50 years and preserve about half of the U.S. sugar market for domestic producers. American consumers pay almost $2 billion annually in extra food costs because of this quota.

Both tariffs and quotas discourage world trade (Figure 7–1). As a result, the major industrialized nations of the world formed the **World Trade Organization** (WTO) in 1995 to address a broad array of world trade issues. The 152 member countries of the WTO, which include the United States, account for more than 97 percent of world trade.[3] The WTO sets rules governing trade between its members through panels of trade experts who decide on trade disputes between members and issue binding decisions. The WTO reviews more than 200 disputes each year.

Rise of Economic Integration

In recent years, a number of countries with similar economic goals have formed transnational trade groups or signed trade agreements for the purpose of promoting free trade among member nations and enhancing their individual economies. Two of the best-known examples are the European Union (or simply EU) and the North American Free Trade Agreement (NAFTA).

FIGURE 7–1

How does protectionism affect world trade? Protectionism hinders world trade through tariff and quota policies of individual countries. Tariffs increase prices and quotas limit supply.

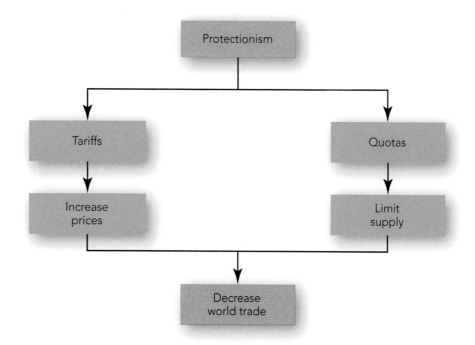

European Union The European Union consists of 27 member countries that have eliminated most barriers to the free flow of goods, services, capital, and labor across their borders (see Figure 7–2 on the next page).[4] This single market houses more than 500 million consumers with a combined gross domestic product larger than that of the United States. In addition, 14 countries have adopted a common currency called the *euro*. Adoption of the euro has been a boon to electronic commerce in the EU by eliminating the need to continually monitor currency exchange rates.

The EU creates abundant marketing opportunities because firms no longer find it necessary to market their products and services on a nation-by-nation basis. Rather, pan-European marketing strategies are possible due to greater uniformity in product and packaging standards; fewer regulatory restriction on transportation, advertising, and promotion imposed by countries; and removal of most tariffs that affect pricing practices. For example, Colgate-Palmolive Company now markets its Colgate toothpaste with one formula and package across EU countries at one price. Black & Decker—the maker of electrical hand tools, appliances, and other consumer products—now produces 8, not 20, motor sizes for the European market, resulting in production and marketing cost savings. These practices were previously impossible with different government and trade regulations. Europeanwide distribution from fewer locations is also feasible given open borders. French tire maker Michelin has closed 180 of its European distribution centers and now uses just 20 to serve all EU countries.

North American Free Trade Agreement The North American Free Trade Agreement (NAFTA) lifted many trade barriers between Canada, Mexico, and the United States and created a marketplace with more than 450 million consumers.[5] NAFTA has stimulated trade flows among member nations as well as cross-border retailing, manufacturing, and investment. For example, NAFTA paved the way for Wal-Mart to move to Mexico and Mexican supermarket giant Gigante to move into the United States. Whirlpool Corporation's Canadian subsidiary stopped making washing machines in Canada and moved that operation to Ohio. Whirlpool then shifted the production of kitchen ranges and compact dryers to Canada. Ford invested $60 million in its Mexico City manufacturing plant to produce smaller cars and light trucks for global sales.

A recent comprehensive free trade agreement among Costa Rica, the Dominican Republic, El Salvador, Guatemala, Honduras, Nicaragua, and the United States extended many NAFTA benefits to Central American countries and the Dominican Republic. Called CAFTA-DR, this agreement is viewed as a step toward a 34-country Free Trade Area of the Americas for the Western Hemisphere.

A New Reality: Global Competition among Global Companies for Global Consumers

The emergence of a largely borderless economic world has created a new reality for marketers of all shapes and sizes. Today, world trade is driven by global competition among global companies for global consumers.

global competition

Occurs when firms originate, produce, and market their products and services worldwide

Global Competition **Global competition** exists when firms originate, produce, and market their products and services worldwide. The automobile, pharmaceutical, apparel, electronics, aerospace, and telecommunication fields represent well-known industries with sellers and buyers on every continent. Other industries that are increasingly global in scope include soft drinks, cosmetics, ready-to-eat cereals, snack chips, and retailing.

Global competition broadens the competitive landscape for marketers. The familiar "cola war" waged by Pepsi-Cola and Coca-Cola in the United States has been repeated

142

Pepsi-Cola, now available in more than 190 countries and territories, accounts for a quarter of all soft drinks sold internationally. This Brazilian ad—"How to make jeans last 10 years"—features the popular Diet Pepsi brand targeted at weight-conscious consumers.

around the world, including India, China, and Argentina. Procter & Gamble's Pampers and Kimberly-Clark's Huggies have taken their disposable diaper rivalry from the United States to Western Europe. Boeing and Europe's Airbus vie for lucrative commercial aircraft contracts on virtually every continent.

Global Companies Three types of companies populate and compete in the global marketplace: (1) international firms, (2) multinational firms, and (3) transnational firms.[6] All three employ people in different countries, and many have administrative, marketing, and manufacturing operations (often called *divisions* or *subsidiaries*) around the world. However, a firm's orientation toward and strategy for global markets and marketing defines the type of company it is.

An *international firm* engages in trade and marketing in different countries as an extension of the marketing strategy in its home country. Generally speaking, these firms market their existing products and services in other countries the same way they do in their home country. Avon, for example, successfully distributes its product line through direct selling in Asia, Europe, and South America, employing virtually the same marketing strategy used in the United States.

A *multinational firm* views the world as consisting of unique parts and markets to each part differently. Multinationals use a **multidomestic marketing strategy**, which means that they have as many different product variations, brand names, and advertising programs as countries in which they do business. For example, Lever Europe, a division of Unilever, markets its fabric softener known as Snuggle in the United States in 10 European countries under seven brand names, including Kuschelweich in Germany, Coccolino in Italy, and Mimosin in France. These products have different packages, different advertising programs, and occasionally different formulas. Procter & Gamble markets Mr. Clean, its popular multipurpose cleaner, in North America and Asia. But you won't necessarily find the Mr. Clean brand in other parts of the world. In many Latin American countries, Mr. Clean is Mastro Limpio. Mr. Clean is Mr. Proper in most parts of Europe, Africa, and the Middle East.

A *transnational firm* views the world as one market and emphasizes universal consumer needs and wants more than differences among cultures. Transnational marketers employ a **global marketing strategy**—the practice of standardizing marketing activities when there are cultural similarities and adapting them when cultures differ.

multidomestic marketing strategy

A multinational firm's offering as many different product variations, brand names, and advertising programs as countries in which it does business

global marketing strategy

Practice of standardizing marketing activities when there are cultural similarities and adapting them when cultures differ

Marketing Matters > > > > > customer value

The Global Teenager—A Market of 500 Million Voracious Consumers with $100 Billion to Spend

The "global teenager" market consists of 500 million 13- to 19-year-olds in Europe, North and South America, and industrialized nations of Asia and the Pacific Rim who have experienced intense exposure to television (MTV broadcasts in 169 countries in 28 languages), movies, travel, the Internet, and global advertising by companies such as Apple, Sony, Nike, and Coca-Cola. The similarities among teens across these countries are greater than their differences. For example, a global study of middle-class teenagers' rooms in 25 industrialized countries indicated it was difficult, if not impossible, to tell whether the rooms were in Los Angeles, Mexico City, Tokyo, Rio de Janeiro, Sidney, or Paris. Why? Teens spend $100 billion annually for a common gallery of products: Sony video games, Tommy Hilfiger apparel, Levi's blue jeans, Nike athletic shoes,

Swatch watches, Apple iPods, Diesel apparel and accessories, and Procter & Gamble Clearasil facial medicine.

Teenagers around the world appreciate fashion and music, and desire novelty and trendier designs and images. They also acknowledge an Americanization of fashion and culture based on another study of 6,500 teens in 26 countries. When asked what country had the most influence on their attitudes and purchase behavior, 54 percent of teens from the United States, 87 percent of those from Latin America, 80 percent of the Europeans, and 80 percent of those from Asia named the United States. This phenomenon has not gone unnoticed by parents. As one parent in India said, "Now the youngsters dress, talk, and eat like Americans."

Global marketing strategies are popular among many business-to-business marketers such as Caterpillar and Komatsu (heavy construction equipment) and Texas Instruments, Intel, Hitachi, and Motorola (semiconductors). Consumer goods marketers such as Timex, Seiko, and Swatch (watches), Coca-Cola and Pepsi-Cola (cola soft drinks), Mattel and Lego (children's toys), Gillette (personal care products), L'Oréal and Shiseido (cosmetics), and McDonald's (quick-service restaurants) successfully execute this strategy.

Each of these companies markets a **global brand**—a brand marketed under the same name in multiple countries with similar and centrally coordinated marketing programs.[7] Global brands have the same product formulation or service concept, deliver the same benefits to consumers, and use consistent advertising across multiple countries and cultures. This isn't to say that global brands are not sometimes tailored to specific cultures or countries. However, adaptation is only used when necessary to better connect the brand to consumers in different markets.

Consider McDonald's.[8] This global marketer has adapted its proven formula of "food, fun, and families" across more than 119 countries on six continents. Although the Golden Arches and Ronald McDonald appear worldwide, McDonald's tailors other aspects of its marketing program. It serves beer in Germany, wine in France, and coconut, mango, and tropical mint shakes in Hong Kong. Hamburgers are made with different meat and spices in Japan, Thailand, India, and the Philippines. But McDonald's world-famous french fry is standardized. Its french fry in Beijing, China, tastes like the one in Paris, France, which tastes like the one in your neighborhood.

Global Consumers Global competition among global companies often focuses on the identification and pursuit of global consumers as described in the accompanying

global brand

A brand marketed under the same name in multiple countries with similar and centrally coordinated marketing programs

Sweden's IKEA is capitalizing on the home-improvement trend sweeping through China. The home-furnishings retailer is courting young Chinese consumers who are eagerly updating their housing with modern, colorful but inexpensive furniture. IKEA entered China in 1998. The company expects to have at least 10 stores open in China by 2010.

global consumers

Customers living around the world who have similar needs or seek similar benefits from products or services

Marketing Matters box.[9] **Global consumers** consist of consumer groups living in many countries or regions of the world who have similar needs or seek similar features and benefits from products or services.

Evidence suggests the presence of a global middle-income class, a youth market, and an elite segment, each consuming or using a common assortment of products and services, regardless of geographic location. A variety of companies have capitalized on the global consumer. Whirlpool, Sony, and IKEA have benefited from the growing global middle-income class desire for kitchen appliances, consumer electronics, and home furnishings, respectively. Levi's, Nike, Coca-Cola, and Apple have tapped the global youth market. DeBeers, Chanel, Gucci, Rolls-Royce, and Sotheby's and Christie's, the world's largest fine art and antique auction houses, cater to the elite segment for luxury goods worldwide.

Emergence of a Networked Global Marketspace

The use of Internet technology as a tool for exchanging goods, services, and information on a global scale is the fourth trend affecting world trade. More than 1 billion businesses, educational institutions, government agencies, and households worldwide are expected to have Internet access by 2010. The broad reach of this technology suggests that its potential for promoting world trade is huge.

The promise of a networked global marketspace is that it enables the exchange of goods, services, and information from companies *anywhere* to customers *anywhere* at *any time* and at a lower cost. This promise has become a reality for buyers and sellers in industrialized countries that possess the telecommunications infrastructure necessary to support Internet technology.

Companies engaged in business-to-business marketing have spurred the growth of global electronic commerce.[10] Ninety percent of global electronic commerce revenue arises from business-to-business transactions among a dozen countries in North America, Western Europe, and the Asia/Pacific Rim region. Industries that have benefited from this technology include industrial chemicals and controls; maintenance, repair, and operating supplies; computer and electronic equipment and components; aerospace parts; and agricultural and energy products. The United States, Canada, United Kingdom, Germany, Sweden, Japan, India, China, and Taiwan are among the most active participants in worldwide business-to-business electronic commerce.

Marketers recognize that the networked global marketspace offers unprecedented access to prospective buyers on every continent. Companies that have successfully capitalized on this access manage multiple country and language websites that customize content and communicate with consumers in their native tongue. Nestlé, the world's largest packaged food manufacturer, coffee roaster, and chocolate maker, is a case in point. The company operates 63 individual country websites in more than 20 languages that span five continents.

Nestlé is an innovator in customizing website content and communicating with consumers in their native tongue. The website shown here is for Hungary.

learning review

1. What is protectionism?

2. The North American Free Trade Agreement was designed to promote free trade among which countries?

3. What is the difference between a multidomestic marketing strategy and a global marketing strategy?

A GLOBAL ENVIRONMENTAL SCAN

LO2

Global companies conduct continuing environmental scans of the five environmental forces described earlier in Figure 3–1 (social, economic, technological, competitive, and regulatory forces). This section focuses on three kinds of uncontrollable environmental variables—cultural, economic, and political-regulatory—that affect global marketing practices in strikingly different ways than those in domestic markets.

Cultural Diversity

cross-cultural analysis
Study of similarities and differences among consumers in two or more nations or societies

values
Socially preferable modes of conduct or states of existence that tend to persist over time

Marketers must be sensitive to the cultural underpinnings of different societies if they are to initiate and consummate mutually beneficial exchange relationships with global consumers. A necessary step in this process is **cross-cultural analysis**, which involves the study of similarities and differences among consumers in two or more nations or societies.[11] A thorough cross-cultural analysis involves an understanding of and an appreciation for the values, customs, symbols, and language of other societies.

Values A society's **values** represent personally or socially preferable modes of conduct or states of existence that tend to persist over time. Understanding and working with these aspects of a society are important factors in global marketing. For example,

- McDonald's does not sell beef hamburgers in its restaurants in India because the cow is considered sacred by almost 85 percent of the population. Instead, McDonald's sells the Maharaja Mac: two all-mutton patties, special sauce, lettuce, cheese, pickles, and onions on a sesame-seed bun.
- Germans have not been overly receptive to the use of credit cards such as Visa or MasterCard and installment debt to purchase goods and services. Indeed, the German word for debt, *Schuld,* is the same as the German word for guilt.

customs

Norms and expectations about the way people do things in a specific country

Foreign Corrupt Practices Act (1977)

Law that makes it a crime for U.S. corporations to bribe an official of a foreign government or political party to obtain or retain business

cultural symbols

Things that represent ideas or concepts

Cultural symbols evoke deep feelings. What cultural lesson did Coca-Cola executives learn when they used the Eiffel Tower and the Parthenon in a global advertising campaign? Read the text to find the answer.

Customs **Customs** are what is considered normal and expected about the way people do things in a specific country. Clearly customs can vary significantly from country to country. Some other customs may seem unusual to Americans. Consider, for example, that in France, men wear more than twice the number of cosmetics than women do and that Japanese women give Japanese men chocolates on Valentine's Day.

The custom of giving token business gifts is popular in many countries where they are expected and accepted. However, bribes, kickbacks, and payoffs offered to entice someone to commit an illegal or improper act on behalf of the giver for economic gain is considered corrupt in any culture. The prevalence of bribery in global marketing has led to an agreement among the world's major exporting nations to make bribery of foreign government officials a criminal offense. This agreement is patterned after the **Foreign Corrupt Practices Act (1977)**, as amended by the *International Anti-Dumping and Fair Competition Act* (1998). These acts make it a crime for U.S. corporations to bribe an official of a foreign government or political party to obtain or retain business in a foreign country. Bribery paid to foreign companies is another matter. In France and Greece, bribes paid to foreign companies are a tax-deductible expense!

Cultural Symbols **Cultural symbols** are things that represent ideas and concepts. Symbols and symbolism play an important role in cross-cultural analysis because different cultures attach different meanings to things. By cleverly using cultural symbols, global marketers can tie positive symbolism to their products, services, and brands to

What does the Nestlé Kit Kat bar have to do with academic achievement in Japan? Read the text to find out.

enhance their attractiveness to consumers. However, improper use of symbols can spell disaster. A culturally sensitive global marketer will know that[12]

- North Americans are superstitious about the number 13, and Japanese feel the same way about the number 4. *Shi,* the Japanese word for four, is also the word for death. Knowing this, Tiffany & Company sells its fine glassware and china in sets of five, not four, in Japan.
- "Thumbs-up" is a positive sign in the United States. However, in Russia and Poland, this gesture has an offensive meaning when the palm of the hand is shown, as AT&T learned. The company reversed the gesture depicted in ads, showing the back of the hand, not the palm.

Cultural symbols evoke deep feelings. Consider how executives at Coca-Cola Company's Italian office learned this lesson. In a series of advertisements directed at Italian vacationers, the Eiffel Tower, Empire State Building, and the Tower of Pisa were turned into the familiar Coca-Cola bottle. However, when the white marble columns in the Parthenon that crowns the Acropolis in Athens were turned into Coca-Cola bottles, the Greeks were outraged. Greeks refer to the Acropolis as the "holy rock," and a government official said the Parthenon is an "international symbol of excellence" and that "whoever insults the Parthenon insults international culture." Coca-Cola apologized for the ad.[13]

Language   Global marketers should not only know the native tongues of countries in which they market their products and services but also the nuances and idioms of a language. Even though about 100 official languages exist in the world, anthropologists estimate that at least 3,000 different languages are spoken. There are 20 official languages spoken in the European Union, and Canada has two official languages (English and French). Seventeen major languages are spoken in India alone.

English, French, and Spanish are the principal languages used in global diplomacy and commerce. However, the best language to communicate with consumers is their own, as any seasoned global marketer will attest to. Unintended meanings of brand names and messages have ranged from the absurd to the obscene:

- When the advertising agency responsible for launching Procter & Gamble's successful Pert shampoo in Canada realized that the name means "lost" in French, it substituted the brand name Pret, which means "ready."
- The Vicks brand name common in the United States is German slang for sexual intimacy; therefore, Vicks is called Wicks in Germany.

back translation

Retranslating a word or phrase back into the original language by a different interpreter to catch errors

Experienced global marketers use **back translation**, where a translated word or phrase is retranslated into the original language by a different interpreter to catch errors. For example, IBM's first Japanese translation of its "Solution for a small planet" advertising message yielded "Answers that make people smaller." The error was caught and corrected. Nevertheless, unintended translations can produce favorable results. Consider Kit Kat bars marketed by Nestlé worldwide. Kit Kat is pronounced "kitto katsu" in Japanese, which roughly translates to "I hope you win." Japanese teens eat Kit Kat bars for good luck, particularly when taking crucial school exams.[14]

Economic Considerations

Global marketing is also affected by economic considerations. Therefore, a scan of the global marketplace should include (1) an assessment of the economic infrastructure in different countries, (2) measurement of consumer income in different countries, and (3) recognition of a country's currency exchange rates.

The Coca-Cola Company has made a huge financial investment in bottling and distribution facilities in Russia.

Economic Infrastructure   The *economic infrastructure*—a country's communications, transportation, financial, and distribution systems—is a critical consideration in determining whether to try to market to a country's consumers and organizations. Parts of the infrastructure that North Americans or Western Europeans take for granted can be huge problems elsewhere—not only in developing nations but even in Eastern Europe, the Indian subcontinent, and China where such an infrastructure is assumed to be in place.[15]

The communication infrastructures in these countries also differ. This infrastructure includes telecommunication systems and networks in use, such as telephones, cable television, broadcast radio and television, computer, satellite, and wireless telephones. In general, the communication infrastructure in many developing countries is limited or antiquated compared with that of developed countries.

Even the financial and legal system can cause problems. Formal operating procedures among financial institutions and the notion of private property is still limited. As a consequence, for example, it is estimated that two-thirds of the commercial transactions in Russia involve nonmonetary forms of payment. The legal red tape involved in obtaining titles to buildings and land for manufacturing, wholesaling, and retailing operations also has been a huge problem. Nevertheless, the Coca-Cola Company invested $750 million to build bottling and distribution facilities in Russia, Frito-Lay spent $60 million to build a plant to make Lay's potato chips, and Mars opened a $200 million candy factory outside Moscow.

Consumer Income and Purchasing Power   A global marketer selling consumer goods must also consider what the average per capita or household income is among a country's consumers and how the income is distributed to determine a nation's purchasing power. Per capita income varies greatly between nations. Average yearly per capita income in EU countries is about $30,000 and is less than $150 in some developing countries such as Liberia. A country's income distribution is important because it gives a more reliable picture of a country's purchasing power. Generally, as the proportion of middle-income households in a country increases, the greater a nation's purchasing power tends to be.[16]

Seasoned global marketers recognize that people in developing countries often have government subsidies for food, housing, and health care that supplement their income. So people with seemingly low incomes are actually promising customers for a variety of products. For instance, a consumer in South Asia earning the equivalent of $250 per year can afford Gillette razors. When that consumer's income rises to $1,000, a Sony television becomes affordable, and a new Volkswagen or Nissan can be bought with an annual income of $10,000. In developing countries of Eastern Europe, a $1,000 annual income makes a refrigerator affordable, and $2,000 brings an automatic washer within reach—good news for Whirlpool, the world's leading manufacturer and marketer of major home appliances.

currency exchange rate
Price of one country's currency expressed in terms of another country's currency

Currency Exchange Rates   A **currency exchange rate** is the price of one country's currency expressed in terms of another country's currency. As economic conditions change, so can the exchange rate between countries. One day the U.S. dollar may be worth 121.7 Japanese yen or 1.5 Swiss francs. But the next day it may be worth 120.5 Japanese yen or 1.3 Swiss francs.

Fluctuations in exchange rates among the world's currencies can affect everyone from international tourists to global companies. For example, when the U.S. dollar is "strong" against the euro, it takes fewer dollars to purchase goods in the EU. As a result, more U.S. tourists will travel to Europe. This is great news for Europe's travel industry, but bad news for European consumers who want to buy U.S. goods, as they will have to pay more for them. And they may choose not to buy. Mattel learned this lesson the hard way. The company was recently unable to sell its popular Holiday Barbie doll and accessories in many international markets because they were too expensive. Why? Barbie prices, expressed in U.S. dollars, were set without regard for how they would translate into other currencies and were too high for many foreign buyers.[17]

Political-Regulatory Climate

The political and regulatory climate for marketing in a country or region of the world means not only identifying the current climate but determining how long a favorable or unfavorable climate will last. An assessment of a country or regional political-regulatory climate includes an analysis of its political stability and trade regulations.

Mattel's Barbie dolls are banned in what country? Read the text to find the answer and the reason why.

Political Stability   Trade among nations or regions depends on political stability. Billions of dollars have been lost in the Middle East and Africa as a result of internal political strife, terrorism, and war. Losses such as these encourage careful selection of politically stable countries and regions of the world for trade.

Political stability in a country is affected by numerous factors, including a government's orientation toward foreign companies and trade with other countries. These factors combine to create a political climate that is favorable or unfavorable for marketing and financial investment in a country or region of the world.

Trade Regulations   Countries have rules that govern business practices within their borders. These rules often serve as trade barriers.[18] For example, Japan has some 11,000 trade regulations. Japanese car safety rules effectively require all automobile replacement parts to be Japanese and not American or European; public health rules make it illegal to sell aspirin or cold medicine without a pharmacist present. The Malaysian government has regulations stating that "advertisements must not project or promote an excessively aspirational lifestyle," Greece bans toy advertising, Sweden outlaws all advertisements to children, and Saudi Arabia bans Mattel's Barbie dolls because they are a symbol of Western decadence.

learning review

4. Cross-cultural analysis involves the study of _____.

5. When foreign currencies can buy more U.S. dollars, are U.S. products more or less expensive for a foreign consumer?

COMPARING GLOBAL MARKET-ENTRY STRATEGIES

LO3

Once a company has decided to enter the global marketplace, it must select a means of market entry. Four general options exist: (1) exporting, (2) licensing, (3) joint venture, and (4) direct investment.[19] As Figure 7–3 demonstrates, the amount of financial commitment, risk, marketing control, and profit potential increases as the firm moves from exporting to direct investment.

Exporting

exporting
Producing goods in one country and selling them in another country

Exporting is producing goods in one country and selling them in another country. This entry option allows a company to make the least number of changes in terms of its product, its organization, and even its corporate goals.

Indirect exporting is when a firm sells its domestically produced goods in a foreign country through an intermediary. It has the least amount of commitment and risk but will probably return the least profit. Indirect exporting is ideal for a company that has no overseas contacts but wants to market abroad. The intermediary is often a distributer that has the marketing know-how and resources necessary for the effort to succeed. Fran Wilson Creative Cosmetics of New York uses an indirect exporting approach to sell its products in Japan. Read the Marketing Matters box on the next page to find out how this innovative marketer and its Japanese distributors sell 20 percent of the lipsticks exported to Japan by U.S. cosmetic companies.[20]

Direct exporting is when a firm sells its domestically produced goods in a foreign country without intermediaries. Most companies become involved in direct exporting when they believe their volume of sales will be sufficiently large and easy to

FIGURE 7–3
A firm's profit potential and control over marketing activities increases as it moves from exporting to direct investment as a global market-entry strategy. But so does the firm's financial commitment and risk. Firms often engage in exporting, licensing, and joint ventures before pursuing a direct investment strategy.

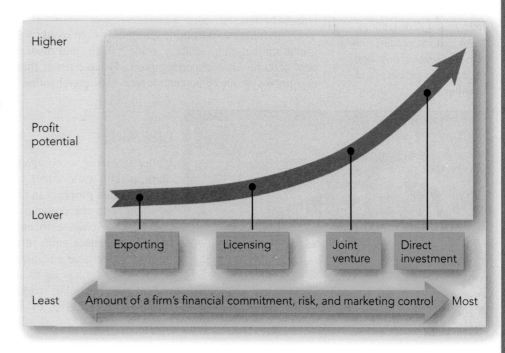

Creative Cosmetics and Creative Export Marketing in Japan

How does a medium-sized U.S. cosmetics firm sell 1.5 million tubes of lipstick in Japan annually? Fran Wilson Creative Cosmetics can attribute its success to a top-quality product, effective advertising, and a novel export marketing program. The firm's Moodmatcher lip coloring comes in green, orange, silver, black, and six other hues that change to a shade of pink, coral, or red, depending on a woman's chemistry when it's applied.

The company does not sell to department stores. According to a company spokesperson, "Shiseido and Kanebo (two large Japanese cosmetics firms) keep all the other Japanese or import brands out of the major department stores." Rather, the company sells its Moodmatcher lipstick through a network of Japanese distributors that reach Japan's 40,000 beauty salons.

The result? The company, with its savvy Japanese distributors, accounts for 20 percent of the lipsticks exported annually to Japan by U.S. cosmetic companies.

McDonald's uses franchising as a market-entry strategy, and about 70 percent of the company's sales come from non-U.S. operations. Note that the golden arches appear prominently—one aspect of its global brand promise.

obtain so that they do not require intermediaries. For example, the exporter may be approached by foreign buyers that are willing to contract for a large volume of purchases. Direct exporting involves more risk than indirect exporting for the company but also opens the door to increased profits. The Boeing Company applies a direct exporting approach. Boeing is the world's largest aerospace company and the largest U.S. exporter.

Even though exporting is commonly employed by large firms, it is the prominent global market-entry strategy among small- and medium-sized companies. Sixty percent of U.S. firms exporting products have fewer than 100 employees. These firms account for about 26 percent of total U.S. merchandise exports.[21]

Licensing

Under *licensing,* a company offers the right to a trademark, patent, trade secret, or other similarly valued items of intellectual property in return for a royalty or a fee. The advantages to the company granting the license are low risk and the chance to enter a foreign market at little cost. The licensee gains information that allows it to start with a competitive advantage. The foreign country gains employment by having the product manufactured locally. For instance, Yoplait yogurt is licensed from Sodima, a French cooperative, by General Mills for sales in the United States.

There are some serious drawbacks to this mode of entry, however. The licensor forgoes control of its product and reduces the potential profits gained from it. In addition, while the relationship lasts, the licensor may be creating its own competition. Some licensees are able to modify the product somehow and enter the market with product and marketing knowledge gained at the expense of the company that got them started. To offset this disadvantage, many companies strive to stay innovative so that the licensee remains dependent on them for improvements and successful operation. Finally, should the licensee prove to be a poor choice, the name or reputation of the company may be harmed.

A variation of licensing is *franchising*. Franchising is one of the fastest-growing market-entry strategies. More than 75,000 franchises of U.S. firms are located in countries throughout the world. Franchises include soft-drink, motel, retailing, fast-food, and car rental operations and a variety of business services. McDonald's is a premier global franchiser. With more than 23,000 units outside the United States, about 70 percent of McDonald's sales come from non-U.S. operations.[22]

Joint Venture

When a foreign company and a local firm invest together to create a local business, it is called a **joint venture**. These two companies share ownership, control, and profits of the new company. For example, Elite Food is a joint venture between Elite Industries and PepsiCo created to market Frito-Lay's Cheetos, Ruffles, and Doritos and other snacks in Israel.

The advantages of this option are twofold. First, one company may not have the necessary financial, physical, or managerial resources to enter a foreign market alone. The joint venture between Ericsson, a Swedish telecommunications firm, and CGCT, a French switch maker, enabled them together to beat out AT&T for a $100 million French contract. Ericsson's money and technology combined with CGCT's knowledge of the French market helped them to win the contract that neither of them could have won alone. Similarly, Ford and Volkswagen formed a joint venture to make four-wheel-drive vehicles in Portugal. Second, a government may require or strongly encourage a joint venture before it allows a foreign company to enter its market. This is the case in China, where thousands of Chinese-foreign joint ventures exist.

The disadvantages arise when the two companies disagree about policies or courses of action for their joint venture or when governmental bureaucracy bogs down the effort. For example, U.S. firms often prefer to reinvest earnings gained, whereas some foreign companies may want to spend those earnings. Or a U.S. firm may want to return profits earned to the United States, while the local firm or its government may oppose this—the problem faced by many potential joint ventures in Eastern Europe, Russia, Latin America, and South Asia.

Elite Food is a joint venture owned equally by Elite Industries Ltd. and PepsiCo. Elite Food markets Frito-Lay's Cheetos, Ruffles, and Doritos and other snacks in Israel.

Direct Investment

The biggest commitment a company can make when entering the global market is **direct investment**, which entails a domestic firm actually investing in and owning a foreign subsidiary or division. Examples of direct investment are Nissan's Smyrna, Tennessee, plant that produces pickup trucks and the Mercedes-Benz factory in Vance, Alabama, that makes the M-class sport-utility vehicle. Many U.S.-based global companies also use this mode of entry. Reebok entered Russia by creating a subsidiary known as Reebok Russia.

For many companies, direct investment often follows one of the other three market-entry strategies. For example, both FedEx and UPS entered

Nestlé has made a sizable direct investment in ice cream manufacturing in China to produce its global brands such as Drumstick. Nestlé operates 26 factories in China.

China through joint ventures with Chinese companies. Each subsequently purchased the interests of its partner and converted the Chinese operations into a division.[23]

The advantages to direct investment include cost savings, better understanding of local market conditions, and fewer local restrictions. Firms entering foreign markets using direct investment believe that these advantages outweigh the financial commitments and risks involved, such as the possible nationalization of assets.

learning review

6. What mode of entry could a company follow if it has no previous experience in global marketing?

7. How does licensing differ from a joint venture?

CRAFTING A WORLDWIDE MARKETING PROGRAM

LO4

The choice of a market-entry strategy is a necessary first step for a marketer when joining the community of global companies. The next step involves the challenging task of designing, implementing, and evaluating marketing programs worldwide.

Successful global marketers standardize global marketing programs whenever possible and customize them wherever necessary. The extent of standardization and customization is often rooted in a careful global environment scan supplemented with judgment based on experience and marketing research.

Product and Promotion Strategies

Global companies have five strategies for matching products and their promotion efforts to global markets. As Figure 7–4 shows, the strategies focus on whether a company extends or adapts its product and promotion message for consumers in different countries and cultures.

Overall, this approach starts with what works in the United States and extends it into new markets, paying close attention to local needs and customs. Throughout the three stages CNS conducts market research and makes financial projections.

As shown in the figure, at each stage of the market development process, performance must be met for the product to enter the next stage. Once success with Breathe Right nasal strips is established in a country, the groundwork is laid and international partners have the ability to introduce other Breathe Right products.

LOOKING FORWARD

"We believe the Breathe Right brand has great potential, both domestically and around the world," says Morfitt. "Growth will come both from further expansion of Breathe Right nasal strips and from other drug-free, better-breathing line extensions," says Morfitt.

Questions

1 What are the advantages and disadvantages for CNS taking Breathe Right strips into international markets?

2 What are the advantages to CNS of (*a*) using its three-stage process to enter new global markets and (*b*) having specific criteria to move through the stages?

3 Using the CNS criteria, with what you know, which countries should have highest priority for CNS?

4 Which single segment of potential Breathe Right strip users would you target to enter new markets?

5 Which marketing mix variables should CNS emphasize the most to succeed in a global arena? Why?

WELCOME TO A WORLD WITHOUT RULES.
CHRISTIAN BALE
MICHAEL CAINE
HEATH LEDGER
GARY OLDMAN
AARON ECKHART
MAGGIE GYLLENHAAL
AND MORGAN FREEMAN
THE DARK KNIGHT
SYNCOPY
WWW.THEDARKKNIGHT.COM
JULY 18

8

Marketing Research: From Customer Insights to Actions

TEST SCREENINGS: HOW LISTENING TO CONSUMERS REDUCES MOVIE RISKS

Batman: The Dark Knight. Indiana Jones and the Kingdom of the Crystal Skull. Harry Potter and the Half Blood Prince. Studios engaged in the fiercely competitive world of filmmaking in 2008 developed blockbuster sequels to help them reduce movie risks.[1]

What's in a Movie Name?
Fixing bad names for movies—like *Shoeless Joe* and *Rope Burns*—can turn potential disasters into hugely successful blockbusters. Don't remember seeing these movies? Well, test screenings—a form of marketing research—found that moviegoers like you had problems with these titles. Here's what happened:

- Shown frequently on television now, *Shoeless Joe* became *Field of Dreams* because audiences thought Kevin Costner might be playing a homeless person.

- *Rope Burns* became *Million Dollar Baby* because audiences didn't like the original name. The movie won the 2005 Academy Award™ for Best Picture and starred Hilary Swank as a woman boxer and Clint Eastwood as her trainer.

  Filmmakers want movie titles that are concise, grab attention, capture the essence of the film, and have no legal restrictions to reduce risk to both the studio and audiences—the same factors that make a good brand name.[2]

The Risks of Today's (and Tomorrow's) Blockbuster Movies
Bad titles, poor scripts, temperamental stars, costly special effects, and several blockbuster movies released at the same time are just a few of the nightmares studios face. Because today's films cost almost $110 million to produce and market,[3] studios try to reduce their risks by:

- *Creating a multiple-episode film series.* Film series like *Batman, Spider-Man, Pirates, Shrek, Harry Potter,* and *Indiana Jones* are relatively "safe" because studios believe that moviegoers liked the first movie and are more likely to attend its sequels. However, there are dangers: (1) Will audiences accept actors who have aged since their last movie episode (Daniel Radcliff as Harry Potter or Harrison Ford as Indiana Jones)? (2) Are the plots of sequels as entertaining as their first

episodes? Some sequels have not achieved the same box office success as their prior episodes due to poor scripts or other factors, like *Jurassic Park: The Lost World* and *Men in Black II*.[4]

- *Conducting test screenings.* In test screenings, 300 to 400 prospective moviegoers are recruited to attend a "sneak preview" of a film before its release. After viewing the movie, the audience fills out an exhaustive survey to critique its title, plot, characters, music, and ending as well as the marketing program (posters, trailers, and so on) to identify improvements to make in the final edit.[5]

  Test screenings resulted in *Fatal Attraction* having one of the most commercially successful "ending-switches" of all time. In sneak previews, audiences liked everything but the ending, which had Alex (Glenn Close) committing suicide and framing Dan (Michael Douglas) as her murderer by leaving his fingerprints on the knife she used. The studio shot $1.3 million of new scenes for the ending that audiences eventually saw. The new ending for *Fatal Attraction* undoubtedly contributed to the movie's box-office success.[6]

- *Using tracking studies.* Immediately before an upcoming film's release, studios will ask prospective moviegoers in the target audience three key questions: (1) Are you aware of the film? (2) Are you interested in seeing the film? and (3) Will you see the film this weekend?[7] Studios then use the data collected to forecast the movie's opening weekend box office sales; if necessary, they will run last-minute ads to increase awareness and interest for the film.

This example shows how marketing research is the link between marketing strategy and decisive marketing actions, the main topic of this chapter. Also, marketing research is often used to help a firm develop its sales forecasts, the final topic of this chapter.

A look at movie risks! Test screenings and tracking studies can help avoid potential dangers, even those faced by *Indiana Jones* sequels.

THE ROLE OF MARKETING RESEARCH

Let's look at (1) what marketing research is, (2) identify some difficulties with it, and (3) describe the five steps marketers use to conduct it.

What Is Marketing Research?

marketing research
The process of collecting and analyzing information in order to recommend actions

Marketing research is the process of defining a marketing problem and opportunity, systematically collecting and analyzing information, and recommending actions.[8] Although imperfect, marketers conduct marketing research to reduce risk of and thereby improve marketing decisions.

Why Good Marketing Research Is Difficult

Marketing researchers often face difficulties in asking consumers questions about new, unknown products. For example:

For how Fisher-Price does marketing research on young children who can't read, see the text.

- Suppose your firm is developing a new product never before seen by consumers. Would they really know whether they are likely to buy a product that they have never thought about before?
- Imagine if you, as a consumer, were asked about your personal hygiene habits. Even though you knew the answer, would you reveal it? When personal or status questions are involved, will people give honest answers?
- Will consumers' actual purchase behavior match their stated interest or intentions? Will they buy the same brand they say they will?

Marketing research must overcome these difficulties and obtain the information needed so that marketers can make reasonable estimates about what consumers will or won't buy.

Five-Step Marketing Research Approach

A *decision* is a conscious choice from among two or more alternatives. All of us make many such decisions daily. At work we choose from alternative ways to accomplish an assigned task. At college we choose from alternative courses. As consumers we choose from alternative brands. No magic formula guarantees correct decisions.

Managers and researchers have tried to improve the outcomes of decisions by using more formal, structured approaches to *decision making*, the act of consciously choosing from alternatives. The systematic marketing research approach used to collect information to improve marketing decisions and actions described in this chapter uses five steps and is shown in Figure 8–1. Although the five-step approach described here focuses on marketing decisions, it provides a systematic checklist for making both business and personal decisions.

FIGURE 8–1

Five-step marketing research approach leading to marketing actions.

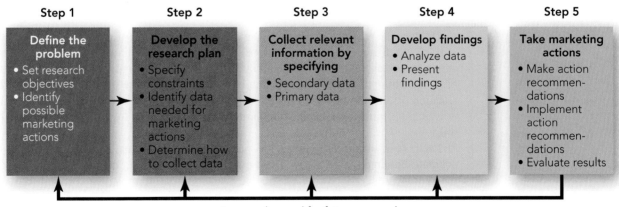

Lessons learned for future research

STEP 1: DEFINE THE PROBLEM

The wheels, noisemaker, and bobbing eyes on Fisher-Price's hugely successful Chatter Telephone resulted from careful marketing research.

Toy designers at Fisher-Price conduct marketing research to discover how children play, how they learn, and what they like to play with.[9] As part of its marketing research, Fisher-Price gets children to play at its state-licensed nursery school in East Aurora, New York. From behind one-way mirrors, toy designers and marketing researchers watch the children use—and abuse—toys, which helps the firm develop better products.

For example, the original model of a classic Fisher-Price toy, the Chatter Telephone™, was simply a wooden phone with a dial that rang a bell. However, observers noted that the children kept grabbing the receiver like a handle to pull the phone along behind them, so a designer added wheels, a noisemaker, and eyes that bobbed up and down.

A careful look at Fisher-Price's toy marketing research shows the two key elements of defining a problem: setting the research objectives and identifying possible marketing actions.

Set the Research Objectives

Research objectives are specific, measurable goals a decision maker—in this case, an executive at Fisher-Price—seeks to achieve in conducting the marketing research. For Fisher-Price, the immediate research objective was to decide whether to market the old or new telephone design.

In setting these research objectives, marketers have to be clear on the purpose of research they are about to do that leads to marketing actions.

Identify Possible Marketing Actions

measures of success

Criteria or standards used in evaluating proposed solutions to a problem

Marketing research isn't perfect. Recently it correctly identified Cybertron Transformers as a "hot toy" . . .

Effective decision makers develop specific **measures of success**, which are criteria or standards used in evaluating proposed solutions to the problem. Different research outcomes—based on the measure of success—lead to different marketing actions. For the Fisher-Price problem, if a measure of success were the total time children spent playing with each of the two telephone designs, the results of observing them would lead to clear-cut actions as follows:

Measure of Success: Playtime	**Possible Marketing Action**
• Children spent more time playing with old design.	• Continue with old design; don't introduce new design.
• Children spent more time playing with new design.	• Introduce new design; drop old design.

One test of whether marketing research should be done is if different outcomes will lead to different marketing actions. If all the research outcomes lead to the same action—such as top management sticking with the older design regardless of what the observed children liked—the research is useless and a waste of money. In this case, research results showed that kids liked the new design, so Fisher-Price introduced its noisemaking pull-toy Chatter Telephone, which became a toy classic and has sold millions.

Each year, *FamilyFun* magazine has dozens of children—and their parents—evaluate hundreds of new toys from over 100 toy manufactures to select its Toy of the Year awards. Over the years, they've been right on the money in selecting Barney the TV dinosaur, Tickle Me Elmo, and Fisher-Price's Love to Dance Bear™ as hot toys—ones that jumped off retailers' shelves. But as shown with the toys in the margin, even careful marketing research can sometimes overlook hot toys. Forecasting which toys are hot and will sell well is critical for retailers, which must place orders to manufacturers 8 to 10 months before holiday shoppers walk into their stores. Bad forecasts can lead to lost sales for understocks and severe losses for overstocks.

Marketing researchers know that defining a problem is an incredibly difficult task. For example, if the objectives are too broad, the problem may not be researchable. If they are too narrow, the value of the research results may be seriously lessened. This is why marketing researchers spend so much time in defining a marketing problem precisely and writing a formal proposal that describes the research to be done.[10]

STEP 2: DEVELOP THE RESEARCH PLAN

The second step in the marketing research process involves (1) specifying the constraints on the marketing research activity, (2) identifying the data needed for marketing decisions, and (3) determining how to collect the data.

Specify Constraints

The *constraints* in a decision are the restrictions placed on potential solutions to a problem. Examples include the limitations on the time and money available to solve the problem. Thus, Fisher-Price might set two constraints on its decision to select either the old or new version of the Chatter Telephone: The decision must be made in 10 weeks and no research budget is available beyond that needed for collecting data in its nursery school.

Identify Data Needed for Marketing Actions

Often marketing research studies wind up collecting a lot of data that are interesting but irrelevant for marketing decisions that result in marketing actions. In the Fisher-Price Chatter Telephone case, it might be nice to know the children's favorite colors, whether they like wood or plastic toys better, and so on. In fact, knowing answers to these questions might result in later modifications of the toy, but right now the problem is to select one of two toy designs. So this study must focus on collecting data that help managers make a clear choice between the two telephone designs.

Determine How to Collect Data

Determining how to collect useful marketing research data is often as important as actually collecting the data—step 3 in the process, which is discussed later. Two key elements in deciding how to collect the data are (1) concepts and (2) methods.

Concepts   In the world of marketing, *concepts* are ideas about products or services. To find out about consumer reaction to a potential new product, marketing researchers frequently develop a *new-product concept,* that is, a picture or verbal description of a product or service the firm might offer for sale. For example, with the Chatter Telephone, Fisher-Price managers developed a new-product concept that involved adding a noisemaker, wheels, and eyes to the basic design, which would make the toy more fun for children and increase sales.

. . . but missed on Hasbro's FurReal Friends Butterscotch Pony and Fisher-Price's TMX™ Elmo.

Methods   *Methods* are the approaches that can be used to collect data to solve all or part of a problem. For example, if you are the marketing researcher at Fisher-Price responsible for the Chatter Telephone, you face a number of methods issues in developing your research plan, including the following:

- Can we actually ask three- or four-year-olds meaningful questions they can answer about their liking or disliking of the two designs?

- Are we better off not asking them questions but simply observing their behavior?
- If we simply observe the children's behavior, how can we do this in a way to get the best information without biasing the results?

Millions of other people have asked similar questions about millions of other products and services. How can you find and use the methodologies that other marketing researchers have found successful? Information on useful methods is available in tradebooks, textbooks, and handbooks that relate to marketing and marketing research. Some periodicals and technical journals, such as the *Journal of Marketing* and the *Journal of Marketing Research* published by the American Marketing Association, summarize methods and techniques valuable in addressing marketing problems.

Special methods vital to marketing are (1) sampling and (2) statistical inference. For example, marketing researchers often use *sampling* by selecting a group of distributors, customers, or prospects, asking them questions, and treating their answers as typical of all those in whom they are interested. They may then use *statistical inference* to generalize the results from the sample to much larger groups of distributors, customers, or prospects to help decide on marketing actions.

---

learning review

1. What is marketing research?
2. What is the five-step marketing research approach?
3. What are constraints, as they apply to developing a research plan?

STEP 3: COLLECT RELEVANT INFORMATION

LO3

Collecting enough relevant information to make a rational, informed marketing decision sometimes simply means using your knowledge to decide immediately. At other times it entails collecting an enormous amount of information at great expense.

Figure 8–2 shows how the different kinds of marketing information fit together. **Data**, the facts and figures related to the problem, are divided into two main parts: secondary data and primary data. **Secondary data** are facts and figures that have already been recorded before the project at hand, whereas **primary data** are facts and figures that are newly collected for the project.

data
Facts and figures related to a problem

secondary data
Facts and figures that have already been recorded before the project at hand

primary data
Facts or figures that are newly collected for a project

Secondary Data: Internal

Secondary data divide into two parts: internal and external. Internal secondary data are data collected inside the organization and include detailed product sales reports as well as customer complaint tabulations. The collection of internal secondary data is often the starting point for a new marketing research study because using this information can result in huge time and cost savings.

Secondary Data: External

Published data from outside the organization are external secondary data. The U.S. Census Bureau publishes a variety of useful reports. Best known is the U.S. Census,

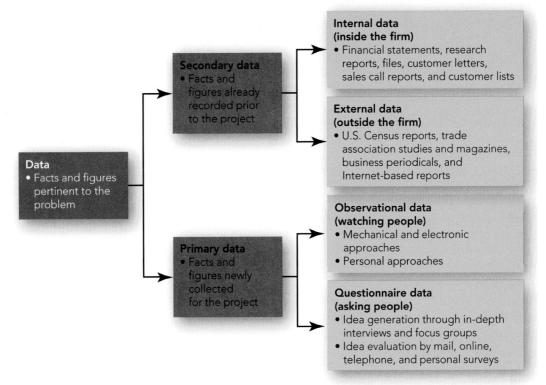

FIGURE 8-2

Types of marketing information. Researchers must choose carefully among these to get the best results, considering time and cost constraints.

which is a count of the U.S. population that occurs every 10 years. Recently, the Census Bureau began collecting data annually from a smaller number of people through the American Community Survey. Both surveys contain detailed information on American households, such as the number of people per household and their age, sex, race/ethnic background, income, occupation, and education. Marketers use these data to identify characteristics and trends of ultimate consumers.

The Census Bureau also publishes other reports that are vital to business firms selling products and services to organizations. The Economic Census, which now encompasses the former U.S. Census of Manufacturers, U.S. Census of Retail Trade, and others, is conducted every five years. The 2007 Economic Census contains data on the number and size of establishments in the United States that produce a good or service on the basis of its North American Industry Classification System (NAICS).

Finally, trade associations, universities, and business periodicals provide detailed data of value to market researchers and planners. These data are now available online via the Internet and can be identified and located using a search engine like Google. The Marketing Matters box provides examples.

Advantages and Disadvantages of Secondary Data

A general rule among marketing people is to obtain secondary data first and then collect primary data. Two important advantages of secondary data are (1) the tremendous time savings if the data have already been collected and published or exist internally and (2) the low cost, such as free or inexpensive Census reports. Furthermore, a greater level of detail is often available through secondary data, especially U.S. Census Bureau data.

However, these advantages must be weighed against some significant disadvantages. First, the secondary data may be out of date, especially if they are U.S. Census

Information contained in online databases available via the Internet consists of indexes to articles in periodicals and statistical or financial data on markets, products, and organizations that are accessed either directly or via Internet search engines or portals through keyword searches.

Online databases of indexes, abstracts, and full-text information from periodicals include:

- LexisNexis™ Academic (www.lexisnexis.com) provides full-text documents from over 6,000 news, business, legal, and reference publications.
- ProQuest databases (www.proquest.com) provide summaries of management, marketing, and other business articles from more than 4,000 journals.

Statistical and financial data on markets, products, and organizations include:

- *The Wall Street Journal* (www.wsj.com), CNBC (www.cnbc.com), and *Fox Business News* (www.foxbusiness.com)

provide up-to-the-minute business news and security prices plus research reports on companies, industries, and countries.

- STAT-USA (www.stat-usa.gov) of the U.S. Department of Commerce provides information on U.S. business, economic, and trade activity collected by the federal government.

Portals and search engines include:

- USA.gov (www.usa.gov) is the portal to all U.S. government websites. Users click on links to browse by topic or enter keywords for specific searches.
- Google (www.google.com) is the most popular portal to the entire Internet. Users click on links to browse by topic or enter keywords for specific searches.

Some of these websites are accessible only if your educational institution has paid a subscription fee. Check with your institution's website.

---

data collected only every 5 or 10 years. Second, the definitions or categories might not be quite right for a researcher's project. For example, the age groupings or product categories might be wrong for the project. Also, because the data are collected for another purpose, they may not be specific enough for the project. In such cases it may be necessary to collect primary data.

---

learning review

4. What is the difference between secondary and primary data?

5. What are some advantages and disadvantages of secondary data?

LO4

Observing people and asking them questions are the two principal ways to collect new or primary data for a marketing study.

Primary Data: Observing Behavior

Observational data can be collected by either mechanical (including electronic) means and personal observation.

observational data

Facts and figures obtained by watching, either mechanically or in person, how people behave

Mechanical Observation   Facts and figures obtained by watching, either mechanically or in person, how people actually behave is the way marketing researchers collect **observational data**. National TV ratings, such as those of Nielsen Media Research shown in Figure 8–3, are an example of mechanical observational data collected

FIGURE 8–3

Nielsen Television Index
Ranking Report for network
TV primetime households,
week of May 19–25, 2008.
The difference of a few share
points in Nielsen TV ratings
affects the cost of a TV ad on
a show and even whether the
show remains on the air.

Source: Copyright 2008,
Nielsen Media Research.

RANK	PROGRAM	NETWORK	RATING	SHARE
1	American Idol—Wednesday	FOX	17.7	28
2	American Idol—Tuesday	FOX	15.1	24
3	Dancing with the Stars—Results	ABC	12.9	20
4	Dancing with the Stars	ABC	12.4	20
5	Grey's Anatomy	ABC	11.8	19
6	CSI: Miami	CBS	10.4	17
7	NCIS	CBS	10.3	16
8	House	FOX	10.0	15
9	Two and a Half Men	CBS	9.0	14
10	Criminal Minds	CBS	8.3	13

Nielsen Media Research is
developing this "Solo Meter"
to measure TV viewing by
those using personal video
devices such as video iPods
and cell phones. The device
is part of Nielsen's A2/M2
Initiative discussed in the text.

by a "people meter." The people meter is a box that (1) is attached to TV sets, VCRs, cable boxes, and satellite dishes in more than 14,000 homes across the country; (2) has a remote that operates the meter when a viewer begins and finishes watching a TV program; and (3) stores and then transmits the viewing information each night to Nielsen Media Research.[11]

Currently, Nielsen employs separate local samples in each of 210 local markets. Ten of the nation's largest markets that reach 30 percent of TV viewing households use the people meter technology to provide viewing information daily. In the rest of the markets, TV viewing is measured using less sophisticated meters or TV diaries (a paper-pencil measurement system). Markets without people meters use this measurement in February, May, July, and November, which are known as "the sweeps."[12]

By 2011, Nielsen will implement a new measurement program dubbed the *Anytime Anywhere Media Measurement (A2/M2) Initiative*. The purpose of A2/M2 is to "follow the video" of twenty-first century viewers. New "active/passive" people meter technology will measure all types of TV viewing behavior from a variety of devices and sources: DVR (digital video recorders), VOD (video on demand), Internet-delivered TV shows on computers via iTunes, streaming media, mobile media devices (cell phones, iPods, etc.), as well as outside the home in bars, fitness clubs, airports, etc. By 2011, Nielsen also planned to expand the people meter service to include the top 25 markets, which account for 50 percent of TV households. For smaller markets Nielsen will use improved people meters and paper-based viewing logs until a better technology, such as personal RFID (radio frequency ID) tags, can be developed.[13]

On the basis of all these observational data, Nielsen Media Research then calculates the rating and share of each TV program. With 112.8 million TV households in the United States, based on the 2000 U.S. Census, a single ratings point equals 1 percent, or 1,128,000 TV households.[14] For TV viewing, a share point is the percentage of TV sets in use tuned to a particular program. Because TV networks and cable sell almost $70 billion annually in advertising[15] and set advertising rates to advertisers on the basis of those data, precision in the Nielsen data is critical. Thus, a change of one percentage point in a rating can mean gaining or losing up to $70 million in advertising revenue because advertisers pay rates on the basis of the size of the audience for a TV program. So as Figure 8–3 shows, we might expect to pay more for a 30-second TV

What determines if *American Idol* stays on the air? For the importance of the TV "ratings game," see the text.

ad on *Grey's Anatomy* than one on *CSI: Miami*. Broadcast and cable networks may change the time slot or even cancel a TV program if its ratings are consistently poor and advertisers are unwilling to pay a rate based on a higher guaranteed rating.

But TV advertisers today have a special problem: with about three out of four TV viewers skipping ads with TiVo or channel surfing during commercials, how many people are actually seeing their TV ad? Now services such as Nielsen Media Research and Media Check offer advertisers minute-by-minute measurement of how many viewers stay tuned during commercials. The viewership data in Figure 8–3 includes not only live TV but also programs taped on digital video recorders (DVRs). With these more precise measures of who is likely to see a TV ad, buying TV ads is becoming a lot more scientific.[16]

Nielsen Online Ratings also uses an electronic meter to record Internet user behavior. These data are collected via a meter installed on computers by tracking the actual mouse clicks made by a large sample of individuals in 13 countries as they surf the Internet. Nielsen Online Ratings identifies the top websites—or "brands"—that have the largest unique audiences and "active reach," which is the percent of total home and office users that visited the website. Figure 8–4, showing the top 10 Internet websites, gives interesting comparisons about Internet usage in terms of time spent at the website per person each week. For example, while Google reaches more people than eBay, the typical eBay user spends almost 50 minutes more per visit than a Google user does.

Personal Observation   Observational data can take some strange twists. Jennifer Voitle, a laid-off investment bank employee with four advanced degrees, responded to an Internet ad and found a new career: *mystery shopper*. Companies pay her to

FIGURE 8–4

Nielsen Online Ratings of the top 10 Internet brands for May 2008

Source: Copyright 2008, Nielsen Online.

RANK	BRAND	UNIQUE AUDIENCE (000s)	ACTIVE REACH (%)	HOURS AND MINUTES PER PERSON PER WEEK
1	Google	121,991	73.3	1:15
2	Yahoo!	114,661	68.9	3:14
3	Microsoft	97,663	58.7	0:44
4	MSN/Windows Live	97,626	58.7	2:07
5	AOL Media Network	89,736	53.9	3:38
6	Fox Interactive Media	70,250	42.2	1:50
7	YouTube	69,329	41.7	0:56
8	Wikipedia	57,285	34.4	0:17
9	eBay	55,633	33.4	1:51
10	Apple	50,531	30.4	1:06

Is this *really* marketing research? A *mystery shopper* at work.

Mforma gets design ideas from teenagers—today's cutting-edge cell phone users.

check on the quality of their products and services and write a detailed report on what she finds. She gets paid to travel to exotic hotels, eat at restaurants, play golf, test-drive new cars, shop for clothes, and play arcade games. But her role posing as a customer gives her client unique marketing research information that can be obtained in no other way. Says Jennifer, "Can you believe they call this work?"[17]

Watching consumers in person or videotaping them are two other observational approaches. For example, Procter & Gamble watched women do their laundry, clean the floor, put on makeup, and so on because they comprise 80 percent of its customers! And Gillette videotaped consumers brushing their teeth in their own bathrooms to see how they really brush—not just how they say they brush. The new-product result: Gillette's Oral-B CrossAction toothbrush.[18]

Ethnographic research is a specialized observational approach where trained observers seek to discover subtle emotional reactions as consumers encounter products in their "natural use environment," such as in their home, car, or hotel. Recently, Kraft launched Deli Creations, which are sandwiches made with its Oscar Mayer meats, Kraft cheeses, and Grey Poupon mustard, after spending several months with consumers in their kitchens. Kraft discovered that consumers wanted complete, ready-to-serve meals that are easy to prepare—and it had the products to create them.[19]

Personal observation is both useful and flexible, but it can be costly and unreliable when different observers report different conclusions when watching the same event. And while observation can reveal *what* people do, it cannot easily determine *why* they do it. This is the principal reason for using questionnaires, our next topic.

Primary Data: Questioning Consumers

How many dozens of times have you filled out some kind of a questionnaire? Maybe a short survey at school or a telephone or e-mail survey to see if you are pleased with the service you received. Asking consumers questions and recording their answers is the second principal way of gathering information.

We can divide this primary data collection task into (1) idea generation methods and (2) idea evaluation methods, although they sometimes overlap and each has a number of special techniques.[20] Each survey method results in valuable **questionnaire data**, which are facts and figures obtained by asking people about their attitudes, awareness, intentions, and behaviors.

Idea Generation Methods—Coming Up with Ideas

"Oh, Dad, you *so* don't get it," is the kind of marketing research feedback Daniel Kranzler often gets when he conducts his *individual interviews* (a single researcher asking questions of one respondent). His company, Mforma, makes games and ring tones for cell phones. With teenagers' ideas often driving the leading-edge designs and features in cell phones, Kranzler wants to connect with their latest thoughts. So for *very direct* input he turns to his 18-year-old daughter, Kat, who tells it like she sees it.[21]

General Mills sought ideas about why Hamburger Helper didn't fare well when introduced. Initial instructions

Listening carefully in focus groups to student and instructor suggestions benefits this text, such as providing answers to the Learning Review questions.

Marketing research by Teenage Research Unlimited involves having teenagers complete a drawing describing themselves.

called for cooking a half-pound of hamburger separately from the noodles or potatoes, which were later mixed with the hamburger. So General Mills researchers used a special kind of individual interview called *depth interviews* in which researchers ask lengthy, free-flowing kinds of questions to probe for underlying ideas and feelings. These depth interviews showed that consumers (1) didn't think it contained enough meat and (2) didn't want the hassle of cooking in two different pots. So the Hamburger Helper product manager changed the recipe to call for a full pound of meat and to allow users to prepare it in one dish. This marketing action converted a potential failure into a success.[22]

Focus groups are informal sessions of 6 to 10 past, present, or prospective customers in which a discussion leader, or moderator, asks their opinions about the firm's and its competitors' products, how they use these products, and special needs they have that these products don't address. Often videorecorded and conducted in special interviewing rooms with a one-way mirror, these groups enable marketing researchers and managers to hear and watch consumer reactions. The informality and peer support in an effective focus group uncover ideas that are often difficult to obtain with individual interviews. For example, 3M ran eight focus groups around the United States and heard consumers complain that standard steel wool pads scratched their expensive cookware. These interviews led to 3M's internationally successful Scotch-Brite® Never Scratch soap pad.[23]

Finding "the next big thing" for consumers has become the obsession not only for consumer product firms but also for firms in many other industries. The result is that marketing researchers have come to rely on other—many would say bizarre—techniques than more traditional individual or focus group interviews. These "fuzzy front end" methods attempt to identify elusive consumer tastes or trends far before typical consumers have recognized them themselves. Examples of unusual ways to collect consumer data and their results include:

- *Having consumers take a photo of themselves every time they snack.* This resulted in General Mills' Homestyle Pop Secret popcorn, which delivers the real butter and bursts of salt in microwave popcorn that consumers thought they could only get from the stovetop variety.[24]

- *Having teenagers complete a drawing.* This is used by researchers at Teenage Research Unlimited (TRU) to help discover what teenagers like, wear, listen to, read, and watch. TRU surveys 3,200 teens and twenty-somethings three times a year to identify their lifestyles, attitudes, trends, and behaviors. With its Favorite Brand Meter™, TRU asks teens to specify the coolest brands within specific product categories, such as sneakers and clothing.[25]

174

New products! To invent them the natural thing is to add more features, new technologies, more glitz. Many new-product successes do just that.

But good marketing research can open huge new markets by taking features away and simplifying the product. Here are some less-is-more new-product breakthroughs that revolutionized national or global markets:

1. *Canon's tabletop copiers.* Canon's marketing research found it couldn't sell its little copiers to big companies, which were happy with their large Xerox machines. So Canon sold its little machines by the zillions to little companies with limited copying needs.

2. *Palm Computing's PalmPilot PDA.* Apple Computer's Newton personal digital assistant (PDA) was a great idea but was too complicated for users. Enter: PalmPilot inventors Donna Dubinsky and Jeff Hawkins, who deleted features to achieve the market breakthrough.

3. *Intuit's QuickBooks accounting software.* Competitors offered complex accounting software containing every feature professional accountants might possibly want. Intuit then introduced QuickBooks, a smaller, cheaper program with less functionality that won 70 percent of the huge market for small-business accounting software within two years.

4. *Swatch watches.* In 1983, a slim plastic watch with only 51 components appeared on the global market. That simplicity—plus top quality, affordable price, and creative designs—is the reason that more than 250 million Swatch watches have been sold.

Sometimes much less is much, much more!

One surprise: Innovation research shows that firms using disruptive innovation and creating newness by simplifying the product are often *not* the industry leaders selling the more sophisticated high-end products with more features.

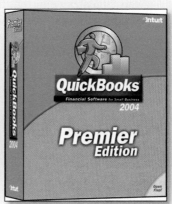

Idea Evaluation Methods—Testing an Idea In idea evaluation, the marketing researcher tries to test ideas discovered earlier to help the marketing manager recommend marketing actions. Marketing research to evaluate new-product ideas is especially difficult because potential buyers can't see or touch what they are asked to comment on. But a huge amount of marketing research is also done to ask users to evaluate and improve existing products. A surprising result is that many products in the marketplace have so many features they overwhelm the users. So effective marketing research often improves products by simplifying them—less is really more—which can greatly expand their products' markets, as discussed in the Marketing Matters box.[26]

Idea evaluation methods often involve conventional questionnaires using personal, mail, telephone, e-mail, fax, or Internet surveys of a large sample of past, present, or prospective consumers. In choosing between these alternatives, the marketing researcher must balance cost against the expected quality of information obtained. Personal interview surveys have a major advantage of enabling the interviewer to be

Wendy's does marketing research continuously to discover changing customer wants, while keeping its "Fresh, hot'n juicy®" image.

flexible in asking probing questions or getting reactions to visual materials, but they are very costly to conduct. Mail surveys are usually biased because those most likely to respond have had especially positive or negative experiences with the product or brand. While telephone interviews allow flexibility, unhappy respondents may hang up on the interviewer, even with the efficiency of computer-assisted telephone interviewing (CATI). E-mail, fax, and Internet surveys are restricted to respondents having the technologies but are expanding rapidly.

The high cost of reaching respondents in their homes using personal interviews has led to a dramatic increase in the use of *mall intercept interviews,* which are personal interviews of consumers visiting shopping centers. These face-to-face interviews reduce the cost of personal visits to consumers in their homes while providing the flexibility to show respondents visual cues such as ads or actual product samples. However, a critical disadvantage of mall intercept interviews is that the people selected for the interviews may not be representative of the consumers targeted, giving a biased result.

Figure 8–5 shows typical problems to guard against when wording questions to obtain meaningful answers from respondents. For example, in a question of whether you eat at fast-food restaurants regularly, the word *regularly* is ambiguous. Two people might answer yes to the question, but one might mean "once a day" while the other means "once or twice a month." Both answers appear as yes to the researcher who tabulates them, but they suggest that dramatically different marketing actions be directed to each of these two prospective consumers. Therefore, it is essential that marketing research questions be worded precisely so that all respondents interpret the same question similarly.

Primary Data: Panels and Experiments

Panels   Two special ways that observations and questionnaires are sometimes used are panels and experiments.

FIGURE 8–5
Typical problems when wording questions

PROBLEM	SAMPLE QUESTION	EXPLANATION OF PROBLEM
Leading question	Why do you like Wendy's fresh meat hamburgers better than those of competitors?	Consumer is led to make statement favoring Wendy's hamburgers.
Ambiguous question	Do you eat at fast-food restaurants regularly? ☐ Yes ☐ No	What is meant by word *regularly*—once a day, once a month, or what?
Unanswerable question	What was the occasion for eating your first hamburger?	Who can remember the answer? Does it matter?
Two questions in one	Do you eat Wendy's hamburgers and chili? ☐ Yes ☐ No	How do you answer if you eat Wendy's hamburgers but not chili?
Nonmutually exclusive answers	What is your age? ☐ Under 20 ☐ 20–40 ☐ 40 and over	What answer does a 40-year-old check?

Marketing researchers often want to know if consumers change their behavior over time, so they take successive measurements of the same people. A *panel* is a sample of consumers or stores from which researchers take a series of measurements. For example, the NPD Group collects data about consumer purchases such as apparel, food, and electronics from its Online Panel, which consists of more than 3 million individuals worldwide. So a firm like General Mills can use descriptive research—counting the frequency of consumer purchases—to measure switching behavior from one brand of its breakfast cereal (Wheaties) to another (Cheerios) or to a competitor's brand (Kellogg's Special K). A disadvantage of panels is that the marketing research firm needs to recruit new members continually to replace those who drop out. These new recruits must match the characteristics of those they replace to keep the panel representative of the marketplace.

Experiments   An *experiment* involves obtaining data by manipulating factors under tightly controlled conditions to test cause and effect, an example of causal research. The interest is in whether changing one of the independent variables (a cause) will change the behavior of the dependent variable that is studied (the result). In marketing experiments, the independent variables of interest—sometimes called the marketing *drivers*—are often one or more of the marketing mix elements, such as a product's features, price, or promotion (like advertising messages or coupons). The ideal dependent variable usually is a change in purchases (incremental unit or dollar sales) of individuals, households, or organizations. For example, food

companies often use *test markets,* which is offering a product for sale in a small geographic area to help evaluate potential marketing actions. So a test market is really a kind of marketing experiment to reduce risks. In 1988, Wal-Mart opened three experimental stand-alone supercenters to gauge consumer acceptance before deciding to open others. Today, Wal-Mart operates 2,500 supercenters around the world.

A potential difficulty with experiments is that outside factors (such as actions of competitors) can distort the results of an experiment and affect the dependent variable (such as sales). A researcher's task is to identify the effect of the marketing variable of interest on the dependent variable when the effects of outside factors in an experiment might hide it.

How might Wal-Mart have done early marketing research to help develop its supercenters, which have achieved international success? For its unusual research, see the text.

Advantages and Disadvantages of Primary Data

Compared with secondary data, primary data have the advantage of being more specific to the problem being studied. The main disadvantages are that primary data are usually far more costly and time consuming to collect than secondary data.

learning review

6. What is the difference between observational and questionnaire data?

7. Which survey provides the greatest flexibility for asking probing questions: mail, telephone, or personal interview?

8. What is the difference between a panel and an experiment?

Syndicated Panel Data and Information Technology

Several market research companies pay households (and businesses) to record all their purchases using a paper or electronic diary. Such *syndicated panel data* economically answer questions that require consistent data collection over time, such as how many times do our customers buy our product in a year? How does that compare to last year and the year before?

For example, one syndicated panel sample has almost 100,000 households. Each household is given an electronic wand to scan the bar-codes on purchases that it makes. Last week's purchases are uploaded every week! This year-versus-year comparison, by asking 100,000 representative households to record all that they buy, is made affordable when lots of companies share the cost of one, syndicated sample. The sample is then used to project statistically the purchase behaviors of all households in the country.

Using Information Technology to Trigger Marketing Actions

LO5

Today's marketing managers can be drowned in such an ocean of data that they need to adopt strategies for dealing with complex, changing views of the competition, the market, and the consumer. The Internet and the PC power of today help make sense out of this data ocean.

The Marketing Manager's View of Sales Drivers   Figure 8–6 shows a marketing manager's view of the product or brand "drivers," the factors that influence buying decisions of a household or organization and, hence, sales. These drivers include both the controllable marketing mix factors like product and distribution as well as uncontrollable factors like competition and the changing tastes of households or organizational buyers.

Understanding these drivers involves managing this ocean of data. Sources feeding this database ocean range from internal data about sales and customers to external data from syndication services and TV ratings. The marketer's task is to convert this data ocean into useful information that leads to marketing actions.

Information technology involves operating computer networks that can store and process data. Today information technology can extract hidden information from large databases such as households' product purchases, TV viewing behavior, and responses to coupon or free-sample promotions. Firms such as Information Resources' InfoScan

FIGURE 8–6

Sales drivers: factors that influence product or brand sales. All these drivers must be considered in designing an effective marketing program.

Source: Ford Consulting Group, Inc.

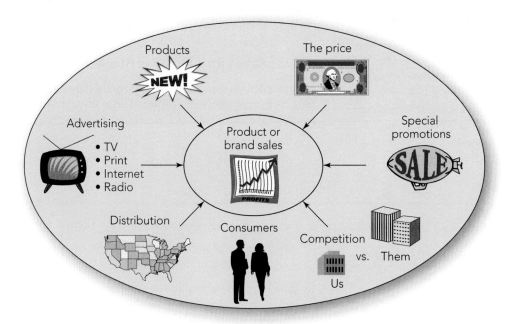

At 10 P.M. what is this man likely to buy besides these diapers? For the curious answer data mining gives, see the text.

and AC Nielsen's ScanTrack collect this information through the bar-code scanners at the checkout counters in supermarket, drug, convenience, and mass merchandise retailers in the United States.[27]

Key Elements of an Information System

Figure 8–7 shows how marketing researchers and managers use information technology to frame questions that provide answers leading to marketing actions. At the bottom of Figure 8–7 the marketer queries the databases in the information system with marketing questions needing answers. These questions go through statistical models that analyze the relationships that exist among the data. The databases form the core, or *data warehouse,* where the ocean of data is collected and stored. After the search of this data warehouse, the models select and link the pertinent data, often presenting them in tables and graphics for easy interpretation. Marketers can also use *sensitivity analysis* to query the database with "what if" questions to determine how a hypothetical change in a driver like advertising can affect sales.

Data Mining: A New Approach to Searching the Data Ocean Traditional marketing research typically involves identifying possible drivers and then collecting data. For example, we might collect data to test the hypothesis that increasing couponing (the driver) during spring will increase trial by first-time buyers (the result).

In contrast, *data mining* is the extraction of hidden predictive information from large databases in order to find statistical links between consumer purchasing patterns and marketing actions. Some of these are common sense: Since many consumers buy peanut butter and grape jelly together, it may be a good idea to run a joint promotion between Skippy peanut butter and Welch's grape jelly. But would you have expected that men buying diapers in the evening sometimes buy a six-pack of beer as well? This

FIGURE 8–7
How marketing researchers and managers use information technology to turn information into action

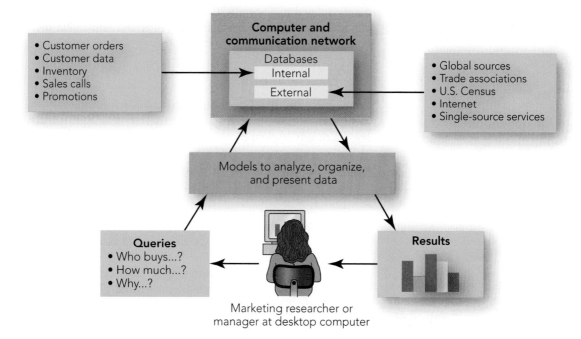

Marketing researcher or manager at desktop computer

is exactly what supermarkets discovered when they mined checkout data from scanners. So they placed diapers and beer near each other, then placed potato chips between them—and increased sales on all three items!

On the near horizon: RFID technology using a "smart tag" microchip on the diapers and beer to tell whether they wind up in the same shopping bag—at 10 in the evening.[28] Still, the success in data mining depends on the judgments of the marketing managers and researchers in how to select, analyze, and interpret the information.

STEP 4: DEVELOP FINDINGS

Mark Twain once observed, "Collecting data is like collecting garbage. You've got to know what you're going to do with the stuff before you collect it." Thus, marketing data and information have little more value than garbage unless they are analyzed carefully and translated into logical findings, step 4 in the marketing research approach.[29]

Analyze the Data

Let's consider the case of Tony's Pizza and Teré Carral, the marketing manager responsible for the Tony's brand. We will use hypothetical data to protect Tony's proprietary information.

Teré is concerned about the limited growth in the Tony's brand over the past four years. She hires a consultant to collect and analyze data to explain what's going on with her brand and to recommend ways to improve its growth. Teré asks the consultant to put together a proposal that includes the answers to two key questions:

1. How are Tony's sales doing on a household basis? For example, are fewer households buying Tony's pizzas, or is each household buying fewer Tony's? Or both?
2. What factors might be contributing to Tony's very flat sales over the past four years?

Facts uncovered by the consultant are vital. For example, is the average household consuming more or less Tony's pizza than in previous years? Is Tony's flat sales performance related to a specific factor? With answers to these questions Teré can identify actions in her marketing plan and implement them over the coming year.

How are sales doing? To see how marketers at Tony's Pizza assessed this question and the reasons they came up with this ad, read the text.

Present the Findings

Findings should be clear and understandable from the way the data are presented. Managers are responsible for *actions*. Often it means delivering the results in clear pictures and, if possible, in a single page.

The consultant gives Teré the answers to her questions using the marketing dashboards in Figure 8–8, a creative way to present findings graphically. Let's look over the shoulders of Teré and the consultant while they interpret these findings:

- Figure 8–8A, the chart showing Annual Sales. This shows the annual growth of the Tony's Pizza brand is stable but virtually flat from 2005 through 2008.
- Figure 8–8B, the chart showing Average Annual Sales per Household. Look closely at this graph. At first glance, it may seem like sales in 2008 are *half* what they were in 2005, right? But be careful to read the numbers on the vertical axis. They show that household

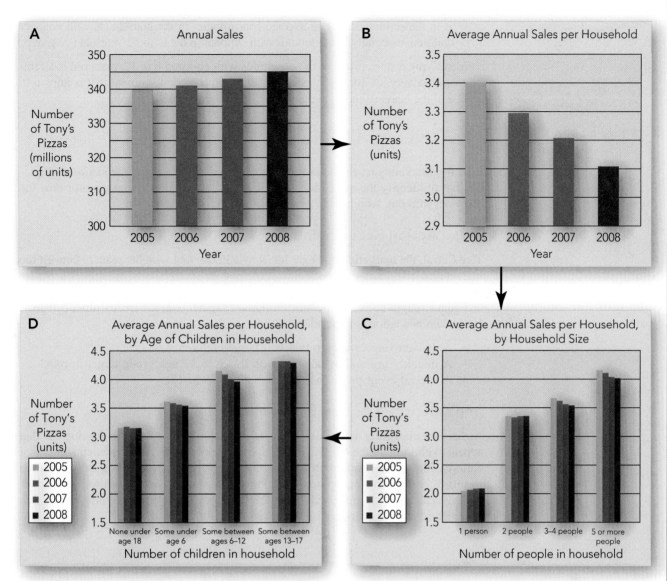

FIGURE 8–8

These marketing dashboards present findings to Tony's marketing manager that lead to recommendations and actions.

Source: Teré Carral, Tony's Pizza.

purchases of Tony's have been steadily declining over the past four years, from an average of 3.4 pizzas per household in 2005 to 3.1 pizzas per household in 2008. (Significant, but hardly a 50 percent drop.) Now the question is, if Tony's annual sales are stable, yet the average individual household is buying fewer Tony's pizzas, what's going on? The answer is, more households are buying pizzas—it's just that each household is buying fewer Tony's pizzas. That households aren't choosing Tony's is a genuine source of concern. But again, here's a classic example of a marketing problem representing a marketing opportunity. The number of households buying pizza is *growing,* and that's good news for Tony's.

• Figure 8–8C, the chart showing Average Annual Sales per Household, by Household Size. This chart starts to show a source of the problem: Even though average sales of pizza to households with only one or two people is stable, households with three or four people and those with five or more are declining in average annual pizza consumption. Which households tend to have more than two people? Answer: Households *with children.* Therefore, we should look more closely at the pizza-buying behavior of households with children.

• Figure 8–8D, the chart showing Average Annual Sales per Household, by Age of Children in the Household. The picture is becoming very clear now: The real problem is in the serious decline in average consumption in the households with younger children, especially in households with children in the 6- to 12-year-old age group.

Identifying a sales problem in households with children 6 to 12 years old is an important discovery, as Tony's sales are declining in a market segment that is known to be one of the heaviest in buying pizzas.

STEP 5: TAKE MARKETING ACTIONS

Effective marketing research doesn't stop with findings and recommendations—someone has to identify the marketing actions, put them into effect, and monitor how the decisions turn out, which is the essence of step 5.

Make Action Recommendations

Teré Carral, the marketing manager for Tony's Pizza, met with her team to convert the market research findings into specific marketing recommendations with a clear objective: Target families with children ages 6 to 12 to reverse the trend among this segment and gain strength in one of the most important segments in the frozen pizza category. Her recommendation is to develop:

- An advertising campaign that will target children 6 to 12.
- A monthly promotion calendar with this 6 to 12 age group target in mind.
- A special event program reaching children 6 to 12.

Implement the Action Recommendations

As her first marketing action, Teré undertakes advertising research to develop ads that appeal to children in the 6 to 12 age group and their families. The research shows that children like colorful ads with funny, friendly characters. She gives these research results to her advertising agency, which develops several sample ads for her review. Teré selects three that are tested on children to identify the most appealing one, which is then used in her next advertising campaign for Tony's Pizza.

learning review

9. How does data mining differ from traditional marketing research?

10. In the marketing research for Tony's Pizza, what is an example of (a) a finding and (b) a marketing action?

SALES FORECASTING TECHNIQUES

LO5

sales forecast

Total sales of a product that a firm expects to sell during a specified time period under specified conditions

Forecasting or estimating potential sales is often a key goal in a marketing research study. Good sales forecasts are important for a firm as it schedules production. The term **sales forecast** refers to the total sales of a product that a firm expects to sell during a specified time period under specified environmental conditions and its own marketing efforts. For example, Betty Crocker might develop a sales forecast of 4 million cases of cake mix for U.S. consumers in 2010, assuming consumers' dessert preferences remain constant and competitors don't change prices.

Three main sales forecasting techniques are often used: (1) judgments of the decision maker, (2) surveys of knowledgeable groups, and (3) statistical methods.

How might a marketing manager at Wilson forecast tennis rackets sales through 2010? Use a lost-horse forecast, as described in the text.

Judgments of the Decision Maker

Probably 99 percent of all sales forecasts are simply the judgment of the person who must act on the results of the forecast—the individual decision maker. A *direct forecast* involves estimating the value to be forecast without any intervening steps. Examples appear daily: How many quarts of milk should I buy? How much money should I get out of the ATM?

A *lost-horse forecast* involves starting with the last known value of the item being forecast, listing the factors that could affect the forecast, assessing whether they have a positive or negative impact, and making the final forecast. The technique gets its name from how you'd find a lost horse: go to where it was last seen, put yourself in its shoes, consider those factors that could affect where you might go (to the pond if you're thirsty, the hayfield if you're hungry, and so on), and go there. For example, a product manager for Wilson's tennis rackets in early 2008 who needed to make a sales forecast through 2010 would start with the known value of 2007 sales and list the positive factors (more tennis courts, more TV publicity) and the negative ones (competition from other sports, high prices of graphite and ceramic rackets) to arrive at the final series of annual sales forecasts.

Surveys of Knowledgeable Groups

If you wonder what your firm's sales will be next year, ask people who are likely to know something about future sales. Two common groups that are surveyed to develop sales forecasts are prospective buyers and the firm's salesforce.

A *survey of buyers' intentions forecast* involves asking prospective customers if they are likely to buy the product during some future time period. For industrial products with few prospective buyers, this can be effective. There are only a few hundred customers in the entire world for Boeing's largest airplanes, so Boeing surveys them to develop its sales forecasts and production schedules.

A *salesforce survey forecast* involves asking the firm's salespeople to estimate sales during a coming period. Because these people are in contact with customers and are likely to know what customers like and dislike, there is logic to this approach. However, salespeople can be unreliable forecasters—painting too rosy a picture if they are enthusiastic about a new product and too grim a forecast if their sales quota and future compensation are based on it.

Statistical Methods

The best-known statistical method of forecasting is *trend extrapolation,* which involves extending a pattern observed in past data into the future. When the pattern is described with a straight line, it is *linear trend extrapolation.* Suppose that in early 2000 you were a sales forecaster for the Xerox Corporation and had actual sales running from 1988 to 1999 (see Figure 8–9 on the next page). Using linear trend extrapolation, you draw a line to fit the past data and project it into the future to give the forecast values shown for 2000 to 2010.

If in 2008 you want to compare your forecasts with actual results, you are in for a surprise—illustrating the strength and weakness of trend extrapolation. Trend extrapolation assumes that the underlying relationships in the past will continue into the future, which is the basis of the method's key strength: simplicity. If this assumption proves correct, you have an accurate forecast. However, if this proves wrong, the forecast is likely to be wrong. In this case your forecasts from 2001 through 2007 were too high, as shown in Figure 8–9, largely because of fierce competition in the photocopying industry.

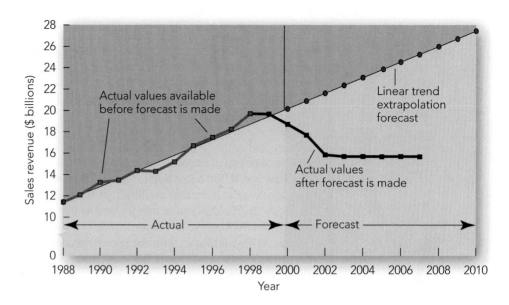

FIGURE 8–9
Linear trend extrapolation of sales revenues at Xerox, made at the start of 2000

Figure labels:
- Actual values available before forecast is made
- Linear trend extrapolation forecast
- Actual values after forecast is made
- Actual
- Forecast
- Sales revenue ($ billions)
- Year

learning review

11. What are the three kinds of sales forecasting techniques?

12. How do you make a lost-horse forecast?

LEARNING OBJECTIVES REVIEW

LO1 *Identify the reason for conducting marketing research.*
To be successful, products and marketing programs must meet the wants and needs of potential customers. So marketing research reduces risk by providing the vital information to help marketing managers understand those wants and needs and translate them into marketing actions.

LO2 *Describe the five-step marketing research approach that leads to marketing actions.*
Marketing researchers engage in a five-step decision-making process to collect information that improves marketing decisions. The first step is to define the problem, which requires setting the research objectives and identifying possible marketing actions. The second step is to develop the research plan, which involves specifying the constraints, identifying data needed for marketing decisions, and determining how to collect the data. The third step is to collect the relevant information, which includes considering pertinent secondary data (both internal and external) and primary data (by observing and questioning consumers) as well as using information technology and data mining to trigger marketing actions. The fourth step is to develop findings from the marketing research data collected. This involves analyzing the data and presenting the findings of the research. The fifth and last step is to take marketing actions, which involves making and implementing the action recommendations.

LO3 *Explain how marketing uses secondary and primary data.*
Secondary data have already been recorded before the start of the project and consist of two parts: (*a*) internal secondary data, which originate from within the organization, such as sales reports and customer comments, and (*b*) external secondary data, which are created by other organizations, such as the U.S. Census Bureau (provides data on the country's population, manufacturers, retailers, and so on) or business and trade publications (provide data on industry trends, market size, etc.). Primary data are collected specifically for the project and are obtained by either observing or questioning people.

LO4 *Discuss the uses of observations, questionnaires, panels, and experiments.*
Marketing researchers observe people in various ways, such as electronically using Nielsen people meters to measure TV viewing behavior or personally using mystery shoppers or ethnographic techniques. Questionnaires involve asking people questions (*a*) in person using interviews or focus groups or (*b*) via a questionnaire using a telephone, fax, print, e-mail, or an Internet survey. Panels involve a sample of consumers or stores that are repeatedly measured through time to see if their behaviors change. Experiments, such as test markets, involve measuring the effect of marketing variables such as price or advertising on sales.

LO5 *Explain how information technology and data mining link marketing information to meaningful marketing actions.*
Today's marketing managers are often overloaded with data—from internal sales and customer data to external data on TV viewing habits or grocery purchases from the scanner data at checkout counters. Information technology enables this massive amount of marketing data to be stored, accessed, and processed. The resulting databases can be queried using data mining to find statistical relationships useful for marketing decisions and actions.

LO6 *Describe three approaches to developing a sales forecast for a company.*
One approach uses subjective judgments of the decision maker, such as direct or lost-horse forecasts. Surveys of knowledgeable groups is a second method. It involves obtaining information such as the intentions of potential buyers or estimates of the salesforce. Statistical methods involving extending a pattern observed in past data into the future is a third example. The best-known statistical method is linear trend extrapolation.

FOCUSING ON KEY TERMS

data p. 168
marketing research p. 164
measures of success p. 166

observational data p. 170
primary data p. 168
questionnaire data p. 173

sales forecast p. 182
secondary data p. 168

APPLYING MARKETING KNOWLEDGE

1 (*a*) Why might a marketing researcher prefer to use secondary data rather than primary data in a study? (*b*) Why might the reverse be true?

2 Suppose your dean of admissions is considering surveying high school seniors about their perceptions of your school to design better informational brochures for them. What are the advantages and disadvantages of doing (*a*) telephone interviews and (*b*) an Internet survey of seniors who have requested information about the school?

3 Nielsen Media Research obtains ratings of local TV stations in small markets by having households fill out diary questionnaires. These give information on (*a*) who is watching TV and (*b*) what program. What are the limitations of this questionnaire method?

4 The format in which information is presented is often vital. (*a*) If you were a harried marketing manager and queried your information system, would you rather see the results in tables or charts and graphs? (*b*) What are one or two strengths and weaknesses of each format?

5 Wisk detergent decides to run a test market to see the effect of coupons and in-store advertising on sales. The index of sales is as follows:

Element in Test Market	Weeks before Coupon	Week of Coupon	Week after Coupon
Without in-store ads	100	144	108
With in-store ads	100	268	203

What are your conclusions and recommendations?

6 Suppose Fisher-Price wants to run a simple experiment to evaluate a proposed chatter telephone design. It has two different groups of children on which to run its experiment for one week each. The first group has the old toy telephone, whereas the second group is exposed to the newly designed pull toy with wheels, a noisemaker, and bobbing eyes. The dependent variable is the average number of minutes during the two-hour play period that one of the children is playing with the toy, and the results are as follows:

Element in Experiment	First Group	Second Group
Independent variable	Old design	New design
Dependent variable	13 minutes	62 minutes

Should Fisher-Price introduce the new design? Why?

7 Which of the following variables would linear trend extrapolation be more accurate for? (*a*) Annual population of the United States or (*b*) annual sales of cars produced in the United States by General Motors. Why?

To help you collect the most useful data for your marketing plan, develop a three-column table:

1 In column 1, list the information you would ideally like to have to fill holes in your marketing plan.
2 In column 2, identify the source for each bit of information in column 1, such as an Internet search, talking to prospective customers, looking at internal data, and so forth.

3 In column 3, set a priority on information you will have time to spend collecting by ranking them: 1 = most important; 2 = next most important, and so forth.

video case 8   Ford Consulting Group Inc.: From Data to Actions

"The fast pace of working as a marketing professional isn't getting any easier," agrees David Ford, as he talks with Mark Rehborg, Tony's Pizza brand manager. "The speed of communication, the availability of real-time market information, and the responsibility for a brand's profit make marketing one of the most challenging professional jobs today."

Mark responds, "Ten years ago, we could reach 80 percent of our target market with 3 television spots—but today, to reach the same 80 percent, we would have to buy 97 spots. We haven't the luxury to be complacent—our core consumer, the 6- to 12-year-old 'big kid,' is part of a savvy, wired culture that is changing rapidly."

DASHBOARDS: DATA INTO ACTIONS

David Ford, president of Ford Consulting Group (FCG), prepares business analysis, often in the form of a dashboard, to assist clients such as Tony's in translating the market and sales information into marketing actions. David works with Mark to grow Tony's sales and profit performance. Mark uses information to choose where to spend his funds to promote his products. Many times, the sales force requests additional promotion funds to help them hit their sales targets.

The information used most often for sales and promotion analysis comes from places like ACNielsen's Scan-Track and Information Resources' InfoScan (IRI) that summarize sales data from grocery stores and other outlets that scan purchases at the checkout.

FCG helps clients make sense of their existing information, *not* in helping clients collect more information. The project that follows is typical of the work Ford Consulting Group (www.fordconsultinggroup.com) undertakes for a client. The data are hypothetical, but the situation is a very typical one in the grocery products industry. Here's a snapshot of some of the terms in the case:

- "You" have just come on the job, as the new marketing person.
- "NE" is the Northeastern sales region of Tony's.
- "SW, NW, SW" are the other sales regions.

PART 1: A TYPICAL QUESTION, ON A TYPICAL DAY

Let's dive into the background of a typical question you might face, on a typical day. On the opposite page are some memos you are given (one from Mark to you) as background.

You dig into data files and develop Table 1 that shows how Tony's is doing in the company's four sales regions and the entire United States on key marketing dimensions. Without reading further, take a deep breath and try to answer question 1.

PART 2: UNCOVERING THE TRUTH

Let's assume your analysis (question 1) shows the NE is a problem, so we need to understand what's going on in the NE. Further effort enables you to develop Table 2. It shows the situation for the four largest supermarket chains in the Northeast sales region that carry Tony's. Now answer question 2.

Questions

1 Study Table 1. (*a*) How does the situation in the Northeast compare with the other regions in the United States? (*b*) What appears to be the reason(s) that sales are soft? (*c*) Write a 150-word e-mail with attachments to Mark Rehborg, your boss, giving your answers to *b*.

2 Study Table 2. (*a*) What do you conclude from this information? (*b*) Summarize your conclusions in a 150-word e-mail with attachments to Mark, who needs them for a meeting tomorrow with Margaret, the Northeast sales region manager. (*c*) What marketing actions might your memo suggest?

TO: Mark Rehborg, Tony's Brand Manager
FROM: Steve Quam, Tony's Field Sales
CC: Margaret Loiaza, NE Sales Region Manager
RE: Feedback on Sales Call at Food-Fast
Hi Mark—

Our sales call at Food-Fast wasn't so great. They don't see how our Tony's is going to sell well enough to justify the additional shelf-space. I also talked to Margaret and she said that second quarter may be weaker than planned across all the NE, and I should give you a heads-up. (She's on vacation this week, Aruba!) She's planning to schedule some time with you to talk about additional promotion money to do catch-up in the third quarter. She'll be there next week.

Steve

TO: You, the New Marketing Person
FROM: Mark Rehborg, Tony's Brand Manager
(Your Boss)
RE: Small Project due Friday
Hi You,

Can you help out here? I've got a meeting with Margaret on Friday afternoon, and she's concerned that Food-Fast and the whole NE is going to need some additional promotion dollars.

Lauretta started the analysis and was hurt in a kick-boxing accident yesterday and won't be back to work for a week. Her files are attached. Can you look through her files and summarize what's going on in the NE and the rest of the U.S.? Does Margaret need more promotion money?

Let's discuss Friday A.M.

Mark

TABLE 1. COMPARISON OF TONY'S PERFORMANCE, BY REGION

Region	Quarterly Change in Volume (%)	Distribution[a] (%)	Price ($)	Price Gap[b] ($)	Promotion Support[c] (%)	Promotion Volume[d] (%)
NE	3%	93%	$1.29	+8	7%	14%
SE	5	95	1.11	−1	9	16
NW	8	98	1.19	+1	8	15
SW	6	96	1.25	0	8	15
U.S.	6	97	1.19	0	8	15

[a] % of outlets carrying Tony's.
[b] Price gap = (Our price) − (Competitor's price).
[c] Promotion support = % of the time brand was promoted.
[d] Promotion volume = % of the volume sold on promotion.

TABLE 2. COMPARISON OF MAJOR SUPERMARKET CHAINS IN THE NORTHEAST

Super-Market Chain	Quarterly Change in Volume (%)	Distribution[a] (%)	Price ($)	Price Gap[b] ($)	Promotion Support[c] (%)	Promotion Volume[d] (%)
Save-a-lot	5%	95%	$1.39	+10	10%	19%
Food-Fast	0	90	1.28	−1	3	4
Get-Fresh	0	90	1.30	+1	3	4
Dollars-Off	7	97	1.34	+5	7	14

9

Segmenting Markets and Positioning Offerings

LEARNING OBJECTIVES

After reading this chapter you should be able to:

LO1 Explain what market segmentation is and when to use it.

LO2 Identify the five steps involved in segmenting and targeting markets.

LO3 Recognize the bases used to segment consumer and organizational markets.

LO4 Develop a market-product grid to identify a target market and recommend resulting actions.

LO5 Explain how marketing managers position products in the marketplace.

ZAPPOS.COM: POWERED BY SERVICE™

Signs of being an entrepreneur can show up early in life. Take the case of Tony Hsieh (opposite page), now chief executive officer (CEO) of shoe retailer Zappos.com. The company name is derived from the Spanish word *zapatos*, which means *shoes*.

At age 12, Hsieh brought in several hundred dollars a month with his button-making business. In college, Hsieh sold pizzas out of his dorm room. Fellow entrepreneur Alfred Lin bought pizzas from Hsieh and then sold them by the slice to other students. And where is pizza-slice marketer Lin today? He's the chief operating *and* chief financial officer at Zappos.com.[1]

A Clear Market Segmentation Strategy

Hsieh, Lin, and founder Nick Swinmurn gave Zappos a clear, specific market segmentation strategy: offer a huge selection of shoes to people who will buy them online. This focus on the segment of online buyers generated $840 million in 2007 sales, with a projected $1 billion plus in 2008.[2]

"With Zappos, the shoe store comes to you," says Pamela Leo, a New Jersey customer. "I can try the shoes in the comfort of my own home. . . . It's fabulous."[3] Besides the in-home convenience, Zappos offers free shipping both ways, 110 percent price protection, and a 365-day return policy. The shoe choices for its online customers are staggering. A recent Zappos home page described "Today at Zappos" as: 1,175 brands, 868,342 UPCs (universal product codes), 2,750,100 total products.

Blue-Ribbon Customer Service

Asked about details of the Zappos website, Tony Hsieh says, "We try to spend most of our time on stuff that will improve customer-service levels."[4] As shown on its home page, Zappos positions itself as "a service company that happens to sell . . . shoes, clothing, bags, accessories, and so on." In addition, the Zappos 1-800 number is displayed prominently on every page of its website. The design of the website lets customers easily search by shoe size. And the Zappos call center is never closed.

This focus on customer service for the Zappos niche of online customers is something the company lives, breathes, and implements. Some examples:

- Customer service and loyalty is so critical both the Zappos call center and headquarters are in the same place—Las Vegas.

- Customer service employees don't use scripts and don't try to keep calls short.

- Every new employee in Las Vegas spends four weeks on the phone as a customer service representative and a week in its Kentucky warehouse.

- Operating the warehouse 24/7 lets customers order shoes as late as 11 p.m. and still get their shoes the next day.

The tender loving care of its customers carries over to Zappos employees: All Zappos call center employees are invited to its Las Vegas vendor appreciation party held before the annual trade show.

The Zappos strategy illustrates successful market segmentation and targeting, the first topics in Chapter 9. The chapter ends with the topic of positioning the organization, product, or brand.

WHY SEGMENT MARKETS?

A business firm segments its markets so it can respond more effectively to the wants of groups of potential buyers and thus increase its sales and profits. Not-for-profit organizations also segment the clients they serve to satisfy client needs more effectively while achieving the organization's goals. Let's describe (1) what market segmentation is and (2) when to segment markets.

What Market Segmentation Means

market segmentation
Combining potential buyers into groups that have common needs and will respond similarly to a marketing action

market segments
Groups of prospective buyers that result from market segmentation

product differentiation
Strategy of using different marketing mix activities, such as product features and advertising, to help consumers perceive a product as being different and better than competing products

People have different needs and wants, even though it would be easier for marketers if they didn't. **Market segmentation** involves aggregating prospective buyers into groups that (1) have common needs and (2) will respond similarly to a marketing action. **Market segments** are the relatively homogeneous groups of prospective buyers that result from the market segmentation process. Each market segment consists of people who are relatively similar to each other in terms of their consumption behavior.

The existence of different market segments has caused firms to use a marketing strategy of **product differentiation**. This strategy involves a firm using different marketing mix activities, such as product features and advertising, to help consumers perceive the product as being different and better than competing products. The perceived differences may involve physical features or nonphysical ones, such as image or price.

Segmentation: Linking Needs to Actions The process of segmenting a market and selecting specific segments as targets is the link between the various buyers' needs and the organization's marketing program, as shown in Figure 9–1. Market segmentation is only a means to an end: to lead to tangible marketing actions that can increase sales and profitability.

FIGURE 9–1
Market segmentation links market needs to an organization's marketing program—specific marketing mix actions to satisfy those needs.

Identify market needs	Link needs to actions	Execute marketing program actions
Benefits in terms of: • Product features • Expense • Quality • Savings in time and convenience	Take steps to segment and target markets	A marketing mix in terms of: • Product • Price • Promotion • Place (Distribution)

Effective market segmentation forms meaningful groupings and develops specific marketing mix actions. People or organizations should be grouped into a market segment according to the similarity of their needs and the benefits they look for in making a purchase. For example, the Zappos target customer segment consists of people who want (1) a wide selection of shoes, (2) to shop online in the convenience of their own home, and (3) to receive the guarantee of quick delivery and free returns.

The market segments must relate to specific marketing actions that the organization can take. These actions may involve separate offerings or other aspects of the marketing mix, such as price, promotion, or distribution strategies. Zappos' actions include offering a huge inventory of shoes and other products, using an online selling strategy, and providing overnight distribution. This enables Zappos to create a positive customer experience and generate repeat purchases.

The Successful Zappos Footwear Segmentation Strategy In 1999, Zappos founder Nick Swinmurn spent an hour in several shoe stores in a mall and went home empty-handed because he couldn't find a pair of shoes with both the right size and style. So Swinmurn quit his day job and decided to start Zappos. Now, on any given day, about 65 percent of Zappos shoppers are repeat customers, and 60 percent of them are female.

In 2007, online sales accounted for $3.5 billion of the $44 billion U.S. shoe market. With $840 million in sales, Zappos achieved an online market share of 24 percent! What about the future? Zappos executives believe that the speed with which a customer receives an online purchase plays a big role in gaining repeat customers. So the company will continue to stress this point of difference, made possible by stocking in its warehouse every item it sells. Zappos' vision for the future:[5]

- One day, 30 percent of all retail transactions in the United States will be online.
- People will buy from the firm with the best service and the best selection.
- Zappos will be that company.

By 2010, footwear sales could reach $5 billion (online) and $50 billion (total) respectively.[6] And if customers associate Zappos with the absolute best service among online sellers with its footwear, clothing and other offerings, Zappos' continued success is highly probable.

When and How to Segment Markets

These *different* covers for the *same* magazine issue show a very effective market segmentation strategy. For which specific one it is and why it works, see the text.

The one-size-fits-all mass markets—like that for Tide laundry detergent of 30 to 40 years ago—no longer exist. The global marketing officer at Procter & Gamble, which

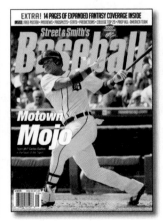

markets Tide, says, "Every one of our brands is targeted." Welcome to today's era of market segmentation and target marketing.[7]

A business firm goes to the trouble and expense of segmenting its markets when it expects that this will increase its sales, profit, and return on investment. When expenses are greater than the potentially increased sales from segmentation, a firm should not attempt to segment its market. Three specific segmentation strategies that illustrate this point are: (1) one product and multiple market segments, (2) multiple products and multiple market segments, and (3) "segments of one," or mass customization.

One Product and Multiple Market Segments

When an organization produces only a single product or service and attempts to sell it to two or more market segments, it avoids the extra costs of developing and producing additional versions of the product. In this case, the incremental costs of taking the product into new market segments are typically those of a separate promotional campaign or a new channel of distribution.

Magazines and books are single products frequently directed to two or more distinct market segments. *Street & Smith's Baseball* annual issue uses different covers for its 16 regions of the U. S. that feature a baseball star for each region. Harry Potter's phenomenal seven-book success is based both on author J. K. Rowling's fiction-writing wizardry and her publishers' creativity in marketing to preteen, teen, and adult segments of readers around the world. By 2008, more than 400 million Harry Potter books had been sold in 64 languages.[8] In the United States, the books were often at the top of *The New York Times* fiction bestseller list—for adults. Although separate covers for magazines or advertisements for books are expensive, they pale compared with the costs of producing multiple magazines or books for multiple market segments.

Multiple Products and Multiple Market Segments

Ford's different lines of cars, SUVs, and pickup trucks are each targeted at a different type of customer—examples of multiple products aimed at multiple market segments. Producing these different vehicles is clearly more expensive than producing only a single vehicle but is effective if it meets customers' needs better, doesn't reduce quality or increase price, and adds to Ford's sales revenues and profits.

Does Harry Potter appeal only to the kids' segment? See the text for the answer to this amazing publishing success.

Marketers increasingly emphasize the two-tier marketing strategies—what some call "Tiffany/Wal-Mart strategies." Many firms are now offering different variations of the same basic offering to high-end and low-end segments. Gap's Banana Republic chain sells blue jeans for $58, whereas its Old Navy stores sell a slightly different version for $22.

Segments of One: Mass Customization

American marketers are rediscovering today what their ancestors running the corner general store knew a century ago: Each customer has unique needs and wants, and desires special tender loving care—the essence of *customer relationship management* (CRM). Economies of scale in manufacturing and marketing during the past century made mass-produced goods so affordable that most customers were willing to compromise their individual tastes and settle for standardized products. Today's Internet ordering and flexible manufacturing and marketing processes have made *mass customization* possible, which means tailoring goods or services to the tastes of individual customers on a high-volume scale.

Mass customization is the next step beyond *build-to-order* (BTO), manufacturing a product only when there is an order from a customer. Dell uses BTO systems that trim work-in-progress inventories and shorten delivery times to customers. To do this, Dell restricts its computer manufacturing line to only a few basic models that can be

Ann Taylor Stores Corp.'s Loft chain tries to reach trendy, casual customers while its flagship Ann Taylor chain targets a more sophisticated woman. Do these store fronts convey this difference? For the potential dangers of this two-segment strategy, see the text.

assembled in four minutes. This gives customers a good choice with quick delivery. But even this system falls a bit short of total mass customization because customers do not have an unlimited number of features they can choose from.[9]

The Segmentation Trade-Off: CRM versus Synergies The key to successful product differentiation and market segmentation strategies is finding the ideal balance between satisfying a customer's individual wants and achieving organizational **synergy**, the increased customer value achieved through performing organizational functions like marketing or manufacturing more efficiently. The "increased customer value" can take many forms: more products, improved quality on existing products, lower prices, easier access to products through improved distribution, and so on. So the ultimate criterion for an organization's marketing success in customer relationship management is that customers should be better off as a result of the increased synergies.

The organization should also achieve increased revenues and profits from the product differentiation and market segmentation strategies it uses. When the increased customer value involves adding new products or a new chain of stores, the product differentiation–market segmentation trade-off raises a critical issue: Are the new products or new chain simply stealing customers and sales from the older, existing ones? This is known as cannibalization.

However, the lines between customer segments can often blur, which can lead to problems, such as the Ann Taylor flagship store competing with its Loft outlets. The flagship Ann Taylor chain targets polished, sophisticated women while its sister Ann Taylor Loft chain targets women wanting moderately priced, trendy, casual clothes they can wear to the office. The nightmare: annual sales of the Loft stores recently passed those of the Ann Taylor chain, which has struggled to reach its target customers. The result: more than 100 stores from both chains are to be closed by 2010.[10]

synergy
The increased customer value achieved through performing organizational functions more efficiently

learning review

1. Market segmentation involves aggregating prospective buyers into groups that have two key characteristics. What are they?

2. In terms of market segments and products, what are the three market segmentation strategies?

STEPS IN SEGMENTING AND TARGETING MARKETS

Figure 9–2 identifies the five-step process used to segment a market and select the target segments on which it wants to focus. Segmenting a market requires both detailed analysis and large doses of common sense and managerial judgment. So market segmentation is both science and art!

Let's have you put on your marketing hat to use market segmentation to choose target markets and take useful marketing actions for the Wendy's restaurant we assume you just bought. Your Wendy's is located next to a large urban university, one that offers both day and evening classes. Your restaurant offers the basic Wendy's fare: hamburgers, chicken and deli sandwiches, salads, french fries, and Frosty desserts. Even though you are part of a chain that has some restrictions on menu and décor, you are free to set your hours of business and to develop local advertising. How can market segmentation help?

Step 1: Group Potential Buyers into Segments

It's not always a good idea to segment a market. Grouping potential buyers into meaningful segments involves meeting some specific criteria that answer the question, "Would segmentation be worth doing and is it possible?" If so, a marketer must find specific variables that can be used to create these various segments.

Criteria to Use in Forming the Segments
A marketing manager should develop segments for a market that meet five essential criteria:[11]

- *Simplicity and cost-effectiveness of assigning potential buyers to segments.* A marketing manager must be able to put a market segmentation plan into effect. This means identifying the characteristics of potential buyers in a market and then cost-effectively assigning them to a segment.
- *Potential for increased profit.* The best segmentation approach is the one that maximizes the opportunity for future profit and return on investment (ROI). If this potential is maximized without segmentation, don't segment. For nonprofit organizations, the criterion is the potential for serving client users more effectively.
- *Similarity of needs of potential buyers within a segment.* Potential buyers within a segment should be similar in terms of a marketing action, such as product features sought or advertising media used.
- *Difference of needs of buyers among segments.* If the needs of the various segments aren't very different, combine them into fewer segments. A different segment usually requires a different marketing action that, in turn, means greater costs. If increased sales don't offset extra costs, combine segments and reduce the number of marketing actions.
- *Potential of a marketing action to reach a segment.* Reaching a segment requires a simple but effective marketing action. If no such action exists, don't segment.

FIGURE 9–2

The five key steps in segmenting and targeting markets link market needs of customers to the organization's marketing program.

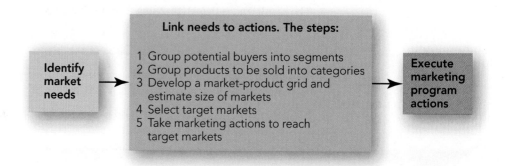

Ways to Segment Consumer Markets Four general bases of segmentation and their respective variables can be used to segment U.S. consumer markets. These four segmentation bases are: (1) *geographic segmentation*, which is based on where prospective customers live or work (region, city size); (2) *demographic segmentation*, which is based on some *objective* physical (gender, race), measurable (age, income), or other classification attribute (birth era, occupation) of prospective customers; (3) *psychographic segmentation*, which is based on some subjective mental or emotional attributes (personality), aspirations (lifestyle), or needs of prospective customers; and (4) *behavioral segmentation*, which is based on some observable actions or attitudes by prospective customers—such as where they buy, what benefits they seek, how frequently they buy, and why they buy. Some examples are:

What special benefit does a MicroFridge offer, and to which market segment might this appeal? The answer appears in the text.

- *Geographic segmentation: region.* Campbell's found that its canned nacho cheese sauce for tortilla chips was too hot for Americans in the East and not hot enough for those in the West and Southwest. The result: today, Campbell's plants in Texas and California produce the hotter sauce and its other plants produce the milder one to better serve these two segments.
- *Demographic segmentation: household size.* More than half of all U.S. households are made up of only one or two persons, so Campbell's packages meals with only one or two servings—from Great Starts breakfasts to L'Orient dinners.
- *Psychographic segmentation: lifestyle.* Claritas' lifestyle segmentation is based on the belief that "birds of a feather flock together." People of similar lifestyles tend to live near one another, have similar interests, and buy similar offerings, which is of great value to marketers. Claritas' PRIZM NE classifies every household in the United States into one of 66 unique market segments.
- *Behavioral segmentation: product features.* Understanding what features are important to different customers is a useful way to segment markets because it can lead directly to specific marketing actions, such as a new product, an ad campaign, or a distribution system. For example, college dorm residents frequently want to keep and prepare their own food to save money or have a late-night snack. However, their dorm rooms are often woefully short of space. MicroFridge understands this and markets a combination microwave, refrigerator, and freezer targeted to these students.

usage rate

Quantity consumed or times visited during a specific period

- *Behavioral segmentation: usage rate.* **Usage rate** is the quantity consumed or patronage—store visits—during a specific period. It varies significantly among different customer groups. Airlines have developed frequent-flyer programs to encourage passengers to use the same airline repeatedly to create loyal customers. This strategy, called *frequency marketing*, focuses on usage rate. One key conclusion: some measure of usage by, or sales obtained from, various segments is central to segmentation analysis.

80/20 rule

Idea that 80 percent of a firm's sales are obtained from 20 percent of its customers

Usage rate is sometimes referred to in terms of the **80/20 rule**, a concept that suggests 80 percent of a firm's sales are obtained from 20 percent of its customers. The percentages in the 80/20 rule are not really fixed at exactly 80 percent and 20 percent but suggest that a small fraction of customers provides a large fraction of a firm's sales.

The Simmons Market Research Bureau semiannually surveys about 25,000 adults to obtain usage rate data. The purpose is to discover how the offerings they buy and the media they watch relate to their behavioral, psychographic, and demographic

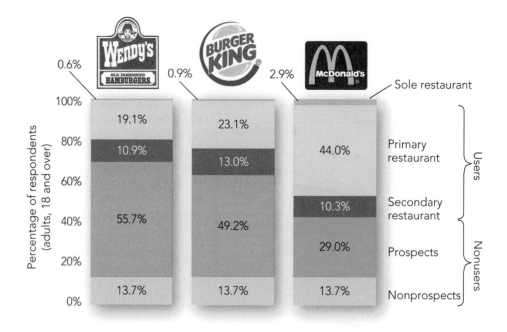

What variables might Xerox use to segment organizational markets for its answer to color copying problems? For the possible answer and related marketing actions, see the text.

characteristics.[12] For example, a recent Simmons survey showed that the 15 percent of the U.S. population who are heavy users of fast-food restaurants provide 35 percent of the consumption volume—more than twice that of the average customer. Thus, as a Wendy's restaurant owner, you want to constantly keep the heavy-user segment in mind and focus most of your marketing efforts on reaching it.

As part of its survey, Simmons asked adults which fast-food restaurant(s) were (1) the sole or only restaurant, (2) the primary one, or (3) one of several secondary ones they went to. As a Wendy's owner, the information depicted in Figure 9–3 should give you some ideas in developing a strategy. For example, the Wendy's bar in Figure 9–3 shows that your sole (0.6 percent), primary (19.1 percent), and secondary (10.9 percent) user segments are somewhat behind Burger King and far behind McDonald's. Thus, a natural strategy is to look at these two competitors and devise a marketing program to win customers from them.

The nonusers part of the Wendy's bar in Figure 9–3 also provides ideas. It shows that 13.7 percent of adult Americans don't go to fast-food restaurants in a typical month and are really nonprospects—unlikely to ever patronize your restaurant. But the 55.7 percent of the Wendy's bar shown as prospects may be worth detailed thought. These adults use the product category (fast food) but do not go to Wendy's. New menu items or promotional strategies may succeed in converting these prospects into users that patronize Wendy's.

Variables to Use in Forming Segments   To help you analyze your Wendy's customers, you need to identify which variables to use to segment them. Because the restaurant is located near a large urban university, the most logical starting point for segmentation is really behavioral: are the prospective customers students or nonstudents?

To segment the students, you could try a variety of (1) geographic variables, such as city or zip code; (2) demographic variables, such as gender, age, year in school, or college major; or (3) psychographic variables, such as personality or needs. But none of these variables really meets the five criteria used to form segments listed previously—particularly, the one about developing marketing actions to reach each segment. However, the behavioral variable of "students" versus "nonstudents" does meet these criteria. Broken down, the "students" variable includes:

- Students living in dormitories (university residence halls, sororities, fraternities).
- Students living near the university in apartments.
- Day commuter students living outside the area.
- Night commuter students living outside the area.

These segmentation variables are a combination of where the student lives and the time he or she is on campus (and near your restaurant). Broken down, the "nonstudents" variable includes:

- Faculty and staff members who work at the university.
- People who live in the area but aren't connected with the university.
- People who work in the area but aren't connected with the university.

People in each of these segments aren't quite as similar as those in the student segments, which makes them harder to reach with a marketing program or action. Think about (1) whether the needs of all these segments are different and (2) how various advertising media can be used to reach these groups effectively.

Ways to Segment Organizational Markets A number of variables can be used to segment organizational markets. For example, a product manager at Xerox responsible for its new line of color printers might use these segmentation bases and corresponding variables:

- *Geographic segmentation: statistical area.* Firms located in a metropolitan statistical area might receive a personal sales call, whereas those in a micropolitan statistical area might be contacted by telephone.
- *Demographic segmentation: NAICS code.* Firms categorized by the North American Industry Classification System code as manufacturers that deal with customers throughout the world might have different document printing needs than do retailers or lawyers serving local customers.
- *Demographic segmentation: number of employees.* The size of the firm is related to the volume of digital documents produced, so firms with varying numbers of employees might be specific target markets for different Xerox systems.
- *Behavioral segmentation: usage rate.* Similar to this segmentation variable for consumer markets, features are often of major importance in organizational markets. So Xerox can target organizations needing fast printing, copying, and scanning in color—the benefits and features emphasized in the ad for its new Xerox WorkCentre 7655 Color MFP system.

learning review

3. The process of segmenting and targeting markets is a bridge between what two marketing activities?

4. What is the difference between the demographic and behavioral bases of market segmentation?

Step 2: Group Products Sold into Categories

What does your Wendy's restaurant sell? The obvious answer is that you sell individual products, such as hamburgers, french fries, and Frostys. But for marketing purposes, you really sell a group of individual products that comprise a "meal." This distinction is critical. Finding a means of grouping the products a firm sells into meaningful categories is as important as grouping customers into segments. If the firm has only one offering, this isn't a problem. But when it has dozens or hundreds, they must be grouped so that buyers can relate to them. This is why department stores and supermarkets organize related products into groups and place them in specific departments or aisles.

Your Wendy's customers are really buying an eating experience—a meal occasion that satisfies a need at a particular time of day. So, the product grouping that makes the most marketing sense is the five "meals" based on the time of day consumers buy them: breakfast, lunch, between-meal snack, dinner, and after-dinner snack. These groupings permit you to market an entire meal and not just individual products like hamburgers or french fries.

LO4

Step 3: Develop a Market-Product Grid and Estimate the Size of Markets

market-product grid
Framework relating the segments of a market to products or marketing actions of the firm

A **market-product grid** is a framework to relate the market segments of potential buyers to products offered or potential marketing actions by an organization. In a complete market-product grid analysis, each cell in the grid can show the estimated market size of a given product sold to a specific market segment. Let's first look at forming a market-product grid for your Wendy's restaurant and then at estimating market sizes.

Forming a Market-Product Grid   Developing a market-product grid means identifying and labeling the markets (or horizontal rows) and product groupings (or vertical columns), as shown in Figure 9–4. From our earlier discussion we've chosen to divide the row market segments as students versus nonstudents, with subdivisions of each. The columns—or "products"—are really the meals (or eating occasions) customers enjoy at the restaurant.

Estimating Market Sizes   Now the size of the market in each cell (the unique market-product combination) of the market-product grid must be estimated. For your Wendy's restaurant, this involves estimating the sales of each kind of meal expected to be sold to each student and nonstudent market segment.

The market size estimates in Figure 9–4 vary from a large market ("3") to no market at all ("0") for each cell in the market-product grid. These may be simple guesstimates

FIGURE 9–4
Selecting a target market for your Wendy's fast-food restaurant next to an urban university. The numbers show the estimated size market in that cell, which leads to selecting the shaded target market shown in the figure.

Market Segments	Break-fast	Lunch	Between-Meal Snack	Dinner	After-Dinner Snack
PRODUCTS: MEALS					
Student					
Dormitory	0	1	3	0	3
Apartment	1	3	3	1	1
Day commuter	0	3	2	1	0
Night commuter	0	0	1	3	2
Nonstudent					
Faculty or staff	0	3	1	1	0
Live in area	0	1	2	2	1
Work in area	1	3	0	1	0

Key: 3 = Large market; 2 = Medium market; 1 = Small market; 0 = No market.

if you don't have the time or money to conduct formal marketing research (as discussed in Chapter 8). But even such crude estimates of the size of specific markets using a market-product grid help determine which target market segments to select and which product groupings to offer.

Step 4: Select Target Markets

A firm must take care to choose its target market segments carefully. If it picks too narrow a set of segments, it may fail to reach the volume of sales and profits it needs. If it selects too broad a set of segments, it may spread its marketing efforts so thin that the extra expense exceeds the increased sales and profits.

Criteria to Use in Selecting the Target Segments   There are two different kinds of criteria in the market segmentation process: those used to (1) divide the market into segments (discussed earlier) and (2) actually pick the target segments. Even experienced marketing executives often confuse these two different sets of criteria. Five criteria can be used to select the target segments for your Wendy's restaurant:

- *Market size.* The estimated size of the market in the segment is an important factor in deciding whether it's worth going after. There is really no market for breakfasts among dormitory students (Figure 9–4), so why devote any marketing effort toward reaching a small or nonexistent segment?
- *Expected growth.* Although the size of the market in the segment may be small now, perhaps it is growing significantly or is expected to grow in the future. Sales of fast-food meals eaten outside the restaurants are projected to exceed those eaten inside. And Wendy's is the fast-food leader in average time to serve a drive-thru order—it is 16.7 seconds faster than McDonald's. This speed and convenience is potentially very important to night commuters in adult education programs.[13]
- *Competitive position.* Is there a lot of competition in the segment now or is there likely to be in the future? The less the competition, the more attractive the segment is. For example, if the college dormitories announce a new policy of "no meals on weekends," this segment is suddenly more promising for your restaurant. Wendy's recently introduced E-Pay pay-by-credit-card service at its restaurants to keep up with this new service at McDonald's.
  - *Cost of reaching the segment.* A segment that is inaccessible to a firm's marketing actions should not be pursued. For example, the few nonstudents who live in the area may not be reachable with ads in newspapers or other media. As a result, do not waste money trying to advertise to them.
  - *Compatibility with the organization's objectives and resources.* If your Wendy's restaurant doesn't yet have the cooking equipment to make breakfasts and has a policy against spending more money on restaurant equipment, then don't try to reach the breakfast segment. As is often the case in marketing decisions, a particular segment may appear attractive according to some criteria and very unattractive according to others.

Choose the Segments   Ultimately, a marketing executive has to use these criteria to choose the segments for special marketing efforts. As shown in Figure 9–4, let's assume you've written off the breakfast product grouping for two reasons: it's too small a market and it's incompatible with your objectives and resources. In terms of competitive position and cost of reaching the segment, you choose to focus on the four

How can Wendy's target different market segments like night customers or commuting college students with different advertising programs? For the answer, see the text and Figure 9–5.

A late night oasis on the highway of hunger.

Wendy's Late Night Pick-up Window is open 'til midnight or later. So, you can get a *hot 'n juicy Classic Single, Classic Double with cheese or Classic Triple with cheese,* and eat great, even late.

student segments and *not* the three nonstudent segments (although you're certainly not going to turn away business from these segments!). Your target market is shaded in Figure 9–4.

Step 5: Take Marketing Actions to Reach Target Markets

The purpose of developing a market-product grid is to trigger marketing actions to increase sales and profits. This means that someone must develop and execute an action plan in the form of a marketing program.

Your Immediate Wendy's Segmentation Strategy You've already reached one significant decision: because there is a limited market for breakfast, you won't open for business until 10:30 a.m. In fact, Wendy's first attempt at a breakfast menu was a disaster and was discontinued in 1986. Wendy's evaluates possible new menu items continuously to compete with not only McDonald's and Burger King but also convenience stores and gas stations that sell reheatable packaged foods and sandwiches.

Another essential decision is where and what meals to advertise to reach specific market segments. An ad in the student newspaper could reach all the student segments, but you might consider this tactic too expensive and want a more focused effort to reach smaller segments. If you choose the three market segment-product grouping combinations shown in Figure 9–5 for special marketing attention, advertising actions to reach them might include:

- *Day commuters* (offer all product groupings or meals). Run ads inside commuter buses and put flyers under the windshield wipers of cars in parking lots used by day commuters. These ads and flyers promote all the meals at your restaurant to a single segment of students, a horizontal cut through the market-product grid.

FIGURE 9–5
Advertising actions to reach specific student segments. These actions can vary from trying to reach an entire market segment or customers for a specific meal to a narrow niche (dinners for night commuters).

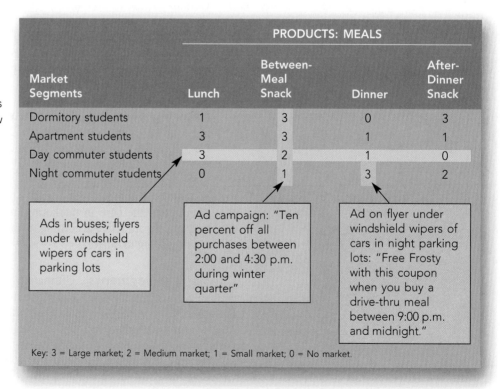

Market Segments	PRODUCTS: MEALS			
	Lunch	Between-Meal Snack	Dinner	After-Dinner Snack
Dormitory students	1	3	0	3
Apartment students	3	3	1	1
Day commuter students	3	2	1	0
Night commuter students	0	1	3	2

Ads in buses; flyers under windshield wipers of cars in parking lots

Ad campaign: "Ten percent off all purchases between 2:00 and 4:30 p.m. during winter quarter"

Ad on flyer under windshield wipers of cars in night parking lots: "Free Frosty with this coupon when you buy a drive-thru meal between 9:00 p.m. and midnight."

Key: 3 = Large market; 2 = Medium market; 1 = Small market; 0 = No market.

- *Between-meal snacks* (target all four student market segments). To promote eating during this downtime for your restaurant, offer "Ten percent off all purchases between 2:00 and 4:30 p.m. during winter quarter." This ad promotes a single meal to all four student segments, a vertical cut through the market-product grid.
- *Dinners to night commuters.* The most focused of all three campaigns, this ad promotes a single meal to the single segment of night commuter students. The campaign might consist of a windshield flyer with a coupon that offers a free Frosty when the customer buys a meal between 9:00 p.m. and midnight.

Depending on how your advertising actions work, you can repeat, modify, or drop them and design new campaigns for other segments you deem are worth the effort. This advertising example is just a small piece of a complete marketing program for your Wendy's restaurant. And Wendy's focus on the after-dinner snack meal occasion (the column highlighted in Figure 9–5 and the Wendy's ad) has been successful because customers like that the late-night pickup window is open until midnight or later.

Future Strategies for Your Wendy's Restaurant Changing customer tastes and competition mean you must alter your strategies when necessary. This involves looking at both (1) what Wendy's headquarters is doing and (2) what might be changing in the area around your restaurant.

How has Apple moved from its 1977 Apple II to today's Mac Pro? The Marketing Matters box and text discussion provide insights into Apple's current market segmentation strategy.

Wendy's plans to focus on high-quality hamburgers and salads and position the chain to be the preferred restaurant for lunch, between-meal snacks, dinner, and late night.[14] Some other innovations now coming off Wendy's drawing boards include:[15]

- Create a new value menu to target younger, 18- to 34-year-old customers.
- Energize the afternoon and late-night snack menus to target the heavy user "Snackers" segments.
- Offer breakfasts with new high-quality, quick-serve menu items to lure commuting breakfast eaters—and overcome the too-slow-to-cook 1980s breakfast disaster.

With these corporate plans, maybe you'd better rethink your market segmentation decisions on hours of operation and breakfasts. Also, if new businesses have moved into your area, what about a new strategy to reach people that work in the area? Or a new promotion for the night owls and early birds—the 8 p.m. to 5 a.m. customers—that now generate one-sixth of revenues at some McDonald's restaurants?[16]

Apple's Ever-Changing Segmentation Strategy Steve Jobs and Steve Wozniak didn't realize they were developing today's multibillion-dollar PC industry when they invented the Apple I in a garage on April Fool's Day in 1976. Hobbyists, the initial target market, were not interested in the product. However, when the Apple II was displayed at a computer trade show in 1977, consumers loved it and Apple Computer was born. Typical of young companies, Apple focused on its products and had little concern for its markets. Its creative, young engineers were often likened to "Boy Scouts without adult supervision."[17]

Steve Jobs left Apple in 1985, the company languished, and it constantly altered its market-product strategies. When Steve Jobs returned in 1997, he detailed his vision for a reincarnated Apple by describing a new market segmentation strategy that he called the "Apple Product Matrix." This strategy consisted of developing two general types of computers (desktops and portables) targeted at two general kinds of market segments—the consumer and professional sectors.

Apple's Segmentation Strategy—Camp Runamok No Longer

Camp Runamok was the nickname given to Apple in the early 1980s because the innovative company had no coherent series of product lines directed at identifiable market segments. Today, Apple has targeted its various lines of Macintosh computers at specific market segments, as shown in the accompanying market-product grid. Because the market-product grid shifts as a firm's strategy changes, the one here is based on Apple's product lines in mid-2008. The grid suggests the market segmentation strategy Steve Jobs is using to compete in the digital age.

MARKETS		HARDWARE PRODUCTS				
SECTOR	SEGMENT	Mac Pro	MacBook Pro	iMac	MacBook	MacBook Air
CONSUMER	Individuals	✓	✓	✓	✓	✓
	Small/home office	✓	✓	✓	✓	✓
	Students			✓	✓	
	Teachers		✓	✓		
PROFESSIONAL	Medium/large business	✓	✓	✓		✓
	Creative	✓	✓	✓		
	College faculty	✓	✓	✓		✓
	College staff			✓	✓	

In most segmentation situations, a single product does not fit into an exclusive market niche. Rather, product lines and market segments overlap. So Apple's market segmentation strategy enables it to offer different products to meet the needs of different market segments, as shown in the Marketing Matters box.

Market-Product Synergies: A Balancing Act

Recognizing opportunities for key synergies—that is, efficiencies—is vital to success in selecting target market segments and making marketing decisions. Market-product grids illustrate where such synergies can be found. How? Let's consider Apple's market-product grid in the accompanying Marketing Matters box and examine the difference between marketing synergies and product synergies shown there.

- *Marketing synergies.* Running horizontally across the grid, each row represents an opportunity for efficiency in terms of a market segment. Were Apple to focus on just one group of consumers, such as the medium/large business segment, its marketing efforts could be streamlined. Apple would not have to spend time learning about the buying habits of students or college faculty. So it could probably create a single ad to reach the medium/large business target segment (the yellow row), highlighting the only products they'd need to worry about developing: the Mac Pro, the MacBook Pro, the iMac, and the MacBook Air. Although clearly not Apple's strategy today, new firms often focus only on a single customer segment.

- *Product synergies.* Running vertically down the market-product grid, each column represents an opportunity for efficiency in research and development (R&D) and production. If Apple wanted to simplify its product line, reduce R&D and production expenses, and manufacture only one computer, which might it choose? Based on the market-product grid, Apple might do well to focus on the iMac (the orange column), because every segment purchases it.

Marketing synergies often come at the expense of product synergies because a single customer segment will likely require a variety of products, each of which will have to be designed and manufactured. The company saves money on marketing but spends more in production. Conversely, if product synergies are emphasized, marketing will have to address the concerns of a wide variety of consumers, which costs more time and money. Marketing managers responsible for developing a company's product line must balance both product and marketing synergies as they try to increase the company's profits.

learning review

5. What are some criteria used to decide which segments to choose for targets?

6. What factor is estimated or measured for each of the cells in a market-product grid?

7. How are marketing and product synergies different in a market-product grid?

POSITIONING THE PRODUCT

LO5

product positioning
The place a product occupies in consumers' minds on important features relative to competing products

product repositioning
Changing the place a product occupies in consumers' minds relative to competitive products

When a company introduces a new product, a decision critical to its long-term success is how prospective buyers view it in relation to those products offered by its competitors. **Product positioning** refers to the place an offering occupies in consumers' minds on important attributes relative to competitive products. By understanding where consumers see a company's product or brand today, a marketing manager can seek to change its future position in their minds. This requires **product repositioning**, *changing* the place an offering occupies in a consumer's mind relative to competitive products.

Two Approaches to Product Positioning

There are two main approaches to positioning a new product in the market. *Head-to-head positioning* involves competing directly with competitors on similar product attributes in the same target market. Using this strategy, Dollar competes directly with Avis and Hertz.

Differentiation positioning involves seeking a less-competitive, smaller market niche in which to locate a brand. McDonald's tried to appeal to the health-conscious segment when it introduced the low-fat McLean Deluxe hamburger to avoid competing directly with Wendy's and Burger King. However, it was eventually dropped from the menu. Companies also follow a differentiation positioning strategy among brands within their own product line to minimize the cannibalization of a brand's sales or market shares.

Writing a Positioning Statement

Marketing managers often convert their positioning ideas for the offering into a succinct written positioning statement. The positioning statement not only is used internally within the marketing department but also for others, outside it, such as research

More "zip" for chocolate milk? The text and Figure 9–7 describe how American dairies have been successfully repositioning chocolate milk to appeal to American adults.

perceptual map
Means of displaying the position of products or brands in consumers' minds

and development engineers or advertising agencies.[18] Here is the Volvo positioning statement for the North American market:

> For upscale American families who desire a carefree driving experience, Volvo is a premium-priced automobile that offers the utmost in safety and dependability.

This focuses Volvo's North American marketing strategy and has led to adding side-door airbags for its cars. Also, Volvo advertising almost always mentions safety and dependability—as seen in its "Volvo for life" campaigns.

Product Positioning Using Perceptual Maps   A key to positioning a product or brand effectively is the perceptions of customers. In determining its position and the preferences of customers, companies obtain three types of data from consumers:

1. Identification of the important attributes for a product class.
2. Judgments of existing products or brands with respect to these attributes.
3. Ratings of an "ideal" product's or brand's attributes.

The firm can then develop market strategies to move its product or brand to an ideal position. From these data, it is possible to develop a **perceptual map**, a means of displaying or graphing in two dimensions the location of products or brands in the minds of consumers to enable a manager to see how consumers perceive competing products or brands and then take marketing actions. Look at Figure 9–6 and develop a positioning strategy to make chocolate milk more appealing to adults.

Repositioning Chocolate Milk for Adults   Figure 9–6 shows the positions that consumer beverages might occupy in the minds of Americans adults. Note that even these positions vary from one consumer to another. But for simplicity, let's assume these are the typical positions on the beverage perceptual map of adult Americans.

U.S. dairies, struggling to increase milk sales, hit on a wild idea: Target adults by positioning chocolate milk to the location of the star shown in the perceptual map in Figure 9–7, the position of letter "B" in Figure 9–6. Their arguments are nutritionally powerful. For women, chocolate milk provides calcium, critically important in female diets. And dieters get a more filling, nutritious beverage than with a soft drink for about

FIGURE 9–6

A perceptual map of the location of beverages in the minds of American adults. Toward which letter would you try to move the perception of chocolate milk to make it more appealing to these adults?

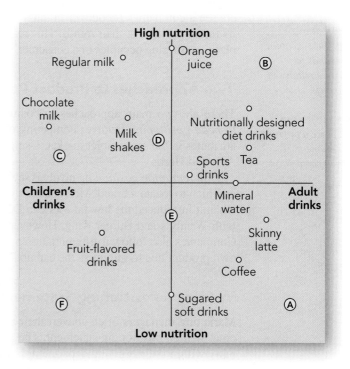

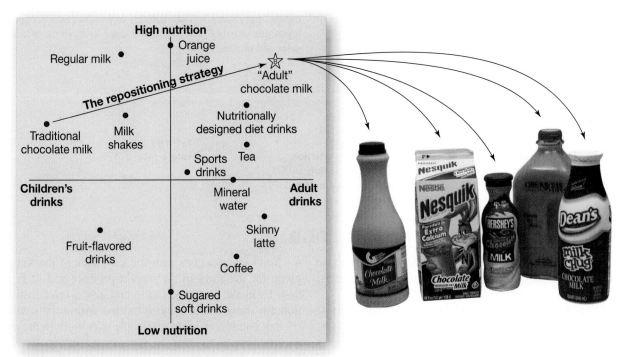

FIGURE 9–7

The strategy American dairies are using to reposition chocolate milk to reach adults: Have adults view chocolate milk both as more nutritional and "more adult."

the same calories.[19] The result: Chocolate milk sales increased dramatically, much of it because of adult consumption.[20] Part of this is due to giving chocolate milk "nutritional respectability" for adults, but another part is due to the innovative packaging that enables many new chocolate milk containers to fit in a car's cup holders.

---

learning review

8. What is the difference between product positioning and product repositioning?

9. Why do marketers use perceptual maps in product positioning decisions?

LEARNING OBJECTIVES REVIEW

LO1 *Explain what market segmentation is and when to use it.*
Market segmentation involves aggregating prospective buyers into groups that (*a*) have common needs and (*b*) will respond similarly to a marketing action. Organizations go to the expense of segmenting their markets when it increases their sales, profits, and ability to serve customers better.

LO2 *Identify the five steps involved in segmenting and targeting markets.*
Step 1 is to group potential buyers into segments. Buyers within a segment should have similar characteristics to each other and respond similarly to marketing actions like a new product or a lower price. Step 2 involves putting related products to be sold into meaningful groups. In step 3, organizations develop a market-product grid with estimated sizes of markets in each of the market-product cells of the resulting table. Step 4 involves selecting the target market segments on which the organization should focus. Step 5

involves taking marketing mix actions—often in the form of a marketing program—to reach the target market segments.

LO3 *Recognize the bases used to segment consumer and organizational markets.*
Bases used to segment consumer markets include geographic, demographic, psychographic, and behavioral ones. Organizational markets use the same bases except for psychographic ones.

LO4 *Develop a market-product grid to identify a target market and recommend resulting actions.*
Organizations use five key criteria to segment markets, whose groupings appear in the rows of the market-product grid. Groups of related products appear in the columns. After estimating the size of market in each cell in the grid, they select the target market segments on which to focus. They then identify marketing mix actions—often in a marketing program—to reach the target market most efficiently.

LO5 *Explain how marketing managers position products in the marketplace.*

Marketing managers often locate competing products on two-dimensional perceptual maps to visualize the products in the minds of consumers. They then try to position new products or reposition existing products in this space to attain the maximum sales and profits.

FOCUSING ON KEY TERMS

80/20 rule p. 195
market-product grid p. 198
market segmentation p. 190
market segments p. 190

perceptual map p. 204
product differentiation p. 190
product positioning p. 203
product repositioning p. 203

synergy p. 193
usage rate p. 195

APPLYING MARKETING KNOWLEDGE

1 What variables might be used to segment these consumer markets? (*a*) lawn mowers, (*b*) frozen dinners, (*c*) dry breakfast cereals, and (*d*) soft drinks.

2 What variables might be used to segment these industrial markets? (*a*) industrial sweepers, (*b*) photocopiers, (*c*) computerized production control systems, and (*d*) car rental agencies.

3 In Figure 9–4, the dormitory market segment includes students living in college-owned residence halls, sororities, and fraternities. What market needs are common to these students that justify combining them into a single segment in studying the market for your Wendy's restaurant?

4 You may disagree with the estimates of market size given for the rows in the market-product grid in Figure 9–4. Estimate the market size, and give a brief justification for these market segments: (*a*) dormitory students, (*b*) day commuters, and (*c*) people who work in the area.

5 Suppose you want to increase revenues for your fast-food restaurant even further. Referring to Figure 9–5, what advertising actions might you take to increase revenues from (*a*) dormitory students, (*b*) dinners, and (*c*) after-dinner snacks from night commuters?

building your marketing plan

Your marketing plan needs (*a*) a market-product grid to focus your marketing efforts and also (*b*) leads to a forecast of sales for the company. Use these steps:

1 Define the market segments (the rows in your grid) using the bases of segmentation used to segment consumer and organizational markets.

2 Define the groupings of related products (the columns in your grid).

3 Form your grid and estimate the size of market in each market-product cell.

4 Select the target market segments on which to focus your efforts with your marketing program.

5 Use the information and the lost-horse forecasting technique to make a sales forecast (company forecast).

video case 9   Rollerblade: Skates to Go Where You Want to Go

4D, TRS, TFS . . . and PLS! Does this look like a spoonful of alphabet soup?

Perhaps. But it really refers to Rollerblade's technologies, programs, and commitment to providing in-line skaters with the best quality of skates and skating experiences possible. Or "by providing benefits beyond what people are expecting to have," as Jeremy Stonier (left in photo), Rollerblade's vice president and general manager, describes it. In fact, more than 265 patents cover Rollerblade's leading-edge technology, with more on the way,

such as the new adjustable Crossfire™ and Activa™ in-line skates.

WHAT'S THE NEXT ACT AFTER LAUNCHING AN INDUSTRY?

What do you do for the next act, for your encore, when you create an entire industry?

That's the challenge facing Rollerblade®, which launched the in-line skate industry over two decades ago. But such success attracts lots of competitors. So what does the company do to grow the sport of in-line skating by providing exciting new products to build and maintain continuing, loyal customer relationships? Let's look at the quarter-century from Rollerblade's launch to its customer-oriented strategy today, which is embodied by Rollerblade's new tagline, "Go Where You Want to Go."

In the early 1700s, a Dutch inventor trying to simulate ice skating in the summer created the first roller skates by attaching spools in a single row to his shoes. His "in-line" arrangement was the standard design until 1863 when the first skates with rollers set as two pairs appeared. This two-pair design became the new standard, and in-line skates virtually disappeared from the market.

In 1980, two Minnesota hockey-playing brothers found an old pair of in-line skates while browsing through a sporting goods store. Working in their garage, they modified the design to add hard plastic wheels, a molded boot shell, and a toe brake. They sold their product, which they dubbed "Rollerblade skates," out of the back of their truck to off-season hockey players and skiers.

In the mid-1980s, Rollerblade marketing executive Mary Horwath concluded that the firm had to market its in-line skates to a broader range of customers. Conversations with in-line skaters convinced Horwath that using Rollerblade skates:

- Was incredible fun.
- Was a great aerobic workout and made the skater stronger and healthier.
- Was quite different from traditional roller skating, which was practiced alone, mostly inside, and mostly by young girls.
- Would appeal to more than just off-season ice hockey skaters and skiers.

Horwath set out to reposition Rollerblade, to change the image in people's minds from in-line skating as off-season training to in-line skating as a new kind of fun exercise that anyone could do. It worked. Horwath and the company succeeded in popularizing in-line skating and actually launched an entirely new industry that by 1997 had more than 27 million U.S. inline skaters.

The marketing problems of Rollerblade today are far different than those it faced in the late 1980s. Rollerblade's success in launching a new industry brought its own dangers: major competition in terms of not only more than 30 other skate manufacturers but also competing sports like skateboarding, biking, and snowboarding.

Yet Rollerblade still has 35 percent of the industry sales, with no other competitor having more than 10 percent. The number of in-line skaters in the U.S. has declined from its 1997 peak, a concern for Rollerblade. If this declining trend continues, Rollerblade can only grow by increasing its share of the number of in-line skates sold annually, requiring innovation and creative marketing strategies to meet customer needs.

ROLLERBLADE'S KEY SEGMENTS

From the outset in-line skaters have been united by a common experience: the thrill and fun of the speed and freedom that comes from almost frictionless wheels on their feet. "As the market has matured, it has settled into four core groups of users," says Stonier. Each requires a number of unique skate features.

"The trickiest segment we sell to is probably the Urban/Street skaters—the 14- to 22-year-old in your neighborhood who is doing tricks you might see on ESPN's X Games," says Stonier. Members of Team Rollerblade, a skating group that gives demonstrations around the country, suggest and test new technologies that find their way first into skates for this segment. The Team Rollerblade Series (or TRS) DT4 in-line skate, which is designed for this segment, contains a "walkable" boot and Training Fit foot liner to keep the skater's feet cool, dry, and comfortable.

Skate buyers overlap somewhat in the Fitness/Recreation segment. The Fitness subgroup skates two or three times a week, at high speeds, and may even aspire to skate in an in-line marathon. As a result, Rollerblade developed the Crossfire 4D skate for men and the Activa 4D skate for women. "No other skate in the industry combines this level of form, function, fit, and aesthetics," exclaims Ronnie Kuliecza, director of product development. The $4D^{TM}$ (D=drive) refers to an innovative, adjustable aluminum frame that when shorter allows for tighter turns and when longer permits more speed. These skates incorporate the new Crossfire Shell for stability and control for turning and 90mm wheels for speed. The skates also use the revolutionary TFS (Total Fit System) Power lacing closure mechanism. Pulling on the TFS disc provides an effortless, quick, and customized fit. Finally, the skates have the PLS (Power Lateral

DT4 in-line skate for the Urban/Street Segment

Crossfire 4D in-line skate for the Fitness/Recreation Segment

Support) to secure the heel and Air Power, inflatable chambers that secure the ankle.

Since most adult skaters are Recreation skaters, Rollerblade designed the new Astro (men) and Wing (women) skates for this larger subsegment. With these skates, both beginner and intermediate skaters get the comfort, reliability, and safety they want.

With the Junior segment, parents are always concerned about having to buy their children new shoes or skates as their feet grow. Not only does the Micro 500 X extendable skate adjust four sizes with a push of a button, but it also has the new TFS Micro closure system. With a simple push of a button and a turn of a dial, a thin cable provides quick closure.

The Race segment is just what the name implies—expert speed skaters wanting the maximum in technical features. The Race Machine Rosso skate has a hyper magnesium frame that holds four 100mm high performance wheels as well as a high tech boot for maximum performance.

The segments don't stop there. While the flagship Rollerblade brand is marketed in sporting goods and skate specialty stores, Rollerblade has a lower-priced Bladerunner line that is sold through mass merchandise (such as Wal-Mart and Target) and sporting goods chain stores. Finally, the global market has enormous potential. With China and South Korea showing high growth today, who knows what new segments could be next?

A FOCUS ON EACH CONSUMER

"One of the big differences between marketing today and in the future is that we will be able to reach each person, such as designing your own personal workout program," says Nicholas Skally (right in photo on previous page), Rollerblade's manager of marketing. Rollerblade's website (www.rollerblade.com) is a step in that direction. "An important benefit of the website is our ability to acquire marketing research data on individual consumers inexpensively," says Skally. This enables Rollerblade to get feedback and ideas directly from its end users.

Website topics include everything from helping you choose which skate is right for you (Product Selector) to helping you brush up on your braking technique though its Animated Skate Lesson. The website's "Skating for Fitness" link provides information on the benefits of in-line skating as well as a workout plan. It also has a Games section targeted for each segment so that "online" skaters can see how fast they can traverse a course or stop without skating into an object! The website allows interested users to subscribe to its newsletter. Finally, Rollerblade developed two "webmercials" designed as viral marketing tools (see Chapter 5) that can be viewed and shared on YouTube.

In the past, Rollerblade often sent out millions of direct-mail pieces or bought commercials on national

Micro 500 X extendable in-line skate for the Junior Segment

Race Machine Rosso in-line skate for the Race Segment

TV networks. Today, Skally points out that Rollerblade now focuses more narrowly by selecting magazines that link directly to the user segments. Rollerblade also offers programs like its (1) Free Skate Lesson program, a coalition of skate schools providing free in-line skating lessons on Free Skate Lesson Day, held each May in major cities across America and (2) Camp Rollerblade, which occurs on Saturdays in selected cities during the spring-fall season.

ROLLERBLADE'S FIRSTS

"If you're going to buy a pair of in-line skates, it only make sense to buy from us," says Stonier, "because we're the ones who started it, perfected it, and continue to push the innovation." As evidence of Rollerblade's innovation, he points to a number of firsts, such as the use of polyurethane boots and wheels, high-tech closure systems, metal frames, dual bearings, and heel brakes. Other firsts include breathable liners, push-button adjustable children's skates, and more importantly, skates designed specifically for women *by women*. Rollerblade employed an engineering team composed of women to develop in-line skates with specially designed lines, cuffs, and footbeds that meets the unique needs of women.

In 2003, Rollerblade was sold to Tecnica of Italy, whose holdings include the Nordica brand of ski equipment. This acquisition provided both firms with huge technology synergies, allowing them to combine their state-of-the-art R&D and manufacturing resources.

Questions

1 What trends in the environmental forces (social, economic, technological, competitive, and regulatory) (*a*) work for and (*b*) work against Rollerblade's potential growth in the twenty-first century?

2 Compare the likely marketing goals for Rollerblade (*a*) in 1986 when Rollerblade was launched and (*b*) today.

3 What kind of focused communication and promotion actions might Rollerblade take to reach the (*a*) Fitness/Recreation and (*b*) Junior market segments? For some starting ideas, visit www.rollerblade.com.

4 In searching for global markets to enter, (*a*) what are some criteria that Rollerblade should use to select countries to enter, and (*b*) what three or four countries meet these criteria best and are the most likely candidates?

10

Developing New Products and Services

LEARNING OBJECTIVES

After reading this chapter you should be able to:

 LO1 Recognize the various terms that pertain to products and services.

 LO2 Identify the ways in which consumer and business products and services can be classified.

 LO3 Describe four unique elements of services.

 LO4 Explain the significance of "newness" in new products and services as it relates to the degree of consumer learning involved.

 LO5 Describe the factors contributing to a new product's or service's success or failure.

 LO6 Explain the purposes of each step of the new-product process.

APPLE'S NEW-PRODUCT REVOLUTIONS

The stage in front of the huge auditorium is empty except for a podium, an iMac, and a huge screen. Then in walks a legend ready for his magic shows in his black turtleneck, jeans, and gray New Balance sneakers.

Apple's Innovation Machine

The legend is Steve Jobs, co-founder and chief executive officer of Apple, Inc., rated *BusinessWeek's* most innovative company on the globe in *both* 2006 and 2007.[1] The magic shows are the annual *Macworld* and developers' conferences in San Francisco where Jobs presents Apple's latest innovations. A sample of Apple's past new-product innovations are:

- Apple II—the first commercial personal computer.
- Macintosh—the first PC with a mouse and a graphical user interface.
- iPod—the first commercially successful MP3 digital music player.
- iPhone—the revolutionary multi-touch mobile phone and MP3 player.
- MacBook Air—the world's thinnest notebook that fits inside an envelope!

And what's next for Apple's innovation machine? The 3G (third generation) iPhone that will enable customers to place video phone calls, use a global positioning system (GPS), access high-speed broadband Internet and data transfer, and enjoy its revolutionary multi-touch interface.

The Revolutionary iPhone

"Everybody hates their phone," says Steve Jobs, "and that's not a good thing." Sample problems: listening to voice-mails and typing text or e-mail messages with small-button keyboards. Several years ago, Jobs put some Apple engineers to work developing touch screens to replace small keyboards common in high-end voice and data mobile phones. This research resulted in 200 new patents that evolved into the innovative iPhone. To build it, Apple sheared off the front of a video iPod and replaced it with a bright, vivid touch screen whose "buttons" appear exactly when you need them.

Armed with this technological wonder, Jobs entered the mobile phone market in June 2007—a market that had almost a *billion* units in annual sales—in which Apple had *none*. Apple planned to sell 10 million iPhones by the end of 2008—18 months after its launch.[2]

The life of an organization depends on how it conceives, produces, and markets *new* products (goods, services, and ideas), the topic of this chapter. Chapter 11 discusses the process of managing *existing* products, services, and brands.

WHAT ARE PRODUCTS AND SERVICES?

LO1

The essence of marketing is in developing products and services to meet buyer needs. A **product** is a good, service, or idea consisting of a bundle of tangible and intangible attributes that satisfies consumers' needs and is received in exchange for money or something else of value. Let's look more carefully at the meanings of goods, services, and ideas.

product

Good, service, or idea consisting of tangible and intangible features that satisfies consumers and is received in exchange for money or something else of value

A Look at Goods, Services, and Ideas

A *good* has tangible attributes that a consumer's five senses can perceive. For example, Apple's latest 3G iPhone can be touched and its contents can be seen and heard. A good also may have intangible attributes consisting of its delivery or warranties and more abstract concepts, such as becoming healthier or wealthier.[3] Goods can also be divided into nondurable goods and durable goods. A *nondurable* good is an item consumed in one or a few uses, such as food products and fuel. A *durable* good is one that usually lasts over many uses, such as appliances, cars, and stereo equipment. This classification method also provides direction for marketing actions. For example, nondurable goods like Wrigley's gum rely heavily on consumer advertising. In contrast, costly durable goods, such as cars, generally emphasize personal selling.

services

Intangible activities or benefits that an organization provides to consumers in exchange for money or something else of value.

Services are intangible activities or benefits that an organization provides to satisfy consumers' needs in exchange for money or something else of value. Services have become a significant part of the U.S. economy, exceeding 40 percent of its gross domestic product. Hence, a good may be the breakfast cereal you eat, whereas a service may be a tax return an accountant fills out for you.

Finally, in marketing, an *idea* is a thought that leads to an action like a concept for a new invention, or getting people out to vote.

Throughout this book "product" generally includes not only physical goods but services and ideas as well. When "product" is used in its narrower meaning of "goods," it should be clear from the example or sentence.

The iPhone's innovative touch screen emerged after Apple engineers studied tablet PCs, portable computers using . . . touch screens.

Classifying Products

Two broad categories of products widely used in marketing relate to the type of user. **Consumer products** are products purchased by the ultimate consumer, whereas **business products** (also called *B2B products or industrial products*) are ones that assist directly or indirectly in providing products for resale. But some products can be considered both consumer and business items. For example, an Apple iMac computer can be sold to consumers for personal use or to business firms for office use. Each classification results in different marketing actions. Viewed as a consumer product, the iMac would be sold through its retail stores or directly from its website. As a business product, an Apple salesperson might contact a firm's purchasing department directly and offer discounts for multiple purchases.

Consumer Products The four types of consumer products shown in Figure 10–1 differ in terms of the (1) effort the consumer spends on the decision, (2) attributes used in making the purchase decision, and (3) frequency of purchase. *Convenience products* are items that the consumer purchases frequently, conveniently, and with a minimum of shopping effort. *Shopping products* are items for which the consumer compares several alternatives on criteria such as price, quality, or style. *Specialty products* are items that the consumer makes a special effort to search out and buy. *Unsought products* are items that the consumer does not know about or knows about but does not initially want.

Figure 10–1 shows how each type of consumer product stresses different marketing mix actions, degrees of brand loyalty, and shopping effort. But how a consumer product is classified depends on the individual. One woman may view a camera as a shopping product and visit several stores before deciding on a brand, whereas her

FIGURE 10–1

How a consumer product is classified significantly affects what products consumers buy and the marketing strategies used.

TYPE OF CONSUMER PRODUCT

BASIS OF COMPARISON	CONVENIENCE	SHOPPING	SPECIALTY	UNSOUGHT
Product	Toothpaste, cake mix, hand soap, ATM cash withdrawal	Cameras, TVs, briefcases, airline tickets	Rolls-Royce cars, Rolex watches, heart surgery	Burial insurance, thesaurus
Price	Relatively inexpensive	Fairly expensive	Usually very expensive	Varies
Place (distribution)	Widespread; many outlets	Large number of selective outlets	Very limited	Often limited
Promotion	Price, availability, and awareness stressed	Differentiation from competitors stressed	Uniqueness of brand and status stressed	Awareness is essential
Brand loyalty of consumers	Aware of brand but will accept substitutes	Prefer specific brands but will accept substitutes	Very brand loyal; will not accept substitutes	Will accept substitutes
Purchase behavior of consumers	Frequent purchases; little time and effort spent shopping	Infrequent purchases; needs much comparison shopping time	Infrequent purchases; needs extensive search and decision time	Very infrequent purchases; some comparison shopping

Specialty goods like Rolex watches require distinct marketing programs to reach narrow target markets.

friend may view a camera as a specialty product and will make a special effort to buy only a Nikon.

Business Products   A major characteristic of business products is that their sales are often the result of *derived demand*; that is, sales of business products frequently result (or are derived) from the sale of consumer products. For example, as consumer demand for Ford cars (a consumer product) increases, the company may increase its demand for paint spraying equipment (a business product).

Business products may be classified as components or support products. *Components* are items that become part of the final product. These include raw materials such as grain or lumber, as well as assemblies or parts, such as a Ford car engine or car door hinges. *Support products* are items used to assist in producing other goods and services. These include:

- *Installations*, such as buildings and fixed equipment.
- *Accessory equipment,* such as tools and office equipment.
- *Supplies,* such as stationery, paper clips, and brooms.
- *Industrial services,* such as maintenance, repair, and legal services.

Strategies to market business products reflect both the complexities of the product involved (paper clips versus computer-machine tools) and the buy-class situations discussed in Chapter 6.

PRODUCT ITEMS, PRODUCT LINES, AND PRODUCT MIXES

product item

Specific product that has a unique brand, size, or price

product line

Group of products that are closely related because they are similar in terms of consumer needs and uses, market segments, sales outlets, or prices

product mix

All the product lines offered by a company

Most organizations offer a range of products and services to consumers. A **product item** is a specific product that has a unique brand, size, or price. For example, Ultra Downy softener for clothes comes in several different sizes. Each size is a separate *stock-keeping unit* (SKU), which is a unique identification number that defines an item for ordering or inventory purposes.

A **product line** is a group of product or service items that are closely related because they satisfy a class of needs, are used together, are sold to the same customer group, are distributed through the same outlets, or fall within a given price range. Nike's product lines include shoes and clothing, whereas the Mayo Clinic's service lines consist of inpatient hospital care and outpatient physician services. Each product line has its own marketing strategy.

The Little Remedies® product line consists of more than a dozen nonprescription medicines for infants and young children. A broad product line enables both consumers and retailers to simplify their buying decisions. If a family has a good experience with one Little Remedies product, it might buy another one in the line. And an extensive line enables Little Remedies to obtain distribution chains like Babies "Я" Us and Wal-Mart, avoiding the need for retailers to deal with many different suppliers.

Many firms offer a **product mix** that consists of all of the product lines offered by an organization. For example, Cray Inc. has a small product mix of four supercomputer lines that are sold mostly to governments and large businesses. Fortune Brands, however, has a large product mix that includes product lines such as sporting equipment (Titleist golf balls) and plumbing supplies (Moen faucets).

Classifying Services

Services can be classified according to whether they are delivered by (1) people or equipment, (2) business firms or nonprofit organizations, or (3) government agencies. Organizations in each of these categories often use significantly different kinds of market-mix strategies to promote their services.

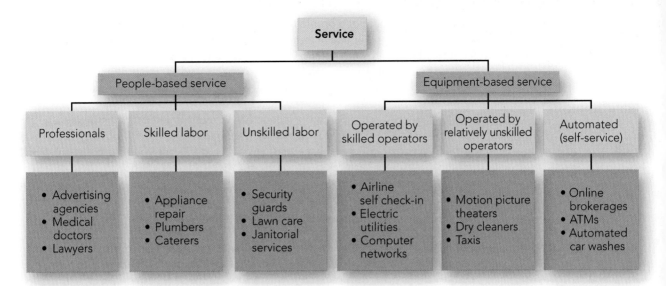

FIGURE 10–2

Services can be classified as equipment-based or people-based.

Delivery by People or Equipment Figure 10–2 shows the great diversity of organizations that offer services. People-based professional services include those offered by advertising agencies or medical doctors. Sears utilizes skilled labor to offer appliance repair services. Brink's uses relatively unskilled labor to provide its security guard services. The quality of all these people-based services can vary significantly depending on the abilities of the person delivering the service.

Figure 10–2 also suggests that equipment-based services do not have the marketing concern of inconsistent quality because employees do not have direct contact when providing the service to consumers. Instead, consumers receive these automated services without interacting with any service employees, such as doing self check-in at Southwest Airlines, watching a movie at a local theater, or using Schwab's online stock trading.[4]

Delivery by Business Firms or Nonprofit Organizations As discussed in Chapter 2, privately owned firms must make profits to survive, while nonprofit organizations seek to satisfy clients and be efficient. The kinds of services each offers affect their marketing activities. Recently, many nonprofit organizations, such as The American Red Cross, have used marketing to improve communications to serve better those in need.

Delivery by Government Agencies Governments at the federal, state, and local levels provide a broad range of services. These organizations also have adopted many marketing practices used by business firms. For example, the United States Postal Service's "Easy Come. Easy Go." marketing campaign is designed to allow it to compete better with UPS, FedEx, DHL, and foreign postal services for global package delivery business.

The Uniqueness of Services

LO3

Four unique elements distinguish services from goods. These are *intangibility, inconsistency, inseparability,* and *inventory*—referred to as the **four I's of services**.

four I's of services
Four unique elements that distinguish services from goods: intangibility, inconsistency, inseparability, and inventory

Intangibility Being intangible, services can't be touched or seen before the purchase decision. Instead, services tend to be a performance rather than an object, which makes them much more difficult for consumers to evaluate. To help consumers assess and compare services, marketers try to make them tangible or show the benefits of using the service.

Inconsistency Services depend on the people who provide them. As a result, their quality varies with each person's capabilities and day-to-day job performance.

Inconsistency is more of a problem in services than it is with tangible goods. Tangible products can be good or bad in terms of quality, but with modern production lines, their quality will at least be consistent. On the other hand, the Philadelphia Phillies baseball team may have great hitting and pitching one day and the next day lose by 10 runs. Organizations attempt to reduce inconsistency through standardization and training.[5]

Inseparability Inseparability means that the consumer cannot distinguish the service provider from the service itself. For example, if the quality of large lectures at your university or college is excellent, but if you don't get your questions answered, find the counseling services poor, or do not receive adequate library assistance, you may not be satisfied with the entire educational experience delivered. Therefore, you probably won't separate your perception of the "educational experience"—the service itself—from all the people delivering the educational services for that institution.

Inventory Many goods have inventory handling costs that relate to their storage, perishability, and movement. With services, these costs are more subjective and are related to **idle production capacity**, which is when the service provider is available but there is no demand for the service. For a service, inventory cost involves paying the service provider along with any needed equipment. If a physician is paid to see patients but no one schedules an appointment, the idle physician's salary must be paid regardless of whether the service was performed. In service businesses that pay employees a commission, such as a part-time clerk at Sears, the sales clerk's work hours can be reduced to lower Sears' idle production capacity.

Today, many businesses find it useful to distinguish between their core product—either a good or a service—and supplementary services. U.S. Bank has both a core service (a checking account) and supplementary services, such as deposit assistance, parking, drive-throughs, and ATMs. Supplementary services often allow service providers to differentiate their offerings from competitors to add value for consumers.[6]

The Goods-Services Continuum

Figure 10–3 shows that many organizations are not strictly goods- or services-based. Is Hewlett-Packard a computer or service firm? Although it manufactures computers,

idle production capacity
When the supply of the service exceeds demand for it

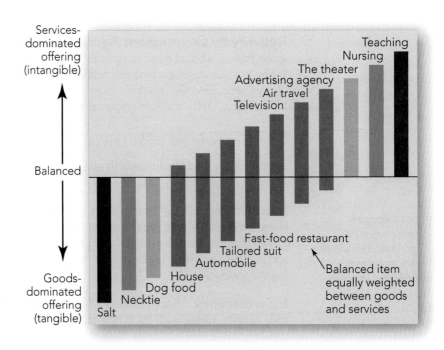

FIGURE 10–3
The goods-services continuum shows how offerings can vary from goods-dominated (salt) to services-dominated (teaching) to many gradations in between.

printers, and other goods, many of the company's employees work in its services division providing systems integration, networking, consulting, and product support.[7] Organizations can offer a range of products from the tangible (goods-dominant) to the intangible (services-dominant), which is referred to as the *goods-services continuum*.

Salt, neckties, and dog food are tangible goods-dominant offerings, whereas teaching, nursing, and the theater are intangible, services-dominant activities. A fast-food restaurant is about half tangible goods (the food) and half intangible services (courtesy, cleanliness, speed, and convenience).

<table>
<tr><td rowspan="3">learning review</td><td>1. What are the four main types of consumer products?</td></tr>
<tr><td>2. What is the difference between a product line and a product mix?</td></tr>
<tr><td>3. What are the 4 I's of services?</td></tr>
</table>

NEW PRODUCTS AND WHY THEY SUCCEED OR FAIL

New products are the lifeblood of a company and keep it growing, but the financial risks can be large. Before discussing how new products reach the market, we'll begin by looking at *what* a new product is.

What Is a New Product?

The term *new* is difficult to define. Is Sony's PlayStation 3 *new* when there was a PlayStation 2? Is Nintendo's Wii *new* when its GameCube launch goes back to 2001? What does *new* mean for new-product marketing? Newness from several points of view are discussed next.

As you read the discussion about what "new" means in new-product development, think about how it affects the marketing strategies of Sony and Nintendo in their *new* video-game launches.

Newness Compared with Existing Products   If a product is functionally different from existing products, it can be defined as new. Sometimes this newness is revolutionary and creates a whole new industry, as in the case of the Apple II computer. At other times additional features are added to an existing product to try to make it appeal to more customers. And as microprocessors now appear not only in computers and cell phones but also in countless applications in vehicles and appliances, consumers' lives get far more complicated. This proliferation of extra features—sometimes called "feature bloat"—overwhelms many consumers. The Marketing Matters box describes how founder Richard Stephens and his Geek Squad are working to address the rise of feature bloat.[8]

Newness in Legal Terms   The U.S. Federal Trade Commission (FTC) advises that the term *new* be limited to use with a product up to six months after it enters regular distribution. The difficulty with this suggestion is in the interpretation of the term *regular distribution*.

Newness from the Organization's Perspective   Successful organizations are starting to view newness and innovation in their products at three levels. At the lowest level, which usually involves the least risk, is a product line extension. This is an incremental improvement of an existing product for the company, such as Cheerios Crunch—an extension of the basic Cheerios. At the next level is a significant jump in the innovation or technology, such as from a regular land-line telephone to a cell phone. The third level is true innovation, a truly revolutionary new product, like the first Apple computer in 1976. Effective new-product programs in large firms deal at all three levels.

Newness from the Consumer's Perspective   A fourth way to define new products is in terms of their effects on consumption. This approach classifies new products according to the degree of learning required by the consumer, as shown in Figure 10–4.

With a *continuous innovation*, consumers don't need to learn new behaviors. Toothpaste manufacturers can add new attributes or features like "whitens teeth" or "removes plaque," as when they introduce a new or improved product. But the extra

FIGURE 10–4
The degree of "newness" in a new product affects the amount of learning effort consumers must exert to use the product and the resulting marketing strategy.

	LOW Degree of New Consumer Learning Needed HIGH		
BASIS OF COMPARISON	**CONTINUOUS INNOVATION**	**DYNAMICALLY CONTINUOUS INNOVATION**	**DISCONTINUOUS INNOVATION**
Definition	Requires no new learning by consumers	Disrupts consumer's normal routine but does not require totally new learning	Requires new learning and consumption patterns by consumers
Examples	New improved shaver or detergent	Electric toothbrush, compact disc player, and automatic flash unit for cameras	VCR, digital video recorder, electric car
Marketing strategy	Gain consumer awareness and wide distribution	Advertise points of difference and benefits to consumers	Educate consumers through product trial and personal selling

Marketing Matters >>>>>>> technology

You Bought a Combination Computer, Lawn Mower, and Dishwasher? Better Call the Geek Squad!

Adding more features to a product to satisfy more consumers seems like a no-brainer strategy.

Feature Bloat

In fact, most marketing research with potential buyers of a product done *before* they buy shows they say they *do want* more features in the product. It's when the new product gets home that the "feature bloat" problems occur—often overwhelming the consumer with mind-boggling complexity.

Computers pose a special problem for homeowners because there's no in-house technical assistance like that existing in large organizations. Also, to drive down prices of home computers, usually little customer support service is available. Call the manufacturers toll-free "help" line? One survey showed that 29 percent of the help-line callers wound up swearing at the customer service representative and 21 percent just screamed.

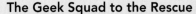

The Geek Squad to the Rescue

Computer feature bloat has given rise to what TV's *60 Minutes* says is "the multibillion-dollar service industry populated by the very people who used to be shunned in the high-school cafeteria: Geeks like Robert Stephens!"

More than over a decade ago he turned his geekiness into the Geek Squad—a group of technically savvy people who can fix almost any computer problem. "There's usually some frantic customer at the door pointing to some device in the corner that will not obey," Stephens explains.

"The biggest complaint about tech support people is rude, egotistical behavior," says Stephens. So he launched the Geek Squad to show some friendly humility by having team members work their wizardry while:

1. Showing genuine concern to customers.
2. Dressing in geeky white shirts, black clip-on ties, and white socks, a "uniform" borrowed from NASA engineers.
3. Driving to customer calls in black-and-white VW "geekmobiles."

Do customers appreciate the 6,000-person Geek Squad, now owned by Best Buy? Robert Stephens answers by explaining, "People will say, 'They saved me . . . they saved my data.'" This includes countless college students working on their paper or thesis with data lost somewhere in their computer—"data they promised themselves they'd back up next week."

For how the kind of innovation present in this ketchup bottle affects marketing strategy, see the text.

features in the new toothpaste do not require buyers to learn new tooth-brushing behaviors, so it is a continuous innovation. The benefit of this simple innovation is that effective marketing mainly depends on generating awareness and not needing to reeducate customers.

With a *dynamically continuous innovation*, only minor changes in behavior are required. Heinz launched its EZ Squirt Ketchup in 2000 in an array of unlikely hues—from green and orange to pink and teal—with kid-friendly squeeze bottles and nozzles.[9] Encouraging kids to write their names on hot dogs or draw dinosaurs on burgers as they use this new product requires only minor behavioral changes. So the marketing strategy here is to educate prospective buyers on the product's benefits, advantages, and proper use.

A *discontinuous innovation* involves making the consumer learn entirely new consumption patterns in order to use the product. Have you bought a wireless router for your computer? Congratulations if you installed it yourself! Recently, one-third of those bought at Best Buy were returned because they were too complicated to set up—the problem with a discontinuous innovation.[10] So marketing efforts for discontinuous innovations usually involve not only gaining initial consumer awareness but also educating consumers on both the benefits and proper use of the innovative product, activities that can cost millions of dollars.

New-product success or failure? For the special problems these two products face, see the text.

Why Products Succeed or Fail

LO5

We all know the giant product successes—such as Apple's iPhone, Swatch watches, CNN. Yet the thousands of product failures every year that slide quietly into oblivion cost American businesses billions of dollars. Research suggests that it takes about 3,000 raw unwritten ideas to produce a single commercially successful new product.[11] To learn marketing lessons and convert potential failures to successes, we can analyze why new products fail and then study several failures in detail. As we go through the new-product process later in the chapter, we can identify ways such failures might have been avoided—admitting that hindsight is clearer than foresight.

Marketing Reasons for New-Product Failures Both marketing and nonmarketing factors contribute to new-product failures. Using the research results from several studies on new-product success and failure, we can identify critical marketing factors—which sometimes overlap—that often separate new-product winners and losers:[12]

1. *Insignificant point of difference.* A distinctive point of difference is essential for a new product to defeat competitive ones—through having superior characteristics that deliver unique benefits to the user. In the mid-1990s, General Mills introduced Fingos, a sweetened cereal flake about the size of a corn chip. Consumers were supposed to snack on them dry, but they didn't.[13] The point of difference was not important enough to get consumers to stop eating competing snacks such as popcorn and potato chips.

2. *Incomplete market and product definition before product development starts.* Ideally, a new product needs a precise *protocol*, a statement that, before product development begins, identifies: (*a*) a well-defined target market; (*b*) specific customers' needs, wants, and preferences; and (*c*) what the product will be and do. Without this protocol, resources are wasted as R&D tries to design a vague product for a phantom market. Apple's early hand-sized Newton personal digital assistant (PDA) fizzled badly because no clear protocol existed and the device was too complicated.

3. *Too little market attractiveness.* Market attractiveness refers to the ideal situation every new-product manager looks for: a large target market with high growth and real buyer need. But often, when looking for ideal market niches, the target market is too small and competitive to warrant the R&D, production,

220

and marketing expenses necessary to reach it. In the early 1990s, Kodak discontinued its Ultralife lithium battery with its 10-year shelf life because its 9-volt size accounted for less than 10 percent of the U.S. battery market.

4. *Poor execution of the marketing mix: name, package, price, promotion, distribution.* Coca-Cola thought its Minute Maid Squeeze-Fresh frozen orange juice concentrate in a squeeze bottle was a hit. The idea was that consumers could make one glass of juice at a time, and the concentrate stayed fresh in the refrigerator for over a month. After two test markets, the product was finished. While consumers loved the idea, the product was too messy, and the advertising and packaging didn't educate them effectively on how much concentrate to mix with water.

5. *Poor product quality.* This factor often results when a product is not thoroughly tested. The costs to an organization for poor quality can be staggering and include the labor, materials, and other expenses to fix the problem—not to mention the lost sales, profits, and market share that usually result. For example, after Microsoft launched its Xbox 360 video game console, millions began to experience the "red ring of death." The problem: its microprocessors ran too hot, causing them to "pop off" their motherboards. Microsoft had to set aside $1.1 billion to extend its warranty and fix any affected console for free—costing it future sales and reducing its market share lead of the $12.5 billion market over rivals Sony and Nintendo.[14]

6. *Not satisfying customer needs on critical factors.* Overlapping somewhat with point 1, this factor stresses that problems on one or two critical factors can kill the product, even though the general quality is high. For example, the Japanese, like the British, drive on the left side of the road. Until 1996, U.S. carmakers sent Japan few right-drive cars—unlike German carmakers who exported right-drive models in several of their brands.[15]

7. *Bad timing.* This results when a product is introduced too soon, too late, or when consumer tastes are shifting dramatically. Bad timing gives new-product managers nightmares. Microsoft, for example, introduced its Zune player a few years after Apple launched its iPod and other competitors offered new MP3 players.

8. *No economical access to buyers.* Grocery products provide an example. Today's mega-supermarkets carry more than 30,000 different SKUs. With about 20,000 new packaged goods products (food, beverage, health and beauty aids, household, and pet items) introduced each year, the cost to gain access to retailer shelf space in huge.[16] Because shelf space is judged in terms of sales per square foot, Thirsty Dog! (a zesty beef-flavored, vitamin-enriched, mineral-loaded, lightly carbonated bottled water for your dog) must displace an existing product on the supermarket shelves, a difficult task with the high sales per square foot demands of these stores. Thirsty Dog! failed to generate enough sales to meet these requirements.

A Look at Some Failures   Before reading the next two paragraphs, study the product failures described in Figure 10–5. Then identify which of the eight reasons listed in the text is the most likely explanation for their failure.

FIGURE 10–5
Why did these two new products fail?

As explained in detail in the text, new products often fail because of one or a combination of eight reasons. Look at the two products described here, and try to identify which reason explains why they failed in the marketplace.

- Kimberly Clark's Avert Virucidal tissues that contained vitamin C derivatives scientifically designed to kill cold and flu germs when users sneezed, coughed, or blew their noses into them.
- OUT! International's Hey! There's A Monster In My Room spray that was designed to rid scary creatures from kids' rooms and had a bubble-gum fragrance.

Compare your insights with those in the text.

The text describes some new-product lessons this iRobot co-founder learned the hard way.

Kimberly Clark's Avert Virucidal tissues lasted 10 months in a test market in upstate New York before being pulled from store shelves. People didn't believe the claims and were frightened by the "-cidal" in the name, which they connected to words like "suicidal." So the tissue probably failed because of not having a clear point of difference and a bad name, and, hence, bad marketing mix execution—probably reasons 1 and 4 in the list in the text.

OUT! International's Hey! There's A Monster In My Room spray was creative and cute when it was introduced. But the name probably kept the kids awake at night more than their fear of the monsters because it suggested the monster was still hiding in the room. Question: wouldn't calling it the Monster-Buster Spray—the secondary name shown at the bottom of the package—have licked the name problem? It looks like the spray was never really defined well in a protocol (reason 2) and definitely had poor name execution (reason 4).[17]

Simple marketing research on consumers should have revealed the problems. Developing successful new products may sometimes involve luck, but more often it involves having a product that really meets a need and has significant points of difference over competitive products.

What *Were* They Thinking? Organizational Problems in New-Product Failure

A number of other organizational problems can cause new-product disasters. Key ones—some that overlap—include:

1. *Not really listening to the "voice of the consumer."* Product managers may believe they "know better" than their customers or feel they "can't afford" the valuable marketing research that could uncover problems.
2. *Skipping steps in the new-product process.* Although details may vary, the seven-step new-product process discussed in the next section is a sequence used in some form by most large organizations. Skipping a step often leads to disaster, the reason that many firms have a "gate" or "milestone" to ensure that one step is completed satisfactorily before going on to the next step.[18]
3. *Pushing a poorly conceived product into the market to generate quick revenue.* Today's marketing managers are under incredible pressure from top management to meet quarterly revenue targets. This focus on speed often results in overlooking the network of services needed to support the physical product.[19]
4. *"Groupthink" in task force and committee meetings.* Someone in the new-product planning meeting knows or suspects the product concept is a dumb idea. But that person is afraid to speak up for fear of being cast as a "negative thinker" and "not a team player" and then being ostracized from real participation in the group. And a strong public commitment to a new product by its key advocate may make it difficult to kill the product even when new negative information comes to light.[20]
5. *Not learning critical takeaway lessons from past failures.* The easiest lessons are from "intelligent failures"—ones that happen early in the new-product process so they are less expensive and that immediately give better understanding of customers' wants and needs.

Helen Greiner, co-founder and chairman of iRobot, talks about lessons she learned from a key product failure. iRobot manufactures a variety of robots—from the Scooba floor washer mentioned in Chapter 1 to the PackBot bomb-disposal robot. Her lessons came from the Ariel, an amphibious mine-clearing robot that was the most advanced walking robot in the world at the time. Helen Greiner notes Ariel didn't satisfy the user's needs because "it couldn't walk far enough, it couldn't carry the payload it would need to carry, and it was too complex." The result: the failure shifted iRobot's focus from "innovation for innovation's sake" to "building practical and affordable robots that help people."[21]

Using Marketing Dashboards

In 2008, you started your own company to sell a nutritious, high-energy snack you developed. It is now January 2010. As a marketer, you ask yourself, "How well is my business growing?"

Your Challenge The snack is sold in all 50 states. Your goal is 10 percent annual growth. To begin 2010, you want to quickly solve any sales problems that occurred during 2009. You know that states whose sales are stagnant or in decline are offset by those with greater than 10 percent growth.

Studying a table of the sales and percent change versus a year ago in each of the 50 states would work but be very time consuming. A good graphic is better. You choose the following marketing metric, where "sales" is measured in units:

Annual %
sales change

$$= \frac{(2009 \text{ Sales} - 2008 \text{ Sales}) \times 100}{2008 \text{ Sales}}$$

You want to act quickly to improve sales. In your map growth that is greater than 10 percent is GREEN, 0 to 10 percent growth is ORANGE, and decline is RED. Notice that you (1) picked a metric and (2) made your own rules that GREEN is good, ORANGE is bad, and RED is very bad.

Your Findings You see that sales growth in the Northeastern states is weaker than the 10 percent target, and sales are actually declining in many of the states.

Your Action Marketing is often about grappling with sales shortfalls. You'll need to start by trying to identify and correct the problems in the largest volume states that are underperforming—in this case in the northeastern United States.

You'll want to do marketing research to see if the problem starts with (1) an external factor like changing consumer tastes or (2) an internal factor like a breakdown in your distribution system.

Annual Percentage Change in Unit Volume, by State

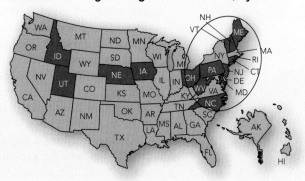

How Marketing Dashboards Can Reduce New-Product Failures

The Using Marketing Dashboards box shows how marketers measure actual market performance versus the goals set in new-product planning. It shows that you have set a goal of 10 percent annual growth for the new snack you developed. You choose a marketing metric of "annual % sales change"—to measure the annual growth rate from 2008 to 2009 for each of the 50 states. Your special concerns in the marketing dashboard are the states shown in red, where sales have actually declined. As shown in the box, having identified the northeastern United States as a problem region, you conduct some in-depth marketing research to lead to corrective actions.

learning review

4. What kind of innovation would an improved electric toothbrush be?

5. Why can an "insignificant point of difference" lead to new-product failure?

THE NEW-PRODUCT PROCESS

LO6

Innovation and new products are the lifeblood of most business firms. To develop new products efficiently, companies like General Electric and 3M use a specific sequence of steps to make their products ready for market. Figure 10–6 shows the **new-product process**, the seven stages an organization goes through to identify business opportunities and convert them to a salable good or service.

Stage 1: New-Product Strategy Development

For companies, *new-product strategy development* is the stage of the new-product process that defines the role for a new product in terms of the firm's overall objectives. Many companies have recently added this step to provide a needed focus for ideas and concepts developed in later stages. During this stage, the firm uses both a SWOT analysis (Chapter 2) and environmental scanning (Chapter 3) to assess its strengths and weaknesses relative to the trends it identifies as opportunities or threats. The outcome not only defines the vital "protocol" for each new-product idea but also identifies the strategic role it might serve in the firm's portfolio.

New-product development in services, like buying a stock or airline ticket or watching a Major League Baseball game, is often difficult. Why? Because services are intangible and performance-oriented. Nevertheless, service innovations can have a huge impact on our lives. For example, the online brokerage firm E*TRADE has revolutionized the financial services industry.

A Major League Baseball park is a study in new-product innovation. If you visit Turner Field, home of the Atlanta Braves, you may be in for a shock about what's going on besides baseball on the field. There's not only the members-only 755 club—honoring Hank Aaron's home run total—but also the Chophouse bar and grill for 20-somethings and a big playground sponsored by Cartoon Network. Each of these attractions become part of the customer experience that the team wants its fans to enjoy—and they are almost as important as fielding a winning team.[22]

Stage 2: Idea Generation

Idea generation is the stage of the new-product process that develops a pool of concepts as candidates for new products, building upon the previous stage's results. Several sources generate new-product ideas.

Customer and Supplier Suggestions   Firms ask their salespeople to talk to their customers and ask their purchasing personnel to talk to their suppliers to discover new-product ideas.[23] Whirlpool gets ideas from customers on ways to standardize

FIGURE 10–6
Carefully using the seven stages in the new-product process increases the chances of new-product success

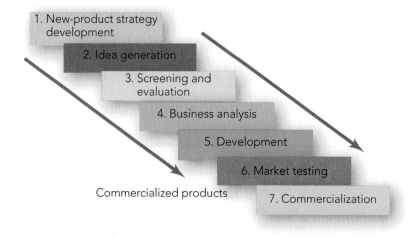

A visit to watch an Atlanta Braves baseball game is often a lot more than the game itself. As described in the text, it may involve a meal at the Chophouse or many other services.

components so that it can cut the number of different product platforms to reduce costs.[24] Business researchers emphasize that firms must actively involve customers and suppliers in the new-product development process.[25] This means the focus should be on what the new product will actually *do* for them rather than simply *what they want.*[26]

A. G. Lafley, CEO of Procter & Gamble (P&G), gave his executives a *revolutionary* thought: "look outside the company for solutions to problems rather than insisting P&G knows best." When he ran P&G's laundry detergent business, he had to redesign the laundry boxes so they were easier to open. Why? While consumers *said* P&G's laundry boxes were "easy to open," cameras they agreed to have installed in their laundry rooms showed they opened the boxes with *screwdrivers!*[27]

Employee and Co-Worker Suggestions   Employees should be encouraged to suggest new-product ideas through suggestion boxes. The idea for Nature Valley Granola Bars from General Mills came when one of its marketing managers observed co-workers bringing granola to work in plastic bags.

Would women *really* help design this car? For how Volvo said "yes," see the text.

Auto industry studies show that women buy about two-thirds of all vehicles and influence about 85 percent of all sales. However, many automakers do marketing research on car-loving, "gear-head" guys to get ideas on new-car features. To bridge the gender gap, Volvo did the *exact opposite*: it obtained ideas on new-car features from all-female focus groups from its Swedish workforce. It then named a five-woman team of Volvo managers to design a "concept car"—what the auto industry uses to test new designs, technical innovations, and consumer reactions. One innovative feature: when pressing an ignition key button, the car's gull-wing doors pop open and the steering wheel pulls in to get into the car easier.[28]

Research and Development Laboratories   A major source of new products is a firm's own R&D laboratories. But Apple, known for its innovative designs, will also go outside its own labs and seek the expertise of others. IDEO, a world-renowned product design firm, helped Apple develop its "mouse" for the Macintosh computer that debuted in 1984. Another source consists of external professional R&D laboratories or "innovation labs" that can also provide new-product ideas.[29] For example, labs at Arthur D. Little helped put the crunch in Cap'n Crunch cereal and the flavor in Carnation Instant Breakfast.

Competitive Products Analyzing the competition can lead to new-product ideas. For six months, the Marriott Corporation sent a six-person intelligence team to travel and stay at economy hotels around the country. The team assessed the competitions' strengths and weaknesses on everything from the soundproof qualities of the rooms to the softness of the towels. Marriott then budgeted $500 million for a new economy hotel chain—Fairfield Inns.

Universities, Inventors, and Small Technology Firms Many firms, such as Texas Instruments, look for visionaries outside their firms that have inventions or innovative ideas that could turn into products. Some sources include:

- *Universities*. Many universities have technology transfer centers that often partner with firms like TI to commercialize inventions of their faculty.
- *Inventors*. Many lone inventors and entrepreneurs develop brilliant ideas—like the Israeli who invented a "tricorder" device like the one seen on the original *Star Trek* TV series: Aim it at a patient and then see his/her vital signs.[30]
- *Small technology firms*. Hewlett-Packard, Google, and the Geek Squad were tiny start-up businesses until a venture capital firm or large corporation found them, invested money in them, and helped them grow.

Stage 3: Screening and Evaluation

Screening and evaluation is the stage of the new-product process that internally and externally evaluates new-product ideas to eliminate those that warrant no further effort.

Internal Approach A firm's employees evaluate the technical feasibility of a proposed new-product idea to determine whether it meets the objectives defined in the new-product strategy development step. For example, 3M scientists develop many world-class innovations in its labs. A recent innovation was its micro-replication technology—one that has 3,000 tiny gripping "fingers" per square inch. An internal assessment showed 3M that this technology could be used to improve the gripping of golf or work gloves.

Organizations that develop service-dominated offerings need to ensure that employees have the commitment and skills to meet customer expectations and sustain customer loyalty—an important criterion in screening a new-service idea. This is the essence of **customer experience management (CEM)**, which is the process of managing the entire customer experience within the firm. Marketers must consider employees' interactions with customers so that the new services are consistently delivered and experienced, clearly differentiated from other service offerings, and relevant and valuable to the target market.

customer experience management (CEM)
Process of managing the entire customer experience within the firm

External Approach Firms use *concept tests*, external evaluations with consumers that consist of preliminary testing of a new-product idea rather than an actual product. Generally, these tests are more useful with minor modifications of existing products than with new, innovative products with which consumers are not familiar.[31] Concept tests rely on written descriptions of the product but may be augmented with sketches, mock-ups, or promotional literature. Key questions for concept testing include: How does the customer perceive the product? Who would use it? and How would it be used?

learning review

6. What step in the new-product process has been added in recent years?

7. What are the main sources of new-product ideas?

8. How do internal and external screening and evaluation approaches differ?

How do you print ink-jet images on Pringles chips safely and inexpensively? The text describes how a global search found the critical technology.

Stage 4: Business Analysis

Business analysis specifies the features of the product and the marketing strategy needed to bring it to market and make financial projections. This is the last checkpoint before significant resources are invested to create a *prototype*—a full-scale operating model of the product. The business analysis stage assesses the total "business fit" of the proposed new product with the company's mission and objectives—from whether the product can be economically developed and manufactured to the marketing strategy needed to have it succeed in the marketplace.

This process requires not only detailed financial projections but also assessments of the marketing and product synergies related to the company's existing operations. Will the new product require a lot of new machinery to produce it or can we use unused capacity of existing machines? Will the new product cannibalize sales of our existing products or increase revenues by reaching new market segments? Can the new product be protected with a patent or copyright? Financial projections of expected profits require estimates of expected prices per unit and units sold, as well as detailed estimates of the costs of R&D, production, and marketing.

For services, business analysis must consider *capacity management*, integrating the service component of the marketing mix with efforts to influence consumer demand. Most services are perishable and have a limited capacity due to the inseparability of the service from its provider. Therefore, a service provider must manage the availability of the offering so that demand matches capacity over the duration of the demand cycle (one day, a week, and so on). For example, airlines and mobile phone service providers use *off-peak pricing* to charge different prices for different times of the day or week to reflect the variations in demand for their services. This enables them to maximize ROI.[32]

Stage 5: Development

Development is the stage of the new-product process that turns the idea on paper into a prototype. This results in a demonstrable, producible product that involves not only manufacturing the product but also performing laboratory and consumer tests to ensure it meets the standards established for it in the protocol. Moreover, the new product must be able to be manufactured at reasonable cost with the required quality.

A brainstorming session at Procter & Gamble produced the idea of printing pop culture images on Pringles chips. But how do you print sharp images using edible dyes on millions of chips—like those for *Spiderman 3?* Internal development would be too long and costly, so P&G circulated a description of its unusual printing need globally. A university professor in Bologna, Italy, had invented an ink-jet method for printing edible images on cakes and cookies. In less than a year, P&G adapted the process and launched its new "Pringle Prints"—at a fraction of the time and cost internal development would have taken.[33]

During development, laboratory tests like this one on Barbie result in safer dolls and toys for children.

For services, developing customer service delivery expectations is critical. This involves analyzing the entire sequence of steps or "service encounters" that make up the service and then developing a flowchart of the points of interaction between consumers and the service provider.[34] High-contact services such as hotels, educational institutions, and car rental agencies use this approach to enhance customer relationships.

Safety tests are also critical for when the product isn't used as planned. To make sure seven-year-olds can't bite Barbie's head off and choke, Mattel clamps her foot in steel jaws in a test stand and then pulls on her head with a wire.

Demographic Characteristic	USA	Wichita Falls, TX
2000 population	281.4 mil.	140,518
Median age (years)	35.3	33.6
% of family households with children under 18	32.8%	33.8%
% Hispanic or Latino of any race	12.5%	11.8%
% African American	12.3%	9.6%
% Asian American	3.6%	1.7%
% Native American	1.5%	1.7%

FIGURE 10–7

Six important U.S. test markets and the "demographics winner": the Wichita Falls, Texas, metropolitan statistical area

Similarly, car manufacturers have done extensive safety tests by crashing their cars into concrete walls.

Stage 6: Market Testing

Market testing is the stage of the new-product process that involves exposing actual products to prospective consumers under realistic purchase conditions to see if they will buy. Often a product is developed, tested, refined, and then tested again to get consumer reactions through either test marketing or simulated test markets.

Test Marketing *Test marketing* involves offering a product for sale on a limited basis in a defined area. This test is done to determine whether consumers will actually buy the product and to try different ways of marketing it. Only about a third of the products test marketed do well enough to go on to the next stage. These market tests are usually conducted in cities that are viewed as being representative of U.S. consumers like the six shown in Figure 10–7. Of these cities, Wichita Falls, Texas, most closely matches the U.S. average found in the 2000 Census. Other criteria used in selecting test market cities include cable systems to deliver different ads to different homes, and tracking systems like those of ACNielsen to measure sales resulting from different advertising campaigns.[35]

This information gives the company an indication of potential sales volume and market share in the test area. Market tests are also used to check other elements of the marketing mix besides the product itself such as price, level of advertising support, and distribution. Because these market tests also are so time consuming and expensive and can alert competitors to a firm's plans, some firms skip test markets or use simulated test markets.

Simulated Test Markets Because of the time, cost, and confidentiality problems of test markets, consumer packaged goods companies often turn to *simulated* (or *laboratory*) *test markets* (*STM*), a technique that simulates a full-scale test market but in a limited fashion. STMs are often run in shopping malls, where consumers are questioned to identify who uses the product class being tested. Next, willing participants are questioned on usage, reasons for purchase, and important product attributes. Qualified persons are then shown TV commercials or print ads for the test product along with competitors' advertising. Finally, they are given money to make a decision to buy or not buy the firm's product—or the competitors' product—from a real or simulated store environment.

Commercializing a new french fry: To learn how Burger King's improved french fries confronted McDonald's fries, see the text.

When Test Markets Don't Work Test marketing is a valuable step in the new-product process, but not all products can use it. Testing a service beyond the concept level is very difficult because the service is intangible and consumers can't see what they are buying. For example, how do you test market a new building for an art museum?

Similarly, test markets for expensive consumer products such as cars or costly industrial products such as jet engines are impractical. For these products, reactions of potential buyers to mockup designs or one-of-a-kind prototypes are all that is feasible.

Stage 7: Commercialization

Finally, the product is brought to the point of *commercialization*—the stage of the new-product process that positions and launches a new product in full-scale production and sales. Companies proceed very carefully at the commercialization stage because this is the most expensive stage for most new products. If competitors introduce a product that leapfrogs the firm's own new product or if cannibalization of its own existing products looks significant, the firm may halt the new-product launch permanently.

Countless other questions arise.[36] Should we make an advance announcement of the new-product introduction to stimulate interest and potential sales?[37] Do we need to add new salespeople?[38] Do the salespeople need extra training?

Large companies use *regional rollouts*, introducing the product sequentially into geographical areas of the United States, to allow production levels and marketing activities to build up gradually to minimize the risk of new-product failure. Grocery product manufacturers and telephone service providers are examples of firms that use this strategy.

Burger King's French Fries: The Complexities of Commercialization
Burger King's "improved french fries" are an example of what can go wrong at the commercialization stage. In the fast-food industry, McDonald's french fries are the gold standard against which all other fries are measured. In 1996, Burger King decided to take on McDonald's fries and spent millions of R&D dollars developing a starch-coated fry designed to retain heat longer and add crispiness. This crispiness was even defined: "An audible crunch that should be present for seven or more chews!"

A 100-person team set to work and developed the starch-coated fry that beat McDonald's fries in taste tests, 57 percent to 35 percent, with 8 percent having no opinion. After "certifrying" 300,000 managers and employees on the new frying procedures, the fries were launched in early 1998 with a $70 million marketing budget. The launch turned into disaster. The reason: The new fry proved too complicated to get right day after day in Burger King restaurants, except under ideal conditions.[39]

By summer 2000, Burger King realized something had to be done. Solution: launch a "new," coated fry in early 2001 that is easier for its kitchens to prepare. A commercialization stage success? You be the judge.

Effective cross-functional teams at Hewlett-Packard have reduced new-product development times significantly—often with the aid of "fences."

The Risks and Uncertainties of the Commercialization Stage New grocery products pose special commercialization problems. Because shelf space is so limited, many supermarkets require a *slotting fee* for new products, a payment a manufacturer makes to place a new item on a retailer's shelf. This can run to several million dollars for a single product. But there's even another potential expense. If a new grocery product does not achieve a predetermined sales target, some retailers require a *failure fee*, a penalty payment a manufacturer makes to compensate a retailer for sales its valuable shelf space failed to make. These costly slotting fees and failure fees are further examples of why large grocery product manufacturers use regional rollouts.

Speed as a Factor in New-Product Success   In recent years, companies have discovered that speed or *time to market* (TtM) is often vital in introducing a new product. Recent studies have shown that high-tech products coming to market on time are far more profitable than those arriving late. So some companies—such as Sony, BMW, 3M, and Hewlett-Packard—have overlapped the sequence of stages described in this chapter.

With this approach, termed *parallel development*, cross-functional team members who conduct the simultaneous development of both the product and the production process stay with the product from conception to production. This has enabled Hewlett-Packard to reduce the development time for notebook computers from 12 months to 7. In software development, *fast prototyping* used a "do it, try it, fix it" approach—encouraging continuing improvement even after the initial design. To speed up time to market many large companies are building "fences" around their new product teams to keep them from getting bogged down in red tape.[40]

---

learning review

9. How does the development stage of the new-product process involve testing the product inside and outside the firm?

10. What is a test market?

11. What is the commercialization of a new product?

LEARNING OBJECTIVES REVIEW

LO1   *Recognize the various terms that pertain to products and services.*

A product is a good, service, or idea consisting of a bundle of tangible and intangible attributes that satisfies consumers and is received in exchange for money or something else of value.

A good has tangible attributes that a consumer's five senses can perceive and intangible ones such as warranties; a laptop computer is an example. Goods can also be divided into nondurable goods, which are consumed in one or a few uses, and durable goods, which usually last over many uses. Services are intangible activities or benefits that an organization provides to satisfy consumer needs in exchange for money or something else of value, such as an airline trip. An idea is a thought that leads to a product or action, such as eating healthier foods.

LO2   *Identify the ways in which consumer and business products and services can be classified.*

By type of user, the major distinctions are consumer products, which are products purchased by the ultimate consumer, and business products, which are products that assist in providing other products for resale.

Consumer products can be broken down based on the effort involved in the purchase decision process, marketing mix attributes used in the purchase, and the frequency of purchase: (*a*) convenience products are items that consumers purchase frequently and with a minimum of shopping effort; (*b*) shopping products are items for which consumers compare several alternatives on selected criteria; (*c*) specialty products are items that consumers make special efforts to seek out and buy; and (*d*) unsought products are items that consumers do not either know about or initially want.

Business products can be broken down into (*a*) components, which are items that become part of the final product, such as raw materials or parts, and (*b*) support products, which are items used to assist in producing other goods and services and include installations, accessory equipment, supplies, and industrial services.

Services can be classified in terms of whether they are delivered by (*a*) people or equipment, (*b*) business firms or nonprofit organizations, or (*c*) government agencies.

Firms can offer a range of products, which involve decisions regarding the product item, product line, and product mix.

LO3   *Describe four unique elements of services.*

The four unique elements or services—the four I's—are intangibility, inconsistency, inseparability, and inventory. Intangibility refers to the tendency of services to be a performance that cannot be held or touched, rather than an object. Inconsistency is a characteristic of services because they depend on people to deliver them, and people vary in their capabilities and in their day-to-day performance. Inseparability refers to the difficulty of separating the deliverer of the services (hair stylist) from the service itself (hair salon). Inventory refers to the need to have service production capability when there is service demand.

LO4   *Explain the significance of "newness" in new products and services as it relates to the degree of consumer learning involved.*

From the important perspective of the consumer, "newness" is often seen as the degree of learning that a consumer must engage in to use the product. With a continuous innovation, no new behaviors must be learned. With a dynamically continuous innovation, only minor behavioral changes are needed. With a discontinuous innovation, consumers must learn entirely new consumption patterns.

LO5 *Describe the factors contributing to a new product's or service's success or failure.*
A new product or service often fails for these marketing reasons: (*a*) insignificant points of difference, (*b*) incomplete market and product definition before product development starts, (*c*) too little market attractiveness, (*d*) poor execution of the marketing mix, (*e*) poor product quality, (*f*) not satisfying customer needs on critical factors, (*g*) bad timing, and (*h*) no economical access to buyers.

LO6 *Explain the purposes of each step of the new-product process.*
The new-product process consists of seven stages a firm uses to develop a salable good or service: (*a*) New-product strategy development involves defining the role for the new product within the firm's overall objectives. (*b*) Idea generation involves developing a pool of concepts from consumers, employees, basic R&D, and competitors to serve as candidates for new products. (*c*) Screening and evaluation involves evaluating new product ideas to eliminate those that are not feasible from a technical or consumer perspective. (*d*) Business analysis involves defining the features of the new product, developing the marketing strategy and marketing program to introduce it, and making a financial forecast. (*e*) Development involves not only producing a prototype product but also testing it in the lab and on consumers to see that it meets the standards set for it. (*f*) Market testing involves exposing actual products to prospective consumers under realistic purchasing conditions to see if they will buy the product. (*g*) Commercialization involves positioning and launching a product in full-scale production and sales with a specific marketing program.

FOCUSING ON KEY TERMS

APPLYING MARKETING KNOWLEDGE

1 Products can be classified as either consumer or business goods. How would you classify the following products? (*a*) Johnson's baby shampoo, (*b*) a Black & Decker two-speed drill, and (*c*) an arc welder.

2 Are Nature Valley Granola bars and Eddie Bauer hiking boots convenience, shopping, specialty, or unsought products?

3 Based on your answer to question 2, how would the marketing actions differ for each product and the classification to which you assigned it?

4 Explain how the four I's of services would apply to a Marriott Hotel.

5 Idle production capacity may be related to inventory or capacity management. How would the pricing component of the marketing mix reduce idle production capacity for (*a*) a car wash, (*b*) a stage theater group, and (*c*) a university?

6 In terms of the behavioral effect on consumers, how would a PC, such as an Apple iMac, be classified? In light of this classification, what actions would you suggest to the manufacturers of these products to increase their sales in the market?

7 What methods would you suggest to assess the potential commercial success for the following new products? (*a*) a new, improved ketchup; (*b*) a three-dimensional television system that took the company 10 years to develop; and (*c*) a new children's toy on which the company holds a patent.

8 Concept testing is an important step in the new-product process. Outline the concept tests for (*a*) an electrically powered car and (*b*) a new loan payment system for automobiles that is based on a variable interest rate. What are the differences in developing concept tests for products as opposed to services?

building your marketing plan

In fine-tuning the product strategy for your marketing plan, do these two things:

1 Develop a simple three-column table in which (*a*) market segments of potential customers are in the first column and (*b*) the one or two key points of differences of the product to satisfy the segment's needs are in the second column.

2 In the third column of your table, write ideas for specific new products for your business in each of the rows in your table.

Vivian Callaway, vice president for the Center for Learning and Experimentation at General Mills, retells the story for the "indulgent, delicious, and gooey" Warm Delights™. She summarizes, "When you want something that is truly innovative, you have to look at the rules you have been assuming in your category and break them all!"

When a new business achieves a breakthrough, it looks easy to outsiders. The creators of Betty Crocker Warm Delights stress that if the marketing decisions had been based on the traditions and history of the cake category, a smaller, struggling business would have resulted. Vivian Callaway (see photo) and her team chose to challenge the assumptions and expectations of accumulated cake category business experience. The team took personal and business risks and Warm Delights is a roaring success.

PLANNING PHASE: INNOVATION, BUT A SHRINKING MARKET

"In the typical grocery store, the baking mix aisle is a quiet place," says Callaway. Shelves sigh with flavors, types, and brands. Prices are low, but there is little consumer traffic. Cake continues to be a tradition

for birthdays and social occasions. But, consumer demand declines. The percentage of U.S. households that bought at least one baking mix in 2000 was 80 percent. Four years later, the percentage of households was 77 percent, a very significant decline of 3 percentage points.

Today, a promoted price of 89 cents to make a 9 × 12 inch cake is common. Many choices, but little differentiation, gradually falling sales, and low uniform prices are the hallmarks of a mature category. But it's not that consumers don't buy cake-like treats. In fact, indulgent treats are growing. The premium prices for ice cream ($3.00 a pint) and chocolate ($3.00 a bar) are not slowing consumer purchases.

The Betty Crocker marketing team challenged the food scientists at General Mills to create a great tasting, easy to prepare, single-serve cake treat. The goal: make it indulgent, delicious, and gooey. The team focused the scientists on a product that would have:

- Consistent great taste.
- Quick preparation.

- A single portion.
- No clean-up.

The food scientists delivered the prototype! Now, the marketing team began hammering out the four P's. They started with a descriptive name "Betty Crocker Dessert Bowls" (see photo) and a plan to shelve it in the "quiet" cake aisle. This practical approach would meet the consumer need for a "small, fast, microwave cake" for dessert. Several marketing challenges emerged:

- *The comparison problem.* The easy shelf price comparison to 9 × 12 inch cakes selling for 89 cents would make it harder to price Dessert Bowls at $2.00.
- *The communication problem.* The product message "a small, faster-to-make cake" wasn't compelling. For example, after-school snacks should be fast and small, but "dessert" sounds too indulgent.
- *The quiet aisle problem.* The cake-aisle shopper is probably not browsing for a cake innovation.
- *The dessert problem.* Consumer's on-the-go, calorie conscious meal plans don't generally include a planned dessert.
- *The microwave problem.* Consumers might not believe it tastes good.

So, the small, fast-cake product didn't resonate with a compelling consumer need. But it would be a safe bet because the Dessert Bowl positioning fit nicely with the family-friendly Betty Crocker brand.

IMPLEMENTATION PHASE: WHO WANTS INDULGENT TREATS?

The consumer insights team really enjoyed the hot, gooey cake product. They feared that it would languish in the cake aisle under the Dessert Bowl name because this didn't capture the essence of what the food delivered. They explored who really are the indulgent treat customers. The data revealed that the heaviest buyers of premium treats are women without children. This focused the team on the key question about the target consumer: "What does she want?" They enlisted an ad agency and consultants to come up with a name that would appeal to "her." Several independently suggested the "Warm Delights" name.

Targeting on-the-go women who want a small, personal treat had marketing advantages:

- The $2.00 Warm Delight price compared favorably to the price of many single-serve indulgent treats.
- The product food message "warm, convenient, delightful" is compelling.
- On-the-go women's meal plans do include the occasional delicious treat.

One significant problem remained: the cake aisle shopper is probably not browsing for an indulgent, single-serve treat.

The marketing team solved this shelving issue by using advertising and product displays outside the cake aisle. This would raise women's awareness of Warm Delights. Television advertising and in-store display programs are costly, so Warm Delights sales would have to be strong to pay back the investment.

Vivian Callaway and the team turned to market research to fine-tune the plan. The research put Warm Delights (and Dessert Bowls) on the shelf in real (different) stores. A few key findings emerged. First, the name "Warm Delights" beat "Dessert Bowls." Second, the Warm Delights with nuts simply wasn't easy to prepare, so nuts were removed. Third, the packaging with a disposable bowl beat the typical cake-mix packaging involving using your own bowl. Finally, by putting the actual product on supermarket shelves and in displays in the stores, sales volumes could be analyzed.

EVALUATION PHASE: TURNING THE PLAN INTO ACTION!

The marketing plan isn't action. Sales for "Warm Delights" required the marketing team to: (1) get the retailers to stock the product, preferably somewhere other than the cake aisle, and (2) appeal to consumers enough to have them buy, like, and re-buy the product.

The initial acceptance of a product by retailers is important. But store managers must experience good sales of Warm Delights to be motivated to keep their shelves restocked with the product.

Did the customer buy one or two Warm Delights? Did the customer return for a second purchase a few weeks later? The syndicated services that sell household panel purchase data provide the answer. The team evaluates these reports to see if the number of people who tried the product matches expectations and how the repeat purchases occur. Often, the 80/20 rule applies. So, in the early months, is there a group of consumers that buys repeatedly and will fill this role?

For ongoing feedback, calls by Warm Delights consumers to the free consumer information line are monitored. This is a great source of real-time feedback. If a pattern emerges and these calls are mostly about the same problem, that is bad. However, when consumers call to say "thank you" or "it's great," that is good. This is an informal quick way to identify if the product is on track or further investigation is warranted.

GOOD MARKETING MAKES A DIFFERENCE

The team took personal and business risks by choosing a Warm Delights plan over the more conservative Dessert Bowl plan. Today, General Mills has loyal Warm Delight consumers who are open to trying new flavors, new sizes, and new forms. What would you do to grow this brand?

Questions

1 What is the competitive set of desserts in which Warm Delights is located?

2 (*a*) Who is the target market? (*b*) What is the point of difference on the positioning for Warm Delights? (*c*) What are the potential opportunities and hindrances of the target market and positioning?

3 (*a*) What marketing research did Vivian Callaway execute? (*b*) What were the critical questions that she sought research and expert advice to get answers to? (*c*) How did this affect the product's marketing mix price, promotion, packaging, and distribution decisions?

4 (*a*) What initial promotional plan directed to consumers in the target market did Callaway use? (*b*) Why did this make sense to Callaway and her team when Warm Delights was launched?

5 If you were a consultant to Vivian Callaway, what product changes would you recommend to increase sales of Warm Delights?product line

11

Managing Products, Services, and Brands

GATORADE: SATISFYING THE UNQUENCHABLE THIRST

The thirst for Gatorade is unquenchable. This brand powerhouse has posted yearly sales gains over four decades and commands about 82 percent of the sports beverage market in the United States.

Like Kleenex in the tissue market, Jello among gelatin desserts, and iPod for digital music players. Gatorade has become synonymous with sports beverages. Concocted in 1965 at the University of Florida as a rehydration beverage for the school's football team, the drink was coined "Gatorade" by an opposing team's coach after watching his team lose to the Florida Gators in the Orange Bowl. The name stuck, and a new beverage product class was born.

Stokely-Van Camp Inc. bought the Gatorade formula in 1967 and commercialized the product. The original Gatorade was a liquid with a lemon-lime flavor. An orange flavor was introduced in 1971 and a fruit punch flavor in 1983. Instant Gatorade arrived in 1979.

The Quaker Oats Company acquired Stokely-Van Camp in 1983. Quaker Oats executives quickly grew sales through a variety of means. More flavors were added and multiple package sizes were offered using different containers—glass and plastic bottles and aluminum cans. Distribution coverage expanded from convenience stores and supermarkets to vending machines, fountain service, and mass merchandisers such as Wal-Mart. Consistent advertising and promotion effectively conveyed the product's unique benefits and links to athletic competition. International opportunities were vigorously pursued. Today, Gatorade is sold in more than 90 countries in North America, Europe, Latin America, the Middle East, Africa, Asia, and Australia and has become a global brand.

Brand development spurred Gatorade's success. Gatorade Frost was introduced in 1997, with a "lighter, crisper" taste aimed at expanding the brand's reach beyond organized sports to other usage occasions. Gatorade Fierce with a "bolder" taste appeared in 1999. In the same year, Gatorade entered the bottled-water category with Propel Fitness Water, a lightly flavored water fortified with vitamins. The Gatorade Performance Series was introduced in 2001, featuring a Gatorade Energy Bar, Gatorade Energy Drink, and Gatorade Nutritional Shake.

Brand development accelerated after PepsiCo Inc. purchased Quaker Oats and the Gatorade brand in 2001. Gatorade All Stars, designed for teens, and Gatorade Xtremo, developed for Latino consumers with an exotic blend of flavors and a bilingual label, were introduced in 2002. Gatorade X-Factor followed in 2003 with three flavors. In 2005, Gatorade Endurance Formula was introduced for serious runners, construction workers, and other people doing long, sweaty workouts. Gatorade Rain, a lighter tasting version of regular Gatorade, arrived

Gatorade's success is a direct result of masterful product and brand management over 45 years.

in 2006 with berry, lime, and tangerine flavors. In 2007, Gatorade A.M. debuted for the morning workout consumer with three morning-friendly flavors and no caffeine. A low-calorie Gatorade drink called G2 was launched in 2008 as well as Gatorade Tiger, named for Tiger Woods. Today, Gatorade is available in over 30 flavors in the United States and more than 50 flavors internationally. Some 45 years after its creation, Gatorade remains a vibrant, multibillion-dollar growth brand with seemingly unlimited potential.[1]

The marketing of Gatorade illustrates effective product and brand management in a dynamic marketplace. This chapter shows how the actions taken by Gatorade executives are typical of those made by successful marketers.

THE PRODUCT LIFE CYCLE

product life cycle

Stages a new product goes through in the marketplace: introduction, growth, maturity, and decline

Products, like people, are viewed as having a life cycle. The concept of the **product life cycle** describes the stages a new product goes through in the marketplace: introduction, growth, maturity, and decline (Figure 11–1).[2] The two curves shown in this figure, total industry sales revenue and total industry profit, represent the sum of sales revenue and profit of all firms producing the product. The reasons for the changes in each curve and the marketing decisions involved are detailed in the following pages.

Introduction Stage

The introduction stage of the product life cycle occurs when a product is introduced to its intended target market. During this period, sales grow slowly, and profit is minimal. The lack of profit is often the result of large investment costs in product development, such as the millions of dollars spent by Gillette to develop the Gillette Fusion razor shaving system. The marketing objective for the company at this stage is to create consumer awareness and stimulate *trial*—the initial purchase of a product by a consumer.

Companies often spend heavily on advertising and other promotion tools to build awareness and stimulate product trial among consumers in the introduction stage. For example, Gillette budgeted $200 million in advertising alone to introduce the Fusion shaving system to male shavers. The result? More than 60 percent of male shavers became aware of the new razor within six months and 26 percent tried the product.[3]

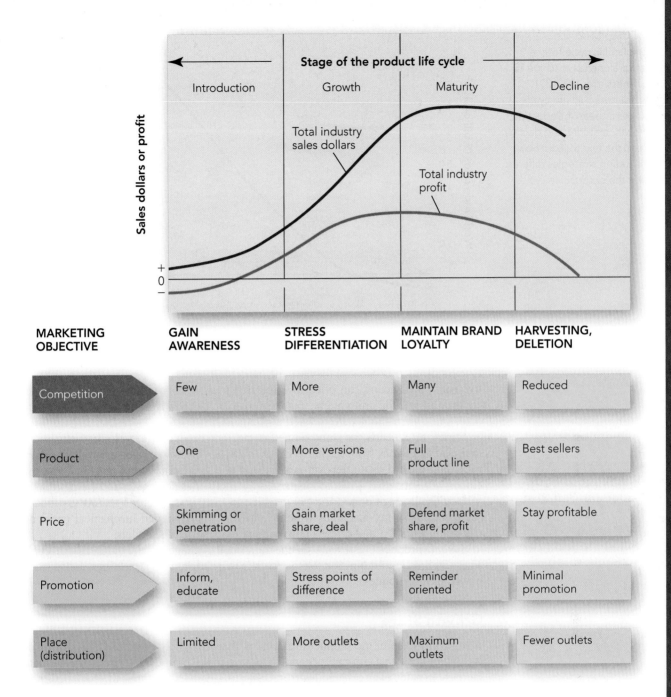

Stage of the product life cycle

	Introduction	Growth	Maturity	Decline

Sales dollars or profit

Total industry sales dollars

Total industry profit

+
0
−

MARKETING OBJECTIVE	GAIN AWARENESS	STRESS DIFFERENTIATION	MAINTAIN BRAND LOYALTY	HARVESTING, DELETION
Competition	Few	More	Many	Reduced
Product	One	More versions	Full product line	Best sellers
Price	Skimming or penetration	Gain market share, deal	Defend market share, profit	Stay profitable
Promotion	Inform, educate	Stress points of difference	Reminder oriented	Minimal promotion
Place (distribution)	Limited	More outlets	Maximum outlets	Fewer outlets

FIGURE 11–1

How stages of the product life cycle relate to a firm's marketing objectives and marketing mix actions

Advertising and promotion expenditures in the introduction stage are often made to stimulate *primary demand,* the desire for the product class rather than for a specific brand, since there are few competitors with the same product. As more competitors launch their own products and the product progresses along its life cycle, company attention is focused on creating *selective demand,* the preference for a specific brand.

Other marketing mix variables also are important at this stage. Gaining distribution can be a challenge because channel intermediaries may be hesitant to carry a new product. Also, a company often restricts the number of variations of the product to ensure control of product quality. Remember that the original Gatorade came in only one flavor—lemon-lime.

During introduction, pricing can be either high or low. A high initial price may be used as part of a *skimming* strategy to help the company recover the costs of development as well as capitalize on the price insensitivity of early buyers. A master of this

FIGURE 11–2

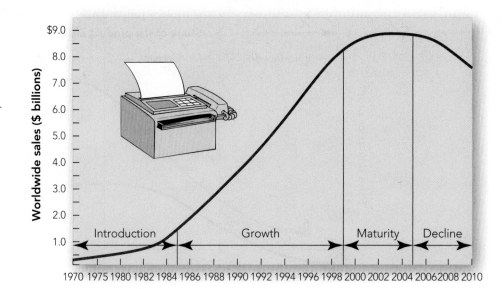

Product life cycle for the
stand-alone fax machine for
business use: 1970–2010.
All four product life-cycle
stages appear: introduction,
growth, maturity, and decline.
Read the text to learn how
marketing strategies differed
over the product life cycle.

strategy is 3M. According to a 3M manager, "We hit fast, price high, and get the heck out when the me-too products pour in."[4] High prices tend to attract competitors eager to enter the market because they see the opportunity for profit. To discourage competitive entry, a company can price low, referred to as *penetration pricing*. This pricing strategy helps build unit volume, but a company must closely monitor costs. These and other pricing techniques are covered in Chapter 12.

Figure 11–2 charts the stand-alone fax machine product life cycle for business use in the United States from the early 1970s to 2010.[5] As shown, sales grew slowly in the 1970s and early 1980s after Xerox pioneered the first portable fax machine. Fax machines were first sold direct to businesses by company salespeople and were premium priced. The average price for a fax machine in 1980 was a hefty $12,700. By today's standards, those fax machines were primitive. They contained mechanical parts, not electronic circuitry, and offered few features seen in today's models.

Several product classes are in the introductory stage of the product life cycle. These include high-definition television (HDTV) and "hybrid" (gasoline- and electric-powered) automobiles.

Growth Stage

The growth stage of the product life cycle is characterized by rapid increases in sales. It is in this stage that competitors appear. For example, Figure 11–2 shows the dramatic increase in sales of fax machines from 1986 to 1998. The number of companies selling fax machines also increased, from one in the early 1970s to four in the late 1970s to seven manufacturers in 1983, which sold nine brands. By 1998 there were some 25 manufacturers and 60 brands from which to choose.

The result of more competitors and more aggressive pricing is that profit usually peaks during the growth stage. For instance, the average price for a fax machine plummeted from $3,300 in 1985 to $500 in 1995. At this stage, the emphasis of advertising shifts to stimulating selective demand, in which product benefits are compared with those of competitors' offerings for the purpose of gaining market share.

Product sales in the growth stage grow at an increasing rate because of new people trying or using the product and a growing proportion of *repeat purchasers*—people who tried the product, were satisfied, and bought again. For the Gillette Fusion razor, over 60 percent of men who tried the razor adopted the product permanently. For successful products, the ratio of repeat to trial purchases grows as the product moves through the life cycle. Durable fax machines meant that replacement purchases were

Hybrid automobiles made by Honda are in the introductory stage of the product life cycle. Digital cameras produced by Panasonic are in the growth stage. Each product and company faces unique challenges based on its product life-cycle stage.

rare. However, it became common for more than one machine to populate a business as their use became more widespread. In 1998, there was one fax machine for every eight people in a business in the United States.

Changes appear in the product in the growth stage. To help differentiate a company's brand from competitors, an improved version or new features are added to the original design, and product proliferation occurs. Changes in fax machines included (1) models with built-in telephones; (2) models that used plain, rather than thermal, paper for copies; (3) models that integrated electronic mail; and (4) models that permitted confidential transmissions.

In the growth stage it is important to gain as much distribution for the product as possible. In the retail store, for example, this often means that competing companies fight for display and shelf space. Expanded distribution in the fax industry is an example. Early in the growth stage, just 11 percent of office machine dealers carried this equipment. By the mid-1990s, more than 70 percent of these dealers sold fax equipment, and distribution was expanded to other stores selling electronic equipment.

Numerous product classes or industries are in the growth stage of the product life cycle. Examples include digital music players and digital cameras.

Maturity Stage

The maturity stage is characterized by a slowing of total industry sales or product class revenue. Also, marginal competitors begin to leave the market. Most consumers who would buy the product are either repeat purchasers of the item or have tried and abandoned it. Sales increase at a decreasing rate in the maturity stage as fewer new buyers enter the market. Profit declines due to fierce price competition among many sellers, and the cost of gaining new buyers at this stage rises.

Marketing attention in the maturity stage is often directed toward holding market share through further product differentiation and finding new buyers. Fax machine manufacturers developed Internet-enabled multifunctional models with new features

Will E-mail Spell Extinction for Fax Machines?

Technological substitution that creates value for customers often causes the decline stage in the product life cycle. Will e-mail replace fax machines?

This question has been debated for years. Even though e-mail continues to grow with broadening Internet access, millions of fax machines are still sold each years. Industry analysts estimate that the number of e-mail mailboxes worldwide will grow to 2.5 billion in 2010. However, the phenomenal popularity of e-mail has not brought fax machines to extinction. Why? The two technologies do not directly compete for the same messaging applications.

E-mail is used for text messages, and faxing is predominately used for communicating formatted documents by business users. Fax usage is expected to increase through 2009, even though unit sales of fax machines have declined on a worldwide basis. Internet technology and e-mail may eventually replace facsimile technology and paper, but not in the immediate future.

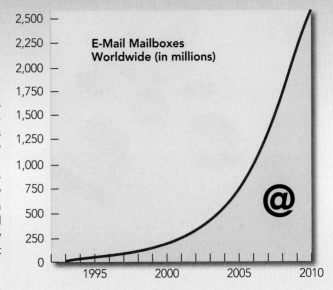

E-Mail Mailboxes Worldwide (in millions)

such as scanning, copying, and color reproduction. They also designed fax machines suitable for small and home businesses, which today represent a substantial portion of sales. Still, a major consideration in a company's strategy in this stage is to control overall marketing cost by improving promotional and distribution efficiency.

Fax machines entered the maturity stage in the late 1990s. At the time, about 90 percent of industry sales were captured by five producers (Hewlett-Packard, Brother, Sharp, Lexmark, and Samsung), reflecting the departure of marginal competitors. By 2004, 200 million stand-alone fax machines were installed throughout the world, sending more than 120 billion faxes annually.

Numerous product classes and industries are in the maturity stage of their product life cycle. These include soft drinks, DVD players, and conventional TVs.

Decline Stage

The decline stage occurs when sales drop. Fax machines for business use moved to this stage in early 2005 and the average price for a fax machine had sunk below $100. Frequently, a product enters this stage not because of any wrong strategy on the part of companies, but because of environmental changes. The word-processing capability of personal computers pushed typewriters into decline. Digital music players are doing the same to compact discs in the recorded music industry. Will Internet technology and e-mail make fax machines extinct any time soon? The accompanying Marketing Matters box offers one perspective on this question.[6]

Products in the decline stage tend to consume a disproportionate share of management and financial resources relative to their future worth. A company will follow one of two strategies to handle a declining product: deletion or harvesting.

Deletion Product *deletion,* or dropping the product from the company's product line, is the most drastic strategy. Because a residual core of consumers still consume or use a product even in the decline stage, product elimination decisions are not taken lightly. For example, Sanford continues to sell its Liquid Paper correction fluid for use with typewriters in the era of word-processing equipment.

Harvesting   A second strategy, *harvesting,* is when a company retains the product but reduces marketing costs. The product continues to be offered to meet customer requests. Coca-Cola, for instance, still sells Tab, its first diet cola, to a small group of die-hard fans. According to Coke's CEO, "It shows you care. We want to make sure those who want Tab, get Tab."[7]

Some Dimensions of the Product Life Cycle

Some important aspects of product life cycles are (1) their length, (2) the shape of their sales curves, and (3) the rate at which consumers adopt products.

Length of the Product Life Cycle   There is no exact time that a product takes to move through its life cycle. As a rule, consumer products have shorter life cycles than business products. For example, many new consumer food products such as Frito-Lay's Baked Lay's potato chips move from the introduction stage to maturity in 18 months. The availability of mass communication vehicles informs consumers quickly and shortens life cycles. Also, technological change tends to shorten product life cycles as new-product innovation replaces existing products.

Shape of the Product Life Cycle   The product life-cycle sales curve shown in Figure 11–1 is the *generalized life cycle,* but not all products have the same shape to their curve. In fact, there are several different life-cycle curves, each type suggesting different marketing strategies. Figure 11–3 shows the shape of life-cycle sales curves for four different types of products: high-learning, low-learning, fashion, and fad products.

A *high-learning product* is one for which significant customer education is required and there is an extended introductory period (Figure 11–3A). Convection ovens, for example, required consumers to learn a new way of cooking and alter familiar recipes used with conventional ovens. As a result, these ovens spent years in the introductory period.

In contrast, for a *low-learning product* sales begin immediately because little learning is required by the consumer, and the benefits of purchase are readily understood (Figure 11–3B). This product often can be easily imitated by competitors, so the marketing strategy is to broaden distribution quickly. In this way, as competitors rapidly enter, most retail outlets already have the innovator's product. It is also important to have the manufacturing

FIGURE 11–3

Alternative product life-cycle curves based on product types. Note the long introduction stage for a high-learning product compared with a low-learning product. Read the text for an explanation of different product life-cycle curves.

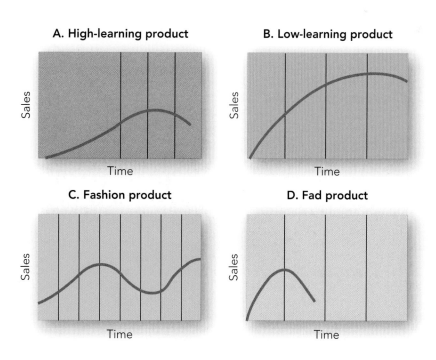

A. High-learning product

B. Low-learning product

C. Fashion product

D. Fad product

capacity to meet demand. An example of a successful low-learning product is Gillette's Fusion razor. This product achieved $1 billion in worldwide sales in less than three years.[8]

A *fashion product* (Figure 11–3C) is a style of the times. Life cycles for fashion products frequently appear in women's and men's apparel. Fashion products are introduced, decline, and then seem to return. The length of the cycles may be months, years, or decades. Consider women's hosiery. Product sales have been declining for years. Women consider it more fashionable to not wear hosiery—bad news for Hanesbrands, the leading marketer of women's sheer hosiery. According to an authority on fashion, "Companies might as well let the fashion cycle take its course and wait for the inevitable return of pantyhose."[9]

A *fad* experiences rapid sales on introduction and then an equally rapid decline (Figure 11–3D). These products are typically novelties and have a short life cycle. They include car tattoos sold in southern California and described as the first removable and reusable graphics for automobiles, and vinyl dresses and fleece bikinis made by a Minnesota clothing company.[10]

The Life Cycle and Consumers The life cycle of a product depends on sales to consumers. Not all consumers rush to buy a product in the introductory stage, and the shapes of the life-cycle curves indicate that most sales occur after the product has been on the market for some time. In essence, a product diffuses, or spreads, through the population, a concept called the *diffusion of innovation.*[11]

Some people are attracted to a product early. Others buy it only after they see their friends or opinion leaders with the item. Figure 11–4 shows the consumer population divided into five categories of product adopters based on when they adopt a new product. Brief profiles accompany each category. For any product to be successful, it must be purchased by innovators and early adopters. This is why manufacturers of new pharmaceuticals try to gain adoption by respected hospitals, clinics, and physicians. Once accepted by innovators and early adopters, the adoption of new products moves on to the early majority, late majority, and laggard categories.

Several factors affect whether a consumer will adopt a new product or not. Common reasons for resisting a product in the introduction stage are usage barriers (the product is not compatible with existing habits), value barriers (the product provides no incentive to change), risk barriers (physical, economic, or social), and psychological barriers (cultural differences or image).[12]

FIGURE 11–4
Five categories and profiles of product adopters. For a product to be successful, it must be purchased by innovators and early adopters.

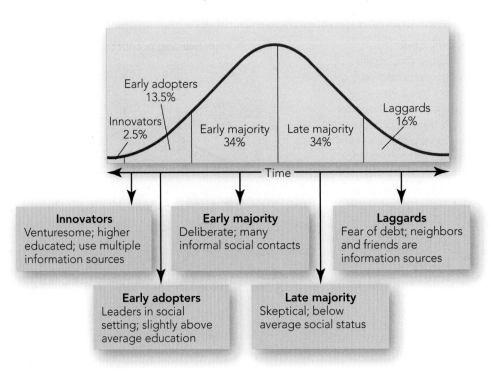

Companies attempt to overcome these barriers in numerous ways. They provide warranties, money-back guarantees, extensive usage instructions, demonstrations, and free samples to stimulate initial trial of new products. For example, software developers offer demonstrations downloaded from the Internet. Maybelline allows consumers to browse through the Cover Girl Color Match system on its website to find out how certain makeup products will look. Free samples are one of the most popular means to gain consumer trial. In fact, 71 percent of consumers consider a sample to be the best way to evaluate a new product.[13]

learning review

1. Advertising plays a major role in the _____ stage of the product life cycle, and _____ plays a major role in maturity.

2. How do high-learning and low-learning products differ?

MANAGING THE PRODUCT LIFE CYCLE

LO2

An important task for a firm is to manage its products through the successive stages of their life cycles. This section describes the role of the product manager who is usually responsible for this and presents three ways to manage a product through its life cycle: modifying the product, modifying the market, and repositioning the product.

Harley-Davidson redesigned some of its motorcycle models to feature smaller hand grips, a lower seat, and an easier-to-pull clutch lever to create a more comfortable ride for women. According to Genevieve Schmitt, founding editor of WomenRidersNow.com, "They realize they are an up-and-coming segment and that they need to accommodate them."

Role of a Product Manager

The product manager, sometimes called *brand manager,* manages the marketing efforts for a close-knit family of products or brands. Introduced by Procter & Gamble in 1928, the product manager style of marketing organization is used by consumer goods firms, such as General Mills, and by industrial firms such as Intel. The U.S. Postal Service also employs product managers.

All product managers are responsible for managing existing products through the stages of the life cycle. Some are also responsible for developing new products. Product managers' marketing responsibilities include developing and executing a marketing program for the product line and approving ad copy, media selection, and package design.

Product managers also engage in extensive data analysis related to their products and brands. Sales, market share, and profit trends are closely monitored. Managers often supplement these data with two measures: (1) a category development index (CDI) and (2) a brand development index (BDI). These indexes help to identify strong and weak market segments (usually demographic or geographic segments) for specific consumer products and brands and provide direction for marketing efforts. The calculation, visual display, and interpretation of these two indexes for Hawaiian Punch are described in the Using Marketing Dashboards box on the next page.

Modifying the Product

Product modification involves altering a product's characteristic, such as its quality, performance, or appearance, to increase the product's value to customers and increase sales. Wrinkle-free and stain-resistant clothing made possible by nanotechnology has revolutionized the men's and women's apparel business and stimulated industry sales of casual pants, shirts, and blouses.

New features, packages, or scents can be used to change a product's characteristics and give the sense of a revised product. Procter & Gamble revamped Pantene shampoo and conditioner with a new vitamin formula and relaunched the brand with

Using Marketing Dashboards
Knowing Your CDI and BDI

Where are sales for my product category and brand strongest and weakest? Data related to this question are often displayed in a marketing dashboard using two indexes: (1) category development index and (2) brand development index.

Your Challenge You have joined the marketing team for Hawaiian Punch, the number 1 fruit punch drink sold in the U.S. The brand has been marketed to mothers with children under 12 years old. The majority of Hawaiian Punch sales are in gallon and 2-liter bottles. Your assignment is to examine the brand's performance and identify growth opportunities for the Hawaiian Punch brand among households that consume prepared fruit drinks (the product category).

Your marketing dashboard displays a category development index and a brand development index provided by a syndicated marketing research firm. Each index is based on the calculations below:

$$\text{Category Development Index (CDI)} = \frac{\substack{\text{Percent of a Product Category's Total} \\ \text{U.S. Sales in a Market Segment}}}{\substack{\text{Percent of the Total U.S. Population in} \\ \text{a Market Segment}}} \times 100$$

$$\text{Brand Development Index (BDI)} = \frac{\substack{\text{Percent of a Brand's Total U.S. Sales in} \\ \text{a Market Segment}}}{\substack{\text{Percent of the Total U.S. Population in} \\ \text{a Market Segment}}} \times 100$$

A CDI over 100 indicates above-average product category purchases by a market segment. A number under 100 indicates below-average purchases. A BDI over 100 indicates a strong brand position in a segment; a number under 100 indicates a weak brand position.

You are interested in CDI and BDI displays for four household segments that consume prepared fruit drinks: (1) households without children, (2) households with children under 6, (3) households with children aged 7 to 12, and (4) households with children aged 13 to 18.

Your Findings The BDI and CDI measures displayed here show that Hawaiian Punch is consumed by households with children, and particularly households with children under age 12. The Hawaiian Punch BDI is over 100 for both segments—not surprising since the brand is marketed to these segments. Households with children 13 to 18 years old evidence high fruit drink consumption with a CDI over 100. But Hawaiian Punch is relatively weak in this segment with a BDI under 100.

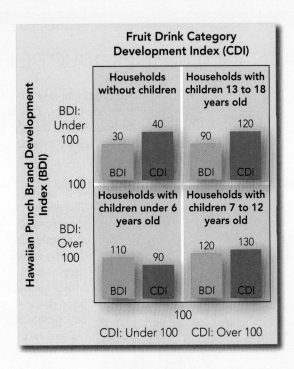

Your Action An opportunity for Hawaiian Punch exists among households with children 13 to 18 years old—teenagers. You might propose that Hawaiian Punch be repositioned for teens. In addition, you might recommend that Hawaiian Punch be packaged in single-serve cans or bottles to attract this segment, much like soft drinks. Teens might also be targeted for advertising and promotions.

a multimillion-dollar advertising and promotion campaign. The result? Pantene, a brand first introduced in the 1940s, is now the top-selling shampoo and conditioner in the United States in an industry with more than 1,000 competitors.

Modifying the Market

With *market modification* strategies, a company tries to find new customers, increase a product's use among existing customers, or create new use situations.

Finding New Customers   Produce companies have begun marketing and packaging prunes as dried plums to attract younger buyers. Harley-Davidson has tailored a marketing program to encourage women to take up cycling, thus doubling the number of potential customers for its motorcycles.[14]

Increasing a Product's Use   Promoting more frequent usage has been a strategy of Campbell Soup Company. Because soup consumption rises in the winter and declines during the summer, the company now advertises more heavily in warm months to encourage consumers to think of soup as more than a cold-weather food. Similarly, the Florida Orange Growers Association advocates drinking orange juice throughout the day rather than for breakfast only.

Creating a New Use Situation   Finding new uses for an existing product has been the strategy behind Dockers, the U.S. market leader in casual pants. Originally intended as a single pant for every situation, Dockers now promotes different looks for different usage situations: work, weekend, dress, and golf.[15] The Milk Processor Education Program suggests new use situations by substituting milk for water or other ingredients when preparing food.

Repositioning the Product

Often a company decides to reposition its product or product line in an attempt to bolster sales. *Product repositioning* changes the place a product occupies in a consumer's mind relative to competitive products. A firm can reposition a product by changing one or more of the four marketing mix elements. Four factors that trigger the need for a repositioning action are discussed next.

Reacting to a Competitor's Position   One reason to reposition a product is because a competitor's entrenched position is adversely affecting sales and market share. New Balance Inc. successfully repositioned its athletic shoes to focus on fit, durability, and comfort rather than competing head-on against Nike and Reebok on fashion and professional sports. The company offers an expansive range of shoes and it networks with podiatrists, not sport celebrities.[16]

Reaching a New Market   When Unilever introduced iced tea in Britain in the mid-1990s, sales were disappointing. British consumers viewed it as leftover hot tea, not suitable for drinking. The company made its tea carbonated and repositioned it as

The Milk Processor Education Program (MilkPEP) promotes the use of milk rather than water or other ingredients in preparing food. According to a MilkPEP executive, "If every household one day a week added milk rather than water to instant coffee and made a caffe latte, it would add [up to] $100 million to the bottom line of the milk industry."

Making Responsible Decisions > > > > > > > > > ethics

Consumer Economics of Downsizing—Get Less, Pay More

For more than 30 years, Starkist put 6.5 ounces of tuna into its regular-sized can. Today, Starkist puts 6.125 ounces of tuna into its can, but charges the same price. Frito-Lay (Doritos and Lay's snack chips), Procter & Gamble (Pampers and Luvs disposable diapers), Nestlé (Poland Spring and Calistoga bottled waters) have whittled away at package contents 5 to 10 percent while maintaining their products' package size, dimensions, and prices. Kimberly-Clark cut its retail price on its jumbo pack of Huggies diapers from $13.50 to $12.50, but reduced the number of diapers per pack from 48 to 42. Georgia-Pacific reduced the content of its Brawny paper towel six-roll pack by 20 percent without lowering the price.

Consumer advocates charge that downsizing the content of packages while maintaining prices is a subtle and unannounced way of taking advantage of consumer buying habits. They also say downsizing is a price increase in disguise and deceptive, but legal. Manufacturers argue that this practice is

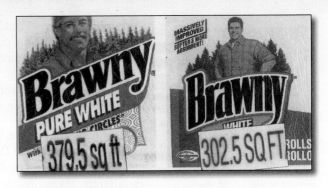

a way of keeping prices from rising beyond psychological barriers for their products.

Is downsizing an unethical practice if manufacturers do not inform consumers that the package contents are less than they were previously?

---

a cold soft drink for teens and sales improved. Johnson & Johnson effectively repositioned St. Joseph Aspirin from one for infants to an adult low-strength aspirin to reduce the risk of heart problems or strokes.[17]

Catching a Rising Trend   Changing consumer trends also lead to repositioning. Growing consumer interest in foods that offer health and dietary benefits is an example.[18] Many products have been repositioned to capitalize on this trend. Calcium-enriched products, such as Kraft American cheese and Uncle Ben's Calcium Plus rice, emphasize healthy bone structure for children and adults. Weight-conscious consumers have embraced low-fat and low-calorie diets in growing numbers. Today, most food and beverage companies offer reduced-fat and low-calorie versions of their products.

Changing the Value Offered   In repositioning a product, a company can decide to change the value it offers buyers and trade up or down. *Trading up* involves adding value to the product (or line) through additional features or higher-quality materials. Michelin and Goodyear have done this with a "run-flat" tire that can travel up to 50 miles at 55 miles per hour after suffering total air loss.

Trading down involves reducing the number of features, quality, or price. For example, some airlines have added more seats, thus reducing legroom, and limited snack service. Trading down exists when companies engage in *downsizing*—reducing the package content without changing package size and maintaining or increasing the package price. Firms are criticized for this practice, as described in the accompanying Making Responsible Decisions box.[19]

---

learning review

3. What does "creating a new use situation" mean in managing a product's life cycle?

4. Explain the difference between trading up and trading down in repositioning.

BRANDING AND BRAND MANAGEMENT

LO3

branding
Organization's use of a name, phrase, design, symbols, or combination of these to identify and distinguish its products

brand name
Any word, device (design, shape, sound, or color), or combination of these used to distinguish a seller's goods or services

brand personality
Set of human characteristics associated with a brand name

Can you describe the brand personality traits for these two brands?

A basic decision in marketing products is **branding**, in which an organization uses a name, phrase, design, symbols, or combination of these to identify its products and distinguish them from those of competitors. A **brand name** is any word, device (design, sound, shape, or color), or combination of these used to distinguish a seller's goods or services. Some brand names can be spoken, such as a Gatorade or Rollerblade. Other brand names cannot be spoken, such as the colored apple (the *logotype* or *logo*) used by Apple.

Consumers may benefit most from branding. Recognizing competing products by distinct trademarks allows them to be more efficient shoppers. Consumers can recognize and avoid products with which they are dissatisfied, while becoming loyal to other, more satisfying brands. As discussed in Chapter 5, brand loyalty often eases consumers' decision making by eliminating the need for an external search.

Brand Personality and Brand Equity

Product managers recognize that brands offer more than product identification and a means to distinguish their products from competitors.[20] Successful and established brands take on a **brand personality**, a set of human characteristics associated with a brand name. Research shows that consumers often assign personality traits to products—traditional, romantic, rugged, sophisticated, rebellious—and choose brands that are consistent with their own or desired self-image. Marketers can and do provide a brand with a personality through advertising that depicts a certain user or usage situation and conveys certain emotions or feelings to be associated with the brand. For example, the personality traits associated with Coca-Cola are all-American and real; with Pepsi, young and exciting; and with Dr Pepper, nonconforming and unique.

brand equity

Added value a brand name gives to a product beyond the functional benefits provided

Brand name importance to a company has led to a concept called **brand equity**, the added value a brand name gives to a product beyond the functional benefits provided. This value has two distinct advantages. First, brand equity provides a competitive advantage. The Sunkist brand implies quality fruit, and the Disney name defines children's entertainment. A second advantage is that consumers are often willing to pay a higher price for a product with brand equity. Brand equity, in this instance, is represented by the premium a consumer will pay for one brand over another when the functional benefits provided are identical. Gillette razors and blades, Bose audio systems, Duracell batteries, Microsoft computer software, and Louis Vuitton luggage all enjoy a price premium arising from brand equity.

Creating Brand Equity Brand equity doesn't just happen. It is carefully crafted and nurtured by marketing programs that forge strong, favorable, and unique customer associations and experiences with a brand. Brand equity resides in the minds of consumers and results from what they have learned, felt, seen, and heard about a brand over time. Marketers recognize that brand equity is not easily or quickly achieved. Rather, it arises from a sequential building process consisting of four steps (Figure 11–5).[21]

- The first step is to develop positive brand awareness and an association of the brand in consumers' minds with a product class or need to give the brand an identity. Gatorade and Kleenex have achieved this in the sports drink and facial tissue product classes, respectively.
- Next, a marketer must establish a brand's meaning in the minds of consumers. Meaning arises from what a brand stands for and has two dimensions—a functional, performance-related dimension and an abstract, imagery-related dimension. Nike has done this through continuous product development and improvement and its links to peak athletic performance in its integrated marketing communications program.
- The third step is to elicit the proper consumer responses to a brand's identity and meaning. Here attention is placed on how consumers think and feel about a brand. Thinking focuses on a brand's perceived quality, credibility, and superiority relative to other brands. Feeling relates to the consumer's emotional reaction to a brand. Michelin elicits both responses for its tires. Not only is Michelin thought of as a credible and superior-quality brand, but consumers also acknowledge a warm and secure feeling of safety, comfort, and self-assurance without worry or concern about the brand.
- The final, and most difficult, step is to create a consumer-brand connection evident in an intense, active loyalty relationship between consumers and the brand. A deep psychological bond characterizes a consumer-brand connection and the personal identification customers have with the brand. Brands that have achieved this status include Harley-Davidson, Apple, and eBay.

FIGURE 11–5

The customer-based brand equity pyramid shows the four-step building process that forges strong, favorable, and unique customer associations with a brand.

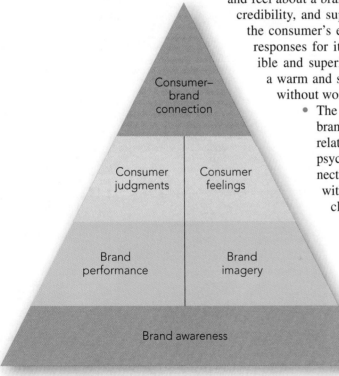

Valuing Brand Equity Brand equity also provides a financial advantage for the brand owner.[22] Successful, established brand names, such as Gillette, Nike, Gatorade, and Nokia, have an economic value in the sense that they are intangible assets. The recognition that brands are assets is apparent in the decision to buy and sell brands. For example, Triarc Companies bought the Snapple brand from Quaker Oats in 1997 for $300 million and sold it to Cadbury Schweppes in 2000 for $900 million. This example illustrates that brands, unlike physical assets that depreciate with time and use, can appreciate in value when effectively marketed. However, brands can lose value when they are not managed properly. Consider the purchase and sale of Lender's Bagels. Kellogg bought the brand for $466 million only to sell it to Aurora Foods for $275 million three years later following deteriorating sales and profits.

Financially lucrative brand licensing opportunities arise from brand equity. *Brand licensing* is a contractual agreement whereby one company (licensor) allows its brand name(s) or trademark(s) to be used with products or services offered by another company (licensee) for a royalty or fee. For example, Disney makes billions of dollars each year licensing its characters for children's toys, apparel, and games. Licensing fees for Winnie the Pooh alone exceed $3 billion annually. General Motors sells more than $2 billion in licensed products each year.[23]

Successful brand licensing requires careful marketing analysis to assure a proper match between the licensor's brand and the licensee's products. World-renowned designer Ralph Lauren earns millions of dollars each year by licensing his Ralph Lauren, Polo, and Chaps brands for dozens of products, including paint by Glidden, furniture by Henredon, footwear by Rockport, and fragrances by L'Oreal. Mistakes, such as Kleenex diapers, Bic perfume, and Domino's fruit-flavored bubble gum, represent a few examples of poor matches and licensing failures.

Picking a Good Brand Name

We take brand names such as Red Bull, iPod, and Adidas for granted, but it is often a difficult and expensive process to pick a good name. Companies will spend between $25,000 and $100,000 to identify and test a new brand name. Five criteria are mentioned most often when selecting a good brand name.[24]

* *The name should suggest the product benefits.* For example, Accutron (watches), Easy Off (oven cleaner), Glass Plus (glass cleaner), Cling-Free (antistatic cloth

General Motors is the worldwide leader in licensed product sales among automakers. One licensing arrangement is for HUMMER® Footwear made by Roper Footwear & Apparel.

IT IS RECOMMENDED THAT YOU CHANGE YOUR SOCKS EVERY 3,000 MILES.

Introducing the only full line of footwear tough enough to be called HUMMER. Now you can sell your customers comfort, style, and performance that's like nothing else.

HUMMER® FOOTWEAR ♦ LIKE NOTHING ELSE.™

for drying clothes), PowerBook (laptop computer), and Tidy Bowl (toilet bowl cleaner) all clearly describe the benefits of purchasing the product.

- *The name should be memorable, distinctive, and positive.* In the auto industry, when a competitor has a memorable name, others quickly imitate. When Ford named a car the Mustang, Pintos, Colts, and Broncos soon followed. The Thunderbird name led to the Phoenix, Eagle, Sunbird, and Firebird.

- *The name should fit the company or product image.* Sharp is a name that can apply to audio and video equipment. Bufferin, Excedrin, Anacin, and Nuprin are scientific-sounding names, good for analgesics. Eveready, Duracell, and DieHard suggest reliability and longevity—two qualities consumers want in a battery.

- *The name should have no legal or regulatory restrictions.* Legal restrictions produce trademark infringement suits, and regulatory restrictions arise through improper use of words. For example, the U.S. Food and Drug Administration discourages the use of the word *heart* in food brand names. This restriction led to changing the name of Kellogg's Heartwise cereal to Fiberwise, and Clorox's Hidden Valley Ranch Take Heart Salad Dressing had to be modified to Hidden Valley Ranch Low-Fat Salad Dressing. Increasingly, brand names need a corresponding address on the Internet. This further complicates name selection because about 140 million domain names are already registered.

- *Finally, the name should be simple* (such as Bold laundry detergent, Axe deodorant and body spray, and Bic pens) *and should be emotional* (such as Joy and Obsession perfumes). In the development of names for international use, having a nonmeaningful brand name has been considered a benefit. A name such as Exxon does not have any prior impressions or undesirable images among a diverse world population of different languages and cultures. The 7Up name is another matter. In Shanghai, China, the phrase means "death through drinking" in the local dialect. Sales have suffered as a result.

multiproduct branding

Manufacturer's branding strategy that uses one name for all products

FIGURE 11–6

Alternative branding strategies are available to marketers. Each has advantages and disadvantages described in the text.

Branding Strategies

Companies can employ several different branding strategies, including multiproduct branding, multibranding, private branding, or mixed branding (Figure 11–6).

Multiproduct Branding Strategy   With **multiproduct branding**, a company uses one name for all its products in a product class. This approach is sometimes

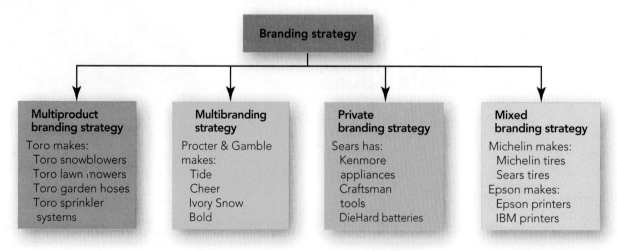

called *family branding,* or *corporate branding* when the company's trade name is used. For example, General Electric, Samsung, Gerber, and Sony engage in corporate branding—the company's trade name and brand name are identical. Church & Dwight uses the Arm & Hammer family brand name for all its products featuring baking soda as the primary ingredient.

Kimberly-Clark was able to leverage the strong Huggies brand equity among mothers when it introduced a full line of baby and toddler toiletries first in the United States and then globally. The success of this brand extension strategy is evident in the $500 million in annual sales generated globally.

There are several advantages to multiproduct branding. Capitalizing again on brand equity, consumers who have a good experience with the product will transfer this favorable attitude to other items in the product class with the same name. Therefore, this brand strategy makes possible *line extensions,* the practice of using a current brand name to enter a new market segment in its product class. Campbell Soup Company employs a multiproduct branding strategy with soup line extensions. It offers regular Campbell soup, home-cooking style, and chunky varieties and more than 100 soup flavors. This strategy can result in lower advertising and promotion costs because the same name is used on all products, thus raising the level of brand awareness. A risk with line extension is that sales of an extension may come at the expense of other items in the company's product line. Line extensions work best when they provide incremental company revenue by taking sales away from competing brands or attracting new buyers.

Some multiproduct branding companies employ *subbranding,* which combines a corporate or family brand with a new brand, to distinguish a part of its product line from others. Gatorade successfully used subbranding with the introduction of Gatorade Frost, Gatorade Rain, and Gatorade A.M. as examples.

A strong brand equity also allows for *brand extension,* the practice of using a current brand name to enter a completely different product class. For instance, equity in the Huggies family brand name has allowed Kimberly-Clark to successfully extend its name to a full line of baby and toddler toiletries.

However, there is a risk with brand extensions. Too many uses for one brand name can dilute the meaning of a brand for consumers. Marketing experts claim this has happened to the Arm & Hammer brand given its use for toothpaste, laundry detergent, gum, cat litter, air freshener, carpet deodorizer, and antiperspirant.[25]

multibranding

Manufacturer's branding strategy that gives each product a distinct name

Multibranding Strategy   Alternately, a company can engage in **multibranding**, which involves giving each product a distinct name. Multibranding is a useful strategy when each brand is intended for a different market segment. P&G makes Camay soap for those concerned with soft skin and Safeguard for those who want deodorant protection. Black & Decker markets its line of tools for the household do-it-yourselfer segment with the Black & Decker name but uses the DeWalt name for its professional tool line. Disney uses the Miramax and Touchstone Pictures names for films directed at adults and its Disney name for children's films.

Multibranding is applied in a variety of ways. Some companies array their brands on the basis of price-quality segments.[26] Marriott International offers 14 hotel and resort brands, each suited for a particular traveler experience and budget. To illustrate, Marriott Marquis hotels and Vacation Clubs offer luxury amenities at a premium price. Marriott and Renaissance hotels offer medium- to high-priced accommodations. Courtyard hotels and Town Place Suites appeal to economy-minded travelers, whereas the Fairfield Inns are for those on a very low travel budget.

Other multibrand companies introduce new product brands as defensive moves to counteract competition. Called *fighting brands,* their chief purpose is to confront competitor brands. For instance, Mattel launched its Flava brand of hip-hop fashion dolls in response to the popularity of Bratz brand dolls sold by MGA Entertainment, which were attracting the 8- to 12-year-old girl segment of Barbie brand sales.

Compared with the multiproduct strategy, advertising and promotion costs tend to be higher with multibranding. The company must generate awareness among consumers and retailers for each new brand name without the benefit of any previous impressions. The advantages of this strategy are that each brand is unique to each market segment and there is no risk that a product failure will affect other products in the line. Still, some large multibrand firms have found that the complexity and expense of implementing this strategy can outweigh the benefits. For example, Liz Claiborne recently pruned 16 of its 36 apparel brands through product deletion and sales to other companies.[27]

Private Branding Strategy A company uses *private branding*, often called *private labeling* or *reseller branding,* when it manufactures products but sells them under the brand name of a wholesaler or retailer. Rayovac, Paragon Trade Brands, and Ralcorp Holdings are major suppliers of private label alkaline batteries, diapers, and grocery products, respectively. Radio Shack, Costco, Sears, Wal-Mart, and Kroger are large retailers that have their own brand names. Private branding is popular because it typically produces high profits for manufacturers and resellers. Consumers also buy them. It is estimated that one of every five items purchased at U.S. supermarkets, drugstores, and mass merchandisers bears a private brand.[28]

Mixed Branding Strategy A fourth branding strategy is *mixed branding*, where a firm markets products under its own name(s) and that of a reseller because the segment attracted to the reseller is different from its own market. Beauty and fragrance marketer Elizabeth Arden is an example. The company sells its Elizabeth Arden brand through department stores and a line of skin care products at Wal-Mart with the "skin-simple" brand name.

PACKAGING AND LABELING PRODUCTS

packaging

Part of a product that refers to any container in which it is offered for sale and on which label information is displayed

The **packaging** component of a product refers to any container in which it is offered for sale and on which label information is displayed. A *label* is an integral part of the package and typically identifies the product or brand, who made it, where and when it was made, how it is to be used, and package contents and ingredients. To a great extent, the customer's first exposure to a product is the package and label and both are an expensive and important part of marketing strategy. For Pez Candy Inc., the character head-on-a-stick plastic container that dispenses a miniature tablet candy is the central element of its marketing strategy as described in the accompanying Marketing Matters box.[29]

Creating Customer Value and Competitive Advantage through Packaging and Labeling

Packaging and labeling cost U.S. companies more than $120 billion annually and account for about 15 cents of every dollar spent by consumers for products.[30] Despite the cost, packaging and labeling are essential because both provide important benefits for the manufacturer, retailer, and ultimate consumer.

Communication Benefits   A major benefit of packaging is the label information on it conveyed to the consumer, such as directions on how, where, and when to use the product and the source and composition of the product, which is needed to satisfy legal requirements of product disclosure. For example, the labeling system for packaged and processed foods in the United States provides a uniform format for

Quick. Name a soft drink.

Can you name this soft-drink brand? If you can, then the package has fulfilled its purpose.

nutritional and dietary information. Many packaged foods contain informative recipes to promote usage of the product. Campbell Soup estimates that the green bean casserole recipe on its cream of mushroom soup can accounts for $20 million in soup sales each year![31] Other information consists of seals and symbols, either government required or commercial seals of approval (such as the Good Housekeeping seal).

Functional Benefits Packaging often plays a functional role, such as storage, convenience, protection, or product quality. Storing food containers is one example, and beverage companies have developed lighter and easier ways to stack products on shelves and in refrigerators. An example is Ocean Spray Cranberries' rectangular juice bottles that allow 10 units per package versus 8 of its former round bottles.

The convenience dimension of packaging is increasingly important. Kraft Miracle Whip salad dressing, Heinz ketchup, and Skippy Squeez'It peanut butter are sold in squeeze bottles and Chicken of the Sea tuna and Folgers coffee are packaged in single-serving portions. Nabisco offers portion-control package sizes for the convenience of weight-conscious consumers. It offers 100-calorie packs of Oreos, Cheese Nips, and other products in individual pouches.

Consumer protection is another important function of packaging, including the development of tamper-resistant containers. Today, companies commonly use safety seals or pop-tops that reveal previous opening. But, no package is truly tamper resistant. U.S. law now provides for maximum penalties of life imprisonment and $250,000 fines for package tampering. Consumer protection through labeling exists in "open dating," which states the expected shelf life of the product.

Functional features of packaging also can affect product quality. Procter & Gamble's Pringles and Frito-Lay's Stax potato crisps with cylindrical packaging offers uniform chips, minimal breakage, and for some consumers, better value for the money than flex-bag packages for chips.

Which chip stacks up better? Frito-Lay's launch of Lay's Stax potato crisps to compete against Procter & Gamble's Pringles illustrates the role of packaging in product and brand management.

Perceptual Benefits A third component of packaging and labeling is the perception created in the consumer's mind. Package and label shape, color, and graphics distinguish one brand from another, convey a brand's positioning, and build brand equity. According to the director of marketing for L'eggs hosiery, "Packaging is important to the positioning and equity of the L'eggs brand."[32] Why? Packaging and labeling have been shown to enhance brand recognition and facilitate the formation of strong, favorable, and unique brand associations.[33] This logic applies to Celestial Seasonings' packaging and labeling, which uses delicate illustrations, soft and warm colors, and quotations about life to reinforce the brand's positioning as a New Age, natural herbal tea.

Successful marketers recognize that changes in packages and labels can update and uphold a brand's image in the customer's mind. For example, Pepsi-Cola has embarked on a packaging change to uphold its image among

The distinctive design of Celestial Seasonings' tea boxes reinforces the brand's positioning as a New Age, natural herbal tea.

teens and young adults. Beginning in 2007, Pepsi-Cola debuted new graphics on its cans and bottles every three or four weeks to reflect the "fun, optimistic, and youthful spirit" of the brand to its customers.[34]

Because labels list a product's source, brands competing in the global marketplace can benefit from "country of origin or manufacture" perceptions as described in Chapter 7. Consumers tend to have stereotypes about country-product pairings that they judge "best"—English tea, French perfume, Italian leather, and Japanese electronics—which can affect a brand's image. Increasingly, Chinese firms are adopting the English language and Roman letters for their brand labels. This is being done because of a common perception in many Asian countries that "things Western are good."[35]

Contemporary Packaging and Labeling Challenges

Package and label designers face four challenges: (1) the continuing need to connect with customers; (2) environmental concerns; (3) health, safety, and security issues; and (4) cost reduction.

Connecting with Customers Packages and labels must be continually updated to connect with customers. The challenge lies in creating aesthetic and functional design features that attract customer attention and deliver customer value in their use. If done right, the rewards can be huge.[36]

For example, the marketing team responsible for Kleenex tissues converted its standard rectangular box into an oval shape with colorful seasonal graphics. Sales soared. After months of in-home research, Kraft product managers discovered that consumers often transferred Chips Ahoy! cookies to jars for easy access and to avoid staleness. The company solved both problems by creating a patented resealable opening on the top of the bag. The result? Sales of the new package doubled that of the old package.

Environmental Concerns Because of widespread worldwide concern about the growth of solid waste and the shortage of viable landfill sites, the amount, composition, and disposal of packaging material continues to receive much attention. Recycling packaging material is a major thrust.[37] Procter & Gamble now uses recycled cardboard in over 70 percent of its paper packaging and is packaging Tide, Cheer, Era, and Dash detergents in jugs that contain 25 percent recycled plastic. Spic and Span liquid cleaner is packaged in 100 percent recycled material. Other firms, such as Wal-Mart, are emphasizing the use of less packaging material. In 2008, the company began working with its 600,000 global suppliers to reduce overall packaging and shipping material by 5 percent by 2013.

Health, Safety, and Security Issues A third challenge involves the growing health, safety, and security concerns of packaging materials. Today, most U.S. and European consumers believe companies should make sure products and their packages are safe and secure, regardless of the cost, and companies are responding in numerous ways. Most butane lighters sold today, like those made by Scripto, contain a child-resistant safety latch to prevent misuse and accidental fire. Child-proof caps on pharmaceutical products and household cleaners and sealed lids on food packages are now common. New packaging technology and materials that extend a product's *shelf life* (the time a product can be stored) and prevent spoilage continue to be developed with special applications for developing countries.

Cost Reduction   About 80 percent of packaging material used in the world consists of paper, plastics, and glass. As the cost of these materials rise, companies are constantly challenged to find innovative ways to cut packaging costs while delivering value to their customers. As an example, Hewlett-Packard reduced the size and weight of its Photosmart product package and shipping container. Through design and material changes, packaging material costs fell by more than 50 percent. Shipping costs per unit dropped 41 percent.[38]

MANAGING THE MARKETING OF SERVICES

Let's use the four Ps framework of the text for discussing the marketing mix for services.[39]

Product (Service)

To a large extent, the concepts of the product component of the marketing mix apply equally well to Cheerios (a good) and to American Express (a service). Yet there are three aspects of the product/service element of the mix that warrant special attention when dealing with services: exclusivity, brand name, and capacity management.

Exclusivity   Chapter 10 pointed out that one favorable dimension in a new product is its ability to be patented. Recall that a patent gives the manufacturer of a product exclusive rights to its production for 17 years. A major difference between products and services is that services cannot be patented. Hence the creator of a successful fast-food hamburger chain could quickly discover the concept being copied by others. Domino's Pizza, for example, has seen competitors copy the quick delivery advantage that propelled the company to success.

Branding   An important aspect in marketing goods is the branding strategy used. However, because services are intangible and, therefore, more difficult to describe, the brand name or identifying logo of the service organization is particularly important in consumer decisions. Brand names help make the abstract nature of services more concrete. Service marketers apply branding concepts in the same way as product marketers. Consider American Express. It has applied subbranding with its American Express Green, Gold, Platinum, Optima, Blue, and Centurian credit cards, with unique service offerings for each.

McDonald's familiar Golden Arches logo is an important part of the company's branding.

Capacity Management   Most services have a limited capacity due to the inseparability of the service from the service provider and the perishable nature of the service. For example, a patient must be in the hospital at the same time as the surgeon to "buy" an appendectomy, and only one patient can be helped at that time. Similarly, no additional surgery can be conducted tomorrow because of an unused operating room or an available surgeon today—the service capacity is lost if it is not used. So the service component of the mix must be integrated with efforts to influence consumer demand. This is referred to as **capacity management**.

capacity management
Integrating the service component of the marketing mix with efforts to influence consumer demand

Price

In the service industries, *price* is referred to in various ways. Hospitals refer to charges; consultants, lawyers, physicians, and accountants to fees; airlines to fares;

and hotels to rates. Regardless of the term used, price plays two essential roles: (1) to affect consumer perceptions and (2) to be used in capacity management. Because of the intangible nature of services, price can indicate the quality of the service. Would you wonder about the quality of a $100 surgery? Studies have shown that when there are few well-known cues by which to judge a product or service quality, consumers use price.[40]

off-peak pricing

Charging different prices during different times of the day or days of the week to reflect variations in demand for the service

The capacity management role of price is also important to movie theaters, airlines, restaurants, and hotels. Many service businesses use **off-peak pricing**, which consists of charging different prices during different times of the day or days of the week to reflect variations in demand for the service. Airlines offer discounts for weekend travel, and movie theaters offer matinee prices.

The United States Postal Service uses advertising to stress the convenience of its service.

Place (Distribution)

Place or distribution is a major factor in developing a service marketing strategy because of the inseparability of services from the producer. Historically, little attention has been paid to distribution in services marketing. But as competition grows, the value of convenient distribution is being recognized. Hairstyling chains such as Cost Cutters Family Hair Care, tax preparation offices such as H&R Block, and accounting firms such as PricewaterhouseCoopers all use multiple locations for the distribution of services. In the banking industry, customers of participating banks using the Cirrus system can access any one of thousands of automatic teller systems throughout the United States. The availability of electronic distribution through the Internet now provides global coverage for travel services, banking, entertainment, and many other information-based services.

Promotion

The value of promotion, specifically advertising, for many services is to show the benefits of purchasing the service. It is valuable to stress availability, location, consistent quality, and efficient, courteous service. In addition, services must be concerned with their image. Promotional efforts, such as Merrill Lynch's use of the bull in its ads, contribute to image and positioning strategies. In most cases promotional concerns of services are similar to those of products.

Another form of promotion, publicity, has played a major role in the promotional strategy of nonprofit services and some professional organizations. Nonprofit organizations such as public school districts, the Chicago Symphony Orchestra, religious organizations, and hospitals have used publicity to disseminate their messages. Because of the heavy reliance on publicity, many services use public service announcements (PSAs), and because PSAs are free, nonprofit groups have tended to rely on them as the foundation of their media plan. However, the timing and location of a PSA are under the control of the medium, not the organization. Thus, the nonprofit service group cannot control who sees the message or when the message is given.

learning review

5. What is the difference between a line extension and a brand extension?

6. Explain the role of packaging in terms of perception.

7. How do service businesses use off-peak pricing?

LEARNING OBJECTIVES REVIEW

LO1 *Explain the product life-cycle concept.*
The product life cycle describes the stages a new product goes through in the marketplace: introduction, growth, maturity, and decline. Product sales growth and profitability differ at each stage, and marketing managers have marketing objectives and marketing mix strategies unique to each stage based on consumer behavior and competitive factors. In the introductory stage, the need is to establish primary demand, whereas the growth stage requires selective demand strategies. In the maturity stage, the need is to maintain market share; the decline stage necessitates a deletion or harvesting strategy. Some important aspects of product life cycles are (*a*) their length, (*b*) the shape of the sales curve, and (*c*) the rate at which consumers adopt products.

LO2 *Identify ways that marketing executives manage a product's life cycle.*
Marketing executives manage a product's life cycle three ways. First, they can modify the product itself by altering its characteristics, such as product quality, performance, or appearance. Second, they can modify the market by finding new customers for the product, increasing a product's use among existing customers, or creating a new use situation for the product. Finally, they can reposition the product using any one or a combination of marketing mix elements. Four factors trigger a repositioning action. They include reacting to a competitor's position, reaching a new market, catching a rising trend, and changing the value offered to consumers.

LO3 *Recognize the importance of branding and alternative branding strategies.*
A basic decision in marketing products is branding, in which an organization uses a name, phrase, design, symbols, or a combination of these to identify its products and distinguish them from those of its competitors. Product managers recognize that brands offer more than product identification and a means to distinguish their products from competitors. Successful and established brands take on a brand personality and acquire brand equity—the added value a given brand name gives to a product beyond the functional benefits provided—that is crafted and nurtured by marketing programs that forge strong, favorable, and unique consumer associations with a brand. A good brand name should suggest the product benefits, be memorable, fit the company or product image, be free of legal restrictions, and be simple and emotional. Companies can and do employ several different branding strategies. With multiproduct branding, a company uses one name for all its products in a product class. A multibranding strategy involves giving each product a distinct name. A company uses private branding when it manufactures products but sells them under the brand name of a wholesaler or retailer. Finally, a company can employ mixed branding, where it markets products under its own name(s) and that of a reseller.

LO4 *Describe the role of packaging and labeling in the marketing of a product.*
Packaging, labeling, and warranties play numerous roles in the marketing of a product. The packaging component of a product refers to any container in which it is offered for sale and on which label information is conveyed. Manufacturers, retailers, and consumers acknowledge that packaging and labeling provide communication, functional, and perceptual benefits. Contemporary packaging and labeling challenges include (*a*) the continuing need to connect with customers, (*b*) environmental concerns, (*c*) health, safety, and security issues, and (*d*) cost reduction.

LO5 *Recognize how the four Ps framework applies to the marketing of services.*
The four Ps framework also applies to services with some adaptations. Because services cannot be patented, unique offerings are difficult to protect. In addition, because services are intangible, brands and logos (which can be protected) are particularly important. The inseparability of production and consumption of services means that capacity management is important to services. The intangible nature of services makes price an important indication of service quality. Distribution has become an important marketing tool for services, and electronic distribution allows some services to provide global coverage. In recent years, service organizations have increased their promotional activities.

FOCUSING ON KEY TERMS

brand equity p. 248	**capacity management** p. 256	**off-peak pricing** p. 257
brand name p. 247	**multibranding** p. 251	**packaging** p. 253
brand personality p. 247	**multiproduct branding** p. 250	**product life cycle** p. 236
branding p. 247		

APPLYING MARKETING KNOWLEDGE

1 Listed here are three different products in various stages of the product life cycle. What marketing strategies would you suggest to these companies? (*a*) Canon digital cameras—growth stage, (*b*) Panasonic high-definition television—introductory stage, and (*c*) handheld manual can openers—decline stage.

2 It has often been suggested that products are intentionally made to break down or wear out. Is this strategy a planned product modification approach?

3 The product manager of GE is reviewing the penetration of trash compactors in American homes. After more than two decades in existence, this product is in relatively few homes. What problems can account for this poor acceptance? What is the shape of the trash compactor life cycle?

4 For years, Ferrari has been known as the manufacturer of expensive luxury automobiles. The company plans to attract the major segment of the car-buying market who purchase medium-priced automobiles. As Ferrari considers this trading-down strategy, what branding strategy would you recommend? What are the trade-offs to consider with your strategy?

building your marketing plan

For the product offering in your marketing plan,

1 Identify (*a*) its stage in the product life cycle and (*b*) key marketing mix actions that might be appropriate, as shown in Figure 11–1.

2 Develop (*a*) branding and (*b*) packaging strategies, if appropriate for your offering.

video case 11 Philadelphia Phillies Inc.: Sports Marketing 101

"Bring everyone in closer. Have fans feel 'I'm not alone here; lots of others are in the seats. This is a *happening!*'" chuckles David Montgomery, president and chief executive officer of the Philadelphia Phillies, Inc.

He continues, "Old Veterans Stadium had too big an inventory of seats for baseball. The new facility and the fact that it's a game played in summer out in the open air really takes you to a much broader audience. Our challenge is to appeal to all the segments in that audience." What Montgomery is referring to is the Phillies' new world-class Citizens Bank Park baseball stadium that opened in 2004. It is a baseball-only ballpark, seating 43,500 fans, where every seat is angled toward home plate to give fans the best view of the action. This contrasts with the 62,000-seat Veterans Stadium that both the Phillies and the Philadelphia Eagles football team shared from 1971 to 2003, where sight lines were always a compromise for the two sports.

The new fan-friendly Phillies stadium is just one element in today's complex strategy to effectively market the Philadelphia Phillies to several different segments of fans—a far different challenge than in the past. A century ago Major League Baseball was pretty simple. You built a stadium. You hired the ballplayers. You printed tickets—hoping and praying a winning team would bring in fans and sell those tickets. And your advertising consisted of printing the team's home schedule in the local newspaper.

THE PHILLIES TODAY: APPEALS, SEGMENTS, AND ACTIVITIES

Baseball, like other sports, is a service whose primary benefit is entertainment. Marketing a Major League Baseball team is far different today.

"How do you market a product that is all over the board?" asks David Buck, the Phillies' vice president of marketing. He first gives a general answer to his question: "The ballpark experience is the key. As long as you project an image of a fun ballpark experience in everything you do, you're going to be in good shape. Our best advertising is word of mouth from happy fans." Next come the specifics. Marketing the appeal of a fun ballpark experience to all segments of fans is critical because the Phillies can't promise a winning baseball team. Every team, even the New York Yankees, has its ups and downs. The Phillies are no different.

Reaching the different segments of fans is a special challenge because each segment attends a game for different reasons and therefore will respond to different special promotions:

- The diehards. Intense baseball fans who are there to watch the strategy and see the Phillies win.
- Kids 14 years and under. At the game with their families, to get bat or bobblehead doll premiums, and have a "run-the-bases" day.
- Women and men 15 years and older. Special "days out," such as Mother's Day or Father's Day.
- Seniors, 60 years and over. A "stroll-the-bases" day.
- 20- and 30-somethings. Meet friends at the ballpark and restaurants for a fun night out.
- Corporate and community groups. At the game to have fun but also to get to know members of their respective organizations better.

It's clear that not all fans are there for exactly the same "fun ballpark experience."

The segments don't stop there. Marisol Lezeano, the Phillies' community outreach coordinator, says, "In the Philadelphia area, we've got a lot of different ethnic groups and we want to make all of them Phillies fans." So she plans special nights for these groups: the Goya Latino Family Celebration night with a Latino Legends poster of Phillies Hispanic players; Asia Pacific night with a giant cloth dragon dancing its way across the outfield; and The Sound of Philadelphia night honoring Black Music Month featuring various African American music groups. "We want all communities to come to the ballpark. We're all fans. It's great. Please be with us," she emphasizes.

The "fun ballpark experience" today also goes beyond simply watching the Phillies play a baseball game. Fans at Citizens Bank Park can also:

- Buy souvenirs at the Phanatic Attic, within the Majestic Clubhouse Store.
- Romp in the Phanatic Phun Zone, the largest soft-play area for kids in Major League Baseball and scale a giant, inflatable baseball rock-climbing wall.
- Test their skills in a pitching game.
- Play the giant Ballpark Pinball game.
- Stroll through Ashburn Alley (named for a famous Phillie), an outdoor food and entertainment area to see the All-Star Walk and the Wall of Fame.
- Eat at McFadden's Restaurant and Saloon year round or Harry the K's Bar & Grill.
- View one of the largest digital video scoreboards in baseball.
- Purchase a luxury suite to experience enhanced amenities.

PROMOTIONAL ACTIVITIES

The range of the Phillies' promotional activities today is mind numbing. Before and during the season, the Phillies run a series of TV ads to generate and/or maintain fan interest. A recent ad campaign targeted kids by showing that the Phillies' players themselves are just like them. The tagline: "There's a little fan in all of us."

The Phillies also use "special promotion days," which typically increase fan attendance by 30 to 35 percent for a game, according to David Buck. These days often generate first-time visits by people who have never seen a Major League Baseball game. They generally fall into three categories: (1) theme nights, (2) event days, and (2) premium gift days.

Theme nights are devoted to special community groups or other fan segments. Examples include College Nights (fellow classmates, alumni, and faculty), dates for families of the military and law enforcement, Rooftop Thursdays (having a luau with friends on the stadium rooftop), and others. Event days can involve camera days where fans can take players' photos—three FUJIFILM Fridays each season for the Phillies. Or they can involve fireworks, an old-timers' game, or running or strolling the bases. Some events are especially memorable. Phillies fans still talk about the ostrich race in which a terrified Phillies' broadcaster wound up in the first row of stands when the ostrich pulling him and his cart panicked due to crowd noise.

"Our premiums or giveaways are directed at specific groups," says Scott Brandreth, the Phillies' merchandising manager. "During the year, we probably have two or three for all fans, six or seven for children 14 years or younger, and maybe one for women over 15, and one for men over 15—often for Mother's Day and Father's Day." These giveaways range from bobble-head dolls and nesting dolls to baseball caps, rally towels, and Louisville Slugger bats. To control expenses, the Phillies try to keep the cost of the premiums in the range of $1 to $3.

Other promotional activities fall in both the traditional and nontraditional categories. Personal appearances at public and charity events by Phillies players and their wives, radio and TV ads, and special events paid for by sponsors have been used by baseball teams for decades. But newer, more nontraditional promotions include the $95 million naming rights for the Citizens Bank Park, Phillies Phantasy Camp (where you can "play ball" with Phillies' legends for a week in January in Florida), special "infield club seats," the Phillies Grand Slam Sweepstakes, where fans can win tickets for a luxury suite, and Phillies youth baseball clubs and leagues. Fans also can now get Phillies updates and order tickets on its website (www.phillies.com).

Probably the best-known mascot in professional sports, the Phillie Phanatic is a Philadelphia legend. This oversized, green furry mascot has been around for over 25 years. It not only appears in the ballpark at all Phillies' home games, but also makes appearances at charity and public events year round. Or rather the *three* Phanatics do so, because the demand is too great for a single Phanatic. "The Phanatic is a great character because he doesn't carry wins or losses," says David Montgomery. "Fans young and old can relate to him . . . he makes you smile, makes you laugh, and adds to the enjoyment of the game."

BOTTOM LINE: REVENUES AND EXPENSES

"We're a private business that serves the public," David Montgomery points out. "And we've got to make sure our revenues more than cover our expenses." He identifies five key sources of revenues and the approximate annual percentages for each:

Sources of Revenue	Approx. %
1. Ticket sales (home and away games)	52%
2. National media (network TV and radio)	13
3. Local media (over-the-air TV, pay TV, radio)	13
4. Advertising (publications, co-sponsorship promotions)	12
5. Concessions (food, souvenirs, restaurants)	10
Total	100

Balanced against these revenues are some major expenses that include players' salaries (about $90 million in 2007) and salaries of more than 150 full-time employees. Other expenses are those for scouting and drafting 40 to 60 new players per year, operating six minor-league farm clubs, and managing a labor force of 400 persons for each of the Phillies' 81 regular season home games at Citizens Bank Park.

David Montgomery never gets bored. "When I finished business school, I had to choose between a marketing research job at a large paper products company or marketing the Philadelphia Phillies," explains Montgomery, who started with the Phillies by selling season and group tickets. "And it was no real decision because there never has been one day on this job that wasn't different and exciting," he says.

Questions

1 (*a*) What is the "product" that the Phillies market? (*b*) What "products" are the Phillies careful not to market?

2 How does the "quality" dimension in marketing the Philadelphia Phillies as an entertainment service differ from that in marketing a consumer product such as a breakfast cereal?

3 When David Montgomery talks about reducing the "inventory of seats" in the new versus old stadium, what does he recognize as (*a*) advantages and (*b*) disadvantages?

4 Considering all five elements of the promotional mix (advertising, personal selling, public relations, sales promotion, and direct marketing), what specific promotional activities should the Phillies use? Which should be used off-season? During the season?

5 What kind of special promotion gift days (with premiums) and event days (no premiums) can the Phillies use to increase attendance by targeting these fan segments: (*a*) 14 and under, (*b*) 15 and over, (*c*) other special fan segments, and (*d*) all fans?

12

Pricing Products and Services

STANDING TALL IN STARBURY SIGNATURE SNEAKERS

How much would you expect to pay for a pair of signature sneakers endorsed by a well-known professional basketball player? $150? $200? How about $14.98?

Stephon Marbury has set about to dismiss the notion that affordable sneakers cannot be a status shoe. How? In 2006, he endorsed the Starbury Collection of basketball shoes priced at $14.98. Within months, *BusinessWeek* featured Starbury shoes as one of the best new products in 2006. *Footwear News* heralded the product as its "Launch of the Year."

But why would a 10-year NBA veteran and New York Knicks point guard with a multiyear, multimillion-dollar contract endorse a $14.98 sneaker? "Kids shouldn't have to feel the pressure to spend so much to feel good about the way they look," Marbury says. "It is very important to me that the Starbury Collection have a strong social component for kids and parents, especially in urban areas." On his website, he declares the Starbury brand is "for the people" and a "movement" that is "bigger than basketball." Marbury added, "The big picture is not having a $200 pair of sneakers when your mother's income is $15,000."

Starbury sneakers were designed in collaboration with Steve & Barry's University Sportswear, which began as a collegiate apparel store at the University of Pennsylvania in 1985. Steve & Barry's operates nearly 276 stores in 39 states with the aim of providing top-quality merchandise at low prices. This aim, coupled with Stephon Marbury's philosophy, led to a professionally designed sneaker with features comparable to shoes endorsed by celebrity athletes priced 10 times higher or more. In Marbury's words, "If you take my shoe and you take a $150 shoe, cut it down in half, and it does the same thing."

So why were Starbury sneakers priced at $14.98 and not a higher price? "It certainly doesn't cost $150 to make a high-performance basketball shoe. The cost of the good is a lot closer to $14.98," said Erin Patton, former architect of Nike's Jordan Brand and principal of TMG, the New York-based brand management consulting firm, who spearheaded the Starbury launch. "When consumers spend $150 for a sneaker, they pay for expensive advertising and promotion, and athlete endorsement contracts. These costs are included in the manufacturer's price of the shoe *before* the retailer markup, which often doubles the retail price to consumers. Steve and Barry's developed an innovative, cost-driven business over a 20-year period to manufacture and sell product exclusively in its stores at rock-bottom prices without passing unnecessary costs on to consumers. That price-value proposition for the masses has always been at the core of the company's philosophy, but partnering with Stephon Marbury placed lightning in the bottle."

Did the $14.98 retail price resonate with consumers? Over 3 million Starbury sneakers were sold within eight months of the product's launch![1]

Welcome to the fascinating—and intense—world of pricing, where many forces come together in the price buyers are asked to pay. This chapter covers important factors used in setting prices.

NATURE AND IMPORTANCE OF PRICE

LO1

The price paid for goods and services goes by many names. You pay *tuition* for your education, *rent* for an apartment, *interest* on a bank credit card, and a *premium* for car insurance. Your dentist or physician charges you a *fee*, a professional or social organization charges *dues,* and airlines charge a *fare*. And what you pay for clothes or a haircut is termed a *price.*

What Is a Price?

price
Money or other considerations exchanged for the ownership or use of a good or service

These examples highlight the many varied ways that price plays a part in our daily lives. From a marketing viewpoint, **price** is the money or other considerations (including other goods and services) exchanged for the ownership or use of a good or service. Recently, Wilkinson Sword exchanged some of its knives for advertising used to promote its razor blades. This practice of exchanging goods and services for other goods and services rather than for money is called *barter*. These transactions account for billions of dollars annually in domestic and international trade.

For most products, money is exchanged. However, the amount paid is not always the same as the list, or quoted, price because of discounts, allowances, and extra fees. While discounts, allowances, and rebates make the effective price lower, other marketing tactics raise the real price. One new 21st century pricing tactic is to use "special fees" and "surcharges." This practice is driven by consumers' zeal for low prices combined with the ease of making price comparisons on the Internet. Buyers are more willing to pay extra fees than a higher list price, so sellers use add-on charges as a way of having the consumer pay more without raising the list price.

All these factors that increase or decrease the price are put together in a "price equation," which is shown for several different products in Figure 12–1. They are

In deciding whether to buy a new $1.5 million Bugatti Veyron, consider incentives, allowances, and extra fees—as well as the original list price!

a key consideration when you buy your next car. As an extreme example, suppose you decide you want to buy a 2008 Bugatti Veyron, the world's fastest production car, that can move you from 0 to 62 mph in 2.5 seconds with a top speed of 253 mph. The Veyron has a list price of $1.5 million. However, if you put $600,000 down now and finance the balance over the next year, you will receive a rebate of $100,000 off the list price. For your 2000 Honda Civic DX four-door sedan that has 80,000 miles and is in fair condition, you are given a trade-in allowance of $4,350.

In addition, you will have to pay sales tax of $98,350, auto registration fees of $1,000 to the state, and a $5,000 destination charge to ship the car from Europe. Finally, your total finance charge is $41,974.

PRICE EQUATION

ITEM PURCHASED	PRICE	= LIST PRICE	INCENTIVES AND − ALLOWANCES	+ EXTRA FEES
New car bought by an individual	Final price	= List price	− Rebate Cash discount Old car trade-in	+ Financing charges Special accessories Destination charges
Term in college bought by a student	Tuition	= Published tuition	− Scholarship Other financial aid Discounts for number of credits taken	+ Special activity fees
Merchandise bought from a wholesaler by a retailer	Invoice price	= List price	− Quantity discount Cash discount Seasonal discount Functional or trade discount	+ Penalty for late payment

FIGURE 12–1

The "price" a buyer pays can take different names, depending on what is purchased.

Applying the price equation (as shown in Figure 12–1) to your purchase, your final price is $1,541,974:

Final price = List price − (Incentives + Allowances) + Extra fees

= $1,500,000 − ($100,000 + $4,350) + ($98,350 + $1,000 + $5,000 + $41,974)

= $1,541,974

Your monthly payment for the one-year loan of $900,000 is $78,498.[2] Are you still interested? Perhaps not. But for the next car you buy, pay attention to the factors beyond the "list price."

Price as an Indicator of Value

From a consumer's standpoint, price is often used to indicate value when it is compared with the perceived benefits such as quality, durability, and so on of a product or service. Specifically, **value** is the ratio of perceived benefits to price, or[3]

$$\text{Value} = \frac{\text{Perceived benefits}}{\text{Price}}$$

value

The ratio of perceived benefits to price

This relationship shows that for a given price, as perceived benefits increase, value increases. For example, if you're used to paying $9.99 for a medium pizza, wouldn't a large pizza at the same price be more valuable? Conversely, for a given price, value decreases when perceived benefits decrease.

For some products, price influences consumers' perception of overall quality and ultimately its value to consumers.[4] In a survey of home furnishing buyers, 84 percent agreed with the statement: "The higher the price, the higher the quality."[5] Kohler introduced a walk-in bathtub that is safer for children and the elderly. Although priced higher than conventional step-in bathtubs, it has proven very successful because buyers are willing to pay more for what they perceive as the benefit of the extra safety.

Here "value" involves the judgment by a consumer of the worth and desirability of a product or service relative to substitutes that satisfy the same need. In this instance a "reference value" emerges, which involves comparing the costs and benefits of substitute items.

Price in the Marketing Mix

Pricing is a critical decision made by a marketing executive because price has a direct effect on a firm's profits. This is apparent from a firm's **profit equation**:

Profit = Total revenue − Total cost

= (Unit price × Quantity sold) − (Fixed cost + Variable cost)

What makes this relationship even more complicated is that price affects the quantity sold, as illustrated with demand curves later in this chapter. Furthermore, since the quantity sold usually affects a firm's costs because of efficiency of production, price also indirectly affects costs. Thus, pricing decisions influence both total revenue (sales) and total cost, which makes pricing one of the most important decisions marketing executives face.

GENERAL PRICING APPROACHES

A key for a marketing manager setting a final price for a product is to find an approximate price level to use as a reasonable starting point. Four common approaches to helping find this approximate price level are (1) demand-oriented, (2) cost-oriented, (3) profit-oriented, and (4) competition-oriented approaches (Figure 12–2). Although these approaches are discussed separately below, some of them overlap, and an effective marketing manager will consider several in selecting an approximate price level.

Demand-Oriented Pricing Approaches

Demand-oriented approaches weigh factors underlying expected customer tastes and preferences more heavily than such factors as cost, profit, and competition when selecting a price level.

Skimming Pricing   A firm introducing a new or innovative product can use *skimming pricing,* setting the highest initial price that customers really desiring the product are willing to pay. These customers are not very price sensitive because they weigh the new product's price, quality, and ability to satisfy their needs against the same characteristics of substitutes. As the demand of these customers is satisfied, the firm lowers the price to attract another, more price-sensitive segment. Thus, skimming pricing gets its name from skimming successive layers of "cream," or customer segments, as prices are lowered in a series of steps.

FIGURE 12–2

Four approaches for selecting an approximate price level

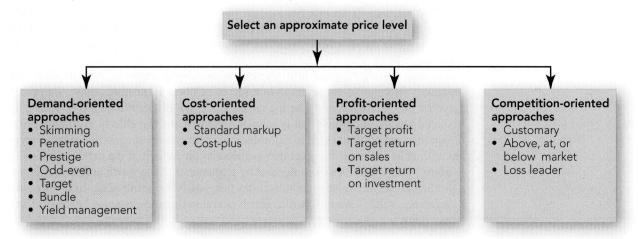

Skimming pricing is an effective strategy when (1) enough prospective customers are willing to buy the product immediately at the high initial price to make these sales profitable, (2) the high initial price will not attract competitors, (3) lowering price has only a minor effect on increasing the sales volume and reducing the unit costs, and (4) customers interpret the high price as signifying high quality. These four conditions are most likely to exist when the new product is protected by patents or copyrights or its uniqueness is understood and valued by consumers. Gillette, for example, adopted a skimming strategy for its five-blade Fusion brand shaving system since many of these conditions applied. The Gillette Fusion shaving system has 70 patents that protect its product technology.[6]

Penetration Pricing Setting a low initial price on a new product to appeal immediately to the mass market is *penetration pricing*, the exact opposite of skimming pricing. Nintendo consciously chose a penetration strategy when it introduced the Nintendo Wii, its popular videogame console.

The conditions favoring penetration pricing are the reverse of those supporting skimming pricing: (1) many segments of the market are price sensitive, (2) a low initial price discourages competitors from entering the market, and (3) unit production and marketing costs fall dramatically as production volumes increase. A firm using penetration pricing may (1) maintain the initial price for a time to gain profit lost from its low introductory level or (2) lower the price further, counting on the new volume to generate the necessary profit.

Prestige Pricing Although consumers tend to buy more of a product when the price is lower, sometimes the reverse is true. If consumers are using price as a measure of the quality of an item, a company runs the risk of appearing to offer a low-quality product if it sets the price below a certain point. *Prestige pricing* involves setting a high price so that quality- or status-conscious consumers will be attracted to the product and buy it. Rolls-Royce cars, Chanel perfume, and Cartier jewelry have an element of prestige pricing in them and may sell worse at lower prices than at higher ones.[7] As described in the Marketing Matters box on the next page, this is the pricing strategy Energizer used with its very successful e^2 high-performance AA batteries.[8]

Odd-Even Pricing Sears offers a Craftsman radial saw for $499.99, the suggested retail price for the Gillette Fusion shaving system is $11.99, and Kmart sells Windex glass cleaner on sale for 99 cents. Why not simply price these items at $500, $12, and $1, respectively? These firms are using *odd-even pricing,* which involves setting prices a few dollars or cents under an even number. The presumption is that consumers see the Sears radial saw as priced at "something over $400" rather than "about $500." In theory, demand increases if the price drops from $500 to $499.99. There is some evidence to suggest this does happen. However, research suggests that overuse of odd-ending prices tends to mute their effect on demand.[9]

Target Pricing Manufacturers will sometimes estimate the price that the ultimate consumer would be willing to pay for a product. They then work backward through markups taken by retailers and wholesalers to determine what price they can charge wholesalers for the product. This practice, called *target pricing,* results in the manufacturer deliberately adjusting the composition and features of a product to achieve the target price to consumers. Canon uses this practice for pricing its cameras, as does Heinz for its complete line of pet foods.[10]

Bundle Pricing A frequently used demand-oriented pricing practice is *bundle pricing*—the marketing of two or more products in a single package price. For example, Delta Air Lines offers vacation packages that include airfare, car rental, and lodging. Bundle pricing is based on the idea that consumers value the package more than the individual items. This is due to benefits received from not having to make

Marketing Matters > > > > > customer value

Energizer's Lesson in Price Perception— Value Lies in the Eye of the Beholder

Battery manufacturers are as tireless as a certain drum-thumping bunny in their efforts to create products that perform better, last longer, and not incidentally, outsell the competition. The commercialization of new alkaline battery technology at a price that creates value for consumers is not always obvious or easy. Just ask the marketing executives at Energizer about their experience with pricing Energizer Advanced Formula and Energizer e^2 AA alkaline batteries.

When Duracell launched its high-performance Ultra brand AA alkaline battery with a 25 percent price premium over standard Duracell batteries, Energizer quickly countered with its own high-performance battery—Energizer Advanced Formula. Believing that consumers would not pay the premium price, Energizer priced its Advanced Formula brand at the same price as its standard AA alkaline battery, expecting to gain market share from Duracell. It did not happen. Why? According to industry analysts, consumers associated Energizer's low price with inferior quality in the high-performance segment. Instead of gaining market share, Energizer lost market share to Duracell and Rayovac, the number three battery manufacturer.

Having learned its lesson, Energizer subsequently released its e^2 high-performance battery, this time priced 4 percent higher than Duracell Ultra and about 50 percent higher than Advanced Formula. The result? Energizer recovered lost sales and market share. The lesson learned? Value lies in the eye of the beholder.

---

separate purchases and enhanced satisfaction from one item given the presence of another. Moreover, bundle pricing often provides a lower total cost to buyers and lower marketing costs to sellers.

Yield Management Pricing   Have you ever been on an airplane and discovered the person next to you paid a lower price for her ticket than you paid? Annoying, isn't it? But what you observed is *yield management pricing*—the charging of different prices to maximize revenue for a set amount of capacity at any given time. Airlines, hotels, and car rental firms engage in capacity management by varying prices based on time, day, week, or season to match demand and supply. American Airlines estimates that yield management pricing produces an annual revenue that exceeds $500 million.[11]

How was the price of the Rock and Roll Hall of Fame and Museum determined? Read the text to find out.

Cost-Oriented Pricing Approaches

With cost-oriented approaches a price setter stresses the cost side of the pricing problem, not the demand side. Price is set by looking at the production and marketing costs and then adding enough to cover direct expenses, overhead, and profit.

Standard Markup Pricing   Managers of supermarkets and other retail stores have such a large number of products that estimating the demand for each product as a means of setting price is impossible. Therefore, they use *standard markup pricing,* which entails adding a fixed percentage to the cost of all items in a specific product class. This percentage markup varies depending on the type of

268

How many picture frames must a store owner sell to make a $7,000 profit? Read the text to find out.

retail store (such as furniture, clothing, or grocery) and on the product involved. High-volume products usually have smaller markups than do low-volume products. Supermarkets such as Kroger, Safeway, and Jewel have different markups for staple items and discretionary items. The markup on staple items like sugar, flour, and dairy products varies from 10 percent to 23 percent, whereas markups on discretionary items like snack foods and candy ranges from 27 percent to 47 percent. These markups must cover all expenses of the store, pay for overhead costs, and contribute something to profits. For supermarkets these markups, which may appear very large, result in only a 1 percent profit on sales revenue.

Cost-Plus Pricing   Many manufacturing, professional services, and construction firms use a variation of standard markup pricing. *Cost-plus pricing* involves summing the total unit cost of providing a product or service and adding a specific amount to the cost to arrive at a price. Cost-plus pricing is the most commonly used method to set prices for business products.[12] For example, this pricing approach was used in setting the price for the $92 million Rock and Roll Hall of Fame and Museum in Cleveland, Ohio.

This method is finding favor among business-to-business marketers in the service sector. For example, the rising cost of legal fees has prompted some law firms to adopt a cost-plus pricing approach. Rather than billing business clients on an hourly basis, lawyers and their clients agree on a fixed fee based on expected costs plus a profit for the law firm. Many advertising agencies now use this approach. Here, the client agrees to pay the agency a fee based on the cost of its work plus some agreed-on profit.[13]

Profit-Oriented Pricing Approaches

A price setter may choose to balance both revenues and costs to set price using profit-oriented approaches. These might either involve a target of a specific dollar volume of profit or express this target profit as a percentage of sales or investment.

Target Profit Pricing   When a firm sets an annual target of a specific dollar volume of profit, this is called *target profit pricing.* For example, if you owned a picture frame store and wanted to achieve a target profit of $7,000, how much would you need to charge for each frame? Because profit depends on revenues and costs, you would have to know your costs and then estimate how many frames you would sell. Let's assume, based on sales in previous years, you expect to frame 1,000 pictures next year. The cost of your time and materials to frame an average picture is $22, while your overhead expenses (rent, manager salaries, etc.) are $26,000. Finally, your goal is to achieve a profit of $7,000. How do you calculate your price per picture?

Profit = Total revenue − Total costs

= (Pictures sold × Price/picture) −
[(Cost/picture × Pictures sold) + overhead cost]

Solving for price per picture, the equation becomes,

$$\text{Price/picture} = \frac{\text{Profit} + [(\text{Cost/picture} \times \text{Pictures sold}) + \text{overhead cost}]}{\text{Pictures sold}}$$

$$= \frac{\$7,000 + [(\$22 \times 1,000) + \$26,000]}{1,000}$$

$$= \frac{\$7,000 + \$48,000}{1,000}$$

$$= \$55 \text{ per picture}$$

Clearly, this pricing method depends on an accurate estimate of demand. Because demand is often difficult to predict, this method has the potential for disaster if the estimate is too high. Generally, a target profit pricing strategy is best for firms offering new or unique products, without a lot of competition. What if other frame stores in your area were charging $40 per framed picture? As a marketing manager, you'd have to offer improved customer value with your more expensive frames, lower your costs, or settle for less profit.

Target Return-on-Sales Pricing Firms such as supermarkets often use *target return-on-sales pricing* to set prices that will give them a profit that is a specified percentage—say, 1 percent—of the sales volume. This price method is often used because of the difficulty in establishing a benchmark of sales or investment to show how much of a firm's effort is needed to achieve the target.

Target Return-on-Investment Pricing Firms such as General Motors and many public utilities use *target return-on-investment pricing* to set prices to achieve a return-on-investment (ROI) target such as a percentage that is mandated by its board of directors or regulators. For example, an electric utility may decide to seek 10 percent ROI. If its investment in plant and equipment is $50 billion, it would need to set the price of electricity to its customers at a level that results in $5 billion a year in profit.

Competition-Oriented Pricing Approaches

Rather than emphasize demand, cost, or profit factors, a price setter can stress what competitors or "the market" is doing.

Customary Pricing For some products where tradition, a standardized channel of distribution, or other competitive factors dictate the price, *customary pricing* is used. Candy bars offered through standard vending machines have a customary price of 75 cents, and a significant departure from this price may result in a loss of sales for the manufacturer. Hershey typically has changed the amount of chocolate in its candy bars depending on the price of raw chocolate rather than vary its customary retail price so that it can continue selling through vending machines.

Above-, At-, or Below-Market Pricing The "market price" of a product is what customers are generally willing to pay, not necessarily the price that the firm sets. For most products it is difficult to identify a specific market price for a product or product class. Still, marketing managers often have a subjective feel for the competitors' price or the market price. Using this benchmark, they then may deliberately choose a strategy of *above-, at-,* or *below-market pricing.*

Among watch manufacturers, Rolex takes pride in emphasizing that it makes one of the most expensive watches you can buy, a clear example of above-market pricing. Manufacturers of national brands of clothing such as Hart Schaffner & Marx and Christian Dior and retailers such as Neiman Marcus deliberately set premium prices for their products.

Large department store chains such as JCPenney generally use at-market pricing. These chains often establish the going market price in the minds of their competitors. Similarly, Revlon cosmetics and Arrow brand shirts are generally priced "at market." They also provide a reference price for competitors that use above- and below-market pricing.

In contrast, a number of firms use below-market pricing. Manufacturers of generic products and retailers that offer their own private brands of products ranging from peanut butter to shampoo deliberately set prices for these products about 8 percent to 10 percent below the prices of nationally branded competitive products such as Skippy peanut butter or Vidal Sassoon shampoo.

Companies use a "price premium" to assess whether its products and brands are above, at, or below the market. An illustration of how the price premium measure is calculated, displayed, and interpreted appears in the Using Marketing Dashboards box.

Using Marketing Dashboards

Are Cracker Jack Prices Above, At, or Below the Market?

How would you determine whether a firm's retail prices are above, at, or below the market? You might visit retail stores and record what prices retailers are charging for products or brands. This laborious activity can be simplified by combining two consumer market share measures to create a "price premium" display on your marketing dashboard.

Your Challenge Frito-Lay is considering whether to buy the Cracker Jack brand of caramel popcorn from Borden Inc. Frito-Lay research shows that Cracker Jack has a strong brand equity. But, Cracker Jack's dollar sales market share and pound volume market share declined recently and trailed the Crunch 'n Munch brand as shown in the table.

Borden's management used an above-market, premium pricing strategy for Cracker Jack. Specifically, Cracker Jack's suggested retail price was set to yield an average price premium per pound of 28 percent relative to Crunch 'n Munch. As a Frito-Lay marketer studying Cracker Jack, your challenge is to calculate and display Cracker Jack's actual price premium relative to Crunch 'n Munch. A price premium is the percentage by which the actual price charged for a specific brand exceeds (or falls short of) a benchmark established for a similar product or basket of products. This premium can be calculated as follows:

$$\text{Price Premium (\%)} = \frac{\text{Dollar Sales Market Share for a Brand}}{\text{Unit Volume Market Share for a Brand}} - 1$$

Brand	Dollar Sales Market Share	Pound Volume Market Share
Crunch 'n Munch	32%	32%
Cracker Jack	26	19
Fiddle Faddle	7	8
Private Brands	4	8
Seasonal, Specialty, and Regional (S,S,R) Brands	31	33
	100%	100%

Your Findings Using caramel popcorn brand market share data, the Cracker Jack price premium is 1.368, or 36.8 percent, calculated as follows: (26 percent ÷ 19 percent) − 1 = 0.368. By comparison, Crunch 'n Munch enjoys no price premium. Its dollar sales market share and unit (pound) market share are equal: (32 percent ÷ 32 percent) − 1 = 0, or zero percent. The price premium, or lack thereof, of other brands can be displayed in a marketing dashboard as shown below.

Your Action Cracker Jack's price premium clearly exceeds the 28 percent Borden benchmark relative to Crunch 'n Munch. Cracker Jack's price premium may have overreached its brand equity. Consideration might be given to assessing Cracker Jack's price premium relative to its market position should Frito-Lay purchase the brand.

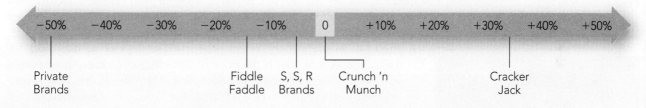

Loss-Leader Pricing For a special promotion retail stores deliberately sell a product below its customary price to attract attention to it. The purpose of this *loss-leader pricing* is not to increase sales but to attract customers in hopes they will buy other products as well, particularly the discretionary items with large markups. For example, Best Buy, Target, and Wal-Mart sell CDs at about half of music companies' suggested retail price to attract customers to their stores.[14]

---

learning review

1. Value is _____.
2. What are the circumstances in pricing a new product that might support skimming or penetration pricing?

ESTIMATING DEMAND AND REVENUE

Basic to setting a product's price is the extent of customer demand for it. Marketing executives must also translate this estimate of customer demand into estimates of revenues the firm expects to receive.

Fundamentals of Estimating Demand

How much money would you pay for your favorite magazine? If the price kept going up, at some point you would probably quit buying it. Conversely, if the price kept going down, you might eventually decide not only to keep buying your magazine but also to get your friend a subscription, too. The lower the price, the higher the demand. The publisher wants to sell more magazines, but will it sell enough additional copies to make up for the lower price per copy? That is an important question for marketing managers. Here's how one firm decided to find out.

Newsweek conducted a pricing experiment at newsstands in 11 cities throughout the United States. At that time, Houston newsstand buyers paid $2.25, while in Fort Worth, New York, Los Angeles, and Atlanta they paid the regular $2.00 price. In San Diego, the price was $1.50, while in Minneapolis–St. Paul, New Orleans, and Detroit it was only $1.00. By comparison, the regular newsstand price for *Time* and *U.S. News & World Report*, *Newsweek*'s competitors, was $1.95. Why did *Newsweek* conduct the experiment? According to a *Newsweek* executive, "We want to figure out what the demand curve for our magazine at the newsstand is."[15]

demand curve

Graph relating quantity sold and price, which shows how many units will be sold at a given price

Read the text to learn how *Newsweek* uses price experiments.

The Demand Curve A **demand curve** is a graph relating the quantity sold and price, which shows the maximum number of units that will be sold at a given price. Demand curve D_1 in Figure 12–3A shows the newsstand demand for *Newsweek* under the existing conditions. Note that as price falls, more people decide to buy and unit sales increase. But price is not the complete story in estimating demand. Economists emphasize three other key factors:

1. *Consumer tastes.* As we saw in Chapter 3, these depend on many factors such as demographics, culture, and technology. Because consumer tastes can change quickly, up-to-date marketing research is essential.

2. *Price and availability of similar products.* The laws of demand work for one's competitors, too. If the price of *Time* magazine falls, more people will buy it. That then means fewer people will buy *Newsweek*. *Time* is considered by economists to be a substitute for *Newsweek*. Online magazines are also a substitute—one whose availability has increased tremendously in recent years. The point to remember is, as the price of substitutes falls or their availability increases, the demand for a product (*Newsweek*, in this case) will fall.

3. *Consumer income.* In general, as real consumer income (allowing for inflation) increases, demand for a product also increases.

The first of these two factors influences what consumers *want* to buy, and the third affects what they *can* buy. Along with price, these are often called *demand factors,* or factors that determine consumers' willingness and ability to pay for goods and services. As discussed earlier in Chapters 8 and 10, it is often very difficult to estimate demand for new products, especially because consumer likes and dislikes are often so difficult to read clearly.

Movement Along versus Shift of a Demand Curve Demand curve D_1 in Figure 12–3A shows that as the price is lowered from $2.00 to $1.50, the quantity demanded increases from 3 million (Q_1) to 4.5 million (Q_2)

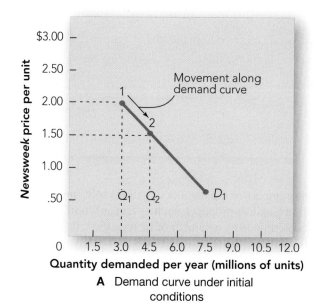

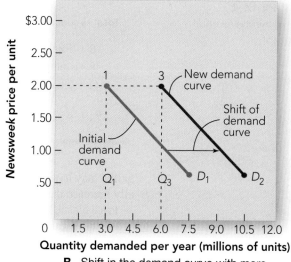

A Demand curve under initial conditions

B Shift in the demand curve with more favorable conditions

FIGURE 12–3

Demand curves for *Newsweek* showing the effect on annual sales (quantity demanded per year) by a change in price caused by (A) a movement along the demand curve and (B) a shift of the demand curve.

units per year. This is an example of a *movement along a demand curve* and assumes that other factors (consumer tastes, price and availability of substitutes, and consumer income) remain unchanged.

What if some of these factors change? For example, if advertising causes more people to want *Newsweek,* newsstand distribution is increased, or if consumer incomes rise, then the demand increases. Now the original curve, D_1 (the blue line in Figure 12–3B), no longer represents the demand; a new curve must be drawn (D_2). Economists call this a *shift in the demand curve*—in this case, a shift to the right, from D_1 to D_2. This increased demand means that more *Newsweek* magazines are wanted for a given price: At a price of $2, the demand is 6 million units per year (Q_3) on D_2 rather than 3 million units per year (Q_1) on D_1.

What price did *Newsweek* select after conducting its experiment? It kept the price at $2.00. However, through expanded newsstand distribution and more aggressive advertising, *Newsweek* was later able to shift its demand curve to the right and charge a price of $2.50 without affecting its newsstand volume.

Price Elasticity of Demand Marketing managers are especially interested in **price elasticity of demand**—a key consideration related to the product's demand curve. Price elasticity of demand is the percentage change in quantity demanded relative to a percentage change in price. It measures how sensitive consumer demand and the firm's revenues are to changes in the product's price.

A product with *elastic demand* is one in which a slight decrease in price results in a relatively large increase in demand, or units sold. The reverse is also true: With elastic demand, a slight increase in price results in a relatively large decrease in demand. Marketing experiments on soft drinks and snack foods show them often to have elastic demand. So marketing managers may cut price to increase the demand, the units sold, and total revenue for one of these products, depending on what competitors' prices are. Recent research studies show that price elasticity for these products is increasing, probably because consumers are more often trying to take advantage of temporary price promotions and deals.

In contrast, a product with *inelastic demand* means that slight increases or decreases in price will not significantly affect the demand, or units sold, for the product. Products and services considered as necessities usually have inelastic demand. What about gasoline for your car? Will an increase of a dollar per gallon cause you to drive fewer miles and buy less gasoline? No? Then you're like millions of other Americans, which is why gasoline has inelastic demand.[16] This means that an increase of a dollar per

price elasticity of demand

The percentage change in the quantity demanded relative to a percentage change in price

FIGURE 12–4

Fundamental revenue concept

Total revenue (TR) is the total money received from the sale of a product. If

    TR = Total revenue

     P = Unit price of the product

     Q = Quantity of the product sold

Then

    TR = P × Q

gallon may have a relatively minor impact on the number of gallons sold, and will actually increase the total revenue of a gasoline producer, such as ExxonMobil.

    Price elasticity of demand is determined by a number of factors. First, the more substitutes a product of service has, the more likely it is to be price elastic. For example, a new sweater, shirt, or blouse has many possible substitutes and is price elastic, but gasoline has almost no substitutes and is price inelastic. Second, products and services considered to be nondiscretionary are price inelastic, so open-heart surgery is price inelastic, whereas airline tickets for a vacation are price elastic. Third, items that require a large cash outlay compared with a person's disposable income are price elastic. Accordingly, cars and yachts are price elastic; pulp fiction books tend to be price inelastic.

Fundamentals of Estimating Revenue

total revenue

Total money received from the sale of a product

While economists may talk about "demand curves," marketing executives are more likely to speak in terms of "revenues generated." Demand curves lead directly to an essential revenue concept critical to pricing decisions: **total revenue**. As summarized in Figure 12–4, total revenue (TR) equals the unit price (P) times the quantity sold (Q). Using this equation, let's recall our picture frame shop and assume our annual demand has improved so we can set a price of $100 per picture and sell 400 pictures per year. So,

    TR = P × Q

       = $100 × 400

       = $40,000

    This combination of price and quantity sold annually will give us a total revenue of $40,000 per year. Is that good? Are you making money, making a profit? Alas, total revenue is only part of the profit equation that we saw earlier:

    Total profit = Total revenue − Total cost

The next section covers the other part of the profit equation: cost.

learning review

3. What three key factors are necessary when estimating consumer demand?

4. Price elasticity of demand is _____.

DETERMINING COST, VOLUME, AND PROFIT RELATIONSHIPS

While revenues are the moneys received by the firm from selling its products or services to customers, costs or expenses are the monies the firm pays out to its employees and suppliers. Marketing managers often use break-even analysis to relate revenues and costs, topics covered in this section.

FIGURE 12–5
Fundamental concepts about "costs," which are the monies the firm pays out to its employees and suppliers: total cost, fixed cost, variable cost, and unit variable cost.

Total cost (TC) is the total expense incurred by a firm in producing and marketing a product. Total cost is the sum of fixed cost and variable cost.

Fixed cost (FC) is the sum of the expenses of the firm that are stable and do not change with the quantity of a product that is produced and sold. Examples of fixed costs are rent on the building, executive salaries, and insurance.

Variable cost (VC) is the sum of the expenses of the firm that vary directly with the quantity of a product that is produced and sold. For example, as the quantity sold doubles, the variable cost doubles. Examples are the direct labor and direct materials used in producing the product and the sales commissions that are tied directly to the quantity sold. As mentioned above,

$$TC = FC + VC$$

Unit variable cost (UVC) is expressed on a per unit basis, or

$$UVC = \frac{VC}{Q}$$

The Importance of Controlling Costs

total cost
Total expenses incurred by a firm in producing and marketing a product; total cost is the sum of fixed cost and variable costs

Understanding the role and behavior of costs is critical for all marketing decisions, particularly pricing decisions. Four cost concepts are important in pricing decisions: **total cost,** *fixed cost, variable cost,* and *unit variable cost* (Figure 12–5).

Many firms go bankrupt because their costs get out of control, causing their total costs to exceed their total revenues over an extended period of time. So firms are increasingly trying to control their fixed costs like insurance and executive salaries and reduce the variable costs in their manufactured items by having production done outside the United States. This is why sophisticated marketing managers make pricing decisions that balance both their revenues and costs.

Break-Even Analysis

break-even analysis
Examines the relationship between total revenue and total cost to determine profitability at different levels of output

Marketing managers often employ an approach that considers cost, volume, and profit relationships based on the profit equation. **Break-even analysis** is a technique that analyzes the relationship between total revenue and total cost to determine profitability at various levels of output. The *break-even point (BEP)* is the quantity at which total revenue and total cost are equal. Profit then comes from all units sold beyond the BEP. In terms of the definitions in Figure 12–5,

$$BEP_{Quantity} = \frac{\text{Fixed cost}}{\text{Unit price} - \text{Unit variable cost}} = \frac{FC}{P - UVC}$$

Calculating a Break-Even Point Consider a picture frame store. Suppose you wish to identify how many pictures you must sell to cover your fixed cost at a given price. Let's assume demand for your framed pictures is strong so the average price customers are willing to pay for each picture is \$120. Also, suppose your fixed cost (FC) is \$32,000 (for real estate taxes, interest on a bank loan, and other fixed expenses) and unit variable cost (UVC) for a picture is now \$40 (for labor, glass, frame, and matting). Your break-even quantity ($BEP_{Quantity}$) is 400 pictures, as follows:

$$\begin{aligned} BEP_{Quantity} &= \frac{\text{Fixed cost}}{\text{Unit price} - \text{Unit variable cost}} = \frac{FC}{P - UVC} \\ &= \frac{\$32{,}000}{\$120 - \$40} \\ &= 400 \text{ pictures} \end{aligned}$$

Quantity of Pictures Sold (Q)	Price Per Picture (P)	Total Revenue (TR) = (P × Q)	Unit Variable Cost (UVC)	Total Variable Cost (VC) = (UVC × Q)	Fixed Cost (FC)	Total Cost (TC) = (FC + VC)	Profit = (TR − TC)
0	$120	$ 0	$40	$ 0	$32,000	$32,000	−$32,000
200	120	24,000	40	8,000	32,000	40,000	−16,000
400	120	48,000	40	16,000	32,000	48,000	0
600	120	72,000	40	24,000	32,000	56,000	16,000
800	120	96,000	40	32,000	32,000	64,000	32,000
1,000	120	120,000	40	40,000	32,000	72,000	48,000
1,200	120	144,000	40	48,000	32,000	80,000	64,000

FIGURE 12–6

Calculating a break-even point for the picture frame store in the text example shows its profit starts at 400 framed pictures per year.

The row shaded in orange in Figure 12–6 shows that your break-even quantity at a price of $120 per picture is 400 pictures. At less than 400 pictures, your picture frame store incurs a loss, and at more than 400 pictures it makes a profit. Figure 12–6 also shows that if you could increase your annual picture sales to 1,000, your store would make a profit of $48,000—the row shaded in green in the figure.

Figure 12–7 shows a graphic presentation of the break-even analysis, called a *break-even chart*. It shows that total revenue and total cost intersect and are equal at a quantity of 400 pictures sold, which is the break-even point at which profit is exactly $0. You want to do better? If your frame store could increase the quantity sold annually to 1,000 pictures, the graph in Figure 12–7 shows you can earn an annual profit of $48,000, just as shown by the row shaded in green in Figure 12–6.

Applications of Break-Even Analysis   Because of its simplicity, break-even analysis is used extensively in marketing, most frequently to study the impact on profit

FIGURE 12–7

Break-even analysis chart for a picture frame store shows the break-even point at 400 pictures and $48,000 in revenue.

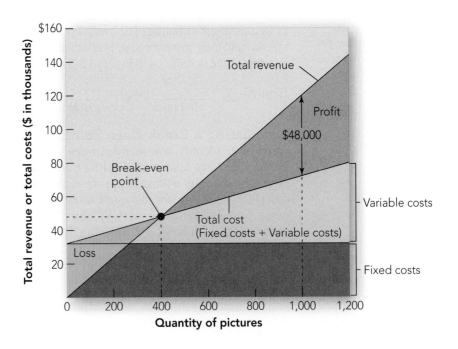

of changes in price, fixed cost, and variable cost. The mechanics of break-even analysis are the basis of the widely used electronic spreadsheets offered by computer programs such as Microsoft Excel that permit managers to answer hypothetical "what if" questions about the effect of changes in price and cost on their profit.

learning review

5. What is the difference between fixed costs and variable costs?
6. What is a break-even point?

PRICING OBJECTIVES AND CONSTRAINTS

LO4

With such a variety of alternative pricing strategies available, a marketing manager must consider the pricing objectives and constraints that will narrow the range of choices. While pricing objectives frequently reflect corporate goals, pricing constraints often relate to conditions existing in the marketplace.

Identifying Pricing Objectives

pricing objectives
Expectations that specify the role of price in an organization's marketing and strategic plans

Pricing objectives specify the role of price in an organization's marketing and strategic plans. To the extent possible, these pricing objectives are carried to lower levels in the organization, such as in setting objectives for marketing managers responsible for an individual brand. These objectives may change depending on the financial position of the company as a whole, the success of its products, or the segments in which it is doing business. H. J. Heinz, for example, has specific pricing objectives for its Heinz ketchup brand that vary by country.

Profit   Three different objectives relate to a firm's profit, which is often measured in terms of return on investment. These objectives have different implications for pricing strategy. One objective is *managing for long-run profits,* in which a company—such as many Japanese car or TV set manufacturers—gives up immediate profit in exchange for achieving a higher market share. Products are priced relatively low compared to their cost to develop, but the firm expects to make greater profits later because of its high market share.

A *maximizing current profit* objective, such as for a quarter or year, is common in many firms because the targets can be set and performance measured quickly. American firms are sometimes criticized for this short-run orientation. As noted earlier, a *target return* objective occurs when a firm sets a profit goal (such as 20 percent for return on investment), usually determined by its board of directors. These three profit objectives have different implications for a firm's pricing objectives.

Another profit consideration for firms such as movie studios and manufacturers is to ensure that those firms in their channels of distribution make adequate profits. Without profits for these channel members, the movie studio or manufacturer is cut off from its customers. For example, Figure 12–8 on the next page shows where each dollar of your movie ticket goes. The 51 cents the movie studio gets must cover its profit plus the cost of making and marketing the movie. Although the studio would like more than 51 cents of your dollar, it settles for this amount to make sure theaters and distributors are satisfied and willing to handle its movies.[17]

FIGURE 12–8
Where each dollar of your movie ticket goes

Labels on figure: Theater 19¢; Distributor 30¢; Movie studio 51¢; 10¢ = Theater expenses; 9¢ = Left for theater; 6¢ = Misc. expenses; 24¢ = Left for distributor; 20¢ = Advertising and publicity expenses; 8¢ = Actors' share of gross; 23¢ = Left for movie studio

Sales   Given that a firm's profit is high enough for it to remain in business, an objective may be to increase sales revenue, which will in turn lead to increases in market share and profit. Objectives related to sales revenue or unit sales have the advantage of being translated easily into meaningful targets for marketing managers responsible for a product line or brand. However, cutting price on one product in a firm's line may increase its sales revenue but reduce those of related products.

Market Share   Market share is the ratio of the firm's sales revenues or unit sales to those of the industry (competitors plus the firm itself). Companies often pursue a market share objective when industry sales are relatively flat or declining. In the late 1990s, Boeing cut prices drastically to try to maintain its 60 percent market share and encountered huge losses. Although increased market share is a primary goal of some firms, others see it as a means to other ends: increasing sales and profits.

Unit Volume   Many firms use unit volume, the quantity produced or sold, as a pricing objective. These firms often sell multiple products at very different prices and need to match the unit volume demanded by customers with price and production capacity. Using unit volume as an objective can be counterproductive if a volume objective is achieved, say, by drastic price cutting that drives down profit.

Survival   In some instances, profits, sales, and market share are less important objectives of the firm than mere survival. Frontier Airlines has attracted passengers with low fares and aggressive promotions to improve the firm's cash flow. This pricing objective has helped Frontier stay alive in the competitive airline industry following its bankruptcy in 2008.

Social Responsibility   A firm may forgo higher profit on sales and follow a pricing objective that recognizes its obligations to customers and society in general. Medtronics followed this pricing policy when it introduced the world's first heart pacemaker. Gerber supplies a specially formulated product free of charge to children who cannot tolerate foods based on cow's milk.

Identifying Pricing Constraints

pricing constraints
Factors that limit the range of price a firm may set

Factors that limit the range of price a firm may set are **pricing constraints**. Consumer demand for the product clearly affects the price that can be charged. Other constraints on price vary from factors within the organization to competitive factors outside it.

Demand for the Product Class, Product, and Brand   The number of potential buyers for a product class (high-definition TVs), product (flat-panel display), and brand (Panasonic) clearly affects the price a seller can charge. So does whether the item is a luxury or a necessity, like bread and a roof over your head. Generally speaking, the higher the demand for a product class and product, the higher the price can be set. Demand for HDTVs and flat-panel displays is high given the switch from analog to digital television signals in 2009.[18]

Newness of the Product: Stage in the Product Life Cycle   The newer the product and the earlier it is in its life cycle, the higher the price that can usually be charged. The high initial price is possible because of patents and limited competition

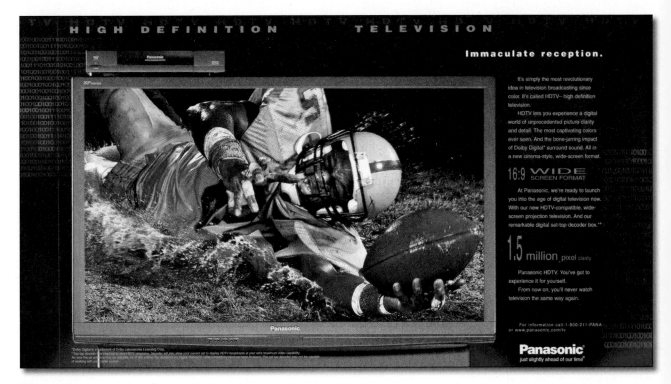

What pricing constraints do high-definition television manufacturers face? Read the text to appreciate the pricing challenges in this market.

in the early stage. HDTVs are in the growth stage of the product life cycle. However, competitors are entering the market, thus leading to greater price competition.

Cost of Producing and Marketing the Product

In the long run, a firm's price must cover all the costs of producing and marketing a product. If the price doesn't cover these costs, the firm will fail; so in the long run, a firm's costs set a floor under its price. The cost to produce HDTVs and flat-panel displays is decreasing by 15 percent per year. However, newer manufacturers have entered the market with aggressive pricing tactics, thus decreasing profit margins.

Competitors' Prices

A firm must know or anticipate what specific price its present and potential competitors are charging now or will charge. And the firm must assess the possibility of dangerous, costly price wars. Some industry forecasters are predicting an HDTV price war by 2011, with many lesser-known companies and brands leaving the market.

Legal and Ethical Considerations

Setting a final price is clearly a complex process. The task is further complicated by legal and ethical issues. Four pricing practices have received special scrutiny over these issues and are described below:

* *Price fixing.* A conspiracy among firms to set prices for a product is termed price fixing. Price fixing is illegal under the Sherman Act. When two or more competitors collude to explicitly or implicitly set prices, this practice is called *horizontal price fixing.* For example, six foreign vitamin companies recently pled guilty to price fixing in the human and animal vitamin industry and paid the largest fine in U.S. history: $335 million.[19] *Vertical price fixing* involves controlling agreements between independent buyers and sellers (a manufacturer and a retailer) whereby sellers are required to not sell products below a minimum retail price. This practice, called *resale price maintenance,* was declared illegal in 1975 under provisions of the Consumer Goods Pricing Act.

- *Price discrimination.* The Clayton Act as amended by the Robinson-Patman Act prohibits price discrimination—the practice of charging different prices to different buyers for goods of like grade and quality. However, not all price differences are illegal; only those that substantially lessen competition or create a monopoly are deemed unlawful.
- *Deceptive pricing.* Price deals that mislead consumers fall into the category of deceptive pricing. Deceptive pricing is outlawed by the Federal Trade Commission. *Bait and switch* is an example of deceptive pricing. This occurs when a firm offers a very low price on a product (the bait) to attract customers to a store. Once in the store, the customer is persuaded to purchase a higher-priced item (the switch) using a variety of tricks, including (1) degrading the promoted item and (2) not having the promised item in stock or refusing to take orders for it.
- *Predatory pricing.* Predatory pricing is charging a very low price for a product with the intent of driving competitors out of business. Once competitors have been driven out, the firm raises its prices. Proving the presence of this practice has been difficult and expensive because it must be shown that the predator explicitly attempted to destroy a competitor and the predatory price was below the defendant's average cost.

It should be clear that laws cannot be passed and enforced to protect consumers and competitors against all of these practices, so it is essential to rely on the ethical standards of those setting prices.

---

learning review

7. What is the difference between pricing objectives and pricing constraints?

8. Explain what bait and switch is and why it is an example of deceptive pricing.

SETTING A FINAL PRICE

LO5

The final price set by the marketing manager serves many functions. It must be high enough to cover the cost of providing the product or service *and* meet the objectives of the company. Yet it must be low enough that customers are willing to pay it. But not too low, or customers may think they're purchasing an inferior product. Dizzy yet? Setting price is one of the most difficult tasks the marketing manager faces, but three generalized steps are useful to follow.

Step 1: Select an Approximate Price Level

Before setting a final price, the marketing manager must understand the market environment, the features and customer benefits of the particular product, and the goals of the firm. A balance must be struck between factors that might drive a price higher (such as a profit-oriented approach) and other forces (such as increased competition from substitutes) that may drive a price down.

Marketing managers consider pricing objectives and constraints first, then choose among the general pricing approaches—demand-, cost-, profit-, or competition-oriented—to arrive at an approximate price level. This price is then analyzed in terms of cost, volume, and profit relationships. Break-even analyses may be run at this point, and finally if this approximate price level "works," it is time to take the next step: setting a specific list or quoted price.

Step 2: Set the List or Quoted Price

A seller must decide whether to follow a one-price or flexible-price policy.

One-Price Policy A *one-price policy*, also called *fixed pricing*, is setting one price for all buyers of a product or service. Saturn Corporation and CarMax use this approach in their stores and feature a "no haggle, one price" price for cars. Some retailers have married this policy with a below-market approach. Dollar Valley Stores and 99¢ Only Stores sell everything in their stores for $1 or less. Family Dollar Stores sell everything for $2.

Flexible-Price Policy In contrast, a *flexible-price policy* involves setting different prices for products and services depending on individual buyers and purchase situation in light of demand, cost, and competitive factors. Dell Inc. uses flexible pricing as it continually adjusts prices in response to changes in its own costs, competitive pressures, and demand from its various personal computer segments (home, small business, corporate, etc.). "Our flexibility allows us to be [priced] different even within a day," says a Dell spokesperson.[20]

What is the best day of the week to shop at Eddie Bauer, Gap, and J. Crew with their flexible-pricing approach? For the answers, see the text.

Chain apparel stores use the beginning of the week to discover what isn't selling well to make plans for the high-traffic weekends. So the best deals in their flexible-price policy come Wednesdays through Fridays, right before the weekend. Some apparel chains have specific days for nationwide price markdowns: Wednesdays for Gap and Thursdays for J. Crew and Eddie Bauer.[21]

Flexible pricing is not without its critics because of its discriminatory potential. For example, car dealers have traditionally used flexible pricing on the basis of buyer–seller negotiations to agree on a final sales price. However, flexible pricing may result in discriminatory practices in car buying as detailed in the Making Responsible Decisions box on the next page.[22]

Step 3: Make Special Adjustments to the List or Quoted Price

When you pay 75 cents for a bag of M&Ms in a vending machine or receive a quoted price of $10,000 from a contractor to renovate a kitchen, the pricing sequence ends with the last step just described: setting the list or quoted price. But when you are a manufacturer of M&M candies and sell your product to dozens or hundreds of wholesalers and retailers in your channel of distribution, you may need to make a variety of special adjustments to the list or quoted price. Wholesalers also must adjust list or quoted prices they set for retailers. Three special adjustments to the list or quoted price are (1) discounts, (2) allowances, and (3) geographical adjustments.

Discounts *Discounts* are reductions from list price that a seller gives a buyer as a reward for some activity of the buyer that is favorable to the seller. Four kinds of discounts are especially important in marketing strategy: (1) quantity, (2) seasonal, (3) trade (functional), and (4) cash.

- *Quantity discounts.* To encourage customers to buy larger quantities of a product, firms at all levels in the channel of distribution offer quantity discounts, which are reductions in unit costs for a larger order. For example, an instant photocopying service might set a price of 10 cents a copy for 1 to 24 copies, 9 cents a copy for 25 to 99, and 8 cents a copy for 100 or more. Because the photocopying service gets more of the buyer's business and has longer production runs that reduce its order-handling costs, it is willing to pass on some of the cost savings in the form of quantity discounts to the buyer.

Making Responsible Decisions > > > > > > ethics

Flexible Pricing—Is There Race and Gender Discrimination in Bargaining for a New Car?

What do 60 percent of prospective buyers dread when looking for a new car? That's right! They dread negotiating the price. Price bargaining demonstrates shortcomings of flexible pricing when purchasing a new car: the potential for minority price discrimination.

A National Bureau of Economic Research study of 750,000 car purchases indicated that Blacks, Hispanics, and women, on average, paid roughly $423, $483, and $105 more, respectively, for a new car in the $21,000 range than the typical purchaser. Smaller price premiums remained after adjusting for income, education, and other factors that may affect price negotiations.

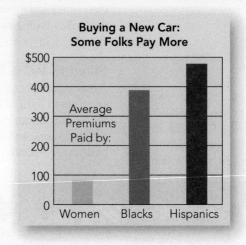

- *Seasonal discounts.* To encourage buyers to stock inventory earlier than their normal demand would require, manufacturers often use seasonal discounts. A firm such as Toro that manufactures lawn mowers and snow throwers offers seasonal discounts to encourage wholesalers and retailers to stock up on lawn mowers in January and February and on snow throwers in July and August—five or six months before the seasonal demand by ultimate consumers. This enables Toro to smooth out seasonal manufacturing peaks and troughs, thereby contributing to more efficient production. It also rewards wholesalers and retailers for the risk they accept in assuming increased inventory carrying costs and having supplies in stock at the time they are wanted by customers.

- *Trade (functional) discounts.* To reward wholesalers and retailers for marketing functions they will perform in the future, a manufacturer often gives trade, or functional, discounts. These reductions off the list or base price are offered to resellers in the channel of distribution on the basis of (1) where they are in the channel and (2) the marketing activities they are expected to perform in the future.

  Traditional trade discounts have been established in various product lines such as hardware, food, and pharmaceutical items. Although the manufacturer may suggest the trade discounts shown in the example just cited, the sellers are free to alter the discount schedule depending on their competitive situation.

- *Cash discounts.* To encourage retailers to pay their bills quickly, manufacturers offer them cash discounts. Suppose a retailer receives a bill quoted at $1,000, 2/10 net 30. This means that the bill for the product is $1,000, but the retailer can take a 2 percent discount ($1,000 × 0.02 = $20) if payment is made within 10 days and send a check for $980. If the payment cannot be made within 10 days, the total amount of $1,000 is due within 30 days. It is usually understood by the buyer that an interest charge will be added after the first 30 days of free credit.

Manufacturers provide a variety of discounts to assist channel members such as for Payless, a retailer promoting its early summer sandals sale.

A retailer like Payless that plans an early summer sale on sandals often tries to take advantage of several of these discounts to increase its revenues and profits.

Allowances   Allowances—like discounts—are reductions from list or quoted prices to buyers for performing some activity.

- *Trade-in allowances.* A new-car dealer can offer a substantial reduction in the list price of that new Toyota Camry by offering you a trade-in allowance of $500 for your Chevrolet. A trade-in allowance is a price reduction given when a used product is part of the payment on a new product. Trade-ins are an effective way to lower the price a buyer has to pay without formally reducing the list price.
- *Promotional allowances.* Sellers in the channel of distribution can qualify for promotional allowances for undertaking certain advertising or selling activities to promote a product. Various types of allowances include an actual cash payment or an extra amount of "free goods" (as with a free case of pizzas to a retailer for every dozen cases purchased). Frequently, a portion of these savings is passed on to the consumer by retailers.

Some companies, such as Procter & Gamble, have chosen to reduce promotional allowances for retailers by using everyday low pricing. *Everyday low pricing* (EDLP) is the practice of replacing promotional allowances with lower manufacturer list prices. EDLP promises to reduce the average price to consumers while minimizing promotional allowances that cost manufacturers billions of dollars every year.

Geographical Adjustments   Geographical adjustments are made by manufacturers or even wholesalers to list or quoted prices to reflect the cost of transportation of the products from seller to buyer. The two general methods for quoting prices related to transportation costs are (1) FOB origin pricing and (2) uniform delivered pricing.

- *FOB origin pricing.* FOB means "free on board" some vehicle at some location, which means the seller pays the cost of loading the product onto the vehicle that is used (such as a barge, railroad car, or truck). FOB origin pricing usually involves the seller's naming the location of this loading as the seller's factory or warehouse (such as "FOB Detroit" or "FOB factory"). The title to the goods passes to the buyer at the point of loading, so the buyer becomes responsible for picking the specific mode of transportation, for all the transportation costs, and for subsequent handling of the product. Buyers farthest from the seller face the big disadvantage of paying the higher transportation costs.
- *Uniform delivered pricing.* When a uniform delivered pricing method is used, the price the seller quotes includes all transportation costs. It is quoted in a contract as "FOB buyer's location," and the seller selects the mode of transportation, pays the freight charges, and is responsible for any damage that may occur because the seller retains title to the goods until delivered to the buyer.

learning review

9. What are the three steps in setting a final price?

10. What is the purpose of (*a*) quantity discounts and (*b*) promotional allowances?

LEARNING OBJECTIVES REVIEW

LO1 *Describe the nature and importance of pricing and the approaches for selecting an approximate price level.*
Price is the money or other considerations (such as barter) exchanged for the ownership or use of a good or service. Although price typically involves money, the amount exchanged is often different from the list or quoted price because of incentives (rebates, discounts, etc.), allowances (trade), and extra fees (finance charges, surcharges, etc.).

Demand, cost, profit, and competition influence the initial consideration of the approximate price level for a product or service. Demand-oriented pricing approaches stress consumer demand and revenue implications of pricing and include seven types: skimming, penetration, prestige, odd-even, target, bundle, and yield management. Cost-oriented pricing approaches emphasize the cost aspects of pricing and include two types: standard markup and cost-plus pricing. Profit-oriented pricing approaches focus on a balance between revenues and costs to set a price and include three types: target profit, target return-on-sales, and target return-on-investment pricing. And finally, competition-oriented pricing approaches stress what competitors or the marketplace are doing and include three types: customary; above-, at-, or below-market; and loss-leader pricing.

LO2 *Explain what a demand curve is and the role of revenues in pricing decisions.*
A demand curve is a graph relating the quantity sold and price, which shows the maximum number of units that will be sold at a given price. Three demand factors affect price: (*a*) consumer tastes, (*b*) price and availability of substitute products, and (*c*) consumer income. These demand factors determine consumers' willingness and ability to pay for goods and services. Assuming these demand factors remain unchanged, if the price of a product is lowered or raised, then the quantity demanded for it will increase or decrease, respectively. The demand curve relates to a firm's total revenue, which is the total money received from sale of a product, or the price of one unit times the quantity of units sold.

LO3 *Explain the role of costs in pricing decisions and describe how combinations of price, fixed cost, and unit variable cost affect a firm's break-even point.*
Four important costs impact a firm's pricing decisions: (*a*) total cost, or total expenses, the sum of fixed cost and variable cost incurred by a firm in producing and marketing a product; (*b*) fixed cost, the sum of expenses of the firm that are stable and do not change with the quantity of a product that is produced and sold; (*c*) variable cost, the sum of expenses of the firm that vary directly with the quantity of a product that is produced and sold; and (*d*) unit variable cost, variable cost expressed on a per unit basis.

Break-even analysis is a technique that analyzes the relationship between total revenue and total cost to determine profitability at various levels of output. The break-even point is the quantity at which total revenue and total cost are equal. Assuming no change in price, if the costs of a firm's product increase due to higher fixed costs (manufacturing or advertising) or variable costs (direct labor or materials), then its break-even point will be higher. And if total cost is unchanged, an increase in price will reduce the break-even point.

LO4 *Recognize the objectives a firm has in setting prices and the constraints that restrict the range of prices a firm can charge.*
Pricing objectives specify the role of price in a firm's marketing strategy and may include profit, sales revenue, market share, unit volume, survival, or some socially responsible price level. Pricing constraints that restrict a firm's pricing flexibility include demand, product newness, production and marketing costs, prices of competitive substitutes, and legal and ethical considerations.

LO5 *Describe the steps taken in setting a final price.*
Three common steps marketing managers often use are: first, select an approximate price level as a starting point; second, set the list or quoted price, choosing between a one-price policy or a flexible-price policy; and third, modify the list or quoted price by considering discounts, allowances, and geographical adjustments.

FOCUSING ON KEY TERMS

break-even analysis p. 275
demand curve p. 272
price p. 264
price elasticity of demand p. 273

pricing constraints p. 278
pricing objectives p. 277
profit equation p. 266

total cost p. 275
total revenue p. 274
value p. 265

APPLYING MARKETING KNOWLEDGE

1 How would the price equation apply to the purchase price of (*a*) gasoline, (*b*) an airline ticket, and (*c*) a checking account?

2 What would be your response to the statement, "Profit maximization is the only legitimate pricing objective for the firm"?

3 Touché Toiletries Inc. has developed an addition to its Lizardman Cologne line tentatively branded Ode d'Toade Cologne. Unit variable costs are 45 cents for a 3-ounce bottle, and heavy advertising expenditures in the first year would result in total fixed costs of $900,000. Ode d'Toade Cologne is priced at $7.50 for a 3-ounce bottle. How many bottles of Ode d'Toade must be sold to break even?

4 Under what conditions would a camera manufacturer adopt a skimming price approach for a new product? A penetration approach?

5 What are some similarities and differences between skimming pricing, prestige pricing, and above-market pricing?

building your marketing plan

1 In starting to set a final price, think about your customers and competitors and set three possible prices.

2 Assume a fixed cost and unit variable cost and (*a*) calculate the break-even points and (*b*) plot a break-even chart for the three prices specified in step 1.

3 Using your best judgment, select one of these prices as your final price.

video case 12 The Starbury Collection: Setting a Price. Making a Difference.

Why would Stephon Marbury, a 10-year NBA veteran and New York Knicks point guard with a multiyear, multimillion-dollar contract, put his seal of approval on a $14.98 basketball sneaker without a lucrative endorsement guarantee?

Why would Steve & Barry's University Sportswear sell a $14.98 sneaker and forgo a meaty retail margin when other stores charge as much as $150 for a pair of signature sneakers?

More to the point, in a world where the average basketball sneaker is priced at $100 and signature shoes are priced much higher, could the Stephon Marbury and Steve & Barry's partnership market $14.98 signature sneakers in a cost-efficient and profitable manner? In a word, yes.

out there who bury their child for a basketball sneaker. We're talking about clothes." He added, "It was very important to me that the Starbury Collection have a strong social component for kids and parents, especially in urban areas."

Steve & Barry's executives enthusiastically embraced Marbury's idea given the retailer's aim of providing top-quality merchandise at low prices at its nearly 200 stores in 33 states. In short order, Steve & Barry's contacted Rocketfish, the athletic gear design firm best known for providing high-performance basketball sneaker concepts to Nike, Reebok, and Converse. It then contracted with a

STEPHON MARBURY + STEVE & BARRY'S = THE STARBURY COLLECTION

In 2005, Stephon Marbury approached executives at Steve & Barry's with a revolutionary idea—market an inexpensive quality basketball sneaker and apparel line with his endorsement and call it the Starbury Collection. Why did Stephon Marbury do this? "Things are crazy out there," Marbury said. "There's kids who are shot over shoes for $150, $100. There's poor mothers

supplier to produce the shoe to tight specifications. Rocketfish worked closely with Marbury and Steve & Barry's to create the Starbury One, a sneaker that delivered all the comfort and stability required for professional basketball players and recreational ballers alike. The retail price—$14.98. In an independent and extensive test conducted at the Parsons School of Design in New York City, Starbury One sneakers were found to be no different in the quality of design and materials from a major sneaker brand that retailed for $150.

BRINGING THE STARBURY COLLECTION TO MARKET: ENTER ERIN PATTON

With a great product at a great price, Steve & Barry's president, Andy Todd, turned to Erin Patton to prepare the Starbury Collection launch and build the brand. Patton was no stranger to brand building. He spent five years as the marketing director for the Air Jordan brand at Nike. According to Patton, "Stephon Marbury understood the difficulty parents and kids face keeping pace with the exorbitant price of sneakers. He knows what it means for inner-city kids and the extreme measures that are sometimes used to get

these products." Patton viewed Marbury's initiative as "an industry changing event"—and one he too wanted to happen. Making it happen was another matter.

With a limited marketing budget, Patton realized that an unconventional launch for the Starbury Collection was necessary. The Starbury Collection was launched on August 17, 2006, followed by a 40-city, 17-day tour of Steve & Barry's stores with Stephon Marbury in the lead. The launch and tour were timed to send a message to parents from lower-income families as they were doing their back-to-school shopping: You can afford to have your kids look and feel like an NBA basketball player. Starbury Collection ads appeared in exclusively urban publications such as *Slam and Dime* and a website (starbury.com) featuring urban phrases, such as "you feel me," which means you understand what I'm saying.

THE RESULT

The result? Over 3 million Starbury sneakers were sold within eight months of the August 2006 launch. In 2007, the Starbury Collection line expanded from 50 products to more than 200. The line includes the Starbury Two sneaker, polo shirts, skateboard shoes, and other lifestyle products; all under $15. "The Starbury Collection is about Steph's vision to eliminate the pressure that parents and kids feel to spend top dollar on the latest sneakers and clothing," said Todd. By setting the right price, the Starbury Collection at Steve & Barry's University Sportswear seeks to make a difference.

Questions

1 What broad pricing objective is most apparent in Stephon Marbury's offer to endorse a signature sneaker for $14.98?

2 In what ways are the demand factors of (*a*) consumer tastes, (*b*) price and availability of substitute products, and (*c*) consumer income important in influencing consumer demand for the Starbury Collection of sneakers and apparel?

3 For analysis purposes only, assume that (*a*) a pair of Starbury One sneakers is delivered to Steve & Barry's from its supplier at a price of $10.00, (*b*) the launch program cost $500,000 including the tour expenses, website development, and print advertising production and placement, and (*c*) these were the only relevant costs. How many pairs of Starbury One sneakers must Steve & Barry's sell to break even given these launch costs? Has Steve & Barry's achieved a 15 percent return on sales given that 3 million pairs of Starbury One sneakers have been sold?

13

Managing Marketing Channels and Supply Chains

LEARNING OBJECTIVES

After reading this chapter you should be able to:

 LO1 Explain what is meant by a marketing channel of distribution and why intermediaries are needed.

 LO2 Distinguish among traditional marketing channels, electronic marketing channels, and different types of vertical marketing systems.

 LO3 Describe factors that marketing executives consider when selecting and managing a marketing channel.

 LO4 Explain what supply chain and logistics management are and how they relate to marketing strategy.

APPLE STORES: CREATING A HIGH-TOUCH CUSTOMER EXPERIENCE IN A HIGH-TECH MARKETING CHANNEL

Apple thrives on innovation . . . in retailing. Yes, retailing! In a short eight-year span, Apple stores have become the gold standard for delivering an unparalleled customer experience. So how did Apple do it?

The vision behind Apple stores was to develop an atmosphere where consumers can experience the thrill of owning and using Apple's complete line of Macintosh computers and an array of digital cameras, camcorders, the entire iPod product family, and more with the assistance of a knowledgeable and customer-friendly staff. In the words of Apple CEO Steven Jobs, Apple stores were to deliver "A buying experience as good as our products." And so they have.

"Apple has changed people's expectations of what retail should be about," says Candace Corlett, a retailing consultant. Product assortments are arranged by customer interests, not product type. Apple products are easily accessible to encourage a customer to "test-drive" them in a shopping environment where clutter is conspicuously absent. Each store's interior design is ultra-modern with a pristine layout and inviting displays. In newer stores, checkout counters have been replaced with Easy Pay, an Apple system that allows salespeople to wander the store with a wireless credit card reader and ask, "Would you like to pay for that?"

The customer experience is enhanced with two novel in-store features. Stores contain a Genius Bar where customers can obtain product information and service on all Apple products from genial technical experts. The Genius Bar is complemented by the Studio in another part of the store. The Studio is staffed by "Creatives" who offer one-to-one training on everything from preparing an iMovie to how to deejay a friend's wedding.

But there is more! The success of Apple stores is also due to the company's commitment to having its world-class products at the right time, at the right place, and in the right form and condition that consumers want them. Apple's network of suppliers that make up its supply chain is considered to be world-class in its own right.

Has the focus on an innovative customer experience and an effective supply chain paid off? Apple stores achieved $1 billion in sales faster than any retail business in history, taking just three years to reach that mark. Equally important, the 240 (and counting) company-owned stores are profitable.[1]

This chapter focuses on marketing channels of distribution and supply chains. Each is an important element in the marketing mix.

NATURE AND IMPORTANCE OF MARKETING CHANNELS

LO1

Reaching prospective buyers, either directly or indirectly, is a prerequisite for successful marketing. At the same time, buyers benefit from distribution systems used by companies.

What Is a Marketing Channel of Distribution?

You see the results of distribution every day. You may have purchased Lay's Potato Chips at a 7-Eleven store, a book through Amazon.com, and Levi's jeans at Sears. Each of these items was brought to you by a marketing channel of distribution, or simply a **marketing channel**, which consists of individuals and firms involved in the process of making a product or service available for use or consumption by consumers or industrial users.

Marketing channels can be compared with a pipeline through which water flows from a source to terminus. Marketing channels make possible the flow of goods from a producer, through intermediaries, to a buyer. Intermediaries go by various names (Figure 13–1) and perform various functions. Some intermediaries actually purchase items from the seller, store them, and resell them to buyers. For example, Celestial Seasonings produces specialty teas and sells them to food wholesalers. The wholesalers then sell these teas to supermarkets and grocery stores, which sell them to consumers. Other intermediaries such as brokers and agents represent sellers but do not actually take title to products—their role is to bring a seller and buyer together. Century 21 real estate agents are examples of this type of intermediary.

Value Is Created by Intermediaries

The importance of intermediaries is made even clearer when we consider the functions they perform and the value they create for buyers.

Important Functions Performed by Intermediaries   Intermediaries make possible the flow of products from producers to ultimate consumers by performing

marketing channel

Individuals and firms involved in the process of making a product or service available for use or consumption by consumers or industrial users.

FIGURE 13–1

A variety of terms is used for marketing intermediaries. They vary in specificity and use in consumer and business markets.

TERM	DESCRIPTION
Middleman	Any intermediary between manufacturer and end-user markets
Agent or broker	Any intermediary with legal authority to act on behalf of the manufacturer
Wholesaler	An intermediary who sells to other intermediaries, usually to retailers; term usually applies to consumer markets
Retailer	An intermediary who sells to consumers
Distributor	An imprecise term, usually used to describe intermediaries who perform a variety of distribution functions, including selling, maintaining inventories, extending credit, and so on; a more common term in business markets but may also be used to refer to wholesalers
Dealer	A more imprecise term than *distributor* that can mean the same as distributor, retailer, wholesaler, and so forth

TYPE OF FUNCTION	ACTIVITIES RELATED TO FUNCTION
Transactional function	• *Buying*: Purchasing products for resale or as an agent for supply of a product • *Selling*: Contacting potential customers, promoting products, and seeking orders • *Risk taking*: Assuming business risks in the ownership of inventory that can become obsolete or deteriorate
Logistical function	• *Assorting*: Creating product assortments from several sources to serve customers • *Storing*: Assembling and protecting products at a convenient location to offer better customer service • *Sorting*: Purchasing in large quantities and breaking into smaller amounts desired by customers • *Transporting*: Physically moving a product to customers
Facilitating function	• *Financing*: Extending credit to customers • *Grading*: Inspecting, testing, or judging products, and assigning them quality grades • *Marketing information and research*: Providing information to customers and suppliers, including competitive conditions and trends

FIGURE 13–2

Marketing channel intermediaries perform three fundamental functions, each of which consists of different activities.

three basic functions (Figure 13–2). Intermediaries perform a transactional function when they buy and sell goods or services. But an intermediary such as a wholesaler also performs the function of sharing risk with the producer when it stocks merchandise in anticipation of sales. If the stock is unsold for any reason, the intermediary—not the producer—suffers the loss.

The logistics of a transaction (described at length later in this chapter) involve the details of preparing and getting a product to buyers. Gathering, sorting, and dispersing products are some of the logistical functions of the intermediary—imagine the several books required for a literature course sitting together on one shelf at your college book-store! Finally, intermediaries perform facilitating functions that, by definition, make a transaction *easier* for buyers. For example, JCPenney issues credit cards to consumers so they can buy now and pay later.

All three functions must be performed in a marketing channel, even though each channel member may not participate in all three. Channel members often negotiate about which specific functions they will perform. Borders, a leading U.S. book retailer, is a case in point. It has negotiated agreements with major book publishers whereby they assume responsibility for choosing books for Borders to buy, displaying the assortment of books on its shelves, and providing information on new titles and consumer reading preferences in specific book categories. For example, HarperCollins has responsibility for cookbooks, Random House for children's books, and Pearson for computer books.[2]

Consumers Also Benefit from Intermediaries   Consumers also benefit from intermediaries. Having the goods and services you want, when you want them, where you want them, and in the form you want them is the ideal result of marketing channels.

In more specific terms, marketing channels help create value for consumers through the four utilities described in Chapter 1: time, place, form, and possession. Time utility refers to having a product or service when you want it. For example, FedEx provides next-morning delivery. Place utility means having a product or service available where consumers want it, such as having a Texaco gas station located on a long stretch of lonely highway. Form utility involves enhancing a product or service to make it more appealing to buyers. Consider the importance of bottlers in the soft-drink industry. Coca-Cola and Pepsi-Cola manufacture the flavor concentrate (cola, lemon-lime) and sell it to bottlers—intermediaries—which then add sweetener and the concentrate to carbonated water and package the beverage in bottles and cans, which are then sold to retailers. Possession utility entails efforts by intermediaries to help buyers take possession of a product or service, such as having airline tickets delivered by a travel agency.

learning review

1. What is meant by a marketing channel?

2. What are the three basic functions performed by intermediaries?

MARKETING CHANNEL STRUCTURE AND ORGANIZATION

A product can take many routes on its journey from a producer to buyers. Marketers continually search for the most efficient route from the many alternatives available. As you'll see, there are some important differences between the marketing channels for consumer goods and those for business goods.

Marketing Channels for Consumer Goods and Services

Figure 13–3 shows the four most common marketing channels for consumer goods and services. It also shows the number of levels in each marketing channel, as evidenced by the number of intermediaries between a producer and ultimate buyers. As the number of intermediaries between a producer and buyer increases, the channel is viewed as increasing in length. Thus, the producer → wholesaler → retailer → consumer channel is longer than the producer → consumer channel.

Direct Channel   Channel A represents a *direct channel* because a producer and ultimate consumers deal directly with each other. Many products and services are distributed this way. A number of insurance companies sell their financial services using a direct channel and branch sales offices. The Schwan Food Company of Marshall, Minnesota, markets a full line of frozen foods in the United States using about 6,500 route salespeople who sell from refrigerated trucks. Because there are no intermediaries with a direct channel, the producer must perform all channel functions.

Indirect Channel   The remaining three channel forms are *indirect channels* because intermediaries are inserted between the producer and consumers and perform

FIGURE 13–3

Common marketing channels for consumer goods and services differ by the kind and number of intermediaries.

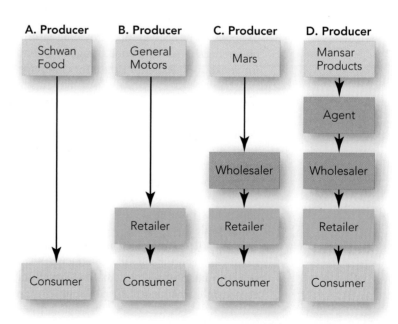

292

numerous channel functions. Channel B, with a retailer added, is most common when a retailer is large and can buy in large quantities from a producer or when the cost of inventory makes it too expensive to use a wholesaler. Automobile manufacturers such as General Motors, Ford, and Toyota use this channel, and a local car dealer acts as a retailer. Why is there no wholesaler? So many variations exist in the product that it would be impossible for a wholesaler to stock all the models required to satisfy buyers; in addition, the cost of maintaining an inventory would be too high. However, large retailers such as Sears, 7-Eleven, Staples, Safeway, and Home Depot buy in sufficient quantities to make it cost effective for a producer to deal with only a retail intermediary.

Adding a wholesaler in Channel C is most common for low-cost, low-unit value items that are frequently purchased by consumers, such as candy, confectionary items, and magazines. For example, Mars sells its line of candies to wholesalers in case quantities, who then break down (sort) the cases so that individual retailers can order in boxes or much smaller quantities.

Channel D, the most indirect channel, is employed when there are many small manufacturers and many small retailers, and an agent is used to help coordinate a large supply of the product. Mansar Products Ltd. is a Belgian producer of specialty jewelry that uses agents to sell to wholesalers in the United States, which then sell to many small independent jewelry retailers.

Marketing Channels for Business Goods and Services

The four most common channels for business goods and services are shown in Figure 13–4. In contrast with channels for consumer products, business channels typically are shorter and rely on one intermediary or none at all because business users are fewer in number, tend to be more concentrated geographically, and buy in larger quantities.

Direct Channel Channel A, represented by IBM's large, mainframe computer business, is a direct channel. Firms using this channel maintain their own salesforce and perform all channel functions. This channel is employed when buyers are large and well defined, the sales effort requires extensive negotiations, and the products are of high unit value and require hands-on expertise in terms of installation or use.

Indirect Channel Channels B, C, and D are indirect channels with one or more intermediaries to reach industrial users. In Channel B an *industrial distributor* performs a variety of marketing channel functions, including selling, stocking, delivering a full product

FIGURE 13–4

Common marketing channels for business goods and services differ by the kind and number of intermediaries.

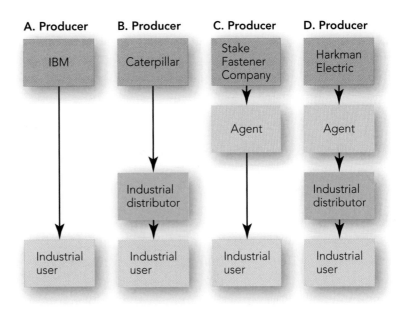

assortment, and financing. In many ways, industrial distributors are like wholesalers in consumer channels. Caterpillar uses industrial distributors to sell its construction and mining equipment in more than 200 countries. In addition to selling, Caterpillar distributors stock 40,000 to 50,000 parts and service equipment using highly trained technicians.

Channel C introduces a second intermediary, an *agent,* who serves primarily as the independent selling arm of producers and represents a producer to industrial users. For example, Stake Fastener Company, a producer of industrial fasteners, has an agent call on industrial users rather than employing its own salesforce.

Channel D is the longest channel and includes both agents and distributors. For instance, Harkman Electric, a producer of electric products, uses agents to call on electrical distributors who sell to industrial users.

Electronic Marketing Channels

These common marketing channels for consumer and business goods and services are not the only routes to the marketplace. Advances in electronic commerce have opened new avenues for reaching buyers and creating customer value.

Interactive electronic technology has made possible *electronic marketing channels,* which employ the Internet to make goods and services available for consumption or use by consumers or business buyers. A unique feature of these channels is that they combine electronic and traditional intermediaries to create time, place, form, and possession utility for buyers.

Figure 13–5 shows the electronic marketing channels for books (Amazon.com), automobiles (Autobytel.com), reservation services (Orbitz.com), and personal computers (Dell.com). Are you surprised that they look a lot like common marketing channels? An important reason for the similarity resides in channel functions detailed in Figure 13–2. Electronic intermediaries can and do perform transactional and facilitating functions effectively and at a relatively lower cost than traditional intermediaries because of efficiencies made possible by information technology. However, electronic intermediaries are incapable of performing elements of the logistical function, particularly for products such as books and automobiles. This function remains with traditional intermediaries or with the producer, as evident with Dell Inc. and its direct channel.

Many services can be distributed through electronic marketing channels, such as car rental reservations marketed by Alamo.com, financial securities by Schwab.com, software by Microsoft.com, and insurance by MetLife.com. However, many other services such as health care and auto repair still involve traditional intermediaries.

FIGURE 13–5

Consumer electronic marketing channels look much like those for consumer goods and services. Read the text to learn why.

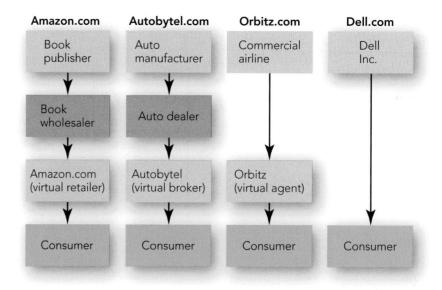

Direct and Multichannel Marketing

Many firms also use direct and multichannel marketing to reach buyers. *Direct marketing channels* allow consumers to buy products by interacting with various advertising media without a face-to-face meeting with a salesperson. Direct marketing channels include mail-order selling, direct-mail sales, catalog sales, telemarketing, interactive media, and televised home shopping (for example, the Home Shopping Network). Some firms sell products almost entirely through direct marketing. These firms include L.L. Bean (apparel), Sharper Image (expensive gifts and novelties), and Newegg.com (consumer electronics). Manufacturers such as Nestlé and Sunkist, in addition to using traditional channels composed of wholesalers and retailers, employ direct marketing through catalogs and telemarketing to reach more buyers.

multichannel marketing
Blending of different communication and delivery channels that are mutually reinforcing in attracting, retaining, and building relationships with consumers

Multichannel marketing is the *blending* of different communication and delivery channels that are *mutually reinforcing* in attracting, retaining, and building relationships with consumers who shop and buy in traditional intermediaries and online. Multichannel marketing seeks to integrate a firm's electronic and delivery channels. At Eddie Bauer, for example, every effort is made to make the apparel shopping and purchase experience for its customers the same in its retail stores, with its catalog, and at its website. According to an Eddie Bauer marketing manager, "We don't distinguish between channels because it's all Eddie Bauer to our customers."[3]

Multichannel marketing also can leverage the value-adding capabilities of different channels. For example, retail stores can leverage their physical presence by allowing customers to pick up their online orders at a nearby store or return or exchange nonstore purchases if they wish. Catalogs can serve as shopping tools for online purchasing, as they do for store purchasing. Websites can help consumers do their homework before visiting a store. Office Depot has leveraged its store, catalog, and website channels with impressive results. The company does more than $4.5 billion in online retail sales annually.

Dual Distribution and Strategic Channel Alliances

dual distribution
Arrangement whereby a firm reaches different buyers by using two or more different types of channels for the same basic product

In some situations producers use **dual distribution**, an arrangement whereby a firm reaches different buyers by using two or more different types of channels for the same basic product. For example, GE sells its large appliances directly to home and apartment builders but uses retail stores, including Lowe's home centers, to sell to consumers. In some instances, firms pair multiple channels with a multibrand strategy. This is done to minimize cannibalization of the firm's family brand and differentiate the channels. For example, Hallmark sells its Hallmark greeting cards primarily through Hallmark stores and select department stores, and its Ambassador brand of cards through discount and drugstore chains.

A recent innovation in marketing channels is the use of *strategic channel alliances,* whereby one firm's marketing channel is used to sell another firm's products. An alliance between Kraft Foods and Starbucks is a case in point. Kraft distributes Starbucks coffee in U.S. supermarkets and internationally. Strategic alliances are popular in global marketing, where the creation of marketing channel relationships is expensive and time consuming. For example, General Motors distributes the Swedish Saab through its Saturn dealers in Canada. General Mills and Nestlé have an extensive alliance that spans more than 130 international markets from Mexico to China. Read the Marketing Matters box on the next page so you won't be surprised when you are served Nestlé (not General Mills) Cheerios when traveling outside North America.[4]

Vertical Marketing Systems

The traditional marketing channels described so far represent a loosely knit network of independent producers and intermediaries brought together to distribute goods and services. However, other channel arrangements exist for the purpose of improving efficiency in performing channel functions and achieving greater marketing

Can you say Nestlé Cheerios *miel amandes*? Millions of French start their day with this European equivalent of General Mills' Honey Nut Cheerios, made possible by Cereal Partners Worldwide (CPW). CPW is a strategic alliance designed from the start to be a global business. It joined the cereal manufacturing and marketing capability of U.S.-based General Mills with the worldwide distribution clout of Swiss-based Nestlé.

From its headquarters in Switzerland, CPW first launched General Mills cereals under the Nestlé label in France, the United Kingdom, Spain, and Portugal in 1991. Today, CPW competes in more than 130 international markets.

The General Mills–Nestlé strategic channel alliance also increased the ready-to-eat cereal worldwide market share of these companies, which are already rated as the two best-managed firms in the world. CPW currently accounts for more than 8 percent of global breakfast cereal sales with about $1.4 billion in annual revenue.

vertical marketing systems
Professionally managed and centrally coordinated marketing channels designed to achieve channel economies and maximum marketing impact

effectiveness. These arrangements are called vertical marketing systems and channel partnerships. **Vertical marketing systems** are professionally managed and centrally coordinated marketing channels designed to achieve channel economies and maximum marketing impact.[5] Figure 13–6 depicts the major types of vertical marketing systems: corporate, contractual, and administered.

Corporate Systems   The combination of successive stages of production and distribution under a single ownership is a *corporate vertical marketing system*. For example, a producer might own the intermediary at the next level down in the channel. This practice, called *forward integration*, is exemplified by Polo/Ralph Lauren, which manufactures clothing and also owns apparel shops. Other examples of forward integration include Goodyear, Apple, and Sherwin-Williams. Alternatively, a retailer might own a manufacturing operation, a practice called *backward integration*. For example, Kroger supermarkets operate 42 manufacturing facilities that produce everything from aspirin to cottage cheese, for sale under the Kroger label. Tiffany & Co., the exclusive jewelry retailer, manufactures about half of the fine jewelry items for sale through its 150 stores and boutiques worldwide.

Companies seeking to reduce distribution costs and gain greater control over supply sources or resale of their products pursue forward and backward integration. However, both types of integration increase a company's capital investment and fixed costs. For this reason, many companies favor contractual vertical marketing systems to achieve channel efficiencies and marketing effectiveness.

Contractual Systems   Under a *contractual vertical marketing system*, independent production and distribution firms integrate their efforts on a contractual basis to obtain greater functional economies and marketing impact than they could achieve alone. Contractual systems are the most popular among the three types of vertical marketing systems.

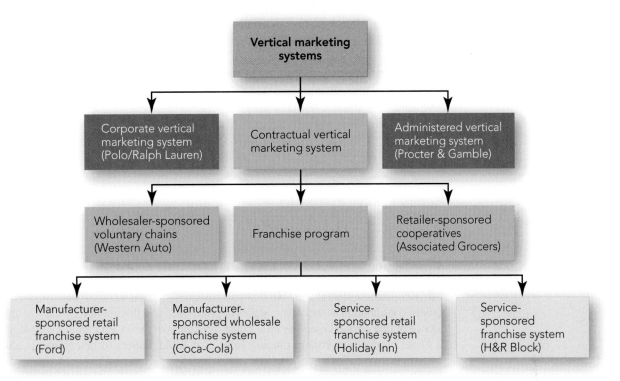

FIGURE 13–6
There are three major types of vertical marketing systems—corporate, contractual, and administered. Contractual systems are the most popular.

Three variations of contractual systems exist. *Wholesaler-sponsored voluntary chains* involve a wholesaler that develops a contractual relationship with small, independent retailers to standardize and coordinate buying practices, merchandising programs, and inventory management efforts. With the organization of a large number of independent retailers, economies of scale and volume discounts can be achieved to compete with chain stores. IGA and Ben Franklin variety and craft stores represent wholesaler-sponsored voluntary chains. *Retailer-sponsored cooperatives* exist when small, independent retailers form an organization that operates a wholesale facility cooperatively. Member retailers then concentrate their buying power through the wholesaler and plan collaborative promotional and pricing activities. Examples of retailer-sponsored cooperatives include Associated Grocers and Ace Hardware.

Tiffany & Co. and H&R Block represent two different types of vertical marketing systems. Read the text to find out how they differ.

The most visible variation of contractual systems is franchising. *Franchising* is a contractual arrangement between a parent company (a franchisor) and an individual or firm (a franchisee) that allows the franchisee to operate a certain type of business under an established name and according to specific rules.

Four types of franchise arrangements are most popular. *Manufacturer-sponsored retail franchise systems* are prominent in the automobile industry, where a manufacturer such as Ford licenses dealers to sell its cars subject to various sales and service conditions. *Manufacturer-sponsored wholesale systems* exist in the soft-drink industry, where Pepsi-Cola licenses wholesalers (bottlers) that purchase concentrate from Pepsi-Cola and then carbonate, bottle, promote, and distribute its products to supermarkets and restaurants. *Service-sponsored retail franchise systems* are provided by firms that have designed a unique approach for performing a service and wish to profit by selling the franchise to others. Holiday Inn, Avis, and McDonald's represent this franchising approach. *Service-sponsored franchise systems* exist when franchisors license individuals or firms to dispense a service under a trade name and specific guidelines. Examples include Snelling and Snelling Inc. employment services and H&R Block tax services.

Administered Systems   In comparison, *administered vertical marketing systems* achieve coordination at successive stages of production and distribution by the size and influence of one channel member rather than through ownership. Procter & Gamble, given its broad product assortment ranging from disposable diapers to detergents, is able to obtain cooperation from supermarkets in displaying, promoting, and pricing its products. Wal-Mart can obtain cooperation from manufacturers in terms of product specifications, price levels, and promotional support, given its position as the world's largest retailer.

---

learning review

3. What is the difference between a direct and an indirect channel?

4. What is the principal distinction between a corporate vertical marketing system and an administered vertical marketing system?

MARKETING CHANNEL CHOICE AND MANAGEMENT

Marketing channels not only link a producer to its buyers but also provide the means through which a firm implements various elements of its marketing strategy. Therefore, choosing a marketing channel is a critical decision.

Factors Affecting Channel Choice and Management

Marketing executives consider three questions when choosing a marketing channel and intermediaries:

1. Which channel and intermediaries will provide the best coverage of the target market?
2. Which channel and intermediaries will best satisfy the buying requirements of the target market?
3. Which channel and intermediaries will be the most profitable?

Target Market Coverage   Achieving the best coverage of the target market requires attention to the density—that is, the number of stores in a geographical area—and type of intermediaries to be used at the retail level of distribution.[6] Three degrees of distribution density exist: intensive, exclusive, and selective.

Intensive distribution means that a firm tries to place its products and services in as many outlets as possible. Intensive distribution is usually chosen for convenience products

intensive distribution

A firm tries to place its products or services in as many outlets as possible

Read the text to learn which buying requirements are satisfied by Jiffy Lube and PETCO.

exclusive distribution
Only one retail outlet in a specific geographical area carries the firm's products

selective distribution
A firm selects a few retail outlets in a specific geographical area to carry its products

or services such as candy, fast food, newspapers, and soft drinks. For example, Coca-Cola's retail distribution objective is to place its products "within an arm's reach of desire."

Exclusive distribution is the extreme opposite of intensive distribution because only one retail outlet in a specified geographical area carries the firm's products. Exclusive distribution is typically chosen for specialty products or services such as automobiles, some women's fragrances, men's and women's apparel and accessories, and yachts. Gucci, one of the world's leading luxury goods companies, uses exclusive distribution in the marketing of its Yves Saint Laurent, Sergio Rossi, Boucheron, Opium, and Gucci brands. Sometimes retailers sign exclusive distribution agreements with manufacturers and suppliers. For instance, Radio Shack sells only Acer, Compaq, and Hewlett-Packard desktop computers in its 6,000 stores.

Selective distribution lies between these two extremes and means that a firm selects a few retail outlets in a specific geographical area to carry its products. Selective distribution weds some of the market coverage benefits of intensive distribution to the control over resale evident with exclusive distribution. For this reason, selective distribution is the most common form of distribution intensity. It is usually associated with shopping goods or services such as Rolex watches, Ben Hogan golf clubs, and Henredon furniture.

Satisfying Buyer Requirements A second consideration in channel choice is gaining access to channels and intermediaries that satisfy at least some of the interests buyers might want fulfilled when they purchase a firm's products or services. These requirements fall into four broad categories: (1) information, (2) convenience, (3) variety, and (4) pre- or postsale services. Each relates to customer experience.

Information is an important requirement when buyers have limited knowledge or desire specific data about a product or service. Properly chosen intermediaries communicate with buyers through in-store displays, demonstrations, and personal selling. Consumer electronics manufacturers such as Sony and Apple have opened their own retail outlets staffed with highly trained personnel, to inform buyers how their products can better satisfy each customer's needs.

Convenience has multiple meanings for buyers, such as proximity or driving time to a retail outlet. For example, 7-Eleven stores, with more than 34,000 outlets worldwide, many of which are open 24 hours a day, satisfy this interest for buyers. Candy and snack-food firms benefit by gaining display space in these stores. For other consumers, convenience means a minimum of time and hassle. Jiffy Lube, which promises to change engine oil and filters quickly, appeals to this aspect of convenience.

Variety reflects buyers' interest in having numerous competing and complementary items from which to choose. Variety is evident in the breadth and depth of products and brands carried by intermediaries, which enhances their attraction to buyers. Thus, manufacturers of pet food and supplies seek distribution through pet superstores such as PETCO and PetSmart, which offer a wide array of pet products.

Pre- or postsale services provided by intermediaries are an important buying requirement for products such as large household appliances that require delivery, installation, and credit. Therefore, Whirlpool seeks dealers that provide such services.

Steven Jobs's decision to distribute Apple products through company-owned stores was motivated by the failure of retailers to deliver on these four consumer interests for Apple. The success of Apple stores speaks for itself.

Profitability   The third consideration in choosing a channel is profitability, which is determined by the margins earned (revenue minus cost) for each channel member and for the channel as a whole. Channel cost is the critical dimension of profitability. These costs include distribution, advertising, and selling expenses associated with different types of marketing channels. The extent to which channel members share these costs determines the margins received by each member and by the channel as a whole.

Companies routinely monitor the performance of their marketing channels. Read the accompanying Using Marketing Dashboards box to see how Charlesburg Furniture views the sales and profit performance of its marketing channels.

Managing Channel Relationships: Conflict and Cooperation

Unfortunately, because channels consist of independent individuals and firms, there is always potential for disagreements concerning who performs which channel functions, how profits are allocated, which products and services will be provided by whom, and who makes critical channel-related decisions. These channel conflicts necessitate measures for dealing with them.

channel conflict

Arises when one channel member believes another channel member is engaged in behavior that prevents it from achieving its goals

Sources of Conflict in Marketing Channels   **Channel conflict** arises when one channel member believes another channel member is engaged in behavior that prevents it from achieving its goals. Two types of conflict occur in marketing channels: vertical conflict and horizontal conflict.

Vertical conflict occurs between different levels in a marketing channel—for example, between a manufacturer and a wholesaler or retailer or between a wholesaler and a retailer. Three sources of vertical conflict are most common.[7] First, conflict arises when a channel member bypasses another member and sells or buys products direct, a practice called **disintermediation**. This conflict emerged when Jenn-Air, a producer of kitchen appliances, decided to terminate its distributors and sell directly to retailers. Second, disagreements over how profit margins are distributed among channel members produce conflict. This happened when the world's biggest music company, Universal Music Group, adopted a pricing policy for CDs that squeezed the profit margins for specialty music retailers. A third conflict situation arises when manufacturers believe wholesalers or retailers are not giving their products adequate attention. For example, Nike stopped shipping popular sneakers such as Nike Shox NZ to Foot Locker in retaliation for the retailer's decision to give more shelf space to shoes costing under $120.

disintermediation

Channel conflict that arises when a channel member bypasses another member and sells or buys products direct

Horizontal conflict occurs between intermediaries at the same level in a marketing channel, such as between two or more retailers (Target and Kmart) or two or more wholesalers that handle the same manufacturer's brands. Two sources of horizontal conflict are common.[8] First, horizontal conflict arises when a manufacturer increases its distribution coverage in a geographical area. For example, a franchised Saturn dealer in Chicago might complain to General Motors that another franchised Saturn dealer has located too close to its dealership. Second, dual distribution causes conflict when different types of retailers carry the same brands. For instance, Goodyear tire dealers

Using Marketing Dashboards

Channel Sales and Profit at Charlesburg Furniture

Charlesburg Furniture is one of 1,000 wood furniture manufacturers in the United States. The company sells its furniture through furniture store chains, independent furniture stores, and department store chains in the southern United States. The company has traditionally allocated its marketing funds for cooperative advertising, in-store displays, and retail sales support on the basis of dollar sales by channel.

Your Challenge As the Vice President of Sales & Marketing at Charlesburg Furniture, you have been asked to review the company's sales and profit in its three channels and recommend a course of action. The question: Should Charlesburg Furniture continue to allocate its marketing funds on the basis of channel dollar sales or profit?

Your Findings Charlesburg Furniture tracks the sales and profit from each channel (and individual store customer) and sales trends on its marketing dashboard. This information is displayed in the marketing dashboard below.

Several findings stand out. Furniture store chains and independent furniture stores account for 85.2 percent of

Charlesburg Furniture sales and 93 percent of company profit. These two channels also evidence growth as measured by annual percentage change in sales. By comparison, department store chains annual percentage sales growth has declined and recorded negative growth in 2007. This channel accounts for 14.8 percent of company sales and 7 percent of company profit.

Your Action Charlesburg Furniture should consider abandoning the practice of allocating marketing funds solely on the basis of channel sales volume. The importance of independent furniture stores to Charlesburg's profitability warrants further spending, particularly given this channel's favorable sales trend. Doubling the percentage allocation for marketing funds for this channel may be too extreme, however. Rather, an objective-task promotional budgeting method should be adopted (see Chapter 16). Charlesburg Furniture might also consider the longer term role of department store chains as a marketing channel.

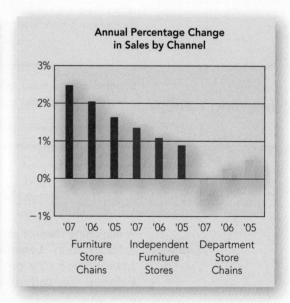

became irate when Goodyear Tire Company decided to sell its brands through Sears, Wal-Mart, and Sam's Clubs. Many switched to competing tire makers.

Securing Cooperation in Marketing Channels Conflict can have destructive effects on the workings of a marketing channel so it is necessary to secure cooperation among channel members. One means is through a *channel captain,* a channel member that coordinates, directs, and supports other channel members. Channel captains can be producers, wholesalers, or retailers. P&G assumes this role because it has a strong consumer

Channel conflict is sometimes visible to consumers. Read the text to learn what antagonized independent Goodyear tire dealers.

following in brands such as Crest, Tide, and Pampers. Therefore, it can set policies or terms that supermarkets will follow. McKesson, a pharmaceutical drug wholesaler, is a channel captain because it coordinates and supports the product flow from numerous small drug manufacturers to drugstores and hospitals nationwide. Wal-Mart is a retail channel captain because of its strong consumer image, number of outlets, and purchasing volume.

A firm becomes a channel captain because it is the channel member with the ability to influence the behavior of other members.[9] Influence can take four forms. First, economic influence arises from the ability of a firm to reward other members given its strong financial position or customer franchise. Microsoft Corporation and Wal-Mart have such influence. Expertise is a second source of influence. For example, American Hospital Supply helps its customers (hospitals) manage inventory and streamline order processing for hundreds of medical supplies. Third, identification with a particular channel member can create influence for that channel member. For instance, retailers may compete to carry the Ralph Lauren line, or clothing manufacturers may compete to be carried by Neiman Marcus, Nordstrom, or Bloomingdale's. In both instances, the desire to be identified with a channel member gives that firm influence over others. Finally, influence can arise from the legitimate right of one channel member to direct the behavior of other members. This situation would occur under contractual vertical marketing systems where a franchisor can legitimately direct how a franchisee behaves.

---

learning review

5. What are the three questions marketing executives consider when choosing a marketing channel and intermediaries?

6. What are the three degrees of distribution density?

LOGISTICS AND SUPPLY CHAIN MANAGEMENT

LO4

logistics

Activities that focus on getting the right amount of the right products to the right place at the right time at the lowest possible cost

A marketing channel relies on logistics to make products available to consumers and industrial users. **Logistics** involves those activities that focus on getting the right amount of the right products to the right place at the right time at the lowest possible cost. The performance of these activities is *logistics management*, the practice of organizing the cost-effective flow of raw materials, in-process inventory, finished goods, and related information from point of origin to point of consumption to satisfy *customer requirements.*

Three elements of this definition deserve emphasis. First, logistics deals with decisions needed to move a product from the source of raw materials to consumption—that is, the *flow* of the product. Second, those decisions have to be *cost effective.* While it is important to drive down logistics costs, there is a limit: a firm needs to drive down logistics costs as long as it can deliver expected *customer service,* which means satisfying customer requirements. The role of management is to see that customer needs are satisfied in the most cost-effective manner. When properly done, the results can be spectacular. Consider Procter & Gamble. Beginning in the 1990s, the company set out to meet consumer needs more effectively by collaborating and partnering with its suppliers and retailers to ensure that the right products reached store shelves at the right time and at a lower cost. The effort was judged a success when, during an 18-month period, P&G's retail customers posted a $65 million savings in logistics costs and customer service increased.[10]

The Procter & Gamble experience is not an isolated incident. Companies now recognize that getting the right items needed for consumption or production to the right place at the right time in the right condition at the right cost is often beyond their individual capabilities and control. Instead, collaboration, coordination, and information sharing among manufacturers, suppliers, and distributors are necessary to create a seamless flow of goods and services to customers. This perspective is represented in the concept of a supply chain and the practice of supply chain management.

Supply Chains versus Marketing Channels

A **supply chain** is a sequence of firms that perform activities required to create and deliver a good or service to consumers or industrial users. It differs from a marketing channel in terms of the firms involved. A supply chain includes suppliers that provide raw material inputs to a manufacturer as well as the wholesalers and retailers that deliver finished goods to consumers. The management process is also different. *Supply chain management* is the integration and organization of information and logistics activities *across firms* in a supply chain for the purpose of creating and delivering goods and services that provide value to consumers. The relation among marketing channels, logistics management, and supply chain management is shown in Figure 13–7. An important feature of supply chain management is its application of sophisticated information technology that allows companies to share and operate systems for order processing, transportation scheduling, and inventory and facility management.

Sourcing, Assembling, and Delivering a New Car: The Automotive Supply Chain

All companies are members of one or more supply chains. A supply chain is essentially a series of linked suppliers and customers in which every customer is, in turn, a supplier to another customer until a finished product reaches the ultimate consumer. Even a simplified supply chain diagram for carmakers shown in Figure 13–8 on the next page illustrates how complex a supply chain can be.[11] A carmaker's supplier network includes thousands of firms that provide the 5,000 or so parts in a typical automobile. They provide items ranging from raw materials such as steel and rubber to components, including transmissions, tires, brakes, and seats, to complex subassemblies and assemblies such as in chassis

FIGURE 13–7
Relating logistics management and supply chain management to supplier networks and marketing channels

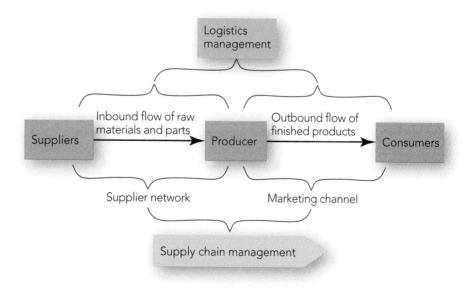

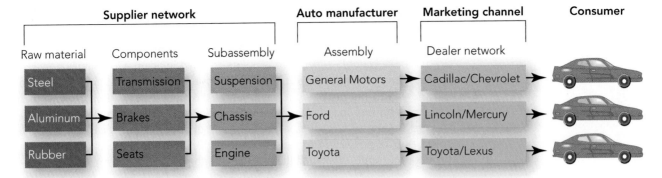

FIGURE 13–8

The automotive supply chain stretches from raw materials to the final consumer.

and suspension systems that make for a smooth, stable ride. Coordinating and scheduling material and component flows for their assembly into actual automobiles by carmakers is heavily dependent on logistical activities, including transportation, order processing, inventory control, materials handling, and information technology. A central link is the carmaker supply chain manager, who is responsible for translating customer requirements into actual orders and arranging for delivery dates and financial arrangements for automobile dealers.

Logistical aspects of the automobile marketing channel are also an important part of the supply chain. Major responsibilities include transportation (which involves the selection and oversight of external carriers—trucking, airline, railroad, and shipping companies—for cars and parts to dealers), the operation of distribution centers, the management of finished goods inventories, and order processing for sales. Supply chain managers also play an important role in the marketing channel. They work with extensive car dealer networks to ensure that the right mix of automobiles is delivered to each location. In addition, they make sure that spare and service parts are available so that dealers can meet the car maintenance and repair needs of consumers. All of this is done with the help of information technology that links the entire automotive supply chain. What does all of this cost? It is estimated that logistics costs represent 25 to 30 percent of the retail price of a typical new car.

Supply Chain Management and Marketing Strategy

The automotive supply chain illustration shows how information and logistics activities are integrated and organized across firms to create and deliver a car for you. What's missing from this illustration is the linkage between a specific company's supply chain and its marketing strategy. Just as companies have different marketing strategies, they also design and manage supply chains differently. The goals to be achieved by a firm's marketing strategy determine whether its supply chain needs to be more responsive or efficient in meeting customer requirements.

Aligning a Supply Chain with Marketing Strategy   There are a variety of supply chain configurations, each of which is designated to perform different tasks well. Marketers today recognize that the choice of a supply chain follows from a clearly defined marketing strategy and involves three steps:[12]

1. *Understand the customer.* To understand the customer, a company must identify the needs of the customer segment being served. These needs, such as a desire for a low price or convenience of purchase, help a company define the relative importance of efficiency and responsiveness in meeting customer requirements.
2. *Understand the supply chain.* Second, a company must understand what a supply chain is designed to do well. Supply chains range from those that emphasize being responsive to customer requirements and demand to those that emphasize efficiency with a goal of supplying products at the lowest possible delivered cost.
3. *Harmonize the supply chain with the marketing strategy.* Finally, a company needs to ensure that what the supply chain is capable of doing well is consistent with the targeted customer's needs and its marketing strategy. If a mismatch

IBM's Integrated Supply Chain—Delivering a Total Solution for Its Customers

IBM is one of the world's great business success stories because of its ability to reinvent itself to satisfy shifting customer needs in a dynamic global marketplace. The company's transformation of its supply chain is a case in point.

Beginning in 2001, IBM set about to build a single integrated supply chain that would handle raw material procurement, manufacturing, logistics, customer support, order entry, and customer fulfillment across all of IBM—something that had never been done before. Why would IBM undertake this task? According to IBM's CEO, Samuel J. Palmisano, "You cannot hope to thrive in the IT industry if you are a high-cost, slow-moving company. Supply chain is one of the new competitive battlegrounds. We are committed to being the most efficient and productive player in our industry."

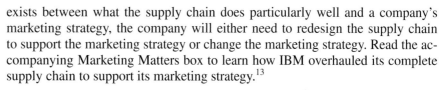

The task wasn't easy. With factories in 10 countries, IBM buys 2 billion parts a year from 33,000 suppliers, offers 78,000 products available in 3 million possible variations, moves over 2 billion pounds of machines and parts annually, processes 1.7 million customer orders annually in North America alone, and operates in 150 countries. Yet with surprising efficiency, IBM overhauled its supply chain from raw material sourcing to postsales support.

Today, IBM is uniquely poised to configure and deliver a tailored mix of hardware, software, and service to provide a total solution for its customers. Not surprisingly, IBM's integrated supply chain is now heralded as one of the best in the world!

---

exists between what the supply chain does particularly well and a company's marketing strategy, the company will either need to redesign the supply chain to support the marketing strategy or change the marketing strategy. Read the accompanying Marketing Matters box to learn how IBM overhauled its complete supply chain to support its marketing strategy.[13]

How are these steps applied and how are efficiency and responsive considerations built into a supply chain? Let's look at how two well-known companies—Dell and Wal-Mart—have harmonized their supply chain and marketing strategy.[14]

Dell: A Responsive Supply Chain   The Dell marketing strategy primarily targets customers who desire having the most up-to-date computer systems customized to their needs. These customers are also willing to (1) wait to have their customized computer system delivered in a few days, rather than picking out a model at a retail store, and (2) pay a reasonable, though not the lowest, price in the marketplace. Given Dell's customer segment, the company has the option of adopting an efficient or responsive supply chain.

An efficient supply chain may use inexpensive, but slower, modes of transportation, emphasize economies of scale in its production process by reducing the variety of system configurations offered, and limit its assembly and inventory storage facilities to a single location, say Austin, Texas, where the company is headquartered. If Dell opted only for efficiency in its supply chain, it would be difficult to satisfy its target customer's desire for rapid delivery and a wide variety of customizable products. Dell instead opted for a responsive supply chain. It relies on more expensive express transportation for receipt of components from suppliers and delivery of finished products to customers. The company achieves product variety and manufacturing efficiency by designing common platforms across several products and using common components. Dell operates manufacturing facilities in Texas, North Carolina, Tennessee, Brazil, Ireland, Malaysia, and China to ensure rapid delivery. Also, Dell has invested heavily in information technology to link itself with suppliers and customers.

Wal-Mart: An Efficient Supply Chain Now let's consider Wal-Mart. Wal-Mart's marketing strategy is to be a reliable, lower-price retailer for a wide variety of mass consumption consumer goods. This strategy favors an efficient supply chain designed to deliver products to consumers at the lowest possible cost. Efficiency is achieved in a variety of ways. For instance, Wal-Mart keeps relatively low inventory levels, and most is stocked in stores available for sale, not in warehouses gathering dust. The low inventory arises from Wal-Mart's innovative use of *cross-docking*—a practice that involves unloading products from suppliers, sorting products for individual stores, and quickly reloading products onto its trucks for a particular store. No warehousing or storing of products occurs, except for a few hours or, at most, a day. Cross-docking allows Wal-Mart to operate only a small number of distribution centers to service its vast network of Wal-Mart stores, Supercenters, Neighborhood Markets, and Sam's Clubs, which contributes to efficiency. On the other hand, the company runs its own fleet of trucks to service its stores. This does increase cost and investment, but the benefits in terms of responsiveness justify the cost in Wal-Mart's case.

Wal-Mart has invested much more than its competitors in information technology to operate its supply chain. The company feeds information about customer requirements and demand from its stores back to its suppliers, which manufacture only what is being demanded. This large investment has improved the efficiency of Wal-Mart's supply chain and made it responsive to customer needs.

Three lessons can be learned from these two examples. First, there is no one best supply chain for every company. Second, the best supply chain is the one that is consistent with the needs of the customer segment being served and complements a company's marketing strategy. And finally, supply chain managers are often called upon to make trade-offs between efficiency and responsiveness on various elements of a company's supply chain.

TWO CONCEPTS OF LOGISTICS MANAGEMENT IN A SUPPLY CHAIN

The objective of logistics management in a supply chain is to minimize total logistics costs while delivering the appropriate level of customer service.

Total Logistics Cost Concept

total logistics cost
Expenses associated with transportation, materials handling and warehousing, inventory, stockouts, order processing, and return goods handling

For our purposes **total logistics cost** includes expenses associated with transportation, materials handling and warehousing, inventory, stockouts (being out of inventory), order processing, and return goods handling. Note that many of these costs are interrelated so that changes in one will impact the others. For example, as the firm attempts to minimize its transportation costs by shipping in larger quantities, it will also experience an increase in inventory levels. Larger inventory levels will not only increase inventory costs but should also reduce stockouts. It is important, therefore, to study the impact on all of the logistics decision areas when considering a change.

FIGURE 13–9

Supply chain managers balance total logistics cost factors against customer service factors.

Total logistics cost factors — Inventory costs, Transportation costs, Materials handling and warehousing costs, Order processing costs, Stockout costs

Customer service factors — Communication, Dependability, Time, Convenience

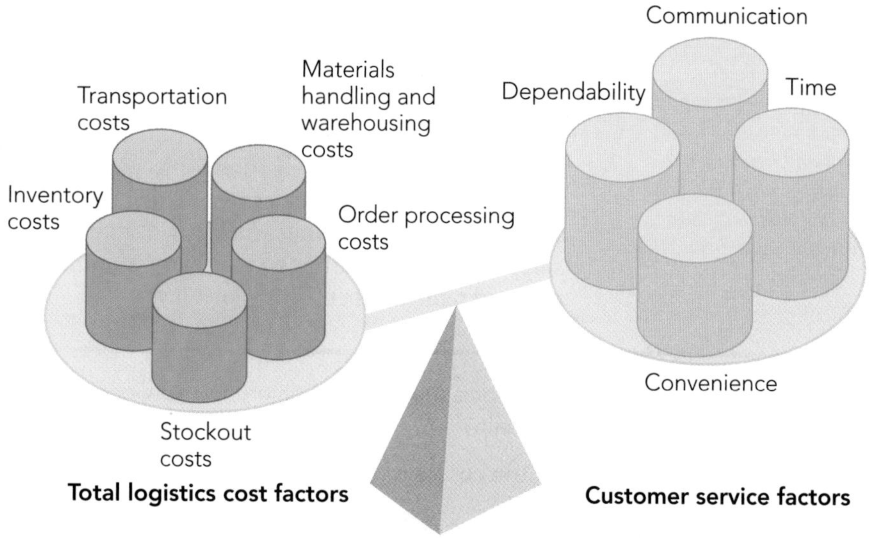

Customer Service Concept

customer service

Ability of logistics management to satisfy users in terms of time, dependability, communication, and convenience

Because a supply chain is a *flow,* the end of it—or *output*—is the service delivered to customers. Within the context of a supply chain, **customer service** is the ability of logistics management to satisfy users in terms of time, dependability, communication, and convenience. As suggested by Figure 13–9, a supply chain manager's key task is to balance these four customer service factors against total logistics cost factors.[15]

Time   In a supply chain setting, time refers to *order cycle* or *replenishment* time for an item, which means the time between the ordering of an item and when it is received and ready for use or sale. The various elements that make up the typical order cycle include recognition of the need to order, order transmittal, order processing, documentation, and transportation. A current emphasis in supply chain management is to reduce order cycle time so that the inventory levels of customers may be minimized. Another emphasis is to make the process of reordering and receiving products as simple as possible, often through inventory systems called *quick response* and *efficient consumer response* delivery systems. For example, at Saks Fifth Avenue, point-of-sale scanner technology records each day's sales. When stock falls below a minimum level, a replenishment order is automatically produced. Vendors such as Donna Karan (DKNY) receive the order, which is processed and delivered within 48 hours.[16]

Dependability   Dependability is the consistency of replenishment. This is important to all firms in a supply chain—and to consumers. How often do you return to a store if it fails to have in stock the item you want to purchase? Dependability can be broken into three elements: consistent lead time, safe delivery, and complete delivery. Consistent service allows planning (such as appropriate inventory levels), whereas inconsistencies create surprises. Intermediaries may be willing to accept longer lead times if they know about them in advance and can thus make plans.

Communication   Communication is a two-way link between buyer and seller that helps in monitoring service and anticipating future needs. Status reports on orders are a typical example of communication between buyer and seller.

Convenience   The concept of convenience for a supply chain manager means that there should be a minimum of effort on the part of the buyer in doing business with the seller. Is it easy for the customer to order? Are the products available from many outlets? Will the seller arrange all necessary details, such as transportation? This customer service factor has promoted the use of **vendor-managed inventory** (VMI), whereby the *supplier* determines the product amount and assortment a customer (such as a retailer) needs and automatically delivers the appropriate items.

Campbell Soup's system illustrates how VMI works.[17] Every morning, retailers electronically inform the company of their demand for all Campbell products and the inventory levels in their distribution centers. Campbell uses that information to forecast future demand and determine which products need replenishment based on upper and lower inventory limits established with each retailer. Trucks leave the Campbell shipping plant that afternoon and arrive at the retailer's distribution centers with the required replenishments the same day.

learning review

7. What is the principal difference between a marketing channel and a supply chain?

8. The choice of a supply chain involves what three steps?

9. A manager's key task is to balance which four customer service factors against which five logistics cost factors?

LEARNING OBJECTIVES REVIEW

LO1 *Explain what is meant by a marketing channel of distribution and why intermediaries are needed.*

A marketing channel of distribution, or simply a marketing channel, consists of individuals and firms involved in the process of making a product or service available for use or consumption by consumers or industrial users. Intermediaries make possible the flow of products from producers to buyers by performing three basic functions. The transactional function involves buying, selling, and risk taking because intermediaries stock merchandise in anticipation of sales. The logistical function involves the gathering, storing, and dispensing of products. The facilitating function assists producers in making goods and services more attractive to buyers. The performance of these functions by intermediaries creates time, place, form, and possession utility for consumers.

LO2 *Distinguish among traditional marketing channels, electronic marketing channels, and different types of vertical marketing systems.*

Traditional marketing channels describe the route taken by products and services from producers to buyers. This route can range from a direct channel with no intermediaries, because a producer and ultimate consumers deal directly with each other, to indirect channels where intermediaries (agents, wholesalers, distributors, or retailers) are inserted between a producer and consumer and perform numerous channel functions. Electronic marketing channels employ the Internet to make goods and services available for consumption or use by consumer or business buyers. Vertical marketing systems are professionally managed and centrally coordinated marketing channels designed to achieve channel economies and maximum marketing impact. There are three major types of vertical marketing systems (VMSs). A corporate VMS combines successive stages of production and distribution under a single ownership. A contractual VMS exists when independent production and distribution firms integrate their efforts on a contractual basis to obtain greater functional economies and

marketing impact than they could achieve alone. An administered VMS achieves coordination at successive stages of production and distribution by the size and influence of one channel member rather than through ownership.

LO3 *Describe factors that marketing executives consider when selecting and managing a marketing channel.*

Marketing executives consider three questions when selecting and managing a marketing channel and intermediaries. First, which channel and intermediaries will provide the best coverage of the target market? Marketers typically choose one of three levels of market coverage: intensive, selective, or exclusive distribution. Second, which channel and intermediaries will best satisfy the buying requirements of the target market? These buying requirements fall into four categories: information, convenience, variety, and attendant services. Finally, which channel and intermediaries will be the most profitable? Here marketers look at the margins earned (revenues minus cost) for each channel member and for the channel as a whole.

LO4 *Explain what supply chain and logistics management are and how they relate to marketing strategy.*

A supply chain is a sequence of firms that perform activities required to create and deliver a good or service to consumers or industrial users. Supply chain management is the integration and organization of information and logistics across firms for the purpose of creating value for consumers. Logistics involves those activities that focus on getting the right amount of the right products to the right place at the right time at the lowest possible cost. Logistics management includes the coordination of the flows of both inbound and outbound goods, an emphasis on making these flows cost effective, and customer service. A company's supply chain follows from a clearly defined marketing strategy. The alignment of a company's supply chain with its marketing strategy involves three steps. First, a supply chain must reflect the needs of the customer segment being served. Second, a company must understand what a supply chain is designed to do well. Supply chains range from those that emphasize being responsive to customer requirements and demands to those that emphasize efficiency with the goal of supplying products at the lowest possible delivered cost. Finally, a supply chain must be consistent with the targeted customer's needs and the company's marketing strategy. The Dell and Wal-Mart examples in the chapter illustrate how this alignment is achieved by two market leaders.

FOCUSING ON KEY TERMS

channel conflict p. 300
customer service p. 307
disintermediation p. 300
dual distribution p. 295
exclusive distribution p. 299

intensive distribution p. 298
logistics p. 302
marketing channel p. 290
multichannel marketing p. 295
selective distribution p. 299

supply chain p. 303
total logistics cost p. 306
vendor-managed inventory p. 308
vertical marketing systems p. 296

APPLYING MARKETING KNOWLEDGE

1 A distributor for Celanese Chemical Company stores large quantities of chemicals, blends these chemicals to satisfy requests of customers, and delivers the blends to a customer's warehouse within 24 hours of receiving an order. What utilities does this distributor provide?

2 Suppose the president of a carpet manufacturing firm has asked you to look into the possibility of bypassing the firm's wholesalers (who sell to carpet, department, and furniture stores) and selling direct to these stores. What caution would you voice on this matter, and what type of information would you gather before making this decision?

3 What type of channel conflict is likely to be caused by dual distribution, and what type of conflict can be reduced by direct distribution? Why?

4 How does the channel captain idea differ among corporate, administered, and contractual vertical marketing systems with particular reference to the use of the different forms of influence available to firms?

5 List the customer service factors that would be vital to buyers in the following types of companies: (*a*) manufacturing, (*b*) retailing, (*c*) hospitals, and (*d*) construction.

building your marketing plan

Does your marketing plan involve selecting channels and intermediaries? If the answer is no, read no further and do not include this element in your plan. If the answer is yes,

1 Identify which channel and intermediaries will provide the best coverage of the target market for your product or service.

2 Specify which channel and intermediaries will best satisfy the important buying requirements of the target market.

3 Determine which channel and intermediaries will be the most profitable.

4 Select your channel(s) and intermediary(ies).

video case 13 Golden Valley Microwave Foods: The Surprising Channel

"We developed the technology that launched the microwave popcorn business and helped make ACT II the number one brand in the world," says Jack McKeon, president of Golden Valley Microwave Foods, a division of ConAgra Foods Inc. "But we were also lucky along the way, as we backed into what has become one of the biggest distribution channels in the industry today, one that no one ever saw coming."

Founded in 1978, today Golden Valley is the global leader in producing and marketing microwave popcorn. Its ACT II brand is tops in the industry. But it hasn't always been easy.

THE LAUNCH: THE IDEA AND THE TECHNOLOGY

In the mid-1980s only about 15 percent of U.S. households had microwave ovens, so launching a microwave foods business was risky. Golden Valley's initial marketing research turned up two key points of difference or benefits that people wanted in their microwave popcorn: (1) fewer unpopped kernels and (2) good popping results in all types of microwave ovens, even low-powered ovens—the kind that many households with microwaves had at the time. Golden Valley's research and development (R&D) staff successfully addressed these wants by developing a microwave popcorn bag utilizing a thin strip of material laminated between layers of paper, which focused the microwave energy to produce high-quality popped corn, regardless of an oven's power. This breakthrough significantly increased the size of the microwave popcorn market (and is still used in all microwave popcorn bags today). Using its revolutionary package, Golden Valley introduced ACT II in 1984.

THE LUCKY DAY: BOTH CAPITAL AND MASS MERCHANDISERS

From its founding in 1978 until a public offering of its stock in September 1986, Golden Valley was privately owned and, like most start-ups, was severely undercapitalized. Due to the cost of developing and introducing ACT II, Golden Valley needed a partner to help develop the business. Its solution was to enter into a licensing agreement to share its technology for packaging microwave popcorn with one of the largest food manufacturers in the industry. The licensing partner would sell the popcorn under its own brand name in grocery stores and supermarkets. In turn, Golden Valley agreed it would not distribute its ACT II brand in U.S. grocery stores or supermarkets for 10 years. This meant that Golden Valley had to find other channels of distribution in which to sell its microwave popcorn.

For the next 10 years the company developed many new channels. ACT II products were sold through vending machines, video stores (e.g., Blockbuster), institutions (e.g., movie theaters, colleges, military bases), drugstores (e.g., Walgreen's, Rite-Aid, Eckerd Drugs), club stores (e.g., Sam's, Costco, and BJ's), and convenience stores. "But the huge opportunity we discovered and developed was the mass merchandiser channel through chains like Wal-Mart and Target," says McKeon. "ACT II microwave popcorn was the first item of any kind to sell a million units in a week for Target, and that happened in 1987. Wal-Mart, too, was on the front end of this market and today is the top seller of microwave popcorn in any channel, selling far more popcorn than the leading grocery chains. Mass merchandisers now account for over a third of all the microwave popcorn sold in the U.S. They created the ACT II business as we know it today, and it was accomplished without a dime of conventional consumer promotions. That's one of the really unique parts of the ACT II story."

THE SITUATION TODAY

In the United States today, more than 90 percent of households own microwave ovens, and more than 60 percent of households are microwave popcorn consumers who spend more than $688 million on the product each year. "Our marketing research shows ACT II is especially strong in young families with kids," says Frank Lynch, vice president of marketing at Golden Valley. This conjures up an image of Mom and Dad watching a movie on TV with the kids and eating ACT II popcorn, a picture close to reality. "ACT II has good market penetration in almost all age, income, urban versus rural, and ethnic segments," he continues.

"From the beginning, Golden Valley has been the leader in the microwave popcorn industry," says McKeon, "and we plan to continue that record." As evidence, he cites a number of Golden Valley's "firsts":

- First mass-marketed microwave popcorn.
- First flavored microwave popcorn.
- First microwave popcorn tub.
- First fat-free microwave popcorn.
- First extra-butter microwave popcorn.
- First one-step sweetened microwave popcorn.

This list highlights a curious market segmentation phenomenon that has emerged in the last five years—the no-butter versus plenty-of-butter consumers. Originally popcorn was seen as junk food. Later studies by nutritionists pointed out its health benefits: low calories and high fiber. This caused Golden Valley to introduce its low-fat popcorn to appeal to the health-conscious segment of consumers. When it comes to eating popcorn while watching a movie at home on TV, however, the more butter on their popcorn, the better. Recently, much of the growth in popcorn sales has been in the spoil-yourself-with-a-lot-of-butter-on-your-popcorn segment.

Because of these diverse consumer tastes in popcorn, Golden Valley has developed a variety of popcorn products around its ACT II brand. Besides the low-fat and extra butter versions, these include the original flavors (natural and butter), sweet glazed products, popcorn in tubs, and Kettle Corn. In 2004, ACT II Big Boy was introduced to appeal to the economy segment. It also has a line of ACT II nonpopcorn snacks such as soft pretzels and snack mixes.

Golden Valley positions ACT II as unpretentious, fun, and youthful—a great product at a reasonable price. By stressing the value aspect of ACT II, Golden Valley has positioned the brand to appeal to today's growing value consciousness of consumers seeking quality products at reasonable prices. In terms of market share, these strategies have enabled ACT II to become the leader in the microwave popcorn market.

OPPORTUNITIES FOR FUTURE GROWTH

For many years the growth of the microwave popcorn industry closely followed the growth of household ownership of microwave ovens—from under 20 percent to more than 90 percent. But now, with a microwave oven in virtually every U.S. home, Golden Valley is trying to identify new market segments, new products, and innovative ways to appeal to all the major marketing channels.

In the United States, Golden Valley's strategy must include finding creative ways to continue to work with existing channels where it has special strength, such as the mass merchandiser channel. It also needs to further develop opportunities in the grocery store and supermarket channel. Now that the 10-year restriction on sales in grocery stores and supermarkets has expired, distribution through wholesalers that reach grocery stores and supermarkets is possible.

Global markets, too, present opportunities. Golden Valley has followed the penetration of microwave ovens in countries around the world, and used brokers to help gain distribution in those markets. Currently, Golden Valley has sales in more than 32 countries and the leading share in most of those markets. However, foreign markets represent foreign tastes, something that does not always lend itself to standardized products. United Kingdom consumers, for example, think of popcorn as a candy or child's food rather than the salty snack it is in the United States. Even in the Disney Park in Paris, American-style popcorn is absent, as French consumers sprinkle sugar on their popcorn. Swedes like theirs very buttery while many Mexicans like jalapeno-flavored popcorn.

Questions

1 Visit ACT II's website at www.ACTII.com and examine the assortment of products offered today. Are (a) the assortment or (b) the packaging related to Golden Valley's distribution channels or the segments they serve?

2 Use Figure 13–3 to create a description of the channels of distribution being used by Golden Valley today.

3 Compared to selling through the nongrocery channels, what kind of product, price, and promotion strategies might Golden Valley use to reach the grocery channel more effectively?

4 What special marketing issues does Golden Valley face as it pursues growth in global markets?

VIEWERS VOTE

HOT! NOT!

8 2

"You look good" "Keep lookin"

VIEWERS SUGGESTIONS
of these? Touch item for details

BlueSky89 Vicki5

BlueSky89 JoanArx

JoanArx MacShana

RESET MIRROR

SÉURA

BlueSky89 totally summer breezy!!!!!

looking great in the green

JoanArx a little to casual for tonights par

14

Retailing and Wholesaling

LEARNING OBJECTIVES

After reading this chapter you should be able to:

 LO1 Identify retailers in terms of the utilities they provide.

 LO2 Explain the alternative ways to classify retail outlets.

 LO3 Describe the many methods of nonstore retailing.

 LO4 Specify retailing mix actions used to implement a retailing strategy.

 LO5 Explain changes in retailing with the wheel of retailing and the retail life-cycle concepts.

 LO6 Describe the types and functions of firms that perform wholesaling activities.

RETAILERS ARE REINVENTING THEIR STORES TO MATCH THE WAY YOU WANT TO SHOP!

Retailers are undergoing a transformation that is designed to make the shopping experience better for you. They are adding bars and restaurants, using technology to allow customers to send images and messages to friends from the fitting rooms, and even building new stores with "open" designs. The combination of being at the mall, interacting with friends who are there, and engaging your personal network online just like you would with MySpace or Facebook will soon be part of the new "social retailing^SM."

For many years luxury department stores such as Barneys New York, Bergdorf Goodman, Neiman Marcus, Nordstrom, and Saks Fifth Avenue have used the same approach—offer expensive, well-known designer clothing in an elegant setting. Young consumers, however, are often looking for a different experience. To adapt to the new preferences many retailers are making changes to their existing stores. Bergdorf Goodman, for example, has added a deejay who will download music onto iPods, Saks has an upscale restaurant for shoppers, and Nordstrom offers live piano music. Some stores are offering "girlfriends" fitting rooms, which have space for as many as five friends, while others are trying fitting rooms with Privalite glass walls that allow privacy when shoppers are trying something on, but become transparent with the touch of a switch!

If friends can't actually be at the store to critique purchases, however, they will soon be able to participate in the shopping through online connections. New interactive fitting-room mirrors at Bloomingdale's allow shoppers to send images to anyone through online, mobile, and live video communication tools and then receive comments back from them. Other new technologies include "virtual" mirrors that project shoes onto customer's feet, and body scanners that collect 200,000 data points to determine exact sizes.

Some retailers are also creating new stores to attract young customers. Neiman Marcus, for example, is opening new stores, called Cusp, that feature "edgy" labels in an open floor plan with exposed ductwork and concrete floors. Sales associates are called "stylists" and a blog (www.blogonthecusp.com) takes the place of advertising. Similarly, Barneys is expanding its Co-op stores, which carry merchandise targeted at those in their 20s and 30s.[1]

Increasing social elements is just one example of the many exciting changes occurring in retailing today. This chapter examines the critical role of retailing in the marketplace and the challenging decisions retailers face as they strive to create value for customers.

What types of products will consumers buy through catalogs, television, the Internet, or by telephone? In what type of store will consumers look for products they don't buy directly? How important is the location of the store? Will customers expect services such as alterations, delivery, installation, or repair? What price should be charged for each product? These are difficult and important questions that are an integral part of retailing. In the channel of distribution, retailing is where the customer meets the product. It is through retailing that exchange (a central aspect of marketing) occurs. **Retailing** includes all activities involved in selling, renting, and providing goods and services to ultimate customers for personal, family, or household use.

retailing
All activities involved in selling, renting, and providing goods and services to ultimate consumers for personal, family, or household use

THE VALUE OF RETAILING

LO1

Retailing is an important marketing activity. Not only do producers and consumers meet through retailing actions, but retailing also creates customer value and has a significant impact on the economy. To consumers, the value of retailing is in the form of utilities provided (Figure 14–1). Retailing's economic value is represented by the people employed in retailing as well as by the total amount of money exchanged in retail sales.

Consumer Utilities Offered by Retailing

The utilities provided by retailers create value for consumers. Time, place, form, and possession utilities are offered by most retailers in varying degrees, but one utility is often emphasized more than others. Look at Figure 14–1 to see how well you can match the retailer with the utility being emphasized in the description.

FIGURE 14–1
Which retailer best provides which utilities?

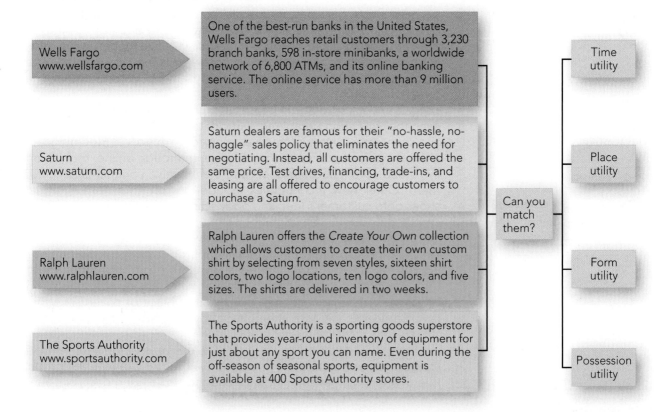

Providing minibanks in supermarkets, as Wells Fargo does, puts the bank's products and services close to the consumer, providing place utility. By providing financing or leasing and taking used cars as trade-ins, Saturn makes the purchase easier and provides possession utility. Form utility—production or alteration of a product—is offered by Polo Ralph Lauren through its online *Create Your Own* program, which offers shirts that meet each customer's specifications. Finding the right sporting equipment during the off-season is the time utility provided by the Sports Authority. Many retailers offer a combination of the four basic utilities. Some supermarkets, for example, offer convenient locations (place utility) and are open 24 hours (time utility). In addition, consumers may seek additional utilities such as entertainment, recreation, or information.[2]

Karstadt is one of the largest retailers outside the U.S.

The Global Economic Impact of Retailing

Retailing is important to the U.S. and global economies. Three of the 30 largest businesses in the United States are retailers (Wal-Mart, Home Depot, and Costco).[3] Wal-Mart's $378 billion of sales in 2007 surpassed the gross domestic product of all but 24 countries for that same year. Wal-Mart, Home Depot, and Costco together have more than 2.4 million employees—more than the combined populations of Austin, Texas; Spokane, Washington; and Ann Arbor, Michigan. Many retailers, including food stores, automobile dealers, and general merchandise outlets, are also significant contributors to the U.S. economy.[4]

Outside the United States large retailers include Daiei in Japan, Carrefour in France, KarstadtQuell in Germany, and Marks & Spencer in Britain.[5] In emerging economies such as China and Mexico, a combination of local and global retailers is evolving. Wal-Mart, for example, has 2,909 stores outside the United States, including stores in Brazil, China, Japan, Mexico, and the United Kingdom.

learning review

1. When Polo makes shirts to a customer's exact preferences, what utility is provided?

2. Two measures of the impact of retailing in the global economy are _____ and _____.

CLASSIFYING RETAIL OUTLETS

LO2

For manufacturers, consumers, and the economy, retailing is an important component of marketing that has several variations. Because of the large number of alternative forms of retailing, it is easier to understand the differences among retail institutions by recognizing that outlets can be classified in several ways. First, *form of ownership* distinguishes retail outlets based on whether individuals, corporate chains, or contractual systems own the outlet. Second, *level of service* is used to describe the degree of service provided to the customer. Three levels of service are provided by self-, limited-, and full-service retailers. Finally, the type of *merchandise line* describes how many different types of products a store carries and in what assortment. The alternative types of outlets are discussed in greater detail in the following pages.

Form of Ownership

There are three general forms of retail ownership—individual, corporate chain, and contractual system.

Independent Retailer One of the most common forms of retail ownership is the independent business, owned by an individual. Small retailers account for most of the 1.5 million retail establishments in the United States and include hardware stores, bakeries, clothing stores, and restaurants. In addition, there are 29,000 jewelry stores, 22,000 florists, and 43,000 sporting good and hobby stores. The advantage of this form of ownership for the owner is that he or she can be his or her own boss.[6] The accompanying Marketing Matters box discusses some of the skills needed to be a successful retailing entrepreneur.[7] For customers, the independent store can offer convenience, quality personal service, and lifestyle compatibility.

Corporate Chain A second form of ownership, the corporate chain, involves multiple outlets under common ownership. Many of the department store names you may know—Bon Marche, Lazurus, Burdines, Famous Barr, Filenes, Foleys, and Marshall Field's—are now one of 850 Macy's stores nationwide. Macy's Inc. also owns 40 Bloomingdale's, which compete with other chains such as Saks Fifth Avenue and Neiman Marcus. In a chain operation, centralization in decision making and purchasing is common. Chain stores have advantages in dealing with manufacturers, particularly as the size of the chain grows. A large chain can bargain with a manufacturer to obtain good service or volume discounts on orders. Consumers also benefit in dealing with chains because there are multiple outlets with similar merchandise and consistent management policies.

Retailing has become a high-tech business for many large chains. Wal-Mart, for example, has developed a sophisticated inventory management and cost control system that allows rapid price changes for each product in every store. In addition, stores such as Wal-Mart and Target are implementing pioneering new technologies such as radio frequency identification (RFID) tags to improve the quality of information available about products.

Contractual Systems Contractual systems involve independently owned stores that band together to act like a chain. The three kinds described in Chapter 13 are retailer-sponsored cooperatives, wholesaler-sponsored voluntary chains, and franchises. One retailer-sponsored cooperative is the Associated Grocers, which consists of neighborhood grocers that all agree with several other independent grocers to buy their meat from the same wholesaler. In this way, members can take advantage of volume discounts commonly available to chains and also give the impression of being a large chain, which may be viewed more favorably by some consumers. Wholesaler-sponsored voluntary chains such as Independent Grocers' Alliance (IGA) try to achieve similar benefits.

As noted in Chapter 13, in a franchise system an individual or firm (the franchisee) contracts with a parent company (the franchisor) to set up a business or retail outlet. The franchisor usually assists in selecting the location, setting up the store or facility, advertising, and training personnel. The franchisee usually pays a onetime franchise fee and an annual royalty, usually tied to franchise's

Subway is a popular business-format franchisor.

sales. There are two general types of franchises: *business-format franchises,* such as McDonald's, Radio Shack, and Blockbuster, and *product-distribution franchises,* such as a Ford dealership or a Coca-Cola distributor. In business-format franchising, the franchisor provides step-by-step procedures for most aspects of the business and guidelines for the most likely decisions a franchisee will face.

Franchise fees paid to the franchisor can range from $15,000 for a Subway franchise to $45,000 for a McDonald's restaurant franchise. When the fees are combined with other costs such as real estate and equipment, however, the total investment can be much higher. Franchisees also pay an ongoing royalty fee that ranges from 5 percent for a UPS Store to 15 percent for a Jackson Hewitt franchise. By selling franchises, an organization reduces the cost of expansion but loses some control. A good franchisor, however, will maintain strong control of the outlets in terms of delivery and presentation of merchandise and try to enhance recognition of the franchise name.[8]

Level of Service

Even though most customers perceive little variation in retail outlets by form of ownership, differences among retailers are more obvious in terms of level of service. In some department stores, such as Loehman's, very few services are provided. Some grocery stores, such as the Cub Foods chain, require customers to bag the food themselves. Other outlets, such as Neiman Marcus, provide a wide range of customer services from gift wrapping to wardrobe consultation.

Self-Service Self-service requires that the customers perform many functions and little is provided by the outlet. Warehouse clubs such as Costco, for example, are usually self-service, with all nonessential customer services eliminated. Similarly most gas stations today are self-service. New forms of self-service are being developed in grocery stores, airlines, camera/photo stores, and hotels. US Airways has installed more than 600 self-service kiosks in all 107 of its U.S. and Caribbean terminals to allow passengers to find a seat and print out a boarding pass without the help of an attendant. Hilton Hotels has self-service kiosks in 170 of its Embassy Suites hotels and all of its domestic Hilton properties. Guests swipe a credit card, select from room options, and receive their room keys. Throughout the United States more than 600,000 self-service kiosks are in use today. In general, the trend is toward retailing experiences that make customers co-creators of the value they receive.[9]

Limited-Service   Limited-service outlets provide some services, such as credit and merchandise return, but not others, such as clothing alterations. General merchandise stores such as Wal-Mart, Kmart, and Target are usually considered limited service outlets. Customers are responsible for most shopping activities, although salespeople are available in departments such as consumer electronics, jewelry, and lawn and garden.

Full-Service   Full-service retailers, which include most specialty stores and department stores, provide many services to their customers. Neiman Marcus, Nordstrom, and Saks Fifth Avenue, for example, all rely on better service to sell more distinctive, higher-margin goods and to retain their customers. Nordstrom offers a wide variety of services, including free exchanges, easy returns, credit cards through Nordstrom bank, a live help line, an online gift finder, catalogs, a four-level loyalty program called Nordstrom Fashion Rewards, and a beauty hotline. Some Nordstrom stores also offer a "Personal Touch" department, which provides shopping assistants for consumers who need help with style, color, and size selection, and a concierge service for assistance with anything else. Nordstrom stores typically have 50 percent more salespeople on the floor than similarly sized stores, and the salespeople are renowned for their professional and personalized attention to customers. Nordstrom also offers RSS feeds to notify customers when new merchandise is available.[10]

Type of Merchandise Line

Retail outlets also vary by their merchandise lines, the key distinction being the breadth and depth of the items offered to customers (Figure 14–2). *Depth of product line* means that the store carries a large assortment of each item, such as a shoe store that offers running shoes, dress shoes, and children's shoes. *Breadth of product line* refers to the variety of different items a store carries, such as appliances and CDs.

Depth of Line   Stores that carry a considerable assortment (depth) of a related line of items are limited-line stores. Oshman's sporting goods stores carry considerable depth in sports equipment ranging from weight-lifting accessories to running shoes. Stores that carry tremendous depth in one primary line of merchandise

FIGURE 14–2
Stores vary in terms of the breadth and depth of their merchandise lines.

Breadth: Number of different product lines

Shoes	Appliances	CDs	Men's clothing
Nike running shoes Florsheim dress shoes Sperry boat shoes Adidas tennis shoes	General Electric dishwashers Panasonic microwave ovens Whirlpool washers Frigidaire refrigerators	Classical Rock Jazz Country R & B Rap	Suits Ties Jackets Overcoats Socks Shirts

Depth: Number of items within each product line

Staples is the category killer in office supplies.

are single-line stores. Victoria's Secret, a nationwide chain, carries great depth in women's lingerie. Both limited- and single-line stores are often referred to as *specialty outlets.*

Specialty discount outlets focus on one type of product, such as electronics (Best Buy), office supplies (Staples), or books (Barnes & Noble) at very competitive prices. These outlets are referred to in the trade as *category killers* because they often dominate the market. Best Buy, for example, controls 17 percent of the consumer electronics market, and Staples is the leader in office supplies.[11]

Breadth of Line Stores that carry a broad product line, with limited depth, are referred to as *general merchandise stores.* For example, large department stores such as Dillard's, Macy's, and Neiman Marcus carry a wide range of different types of products but not unusual sizes. The breadth and depth of merchandise lines are important decisions for a retailer. Traditionally, outlets carried related lines of goods. Today, however, **scrambled merchandising**, offering several unrelated product lines in a single store, is common. The modern drugstore carries food, camera equipment, magazines, paper products, toys, small hardware items, and pharmaceuticals. Supermarkets rent videos, print photos, and sell flowers.

learning review

3. Centralized decision making and purchasing are an advantage of _____ ownership.

4. What are some examples of new forms of self-service retailers?

5. Would a shop for big men's clothes carrying pants in sizes 40 to 60 have a broad or deep product line?

NONSTORE RETAILING

LO3

Most of the retailing examples discussed earlier in the chapter, such as corporate chains, department stores, and limited- and single-line specialty stores, involve store retailing. Many retailing activities today, however, are not limited to sales in a store. Nonstore retailing occurs outside a retail outlet through activities that involve varying levels of customer and retailer involvement. The six forms of nonstore retailing include automatic vending, direct mail and catalogs, television home shopping, online retailing, telemarketing, and direct selling.

Automatic Vending

Vending machines offer many products found in convenience stores.

Nonstore retailing includes vending machines, which make it possible to serve customers when and where stores cannot. Machine maintenance, operating costs, and location leases can add to the cost of the products, so prices in vending machines tend to be higher than those in stores. About 29 percent of the products sold from vending machines are cold beverages, another 19 percent are candy and snacks, and 36 percent are food. Many other products are quickly becoming available in vending machines. Zoom Systems is putting machines with MP3 players, skin cream, cell phones, and cameras in shopping malls, hotels, and airports across the country. The 5.6 million vending machines currently in use in the United States generate more than $21 billion in annual sales.[12]

Specialty catalogs appeal to market niches.

Improved technology is making vending machines easier to use by reducing the need for cash. Many machines already accept credit cards, and some machines in Japan allow cashless purchases using cell phones. Japan's largest mobile phone company, DoCoMo, has introduced cell phones equipped with an electronic cash system that will allow consumers to charge vending machine purchases to their cell phone accounts. Another improvement in vending machines is the use of wireless technology to notify vendors when their machines are empty. Nestlé, for example, is installing hundreds of ice cream vending machines in France and England that send wireless messages to drivers of supply trucks. Finally, one of the biggest developments in vending is the trend toward fully automated stores. Get and Go Express stores now open in Florida feature 16 vending machines that offer many of the products typically found in a convenience store, and Moviebank USA recently opened a completely automated video rental store in Reno, Nevada.[13]

Direct Mail and Catalogs

Direct-mail and catalog retailing is attractive because it eliminates the cost of a store and clerks. For example, it costs a traditional retail store $34 to acquire a new customer, whereas catalog customers are acquired for approximately $14. In addition, direct mail and catalogs improve marketing efficiency through segmentation and targeting, and they create customer value by providing a fast and convenient means of making a purchase. The average U.S. household now receives 18 direct-mail items or catalogs each week, and research indicates that 85 percent of the households read some or all of their mail. The Direct Marketing Association estimates that direct-mail and catalog retailing creates 1.7 million jobs and $1.9 trillion in sales. Direct-mail and catalog retail is popular outside of the United State also. Furniture retailer IKEA delivered 160 million copies of its catalog in 25 languages last year.[14]

One reason for the growth in catalog sales is that traditional retailers such as Crate and Barrel and OfficeMax are adding catalog operations. As consumer's direct-mail purchases have increased, the number of catalogs and the number of products sold through catalogs have increased. The competition, combined with increases in postal rates, however, have caused catalog retailers to focus on proven customers rather than prospective customers. Another successful approach used by many catalog retailers is to send specialty catalogs to market niches identified in their databases. L. L. Bean, a long-standing catalog retailer, has developed an individual catalog for fly-fishing enthusiasts. Similarly, Lillian Vernon Corporation sends a specialty catalog called "Lilly's Kids" to customers with children or grandchildren, and JCPenney sends a catalog called "Big & Tall" to customers who have purchased large-size clothing.[15]

Television home shopping programs serve millions of customers each year.

Television Home Shopping

Television home shopping is possible when consumers watch a shopping channel on which products are displayed; orders are then placed over the telephone or the Internet. Currently, the three largest programs are QVC, HSN, and ShopNBC. QVC ("quality, value, convenience") broadcasts live 24 hours each day, 364 days a year, and reaches 151 million households in the United States, United Kingdom, Germany, and Japan. The company generates sales of more than $6.5 billion from its 42 million customers by offering 250 new products each week and shipping more than 100 million packages each year.[16]

In the past, television home shopping programs have attracted mostly 40- to 60-year-old women. To begin to attract a younger audience QVC has invited celebrities onto the show. For example, *American Idol* judge Paula Abdul, supermodel Heidi Klum, and singer Carly Simon have all been on the show selling jewelry and CDs. New partnerships, such as QVC's agreement to be the NFL's "official television retailer," also help attract new customers. The shopping programs are also using other forms of retailing. QVC now has three types of retail stores: a studio store at its headquarters, QVC @ the Mall in the Mall of America in Minnesota, and five outlet stores. Similarly, the Home Shopping Network has added catalogs to its online and television offerings. Finally, several television shopping programs are testing interactive technology that allows viewers to place orders with their remote control rather than the telephone.[17]

Online Retailing

Online retailing allows consumers to search for, evaluate, and order products through the Internet. For many consumers the advantages of this form of retailing are the 24-hour access, the ability to comparison shop, in-home privacy, and variety. Studies of online shoppers indicated that men were initially more likely than women to buy something online. As the number of online households increased, however, the profile of online shoppers changed to include all shoppers. In addition, the number of online retailers grew rapidly for several years and then declined as many stand-alone, Internet-only businesses failed or consolidated. Today, there has been a melding of traditional and online retailers—"bricks and clicks"—that are using experiences from both approaches to create better value and experiences for customers. Wal-Mart (www.walmart.com) and JCPenney (www.jcp.com) have recently introduced "site-to-store" service that allows customers to order online and pick up the order without a shipping fee at the store of their choice. Experts predict that online sales will reach $328 billion by 2010.[18]

Shopping "bots" find the best prices for products consumers specify.

Online retail purchases can be the result of several very different approaches. First, consumers can pay dues to become a member of an online discount service such as www.netMarket.com. The service offers tens of thousands of products and more than 1,200 brand names at very low prices to its 25 million subscribers. Another approach to online retailing is to use a shopping "bot" such as www.mysimon.com. This site searches the Internet for a product specified by the consumer and provides a report on the locations of the best prices available. Consumers can also use the Internet to go directly to online malls (www.fashionmall.com), apparel retailers (www.gap.com), bookstores (www.amazon.com), computer manufacturers (www.dell.com), grocery stores (www.peapod.com), music and video stores (www.cdnow.com), and travel agencies (www.travelocity.com). A final approach to online retailing is the online auction, such as www.ebay.com, where consumers bid on more than 1,000 categories of products.[19]

One of the biggest problems online retailers face is that nearly two-thirds of online shoppers make it to "checkout" and then leave the website to compare shipping costs and prices on other sites. Of the shoppers who leave, 70 percent do not return. One way online retailers are addressing this issue is to offer consumers a comparison of competitors' offerings. At Booksamillion.com, for example, consumers can use a "comparison engine" to compare prices with Amazon.com, Barnesandnoble.com, and Borders.com.[20] Experts suggest that online retailers should think of their websites as dynamic billboards if they are to attract and retain customers.[21] Online retailers are also trying to improve the online retailing experience by adding experiential or interactive activities to their websites. Similarly, car manufacturers such as BMW, Mercedes, and Jaguar encourage website visitors to "build" a vehicle by selecting interior and exterior colors, packages, and options and then view the customized virtual car. In addition, the merger of television home shopping and online retailing will be possible through TV-based Internet platforms such as Microsoft's MSN TV, which uses an Internet appliance attached to a television to connect to the Internet.

Telemarketing

telemarketing

Using the telephone to interact with and sell directly to consumers

Another form of nonstore retailing, called **telemarketing**, involves using the telephone to interact with and sell directly to consumers. Compared with direct mail, telemarketing is often viewed as a more efficient means of targeting consumers. Insurance companies, brokerage firms, and newspapers have often used this form of retailing as a way to cut costs but still maintain access to their customers. According to the Direct Marketing Association, annual telemarketing sales exceed $500 billion.[22]

The telemarketing industry has recently gone through dramatic changes as a result of new legislation related to telephone solicitations. Issues such as consumer privacy, industry standards, and ethical guidelines have encouraged discussion among consumers, Congress, the Federal Trade Commission, and businesses. The result was legislation that created the National Do-Not-Call registry (www.donotcall.gov) for consumers who do not want to receive telephone calls related to company sales efforts. Recent surveys indicate that 76 percent of U.S. adults have signed up for the registry. Companies that use telemarketing have already adapted by adding compliance software to ensure that numbers on the list are not called. In addition, some firms are considering shifting their telemarketing budgets to direct-mail and door-to-door techniques.[23]

Direct Selling

Direct selling, sometimes called door-to-door retailing, involves direct sales of goods and services to consumers through personal interactions and demonstrations in their home or office. A variety of companies, including familiar names such as Avon, Fuller Brush, Mary Kay Cosmetics, and World Book, have created an industry with more than $22 billion in sales by providing consumers with personalized service and convenience. In the United States, there are more than 14 million direct salespeople working full-time and part-time in 70 product categories.[24]

Growth in the direct selling industry is the result of two trends. First, many direct selling retailers are expanding into markets outside of the United States. Avon, for example, has 5 million sales representatives in 114 countries and is hiring an additional 399,000 new salespeople in China alone. The second trend is the growing number of companies that are using direct selling to reach consumers who prefer one-on-one customer service and a social shopping experience rather than online shopping or big discount stores. The Direct Selling Association reports that the number of companies using direct selling has increased by 30 percent in the past five years. Companies such as Pampered Chef, Crayola, Jockey, and the Body Shop have all recently started using direct selling to broaden their customer base.[25]

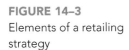

learning review

6. Successful catalog retailers often send _____ catalogs to _____ markets identified in their databases.

7. How are retailers increasing consumer interest and involvement in online retailing?

8. Where are direct selling retail sales growing? Why?

RETAILING STRATEGY

LO4

This section describes how a retailer develops and implements a retailing strategy. In developing retailing strategy, managers work with the **retailing mix**, which includes activities related to managing the store and the merchandise in the store. The retailing mix shown in Figure 14–3 is similar to the marketing mix and includes retail pricing, store location, retail communication, and merchandise.

retailing mix
The activities related to managing the store and the merchandise in the store, which includes retail pricing, store location, retail communication, and merchandise

Retail Pricing

In setting prices for merchandise, retailers must decide on the markup, markdown, and timing for markdowns. The *markup* refers to how much should be added to the cost the retailer paid for a product to reach the final selling price. Retailers decide on the *original markup,* but by the time the product is sold, they end up with a *maintained markup.* The original markup is the difference between retailer cost and initial selling price. When products do not sell as quickly as anticipated, their price is reduced. The difference between the final selling price and retailer cost is the maintained markup, which is also called the *gross margin.*

Discounting a product, or taking a *markdown,* occurs when the product does not sell at the original price and an adjustment is necessary. Often new models or styles force the price of existing models to be marked down. Discounts may also be used to increase demand for complementary products.[26] For example, retailers might take a markdown on CD players to increase sales of CDs or reduce the price of cake mix to generate frosting purchases. The *timing* of a markdown can be important. Many retailers take a markdown as soon as sales fall off to free up valuable selling space and cash. However, other stores delay markdowns to discourage bargain hunters and maintain an image of quality. There is no clear answer, but retailers must consider how the timing might affect

FIGURE 14–3
Elements of a retailing strategy

T.J. Maxx is a popular off-price retailer. Off 5th provides an outlet for excess merchandise from Saks Fifth Avenue.

future sales. Recent research indicates that frequent promotions increase consumers' ability to remember regular prices.[27]

Although most retailers plan markdowns, many retailers use price discounts as a part of their regular merchandising policy. Wal-Mart and Home Depot, for example, emphasize consistently low prices and eliminate most markdowns with a strategy often called *everyday low pricing.*[28] Because consumers often use price as an indicator of product quality, however, the brand name of the product and the image of the store become important decision factors in these situations.[29] Another strategy, *everyday fair pricing,* is advocated by retailers that may not offer the lowest price but try to create value for customers through service and the total buying experience.[30] Consumers often use the prices of *benchmark* or *signpost* items, such as a can of Coke, to form an overall impression of the store's prices.[31] In addition, price is the most likely to influence consumers' assessment of merchandise value.[32] When store prices are based on rebates, retailers must be careful to avoid negative consumer perceptions if the rebate processing time is long (e.g., six weeks).[33]

Off-price retailing is a retail pricing practice that is used by retailers such as T.J. Maxx, Burlington Coat Factory, and Ross Stores. *Off-price retailing* involves selling brand-name merchandise at lower than regular prices. The difference between the off-price retailer and a discount store is that off-price merchandise is bought by the retailer from manufacturers with excess inventory at prices below wholesale prices, while the discounter buys at full wholesale price (but takes less of a markup than do traditional department stores). Because of this difference in the way merchandise is purchased by the retailer, selection at an off-price retailer is unpredictable, and searching for bargains has become a popular activity for many consumers. "It's more like a sport than it is like ordinary shopping," says Christopher Boring of Columbus, Ohio's Retail Planning Associates.[34] Savings to the consumer at off-price retailers are reported as high as 70 percent off the prices of a traditional department store. A variation of off-price retailing includes outlet stores such as Nordstrom Rack and Off 5th (Saks Fifth Avenue outlet), which allow retailers to sell excess merchandise and still maintain an image of offering merchandise at full price in their primary store.

Store Location

A second aspect of the retailing mix involves deciding where to locate the store and how many stores to have. Department stores, which started downtown in most cities, have followed customers to the suburbs, and in recent years more stores have been opened in large regional malls. Most stores today are near several others in one of four settings: the central business district, the regional center, the strip, or the power center.

The *central business district* is the oldest retail setting, the community's downtown area. Until the regional outflow to suburbs, it was the major shopping area, but the suburban population has grown at the expense of the downtown shopping area. Consumers often view central business district shopping as less convenient because of lack of parking, higher crime rates, and exposure to the weather. Many cities such as Cincinnati, Denver, and San Antonio have implemented plans to revitalize shopping in central business districts by attracting new offices, entertainment, and residents to downtown locations.

Regional shopping centers consist of 50 to 150 stores that typically attract customers who live or work within a 5- to 10-mile range. These large shopping areas often contain two or three *anchor stores,* which are well-known national or regional stores such as Sears, Saks Fifth Avenue, and Bloomingdale's. The largest variation of a regional center is the West Edmonton Mall in Alberta, Canada. The shopping center is a conglomerate of 800 stores, nine amusement centers, 110 restaurants, and a 355-room Fantasyland hotel.[35]

Not every suburban store is located in a shopping mall. Many neighborhoods have clusters of stores, referred to as a *strip location,* to serve people who are within a 5- to 10-minute drive. Gas station, hardware, laundry, grocery, and pharmacy outlets are commonly found in a strip location. Unlike the larger shopping centers, the composition of these stores is usually unplanned. A variation of the strip shopping location is called the *power center,* which is a huge shopping strip with multiple anchor (or national) stores. Power centers are seen as having the convenient location found in many strip centers and the additional power of national stores. These large strips often have two to five anchor stores and often contain a supermarket, which brings the shopper to the power center on a weekly basis.[36]

The many forms of retail distribution described in this section and previously in this chapter represent an exciting menu of choices for creating customer value in the marketplace. Each format allows retailers to offer unique benefits and meet particular needs of various customer groups. Today, retailers combine many of the forms of distribution to offer a broader spectrum of benefits and experiences.[37] These **multichannel retailers** utilize and integrate a combination of traditional store formats and nonstore formats such as catalogs, television, and online retailing.[38] Barnes & Noble, for example, created Barnesandnoble.com to compete with Amazon.com. Similarly, Office Depot has integrated its store, catalog, and Internet operations to make shopping simpler and more convenient.

multichannel retailers
Use a combination of traditional store formats and nonstore formats such as catalogs, television, and online retailing

Retail Communication

A retailer's communication activities can play an important role in positioning a store and creating its image. While the traditional elements of communication and promotion are discussed in Chapter 16 on advertising and Chapter 17 on personal selling, the message communicated by the many other elements of the retailing mix are also important.

Deciding on the image of a retail outlet is an important retailing mix factor that has been widely recognized and studied since the late 1950s. Pierre Martineau described image as "the way in which the store is defined in the shopper's mind," partly by its functional qualities and partly by an aura of psychological attributes.[39] In this definition, *functional* refers to mix elements such as price ranges, store layouts, and breadth and depth of merchandise lines. The psychological attributes are the intangibles such as a sense of belonging, excitement, style, or warmth. Image has been found to include impressions of the corporation that operates the store, the category or type of store, the product categories in the store, the brands in each category, merchandise and service quality, and the marketing activities of the store.[40]

Closely related to the concept of image is the store's atmosphere or ambiance. Many retailers believe that sales are affected by layout, color, lighting, and music in the store as well as by how crowded it is. In addition, the physical surroundings that influence customers may affect the store's employees.[41] In creating the right image and atmosphere, a retail store tries to attract its target audience with what those consumers seek from the buying experience, so the store will fortify the beliefs and the emotional reactions buyers are seeking.[42] While store image perceptions can exist independently of shopping experiences, consumers' shopping experiences can also influence store perceptions.[43]

Merchandise

A final element of the retailing mix is the merchandise offering. Managing the breadth and depth of the product line requires retail buyers who are familiar with the needs of the target market and the alternative products available from the many manufacturers that might be interested in having a product available in the store. A popular approach to managing the assortment of merchandise today is called **category management**. This approach assigns a manager with the responsibility for selecting all products that consumers in a market segment might view as substitutes for each other, with the objective of maximizing sales and profits in the category. For example, a category manager might be responsible for shoes in a department store or paper products in a grocery store.

category management
An approach to managing the assortment of merchandise which maximizes sales and profits

Using Marketing Dashboards
Why Apple Stores May Be the Best in the United States!

How effective is my retail format compared to other stores? How are my stores performing this year compared to last year? Information related to this question is often displayed in a marketing dashboard using two measures: (1) sales per square foot and (2) same store sales growth.

Your Challenge You have been assigned to evaluate the Apple store retail format. The store's simple, inviting, open atmosphere has been the topic of discussion among many retailers. Apple, however, is new to the retailing business and many experts have been skeptical of the format. To allow an assessment of Apple stores, use *sales per square foot* as an indicator of how effectively retail space is used to generate revenue and *same store growth* to compare the increase in sales of stores that have been open for the same period of time. The calculations for these indicators are:

Sales per square foot
= Total sales/Selling area in square feet

Same store growth
= (Store sales in year 2 − Store sales in year 1)/
  Store sales in year 1

Your Findings You decide to collect sales information for Saks, Neiman Marcus, Best Buy, Tiffany, and Apple stores to allow comparisons with other successful retailers. The information you collect allows the calculation of *sales per square foot* and *same store growth* for each store. The results are then easy to compare in the accompanying graphs.

Your Action The results of your investigation indicate that Apple stores' sales per square foot are higher than any of the comparison stores at $4,000. In addition, Apple's same store growth rate of 45 percent is higher than all of the other stores. You conclude that the elements of Apple's format are very effective and even indicate that Apple may currently be the best retailer in the United States.

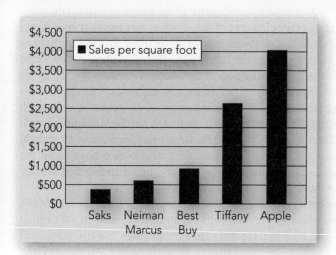

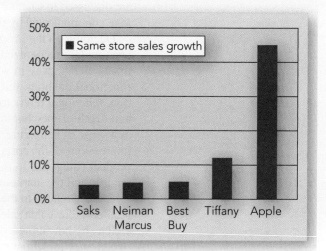

Many retailers are developing an advanced form of category management called *consumer marketing at retail* (CMAR). Recent surveys show that, as part of their CMAR programs, retailers are conducting research, analyzing the data to identify shopper problems, translating the data into retailing mix actions, executing shopper-friendly in-store programs, and monitoring the performance of the merchandise. Wal-Mart, for example, has used the approach to test baby-product and dollar-product categories. Grocery stores such as Safeway and Kroger use the approach to determine the appropriate mix of brand name and private label products. Specialty retailer Barnes & Noble recently won a best practice award for its application of the approach to the selection, presentation, and promotion of magazines.[44]

Retailers have a variety of metrics that can be used to assess the effectiveness of a store or retail format. First, there are measures related to customers such as the number of transactions per customer, the average transaction size per customer, the number of customers per day or per hour, and the average length of a store visit. Second, there are measures related to products such as number of returns, inventory turnover, inventory carrying cost, and average number of items per transaction. Finally, there are financial measures, such as gross margin, sales per employee, return on sales, and markdown percentage.[45] The two most popular measures for retailers are *sales per square foot* and *same store growth rate*. The accompanying Using Marketing Dashboards box describes the calculation of these measures for Apple stores.[46]

learning review

9. How does original markup differ from maintained markup?

10. A huge shopping strip with multiple anchor stores is a _____ center.

11. What is a popular approach to managing the assortment of merchandise in a store?

THE CHANGING NATURE OF RETAILING

LO5

Retailing is the most dynamic aspect of a channel of distribution. New types of retailers are always entering the market, searching for a new position that will attract customers. The reason for this continual change is explained by two concepts: the wheel of retailing and the retail life cycle.

The Wheel of Retailing

wheel of retailing

A concept that describes how new forms of retail outlets enter the market

The **wheel of retailing** describes how new forms of retail outlets enter the market.[47] Usually they enter as low-status, low-margin stores such as a drive-in hamburger stand with no indoor seating and a limited menu (Figure 14–4, box 1). Gradually these outlets add fixtures and more embellishments to their stores (in-store seating, plants, and chicken sandwiches as well as hamburgers) to increase the attractiveness for customers.

FIGURE 14–4
The wheel of retailing describes how retail outlets change.

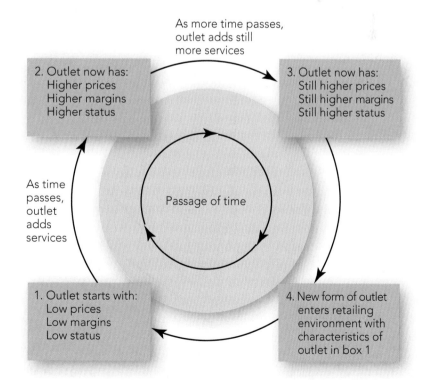

As more time passes, outlet adds still more services

2. Outlet now has:
   Higher prices
   Higher margins
   Higher status

3. Outlet now has:
   Still higher prices
   Still higher margins
   Still higher status

As time passes, outlet adds services

Passage of time

1. Outlet starts with:
   Low prices
   Low margins
   Low status

4. New form of outlet enters retailing environment with characteristics of outlet in box 1

The wheel of retailing has come full circle for Taco Bell.

With these additions, prices and status rise (box 2). As time passes, these outlets add still more services and their prices and status increase even further (box 3). These retail outlets now face some new form of retail outlet that again appears as a low-status, low-margin operator (box 4), and the wheel of retailing turns as the cycle starts to repeat itself.

When Ray Kroc started the first McDonald's in 1955 it opened shortly before lunch and closed just after dinner, offering a limited menu for the two meals without any inside seating for customers. Over time, the wheel of retailing has led to new products and services. In 1975, McDonald's introduced the Egg McMuffin and turned breakfast into a fast-food meal. Today, McDonald's has an extensive menu, seating, and services such as wireless Internet connections. For the future, McDonald's is testing new products such as premium-blend coffee, frying oil without trans fats, and fruit smoothies; new formats such as its coffee, pastry, and sandwich outlets called McCafe, and seating "zones" for different types of customers; and 24/7 "always open" hours.

The changes are leaving room for new forms of outlets such as Checker Drive-In Restaurants. The chain opened fast-food stores that offered only basics—burgers, fries, and cola, a drive-through window and no inside seating—and now has more than 800 stores. The wheel is turning for other outlets too—Boston Market has added pick-up, delivery, and full-service catering to its original restaurant format, and it also provides Boston Market meal solutions through supermarket delis and Boston Market frozen meals in the frozen food sections. For still others, the wheel has come full circle. Taco Bell is now opening small, limited-offering outlets in gas stations, discount stores, or "wherever a burrito and a mouth might possibly intersect."[48]

The Retail Life Cycle

retail life cycle

The process of growth and decline that retail outlets, like products, experience over time

The process of growth and decline that retail outlets, like products, experience is described by the **retail life cycle**.[49] Figure 14–5 shows the retail life cycle and the position of various current forms of retail outlets on it. Early growth is the stage of

FIGURE 14–5
The retail life cycle describes stages of growth and decline for retail outlets.

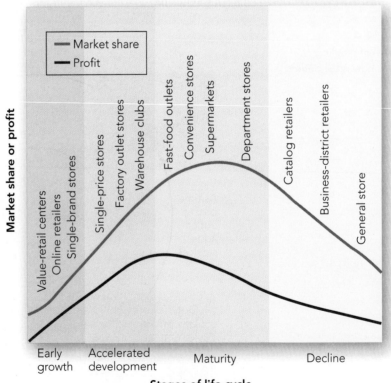

emergence of a retail outlet, with a sharp departure from existing competition. Market share rises gradually, although profits may be low because of start-up costs. In the next stage, accelerated development, both market share and profit achieve their greatest growth rates. Usually multiple outlets are established as companies focus on the distribution element of the retailing mix. In this stage, some later competitors may enter. Wendy's, for example, appeared on the hamburger chain scene almost 20 years after McDonald's had begun operations. The key goal for the retailer in this stage is to establish a dominant position in the fight for market share.

The battle for market share is usually fought before the maturity stage, and some competitors drop out of the market. In the wars among hamburger chains, Jack in the Box, Gino Marchetti's, and Burger Chef used to be more dominant outlets. New retail forms enter in the maturity stage, stores try to maintain their market share, and price discounting occurs.

WHOLESALING

Many retailers depend on intermediaries that engage in wholesaling activities—selling products and services for the purposes of resale or business use. There are several types of intermediaries, including wholesalers and agents (described briefly in Chapter 13), as well as manufacturers' sales offices, which are important to understand as part of the retailing process.

Merchant Wholesalers

merchant wholesalers
Independently owned firms that take title to the merchandise they handle

Merchant wholesalers are independently owned firms that take title to the merchandise they handle. They go by various names, including industrial distributor (described earlier). More than 80 percent of the firms engaged in wholesaling activities are merchant wholesalers.

Merchant wholesalers are classified as either full-service or limited-service wholesalers, depending on the number of functions performed. Two major types of full-service wholesalers exist. *General merchandise* (or *full-line*) *wholesalers* carry a broad assortment of merchandise and perform all channel functions. This type of wholesaler is most prevalent in the hardware, drug, and clothing industries. However, these wholesalers do not maintain much depth of assortment within specific product lines. *Specialty merchandise* (or *limited-line*) *wholesalers* offer a relatively narrow range of products but have an extensive assortment within the product lines carried. They perform all channel functions and are found in the health foods, automotive parts, and seafood industries.

Four major types of limited-service wholesalers exist. *Rack jobbers* furnish the racks or shelves that display merchandise in retail stores, perform all channel functions, and sell on consignment to retailers, which means they retain the title to the products displayed and bill retailers only for the merchandise sold. Familiar products such as hosiery, toys, housewares, and health and beauty items are sold by rack jobbers. *Cash and carry wholesalers* take title to merchandise but sell only to buyers who call on them, pay cash for merchandise, and furnish their own transportation for merchandise. They carry a limited product assortment and do not make deliveries, extend credit, or supply market information. This wholesaler is common in electric supplies, office supplies, hardware products, and groceries.

Drop shippers, or desk jobbers, are wholesalers that own the merchandise they sell but do not physically handle, stock, or deliver it. They simply solicit orders from retailers and other wholesalers and have the merchandise shipped directly from a producer to a buyer. Drop shippers are used for bulky products such as coal, lumber, and chemicals, which are sold in extremely large quantities. *Truck jobbers* are small wholesalers that have a small warehouse from which they stock their trucks for distribution to retailers. They usually handle limited assortments of fast-moving or perishable items that are sold for cash directly from trucks in their original packages. Truck jobbers handle products such as bakery items, dairy products, and meat.

Agents and Brokers

Unlike merchant wholesalers, agents and brokers do not take title to merchandise and typically perform fewer channel functions. They make their profit from commissions or fees paid for their services, whereas merchant wholesalers make their profit from the sale of the merchandise they own.

Manufacturer's agents and selling agents are the two major types of agents used by producers. **Manufacturer's agents**, or *manufacturer's representatives,* work for several producers and carry noncompetitive, complementary merchandise in an exclusive territory. Manufacturer's agents act as a producer's sales arm in a territory and are principally responsible for the transactional channel functions, primarily selling. They are used extensively in the automotive supply, footwear, and fabricated steel industries.

By comparison, *selling agents* represent a single producer and are responsible for the entire marketing function of that producer. They design promotional plans, set prices, determine distribution policies, and make recommendations on product strategy. Selling agents are used by small producers in the textile, apparel, food, and home furnishing industries.

Brokers are independent firms or individuals whose principal function is to bring buyers and sellers together to make sales. Brokers, unlike agents, usually have no continuous relationship with the buyer or seller but negotiate a contract between two parties and then move on to another task. Brokers are used extensively by producers of seasonal products (such as fruits and vegetables) and in the real estate industry.

A unique broker that acts in many ways like a manufacturer's agent is a food broker, representing buyers and sellers in the grocery industry. Food brokers differ from conventional brokers because they act on behalf of producers on a permanent basis and receive a commission for their services. For example, Nabisco uses food brokers to sell its candies, margarine, and Planters peanuts, but it sells its line of cookies and crackers directly to retail stores.

Manufacturer's Branches and Offices

Unlike merchant wholesalers, agents, and brokers, manufacturer's branches and sales offices are wholly owned extensions of the producer that perform wholesaling activities. Producers assume wholesaling functions when there are no intermediaries to perform these activities, customers are few in number and geographically concentrated, or orders are large or require significant attention. A *manufacturer's branch office* carries a producer's inventory and performs the functions of a full-service wholesaler. A *manufacturer's sales office* does not carry inventory, typically performs only a sales function, and serves as an alternative to agents and brokers.

---

manufacturer's agents
Work for several producers and carry noncompetitive, complementary merchandise in an exclusive territory

brokers
Independent firms or individuals whose main function is to bring buyers and sellers together to make sales

---

learning review

12. According to the wheel of retailing, when a new retail form appears, how would you characterize its image?

13. Market share is usually fought out before the _____ stage of the retail life cycle.

14. What is the difference between merchant wholesalers and agents?

LEARNING OBJECTIVES REVIEW

LO 1 *Identify retailers in terms of the utilities they provide.*
Retailers provide time, place, form, and possession utilities. Time utility is provided by stores with convenient time-of-day (e.g., open 24 hours) or time-of-year (e.g., seasonal sports equipment available all year) availability. Place utility is provided by the number and location of the stores. Possession utility is provided by making a purchase possible (e.g., financing) or easier (e.g., delivery). Form utility is provided by producing or altering a product to meet the customer's specifications (e.g., custom-made shirts).

LO 2 *Explain the alternative ways to classify retail outlets.*
Retail outlets can be classified by their form of ownership, level of service, and type of merchandise line. The forms of ownership include independent retailers, corporate chains, and contractual systems that include retailer-sponsored cooperatives, wholesaler-sponsored voluntary chains, and franchises. The levels of service include self-service, limited-service, and full-service outlets. Stores classified by their merchandise line include stores with depth, such as sporting good specialty stores, and stores with breadth, such as large department stores.

LO 3 *Describe the many methods of nonstore retailing.*
Nonstore retailing includes automatic vending, direct mail and catalogs, television home shopping, online retailing, telemarketing, and direct selling. The methods of nonstore retailing vary by the level of involvement of the retailer and the level of involvement of the customer. Vending, for example, has low involvement, whereas both the consumer and the retailer have high involvement in direct selling.

LO 4 *Specify retailing mix actions used to implement a retailing strategy.*
Retailing mix actions are used to manage a retail store and the merchandise in a store. The mix variables include pricing, store location, communication activities, and merchandise. Two common forms of assessment for retailers are "sales per square foot" and "same store growth."

LO 5 *Explain changes in retailing with the wheel of retailing and the retail life-cycle concepts.*
The wheel of retailing concept explains how retail outlets typically enter the market as low-status, low-margin stores. Over time, stores gradually add new products and services, increasing their prices, status, and margins, and leaving an opening for new low-status, low-margin stores. The retail life cycle describes the process of growth and decline for retail outlets through four stages: early growth, accelerated development, maturity, and decline.

LO 6 *Describe the types and functions of firms that perform wholesaling activities.*
There are three types of firms that perform wholesaling functions. First, merchant wholesalers are independently owned and take title to merchandise. They include general merchandise wholesalers, specialty merchandise wholesalers, rack jobbers, cash and carry wholesalers, drop shippers, and truck jobbers and can perform a variety of channel functions. Second, agents and brokers do not take title to merchandise and primarily perform marketing functions. Finally, manufacturer's branches, which may carry inventory, and sales offices, which perform sales functions, are wholly owned by the producer.

FOCUSING ON KEY TERMS

brokers p. 330
category management p. 325
manufacturer's agents p. 330
merchant wholesalers p. 329

multichannel retailers p. 325
retail life cycle p. 328
retailing p. 314
retailing mix p. 323

scrambled merchandising p. 319
telemarketing p. 322
wheel of retailing p. 327

APPLYING MARKETING KNOWLEDGE

1 Discuss the impact of the growing number of dual-income households on (*a*) nonstore retailing and (*b*) the retail mix.

2 In retail pricing, retailers often have a maintained markup. Explain how this maintained markup differs from original markup and why it is so important.

3 What are the similarities and differences between the product and retail life cycles?

4 How would you classify Wal-Mart in terms of its position on the wheel of retailing versus that of an off-price retailer?

5 Develop a chart to highlight the role of each of the four main elements of the retailing mix across the four stages of the retail life cycle.

6 Breadth and depth are two important components in distinguishing among types of retailers. Discuss the breadth and depth implications of the following retailers discussed in this chapter: (*a*) Nordstrom, (*b*) Wal-Mart, (*c*) L. L. Bean, and (*d*) Best Buy.

7 According to the wheel of retailing and the retail life cycle, what will happen to factory outlet stores?

8 The text discusses the development of online retailing in the United States. How does the development of this retailing form agree with the implications of the retail life cycle?

9 Comment on this statement: The only distinction among merchant wholesalers, and agents and brokers is that merchant wholesalers take title to the products they sell.

Does your marketing plan involve using retailers? If the answer is no, read no further and do not include a retailing element in your plan. If the answer is yes,

1 Use Figure 14–3 to develop your retailing strategy by (*a*) selecting a position in the retail positioning matrix and (*b*) specifying the details of the retailing mix.

2 Develop a positioning statement describing the breadth of the product line (broad versus narrow) and value added (low versus high).

3 Describe an appropriate combination of retail pricing, store location, retail communication, and merchandise assortment.

video case 14   Mall of America: Shopping and a Whole Lot More

"If you build it, they will come" not only worked in the movie *Field of Dreams* but also applies—big time—to Mall of America.

Located in a suburb of Minneapolis, Mall of America (www.mallofamerica.com) is the largest completely enclosed retail and family-entertainment complex in the United States. "We're more than a mall, we're a destination," explains Maureen Cahill, an executive at Mall of America. More than 100,000 people each day—40 million visitors each year—visit the one-stop complex offering retail shopping, guest services, convenience, a huge variety of entertainment, and fun for all. "Guest services" include everything from high school and college classrooms to a doctor's office and a wedding chapel.

THE CONCEPT AND CHALLENGE

The idea for the Mall of America came from the West Edmonton Mall in Alberta, Canada. The Ghermezian Brothers, who developed that mall, sought to create a unique mall that would attract not only local families but also tourists from the Upper Midwest, the nation, and even from abroad.

The two challenges for Mall of America: How can it (1) attract and keep the large number of retail establishments needed to (2) continue to attract even more millions of visitors than today? A big part of the answer is in Mall of America's positioning—"There is a place for fun in your life!"

THE STAGGERING SIZE AND OFFERINGS

Opened August 1992 amid tremendous worldwide publicity, Mall of America faced skeptics who had their doubts because of its size, its unique retail-entertainment mix, and the nationwide recession. Despite these concerns, it opened with more than 80 percent of its space leased and attracted more than 1 million visitors its first week.

Mall of America is 4.2 million square feet, the equivalent of 88 football fields. This makes it three to four times the size of most other regional malls. It includes four anchor department stores: Nordstrom, Macy's, Bloomingdale's, and Sears. It also includes more than 520 specialty stores, from Brooks Brothers and Sharper Image to Marshall's and DSW Shoe Warehouse. Approximately 36 percent of Mall of America's space is devoted to anchors and 64 percent to specialty stores. This makes the space allocation the reverse of most regional malls.

The retail-entertainment mix of Mall of America is incredibly diverse. For example, there are more than 100 apparel and accessory stores, 18 jewelry stores, and 33 shoe stores. Two food courts with 27 restaurants plus more than 30 other restaurants scattered throughout the building meet most food preferences of visitors. Another surprise: Mall of America is home to many "concept stores," where retailers introduce a new type of store or design. Because of its incredible size, the mall has 194 stores not found at competing regional malls. In addition, it has an entrepreneurial program for people with an innovative retail idea and limited resources. They can open up a kiosk, wall unit, or small store for a specified time period or as a temporary seasonal tenant.

Unique features of Mall of America include:

- A seven-acre theme park with more than 50 attractions and rides, including a roller coaster, Ferris wheel, and games in a glass-enclosed, skylighted area with more than 400 trees.
- Underwater Adventures, where visitors are surrounded by sharks, stingrays, and sea turtles; can adventure among fish native to the north woods; and can discover what lurks at the bottom of the Mississippi River.
- Entertainment choices that include a 14-screen theater, A.C.E.S. Flight Simulation, NASCAR Silicon Motor Speedway, and Dinosaur Walk Museum.
- The LEGO Land Imagination Center, a 6,000-square-foot showplace with more than 30 full-sized models.

As a host to corporate events and private parties, Mall of America has a rotunda that opens to all four floors that facilitates presentations, demonstrations, and exhibits. Organizations such as PepsiCo, Visa-USA, and Chevrolet have used the facilities to gain shopper awareness. Mall of America is a rectangle with the anchor department stores at the corners and amusement park in the skylighted central area, making it easy for shoppers to understand and navigate. It has 12,550 free parking ramp spaces on site and another 7,000 spaces nearby during peak times.

THE MARKET

The Minneapolis–St. Paul metropolitan area is a market with more than 3 million people. A total of 30 million people live within a day's drive of Mall of America. A survey of its shoppers showed that 32 percent of the shoppers travel 150 miles or more and account for more than 50 percent of the sales revenues. Located three miles from the Minneapolis/St. Paul International Airport, Mall of America provides a shuttle bus from the airport every half hour. Light-rail service from the airport and downtown Minneapolis is also available.

Tourism accounts for four out of ten visits to Mall of America. About 6 percent of visitors come from outside the United States. Some come just to see and experience Mall of America, while others take advantage of the cost savings available on goods (Japan) or taxes (Canada and states with sales taxes on clothing).

THE FUTURE: FACING THE CHALLENGES

Where does Mall of America head in the future?

"We just did a brand study and found that Mall of America is one of the most recognized brands in the world," says Cahill. "They might not know where we are sometimes, but they've heard of Mall of America and they know they want to come."

"What we've learned since 1992 is to keep the Mall of America fresh and exciting," she explains. "We're constantly looking at what attracts people and adding to that. We're adding new stores, new attractions, and new events. We hold more than 350 events a year and with everyone from Garth Brooks to Sarah Ferguson to N Sync."

Mall of America recently announced a plan for a 5.6 million-square-foot expansion, the area of another 117 football fields, connected by pedestrian skyway to the present building. "The second phase will not be a duplicate of what we have," says Cahill. "We have plans for at least three hotels, a performing arts center, a business office complex, an art or history museum, and possibly even a television broadcast facility."

One of the first elements of the expansion includes a recently opened 306,000-square-foot IKEA store. Other new elements will include a 13,000-square-foot restaurant called Cantina Corona, a 6,000-seat performing arts auditorium created by AEG, a 300,000-square-foot Bass Pro store, and a 200-room Kimpton Hotel. All of these new additions and the many offerings of the current mall reinforce that Mall of America is a shopping destination and a whole lot more!

Questions

1 Why has Mall of America been such a marketing success so far?

2 What (*a*) retail and (*b*) consumer trends have occurred since Mall of America was opened in 1992 that it should consider when making future plans?

3 (*a*) What criteria should Mall of America use in adding new facilities to its complex? (*b*) Evaluate (*i*) retail stores, (*ii*) entertainment offerings, and (*iii*) hotels on these criteria.

4 What specific marketing actions would you propose that Mall of America managers take to ensure its continuing success in attracting visitors (*a*) from the local metropolitan area and (*b*) from outside of it?

15

Integrated Marketing Communications and Direct Marketing

LEARNING OBJECTIVES

After reading this chapter you should be able to:

LO1 Discuss integrated marketing communication and the communication process.

LO2 Describe the promotional mix and the uniqueness of each component.

LO3 Select the promotional approach appropriate to a product's target audience and life-cycle stage, as well as channel strategies.

LO4 Describe the elements of the promotion decision process.

LO5 Explain the value of direct marketing for consumers and sellers.

HOW DO MARKETERS FIGHT THE GAME CONSOLE WARS? WITH INTEGRATED MARKETING COMMUNICATIONS!

Chances are that sometime recently you've played, or seen others playing, one of the three popular video entertainment systems. Sony's PlayStation, Microsoft's Xbox, and Nintendo's Wii are all in a dogfight for your gaming time and budget. The battle is being fought with complex integrated marketing communications campaigns that include almost every form of media. "All the media focus is on next-gen consoles and games," explains Erik Whiteford, marketing director at game software developer 2K Sports.

The stakes are high because so many worldwide consumers have one or more of the systems. Since 2000, Sony has shipped more than 110 million units of its PS2 model, which is now being replaced by the new PS3 and competing with the Xbox 360 and the Wii. Recently, the industry reached $7.4 billion in sales. Experts believe consumers will continue to purchase more than 6 million of each of the new systems each year, and by 2011 Sony will have about 44 percent of the market, compared to 40 percent for Xbox and 16 percent for Wii.

Sony's integrated campaign features a variety of components including television ads on broadcast and cable networks; print ads in monthly, weekly, and daily publications; online advertising on gaming, sports, and lifestyle websites; and billboard and bus shelter ads in metropolitan areas. The campaign also includes interactive elements at its Playbeyond.com website, 14,000 kiosks at retailers, and a huge truck called the "PlayStation Experience" that stops at concerts to let visitors play the Sony system and games on location. In Europe the launch campaign also includes short films shown in movie theaters.

Microsoft's Xbox campaign also integrates many communication elements. In addition to television ads and short online movies, Xbox has advertising with partner retailers including Target, Wal-Mart, and Sears. The Nintendo Wii campaign includes TV advertising; a promotion with Coca-Cola on the packaging of its Fanta, Sprite, and Dr Pepper brands; and live stunts by actors playing Wii tennis in front of a huge screen.

While the messages in the many forms of media may vary slightly, the campaigns are designed to emphasize a single theme. Sony is trying to communicate a message that the PS3 is "an experience 'beyond' games, harnessing the power of imagination." Microsoft's message for the Xbox 360 is "Jump In" and move to the next generation of gaming. Nintendo is positioning its Wii as a gaming system for the entire family.

What are some of the most innovative elements of these integrated campaigns? Sony included Blu-ray discs of *Talladega Nights: The Ballad of Ricky Bobby* in 500,000 PS3 boxes. Kellogg put Xbox 360 cartridges in 80 million cereal boxes in its highest-value promotion ever. At the Los Angeles launch of the Wii, videos of people singing songs about the Wii were posted on YouTube.com. Perhaps you've seen some of the promotions, and you are certain to see more in the future as the console wars continue.[1]

The many types of promotion used by Sony, Microsoft, and Nintendo demonstrate the opportunity for creativity in communicating with potential customers and the importance of integrating the various elements of a communication program. Promotion represents the fourth element in the marketing mix. The promotional element consists of communication tools, including advertising, personal selling, sales promotion, public relations, and direct marketing. The combination of one or more of these communication tools is called the **promotional mix**. All of these tools can be used to (1) inform prospective buyers about the benefits of the product, (2) persuade them to try it, and (3) remind them later about the benefits they enjoyed by using the product. In the past, marketers often viewed the communication tools as separate and independent. The advertising department, for example, often designed and managed its activities without consulting departments or agencies that had responsibility for sales promotion or public relations. The result was often an overall communication effort that was uncoordinated and, in some cases, inconsistent. Today, the concept of designing marketing communications programs that coordinate all promotional activities—advertising, personal selling, sales promotion, public relations, and direct marketing—to provide a consistent message across all audiences is referred to as **integrated marketing communications (IMC)**. In addition, by taking consumer expectations into consideration, IMC is a key element in a company's customer experience management strategy.[2]

This chapter provides an overview of the communication process, a description of the promotional mix elements, several tools for integrating the promotional mix, and a process for developing a comprehensive promotion program. One of the promotional mix elements, direct marketing, is also discussed in this chapter. Chapter 16 covers advertising, sales promotion, and public relations, and Chapter 17 discusses personal selling.

THE COMMUNICATION PROCESS

LO1

communication
Process of conveying a message to others

Communication is the process of conveying a message to others and it requires six elements: a source, a message, a channel of communication, a receiver, and the processes of encoding and decoding[3] (Figure 15–1). The *source* may be a company or person who has information to convey. The information sent by a source, such as a description of a new cellular telephone, forms the *message*. The message is conveyed by means of a *channel of communication* such as a salesperson, advertising media, or public relations tools. Consumers who read, hear, or see the message are the *receivers*.

Encoding and Decoding

Encoding and decoding are essential to communication. *Encoding* is the process of having the sender transform an idea into a set of symbols. *Decoding* is the reverse, or the process of having the receiver take a set of symbols, the message, and transform the symbols back to an idea. Look at the accompanying automobile advertisement: Who is the source, and what is the message?

Decoding is performed by the receivers according to their own frame of reference: their attitudes, values, and beliefs.[4] Jaguar is the source and the advertisement is the message, which appeared in *Wired* magazine (the channel). How would you interpret

promotional mix
Combination of one or more of the communication tools used to inform, persuade, or remind prospective buyers

integrated marketing communications
Concept of designing marketing communications programs that coordinate all promotional activities to provide a consistent message across all audiences

FIGURE 15–1
The communication process
consists of six key elements.

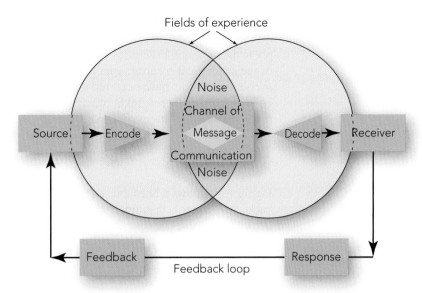

(decode) this advertisement? The picture and text in the advertisement show that the source's intention is to generate interest in a vehicle with "The undeniable beauty of speed"—a statement the source believes will appeal to the readers of the magazine.

The process of communication is not always a successful one. Errors in communication can happen in several ways. The source may not adequately transform the abstract idea into an effective set of symbols, a properly encoded message may be sent through the wrong channel and never make it to the receiver, the receiver may not properly transform the set of symbols into the correct abstract idea, or finally, feedback may be so delayed or distorted that it is of no use to the sender. Although communication appears easy to perform, truly effective communication can be very difficult.

How would you decode this ad?

For the message to be communicated effectively, the sender and receiver must have a mutually shared *field of experience*—a similar understanding and knowledge they apply to the message. Figure 15–1 shows two circles representing the fields of experience of the sender and receiver, which overlap in the message. Some of the better-known message problems have occurred when U.S. companies have taken their messages to cultures with different fields of experience. Many misinterpretations are merely the result of bad translations. For example, KFC made a mistake when its "finger-lickin' good" slogan was translated into Mandarin Chinese as "eat your fingers off!"[5]

Feedback

Figure 15–1 shows a line labeled *feedback loop,* which consists of a response and feedback. A *response* is the impact the message had on the receiver's knowledge, attitudes, or behaviors. *Feedback* is the sender's interpretation of the response and indicates whether the message was decoded and understood as intended. Chapter 16 reviews approaches called *pretesting* that ensure that messages are decoded properly.

Noise

Noise includes extraneous factors that can work against effective communication by distorting a message or the feedback received (Figure 15–1). Noise can be a simple error, such as a printing mistake that affects the meaning of a newspaper advertisement, or using words or pictures that fail to communicate the message clearly. Noise can also occur when a salesperson's message is misunderstood by a prospective buyer, such as when a salesperson's accent, use of slang terms, or communication style make hearing and understanding the message difficult.

---

learning review

1. What are the six elements required for communication to occur?

2. A difficulty for U.S. companies advertising in international markets is that the audience does not share the same _____.

3. A misprint in a newspaper ad is an example of _____.

THE PROMOTIONAL ELEMENTS

LO2

To communicate with consumers, a company can use one or more of five promotional alternatives: advertising, personal selling, public relations, sales promotion, and direct marketing. Figure 15–2 summarizes the distinctions among these five elements. Three of these elements—advertising, sales promotion, and public relations—are often said to use *mass selling* because they are used with groups of prospective buyers. In contrast, personal selling uses *customized interaction* between a seller and a prospective buyer. Personal selling activities include face-to-face, telephone, and interactive electronic communication. Direct marketing also uses messages customized for specific customers.

Advertising

advertising
Any paid form of nonpersonal communication about an organization, good, service, or idea by an identified sponsor

Advertising is any paid form of nonpersonal communication about an organization, good, service, or idea by an identified sponsor. The *paid* aspect of this definition is important because the space for the advertising message normally must be bought. An occasional exception is the public service announcement, where the advertising time or space is donated. A full-page, four-color ad in *Time* magazine, for example, costs $255,840. The *nonpersonal* component of advertising is also important. Advertising involves mass media (such as TV, radio, and magazines), which are nonpersonal and do not have

PROMOTIONAL ELEMENT	MASS OR CUSTOMIZED	PAYMENT	STRENGTHS	WEAKNESSES
Advertising	Mass	Fees paid for space or time	• Efficient means for reaching large numbers of people	• High absolute costs • Difficult to receive good feedback
Personal selling	Customized	Fees paid to salespeople as either salaries or commissions	• Immediate feedback • Very persuasive • Can select audience • Can give complex information	• Extremely expensive per exposure • Messages may differ between salespeople
Public relations	Mass	No direct payment to media	• Often most credible source in the consumer's mind	• Difficult to get media cooperation
Sales promotion	Mass	Wide range of fees paid, depending on promotion selected	• Effective at changing behavior in short run • Very flexible	• Easily abused • Can lead to promotion wars • Easily duplicated
Direct marketing	Customized	Cost of communication through mail, telephone, or computer	• Messages can be prepared quickly • Facilitates relationship with customer	• Declining customer response • Database management is expensive

FIGURE 15–2

The five elements of the promotional mix

an immediate feedback loop as does personal selling. So before the message is sent, marketing research plays a valuable role; for example, it determines that the target market will actually see the medium chosen, and that the message will be understood.

There are several advantages to a firm using advertising in its promotional mix. It can be attention-getting—as with the Diet Coke ad shown on the next page—and also can communicate specific product benefits to prospective buyers. By paying for the advertising space, a company can control *what* it wants to say and, to some extent, to *whom* the message is sent. Advertising also allows the company to decide *when* to send its message (which includes how often). The nonpersonal aspect of advertising also has its advantages. Once the message is created, the same message is sent to all receivers in a market segment. If the pictorial, text, and brand elements of an advertisement are properly pretested, an advertiser can ensure the ad's ability to capture consumers' attention[6] and trust that the same message will be decoded by all receivers in the market segment.

Advertising has some disadvantages. As shown in Figure 15–2 and discussed in depth in Chapter 16, the costs to produce and place a message are significant, and the lack of direct feedback makes it difficult to know how well the message was received.

Personal Selling

The second major promotional alternative is **personal selling**, defined as the two-way flow of communication between a buyer and seller, designed to influence a person's or group's purchase decision. Unlike advertising, personal selling is usually face-to-face communication between the sender and receiver. Why do companies use personal selling?

personal selling

Two-way flow of communication between a buyer and seller, often in a face-to-face encounter, designed to influence a person's or group's purchase decision

There are important advantages to personal selling, as summarized in Figure 15–2. A salesperson can control to *whom* the presentation is made, reducing the amount of *wasted coverage,* or communication with consumers who are not in the target audience. The personal component of selling has another advantage in that the seller can see or hear the potential buyer's reaction to the message. If the feedback is unfavorable, the salesperson can modify the message.

The flexibility of personal selling can also be a disadvantage. Different salespeople can change the message so that no consistent communication is given to all customers. The high cost of personal selling is probably its major disadvantage. On a cost-per-contact basis, it is generally the most expensive of the five promotional elements.

Public Relations

public relations

Form of communication management that seeks to influence the feelings, opinions, or beliefs held by customers, potential customers, stockholders, suppliers, employees, and others about a company and its products or services

publicity

Nonpersonal, indirectly paid presentation of an organization, good, or service

Public relations is a form of communication management that seeks to influence the feelings, opinions, or beliefs held by customers, prospective customers, stockholders, suppliers, employees, and other publics about a company and its products or services.[7] Many tools such as special events, lobbying efforts, annual reports, press conferences,[8] RSS feeds, and image management may be used by a public relations department, although publicity often plays the most important role. **Publicity** is a nonpersonal, indirectly paid presentation of an organization, good, or service. It can take the form of a news story, editorial, or product announcement. A difference between publicity and both advertising and personal selling is the "indirectly paid" dimension. With publicity a company does not pay for space in a mass medium (such as television or radio) but attempts to get the medium to run a favorable story on the company. In this sense, there is an indirect payment for publicity in that a company must support a public relations staff.

An advantage of publicity is credibility. When you read a favorable story about a company's product (such as a glowing restaurant review), there is a tendency to believe it. Travelers throughout the world have relied on Frommer's guides such as *Australia from $60 a Day*. These books outline out-of-the-way, inexpensive restaurants and hotels, giving invaluable publicity to these establishments. Such businesses do not (nor can they) buy a mention in the guide.

The disadvantage of publicity relates to the lack of the user's control over it. A company can invite media to cover an interesting event such as a store opening or a new product release, but there is no guarantee that a story will result, if it will be positive, or who will be in the audience. Social media, such as blogs, have grown dramatically and allow uncontrollable public discussions of almost any company activity. Many public relations departments now focus on facilitating and responding to

Advertising, public relations, and sales promotion are three elements of the promotional mix.

online discussions. McDonald's, for example, responds to comments about McDonald's products and promotions on the blog, *Open for Discussion.*[9] Generally, publicity is an important element of most promotional campaigns, although the lack of control means that it is rarely the primary element. Research related to the sequence of IMC elements, however, indicates that publicity followed by advertising with the same message increases the positive response to the message.[10]

Sales Promotion

sales promotion
A short-term offer designed to arouse interest in buying a good or service

A fourth promotional element is **sales promotion**, a short-term inducement of value offered to arouse interest in buying a good or service. Used in conjunction with advertising or personal selling, sales promotions are offered to intermediaries as well as to ultimate consumers. Coupons, rebates, samples, and contests such as Dairy Queen's "Freeze! Click! Win!" promotion are just a few examples of sales promotions discussed later in this chapter.[11]

The advantage of sales promotion is that the short-term nature of these programs (such as a coupon or sweepstakes with an expiration date) often stimulates sales for their duration. Offering value to the consumer in terms of a cents-off coupon or rebate may increase store traffic from consumers who are not store-loyal.[12]

Sales promotions cannot be the sole basis for a campaign because gains are often temporary and sales drop off when the deal ends.[13] Advertising support is needed to convert the customer who tried the product because of a sales promotion into a long-term buyer.[14] If sales promotions are conducted continuously, they lose their effectiveness. Customers begin to delay purchase until a coupon is offered, or they question the product's value. Some aspects of sales promotions also are regulated by the federal government. These issues are reviewed in detail in Chapter 16.

Direct Marketing

direct marketing
Promotional element that uses direct communication with consumers to generate a response in the form of an order, a request for further information, or a visit to a retail outlet

Another promotional alternative, **direct marketing**, uses direct communication with consumers to generate a response in the form of an order, a request for further information, or a visit to a retail outlet.[15] The communication can take many forms including face-to-face selling, direct mail, catalogs, telephone solicitations, direct response advertising (on television and radio and in print), and online marketing. Like personal selling, direct marketing often consists of interactive communication. It also has the advantage of being customized to match the needs of specific target markets. Messages can be developed and adapted quickly to facilitate one-to-one relationships with customers.

While direct marketing has been one of the fastest-growing forms of promotion, it has several disadvantages. First, most forms of direct marketing require a comprehensive and up-to-date database with information about the target market. Developing and maintaining the database can be expensive and time consuming. In addition, growing concern about privacy has led to a decline in response rates among some customer groups. Companies with successful direct marketing programs are sensitive to these issues and often use a combination of direct marketing alternatives together, or direct marketing combined with other promotional tools, to increase value for customers.

learning review

4. Explain the difference between advertising and publicity when both appear on television.

5. Which promotional element should be offered only on a short-term basis?

6. Cost per contact is high with the _____ element of the promotional mix.

INTEGRATED MARKETING COMMUNICATIONS— DEVELOPING THE PROMOTIONAL MIX

A firm's promotional mix is the combination of one or more of the promotional tools it chooses to use. In putting together the promotional mix, a marketer must consider two issues. First, the balance of the elements must be determined. Should advertising be emphasized more than personal selling? Should a promotional rebate be offered? Would public relations activities be effective? Several factors affect such decisions: the target audience for the promotion,[16] the stage of the product's life cycle, characteristics of the product, decision stage of the buyer, and even the channel of distribution. Second, because the various promotional elements are often the responsibility of different departments, coordinating a consistent promotional effort is necessary. A promotional planning process designed to ensure integrated marketing communications can facilitate this goal.

Publications such as *Restaurant News* reach business buyers.

The Target Audience

Promotional programs are directed to the ultimate consumer, to an intermediary (retailer, wholesaler, or industrial distributor), or to both. Promotional programs directed to buyers of consumer products often use mass media because the number of potential buyers is large. Personal selling is used at the place of purchase, generally the retail store. Direct marketing may be used to encourage first-time or repeat purchases. Combinations of many media alternatives are a necessity for some target audiences today. The Marketing Matters box describes how Generation Y consumers can be reached through mobile marketing programs.[17]

Advertising directed to business buyers is used selectively in trade publications, such as *Restaurant News* magazine for buyers of restaurant equipment and supplies. Because business buyers often have specialized needs or technical questions, personal selling is particularly important. The salesperson can provide information and the necessary support after sales.

Intermediaries are often the focus of promotional efforts. As with business buyers, personal selling is the major promotional ingredient. The salespeople assist intermediaries in making a profit by coordinating promotional campaigns sponsored by the manufacturer and by providing marketing advice and expertise. Intermediaries' questions often pertain to the allowed markup, merchandising support, and return policies.

The Product Life Cycle

LO3

All products have a product life cycle (see Chapter 11), and the composition of the promotional mix changes over the four life-cycle stages:

- *Introduction stage.* Informing consumers in an effort to increase their level of awareness is the primary promotional objective in the introduction stage of the product life cycle. In general, all the promotional mix elements are used at this time.
- *Growth stage.* The primary promotional objective of the growth stage is to persuade the consumer to buy the product. Advertising is used to communicate brand differences, and personal selling is used to solidify the channel of distribution.
- *Maturity stage.* In the maturity stage the need is to maintain existing buyers. Advertising's role is to remind buyers of the product's existence. Sales promotion, in the form of discounts, coupons, and events, is important in maintaining loyal buyers.

- *Decline stage.* The decline stage of the product life cycle is usually a period of phase-out for the product, and little money is spent in the promotional mix.

Figure 15–3 shows how the promotional mix for Purina Dog Chow might change through the product life cycle.

FIGURE 15–3

Promotional tools used over the product life cycle of Purina Dog Chow

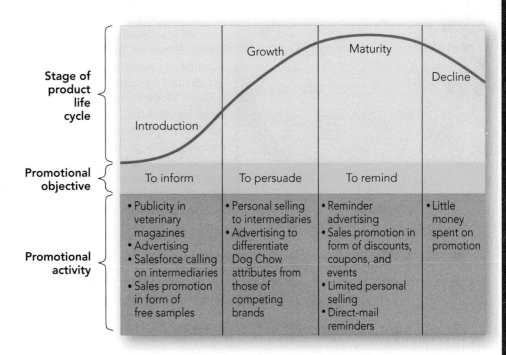

Stage of product life cycle	Introduction	Growth	Maturity	Decline
Promotional objective	To inform	To persuade	To remind	
Promotional activity	• Publicity in veterinary magazines • Advertising • Salesforce calling on intermediaries • Sales promotion in form of free samples	• Personal selling to intermediaries • Advertising to differentiate Dog Chow attributes from those of competing brands	• Reminder advertising • Sales promotion in form of discounts, coupons, and events • Limited personal selling • Direct-mail reminders	• Little money spent on promotion

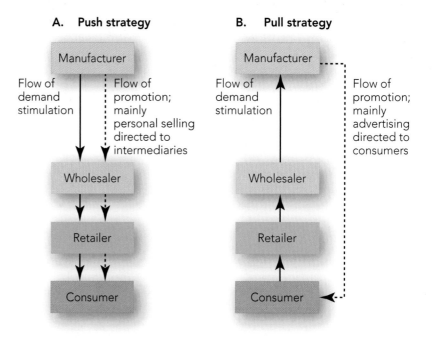

FIGURE 15–4

A comparison of push and pull promotional strategies

A. Push strategy

Manufacturer

Flow of demand stimulation

Flow of promotion; mainly personal selling directed to intermediaries

Wholesaler

Retailer

Consumer

B. Pull strategy

Manufacturer

Flow of demand stimulation

Flow of promotion; mainly advertising directed to consumers

Wholesaler

Retailer

Consumer

Channel Strategies

Chapter 13 discussed the channel flow from a producer to intermediaries to consumers. Achieving control of the channel is often difficult for the manufacturer, and promotional strategies can assist in moving a product through the channel of distribution. This is where a manufacturer has to make an important decision about whether to use a push strategy, pull strategy, or both in its channel of distribution.[18]

Push Strategy   Figure 15–4A shows how a manufacturer uses a **push strategy**, directing the promotional mix to channel members to gain their cooperation in ordering and stocking the product. In this approach, personal selling and sales promotions play major roles. Salespeople call on wholesalers to encourage orders and provide sales assistance. Sales promotions, such as case discount allowances (20 percent off the regular case price), are offered to stimulate demand. By pushing the product through the channel, the goal is to get channel members to push it to their customers.

Ford Motor Company, for example, provides support and incentives for its 4,200 Ford and Lincoln-Mercury dealers. Through a multi-level program, Ford provides incentives to reward dealers for meeting sales goals. Dealers receive an incentive when they are near a goal, another when they reach a goal, and a larger incentive if they exceed sales projections. Ford also offers some dealers special incentives for maintaining superior facilities or improving customer service. All of these actions are intended to encourage Fords dealers to "push" the Ford products through the channel to consumers.[19]

Pull Strategy   In some instances, manufacturers face resistance from channel members who do not want to order a new product or increase inventory levels of an existing brand. As shown in Figure 15–4B, a manufacturer may then elect to implement a

pull strategy

Directing the promotional mix at ultimate consumers to encourage them to ask the retailer for the product

pull strategy by directing its promotional mix at ultimate consumers to encourage them to ask the retailer for a product. Seeing demand from ultimate consumers, retailers order the product from wholesalers and thus the item is pulled through the intermediaries. Pharmaceutical companies, for example, now spend more than $4 billion annually on *direct-to-consumer* prescription drug advertising, to complement traditional personal selling and free samples directed only at doctors.[20] The strategy is designed to encourage consumers to ask their doctor for a specific drug by name—pulling it through the channel. Successful campaigns such as the print ad on the opposite page, which says "Ask your doctor about new Juvéderm," can have dramatic effects on the sales of a product.

---

learning review

7. Promotional programs can be directed to _____, to _____, or to both.

8. Describe the promotional objective for each stage of the product life cycle.

9. Explain the differences between a push strategy and a pull strategy.

DEVELOPING AN IMC PROGRAM

Because media costs are high, promotion decisions must be made carefully, using a systematic approach. Paralleling the planning, implementation, and evaluation steps described in the strategic marketing process (Chapter 2), the promotion decision process is divided into (1) developing, (2) executing, and (3) assessing the promotion program (Figure 15–5).

Identifying the Target Audience

The first decision in developing the promotion program is identifying the *target audience,* the group of prospective buyers toward which a promotion program is directed. To the extent that time and money permit, the target audience for the promotion program is the target market for the firm's product, which is identified from marketing

FIGURE 15–5

The promotion decision process includes planning, implementation, and evaluation.

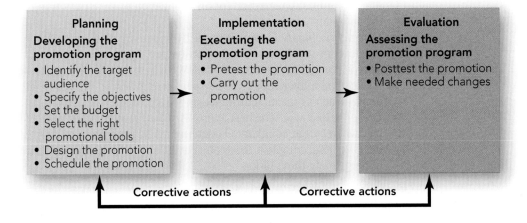

research and market segmentation studies. The more a firm knows about its target audiences—including their lifestyle, attitudes, and values—the easier it is to develop a promotion program. If a firm wanted to reach you with television and magazine ads, for example, it would need to know what TV shows you watch and what magazines you read.

Specifying Promotion Objectives

hierarchy of effects
Sequence of stages a prospective buyer goes through: awareness, interest, evaluation, trial, and adoption

After the target audience is identified, a decision must be reached on what the promotion should accomplish. Consumers can be said to respond in terms of a **hierarchy of effects**, which is the sequence of stages a prospective buyer goes through from initial awareness of a product to eventual action (either trial or adoption of the product).[21] The five stages are:

- *Awareness*—the consumer's ability to recognize and remember the product or brand name.
- *Interest*—an increase in the consumer's desire to learn about some of the features of the product or brand.
- *Evaluation*—the consumer's appraisal of the product or brand on important attributes.
- *Trial*—the consumer's actual first purchase and use of the product or brand.
- *Adoption*—through a favorable experience on the first trial, the consumer's repeated purchase and use of the product or brand.

For a totally new product, the sequence applies to the entire product category, but for a new brand competing in an established product category it applies to the brand itself. These steps can serve as guidelines for developing promotion objectives.

Setting the Promotion Budget

After setting the promotion objectives, a company must decide how much to spend. The promotion expenditures needed to reach U.S. households are enormous. Four companies—Procter & Gamble, AT&T, General Motors, and Time Warner—each spend a total of more than $3 billion annually on promotion.[22] Determining the ideal amount for the budget is difficult because there is no precise way to measure the exact results of spending promotion dollars. However, several methods can be used to set the promotion budget:[23]

- *Percentage of sales.* In the percentage of sales budgeting approach, the amount of money spent on promotion is a percentage of past or anticipated sales. A common budgeting method,[24] this approach is often stated in terms such as "our promotion budget for this year is 3 percent of last year's gross sales." See the Using Marketing Dashboards box for an application of the promotion-to-sales ratio to the automotive industry.
- *Competitive parity.* Competitive parity budgeting matches the competitor's absolute level of spending or the proportion per point of market share.[25]
- *All you can afford.* Common to many businesses, the all-you-can-afford budgeting method allows money to be spent on promotion only after all other budget items—such as manufacturing costs—are covered.
- *Objective and task.* The best approach to budgeting is objective and task budgeting, whereby the company (1) determines its promotion objectives, (2) outlines the tasks to accomplish these objectives, and (3) determines the promotion cost of performing these tasks.[26]

Of the various methods, only the objective and task method takes into account what the company wants to accomplish and requires that the objectives be specified.[27]

Using Marketing Dashboards

How Much Should You Spend on IMC?

Integrated marketing communications programs coordinate a variety of promotion alternatives to provide a consistent message across audiences. The amount spent on the various promotional elements, or on the total campaign, may vary depending on the target audience, the type of product, where the product is in the product life cycle, and the channel strategy selected. Managers often use the promotion-to-sales ratio on their marketing dashboard to assess how effective the IMC program expenditures are at generating sales.

Your Challenge As a manager at General Motors you've been asked to assess the effectiveness of all promotion expenditures during the past year. The promotion-to-sales ratio can be used by managers to make year-to-year comparisons of their programs, to compare the effectiveness of their program with competitor's programs, or to make comparisons with industry averages. You decide to calculate the promotion-to-sales ratio for General Motors. In addition, to allow a comparison, you decide to make the same calculation for one of your competitors, Ford, and for the entire automobile industry. The ratio is calculated as follows:

Promotion-to-sales ratio =
Total promotion expenditures/Total sales

Your Findings The information needed for these calculations is readily available from trade publications and annual reports. The following graph shows the promotion-to-sales

ratio for General Motors and Ford and the automotive industry. General Motors spent $3.296 billion on its IMC program to generate $129 billion in U.S. sales for a ratio of 2.6 (percent). Ford's ratio was 3.2, and the industry average was 2.7.

Your Action General Motor's promotion-to-sales ratio is substantially lower than Ford's and slightly lower than the industry average. This suggests that the current mix of promotional activities and the level of expenditures are both creating an effective IMC program. In the future you will want to monitor the factors that may influence the ratio. The average ratio for the beverage industry has risen to 9 while the average for grocery stores is about 1.

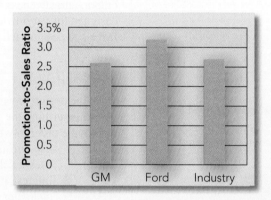

Selecting the Right Promotional Tools

Once a budget has been determined, the combination of the five basic IMC tools—advertising, personal selling, sales promotion, public relations, and direct marketing—

The Olympics use a comprehensive IMC program.

can be specified. While many factors provide direction for selection of the appropriate mix, the large number of possible combinations of the promotional tools means that many combinations can achieve the same objective. Therefore, an analytical approach and experience are particularly important in this step of the promotion decision process. The specific mix can vary from a simple program using a single tool to a comprehensive program using all forms of promotion. The Olympics have become a very visible example of a comprehensive integrated communication program. Because the Games are repeated every two years, the promotion is almost continuous. Included in the program are advertising campaigns, personal selling efforts by the Olympic committee and organizers, sales promotion activities such as product tie-ins and sponsorships, public relations programs managed by the host cities, and direct marketing efforts targeted at a variety of audiences including governments, organizations, firms, athletes, and individuals.[28] At this stage, it is also important to assess the relative importance of the various tools. While it may be desirable to utilize and integrate several forms of promotion, one may deserve emphasis. The Olympics, for example, place exceptional importance on public relations and publicity.

Designing the Promotion

The central element of a promotion program is the promotion itself. Advertising consists of advertising copy and the artwork that the target audience is intended to see or hear. Personal selling efforts depend on the characteristics and skills of the salesperson. Sales promotion activities consist of the specific details of inducements such as coupons, samples, and sweepstakes. Public relations efforts are readily seen in tangible elements such as news releases, and direct marketing actions depend on written, verbal, and electronic forms of delivery. The design of the promotion will play a primary role in determining the message that is communicated to the audience. This design activity is frequently viewed as the step requiring the most creativity. In addition, successful designs are often the result of insight regarding consumer's interests and purchasing behavior. All of the promotion tools have many design alternatives. Advertising, for example, can utilize fear, humor, attractiveness, or other themes in its appeal.[29] Similarly, direct marketing can be designed for varying levels of personal or customized appeals. One of the challenges of IMC is to design each promotional activity to communicate the same message.

Scheduling the Promotion

Videogames based on movies are often part of a movie promotion program.

Once the design of each of the promotional program elements is complete, it is important to determine the most effective timing of their use. The promotion schedule describes the order in which each promotional tool is introduced and the frequency of its use during the campaign. Movie studio Paramount Pictures, for example, uses a schedule of several promotional tools for its movies. To generate interest in *Iron Man,* an official movie website offered movie clips and character information, and a movie "trailer" was shown on television and in theaters before the movie was released. Paramount's partner, Marvel Comics, offered *Iron Man* digital wallpaper and other fan art. In addition, videogames based on the movie characters were produced and released with the movie. Then movie-related products such as Slurpee beverage cups available at 7-Eleven convenience stores and action figures available in Burger King Kids Meals were offered. After the movie was released, an online contest encouraged fans to enter to win a limited edition LG phone that was used in the movie, and Audi promoted the Audi R8 sports car driven in the movie.[30]

Overall, the scheduling of the various promotions was designed to generate interest, bring consumers into theaters, and then encourage additional purchases after seeing the movie. Several factors such as seasonality and competitive promotion activity can also influence the promotion schedule. Businesses such as ski resorts, airlines, and professional sports teams are likely to reduce their promotional activity during the "off" season. Similarly, restaurants, retail stores, and health clubs are likely to increase their promotional activity when new competitors enter the market.

EXECUTING AND ASSESSING THE PROMOTION PROGRAM

As shown earlier in Figure 15–5, the ideal execution of a promotion program involves pretesting each design before it is actually used to allow for changes and modifications that improve its effectiveness. Similarly, posttests are recommended to evaluate the impact of each promotion and the contribution of the promotion toward achieving the program objectives. The most sophisticated pretest and posttest procedures have been developed for advertising and are discussed in Chapter 16. Testing procedures for sales promotion and direct marketing efforts currently focus on comparisons of different designs or responses of different segments. To fully benefit from IMC programs, companies must create and maintain a test-result database that allows comparisons of the relative impact of the promotional tools and their execution options in varying situations. Information from the database will allow informed design and execution decisions and provide support for IMC activities during internal reviews by financial or administrative personnel. The San Diego Padres baseball team, for example, developed a database of information relating attendance to its integrated campaign using a new logo, special events, merchandise sales, and a loyalty program.

Carrying out the promotion program can be expensive and time consuming. One researcher estimates that "an organization with sales less than $10 million can successfully implement an IMC program in one year, one with sales between $200 million and $500 million will need about three years, and one with sales between $2 billion and $5 billion will need five years." In addition, firms with a market orientation are more likely to implement an IMC program.[31] To facilitate the transition, there are approximately 200 integrated marketing communications agencies in operation. In addition, some of the largest agencies are adopting approaches that embrace "total communications solutions." Starcom USA, which recently won *Advertising Age* magazine's Media Agency of the Year award, for example, is part of an integrated network of 5,800 global media professionals in 110 offices in 67 countries. The agency's services include media management, direct response media planning, Internet and digital communications, sports sponsorships, gaming, and multicultural, entertainment, and event marketing. One of its integrated campaigns for Allstate Insurance Company created a partnership with Discovery Channel's *It Takes a Thief* series, and utilized sweepstakes, a website, and print advertising, in addition to its traditional personal selling by Allstate agents. While many agencies still have departments dedicated to promotion, direct marketing, and other specialties, the trend today is clearly toward a long-term perspective in which all forms of promotion are integrated.[32]

An important factor in developing successful IMC programs is to create a process that facilitates their design and use. A tool used to evaluate a company's current process is the IMC audit. The audit analyzes the internal communication network of the company; identifies key audiences; evaluates customer databases; assesses messages in recent advertising, public relations releases, packaging, websites, and e-mail communication, signage, sales promotions, and direct mail; and determines the IMC expertise of company and agency personnel.[33] This process is becoming increasingly important as consumer-generated media such as blogs, RSS, podcasts, and social networks become more popular. Now, in addition to ensuring that traditional forms of communication are integrated, companies must be able to monitor consumer content, respond to inconsistent messages, and even answer questions from individual customers.[34]

learning review

10. What are the stages of the hierarchy of effects?

11. What are four approaches to setting the promotion budget?

12. How have advertising agencies changed to facilitate the use of IMC programs?

DIRECT MARKETING

LO5

Direct marketing has many forms and utilizes a variety of media. Several forms of direct marketing—direct mail and catalogs, television, telemarketing, and direct selling—were discussed as methods of nonstore retailing in Chapter 14. In addition, although advertising is discussed in Chapter 16, a form of advertising—direct response advertising—is an important form of direct marketing. Finally, interactive or online marketing is discussed in detail in Chapter 18. In this section, the growth of direct marketing, its value for consumers and sellers, and key global, technological, and ethical issues are discussed.

The Growth of Direct Marketing

The increasing interest in customer relationship management is reflected in the dramatic growth of direct marketing. The ability to customize communication efforts and create one-to-one interactions is appealing to most marketers, particularly those with IMC programs. While many direct marketing methods are not new, the ability to design and use them has increased with the availability of customer information databases and new printing technologies. In recent years, direct marketing growth has outpaced total economic growth. Direct marketing expenditures of $166 billion are expected to grow at a rate of 6 percent. Similarly, 2007 revenues of $2.06 trillion are expected to grow to $2.63 trillion by 2011. The percentage of total U.S. revenues that are the result of direct marketing is currently 7 percent and growing! Direct mail is the most popular form of direct marketing. It is used by 69 percent of marketers and generates a 2.18 percent response rate.[35] Another component of the growth in direct marketing is the increasing popularity of the newest direct marketing channel—the Internet. Total online sales have risen from close to nothing in 1996 to projections of $340 billion in 2011. Continued growth in the number of consumers with Internet access and the number of businesses with websites and electronic commerce offerings is likely to contribute to the future growth of direct marketing.

The Value of Direct Marketing

One of the most visible indicators of the value of direct marketing for consumers is the level of use of various forms of direct marketing. For example, 43 percent of the U.S. population has ordered merchandise or services by mail, phone, or Internet; more than 12 million adults have purchased items from a television offer; the average adult spends more than 30 hours per year accessing online services; and more than 21 percent of all adults make three to five purchases from a catalog each year. Consumers report many benefits, including the following: They don't have to go to a store, they can usually shop 24 hours a day, buying direct saves time, they avoid hassles with salespeople, they can save money, it's fun and entertaining, and direct marketing offers more privacy than in-store shopping. Many consumers also believe that direct marketing provides excellent customer service. Toll-free telephone numbers, customer service representatives with access to information regarding purchasing preferences, overnight delivery services, and unconditional guarantees all help create value for direct marketing customers. At Landsend.com, when customers need assistance they can click the "Lands' End Live" icon to receive help from a sales representative on the phone or online until the correct product is found. "It's like we were walking down the aisle in a store," says one Lands' End customer![36]

The value of direct marketing for sellers can be described in terms of the responses it generates.[37] **Direct orders** are the result of offers that contain all the information necessary for a prospective buyer to make a decision to purchase and complete the

direct orders
The result of direct marketing offers that contain all the information necessary for a potential buyer to make a decision to purchase and complete the transaction

Four Seasons uses direct mail to generate leads for its private residences.

transaction. Priceline.com, for example, will send *PriceBreaker* e-mail alerts to people in its database. The messages offer discounted fares and rates to customers who can travel on very short notice. **Lead generation** is the result of an offer designed to generate interest in a product or service and a request for additional information. Four Seasons Hotels now sell private residences in several of their properties and send direct mail to prospective residents asking them to request additional information on the telephone or through a website. Finally, **traffic generation** is the outcome of an offer designed to motivate people to visit a business. General Motors recently mailed a sweepstakes to 5 million prospective car buyers inviting them to match a number on the mailing with a number on display in the dealer showrooms for a chance to win a new car. Nearly 400,000 customers visited GM dealers, and 40,000 of those purchased new cars![38]

Technological, Global, and Ethical Issues in Direct Marketing

The information technology and databases described in Chapter 8 are key elements in any direct marketing program. Databases are the result of organizations' efforts to collect demographic, media, and consumption profiles of customers so that direct marketing tools, such as catalogs, can be directed at specific customers. For example, Lillian Vernon started her very successful mail-order company four decades ago at her kitchen table by putting all her merchandise in a single catalog: Laundry baskets and men's slippers on one page might be followed by toys on the next. But in the last few years Lillian Vernon has shifted to a database approach with the 150 million catalogs mailed annually. There are now home-oriented, children's, and Christmas-ornament catalogs targeted at customers who have purchased these kinds of merchandise from the main catalog in the past.[39]

Direct marketing faces several challenges and opportunities in global markets today. Several countries such as Italy and Denmark, for example, have requirements for mandatory "opt-in"—that is, potential customers must give permission to include their name on a list for direct marketing solicitations. In addition, the availability of international mailing lists has declined because publications such as *Forbes* Global Edition and *BusinessWeek* European Edition have been discontinued. Replacing postal lists with e-mail lists is a potential solution although obtaining e-mail addresses is difficult also. In other countries, the mail, telephone, and Internet systems are not as well developed as they are in the United States. The need for improved reliability and security of the postal system in South Africa, for example, has slowed the growth of direct mail, while the dramatic growth of mobile phone penetration has created an opportunity for direct mobile marketing campaigns. Another issue for global direct marketers is payment. The availability of credit and credit cards varies throughout the world, creating the need for alternatives such as C.O.D., bank deposits, and online payment accounts.[40]

Global and domestic direct marketers both face challenging ethical issues today. Considerable attention has been given to some annoying direct marketing activities such as telephone solicitations during dinner and evening hours. Concerns about privacy, however, have led to various attempts to provide guidelines that balance consumer and business interests. The European Union passed a consumer privacy law, called the Data Protection Directive, after several years of discussion with the Federation of European Direct Marketing and the U.K.'s Direct Marketing Association. In the United States, the Federal Trade Commission and many state legislatures have also been concerned about privacy. Several bills that call for a do-not-mail registry similar to the do-not-call registry are being discussed.[41] Another issue, the proliferation of e-mail advertising, has received increasing attention from consumers and marketers recently. The Making Responsible Decisions box on the next page offers some details of the debate.[42]

Making Responsible Decisions > > > > > > > > > > ethics

Is Spam Out of Control?

More than 1 billion e-mail messages are sent each day in the United States. Experts estimate that about three-fourths of them are direct marketing messages—personalized offers from companies such as Pepsi, Victoria's Secret, Toyota, and the Phoenix Suns. In fact, e-mail advertisers spend more than $2 billion on their campaigns each year. One reason is that e-mail offers one-to-one conversations with each prospective consumer. Another reason is that the average cost per e-mail message is less than $0.01 compared to $0.75 to $2.00 for direct mail and $1 to $3 for telemarketing.

Some consumers have complained that they are inundated with unsolicited messages, sometimes called "spam," and ignore them, while marketers believe that better management of e-mail campaigns will improve the value of e-mail advertising for customers. Two general approaches to man-aging e-mail are being discussed. The "opt-out" system allows recipients to decline future messages after the first contact. The "opt-in" system requires advertisers to obtain e-mail addresses from registration questions on websites, business-reply cards, and even entry forms for contests or sweepstakes. Surveys indicate that about 77 percent of the unsolicited e-mails are deleted without being read, while only 2 percent of the e-mails received with the consumer's permission are deleted.

In the United States, the *Controlling the Assault of Non-Solicited Pornography and Marketing Act* (CAN-SPAM) requires e-mail be truthful and to provide an opt-out return e-mail address. In Japan, new regulations that require opt-in procedures are being discussed. What is your opinion? Why?

---

learning review

13. The ability to design and use direct marketing programs has increased with the availability of _____ and _____.

14. What are the three types of responses generated by direct marketing activities?

LEARNING OBJECTIVES REVIEW

LO1 *Discuss integrated marketing communication and the communication process.*

Integrated marketing communication is the concept of designing marketing communications programs that coordinate all promotional activities—advertising, personal selling, sales promotion, public relations, and direct marketing—to provide a consistent message across all audiences. The communication process conveys messages with six elements: a source, a message, a channel of communication, a receiver, and encoding and decoding. The communication process also includes a feedback loop and can be distorted by noise.

LO2 *Describe the promotional mix and the uniqueness of each component.*

There are five promotional alternatives. Advertising, sales promotion, and public relations are mass selling approaches, whereas personal selling and direct marketing use customized messages. Advertising can have high absolute costs but reaches large numbers of people. Personal selling has a high cost per contact but provides immediate feedback. Public relations is often difficult to obtain but is very credible. Sales promotion influences short-term consumer behavior. Direct marketing can help develop customer relationships although maintaining a database can be very expensive.

LO3 *Select the promotional approach appropriate to a product's target audience and life-cycle stage, as well as channel strategies.*

The promotional mix depends on the target audience. Programs for consumers, business buyers, and intermediaries might emphasize advertising, personal selling, and sales promotion, respectively. The promotional mix also changes over the product life-cycle stages. During the introduction stage, all promotional mix elements are used. During the growth stage advertising is emphasized, while the maturity stage utilizes sales promotion and direct marketing. Little promotion is used during the decline stage. Finally, the promotional mix can depend on the channel strategy. Push strategies require personal selling and sales promotions directed at channel members, while pull strategies depend on advertising and sales promotion directed at consumers.

LO4 *Describe the elements of the promotion decision process.* The promotional decision process consists of three steps: planning, implementation, and evaluation. The planning step consists of six elements: identify the target audience, specify the objectives, set the budget, select the right promotional elements, design the promotion, and schedule the promotion. The implementation step includes pretesting. The evaluation step includes posttesting.

LO5 *Explain the value of direct marketing for consumers and sellers.* The value of direct marketing for consumers is indicated by its level of use. For example, 43 percent of them have made a purchase by phone, mail, or Internet, and 12 million people have purchased items from a television offer. The value of direct marketing for sellers can be measured in terms of three types of responses: direct orders, lead generation, and traffic generation.

FOCUSING ON KEY TERMS

advertising p. 338
communication p. 336
direct marketing p. 341
direct orders p. 350
hierarchy of effects p. 346
integrated marketing communications
(IMC) p. 336

lead generation p. 351
personal selling p. 339
promotional mix p. 336
public relations p. 340
publicity p. 340

pull strategy p. 344
push strategy p. 345
sales promotion p. 341
traffic generation p. 351

APPLYING MARKETING KNOWLEDGE

1 After listening to a recent sales presentation, Mary Smith signed up for membership at the local health club. On arriving at the facility, she learned there was an additional fee for racquetball court rentals. "I don't remember that in the sales talk; I thought they said all facilities were included with the membership fee," complained Mary. Describe the problem in terms of the communication process.

2 Develop a matrix to compare the five elements of the promotional mix on three criteria—to *whom* you deliver the message, *what* you say, and *when* you say it.

3 Explain how the promotional tools used by an airline would differ if the target audience were (*a*) consumers who travel for pleasure and (*b*) corporate travel departments that select the airlines to be used by company employees.

4 Suppose you introduced a new consumer food product and invested heavily both in national advertising (pull strategy) and in training and motivating your field salesforce to sell the product to food stores (push strategy). What kinds of feedback would you receive from both the advertising and your salesforce? How could you increase both the quality and quantity of each?

5 Fisher-Price Company, long known as a manufacturer of children's toys, has introduced a line of clothing for children. Outline a promotional plan to get this product introduced in the marketplace.

6 Many insurance companies sell health insurance plans to companies. In these companies the employees pick the plan, but the set of offered plans is determined by the company. Recently Blue Cross–Blue Shield, a health insurance company, ran a television ad stating, "If your employer doesn't offer you Blue Cross–Blue Shield coverage, ask why." Explain the promotional strategy behind the advertisement.

7 Identify the sales promotion tools that might be useful for (*a*) Tastee Yogurt, a new brand introduction, (*b*) 3M self-sticking Post-it Notes, and (*c*) Wrigley's Spearmint Gum.

8 Design an integrated marketing communications program—using each of the five promotional elements—for Rhapsody, the online music service.

9 BMW introduced its first sport utility vehicle, the X5, to compete with other popular all-wheel-drive vehicles such as the Mercedes-Benz M-class and Jeep Grand Cherokee. Design a direct marketing program to generate (*a*) leads, (*b*) traffic in dealerships, and (*c*) direct orders.

10 Develop a privacy policy for database managers that provides a balance of consumer and seller perspectives. How would you encourage voluntary compliance with your policy? What methods of enforcement would you recommend?

To develop the promotion strategy for your marketing plan, follow the steps suggested in the planning phase of the promotion decision process described in Figure 15–5.

1 You should (*a*) identify the target audience, (*b*) specify the promotion objectives, (*c*) set the promotion budget, (*d*) select the right promotion tools, (*e*) design the promotion, and (*f*) schedule the promotion.

2 Also specify the pretesting and posttesting procedures needed in the implementation and control phases.

3 Finally, describe how each of your promotion tools are integrated to provide a consistent message.

video case 15   Las Vegas: Creating a Brand with IMC

"We made a decision collectively with the agency that we needed to go into the branding of Las Vegas," observes Rossi Ralenkotter, president and CEO of the Las Vegas Convention and Visitors Authority (LVCVA). The mission of LVCVA is to attract visitors to Las Vegas through its many promotional activities. Although Las Vegas has grown from its early days as a destination for southern California residents, branding provides an opportunity for additional growth. Now the LVCVA is undertaking the challenge of creating a campaign that utilizes all of its resources and delivers a consistent message. As Ralenkotter explained, "We need to have a fully integrated program."

A HISTORY OF LAS VEGAS

The first settlers to the area that is now Las Vegas arrived in 1855. The population grew and the city of Las Vegas was incorporated in 1911. To encourage tourism, gaming was legalized in 1931, and one of the first hotels, the Flamingo, opened in 1946. Other hotels soon followed, including the Sahara, the Sands, the New Frontier, the Royal Nevada, The Showboat, The Riviera, The Fremont, Binion's Horseshoe, and The Tropicana. Although gaming was the primary attraction, entertainment by the biggest stars of films and music like Elvis Presley, Frank Sinatra, Dean Martin, Abbott and Costello, Bing Crosby, and Carol Channing also became popular. By 1975 Nevada gaming revenues were $1 billion and growing.

Las Vegas entered a new era with the construction of large resort hotels. Each development became larger or more expensive than its predecessors, including the 3,000-room Mirage in 1989, the 5,000-room MGM Grand in 1993, the $1.7 billion Bellagio in 1998, and megaresort Wynn Las Vegas in 2005. The hotels developed elaborate casinos and competed for visitors with performances by entertainers. Wayne Newton, for example, eventually gave more than 25,000 Las Vegas performances and Sigfried and Roy gave 15,000. New forms of entertainment such as *Star Trek: The Experience* and *Cirque du Soleil* became popular. In an effort to become a place with more than gaming and live performances, Las Vegas built theme parks, roller coasters, and childrens' activities to position itself as a family-friendly destination. Generally, these marketing efforts were not successful and Las Vegas Convention and Visitors Authority decided to consider other approaches to attracting visitors.

In short order, the MGM Grand replaced its amusement park with night clubs, the Hard Rock Hotel began offering blackjack in its pools, and Treasure Island replaced its child-themed pirate show with a version targeted at adults. Dining experiences changed as "celebrity" chefs such as Emeril Lagasse, Charlie Palmer, and Wolfgang Puck opened sophisticated restaurants. Hotels added extravagant spas and designer shops, and there is also the Guggenheim Hermitage Museum and a gallery of works from the Boston Museum of Fine Arts. Finally, traditional events such as automobile racing at the Las Vegas Motor Speedway, national events such as the NBA All-Star game, and relatively new events such as the Ultimate Fighting Championship became popular attractions. All of the activities proved to be incredibly popular. In fact, while gaming revenue reached $7 billion, shows, hotels, restaurants, clubs and shops generated another $23 billion!

THE LAS VEGAS CONVENTION AND VISITORS AUTHORITY

The Las Vegas Convention and Visitors Authority was created by the Nevada State Legislature to manage the cyclical nature of tourism. Officials noticed that the number of visitors to Las Vegas declined during weekdays, summer months, and holiday seasons. The marketing division of the LVCVA became responsible for increasing leisure travel visits, and convention and meeting attendance. The marketing division created three departments to be responsible for advertising, sports and sponsorships, and Internet marketing. The advertising department uses a variety of media to reach potential visitors. The sports and sponsorship department helps create the Las Vegas brand by communicating messages about local events to millions of participants and fans. The Internet marketing department is responsible for ensuring relevant and timely Web content, responding to website inquiries, and monitoring the performance of Web promotions. The marketing division serves as a liaison with the LVCVA's advertising and promotion agency. It also facilitates the correct and timely use of strategy and content in all promotional campaigns and branding efforts.

Ralenkotter asked advertising and promotion agency R&R Partners to identify a new campaign for Las Vegas. The agency had a philosophy of using marketing research to develop a deep understanding of customers, and of using innovative thinking to create effective solutions to marketing challenges. R&R Partners also believed that it was important to manage a consistent brand message across all audiences and all media. After their initial research, they initiated a discussion with the LVCVA to begin a shift from product advertising which emphasized specific features of the city and its hotels to a brand campaign that emphasized the emotions that visitors experience when they are in Las Vegas. Over time an idea emerged. "The idea 'What Happens Here, Stays Here' was two or three or four years in the making," explains Randy Snow, executive vice president and creative director at R&R Partners. He added, "We conducted a year-long account planning exercise and discovered the emotional connection between Las Vegas and its customers." Ralenkotter agreed to the concept and authorized a $58 million, 20-month integrated marketing communications campaign.

THE LAS VEGAS IMC CAMPAIGN

The emotional element that the research had uncovered was the idea that people often feel free to do or see things in Las Vegas that they might not do or see anywhere else. R&R Partners continued to conduct research and many of the ideas for the campaign came from actual visitors. The agency was careful to include men and women, business and leisure travelers, and visitors from different parts of the United States. Additional findings from the research made it clear that the campaign would need to be fully integrated to include advertising, public relations, personal selling, and promotional efforts. First, the diversity of the visitors to Las Vegas meant that they used many different types of media in their travel decisions. Second, several of the segments that visited Las Vegas were "multitaskers" and used multiple sources of information at the same time. The agency also knew that an integrated marketing communication campaign would multiply the effectiveness of its budget.

Advertising

The initial "Vegas Stories" campaign ran television ads that told stories about enticing experiences a visitor might have in Las Vegas and concluded with "What Happens Here, Stays Here." Print ads with the same message also began running in magazines. The slogan became an instant hit, and soon became a pop-culture catchphrase. For example, flight attendants were heard welcoming airline travelers to Las Vegas and then saying "And remember folks, what happens here, stays here." Similarly, the tagline was used on Jay Leno's *Tonight Show*, newscasts, talk shows, and TV sitcoms. Billy Crystal even closed the Academy Awards by saying, "And remember. What happens at the Oscars, stays at the Oscars." By the end of the year the campaign was ranked as one of the top 10 most likeable campaigns according to *USA Today*'s Ad Tracker.

Public Relations and Promotions

The public relations department was able to obtain coverage in newspapers and evening news programs when the NFL refused to run one of the new campaign ads during the Super Bowl. New television series programming such as *CSI* and *Las Vegas* became popular and added to the visibility of Las Vegas. Poker programs such as ESPN's *United States Poker Championship,* the Travel Channel's *World Poker Tour,* and Fox Sports Net's *Poker Superstars Invitational Tournament* made the gaming experience easily accessible. R&R Partners also worked with *Time* magazine on an article that became a cover story.

Other promotional elements also contributed to the success of the campaign. Sweepstakes offered the chance to win special experiences such as New Year's Eve in Las Vegas, and the LVCVA also facilitated sports sponsorships, including many golf tournaments.

Online

Another element of the integrated campaign included Web offerings. The LVCVA created a tourism website (www.visitlasvegas.com) with information about hotels and activities, and links to special offers. The website also integrated the new campaign by providing interactive links such as "Be Anyone in Las Vegas." The humorous link allows visitors to create an identity that includes a name (e.g., Vinny) and a profession (e.g., Double Agent) and "everything you need to back up your story, including a brief history, a printable business card, a prerecorded 1-800 number, and a website." Another link allows potential visitors to send personalized video e-mail messages to friends with the tagline, "What Happens Here, Stays Here." Banner ads and paid search engine advertising help generate more than 500,000 "hits" each month.

Personal Selling

In addition, a personal selling staff follows up on the awareness created by other elements of the campaign by calling on travel agents, corporate meeting planners, and trade show producers. Overall, each element of the campaign is designed to provide a message consistent with other elements.

FUTURE STRATEGY

How can the LVCVA and R&R Partners assess the success of their campaign? One important measure is the essence of the LVCVA mission—number of visitors. Other measures might include the revenue produced by visitors to Las Vegas, the amount of gaming revenue, the number of convention delegates, and the number of airline passengers arriving in Las Vegas. Table 1 shows information about each of these measures prior to the introduction of the campaign in 2003 (shown in black), and following the campaign (shown in pink). Each of the measures had a dramatic increase, suggesting that the campaign was a huge success!

So where does Ralenkotter go from here? A variation of the campaign will begin to focus on visitor stories that use Las Vegas experiences such as Broadway shows or extraordinary restaurants as an "alibi." Las Vegas is also likely to get bigger and better as new developments such as MGM Mirage's $7 billion Project CityCenter and Boyd Gaming's $4 billion Echelon Place are completed. Finally, Vegas is going global. American-run casinos such as the Mirage have announced plans to build casinos in China, and others are looking at Britain, Thailand, and even Singapore. The success of the campaign is likely to lead to other new ventures also. As Ralenkotter observes, "We are the talk of the travel industry!"

TABLE 1: LAS VEGAS VISITOR STATISTICS					
	Number of Visitors	Revenue from Visitors	Gaming Revenue from Visitors	Number of Convention Delegates	Number of Airline Passengers
2000	35,859,691	31,462,337,364	7,671,252,000	3,853,363	36,865,866
2001	35,017,317	31,907,491,818	7,636,547,000	5,014,240	35,179,960
2002	35,071,505	31,613,937,641	7,630,562,000	5,105,450	35,009,011
2003	35,540,126	32,777,906,318	7,830,856,000	5,657,796	36,265,932
2004	37,388,781	33,724,467,453	8,711,426,000	5,724,864	41,441,531
2005	38,566,717	36,733,452,851	9,717,322,000	6,166,194	44,267,370
2006	38,914,889	39,419,205,580	10,643,206,000	6,307,961	46,193,329

Questions

1 What information about consumers led the advertising agency to suggest a shift from product advertising to brand marketing? How are the two approaches different?

2 What characteristics of Las Vegas visitors suggested that an integrated marketing communications campaign would be necessary?

3 Which of the promotional elements described in Figure 15–2 were used by the Las Vegas Convention and Visitors Authority in the "What Happens Here, Stays Here" campaign? What measures indicate that the campaign was a success?

4 What are several new strategies Las Vegas might pursue as it continues its brand marketing activities? Will the program elements that worked in the U.S. also work in China and other countries?

16

Advertising, Sales Promotion, and Public Relations

LEARNING OBJECTIVES

After reading this chapter you should be able to:

LO1 Explain the differences between product advertising and institutional advertising and the variations within each type.

LO2 Describe the steps used to develop, execute, and evaluate an advertising program.

LO3 Explain the advantages and disadvantages of alternative advertising media.

LO4 Discuss the strengths and weaknesses of consumer-oriented and trade-oriented sales promotions.

LO5 Recognize public relations as an important form of communication.

ADVERTISERS HAVE ANOTHER LIFE ON SECOND LIFE!

Do you have a second life online? Do you have a Web ID? An avatar? If you do, you are one of many, and advertisers are eager to meet you in your virtual world.

The world of advertising has changed dramatically in just the past few years. First, there are many new forms of media, such as social networking sites, blogs, and podcasts, to compete with traditional media. Some experts have suggested that MySpace and YouTube may have been the most influential new media in decades. Second, consumers have changed their behavior to use more than one source of advertising at the same time. Gregg Hanno, a former magazine publisher, observed that watching TV, while listening to music, flipping through a magazine, and surfing the Internet is the new "normal." Finally, technology, such as digital video recorders and TiVo, that allows consumers to skip or "zap" commercials has put consumers in control.

So what is an advertiser to do? One answer has been to create a presence in a virtual world. Second Life is a game-like virtual world where users live as online versions of themselves while interacting with real-life brands. Wells Fargo was one of the first to use this media alternative when it launched a virtual environment called Stagecoach Island in Second Life to attract young, tech-savvy customers and teach them about banking. Since then many other companies such as Coca-Cola, Coldwell Banker, Adidas, and Reebok have created islands and stores on Second Life.

As advertisers and consumers have become more familiar with virtual worlds, many new approaches are being developed. Coca-Cola, for example, is also using a MySpace social-networking page, del.icio.us keyword tagging, a Flickr photo page, and a YouTube video clip. MTV was on Second Life but then decided to create its own online environments to accompany its TV series such as *Pimp My Ride*. Each site weaves the TV show story line into the digital world. Disney created its own Virtual Magic Kingdom that replicates Disney's amusement parks online. All of the options represent varying levels of security, customization, and control for the advertisers.

What's next? One possibility is adding more functionality to the interactivity of current sites. At Zwinky.com, for example, rapper 50 Cent created a fully functioning avatar that fans can customize and use as their own. Similarly, musician Avril Lavigne partnered with Stardoll, a site that creates virtual likenesses of celebrities, just before the release of a new album. Another site, Doppelganger, now hosts the Pussycat Dolls Music Lounge. Advertisers are also likely to try to improve traditional advertising. New research suggests that TiVo users are less likely to fast-forward through ads if they are very engaging and entertaining or if they ask for a direct response. To accommodate the fast pace and short attention of most consumers today, many advertisers are simply moving to shorter ads.[1]

Virtual advertising, and the use of new media, are just a few of the many exciting changes taking place in the field of advertising today. Chapter 15 described **advertising** as any paid form of nonpersonal communication about an organization, a good, a service, or an idea by an identified sponsor. This chapter describes three of the promotional mix elements—advertising, sales promotion, and public relations.

advertising
Any paid form of nonpersonal communication about an organization, good, service, or idea by an identified sponsor

TYPES OF ADVERTISEMENTS

As you look through any magazine, watch television, listen to the radio, or browse the Internet, the variety of advertisements you see or hear may give you the impression that they have few similarities. Advertisements are prepared for different purposes, but they basically consist of two types: product advertisements and institutional advertisements.

Product Advertisements

product advertisements
Advertisements that focus on selling a good or service; forms include pioneering (informational), competitive (persuasive), and reminder

Focused on selling a good or service, **product advertisements** take three forms: (1) pioneering (or informational), (2) competitive (or persuasive), and (3) reminder. Look at the ads for Verizon, Sony, and M&Ms to determine the type and objective of each ad.

Used in the introductory stage of the product life cycle, *pioneering* advertisements tell people what a product is, what it can do, and where it can be found. The key objective of a pioneering advertisement (such as the ad for Verizon's new BlackBerry World Edition) is to inform the target market. Informative ads have been found to be interesting, convincing, and effective.[2]

Advertising that promotes a specific brand's features and benefits is *competitive.* The objective of these messages is to persuade the target market to select the firm's brand rather than that of a competitor. An increasingly common form of competitive advertising is *comparative* advertising, which shows one brand's strengths relative to those of competitors.[3] The Sony ad, for example, highlights the competitive advantage of the Sony camera over its primary competitors Canon and Nikon. Studies indicate that comparative ads attract more attention and increase the perceived quality of the advertiser's brand.[4] Firms that use comparative advertising need market research to provide legal support for their claims.[5]

Advertisements serve varying purposes. Which ad would be considered a (1) pioneering, (2) competitive, and (3) reminder ad?

Reminder advertising is used to reinforce previous knowledge of a product. The M&Ms ad shown reminds consumers about a special event, in this case, Valentine's Day. Reminder advertising is good for products that have achieved a well-recognized position and are in the mature phase of their product life cycle. Another type of reminder ad, *reinforcement,* is used to assure current users they made the right choice. One example: "Aren't you glad you use Dial. Don't you wish everybody did?"

Institutional Advertisements

institutional advertisements

Advertisements designed to build goodwill or an image for an organization, rather than promote a specific good or service

The objective of **institutional advertisements** is to build goodwill or an image for an organization rather than promote a specific good or service. Institutional advertising has been used by companies such as Texaco, Pfizer, and IBM to build confidence in the company name.[6] Often this form of advertising is used to support the public relations plan or counter adverse publicity. Four alternative forms of institutional advertisements are often used:

A competitive institutional ad by dairy farmers tries to increase demand for milk.

1. *Advocacy* advertisements state the position of a company on an issue. Lorillard Tobacco Company places ads discouraging teenagers from smoking. Another form of advocacy advertisement is used when organizations make a request related to a particular action or behavior, such as a request by American Red Cross for blood donations.
2. *Pioneering institutional* advertisements, like the pioneering ads for products discussed earlier, are used for announcements about what a company is, what it can do, or where it is located. Recent Bayer ads, stating "We cure more headaches than you think," are intended to inform consumers that the company produces many products in addition to aspirin. When Travelers decided to begin using the umbrella logo again, and changed its stock symbol and official name, it ran pioneering institutional ads to inform consumers.
3. *Competitive institutional* advertisements promote the advantages of one product class over another and are used in markets where different product classes compete for the same buyers. America's milk processors and dairy farmers use their "Got Milk?" campaign to increase demand for milk as it competes against other beverages.
4. *Reminder institutional* advertisements, like the product form, simply bring the company's name to the attention of the target market again. The Army branch of the U.S. military sponsors a campaign to remind potential recruits of the opportunities in the Army.

learning review

1. What is the difference between pioneering and competitive ads?
2. What is the purpose of an institutional advertisement?

DEVELOPING THE ADVERTISING PROGRAM

The promotion decision process described in Chapter 15 can be applied to each of the promotional elements. Advertising, for example, can be managed by following the three steps (developing, executing, and evaluating) of the process.

Identifying the Target Audience

To develop an effective advertising program advertisers must identify the target audience. All aspects of an advertising program are likely to be influenced by the characteristics of the prospective consumer. Understanding the lifestyles, attitudes, and demographics of the target market is essential. When Under Armour began advertising to women, the ads did not have the same ending as the men's ads: "We must protect this house!" Women said they wanted similar ads so Under Armour introduced a new "hard-core athlete" campaign for women.[7] Even scheduling can depend on the audience. Claritin, a popular allergy medication, schedules its use of brochures, in-store displays, coupons, and advertising to correspond to the allergy season, which varies by geographic region.[8] To eliminate possible bias that might result from subjective judgments about some population segments, the Federal Communications Commission suggests that advertising program decisions be based on market research about the target audience.[9]

Specifying Advertising Objectives

The guidelines for setting promotion objectives described in Chapter 15 also apply to setting advertising objectives. This step helps advertisers with other choices in the promotion decision process such as selecting media and evaluating a campaign. Advertising with an objective of creating awareness, for example, would be better matched with a magazine than a directory such as the Yellow Pages.[10] The Magazine Publishers of America believe objectives are so important that they offer a $100,000 prize each year to the campaign that best meets its objectives. The last winner, MINI USA, won with its "Covert" campaign, which increased online traffic 75 percent and surpassed goals by 200 percent.[11] Similarly, the Advertising Research Foundation is collecting information about the effectiveness of advertising, particularly new forms such as online advertising.[12]

Setting the Advertising Budget

Do you remember this Sierra Mist ad from the Super Bowl?

During the 1990 Super Bowl, it cost companies $700,000 to place a 30-second ad. By 2008, the cost of placing a 30-second ad during Super Bowl XLII was $2.7 million. The reason for the escalating cost is the growing number of viewers: more than 45 million homes and 97.5 million people tune in. In addition, the audience is attractive to advertisers because research indicates that it is equally split between men and women and that before the game 54 percent of survey respondents were "looking forward" to watching the 59 spots. The ads are effective too: Movies promoted during the Super Bowl achieve 40 percent more revenue than movies not promoted on the Super Bowl broadcast. As a result, the Super Bowl attracts relatively new advertisers such as Van Heusen and Garmin and regular advertisers such as Anheuser-Busch and Chevrolet. Which ads were rated the highest? E*TRADE, Tide to Go, Bud Light, and Audi.[13]

Designing the Advertisement

An advertising message usually focuses on the key benefits of the product that are important to a prospective buyer in making trial and adoption decisions. The message depends on the general form or appeal used in the ad and the actual words included in the ad.

Message Content Most advertising messages are made up of both informational and persuasional elements. Information and persuasive content can be combined in the form of an appeal to provide a basic reason for the consumer to act. Although the marketer can use many different types of appeals, common advertising appeals include fear appeals,[14] sex appeals, and humorous appeals.

Fear appeals suggest to the consumer that he or she can avoid some negative experience through the purchase and use of a product or service, a change in behavior, or a reduction in the use of a product. Examples with which you may be familiar include: fire or smoke detector ads that depict a home burning; political candidate endorsements that warn against the rise of other, unpopular ideologies; or social cause ads warning of the

Sex appeals can be found in almost any product category.

serious consequences of drug and alcohol use or AIDS. When using fear appeals, the advertiser must be sure that the appeal is strong enough get the audience's attention and concern but not so strong that it will lead them to tune out the message. In fact, recent research on antismoking ads indicates that stressing the severity of long-term health risks may actually enhance smoking's allure among youth.[15]

In contrast, *sex appeals* suggest to the audience that the product will increase the attractiveness of the user. Sex appeals can be found in almost any product category, from automobiles to toothpaste. The contemporary women's clothing store Bebe, for example, designs its advertising to "attract customers who are intrigued by the playfully sensual and evocative imagery of the Bebe lifestyle." Unfortunately, many commercials that use sex appeals are only successful at gaining the attention of the audience; they have little impact on how consumers think, feel, or act. Some advertising experts even argue that such appeals get in the way of successful communication by distracting the audience from the purpose of the ad.[16]

Humorous appeals imply either directly or subtly that the product is more fun or exciting than competitors' offerings. As with fear and sex appeals, the use of humor is widespread in advertising and can be found in many product categories. You may have smiled at the popular GEICO "So easy a caveman can do it" campaign, which was designed to generate traffic to GEICO's website. The ads have been so popular that people started asking GEICO where the cavemen lived, what they liked to eat, and what their hobbies were. The consumer interest led GEICO to introduce a website, www.cavemanscrib.com, where millions of visitors have learned more about the caveman and GEICO.[17] You may have a favorite humorous ad character, such as the Energizer battery bunny, the AFLAC duck, or the GEICO gecko. Unfortunately for the advertiser, humor tends to wear out quickly, eventually boring the consumer. Another problem with humorous appeals is that their effectiveness may vary across cultures if used in a global campaign.[18]

Creating the Actual Message Copywriters are responsible for creating the text portion of the messages in advertisements. Translating the copywriter's ideas into an actual advertisement is a complex process.

Designing quality artwork, layout, and production for the advertisements is costly and time consuming. High-quality TV commercials typically cost about $335,000 to

Samsung uses a strong visual component to create a message.

produce a 30-second ad, a task done by about 2,000 small commercial production companies across the United States. One reason for the high costs is that as companies have developed global campaigns, the need to shoot commercials in exotic locations has increased. Audi recently filmed commercials in Germany, Australia, and Morocco. Actors are expensive also. The Screen Actors Guild reports that an actor in a typical network TV car ad would earn between $12,000 and $15,000.[19]

Advertising agency Berlin Cameron was recently designated as *Advertising Age* magazine's U.S. Agency of the Year for its "rare combination of new-business savvy, strategic insight, creative prowess, and big personality." Examples of the agency's approach include the "Treat yourself well. Everyday" campaign for Dasani bottled water, the "Imagine" campaign for Samsung consumer electronics, and the "Real" campaign for Coca-Cola.[20]

learning review

3. The Federal Communications Commission suggests that advertising program decisions be based on _____.

4. Describe three common forms of advertising appeals.

Selecting the Right Media

Every advertiser must decide where to place its advertisements. The alternatives are the *advertising media,* the means by which the message is communicated to the target audience. Newspapers, magazines, radio, and TV are examples of advertising media. This decision on media selection is related to the target audience, type of product, nature of the message, campaign objectives, available budget, and the costs of the alternative media. Figure 16–1 shows the distribution of the $280 billion spent on advertising among the many media alternatives.[21]

In deciding where to place advertisements, a company has several media to choose from and a number of alternatives, or vehicles, within each medium. Often advertisers use a mix of media forms and vehicles to maximize the exposure of the message to the target audience while at the same time minimizing costs. These two conflicting

FIGURE 16–1

Advertising expenditures (in $ millions) vary among many media alternatives.

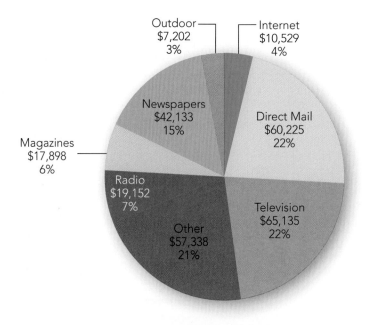

Using Marketing Dashboards

What Is the Best Way to Reach 1,000 Customers?

Marketing managers must choose from many advertising options as they design a campaign to reach potential customers. Because there are so many media alternatives (television, radio, magazines, etc.) and multiple options within each of the media, it is important to monitor the efficiency of advertising expenditures on your marketing dashboard.

Your Challenge As the marketing manager for a company about to introduce a new soft drink into the U.S. market, you are preparing a presentation in which you must make recommendations for the advertising campaign. You have observed that competitors use magazine ads, newspaper ads, and even Super Bowl ads! To compare the cost of some of the alternatives you decide to use one of the most common measures in advertising: cost per thousand impressions (CPM). The CPM is calculated as follows:

Cost per thousand impressions =
   Advertising cost ($)/Impressions generated (in 1000s)

Your challenge is to determine the most efficient use of your advertising budget.

Your Findings Your research department helps you collect cost and audience size information for three options: a two-page color ad in *USA Today* newspaper, a full-page color ad in *Sports Illustrated* magazine, and a 30-second television ad during the Super Bowl. With this information you are able to calculate the cost per thousand impressions for each alternative.

Media Alternative	Cost of Ad	Audience Size	Cost per Thousand Impressions
USA Today (newspaper)	$451,440	2,627,881	$172
Sports Illustrated (magazine)	$320,000	3,150,000	$102
Super Bowl (television)	$2,700,000	97,500,000	$28

Your Action Based on the calculations for these options you see that there is a large variation in the cost of reaching 1,000 potential customers (CPM) and also in the absolute cost of the advertising. Although advertising on the Super Bowl has the lowest CPM, $28 for each 1,000 impressions, it also has the largest absolute cost! Your next step will be to consider other factors such as your total available budget, the profiles of the audiences each alternative reaches, and whether the type of message you want to deliver is better communicated in print or on television.

goals of (1) maximizing exposure and (2) minimizing costs are of central importance to media planning.

Because advertisers try to maximize the number of individuals in the target market exposed to the message, they must be concerned with reach. *Reach* is the number of different people or households exposed to an advertisement. The exact definition of reach sometimes varies among alternative media. Newspapers often use reach to describe their total circulation or the number of different households that buy the paper. Television and radio stations, in contrast, describe their reach using the term *rating*—the percentage of households in a market that are tuned to a particular TV show or radio station. In general, advertisers try to maximize reach in their target market at the lowest cost.

Although reach is important, advertisers are also interested in exposing their target audience to a message more than once. This is because consumers often do not pay close attention to advertising messages, some of which contain large amounts of relatively complex information. When advertisers want to reach the same audience more than once, they are concerned with *frequency*, the average number of times a person in the target audience is exposed to a message or advertisement. Like reach, greater frequency is generally viewed as desirable.[22] Studies indicate that with repeated exposure to advertisements consumers respond more favorably to brand extensions.[23]

When reach (expressed as a percentage of the total market) is multiplied by frequency, an advertiser will obtain a commonly used reference number called *gross rating points* (GRPs). To obtain the appropriate number of GRPs to achieve an advertising campaign's objectives, the media planner must balance reach and frequency. The balance will also be influenced by cost. *Cost per thousand* (CPM) refers to the cost of reaching 1,000 individuals or households with the advertising message in a given medium (*M* is the Roman numeral for 1,000). See the Using Marketing Dashboards box on the previous page for an example of the use of CPM in media selection.

Different Media Alternatives

Figure 16–2 summarizes the advantages and disadvantages of the major advertising media, which are described in more detail below. Direct mail was discussed in Chapter 15.

Cable channels can reach narrowly defined audiences.

Television Television is a valuable medium because it communicates with sight, sound, and motion. Print advertisements alone could never give you the sense of a sports car accelerating from a stop or cornering at high speed. In addition, network television is the only medium that can reach 95 percent of the homes in the United States.[24] *Out-of-home* TV also reaches millions of viewers in bars, hotels, offices, and college campuses each week.[25]

Television's major disadvantage is cost: The price of a prime-time, 30-second ad run on *Grey's Anatomy* is $419,000 and the average price for all prime-time programs is $127,990.[26] Because of these high charges, many advertisers choose less expensive "spot" ads, which run between programs in 10-, 15-, 30-, or 60-second lengths. Shorter ads reduce costs but severely restrict the amount of information and emotion that can be conveyed. Research indicates, however, that two different versions of a 15-second commercial, run back-to-back, will increase recall over long intervals.[27]

Another problem with television advertising is the likelihood of *wasted coverage*—having people outside the market for the product see the advertisement. The cost and wasted coverage problems of TV advertising can be reduced through the specialized cable and direct broadcast (satellite) channels. Advertising time is often less expensive on cable and direct broadcast channels than on the major networks. There are currently about 150 options—such as ESPN, MTV, Lifetime, Oxygen, the Speed Channel, the History Channel, the Science Channel, and the Food Network—that reach very narrowly defined audiences. Other forms of television are changing television advertising also. Pay-per-view and downloadable movie services and digital video recorders (DVRs), for example, offer the potential of commercial-free viewing. Many cable and satellite TV services now offer boxes with built-in DVRs and remotes with "30-second skip" buttons for ad-zapping.

infomercials
Program-length (30-minute) advertisements that take an educational approach to communication with potential customers

Another popular form of television advertising is the infomercial. **Infomercials** are program-length (30-minute) advertisements that take an educational approach to communication with potential customers. Today, more than 90 percent of all TV stations air infomercials, and more than 25 percent of all consumers have purchased a product as a result of seeing an infomercial.

Radio There are seven times as many radio stations as television stations in the United States. The major advantage of radio is that it is a segmented medium. There are the Farm Radio Network, the Physicians' Network, all-talk shows, and hard rock stations, all listened to by different market segments. The average college student is a surprisingly heavy radio listener and spends more time during the day listening to radio than watching network television—2.2 hours versus 1.6 hours. Thus, advertisers with college students as their target market must consider radio.

The disadvantage of radio is that it has limited use for products that must be seen. Another problem is the ease with which consumers can tune out a commercial by

MEDIUM	ADVANTAGES	DISADVANTAGES
Television	Reaches extremely large audience; uses picture, print, sound, and motion for effect; can target specific audiences	High cost to prepare and run ads; short exposure time and perishable message; difficult to convey complex information
Radio	Low cost; can target specific local audiences; ads can be placed quickly; can use sound, humor, and intimacy effectively	No visual element; short exposure time and perishable message; difficult to convey complex information
Magazines	Can target specific audiences; high-quality color; long life of ad; ads can be clipped and saved; can convey complex information	Long time needed to place ad; relatively high cost; competes for attention with other magazine features
Newspapers	Excellent coverage of local markets; ads can be placed and changed quickly; ads can be saved; quick consumer response; low cost	Ads compete for attention with other newspaper features; short life span; poor color
Yellow Pages	Excellent coverage of geographic segments; long use period; available 24 hours/365 days	Proliferation of competitive directories in many markets; difficult to keep up-to-date
Internet	Video and audio capabilities; animation can capture attention; ads can be interactive and link to advertiser	Animation and interactivity require large files and more time to load; effectiveness is still uncertain
Outdoor	Low cost; local market focus; high visibility; opportunity for repeat exposures	Message must be short and simple; low selectivity of audience; criticized as a traffic hazard
Direct mail	High selectivity of audience; can contain complex information and personalized messages; high-quality graphics	High cost per contact; poor image (junk mail)

FIGURE 16–2

Advertisers must consider the advantages and disadvantages of the many media alternatives.

switching stations. A new form of radio available through satellite services offers up to 300 digital-quality coast-to-coast radio channels to consumers for a monthly subscription fee. Sirius XM Radio offers commercial-free channels and channels with only about 6 minutes of advertising per hour compared with 15 to 20 minutes heard on "free" channels.[28] Radio is also a medium that competes for people's attention as they do other activities such as driving, working, or relaxing. Peak radio listening time is during the drive times (6 to 10 A.M. and 4 to 7 P.M.).

Magazines Magazines have become a very specialized medium, primarily because there are currently more than 19,532 magazines. New magazines are introduced each year, such as *Cookie,* a lifestyle-parenting magazine targeted at modern mothers; *All You,* a general topics magazine sold only through Wal-Mart; and *American Thunder,* a magazine about NASCAR racing for men. The marketing advantage of this medium is the great number of special-interest publications that appeal to

Magazines such as *CosmoGirl* appeal to narrowly defined segments.

narrowly defined segments. Runners read *Runner's World,* sailors buy *Yachting,* gardeners subscribe to *Garden Design,* and teenagers peruse *CosmoGirl.* More than 441 publications focus on computers and automation, 645 are dedicated to travel, and 383 magazine titles are related to music.[29] Each magazine's readers often represent a unique profile. Take the *Rolling Stone* reader, who tends to listen to music more than most people—so Sony knows an ad for its MP3 Walkman in *Rolling Stone* is reaching the desired target audience. In addition to the distinct audience profiles of magazines, good color production is an advantage that allows magazines to create strong images.[30]

The cost of advertising in national magazines is a disadvantage, but many national publications publish regional and even metro editions, which reduces the absolute cost and wasted coverage. *Time* publishes well over 400 different editions, including Latin American, Canadian, Asian, South Pacific, European, and U.S. editions. The U.S. editions include national, demographic, regional, state, and city options.

Newspapers   Newspapers are an important local medium with excellent reach potential. Daily publication allows advertisements to focus on specific current events, such as a 24-hour sale. Local retailers often use newspapers as their sole advertising medium. Newspapers are rarely saved by the purchaser, however, so companies are generally limited to ads that call for an immediate customer response (although customers can clip and save ads they select). Companies also cannot depend on newspapers for color reproduction as good as that in most magazines.

National advertising campaigns rarely include this medium except in conjunction with local distributors of their products. In these instances, both parties often share the advertising costs using a cooperative advertising program, which is described later in this chapter. Another exception is the use of newspapers such as *The Wall Street Journal* and *USA Today,* each of which have national distribution of more than 2 million readers.

Yellow Pages   Yellow pages represent an advertising media alternative comparable to radio and magazines in terms of expenditures—about $17 billion in the United States and $31 billion globally. According to the Yellow Pages Integrated Media Association, consumers turn to print yellow pages more than 13.4 billion times annually and online yellow pages an additional 3.8 billion times per year. One reason for this high level of use is that the 7,000 yellow pages directories reach almost all households with telephones. Yellow pages are a directional medium because they help consumers know where purchases can be made after other media have created awareness and demand. A disadvantage is the lack of timeliness, because yellow pages can only be updated with new information once each year.[31]

Yellow Pages have many advantages including a long life span.

Internet   The Internet represents a relatively new medium for advertisers although it has already attracted a wide variety of industries. Online advertising is similar to print advertising in that it offers a visual message. It has additional advantages, however, because it can also use the audio and video capabilities of the Internet. Sound and movement may simply attract more attention from viewers, or they may provide an element of entertainment to the message. Online advertising also has the unique feature of being interactive. Called *rich media,* these interactive ads have drop-down menus, built-in games, or search engines to engage viewers.[32] Although online advertising is relatively small compared to other traditional media, it offers an opportunity to reach younger consumers who have developed a preference for online communication.[33]

Who Is Responsible for Click Fraud?

Spending on Internet advertising is expected to reach $29 billion in 2010 as many advertisers shift their budgets from print and TV to the Internet. For most advertisers one advantage of online advertising is that they only pay when someone clicks on their ad. Unfortunately, the growth of the medium has led to "click fraud," which is the deceptive clicking of ads solely to increase the amount advertisers must pay. There are several forms of click fraud. One method is the result of Paid-to-Read (PTR) websites that recruit and pay members to simply click on ads. Another method is the result of "clickbots," which are software programs that produce automatic clicks on ads. While the activity is difficult to detect and stop, experts estimate that up to 15% of clicks may be the result of fraud, and may be costing advertisers as much as $500 million each year!

Two of the largest portals for Internet advertising are Google and Yahoo! Both firms try to filter out illegitimate clicks although some advertisers claim that they are still being charged for PTR and clickbot traffic. Although the laws that may govern click fraud are not very clear, Google and Yahoo! have each settled class action lawsuits and agreed to provide rebates or credits to advertisers who were charged for fraudulent clicks.

Investigations of the online advertising industry have discovered a related form of click fraud which occurs when legitimate website visitors click on ads without any intention of looking at the site. As one consumer explains, "I always try and remember to click on the ad banners once in a while to try and keep the sites free." Stephen Dubner calls this "webtipping"!

As the Internet advertising industry grows it will become increasingly important to resolve the issue of click fraud. Consumers, advertisers, websites that carry paid advertising, and the large web portals are all involved in a complicated technical, legal, and social situation. Who do you think is responsible for click fraud? Who should lead the way in the effort to find a solution?

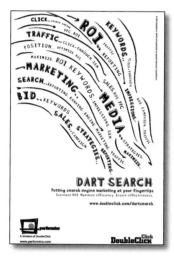

DoubleClick's Dart Search service can provide an assessment of the effectiveness of a website.

A disadvantage to online advertising is the difficulty of measuring impact. Online advertising lags behind radio, TV, and print in offering advertisers proof of effectiveness. To address this issue several companies are testing methods of tracking where viewers go on their computer in the days and weeks after seeing an ad. Nielsen's Online rating service, for example, measures actual click-by-click behavior through meters installed on the computers of 225,000 individuals in 26 countries both at home and at work (see www.nielsen-online.com for recent ratings). The accompanying Making Responsible Decisions box describes how click fraud is increasing the necessity of assessing online advertising effectiveness.[34] Another suggestion being tested by Volvo and Unilever is *permission-based* advertising, where viewers agree to watch a commercial online in exchange for points, samples, or access to premium content, and advertisers only pay for completed views.[35]

Outdoor   A very effective medium for reminding consumers about your product is outdoor advertising, such as the scoreboard at San Diego's Qualcomm Stadium. The most common form of outdoor advertising, called *billboards,* often results in good reach and frequency and has been shown to increase purchase rates.[36] The visibility of this medium is good supplemental reinforcement for well-known products, and it is a relatively low-cost, flexible alternative. A company can buy space just in the desired geographical market. A disadvantage to billboards, however, is that no opportunity exists for lengthy advertising copy. Also, a good billboard site depends on traffic patterns and sight lines. In many areas, environmental laws have limited the use of this medium.

If you have ever lived in a metropolitan area, chances are you might have seen another form of outdoor advertising, *transit advertising.* This medium includes messages on the interior and exterior of buses, subway cars, and taxis. As use of mass transit grows, transit advertising may become increasingly important. Selectivity is available to advertisers, who can buy space by neighborhood or bus route. One disadvantage to this medium is that the heavy travel times, when the audiences are the largest, are not conducive to reading advertising copy. People are standing shoulder to shoulder on the subway, hoping not to miss their stop, and little attention is paid to the advertising.

Outdoor advertising can be an effective medium for reminding consumers about a product, and out-of-home advertising is becoming interactive.

Other Media As traditional media have become more expensive and cluttered, advertisers have been attracted to a variety of nontraditional advertising options called out-of-home advertising, or *place-based media.* Messages are placed in locations that attract a specific target audience such as airports, doctors' offices, health clubs, theaters (where ads are played on the screen before the movies are shown), even bathrooms of bars, restaurants, and nightclubs.[37] Soon there will be advertising on video screens on gas pumps, ATMs, and in elevators, and increasingly it will be interactive. New York's La Guardia airport has started putting ads on baggage conveyors, and Beach'n Billboard will even imprint ads in the sand on a beach.[38]

Scheduling the Advertising

There is no correct schedule to advertise a product, but three factors must be considered. First is the issue of *buyer turnover,* which is how often new buyers enter the market to buy the product. The higher the buyer turnover, the greater is the amount of advertising required. A second issue in scheduling is the *purchase frequency;* the more frequently the product is purchased, the less repetition is required. Finally, companies must consider the *forgetting rate,* the speed with which buyers forget the brand if advertising is not seen.

Setting schedules requires an understanding of how the market behaves. Most companies tend to follow one of three basic approaches:

1. *Continuous (steady) schedule.* When seasonal factors are unimportant, advertising is run at a continuous or steady schedule throughout the year.
2. *Flighting (intermittent) schedule.* Periods of advertising are scheduled between periods of no advertising to reflect seasonal demand.
3. *Pulse (burst) schedule.* A flighting schedule is combined with a continuous schedule because of increases in demand, heavy periods of promotion, or introduction of a new product.

For example, products such as dry breakfast cereals have a stable demand throughout the year and would typically use a continuous schedule of advertising. In contrast, products such as snow skis and suntan lotions have seasonal demands and receive flighting-schedule advertising during the seasonal demand period. Some products such as toys or automobiles require pulse-schedule advertising to facilitate sales throughout the year and during special periods of increased demand (such as holidays or new car introductions).

Some evidence suggests that pulsing schedules are superior to other advertising strategies.[39] In addition, recent research findings indicate that the effectiveness of a particular ad wears out quickly and, therefore, many alternative forms of a commercial may be more effective.[40]

learning review

5. You see the same ad in *Time* and *Fortune* magazines and on billboards and TV. Is this an example of reach or frequency?

6. Why has the Internet become a popular advertising medium?

7. Describe three approaches to scheduling advertising.

EXECUTING THE ADVERTISING PROGRAM

Executing the advertising program involves pretesting the advertising copy and actually carrying out the advertising program. John Wanamaker, the founder of Wanamaker's Department Store in Philadelphia, remarked, "I know half my advertising is wasted, but I don't know what half." By evaluating advertising efforts, marketers can try to ensure that their advertising expenditures are not wasted.[41] Evaluation is done usually at two separate times: before and after the advertisements are run in the actual campaign. Several methods used in the evaluation process at the stages of idea formulation and copy development are discussed below. Posttesting methods are reviewed in the section on assessment.

Pretesting the Advertising

pretests

Tests conducted before an advertisement is placed to determine whether it communicates the intended message or to select among alternative versions of an advertisement

To determine whether the advertisement communicates the intended message or to select among alternative versions of the advertisement, **pretests** are conducted before the advertisements are placed in any medium.

Portfolio Tests   Portfolio tests are used to test copy alternatives. The test ad is placed in a portfolio with several other ads and stories, and consumers are asked to read through the portfolio. Afterward, subjects are asked for their impressions of the ads on several evaluative scales, such as from "very informative" to "not very informative."

Jury Tests   Jury tests involve showing the ad copy to a panel of consumers and having them rate how they liked it, how much it drew their attention, and how attractive they thought it was. This approach is similar to the portfolio test in that consumer reactions are obtained. However, unlike the portfolio test, a test advertisement is not hidden within other ads.

Theater Tests   Theater testing is the most sophisticated form of pretesting. Consumers are invited to view new television shows or movies in which test commercials are also shown. Viewers register their feelings about the advertisements either on handheld electronic recording devices used during the viewing or on questionnaires afterward.

Carrying Out the Advertising Program

The responsibility for actually carrying out the advertising program can be handled by one of three types of agencies. The *full-service agency* provides the most complete range of services, including market research, media selection, copy development, artwork, and production. Agencies that assist a client by both developing and placing advertisements have traditionally charged a commission of 15 percent of media costs. As corporations have introduced integrated marketing approaches, however, most advertisers (70 percent) have switched from paying commissions to incentives or fees based on performance. Brad Brinegar, former CEO of advertising agency Leo Burnett USA, says, "A lot of value we offer is in strategic thinking, and how to pay for that is very different from traditional media spending." The most common performance criteria used are sales, brand and ad awareness, market share, and copy test results. *Limited-service agencies* specialize in one aspect of the advertising process such as providing creative services to develop the advertising copy, buying previously unpurchased media (media agencies), or providing Internet services (Internet agencies). Limited-service agencies that deal in creative work are compensated by a contractual agreement for the services performed. Finally, *in-house agencies* made up of the company's own advertising staff may provide full services or a limited range of services.

ASSESSING THE ADVERTISING PROGRAM

The advertising decision process does not stop with executing the advertising program. The advertisements must be posttested to determine whether they are achieving their intended objectives, and results may indicate that changes must be made in the advertising program.

Posttesting the Advertising

posttests

Tests conducted after an advertisement has been shown to the target audience to determine whether it has accomplished its intended purpose

An advertisement may go through **posttests** after it has been shown to the target audience to determine whether it accomplished its intended purpose. Five approaches common in posttesting are discussed here.[42]

Aided Recall After being shown an ad, respondents are asked whether their previous exposure to it was through reading, viewing, or listening. The Starch test shown in the accompanying photo uses aided recall to determine the percentage of those (1) who remember seeing a specific magazine ad (*noted*), (2) who saw or read any part of the ad identifying the product or brand (*seen-associated*), and (3) who read at least half of the ad (*read most*). Elements of the ad are then tagged with the results, as shown in the picture.

Starch uses aided recall to posttest an advertisement.

Unaided Recall A question such as "What ads do you remember seeing yesterday?" is asked of respondents without any prompting to determine whether they saw or heard advertising messages.

Attitude Tests Respondents are asked questions to measure changes in their attitudes after an advertising campaign, such as whether they have a more favorable attitude toward the product advertised.[43]

Inquiry Tests Additional product information, product samples, or premiums are offered to an ad's readers or viewers. Ads generating the most inquiries are presumed to be the most effective.

Sales Tests Sales tests involve studies such as controlled experiments (e.g., using radio ads in one market and newspaper ads in another and comparing the results) and consumer purchase tests (measuring retail sales that result from a given advertising campaign). The most sophisticated experimental methods today allow a manufacturer, a distributor, or an advertising agency to manipulate an advertising variable (such as schedule or copy) through cable systems and observe subsequent sales effects by monitoring data collected from checkout scanners in supermarkets.[44]

learning review

8. Explain the difference between pretesting and posttesting advertising copy.

9. What is the difference between aided and unaided recall posttests?

SALES PROMOTION

LO4

Sales promotion has become a key element of the promotional mix, which now accounts for more than $342 billion in annual expenditures. In a recent survey by *PROMO* magazine, marketing professionals reported that approximately 41 percent of their budgets were allocated to advertising, 28 percent to consumer promotion, 28 percent to trade promotion, and 3 percent to other marketing activities.[45] The allocation of marketing expenditures reflects the trend toward integrated promotion programs, which include a variety of promotion elements. Selection and integration of the many promotion techniques require a good understanding of the advantages and disadvantages of each kind of promotion.[46]

Consumer-Oriented Sales Promotions

consumer-oriented sales promotions

Sales tools, such as coupons, sweepstakes, and samples, used to support a company's advertising and personal selling efforts directed to ultimate consumers

Directed to ultimate consumers, **consumer-oriented sales promotions**, or simply *consumer promotions*, are sales tools used to support a company's advertising and personal selling. The alternative consumer-oriented sales promotion tools include coupons, deals, premiums, contests, sweepstakes, samples, loyalty programs, point-of-purchase displays, rebates, and product placement.

Coupons Coupons are sales promotions that usually offer a discounted price to the consumer, which encourages trial. Approximately 286 billion coupons are distributed in the United States each year. Coupon redemptions have been declining since 1992 and are now at 2.6 billion coupons, or approximately .9 percent. One explanation for the decline is that the average expiration period has been declining—to about three months—giving consumers less time to redeem coupons. The average face value of redeemed coupons is about $1.27. Companies that have increased their use of coupons include Procter & Gamble, H.J. Heinz, Nestlé, ConAgra, and Kraft. In addition, the number of coupons generated at Internet sites (e.g., www.valpak. com and www.couponsonline.com) and over cell phones has been increasing. Coupons are often viewed as a key element of an integrated marketing program. When Duracell signed Jon Bon Jovi as a spokesperson, for example, coupons on Duracell battery packs offered $3 to $5 off Bon Jovi CDs and coupons on the CDs offered discounts on batteries.[47]

Coupons are often far more expensive than the face value of the coupon; a 25-cent coupon can cost three times that after paying for the advertisement to deliver it, dealer handling, clearinghouse costs, and redemption. In addition, misredemption, or paying the face value of the coupon even though the product was not purchased, should be added to the cost of the coupon. The Coupon Information Corporation estimates that companies pay out refunds of more than $500 million each year as a result of coupon fraud.[48]

Coupons encourage trial by offering a discounted price.

Deals Deals are short-term price reductions, commonly used to increase trial among potential customers or to retaliate against a competitor's actions. For example, if a rival manufacturer introduces a new cake mix, the company responds with a "two packages for the price of one" deal. This short-term price reduction builds up the stock on the kitchen shelves of cake mix buyers and makes the competitor's introduction more difficult.

Premiums A promotional tool often used with consumers is the premium, which consists of merchandise offered free or at a significant savings over its retail price. This latter type of premium is called *self-liquidating* because the cost charged to the consumer covers the cost of the item. McDonald's, for example, used a free premium in a promotional partnership with DreamWorks during the release of the movies *Shrek the Third* and *Bee Movie*. Collectible toys that portrayed movie characters were given away free with the purchase of a Happy Meal. Milk-Bone dog biscuits used a self-liquidating premium when it offered a ball toy for $8.99 and two proofs of purchase.[49] By offering a premium, companies encourage customers to return frequently or to use more of the product.

Contests A fourth sales promotion is the contest, where consumers apply their skill or analytical or creative thinking to try to win a prize. This form of promotion has been growing as requests for videos, photos, and essays are a good match with the trend toward consumer-generated content. For example, Doritos sponsored the "Crash the Super Bowl" contest, asking people to create their own 30-second ad about Doritos. A panel of judges selected five finalists from the 1,070 entries, and the public voted online for its favorite. The ads were viewed more than 3 million times, and the top two ads aired on the Super Bowl.[50] If you like contests, you can even enter online now at websites such as www.playhere.com.

Sweepstakes *Reader's Digest* and Publisher's Clearing House are two well-known sweepstakes. These sales promotions require participants to submit some kind of entry but are purely games of chance requiring no analytical or creative effort by the consumer. Two variations of sweepstakes are popular now. First is the sweepstake that offers products that consumers value. ConAgra Foods, for example, created the "Shrek's Quest for the Crown" instant-win promotion. The game offered a chance to win a $1,000 Visa gift card by entering UPC codes from ConAgra products tied to the *Shrek the Third* DVD release at a promotion website. Coca-Cola has a similar sweepstakes called "My Coke Rewards" which allows consumers to use codes from bottle caps to enter to win prizes or to collect points to be redeemed for rewards. The second is the sweepstake that offers an "experience" as the prize. For example, one of television's most popular series, *American Idol,* sponsors a 53-city live concert tour of the show's finalists. Concert attendees can enter a sweepstakes to win a trip for two to the season finale of *American Idol* in Los Angeles.[51] Federal laws, the Federal Trade Commission, and state legislatures have issued rules covering sweepstakes, contests, and games to regulate fairness, ensure that the chance for winning is represented honestly, and guarantee that the prizes are actually awarded.[52]

Samples Another common consumer sales promotion is sampling, which is offering the product free or at a greatly reduced price. Often used for new products, sampling puts the product in the consumer's hands. A trial size is generally offered that is smaller than the regular package size. If consumers like the sample, it is hoped they will remember and buy the product. When Mars changed its Milky Way Dark to Milky Way Midnight, it gave away more than 1 million samples to college students at night clubs, several hundred campuses, and popular spring break locations. Awareness of the candy bar rose to 60 percent, trial rose 166 percent, and sales rose 25 percent. Recent research indicates that 63 percent of college students who receive a sample will also purchase the product. Overall, companies invest more than $2 billion in sampling programs each year.[53]

Loyalty Programs Loyalty programs are a sales promotion tool used to encourage and reward repeat purchases by acknowledging each purchase made by a consumer and offering a premium as purchases accumulate. The most popular loyalty programs today are the frequent-flier and frequent-traveler programs used by airlines, hotels, and car rental services to reward loyal customers. American Airlines customers, for example, earn points for each mile they fly and can then redeem the accumulated points for free tickets or upgrades on the airline.

Point-of-Purchase Displays In a store aisle, you often encounter a sales promotion called a *point-of-purchase display*. These product displays take the form of advertising signs, which sometimes actually hold or display the product, and are often located in high-traffic areas near the cash register or the end of an aisle. The point-of-purchase display for Nabisco's annual back-to-school program is designed to maximize the consumer's attention to lunch box and after-school snacks, and to provide storage for the products. Annual expenditures on point-of-purchase promotions now exceed $19 billion and are expected to grow as point-of-purchase becomes integrated with all forms of promotion.[54]

Rebates Another consumer sales promotion, the cash rebate, offers the return of money based on proof of purchase. This tool has been used heavily by car manufacturers facing increased competition. For example, Ford offers recent college graduates a $500 rebate on many of its vehicles, as part of its College Student Purchase Program.[55] When a rebate is offered on lower-priced items, the time and trouble of mailing in a proof of purchase to get the rebate check often means that many buyers never take advantage of it. However, this "slippage" is less likely to occur with frequent users of rebate promotions.[56] In addition, online consumers are more likely to take advantage of rebates.

Product Placement A final consumer promotion, **product placement**, involves the use of a brand-name product in a movie, television show, video, or commercial for another product. It was Steven Spielberg's placement of Hershey's Reese's Pieces in *E.T.* that first brought a lot of interest to the candy. Similarly, when Tom Cruise wore Bausch and Lomb's Ray-Ban sunglasses in *Risky Business* and its Aviator glasses in *Top Gun,* sales skyrocketed from 100,000 pairs to 7,000,000 pairs in five years. After *Toy Story*, Etch-A-Sketch sales increased 4,500 percent and Mr. Potato Head sales increased 800 percent. More recently, you might remember seeing the Aston Martin and the Range Rover, both Ford products, in *Casino Royale,* or the Dairy Queen brand

Can you identify these product placements?

on episodes of *The Apprentice.* In the television show *Survivor,* participants often receive Doritos and Mountain Dew as rewards.[57] A variation of this form of promotion, called *reverse product placement*, brings fictional products to the marketplace. Bertie Bott's Every Flavor Beans, for example, began as an imaginary brand in Harry Potter books. Similarly, the movie *Forrest Gump* led to the Bubba Gump Shrimp Company restaurant chain. Finally, 7-Eleven converted 12 of its stores into Kwik-E-Marts, the imaginary convenience stores in the television cartoon series, *The Simpsons*, to coincide with the release of *The Simpsons Movie.*[58]

Trade-Oriented Sales Promotions

Trade-oriented sales promotions, or simply *trade promotions,* are sales tools used to support a company's advertising and personal selling directed to wholesalers, distributors, or retailers. Some of the sales promotions just reviewed are used for this purpose, but there are three other common approaches targeted uniquely to these intermediaries: (1) allowances and discounts, (2) cooperative advertising, and (3) training of distributors' salesforces.

Allowances and Discounts   Trade promotions often focus on maintaining or increasing inventory levels in the channel of distribution. An effective method for encouraging such increased purchases by intermediaries is the use of allowances and discounts. However, overuse of these price reductions can lead to retailers changing their ordering patterns in the expectation of such offerings. Although there are many variations that manufacturers can use with discounts and allowances, three common approaches are the merchandise allowance, the case allowance, and the finance allowance.[59]

Reimbursing a retailer for extra in-store support or special featuring of the brand is a *merchandise allowance.* Performance contracts between the manufacturer and trade member usually specify the activity to be performed, such as a picture of the product in a newspaper with a coupon good at only one store. The merchandise allowance then consists of a percentage deduction from the list case price ordered during the promotional period. Allowances are not paid by the manufacturer until it sees proof of performance (such as a copy of the ad placed by the retailer in the local newspaper).

A second common trade promotion, a *case allowance,* is a discount on each case ordered during a specific time period. These allowances are usually deducted from the invoice. A variation of the case allowance is the "free goods" approach, whereby retailers receive some amount of the product free based on the amount ordered, such as 1 case free for every 10 cases ordered.[60]

A final trade promotion, the *finance allowance,* involves paying retailers for financing costs or financial losses associated with consumer sales promotions. This trade promotion is regularly used and has several variations. One type is the floor stock protection program—manufacturers give retailers a case allowance price for products in their warehouse, which prevents shelf stock from running down during the promotional period. Also common are freight allowances, which compensate retailers that transport orders from the manufacturer's warehouse.

Cooperative Advertising   Resellers often perform the important function of promoting the manufacturer's products at the local level. One common sales promotional activity is to encourage both better quality and greater quantity in the local advertising efforts of resellers through **cooperative advertising**. These are programs by which a manufacturer pays a percentage of the retailer's local advertising expense for advertising the manufacturer's products.

Usually the manufacturer pays a percentage, often 50 percent, of the cost of advertising up to a certain dollar limit, which is based on the amount of the purchases the retailer makes of the manufacturer's products. In addition to paying for the advertising, the manufacturer often furnishes the retailer with a selection of different ad executions, sometimes suited for several different media. A manufacturer may provide, for example, several different print layouts as well as a few broadcast ads for the retailer to adapt and use.[61]

Training of Distributors' Salesforces

One of the many functions the intermediaries perform is customer contact and selling for the producers they represent. Both retailers and wholesalers employ and manage their own sales personnel. A manufacturer's success often rests on the ability of the reseller's salesforce to represent its products.

Thus, it is in the best interest of the manufacturer to help train the reseller's salesforce. Because the reseller's salesforce is often less sophisticated and knowledgeable about the products than the manufacturer might like, training can increase their sales performance. Training activities include producing manuals and brochures to educate the reseller's salesforce. The salesforce then uses these aids in selling situations.

PUBLIC RELATIONS

LO5

publicity tools
Methods of obtaining nonpersonal presentation of an organization, good, or service without direct cost

As noted in Chapter 15, public relations is a form of communication management that seeks to influence the image of an organization and its products and services. In developing a public relations campaign, several methods of obtaining nonpersonal presentation of an organization, good, or service without direct cost—**publicity tools**—are available to the public relations director. Many companies frequently use the *news release,* consisting of an announcement regarding changes in the company or the product line. The objective of a news release is to inform a newspaper, radio station, or other medium of an idea for a story. A recent study found that more than 40 percent of all free mentions of a brand name occur during news programs.[62]

A second common publicity tool is the *news conference.* Representatives of the media are all invited to an informational meeting, and advance materials regarding the content are sent. This tool is often used when negative publicity—as in the cases of the options backdating scandals, the recalls of unsafe Chinese-made products, and the San Francisco Bay oil spill—requires a company response.[63]

Nonprofit organizations rely heavily on *public service announcements* (PSAs), which are free space or time donated by the media. For example, the charter of the American Red Cross prohibits any local chapter from advertising, so to solicit blood donations local chapters often depend on PSAs on radio or television to announce their needs.

---

learning review

10. Which sales promotional tool is most common for new products?

11. Which trade promotion is used to encourage local advertising efforts of resellers?

12. What is a news release?

LEARNING OBJECTIVES REVIEW

LO1 *Explain the differences between product advertising and institutional advertising and the variations within each type.* Product advertisements focus on selling a good or service and take three forms: Pioneering advertisements tell people what a product is, what it can do, and where it can be found; competitive advertisements persuade the target market to select the firm's brand rather than a competitor's; and reminder advertisements reinforce previous knowledge of a product. Institutional advertisements are used to build goodwill or an image for an organization. They include advocacy advertisements, which state the position of a company on an issue, and pioneering, competitive, and reminder advertisements, which are similar to the product ads but focused on the institution.

LO2 *Describe the steps used to develop, execute, and evaluate an advertising program.*
The promotion decision process can be applied to each of the promotional elements. The steps to develop an advertising program include identifying the target audience, specifying the advertising objectives, setting the advertising budget, designing the advertisement, creating the message, selecting the media, and scheduling the advertising. Executing the program requires pretesting, and assessing the program requires posttesting.

LO3 *Explain the advantages and disadvantages of alternative advertising media.*
Television advertising reaches large audiences and uses picture, print, sound, and motion; its disadvantages, however, are that it is expensive and perishable. Radio advertising is inexpensive and can be placed quickly, but it has no visual element and is perishable. Magazine advertising can target specific audiences but it is relatively expensive. Newspapers provide excellent coverage of local markets and can be changed quickly, but they have a short life span and poor color. Yellow pages advertising reaches almost all households with telephones; its disadvantages, however, are that there is a proliferation of directories and they cannot be updated frequently. Internet advertising can be interactive, but its effectiveness is difficult to measure. Outdoor advertising provides repeat exposures, but its message must be very short and simple. Direct mail can be targeted at very selective audiences, but its cost per contact is high.

LO4 *Discuss the strengths and weaknesses of consumer-oriented and trade-oriented sales promotions.*
Coupons encourage consumer trial but are often more expensive than the face value of the coupon. Deals also increase trial and may be used during a competitor's promotion. Premiums offer consumers additional merchandise free with a purchase, or at a significant savings over its retail price. Contests create involvement but require creative thinking. Sweepstakes encourage repeat purchases and require no creative effort by the consumer. Samples are often used for new products and encourage purchase of the product. Loyalty programs encourage and reward repeat purchases. Displays provide visibility in high-traffic areas. Rebates offer a return of money based on proof of purchase. Product placement involves the use of a brand-name product in a movie, TV show, or commercial. Trade-oriented sales promotions include (*a*) allowances and discounts, which increase purchases but may change retailer ordering patterns, (*b*) cooperative advertising, which encourages local advertising, and (*c*) salesforce training, which helps increase sales by providing the salespeople with product information and selling skills.

LO5 *Recognize public relations as an important form of communication.*
Public relations activities seek to influence the image of an organization and its products and services. A frequently used public relations tool is publicity. Publicity tools include new releases and news conferences. Nonprofit organization often use public service announcements.

FOCUSING ON KEY TERMS

advertising p. 360
**consumer-oriented sales
   promotions** p. 373
cooperative advertising p. 376

infomercials p. 367
institutional advertisements p. 361
posttests p. 372
pretests p. 371

product advertisements p. 360
product placement p. 375
publicity tools p. 377
trade-oriented sales promotions p. 376

APPLYING MARKETING KNOWLEDGE

1 How does competitive product advertising differ from competitive institutional advertising?

2 Suppose you are the advertising manager for a new line of children's fragrances. Which form of media would you use for this new product?

3 You have recently been promoted to be director of advertising for the Timkin Tool Company. In your first meeting with Mr. Timkin, he says, "Advertising is a waste! We've been advertising for six months now and sales haven't increased. Tell me why we should continue." Give your answer to Mr. Timkin.

4 A large life insurance company has decided to switch from using a strong fear appeal to a humorous approach. What are the strengths and weaknesses of such a change in message strategy?

5 Which medium has the lowest cost per thousand?

Medium	Cost	Audience
TV show	$5,000	25,000
Magazine	2,200	6,000
Newspaper	4,800	7,200
FM radio	420	1,600

6 Some national advertisers have found that they can have more impact with their advertising by running a large number of ads for a period and then running no ads at all for a period. Why might such a flighting schedule be more effective than a continuous schedule?

7 Each year managers at Bausch & Lomb evaluate the many advertising media alternatives available to them as they develop their advertising program for contact lenses. (*a*) What advantages and disadvantages of each alternative should they consider? (*b*) Which media would you recommend to them?

8 What are two advantages and two disadvantages of the advertising posttests described in the chapter?

9 Federated Banks is interested in consumer-oriented sales promotions that would encourage senior citizens to direct deposit their Social Security checks with the bank. Evaluate the sales promotion options, and recommend two of them to the bank.

10 How can public relations be used by Firestone and Ford following investigations into complaints about tire failures?

building your marketing plan

To augment your promotion strategy from Chapter 15:

1 Use Figure 16–2 to select the advertising media you will include in your plan by analyzing how combinations of media (e.g., television and Internet advertising, radio and yellow pages advertising) can complement each other.

2 Select your consumer-oriented sales promotion activities.

3 Specify which trade-oriented sales promotions and public relations activities you will use.

video case 16 Fallon Worldwide: In the *Creativity* Business

"Most people think of Fallon as being in the advertising business, but we don't really think of ourselves that way," says Rob White, president of Fallon Worldwide. "We believe that we are a creativity company that happens to do some advertising," he continues. As an example, he points out that Fallon starts upstream of a firm's communication issues to identify the key business problem and uses creativity to help solve it. Sometimes this involves a heavy dose of advertising and other times almost none. But it always takes a very creative flair.

Founded in 1981, Fallon Worldwide—or simply Fallon—has won dozens of advertising awards. This includes two Agency of the Year awards given by *Advertising Age* magazine. "I think Fallon's success is due to two important things," says White. "One is the people and the other one is the culture that bonds the people together. When you create a special kind of culture with collaboration and teamwork from a very high level and people with different backgrounds, amazing things can happen," he explains.

Bruce Bildsten, Fallon creative group director, echoes this focus on creativity: "It's always a challenge as creative director to try to stay at the forefront and come up with something that people haven't seen. I desperately try not to look at other advertising for ideas. I always challenge our people to look at work from other parts of the world—film, novels, music—for inspiration."

A look at two promotional campaigns developed at Fallon show how creativity, teamwork, and not looking at traditional ads from other agencies come together to build award-winning campaigns. Both campaigns discussed below have been recognized for their creativity and their success at achieving the clients' objectives.

CITIBANK: ATTRACTING BALANCE SEEKERS

Citibank approached Fallon because it knew it had a problem. Citi had been successful in the past by being a low-cost provider, having great service, and by focusing on direct marketing. Suddenly that wasn't

enough. Competition had increased significantly and customer perceptions of banks and credit card companies had changed. Laurel Flatt, Fallon account director on the Citibank account, describes the challenge: "New banks were springing up all over the place. There were new credit card companies. Consumers looked at financial services as simply a commodity. Your relationship with your bank, your credit card company was once a very, very special relationship." Now, however, consumers viewed one bank as being no different than another.

When Citibank came to Fallon, it said that it really wanted to be "un-banklike," it wanted to be different. Fallon asked the question, "What is the right way to be un-banklike in a way that will generate results for the Citi brand?" Qualitative and quantitative research identified a segment of consumers that Fallon labeled "balance seekers." This group amounted to about 50 percent of the market for financial services. Balance seekers viewed financial services and money as a means to an end, something that helps them lead the life they live. This segment also shared an attitude that was receptive to the idea of an un-banklike message, though they had different income levels, assets, ages, and other demographic characteristics.

Fallon translated un-banklike to mean very friendly, human, and a little bit quirky—very different from the serious tone of traditional bank and financial services companies. In addition, Fallon wanted the Citi brand to represent a healthy approach to money. Finally, Fallon wanted to communicate that the credit card protects consumers and their purchases.

Fallon's ad executions were funny and engaging. One ad shows a middle-aged woman from Minnesota getting a tattoo. The tag line is "It didn't seem right to us, either" and talks about Citi's Fraud Early Warning system to identify unusual spending behavior. Another ad shows a truck driver from Iowa asleep under a hair dryer at La Petite Lily Day Spa with the same tag line and message about how Citi's identity theft solutions can help make things right. The Citi campaign utilized billboards and wall advertising, bus shelter kiosks, magazines, and television.

Fallon used brand-tracking to chart the degree of differentiation of the Citi brand. Over time, the differentiation climbed as more and more people perceived Citi as different from other banks yet relevant in their lives. Sales results were also positive. Card acquisition and card usage increased dramatically!

HOLIDAY INN EXPRESS: ATTRACTING "SMART" CONSUMERS

When Holiday Inn decided to enter the limited-service hotel segment with its Holiday Inn Express hotels, it hired Fallon Worldwide to develop the campaign. Holiday Inn had a long history with American consumers who remembered it as the hotel for family road trips. Most of the growth in the hotel industry, however, was related to business travel, and that segment already had two strong competitors—Courtyard by Marriott and Hampton Inns. Holiday Inn Express was starting with a budget that was much smaller than its competitors, so Fallon knew it needed to "outsmart rather than outspend" them.

The agency's first step was to identify the target market. It conducted extensive research to understand the psychological profile of users of that type of hotel and the motivations for their lodging choices. Fallon decided to focus on a specific group of travelers who seldom made reservations. "In this case it was males 25–54 that tend to travel by car when they do business, so they were true 'road warriors,'" explains Mike Buchner, chief operating officer and client services director at Fallon. The research revealed another insight about these travelers. They only wanted the necessities, but they felt savvy for making a practical choice. This emotional benefit became the creative focus of the discussions at Fallon and resulted in the Holiday Inn Express "Stay Smart" campaign.

The campaign used television ads designed to create awareness and differentiate Holiday Inn Express by showing how Holiday Inn Express makes guests feel smart about their hotel selection. One ad, for example, shows a man giving advice to a tourist who is being confronted by a bear. When asked if he is a forest ranger, the man responds, "No, but I did stay in a Holiday Inn Express last night." A similar ad shows a man dressed as a clown giving advice to a bull rider at a rodeo. Then the man explains that he is not a rodeo clown but a children's birthday party clown, and the conclusion is the same: "But I did stay at a Holiday Inn Express last night." To create the greatest impact with the limited budget, Fallon only ran the ads on Sundays and Mondays—days that the target market typically did not travel. In addition, they only ran the ads on cable networks such as CNN, ESPN, and Fox Sports—programs that research showed were very popular with road warriors.

The Stay Smart advertising theme eventually became the basis for an entire branding effort. Holiday Inn Express now offers SimplySmart bathroom designs, SimplySmart bedding collections, Smart Roast coffee, and even a webcast about activities in America called The Smart Show. The result has been very positive as the number of visitors, sales, and operating profits have increased. According to Verchele Wiggins, vice president of brand management at Holiday Inn Express, "the extent to which the popular phrase 'No, but I did stay at a Holiday Inn Express last night' has penetrated pop culture has far exceeded anything that we would have ever imagined." In fact, the campaign is so successful that Holiday Inn Express now has 1,583 hotels and is the fastest growing hotel brand in the United States, adding two new hotels each week!

Verchele Wiggins
Vice-President of Brand Management, Holiday Inn Express

PUSHING THE CREATIVE BARRIERS

How does Fallon keep the creative juices flowing—from developing new promotional campaigns to using new media? The founders of Fallon Worldwide, Pat Fallon and Fred Senn, explain how they do it in their new book titled *Juicing the Orange.* Generally, they emphasize the "need to build a culture of creativity." They believe that "only a campaign that makes a genuine human connection with the audience can invite the consumer to participate in your message." So, watch for the creativity that led Fallon to such success with Citibank and Holiday Inn Express to continue to develop award-winning commercials for its many other clients, including Sony, Garmin, NBC, Purina, Nordstrom, *Time* magazine, and Volkswagen!

Questions

1 Fallon Worldwide stresses its creativity, as shown by the comments from the Fallon people in the case. (*a*) In what ways do the Citi and Holiday Inn Express campaigns reflect their creativity? (*b*) What were the sources of the ideas in the two campaigns?
2 In the Citi and Holiday Inn Express campaigns what were (*a*) the target markets, and (*b*) each brand's positioning?
3 Compare the media used for the Citi and the Holiday Inn Express campaigns. (*a*) Why were these media chosen? (*b*) Do you expect the use of these media to change in the future?
4 How might Fallon and its clients measure the success of (*a*) the Citi, and (*b*) the Holiday Inn Express campaigns?

17 Personal Selling and Sales Management

LEARNING OBJECTIVES

After reading this chapter you should be able to:

LO1 Discuss the nature and scope of personal selling and sales management in marketing.

LO2 Identify the different types of personal selling.

LO3 Explain the stages in the personal selling process.

LO4 Describe the major functions of sales management.

XEROX DELIVERS AN EXCEPTIONAL CUSTOMER EXPERIENCE BY SELLING THE WAY CUSTOMERS WANT TO BUY

Anne Mulcahy has a challenging assignment. As the chairman of the board and chief executive officer at Xerox Corporation, she is in the midst of successfully managing one of the greatest feats in the annals of business history: restoring Xerox's legendary marketing and financial vitality.

Her success to date can be attributed to staying in sync with Xerox customers and employees. "I believe strongly that my success as a leader is driven by my commitment to understanding and meeting customers' requirements, as well as developing and nurturing a motivated and proud workforce," says Mulcahy.

Mulcahy is ideally suited to the task. She began her 33-year Xerox career as a field sales representative and assumed increasingly responsible management and executive positions. These included chief staff officer, president of Xerox's General Markets Operations, and president and chief operating officer of Xerox. As chairman and CEO, Mulcahy had to muster the knowledge and experience gained from this varied background. Not surprisingly, her field sales background played a pivotal role.

"We will win back market share one customer at a time, one sale at a time," Mulcahy says. "We'll do that by providing greater value than our competitors—and that means selling the way customers want to buy." She adds, "Doing what's right for the customer—that's our guiding principle." And attention to the customer buying experience has paid huge dividends. Xerox sales revenue and net income have soared during Mulcahy's tenure as chairman and CEO. Her dedicated customer focus and field sales experience bodes well for the continued success of Xerox.[1]

This chapter describes the scope and significance of personal selling and sales management in marketing and creating value for customers. It first highlights the many forms of personal selling. Next, the major steps in the selling process are outlined with an emphasis on building buyer-seller relationships. Attention is then focused on salesforce management and its critical role in achieving a company's broader marketing objectives. Three major salesforce management functions are then detailed. They are sales plan formulation, sales plan implementation, and salesforce evaluation. Finally, technology's persuasive influence on how selling is done and how salespeople are managed is described.

SCOPE AND SIGNIFICANCE OF PERSONAL SELLING AND SALES MANAGEMENT

LO1

personal selling
The two-way flow of communication between a buyer and seller, often in a face-to-face encounter, designed to influence a person's or group's purchase decision

sales management
Planning the selling program, and implementing and evaluating the personal selling effort of the firm

Chapter 15 described personal selling and management of the sales effort as being part of the firm's promotional mix. Although it is important to recognize that personal selling is a useful vehicle for communicating with present and potential buyers, it is much more.

Nature of Personal Selling and Sales Management

Personal selling involves the two-way flow of communication between a buyer and seller, often in a face-to-face encounter, designed to influence a person's or group's purchase decision. However, with advances in telecommunications, personal selling also takes place over the telephone, through video teleconferencing and Internet-enabled links between buyers and sellers.

Personal selling remains a highly human-intensive activity despite the use of technology. Accordingly, the people involved must be managed. **Sales management** involves planning the selling program, and implementing and evaluating the personal selling effort of the firm. The tasks involved in managing personal selling include setting objectives; organizing the salesforce; recruiting, selecting, training, and compensating salespeople; and evaluating the performance of individual salespeople.

Selling Happens Almost Everywhere

"Everyone lives by selling something," wrote author Robert Louis Stevenson a century ago. His observation still holds true today. The Bureau of Labor Statistics reports that about 14 million people are employed in sales positions in the United States. Included in this number are manufacturing sales personnel, real estate brokers, stockbrokers, and salesclerks who work in retail stores. In reality, however, virtually every occupation that involves customer contact has an element of personal selling. For example, attorneys, accountants, bankers, and company personnel recruiters perform sales-related activities, whether or not they acknowledge it.

About 20 percent of chief executive officers in the largest U.S. corporations have significant sales experience in their work history like Anne Mulcahy at Xerox.[2] Thus, selling often serves as a stepping-stone to top management, as well as being a career path itself.

Could this be a salesperson in the operating room? Read the text to find why Medtronic salespeople visit hospital operating rooms.

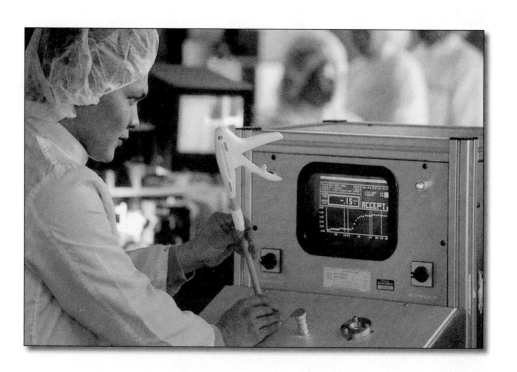

Personal Selling in Marketing

Personal selling serves three major roles in a firm's overall marketing effort. First, salespeople are the critical link between the firm and its customers. This role requires that salespeople match company interests with customer needs to satisfy both parties in the exchange process. Second, salespeople *are* the company in a consumer's eyes. They represent what a company is or attempts to be and are often the only personal contact a customer has with the company. For example, the "look" projected by Gucci salespeople is an important factor in communicating the style of the company's apparel line. Third, personal selling may play a dominant role in a firm's marketing program. This situation typically arises when a firm uses a push marketing strategy, described in Chapter 15. Avon, for example, pays almost 40 percent of its total sales dollars for selling expenses.

Creating Customer Solutions and Value through Salespeople: Relationship Selling

As the critical link between the firm and its customers, salespeople can create customer value in many ways. For instance, by being close to the customer, salespeople can identify creative solutions to customer problems. Salespeople at Medtronic Inc., the world leader in the heart pacemaker market, are in the operating room for more than 90 percent of the procedures performed with their product and are on call, wearing pagers, 24 hours a day. "It reflects the willingness to be there in every situation, just in case a problem arises—even though nine times out of ten the procedure goes just fine," notes a satisfied customer.[3] Salespeople can create value by easing the customer buying process. This happened at AMP Inc., a producer of electrical products. Salespeople and customers had a difficult time getting product specifications and performance data on AMP's 70,000 products quickly and accurately. The company now records all information on CD-ROM disks that can be scanned instantly by salespeople and customers. Customer value is also created by salespeople who follow through after the sale. At Jefferson Smurfit Corporation, a multibillion-dollar supplier of packaging products, one of its salespeople juggled production from three of the company's plants to satisfy an unexpected demand for boxes from General Electric. This person's action led to the company being given GE's Distinguished Supplier Award.

relationship selling

Practice of building ties to customers based on a salesperson's attention and commitment to customer needs over time

Customer value creation is made possible by **relationship selling**, the practice of building ties to customers based on a salesperson's attention and commitment to customer needs over time. Relationship selling involves mutual respect and trust among buyers and sellers. It focuses on creating long-term customers, not a onetime sale. A survey of 300 senior sales executives revealed that 96 percent consider "building long-term relationships with customers" to be the most important activity affecting sales performance. Companies such as Xerox, American Express, Electronic Data Systems, Motorola, and Owens-Corning have made relationship building a core focus of their sales effort.[4]

Relationship selling represents another dimension of customer relationship management. Both emphasize the importance of learning about customer needs and wants and tailoring solutions to customer problems as a means to customer value creation.

---

learning review

1. What is personal selling?

2. What is involved in sales management?

THE MANY FORMS OF PERSONAL SELLING

LO2

Personal selling assumes many forms based on the amount of selling done and the amount of creativity required to perform the sales task. Broadly speaking, two types of personal selling exist: order taking and order getting. While some firms use only one of these types of personal selling, others use a combination of both.

Order Taking

Typically, an **order taker** processes routine orders or reorders for products that were already sold by the company. The primary responsibility of order takers is to preserve an ongoing relationship with existing customers and maintain sales.

Two types of order takers exist. *Outside order takers* visit customers and replenish inventory stocks of resellers, such as retailers or wholesalers. For example, Frito-Lay salespeople call on supermarkets, convenience stores, and other establishments to ensure that the company's line of snack products (such as Doritos and Tostitos tortilla chips) is in adequate supply. In addition, outside order takers often provide assistance in arranging displays.

Inside order takers, also called *order clerks* or *salesclerks,* typically answer simple questions, take orders, and complete transactions with customers. Many retail clerks are inside order takers. Inside order takers are often employed by companies that use *inbound telemarketing,* the use of toll-free telephone numbers that customers can call to obtain information about products or services and make purchases. In business-to-business settings, order taking arises in straight rebuy situations as described in Chapter 6.

Order takers generally do little selling in a conventional sense and engage in only modest problem solving with customers. They often represent products that have few options, such as magazine subscriptions and highly standardized industrial products. Inbound telemarketing is also an essential selling activity for more "customer service" driven firms, such as Dell Inc. At these companies, order takers undergo extensive training so that they can better assist callers with their purchase decisions.

Order Getting

An **order getter** sells in a conventional sense and identifies prospective customers, provides customers with information, persuades customers to buy, closes sales, and follows up on customers' use of a product or service. Like order takers, order getters can be inside (an automobile salesperson) or outside (a Xerox salesperson). Order getting involves a high degree of creativity and customer empathy and is typically required for selling complex or technical products with many options, so considerable product knowledge and sales training are necessary. In modified rebuy or new-buy

A Frito-Lay salesperson takes inventory of snacks for the store manager to sign. In this situation, the manager will make a straight rebuy decision.

FIGURE 17–1

How do outside order-getting salespeople spend their time each week? You might be surprised after reading the text.

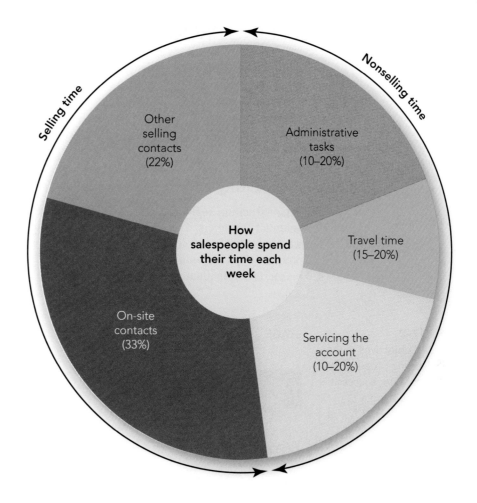

purchase situations in business-to-business selling, an order getter acts as a problem solver who identifies how a particular product may satisfy a customer's need. Similarly, in the purchase of a service, such as insurance, a Metropolitan Life insurance agent can provide a mix of plans to satisfy a buyer's needs depending on income, stage of the family's life cycle, and investment objectives.

Order getting is not a 40-hour-per-week job. Industry research shows that outside order getters, or field service representatives, often work over 50 hours per week. As shown in Figure 17–1, 55 percent of their time is spent selling. Another 10 to 20 percent is devoted to customer service calls. The remainder of their workweek is occupied by getting to customers and performing administrative tasks.[5]

Order getting by outside salespeople is also expensive. It is estimated that the average cost of a single field sales call on a business customer is about $350, factoring in salespeople compensation, benefits, and travel-and-entertainment expenses. This cost illustrates why outbound telemarketing is popular. *Outbound telemarketing* is the practice of using the telephone rather than personal visits to contact current and prospective customers. A much lower cost per sales call (from $20 to $25) and little or no field expense accounts for its widespread appeal. More than 100 million outbound telemarketing calls are made to homes and businesses each year in the United States.[6]

learning review

3. What is the principal difference between an order taker and an order getter?

4. What percentage of an order-getting salesperson's time is spent selling?

THE PERSONAL SELLING PROCESS: BUILDING RELATIONSHIPS

LO3

personal selling process
Sales activities occurring before and after the sale itself, consisting of six stages: (1) prospecting, (2) preapproach, (3) approach, (4) presentation, (5) close, and (6) follow-up

Selling, and particularly order getting, is a complicated activity that involves building buyer–seller relationships. Although the salesperson–customer interaction is essential to personal selling, much of a salesperson's work occurs before this meeting and continues after the sale itself. The **personal selling process** consists of six stages: (1) prospecting, (2) preapproach, (3) approach, (4) presentation, (5) close, and (6) follow-up (see Figure 17–2).

Prospecting

Personal selling begins with the *prospecting* stage—the search for and qualification of potential customers. There are three types of prospects. A *lead* is the name of a person who may be a possible customer. A *prospect* is a customer who wants or needs the product. If an individual wants the product, can afford to buy it, and is the decision maker, this individual is a *qualified prospect*.

FIGURE 17–2
Stages and objectives of the personal selling process. Each stage is critical for successful selling and building a relationship.

STAGE	OBJECTIVE	COMMENTS
1. Prospecting	Search for and qualify prospects	Start of the selling process; prospects produced through advertising, referrals, and cold canvassing
2. Preapproach	Gather information and decide how to approach the prospect	Information sources include personal observation, other customers, and own salespeople
3. Approach	Gain prospect's attention, stimulate interest, and make transition to the presentation	First impression is critical; gain attention and interest through reference to common acquaintances, a referral, or product demonstration
4. Presentation	Begin converting a prospect into a customer by creating a desire for the product or service	Different presentation formats are possible; however, involving the customer in the product or service through attention to particular needs is critical; important to deal professionally and ethically with prospect skepticism, indifference, or objections
5. Close	Obtain a purchase commitment from the prospect and create a customer	Salesperson asks for the purchase; different approaches include the trial close and assumptive close
6. Follow-up	Ensure that the customer is satisfied with the product or service	Resolve any problems faced by the customer to ensure customer satisfaction and future sales possibilities

Trade shows are a popular source for leads and prospects. Companies like TSCentral provide comprehensive trade show information.

Leads and prospects are generated using several sources. For example, advertising may contain a coupon or a toll-free number to generate leads. Some companies use exhibits at trade shows, professional meetings, and conferences to generate leads or prospects. Staffed by salespeople, these exhibits are used to attract the attention of prospective buyers and disseminate information. Others utilize the Internet for generating leads and prospects. Today, salespeople are using websites, e-mail, bulletin boards, and newsgroups to connect to individuals and companies that may be interested in their products or services.

Another approach for generating leads is through *cold canvassing* or *cold calling,* either in person or by telephone. This approach simply means that a salesperson may open a directory, pick a name, and contact that individual or business. Even with a high refusal rate, cold canvassing can be successful.[7] For example, on one occasion, 41 brokers at Lehman Brothers identified 18,004 prospects, qualified 1,208 of them, made 659 sales presentations, and opened 40 new accounts in four working days.

Cold canvassing is often criticized by U.S. consumers and is now regulated. A recent survey reported that 75 percent of U.S. consumers consider this practice an intrusion on their privacy, and 72 percent find it distasteful.[8] *The Telephone Consumer Protection Act* (1991) contains provisions to curb abuses such as early morning or late night calling. Additional federal regulations require more complete disclosure regarding solicitations, include provisions that allow consumers to avoid being called at any time through the Do Not Call Registry, and impose fines for violations. For example, satellite television provider DirecTV was fined $5.3 million for making thousands of calls to consumers who had put their telephone numbers on the Do Not Call Registry.[9]

Preapproach

Once a salesperson has identified a qualified prospect, preparation for the sale begins with the preapproach. The *preapproach* stage involves obtaining further information on the prospect and deciding on the best method of approach. Knowing how the prospect prefers to be approached, and what the prospect is looking for in a product or service, is essential.

For instance, a Merrill Lynch stockbroker will need information on a prospect's discretionary income, investment objectives, and preference for discussing brokerage services over the telephone or in person. For business product companies such as Texas Instruments, the preapproach involves identifying the buying role of a prospect (e.g., influencer or decision maker), important buying criteria, and the prospect's receptivity to a formal or informal presentation. Identifying the best time to contact a prospect is also important. Northwestern Mutual Life Insurance Company suggests the best times to call on people in different occupations: dentists before 9:30 A.M., lawyers between 11:00 A.M. and 2:00 P.M., and college professors between 7:00 P.M. and 8:00 P.M.

Successful salespeople recognize that the preapproach stage should never be shortchanged. Their experience coupled with research on customer complaints indicate that failure to learn as much as possible about the prospect is unprofessional and the ruin of a sales call.

Approach

The *approach* stage involves the initial meeting between the salesperson and prospect, where the objectives are to gain the prospect's attention, stimulate interest, and build the foundation for the sales presentation itself and the basis for a working relationship. The first impression is critical at this stage, and it is common for salespeople to begin the conversation with a reference to common acquaintances, a referral, or even the product or service itself. Which tactic is taken will depend on the information obtained in the prospecting and preapproach stages.

How business cards are exchanged with Asian customers is very important. Read the text to learn the appropriate protocol in the approach stage of the personal selling process.

The approach stage is very important in international settings. In many societies outside the United States, considerable time is devoted to nonbusiness talk designed to establish a rapport between buyers and sellers. For instance, it is common for two or three meetings to occur before business matters are discussed in the Middle East and Asia. Gestures are also very important. The initial meeting between a salesperson and a prospect in the United States customarily begins with a firm handshake. Handshakes also apply in France, but they are gentle, not firm. Forget the handshake in Japan. An appropriate bow is expected. What about business cards? Business cards should be printed in English on one side and the language of the prospective customer on the other. Knowledgeable U.S. salespeople know that their business cards should be handed to Asian customers using both hands, with the name facing the receiver. In Asia, anything involving a person's name demands respect.

Presentation

The *presentation* stage is at the core of the order-getting selling process, and its objective is to convert a prospect into a customer by creating a desire for the product or service. Three major presentation formats exist: (1) stimulus-response format, (2) formula selling format, and (3) need-satisfaction format.

Stimulus-Response Format The *stimulus-response presentation* format assumes that given the appropriate stimulus by a salesperson, the prospect will buy. With this format the salesperson tries one appeal after another, hoping to hit the right button. A counter clerk at McDonald's is using this approach when he or she asks whether you'd like an order of french fries or a dessert with your meal. The counter

clerk is engaging in what is called *suggestive selling*. Although useful in this setting, the stimulus-response format is not always appropriate, and for many products a more formalized format is necessary.

Formula Selling Format   The *formula selling presentation* format is based on the view that a presentation consists of information that must be provided in an accurate, thorough, and step-by-step manner to inform the prospect. A popular version of this format is the *canned sales presentation,* which is a memorized, standardized message conveyed to every prospect. Used frequently by firms in telephone and door-to-door selling of consumer products (e.g., Kirby vacuum cleaners), this approach treats every prospect the same, regardless of differences in needs or preference for certain kinds of information.

Canned sales presentations can be advantageous when the differences between prospects are unknown or with novice salespeople who are less knowledgeable about the product and selling process than experienced salespeople. Although it guarantees a thorough presentation, it often lacks flexibility and spontaneity and, more important, does not provide for feedback from the prospective buyer—a critical component in the communication process and the start of a relationship.

Need-Satisfaction Format   The stimulus-response and formula selling formats share a common characteristic: The salesperson dominates the conversation. By comparison, the *need-satisfaction presentation* format emphasizes probing and listening by the salesperson to identify needs and interests of prospective buyers. Once these are identified, the salesperson tailors the presentation to the prospect and highlights product benefits that may be valued by the prospect. The need-satisfaction format, which emphasizes problem solving and customer solutions, is the most consistent with the marketing concept and relationship building.

Rockport sales representatives are adept at adaptive selling to retail buyers.

Two selling styles are common with this format.[10] **Adaptive selling** involves adjusting the presentation to fit the selling situation, such as knowing when to offer solutions and when to ask for more information. Sales research and practice show that knowledge of the customer and sales situation are key ingredients for adaptive selling. Many consumer service firms such as brokerage and insurance firms and consumer product firms like Rockport, AT&T, and Gillette effectively apply this selling style.

Consultative selling focuses on problem identification, where the salesperson serves as an expert on problem recognition and resolution. With consultative selling, problem solution options are not simply a matter of choosing from an array of existing products or services. Rather, novel solutions often arise, thereby creating unique value for the customer.

Consultative selling is prominent in business-to-business marketing. Johnson Controls' Automotive Systems Group, IBM's Global Services, and DHL Worldwide Express offer customer solutions through their consultative selling style, as does Xerox. According to a senior Xerox sales executive, "Our business is no longer about selling boxes. It's about selling digital, networked-based information management solutions, and this requires a highly customized and consultative selling process." But what does a customer solution really mean? The Marketing Matters box on the next page offers a unique answer.[11]

Handling Objections   A critical concern in the presentation stage is handling objections. *Objections* are excuses for not making a purchase commitment or decision.

Solutions for problems are what companies are looking for from suppliers. At the same time, suppliers focus on customer solutions to differentiate themselves from competitors. So what is a customer solution and what does it have to do with selling?

Sellers view a solution as a customized and integrated combination of products and services for meeting a customer's business needs. But what do buyers think? From a buyer's perspective, a solution is one that (1) meets their requirements, (2) is designed to uniquely solve their problem, (3) can be implemented, and (4) ensures follow-up. This insight arose from a field study conducted by three researchers at Emory University. Their in-depth study also yielded insight into what an effective

customer solution offers. According to one buyer interviewed in their study:

They (the supplier) make sure that their sales and marketing guys know what's going on. The sales and technical folks know what's going on, and the technical and support guys know what's going on with me. All these guys are in the loop, and it's not a puzzle for them.

So what does putting the customer into customer solutions have to do with selling? Three things stand out. First, considerable time and effort is necessary to fully understand a specific customer's requirements. Second, effective customer solutions are based on relationships among sellers and buyers. And finally, consultative selling is central to providing novel solutions for customers, thereby creating value for them.

Some objections are valid and are based on the characteristics of the product or service or price. However, many objections reflect prospect skepticism or indifference. Whether valid or not, experienced salespeople know that objections do not put an end to the presentation. Rather, techniques can be used to deal with objections in a courteous, ethical, and professional manner. The following six techniques are the most common:[12]

1. *Acknowledge and convert the objection.* This technique involves using the objection as a reason for buying. For example, a prospect might say, "The price is too high." The reply: "Yes, the price is high because we use the finest materials. Let me show you. . . ."
2. *Postpone.* The postpone technique is used when the objection will be dealt with later in the presentation: "I'm going to address that point shortly. I think my answer would make better sense then."
3. *Agree and neutralize.* Here a salesperson agrees with the objection, then shows that it is unimportant. A salesperson would say, "That's true. Others have said the same. But, they thought that issue was outweighed by other benefits."
4. *Accept the objection.* Sometimes the objection is valid. Let the prospect express such views, probe for the reason behind it, and attempt to stimulate further discussion on the objection.
5. *Denial.* When a prospect's objection is based on misinformation and clearly untrue, it is wise to meet the objection head on with a firm denial.
6. *Ignore the objection.* This technique is used when it appears that the objection is a stalling mechanism or is clearly not important to the prospect.

Each of these techniques requires a calm, professional interaction with the prospect and is most effective when objections are anticipated in the preapproach stage. Handling objections is a skill requiring a sense of timing, appreciation for the prospect's state of mind, and adeptness in communication. Objections also should be handled ethically. Lying or misrepresenting product or service features is an unethical practice.

Close

The *closing* stage in the selling process involves obtaining a purchase commitment from the prospect. This stage is the most important and the most difficult because the salesperson must determine when the prospect is ready to buy. Telltale signals indicating a readiness to buy include body language (prospect reexamines the product or contract closely), statements ("This equipment should reduce our maintenance costs"), and questions ("When could we expect delivery?").

The close itself can take several forms. Three closing techniques are used when a salesperson believes a buyer is about ready to make a purchase: (1) trial close, (2) assumptive close, and (3) urgency close. A *trial close* involves asking the prospect to make a decision on some aspect of the purchase: "Would you prefer the blue or gray model?" An *assumptive close* entails asking the prospect to consider choices concerning delivery, warranty, or financing terms under the assumption that a sale has been finalized. An *urgency close* is used to commit the prospect quickly by making reference to the timeliness of the purchase: "The low interest financing ends next week," or "That is the last model we have in stock." Of course, these statements should be used only if they accurately reflect the situation; otherwise, such claims would be unethical. When a prospect is clearly ready to buy, the *final close* is used, and a salesperson asks for the order.

Follow-Up

The selling process does not end with the closing of a sale; rather, professional selling requires customer follow-up. One marketing authority equated the follow-up with courtship and marriage, by observing, "the sale merely consummates the courtship. Then the marriage begins. How good the marriage is depends on how well the relationship is managed."[13] The *follow-up* stage includes making certain the customer's purchase has been properly delivered and installed and difficulties experienced with the use of the item are addressed. Attention to this stage of the selling process solidifies the buyer–seller relationship. Research shows that the cost and effort to obtain repeat sales from a satisfied customer is roughly half of that necessary to gain a sale from a new customer.[14] In short, today's satisfied customers become tomorrow's qualified prospects or referrals.

---

learning review

5. What are the six stages in the personal selling process?

6. Which presentation format is most consistent with the marketing concept? Why?

THE SALES MANAGEMENT PROCESS

Selling must be managed if it is going to contribute to a firm's marketing objectives. Although firms differ in the specifics of how salespeople and the selling effort are managed, the sales management process is similar across firms. Sales management consists of three interrelated functions: (1) sales plan formulation, (2) sales plan implementation, and (3) salesforce evaluation (Figure 17–3 on the next page).

Sales Plan Formulation: Setting Direction

Formulating the sales plan is the most basic of the three sales management functions. According to the vice president of the Harris Corporation, a global communications

FIGURE 17–3

The sales management process involves sales plan formulation, sales plan implementation, and evaluation of the salesforce.

sales plan

Statement describing what is to be achieved and where and how the selling effort of salespeople is to be deployed

company, "If a company hopes to implement its marketing strategy, it really needs a detailed sales planning process."[15] The **sales plan** is a statement describing what is to be achieved and where and how the selling effort of salespeople is to be deployed. Sales plan formulation involves three tasks: (1) setting objectives, (2) organizing the salesforce, and (3) developing account management policies.

Setting Objectives Setting objectives is central to sales management because this task specifies what is to be achieved. In practice, objectives are set for the total salesforce and for each salesperson. Selling objectives can be output related and focus on dollar or unit sales volume, number of new customers added, and profit. Alternatively, they can be input related and emphasize the number of sales calls and selling expenses. Output- and input-related objectives are used for the salesforce as a whole and for each salesperson. A third type of objective that is behaviorally related is typically specific for each salesperson and includes his or her product knowledge, customer service, and selling and communication skills.

Organizing the Salesforce Establishing a selling organization is the second task in formulating the sales plan. Companies organize their salesforce on the basis of (1) geography, (2) customer, or (3) product or service. A geographical structure is the simplest organization, where the United States, or indeed the globe, is first divided into regions and each region is divided into districts or territories. Salespeople are assigned to each district with defined geographical boundaries and call on all customers and represent all products sold by the company. The main advantage of this structure is that it can minimize travel time, expenses, and duplication of selling effort. However, if a firm's products or customers require specialized knowledge, then a geographical structure is not suitable.

A customer sales organizational structure is used when different types of buyers have different needs. In practice this means that a different salesforce calls on each separate type of buyer or marketing channel. For example, Kodak recently switched from a geographical to a marketing channel structure with different sales teams serving specific retail channels: mass merchandisers, photo specialty outlets, and food and drug stores. The rationale for this approach is that more effective, specialized customer support and knowledge are provided to buyers. However, this structure often leads to higher administrative costs and some duplication of selling effort, because two separate salesforces are used to represent the same products.

major account management

Practice of using team selling to focus on important customers so as to build mutually beneficial, long-term, cooperative relationships; also called key account management

A variation of the customer organizational structure is **major account management**, or *key account management,* the practice of using team selling to focus on important customers so as to build mutually beneficial, long-term, cooperative relationships. Major account management involves teams of sales, service, and often technical personnel who work with purchasing, manufacturing, engineering, logistics, and financial executives in customer organizations. This approach, which often assigns company personnel to a customer account, results in "customer specialists" who can provide exceptional service. Procter & Gamble uses this approach with Wal-Mart as does Black & Decker with Home Depot. Other companies have embraced this practice as described in the accompanying Marketing Matters box.[16]

Creating and Sustaining Customer Value through Cross-Functional Team Selling

The day of the lone salesperson calling on a customer is rapidly becoming history. Today, 75 percent of companies employ cross-functional teams of professionals to work with customers to improve relationships, find better ways of doing things, and, of course, create and sustain value for their customers.

Xerox and IBM pioneered cross-functional team selling, but other firms were quick to follow as they spotted the potential to create and sustain value for their customers. Recognizing that corn growers needed a herbicide they could apply less often, a DuPont team of chemists, sales and marketing executives, and regulatory specialists created just the right product that recorded sales of $57 million in its first year. Procter & Gamble uses teams of marketing, sales, advertising, computer systems, and supply chain personnel to work with its major retailers, such as Wal-Mart, to identify ways to develop, promote, and deliver products. Pitney Bowes Inc., which produces sophisticated computer systems that weigh, rate, and track packages for firms such as UPS and FedEx, also uses sales teams to meet customer needs. These teams consist of sales personnel, "carrier management specialists," and engineering and administrative executives who continually find ways to improve the technology of shipping goods across town and around the world.

Efforts to create and sustain customer value through cross-functional team selling have become a necessity as customers seek greater value for their money. According to the vice president for procurement of a *Fortune* 500 company, "Today, it's not just getting the best price but getting the best value—and there are a lot of pieces to value."

A product sales organization is used when specific knowledge is required to sell a product. For example, Lone Star Steel has a salesforce that sells drilling pipe to oil companies and another that sells specialty steel products to manufacturers. The primary advantage of this structure is that salespeople can develop expertise with technical characteristics, applications, and selling methods associated with a particular product or family of products. However, this structure also produces high administrative costs and duplication of selling effort because two company salespeople may call on the same customer.

In short, there is no one best sales organization for all companies in all situations. The organization of the salesforce should reflect the marketing strategy of the firm.

Developing Account Management Policies

account management policies

Policies that specify whom salespeople should contact, what kinds of selling and customer service activities should be engaged in, and how these activities should be carried out

The third task in formulating a sales plan involves developing **account management policies** specifying whom salespeople should contact, what kinds of selling and customer service activities should be engaged in, and how these activities should be carried out. These policies might state which individuals in a buying organization should be contacted, the amount of sales and service effort that different customers should receive, and the kinds of information salespeople should collect before or during a sales call.

An example of an account management policy grid in Figure 17–4 on the next page shows how different accounts or customers can be grouped by level of opportunity and the firm's competitive sales position. When specific account names are placed in each cell, salespeople clearly see which accounts should be contacted, with what level of selling and service activity, and how to deal with them. Accounts in cells 1 and 2 might

Competitive position of sales organization

High · Low

	High	**Low**
High	**1** *Attractiveness:* Accounts offer a good opportunity because they have high potential and the sales organization has a strong position. *Account management policy:* Accounts should receive high level of sales calls and service to retain and possibly build accounts.	**3** *Attractiveness:* Accounts may offer a good opportunity if the sales organization can overcome its weak position. *Account management policy:* Emphasize a heavy sales organization position or shift resources to other accounts if a stronger sales organization position is impossible.
Low	**2** *Attractiveness:* Accounts are somewhat attractive because the sales organization has a strong position, but future opportunity is limited. *Account management policy:* Accounts should receive moderate level of sales and service to maintain current position of sales organization.	**4** *Attractiveness:* Accounts offer little opportunity, and the sales organization position is weak. *Account management policy:* Consider replacing personal calls with telephone sales or direct mail to service accounts. Consider dropping account if unprofitable.

(Account opportunity — High / Low, vertical axis)

FIGURE 17–4

An account management policy grid grouping customers according to the level of opportunity and a firm's competitive sales position

have high frequencies of personal sales calls and increased time spent on a call. Cell 3 accounts will have lower call frequencies. Cell 4 accounts might be contacted through telemarketing or direct mail rather than in person. For example, Union Pacific Railroad recently put its 20,000 smallest accounts on a telemarketing program. A subsequent survey of these accounts indicated that 84 percent rated Union Pacific's sales effort "very effective" compared with 67 percent before the switch.

Sales Plan Implementation: Putting the Plan into Action

The sales plan is put into practice through the tasks associated with sales plan implementation. Whereas sales plan formulation focuses on "doing the right things," implementation emphasizes "doing things right." The three major tasks involved in implementing a sales plan are: (1) salesforce recruitment and selection, (2) salesforce training, and (3) salesforce motivation and compensation.

Salesforce Recruitment and Selection

Effective recruitment and selection of salespeople is one of the most crucial tasks of sales management.[17] It entails finding people who match the type of sales position required by a firm. Recruitment and selection practices would differ greatly between order-taking and order-getting sales positions, given the differences in the demands of these two jobs. Therefore, recruitment and selection begin with a carefully crafted job analysis and job description followed by a statement of job qualifications.

A *job analysis* is a study of a particular sales position, including how the job is to be performed and the tasks that make up the job. Information from a job analysis is used to write a *job description*, a written document that describes job relationships and requirements that characterize each sales position. It explains (1) to whom a salesperson reports, (2) how a salesperson interacts with other company personnel, (3) the customers to be called on, (4) the specific activities to be carried out, (5) the physical and mental demands of the job, and (6) the types of products and services to be sold. The job description is then translated into a statement of job qualifications, including the aptitudes, knowledge, skills, and a variety of behavioral characteristics considered necessary to perform the job successfully. Qualifications for order-getting sales positions often mirror the expectations of buyers: (1) imagination and problem-solving ability, (2) honesty, (3) intimate product knowledge, and (4) attentiveness reflected in responsiveness to buyer needs, customer loyalty, and follow-up. Firms use a variety of methods for evaluating prospective salespeople. Personal interviews, reference checks, and background information provided on application forms are the most frequently used methods.

Salesforce Training   Whereas recruitment and selection of salespeople is a onetime event, salesforce training is an ongoing process that affects both new and seasoned salespeople.[18] Sales training covers much more than selling practices. For example, IBM Global Services salespeople, who sell consulting and various information technology services, take at least two weeks of in-class and Internet-based training on both consultative selling and the technical aspects of business.

On-the-job training is the most popular type of training, followed by individual instruction taught by experienced salespeople. Formal classes, seminars taught by sales trainers, and computer-based training are also popular.

Salesforce Motivation and Compensation   A sales plan cannot be successfully implemented without motivated salespeople. Research on salesperson motivation suggests that (1) a clear job description; (2) effective sales management practices; (3) a personal need for achievement; and (4) proper compensation, incentives, or rewards will produce a motivated salesperson.[19]

The importance of compensation as a motivating factor means that close attention must be given to how salespeople are financially rewarded for their efforts. Salespeople are paid using one of three plans: (1) straight salary, (2) straight commission, or (3) a combination of salary and commission. Under a *straight salary compensation plan,* a salesperson is paid a fixed fee per week, month, or year. With a *straight commission compensation plan,* a salesperson's earnings are directly tied to the sales or profit generated. For example, an insurance agent might receive a 2 percent commission of $2,000 for selling a $100,000 life insurance policy. A *combination compensation plan* contains a specified salary plus a commission on sales or profit generated.

Each compensation plan has its advantages and disadvantages.[20] A straight salary plan is easy to administer and gives management a large measure of control over how salespeople allocate their efforts. However, it provides little incentive to expand sales volume. This plan is used when salespeople engage in many nonselling activities, such as account or customer servicing. A straight commission plan provides the maximum amount of selling incentive but can detract salespeople from providing customer service. This plan is common when nonselling activities are minimal. Combination plans are most preferred by salespeople and attempt to build on the advantages of salary and commission plans while reducing potential shortcomings of each.

Why is Jill Moore, a successful Mary Kay Cosmetics national sales director, posing with a new pink Cadillac Escalade before the company's annual sales meeting? Read the text to learn how Mary Kay rewards its top sales performers.

Nonmonetary rewards are also given to salespeople for meeting or exceeding objectives. These rewards include trips, honor societies, distinguished salesperson awards, and letters of commendation. Some unconventional rewards include the new pink Cadillacs and Pontiacs and jewelry given by Mary Kay Cosmetics to outstanding salespeople. Mary Kay, with 12,000 cars, has the largest fleet of General Motors cars in the world.[21]

Effective recruitment, selection, training, motivation, and compensation programs combine to create a productive salesforce. Ineffective practices often lead to costly salesforce turnover. The expense of replacing and training a new salesperson, including the cost of lost sales, can be high. Also, new recruits are often less productive than seasoned salespeople.

Salesforce Evaluation: Measuring Results

The final function in the sales management process involves evaluating the salesforce. It is at this point that salespeople are assessed as to whether sales objectives were met and account management policies were followed. Both quantitative and behavioral measures are used to assess different selling dimensions.

Quantitative Assessments

Quantitative assessments are based on input- and output-related objectives set forth in the sales plan. Input-related measures focus on the actual activities performed by salespeople such as those involving sales calls, selling expenses, and account management policies. The number of sales calls made, selling expense related to sales made, and the number of reports submitted to superiors are frequently used input measures.

Output measures often appear in a sales quota. A **sales quota** contains specific goals assigned to a salesperson, sales team, branch sales office, or sales district for a stated time period. Dollar or unit sales volume, last year/current sales ratio, sales of specific products, new accounts generated, and profit achieved are typical goals. The time period can range from one month to one year.

sales quota

Specific goals assigned to a salesperson, sales team, branch sales office, or sales district for a stated period

Behavioral Evaluation

Behavioral measures are also used to evaluate salespeople. These include assessments of a salesperson's attitude, attention to customers, product knowledge, selling and communication skills, appearance, and professional demeanor.[22]

About 60 percent of U.S. companies now include customer satisfaction as a behavioral measure of salesperson performance. Indianapolis Power & Light, for example, asks major customers to grade its salespeople from A to F. IBM Siebel Systems has been the most aggressive in using this behavioral measure. Forty percent of a Siebel salesperson's evaluation is linked to customer satisfaction; the remaining 60 percent is linked to profits achieved.

Increasingly, companies are using marketing dashboards to track salesperson performance for evaluation purposes. An illustration appears in the accompanying Using Marketing Dashboards box.

Salesforce Automation and Customer Relationship Management

Personal selling and sales management have undergone a technological revolution with the integration of salesforce automation into customer relationship management processes. In fact, the convergence of computer, information, communication, and Internet technologies has transformed the sales function in many companies and made the promise of customer relationship management a reality. **Salesforce automation (SFA)** is the use of these technologies to make the sales function more effective and efficient. SFA applies to a wide range of activities, including each stage in the personal selling process and management of the salesforce itself.[23]

Salesforce automation exists in many forms. Examples of SFA applications include computer hardware and software for account analysis, time management, order processing and follow-up, sales presentations, proposal generation, and product and sales training. Each application is designed to ease administrative tasks and free up time for salespeople to be with customers building relationships, designing solutions, and providing service.

salesforce automation (SFA)

Use of technology to make the sales function more effective and efficient

Salesforce Technology

Technology has become an integral part of field selling. Today, most companies supply their field salespeople with laptop computers.

Using Marketing Dashboards

Tracking Salesperson Performance at Moore Chemical & Sanitation Supply Inc.

Moore Chemical & Sanitation Supply Inc. (MooreChem) is a large midwestern supplier of cleaning chemicals and sanitary products. MooreChem sells to janitorial companies that clean corporate and professional office buildings.

MooreChem recently installed a sales and account management planning software package that included a dashboard for each of its sales representatives. Salespeople had access to their dashboards as well. These dashboards included seven measures—sales revenue, gross margin, selling expense, profit, average order size, new customers, and customer satisfaction. Each measure was gauged to show actual salesperson performance relative to target goals.

Your Challenge As a newly promoted district sales manager at MooreChem, your responsibilities include tracking each salesperson's performance in your district. You are also responsible for directing the sales activities and practices of district salespeople.

In anticipation of a performance review with one of your salespeople, Brady Boyle, you review his dashboard for the previous quarter. Provide a constructive review of his performance.

Your Findings Brady Boyle's quarterly performance is displayed below. Boyle has exceeded targeted goals for sales revenue, selling expenses, and customer satisfaction. All of these measures show an upward trend. He has met his target for gaining new customers and average order size. But, Boyle's gross margin and profit are below targeted goals. These measures evidence a downward trend as well. Brady Boyle's mixed performance requires a constructive and positive correction.

Your Action Brady Boyle should already know how his performance compares with targeted goals. Remember, Boyle has access to his dashboard. Recall that he has exceeded his sales target, but is considerably under his profit target. Boyle's sales trend is up, but his profit trend is down.

You will need to focus attention on Boyle's gross margin and selling expense results and trend. Boyle, it seems, is spending time and money selling lower margin products that produce a targeted average order size. It may very well be that Boyle is actually expending effort selling more products to his customers. Unfortunately, the product mix yields lower gross margins, resulting in a lower profit.

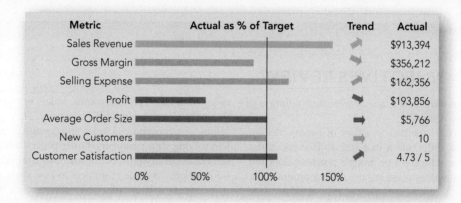

Metric	Actual as % of Target	Trend	Actual
Sales Revenue		↗	$913,394
Gross Margin		↘	$356,212
Selling Expense		↗	$162,356
Profit		↘	$193,856
Average Order Size		→	$5,766
New Customers		→	10
Customer Satisfaction		↗	4.73 / 5

For example, salespeople for Godiva Chocolates use their laptop computers to process orders, plan time allocations, forecast sales, and communicate with Godiva personnel and customers. While in a department store candy buyer's office, such as Neiman Marcus, a salesperson can calculate the order cost (and discount), transmit the order, and obtain a delivery date within minutes from Godiva's order processing department.[24]

Toshiba America Medical System salespeople use laptop computers with built-in CD-ROM capabilities to provide interactive presentations for their computerized tomography (CT) and magnetic resonance imaging (MRI) scanners. In it the customer sees elaborate three-dimensional animations, high-resolution scans, and video clips of the company's products in operation as well as narrated testimonials from satisfied customers. Toshiba has found this application to be effective both for sales presentations and for training its salespeople.[25]

Salesforce Communication   Technology has changed the way salespeople communicate with customers, other salespeople and sales support personnel, and management. Facsimile, electronic mail, and voice mail are common communication technologies used by salespeople today. Cellular (phone) technology, which now allows salespeople to exchange data, text, and voice transmissions, is also popular. Whether traveling or in a customer's office, these technologies provide information at the salesperson's fingertips to answer customer questions and solve problems.

Perhaps the greatest impact on salesforce communication is the application of Internet technology. Today, salespeople are using their company's intranet for a variety of purposes. At EDS, a professional services firm, salespeople access its intranet to download client material, marketing content, account information, technical papers, and competitive profiles. In addition, EDS offers 7,000 training classes that salespeople can take anytime and anywhere.

Salesforce automation is clearly changing how selling is done and how salespeople are managed. Its numerous applications promise to boost selling productivity, improve customer relationships, and decrease selling cost.

Salespeople rely upon multiple communication technologies to perform their selling and nonselling tasks today.

---

learning review

7. What are the three types of selling objectives?

8. What three factors are used to structure sales organizations?

LEARNING OBJECTIVES REVIEW

LO1   *Discuss the nature and scope of personal selling and sales management in marketing.*

Personal selling involves the two-way flow of communication between a buyer and seller, often in a face-to-face encounter, designed to influence a person's or group's purchase decision. Sales management involves planning the selling program and implementing and controlling the personal selling effort of the firm. The scope of selling and sales management is apparent in three ways. First, virtually every occupation that involves customer contact has an element of personal selling. Second, selling plays a significant role in a company's overall marketing effort. Salespeople occupy a boundary position between buyers and sellers; they *are* the company to many buyers and account for a major cost of marketing in a variety of industries; and they can create value for customers. Finally, through relationship selling, salespeople play a central role in tailoring solutions to customer problems as a means to customer value creation.

LO2   *Identify the different types of personal selling.*

Two types of personal selling exist: (*a*) order taking and (*b*) order getting. Each type differs from the others in terms of actual selling done and the amount of creativity required to perform the sales

task. Order takers process routine orders or reorders for products that were already sold by the company. They generally do little selling in a conventional sense and engage in only modest problem solving with customers. Order getters sell in a conventional sense and identify prospective customers, provide customers with information, persuade customers to buy, close sales, and follow up on customers' use of a product or service. Order getting involves a high degree of creativity and customer empathy and is typically required for selling complex or technical products with many options. Customer sales support personnel augment the sales effort of order getters by performing a variety of services.

LO3   *Explain the stages in the personal selling process.*

The personal selling process consists of six stages: (*a*) prospecting, (*b*) preapproach, (*c*) approach, (*d*) presentation, (*e*) close, and (*f*) follow-up. Prospecting involves the search for and qualification of potential customers. The preapproach stage involves obtaining further information on the prospect and deciding on the best method of approach. The approach stage involves the initial meeting between the salesperson and prospect. The presentation stage involves converting a prospect into a customer by creating a desire for the product or service. The close involves obtaining a purchase commitment from the prospect. The follow-up stage involves making certain that the customer's purchase has been properly delivered and installed and difficulties experienced with the use of the item are addressed.

LO4 *Describe the major functions of sales management.*
Sales management consists of three interrelated functions: (*a*) sales plan formulation, (*b*) sales plan implementation, and (*c*) evaluation of the salesforce. Sales plan formulation involves setting objectives, organizing the salesforce, and developing account management policies. Sales plan implementation involves salesforce recruitment, selection, training, motivation, and compensation. Finally, salesforce evaluation focuses on quantitative assessments of sales performance and behavioral measures such as customer satisfaction that are linked to selling objectives and account management policies.

FOCUSING ON KEY TERMS

account management policies p. 395	**order taker** p. 386	**sales management** p. 384
adaptive selling p. 391	**personal selling** p. 384	**sales plan** p. 394
consultative selling p. 391	**personal selling process** p. 388	**sales quota** p. 398
major account management p. 394	**relationship selling** p. 385	
order getter p. 386	**salesforce automation** p. 398	

APPLYING MARKETING KNOWLEDGE

1 Jane Dawson is a new sales representative for the Charles Schwab brokerage firm. In searching for clients, Jane purchased a mailing list of subscribers to *The Wall Street Journal* and called them all regarding their interest in discount brokerage services. She asked if they have any stocks and if they have a regular broker. Those people without a regular broker were asked their investment needs. Two days later Jane called back with investment advice and asked if they would like to open an account. Identify each of Jane Dawson's actions in terms of the steps of selling.

2 For the first 50 years of business the Johnson Carpet Company produced carpets for residential use. The salesforce was structured geographically. In the past five years, a large percentage of carpet sales has been to industrial users, hospitals, schools, and architects. The company also has broadened its product line to include area rugs, Oriental carpets, and wall-to-wall carpeting. Is the present salesforce structure appropriate, or would you recommend an alternative?

3 Where would you place each of the following sales jobs on the order-taker/order-getter continuum shown below? (*a*) Burger King counter clerk, (*b*) automobile insurance salesperson, (*c*) IBM computer salesperson, (*d*) life insurance salesperson, and (*e*) shoe salesperson.

Order taker ————————————————— Order getter

4 Listed here are two different firms. Which compensation plan would you recommend for each firm, and what reasons would you give for your recommendations? (*a*) A newly formed company that sells lawn care equipment on a door-to-door basis directly to consumers; and (*b*) the Nabisco Company, which sells heavily advertised products in supermarkets by having the salesforce call on these stores and arrange shelves, set up displays, and make presentations to store buying committees.

5 Suppose someone said to you, "The only real measure of a salesperson is the amount of sales produced." How might you respond?

building your marketing plan

Does your marketing plan involve a personal selling activity? If the answer is no, read no further and do not include a personal selling element in your plan. If the answer is yes:

1 Identify the likely prospects for your product or service.
2 Determine what information you should obtain about the prospect.

3 Describe how you would approach the prospect.
4 Outline the presentation you would make to the prospect for your product or service.
5 Develop a sales plan, focusing on the organizational structure you would use for your salesforce (geography, product, or customer).

"I'm like the quarterback of the team. I manage 250 accounts, and anything from billing issues, to service issues, to selling the products. I'm really the face to the customer," says Alison Capossela, a Washington, D.C.–based Xerox sales representative.

As the primary company contact for Xerox customers, Alison is responsible for developing and maintaining customer relationships. To accomplish this she uses a sophisticated selling process which requires many activities from making presentations, to attending training sessions, to managing a team of Xerox personnel, to monitoring competitors' activities. The face-to-face interactions with customers, however, are the most rewarding for Capossela. "It's an amazing feeling; the more they challenge me the more I fight back. It's fun!" she explains.

THE COMPANY

Xerox Corporation's mission is to "help people find better ways to do great work by constantly leading in document technologies, products, and services that improve customers' work processes and business results." To accomplish this mission Xerox employs 53,700 people in 160 countries. With annual sales of $16 billion, Xerox is the world's leading document management enterprise and a *Fortune* 500 company. Xerox offers a wide range of products and services. These include printers, copiers and fax machines, multifunction and network devices, high-speed color presses, digital imaging and archiving products and services, and supplies such as toner, paper, and ink. The entire company is guided by customer-focused and employee-centered core values (e.g., "We succeed through satisfied customers") and a passion for innovation, speed, and adaptability.

Xerox was founded in 1906 as a manufacturer of photographic paper called The Haloid Company. In 1947, the company purchased the license to basic xerographic patents. The following year it received a trademark for the word "Xerox." By 1973 Xerox had introduced the automatic, plain-paper copier, opened offices in Japan, and its Palo Alto Research Center (PARC) had invented the world's first personal computer (the Alto), the "mouse," and graphical user interface software. In 1994, Xerox adopted "The Document Company" as its signature and the partially digitized red "X" as its corporate symbol. Despite this extraordinary history of success, Xerox was $19 billion in debt by 2000 and was losing business rapidly. Many experts predicted that the company would fail.

The Xerox board of directors knew a change was needed and it asked Anne M. Mulcahy to serve as the company's CEO. Mulcahy had begun her career as a sales representative at Xerox and observed that "we had lost our way in terms of delivering value to customers." Mulcahy reduced the size of the workforce by one-third and invested in new technologies, while keeping the Xerox culture and values. The changes, coupled with Mulcahy's commitment to a sales organization that focused on customer relationships, reversed Xerox's decline. As Kevin Warren, vice president of sales explains: "One of the reasons she has been so successful is that she absolutely resonates with all the people. I think [because of] the fact that she started out as a sales rep, people feel like she is one of them." The turnaround has been such an extraordinary success that Mulcahy was recently recognized by *Forbes* magazine as the tenth most powerful woman in the world!

THE SELLING PROCESS AT XEROX

When Mulcahy became CEO, Xerox began a shift to a consultative selling model that focused on helping customers solve their business problems rather than just placing more equipment in their office. The shift meant that sales reps needed to be less product-oriented and more relationship- and value-oriented. Xerox wanted to be a provider of total solutions. Today, Xerox has more than 8,000 sales professionals throughout the world who spend a large amount of their day developing customer relationships. Capossela explains: "Fifty percent of my day is spent with my customers, twenty-five percent is following up with phone calls or e-mails, and another twenty-five percent involves preparing proposals." The approach has helped Xerox attract new customers and keep existing customers.

The sales process at Xerox typically follows the six stages of the personal selling process identified in Figure 17–2: (1) Xerox identifies potential clients through responses to advertising, referrals, and telephone calls; (2) the salesforce prepares for a presentation by familiarizing themselves with the potential client and its document needs; (3) a Xerox sales representative approaches the prospect and suggests a meeting and presentation; (4) as the presentation begins, the salesperson summarizes relevant information about potential solutions Xerox can offer, states what he or she hopes to get out of the meeting, explains how the products and services work, and reinforces the benefits of working with Xerox; (5) the salesperson engages in an action close (gets a signed document or a firm confirmation of the sale); and then (6) continues to meet and communicate with the client to provide assistance and monitor the effectiveness of the installed solution.

Xerox sales representatives also use the selling process to maintain relationships with existing customers.

In today's competitive environment it is not unusual to have customers who have been approached by competitors or who are required to obtain more than one bid before renewing a contract. Xerox has teams of people who collect and analyze information about competitors and their products. The information is sent out to sales reps or offered to them through workshops and seminars. The most difficult competitors are the ones that have also invested in customer relationships. The selling process allows Xerox to continually react and respond to new information and take advantage of opportunities in the marketplace.

of the program consisted of interactive training sessions and distance-learning Webinars. Every new sales representative at Xerox receives eight weeks of training development in the field and at the Xerox Corporate University in Virginia. "The training program is phenomenal!" according to Capossela. The training and its focus on the customer is part of the Xerox culture outside of the sales organization also. Every senior executive at Xerox is responsible for working with at least one customer. They also spend a full day every month responding to incoming customer calls and inquiries.

THE SALES MANAGEMENT PROCESS AT XEROX

The Xerox salesforce is divided into four geographic organizations: North America, which includes the United States and Canada; Europe, which includes 17 countries; Global Accounts, which manages large accounts that operate in multiple locations; and Developing Markets, which includes all other geographic territories that may require Xerox products and services. Within each geographic area, the majority of Xerox products and services are typically sold through its direct salesforce. Xerox also utilizes a variety of other channels, including value-added resellers, independent agents, dealers, systems integrators, telephone, and Internet sales channels.

Motivation and compensation is an important aspect of any salesforce. At Xerox there is a passion for winning that provides a key incentive for sales reps. In addition, the compensation plan plays an important role. As Warren explains, "Our compensation plans are a combination of salary as well as an opportunity to leverage earnings through sales commissions and bonuses." Xerox also has a recognition program called the President's Club where the top performers are awarded a five-day trip to one of the top resorts in the world. The program has been a huge success and has now been offered for more than 30 years.

Perhaps the most well-known component of Xerox's sales management process is its sales representative training program. For example, Xerox developed the "Create and Win" program to help sales reps learn the new consultative selling approach. The components

WHAT IS IN THE FUTURE FOR THE XEROX SALESFORCE?

The recent growth and success at Xerox is creating many opportunities for the company and for its sales representatives. For example, Xerox is accelerating the development of its top salespeople. Mentors are used to provide advice for day-to-day issues and long-term career planning. In addition, globalization has become such an important initiative at Xerox that experienced and successful sales representatives are quickly given opportunities to manage large global accounts. Xerox is also moving toward an approach that empowers sales representatives to make decisions about how to handle accounts. The large number of Xerox customers means there are a variety of different corporate styles, and the sales reps are increasingly the best qualified to manage the relationship. This approach is just one more example of Xerox's commitment to customers and creating customer value.

Questions

1 Why was Anne Mulcahy's experience as a sales representative an important part of Xerox's growth in recent years?

2 How did the sales approach change after Mulcahy became the CEO of Xerox?

3 How does Xerox create customer value though its personal selling process? How does Alison Capossela provide solutions for Xerox customers?

4 Why is the Xerox training program so important to the company's success?

18

Implementing Interactive and Multichannel Marketing

LEARNING OBJECTIVES

After reading this chapter you should be able to:

LO1 Describe what interactive marketing is and how it creates customer value, customer relationships, and customer experiences.

LO2 Explain why certain types of products and services are particularly suited for interactive marketing.

LO3 Describe why consumers shop and buy online and how marketers influence online purchasing behavior.

LO4 Define cross-channel shoppers and the role of transactional and promotional websites in reaching these shoppers.

SEVEN CYCLES. ONE BIKE. YOURS.

"One bike. Yours" is the company motto for Seven Cycles Inc., located in Watertown, Massachusetts. And for good reason.

Seven Cycles is the largest custom bicycle frame builder in the world. The company produces a huge range of road, mountain, cyclo-cross, triathlon, single-speed, and tandem bikes annually, and no two bikes are exactly alike. At Seven Cycles, attention is focused on each customer's unique cycling experience through the optimum fit, function, performance, and comfort of his or her very own bike. According to one satisfied customer, "Getting a Seven is more of a creation than a purchase."

The marketing success of Seven Cycles is due certainly to its state-of-the-art bicycle frames. But as Rob Vandermark, company founder and president, says, "Part of our success is that we are tied to a business model that includes the Internet."

Seven Cycles uses its multi-language (English, German, Chinese, Japanese, and Korean) website (www.sevencycles.com) to let customers get deeply involved in the frame-building process and the selection of wheels, drive train components, saddle, and handlebars to complete the bike. It enables customers to design their own bike using the company's Custom Kit™ fitting system that considers the rider's size and riding habits. Then, customers can track their custom bike all the way through the development and production process by clicking "Where's My Frame?" on the Seven Cycles website.

This customization process and continuous feedback makes for a collaborative relationship between Seven Cycles, its 230 authorized dealers and distributors, and customers in 40 countries. "It also results in a customer experience as unique as each bike made," says Jennifer Miller, director of marketing at Seven Cycles.[1]

This chapter describes how companies design and implement interactive marketing programs that capitalize on the unique value-creation capabilities of Internet technology. We begin by explaining how this technology can create customer value, build customer relationships, and produce customer experiences in novel ways. Next, we describe how Internet technology affects and is affected by consumer behavior and marketing practice. Finally, we show how marketers integrate and leverage their communication and delivery channels using Internet technology to implement multichannel marketing programs.

CREATING CUSTOMER VALUE, RELATIONSHIPS, AND EXPERIENCES IN MARKETSPACE

LO1

Consumers and companies populate two market environments today. One is the traditional *marketplace.* Here buyers and sellers engage in face-to-face exchange relationships in a material environment characterized by physical facilities (stores and offices) and mostly tangible objects. The other is the *marketspace,* an Internet-enabled digital environment characterized by face-to-screen exchange relationships and electronic images and offerings.

The existence of two market environments has been a boon for consumers. Today, consumers can shop for and purchase a wide variety of products and services in either market environment. Actually, many consumers now browse and buy in both market environments, and more are expected to do so in the future. Figure 18–1 shows the growth in online shoppers and estimated retail sales in the United States since 2000.[2] By 2011, 156 million individuals, or 80 percent of Internet users ages 14 and older, will shop online in the United States. They are projected to buy $340 billion worth of products and services in 2011.

Customer Value Creation in Marketspace

Why has the marketspace captured the eye and imagination of marketers worldwide? Recall from Chapter 1 that marketing creates time, place, form, and possession utilities, thereby providing value. Marketers believe that the possibilities for customer value creation are greater in the digital marketspace than in the physical marketplace.

In marketspace, the provision of direct, on-demand information is possible from marketers *anywhere* to customers *anywhere at any time.* Why? Operating hours and geographical constraints do not exist in marketspace. For example, Recreational Equipment (www.rei.com), an outdoor gear marketer, reports that 35 percent of its orders are placed between 10:00 P.M. and 7:00 A.M., long after and before retail stores are open for business. This isn't surprising. About 58 percent of Internet users prefer to shop and buy in their pajamas.[3] Similarly, a U.S. consumer from Chicago can access Marks & Spencer (www.marks-and-spencer.co.uk), the well-known British department store, to shop for clothing as easily as a person living near London's Piccadilly Square.

Possession utility—getting a product or service to consumers so they can own or use it—is accelerated. Airline, car rental, and lodging electronic reservation systems such as Orbitz (www.orbitz.com) allow comparison shopping for the lowest fares, rents, and rates and almost immediate access to and confirmation of travel arrangements and accommodations. Not surprisingly, Internet usage among people who travel on a regular basis is 20 percent higher than those who travel infrequently.[4]

FIGURE 18–1

Trend in online shoppers and online retail sales revenue in the United States

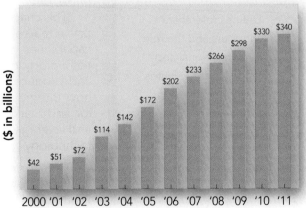

No matter what form your two-wheeled passion takes. Whatever road, trail, or entirely improvised route you follow. There is a Seven for you. Expertly designed and handcrafted for who you are and the way you ride.

www.sevencycles.com   **telephone** 617.923.7774   **email** info@sevencycles.com   **One Bike. Yours.**

Seven Cycles creates form utility in the creation of customized bikes for its customers in 40 countries.

The greatest marketspace opportunity for marketers, however, lies in its potential for creating form utility. Interactive two-way Internet-enabled communication capabilities in marketspace invite consumers to tell marketers specifically what their requirements are, making customization of a product or service to fit the buyer's exact needs possible. For instance, at Godiva.com, customers can choose an assortment of their favorite chocolates from an online catalog for a gift or a delectable self-indulgent treat. Or, consumers can arrange for a custom-made mountain bike from Seven Cycles as described in the chapter-opening example.

Interactivity, Individuality, and Customer Relationships in Marketspace

Marketers also benefit from two unique capabilities of Internet technology that promote and sustain customer relationships. One is *interactivity;* the other is *individuality.*[5] Both capabilities are important building blocks for buyer–seller relationships. For these relationships to occur, companies need to interact with their customers by listening and responding to their needs. Marketers must also treat customers as individuals and empower them to (1) influence the timing and extent of the buyer–seller interaction and (2) have a say in the kind of products and services they buy, the information they receive, and in some cases, the prices they pay.

Internet technology allows for interaction, individualization, and customer relationship building to be carried out on a scale never before available and makes interactive marketing possible. **Interactive marketing** involves two-way buyer–seller electronic communication in a computer-mediated environment in which the buyer controls the kind and amount of information received from the seller. Interactive

interactive marketing

Two-way buyer–seller electronic communication in a computer-mediated environment in which the buyer controls the kind and amount of information received from the seller

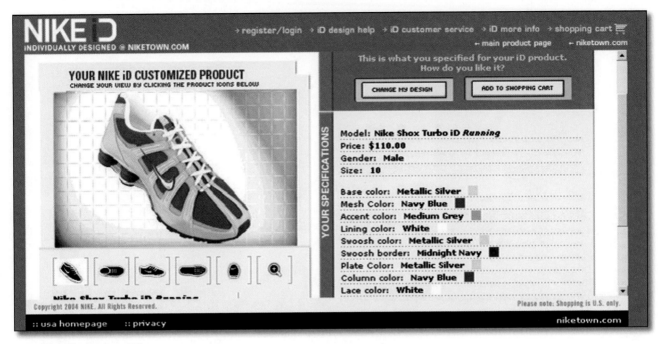

Nike has effectively used choiceboard technology for customizing athletic shoes.

choiceboard
Interactive, Internet-enabled system that allows individual customers to design their own products and services

collaborative filtering
Process that automatically groups people with similar buying intentions, preferences, and behaviors, and predicts future purchases

marketing is characterized by sophisticated choiceboard and personalization systems that transform information supplied by customers into customized responses to their individual needs.

Choiceboards   A **choiceboard** is an interactive, Internet-enabled system that allows individual customers to design their own products and services by answering a few questions and choosing from a menu of product or service attributes (or components), prices, and delivery options.[6] Customers today can design their own computers with Dell's online configurator, style their own athletic shoe at NikeID. com, assemble their own investment portfolios with Schwab's mutual funds evaluator, build their own bicycle at SevenCycles.com, and create a diet and fitness program at ediet.com that fits their lifestyle. Because choiceboards collect precise information about preferences and behavior of individual buyers, a company becomes more knowledgeable about a customer and better able to anticipate and fulfill that customer's needs.

Most choiceboards are essentially transaction devices. However, companies such as Dell have expanded the functionality of choiceboards using collaborative filtering technology. **Collaborative filtering** is a process that automatically groups people with similar buying intentions, preferences, and behaviors, and predicts future purchases.[7] For example, say two people who have never met buy a few of the same CDs over time. Collaborative filtering software is programmed to reason that these two buyers might have similar musical tastes: If one buyer likes a particular CD, then the other will like it as well. The outcome? Collaborative filtering gives marketers the ability to make a dead-on sales recommendation to a buyer in *real time*. You see collaborative filtering applied each time you view a selection at Amazon.com and see "Customers who bought this (item) also bought. . . ."

Choiceboards and collaborative filtering represent two important capabilities of Internet technology and have changed the way companies operate today. According to an electronic commerce manager at IBM, "The business model of the past was make and sell. Now instead of make and sell, it's sense and respond."[8]

Personalization   Choiceboards and collaborative filtering are marketer-initiated efforts to provide customized responses to the needs of individual buyers. Personalization

personalization

Consumer-initiated practice of generating content on a marketer's website that is custom tailored to an individual's specific needs and preferences

permission marketing

Asking for a consumer's consent (called opt-in) *to receive e-mail and advertising based on personal data supplied by the consumer*

systems are typically buyer-initiated efforts. **Personalization** is the consumer-initiated practice of generating content on a marketer's website that is custom tailored to an individual's specific needs and preferences. For example, Yahoo! (www.yahoo.com) allows users to create personalized MyYahoo pages. Users can add or delete a variety of types of information from their personal pages, including specific stock quotes, weather conditions in any city in the world, and local television schedules. In turn, Yahoo! can use the buyer profile data entered when users register at the site to tailor e-mail messages, advertising, and content to the individual—and even post a happy birthday greeting on the user's special day.

An aspect of personalization is a buyer's willingness to have tailored communications brought to his or her attention. Obtaining this approval is called **permission marketing**—the solicitation of a consumer's consent (called *opt-in*) to receive e-mail and advertising based on personal data supplied by the consumer. Permission marketing is a proven vehicle for building and maintaining customer relationships, provided it is properly used.

Companies that successfully employ permission marketing adhere to three rules.[9] First, they make sure opt-in customers only receive information that is relevant and meaningful to them. Second, their customers are given the option of *opting out,* or changing the kind, amount, or timing of information sent to them. Finally, their customers are assured that their name or buyer profile data will not be sold or shared with others. This assurance is important. Nearly half of adult Internet users voice concern about the privacy of their personal information.[10]

Creating an Online Customer Experience

A continuing challenge for companies is the design and execution of marketing programs that capitalize on the unique and evolving customer value-creation capabilities of Internet technology. Companies now realize that applying Internet technology to create time, place, form, and possession utility is just a starting point for creating a meaningful marketspace presence. Today, the quality of the customer experience produced by a company is the standard by which a meaningful marketspace presence is measured.

From an interactive marketing perspective, *customer experience* is defined as the sum total of the interactions that a customer has with a company's website, from the initial look at a homepage through the entire purchase decision process.[11] Companies produce a customer experience through seven website design elements. These elements are context, content, community, customization, communication, connection, and commerce, each of which is summarized in Figure 18–2 on the next page. A closer look at these elements illustrates how each contributes to customer experience.

Harley-Davidson pays close attention to creating a favorable customer experience by employing all seven website design elements.

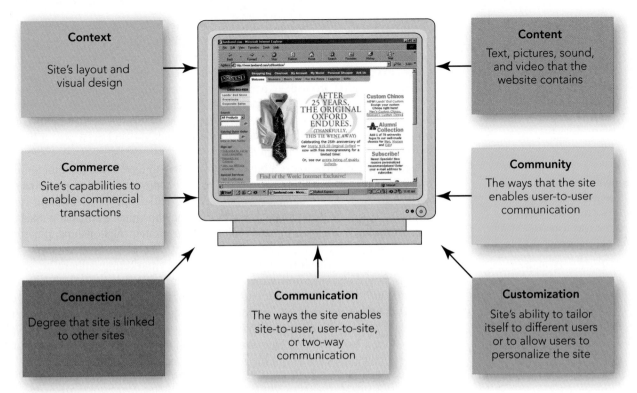

FIGURE 18–2
Seven website design elements that drive customer experience

The boxes in the figure read:

Context — Site's layout and visual design

Content — Text, pictures, sound, and video that the website contains

Commerce — Site's capabilities to enable commercial transactions

Community — The ways that the site enables user-to-user communication

Connection — Degree that site is linked to other sites

Communication — The ways the site enables site-to-user, user-to-site, or two-way communication

Customization — Site's ability to tailor itself to different users or to allow users to personalize the site

Context refers to a website's aesthetic appeal and functional look and feel reflected in site layout and visual design. A functionally oriented website focuses largely on the company's offering, be it products, services, or information. Travel websites, such as Travelocity.com, tend to be functionally oriented and emphasize destinations, scheduling, and prices. In contrast, beauty websites, such as Revlon.com, are more aesthetically oriented. As these examples suggest, context attempts to convey the core consumer benefit provided by the company's offerings. *Content* applies to all digital information on a website, including the presentation form—text, video, audio, and graphics. Content quality and presentation along with context dimensions combine to engage a website visitor and provide a platform for the five remaining design elements.

Website *customization* is the ability of a site to modify itself to, or be modified by, each individual user. This design element is prominent in websites that offer personalized content, such as MyeBay and MyYahoo! The *connection* element in website design is the network of formal linkages between a company's site and other sites. These links are embedded in the website; appear as highlighted words, a picture, or graphic; and allow a user to effortlessly visit other sites with a mouse click. Connection is a major design element for informational websites such as *The New York Times.* Users of NYTimes.com can access the book review section and link to Barnes & Noble to order a book or browse related titles without ever visiting a store.

Communication refers to the dialogue that unfolds between the website and its users. Consumers—particularly those who have registered at a site—now expect that communication be interactive and individualized in real time much like a personal conversation. In fact, some websites now enable a user to talk directly with a customer representative while shopping the site. For example, two-thirds of the sales through Dell.com involve human sales representatives. In addition, an increasing number of company websites encourage user-to-user communications hosted by the company to

410

Using Marketing Dashboards

Sizing Up Site Stickiness at Sewell Automotive Companies

Automobile dealerships have invested significant time, effort, and money in their websites. Why? Car browsing and shopping on the Internet is now commonplace.

Dealerships commonly measure website performance by tracking visit, visitor traffic, and "stickiness"—the amount of time per month visitors spend on their website. Website design, easy navigation, involving content, and visual appeal combine to enhance the interactive customer experience and website stickiness.

To gauge stickiness, companies monitor the average time spent per unique visitor (in minutes) on their websites. This is done by tracking and displaying the average visits per monthly unique visitor and the average time spent per visit, in minutes, in their marketing dashboards. The relationship is as follows:

$$\text{Average time spent per unique visitor (minutes)} = \left(\begin{array}{c}\text{Average visits per} \\ \text{monthly unique visitor}\end{array}\right) \times \left(\begin{array}{c}\text{Average time spent} \\ \text{per visit (minutes)}\end{array}\right)$$

Your Challenge As the manager responsible for Sewell.com, the Sewell Automotive Companies website, you have been asked to report on the effect recent improvements in the company's website have had on the amount of time per month visitors spend on the website. Sewell ranks among the largest U.S. dealerships and is a recognized customer service leader in the automotive industry. Its website reflects the company's commitment to an unparalleled customer experience at its family of Cadillac, HUMMER, Saab, Lexus, Pontiac, Buick, GMC, and Infiniti dealerships.

Your Findings Examples of monthly marketing dashboard traffic and time measures are displayed below for June 2006, three months before the website improvements (green arrow), and June 2007, three months after the improvements were made (red arrow).

The average time spent per unique monthly visitor increased from 8.5 minutes in June 2006 to 11.9 minutes in June 2007—a sizable jump. The increase is due primarily to the upturn in the average time spent per visit from 7.1 minutes to 8.5 minutes. The average number of visits also increased, but the percentage change was much less.

Your Action Improvements in the website have noticeably "moved the needle" for average time spent per unique visitor metric. Still, additional action may be required to increase average visits per monthly unique visitor. These actions might include an analysis of Sewell's Internet advertising program, search engine initiatives with Google, links to automobile manufacturer websites, and broader print and electronic media advertising.

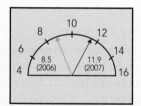

Average Time Spent per Unique Visitor (minutes)

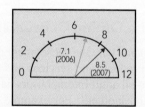

Average Time Spent per Visit (minutes)

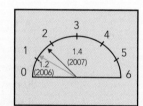

Average Visits per Monthly Unique Visitor

create virtual communities, or simply, *community*. This design element is growing in popularity because it has been shown to enhance customer experience and build favorable buyer–seller relationships. Examples of communities range from the Huggies Baby Network hosted by Kimberly-Clark (www.huggies.com) to the Harley Owners Group (HOG) sponsored by Harley-Davidson (www.harley-davidson.com).

The seventh design element is *commerce*—the website's ability to conduct sales transactions for products and services. Online transactions are quick and simple in well-designed websites. Amazon.com has mastered this design element with "one-click shopping," a patented feature that allows users to place and order products with a single mouse click.

All websites do not include every design element. Although every website has context and content, they differ in the use of the remaining five elements. Why? Websites have different purposes. For example, only websites that emphasize the actual sale of products and services include the commerce element. Websites that are used primarily for advertising and promotion purposes emphasize the communication element. The difference between these two types of websites is discussed later in the chapter in the description of multichannel marketing.

Companies use a broad array of measures to assess website performance. Increasingly, the amount of time per month visitors spend on their website, or "stickiness," is used to gauge customer experience. Read the Using Marketing Dashboards box on the previous page to learn how stickiness is measured and interpreted at Sewell Automotive Companies.

learning review

1. The consumer-initiated practice of generating content on a marketer's website that is custom tailored to an individual's specific needs and preferences is called _____.

2. Companies produce a customer experience through what seven website design elements?

ONLINE CONSUMER BEHAVIOR AND MARKETING PRACTICE IN MARKETSPACE

Who are online consumers, and what do they buy? Why do they choose to shop and purchase products and services in the digital marketspace rather than or in addition to the traditional marketplace? Answers to these questions have a direct bearing on marketspace marketing practices.

Who Is the Online Consumer?

Online consumers are the subsegment of all Internet users who employ this technology to research products and services and make purchases. Research indicates that about 90 percent of all adult Internet users have sought online product or service information at one time or another.[12] For example, some 70 percent of prospective travelers have researched travel information online, even though fewer than 25 percent have actually made online travel reservations. More than 60 percent have researched automobiles before making a purchase, but less than 5 percent of users actually bought a vehicle online. Almost 70 percent of adult Internet users have actually purchased a product or service online at one time or another.

As a group, online consumers are more likely to be women than men and tend to be better educated, younger, and more affluent than the general U.S. population, which makes them an attractive market.[13] Even though online shopping and buying is growing in popularity, a small percentage of online consumers still account for a disproportionate share of online retail sales in the United States. It is estimated that 20 percent of online consumers who spend $1,000-plus per year online account for 87 percent of total consumer online sales.[14] Also, women tend to purchase more goods and services online than men.

Numerous marketing research firms have studied the lifestyles and shopping habits of online consumers. A recurrent insight is that online consumers are diverse and represent different kinds of people seeking different kinds of online experiences. As an illustration, the Marketing Matters box provides an in-depth look at life styles and shopping habits of today's "Internet mom."[15]

Do you have fond childhood memories of surfing the Internet with your mother? Today's children probably will.

Recent research indicates that almost 40 million mothers with children under 18 years of age are online regularly. They're typically 38 years old and tend to be married, college educated, and working outside the home. A study conducted by C&R Research on behalf of Disney Online has identified four segments of mothers based on their Internet usage.

The *Yes Mom* segment represents 14 percent of online moms. They work outside the home, go online eight hours per week, and value the convenience of obtaining information about products and services. The *Mrs. Net Skeptic* segment accounts for 31 percent of online moms. They tend to be stay-at-home moms, are extremely family-oriented, and go online six hours per week for parenting and children's education information and food and cooking tips. The *Tech Nester* mom (32 percent of online moms) believes the Internet brings their family closer together. They average 10 hours per week online and prefer online shopping to in-store shopping. The fourth segment—*Passive Under Pressure* moms—tend to be Internet newbies and go online, but infrequently.

The first three segments, which account for 77 percent of online moms, agree that the Internet has simplified their lives. They also say that the Internet has been an invaluable information source for vacation travel, financial products, and automobiles and for useful ideas and suggestions on family-related topics. Online moms ranked weather, food and cooking, entertainment, news, health, and parenting as the most popular websites to visit.

What Online Consumers Buy

LO2

Much still needs to be learned about online consumer purchase behavior. Although research has documented the most frequently purchased products and services bought online, marketers also need to know why these items are popular in the digital marketspace.

There are six general product and service categories that dominate online consumer buying today and for the foreseeable future as shown in Figure 18–3 on the next page.[16] One category consists of items for which product information is an important part of the purchase decision, but prepurchase trial is not necessarily critical. Items such as computers, computer accessories, and consumer electronics sold by Dell.com fall into this category. So do books, which accounts for the sales growth of Amazon.com and Barnes & Noble (www.barnesandnoble.com). Both booksellers publish short reviews of new books that visitors to their websites can read before making a purchase decision.

A second category includes items for which audio or video demonstration is important. This category consists of CDs, videos, and DVDs sold by Columbia House.com. The third category contains items that can be delivered digitally, including computer software, travel and lodging reservations and confirmations, financial brokerage services, and electronic ticketing. Popular websites for these items include Travelocity. com, Schwab.com. and Ticketmaster.com.

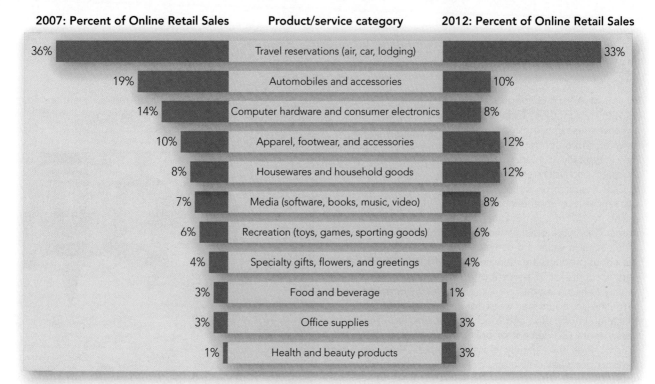

2007: Percent of Online Retail Sales	Product/service category	2012: Percent of Online Retail Sales
36%	Travel reservations (air, car, lodging)	33%
19%	Automobiles and accessories	10%
14%	Computer hardware and consumer electronics	8%
10%	Apparel, footwear, and accessories	12%
8%	Housewares and household goods	12%
7%	Media (software, books, music, video)	8%
6%	Recreation (toys, games, sporting goods)	6%
4%	Specialty gifts, flowers, and greetings	4%
3%	Food and beverage	1%
3%	Office supplies	3%
1%	Health and beauty products	3%

FIGURE 18–3
Estimated percentage of online retail sales by product/service category: 2007 and 2012

Unique items, such as collectibles, specialty goods, and foods and gifts, represent a fourth category. Collectible auction houses (www.sothebys.com), food merchants (www.harryanddavid.com), and flower marketers (www.1800flowers.com) sell these products. A fifth category includes items that are regularly purchased and where convenience is very important. Many consumer-packaged goods, such as grocery products, fall into this category. A final category of items consists of highly standardized products and services for which information about price is important. Certain kinds of insurance (auto and homeowners), home improvement products, casual apparel, and toys make up this category.

Why Consumers Shop and Buy Online

Marketers emphasize the customer value-creation possibilities, the importance of interactivity, individuality and relationship building, and producing customer experience in the new marketspace. However, consumers typically refer to six reasons they shop and buy online: convenience, choice, customization, communication, cost, and control (Figure 18–4).

Convenience Online shopping and buying is *convenient.* Consumers can visit Wal-Mart at www.walmart.com to scan and order from among thousands of displayed products without fighting traffic, finding a parking space, walking through long aisles, and standing in store checkout lines. Alternatively, online consumers can use **bots**, electronic shopping agents or robots, such as mysimon.com, that comb websites to compare prices and product or service features. In either instance, an online consumer has never ventured from his or her computer monitor. However, for convenience to remain a source of customer value creation, websites must be easy to locate and navigate, and image downloads must be fast.

Choice *Choice,* the second reason consumers shop and buy online, has two dimensions. First, choice exists in the product or service selection offered to consumers.

bots
Electronic shopping agents or robots that comb websites to compare prices and product or service features

FIGURE 18–4

Why do consumers shop and buy online? Read the text to learn how convenience, choice, customization, communication, cost, and control result in a favorable customer experience.

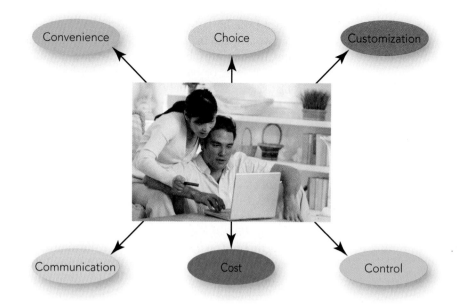

Buyers desiring selection can avail themselves of numerous websites for almost anything they want. For instance, online buyers of consumer electronics can shop individual manufacturers such as Sony (www.sony.com) and QVC.com, a general merchant that offers more than 100,000 products.

Choice assistance is the second dimension. Here, the interactive capabilities of Internet-enabled technologies invite customers to engage in an electronic dialogue with marketers for the purpose of making informed choices. Lands' End (www.landsend.com) provides choice assistance with its "Chat online" service. Potential customers can connect with an online customer service representative to help them with sizes, fit, or other questions they might have.

Customization Even with a broad selection and choice assistance, some customers prefer one-of-a-kind items that fit their specific needs. *Customization* arises from Internet-enabled capabilities that make possible a highly interactive and individualized information and exchange environment for shoppers and buyers. Remember the earlier NikeID, Schwab, Dell, and SevenCycles examples? To varying degrees, online consumers also benefit from *customerization*—the growing practice of not only customizing a product or service but also personalizing the marketing and overall shopping and buying interaction for each customer.[17] Customerization seeks to do more than offer consumers the right product, at the right time, at the right price. It combines choiceboard and personalization systems to expand the exchange environment beyond a transaction and makes shopping and buying an enjoyable, personal experience.

Communication Online consumers particularly welcome the *communication* capabilities of Internet-enabled technologies. This communication can take three forms: (1) marketer-to-consumer e-mail notification, (2) consumer-to-marketer buying and service requests, and (3) consumer-to-consumer chat rooms and instant messaging, plus social networking websites such as MySpace and Facebook.

Communication has proven to be a double-edged sword for online consumers. On the one hand, the interactive communication capabilities of Internet-enabled technologies increase consumer convenience, reduce information search costs, and make choice assistance and customization possible. Communication also promotes the development of company-hosted and independent **web communities**—websites that allow people to congregate online and exchange views on topics of common interest. For instance,

web communities
Websites that allow people to meet online and exchange views on topics of common interest

Coca-Cola hosts MyCoke.com, and iVillage.com is an independent web community for women and includes topics such as career management, personal finances, parenting, relationships, beauty, and health.

Web logs, or blogs, are another form of communication. A **blog** is a web page that serves as a publicly accessible personal journal for an individual or organization. Blogs have grown in popularity because they provide online forums on a wide variety of subjects ranging from politics to car repair. It is estimated that the 5,000-plus comments a week on gmblogs.com is worth $100,000 in marketing research each week to General Motors.[18]

On the other hand, communications can take the form of electronic junk mail or unsolicited e-mail, called **spam**. The prevalence of spam has prompted many online services to institute policies and procedures to prevent spammers from spamming their subscribers, and several states have antispamming laws. In 2004, the *CAN-SPAM (Controlling the Assault of Non-Solicited Pornography and Marketing) Act* became effective and restricts information collection and unsolicited e-mail promotions on the Internet.

Internet-enabled communication capabilities also make possible *buzz,* a popular term for word-of-mouth behavior in marketspace. Chapter 5 described the importance of word of mouth in consumer behavior. Internet technology has magnified its significance. According to Jeff Bezos, president of Amazon.com, "If you have an unhappy customer on the Internet, he doesn't tell his six friends, he tells his 6,000 friends![19] Buzz is particularly influential for toys, cars, sporting goods, motion pictures, apparel, consumer electronics, pharmaceuticals, health and beauty products, and health care services. Some marketers have capitalized on this phenomenon by creating buzz through viral marketing.

Viral marketing is an Internet-enabled promotional strategy that encourages individuals to forward marketer-initiated messages to others via e-mail. There are three approaches to viral marketing. Marketers can embed a message in the product or service so that customers hardly realize they are passing it along. The classic example was Hotmail, which was one of the first companies to provide free, Internet-based e-mail. Each outgoing e-mail message had the tagline: "Get Your Private, Free Email from MSN Hotmail." Today, Windows Live Hotmail has more than 100 million users.

Marketers can also make the website content so compelling that viewers want to share it with others. De Beers has done this at www.adiamondisforever.com, where users can design their own rings and show them to others. One out of five website visitors e-mail their ring design to friends and relatives who visit the site. Similarly, eBay reports that more than half its visitors are referred by other visitors. Finally, marketers can offer incentives (discounts, sweepstakes, or free merchandise) for referrals.

De Beers effectively applies viral marketing at its custom ring website. How? Users of the custom ring feature can show what they have designed to friends and relatives.

dynamic pricing

Practice of changing prices for products and services in real time in response to supply and demand conditions

Cost Consumer *cost* is a fifth reason for online shopping and buying. Many popular items bought online can be purchased at the same price or cheaper than in retail stores.[20] Lower prices also result from Internet-enabled software that permits **dynamic pricing**, the practice of changing prices for products and services in real time in response to supply and demand conditions. Dynamic pricing is a form of flexible pricing (see Chapter 12) and can often result in lower prices. It is typically used for pricing time-sensitive items like airline seats, scarce items found at art or collectible auctions, and out-of-date items such as last year's models of computer equipment and accessories. A consumer's cost of external information search, including time spent and often the hassle of shopping, is also reduced. Greater shopping convenience and lower external search costs are two major reasons for the popularity of online shopping and buying among women, and particularly for those who work outside the home.

Control The sixth reason consumers prefer to buy online is the *control* it gives them over their shopping and purchase decision process. Online shoppers and buyers are empowered consumers. They deftly use Internet technology to seek information, evaluate alternatives, and make purchase decisions on their own time, terms, and conditions. For example, studies show that shoppers spend an average of five hours researching cars online before setting foot in a showroom.[21] The result of these activities is a more informed consumer and discerning shopper. In the words of one marketing consultant, "In the marketspace, the customer is in charge."[22]

Even though consumers have many reasons for shopping and buying online, a segment of Internet users refrain from making purchases for privacy and security reasons. These consumers are concerned about a rarely mentioned seventh C—cookies. **Cookies** are computer files that a marketer can download onto the computer of an online shopper who visits the marketer's website. Cookies allow the marketer's website to record a user's visit, track visits to other websites, and store and retrieve this information in the future. Cookies also contain visitor information such as expressed product preferences, personal data, passwords, and financial information, including credit card numbers. Clearly, cookies make possible customized and personalized content for online shoppers. The controversy surrounding cookies is summed up by an authority on the technology: "At best a cookie makes for a user-friendly Web world: like a doorman or salesclerk who knows who you are. At worst, cookies represent a potential loss of privacy."[23] Read the Making Responsible Decisions box on the next page to learn more about privacy and security issues in the digital marketplace.[24]

cookies

Computer files that a marketer can download onto the computer of an online shopper who visits the marketer's website

When and Where Online Consumers Shop and Buy

Shopping and buying also happen at different times in marketspace than in the traditional marketplace.[25] About 80 percent of online retail sales occur Monday through Friday. The busiest shopping day is Wednesday. By comparison, 35 percent of retail store sales are registered on the weekend. Saturday is the most popular shopping day. Monday through Friday online shopping and buying often occur during normal work hours—some 70 percent of online consumers say they visit websites from their place of work, which partially accounts for the sales level during the workweek. Favorite websites for workday shopping and buying include those featuring event tickets, auctions, online periodical subscriptions, flowers and gifts, consumer electronics, and travel. Websites offering health and beauty items, apparel and accessories, and music and video tend to be browsed and bought from a consumer's home.

learning review

3. What is viral marketing?

4. What are the six reasons consumers prefer to shop and buy online?

Let the E-Buyer Beware

Privacy and security are two key reasons consumers are leery of online shopping and buying. A recent Gartner Research poll reported that 46 percent of online consumers have privacy and security concerns about the Internet. Even more telling, many have stopped shopping a website or forgone an online purchase because of these concerns. Industry analysts estimate that about $913 million in e-commerce sales are lost annually because of security concerns among online shoppers. Another $1 billion is lost because of shoppers who refuse to shop online at all because of privacy and security concerns.

Consumer concerns are not without merit. According to the Federal Trade Commission, 46 percent of fraud complaints are Internet related. In addition, consumers lose millions of dollars each year due to identity theft resulting from breaches in company security systems. A percolating issue is whether the U.S. government should pass more stringent Internet privacy and security laws. About 70 percent of online consumers favor such action.

Companies, however, favor self-regulation. For example, TRUSTe (www.truste.com) awards its trademark to company websites that comply with standards of privacy protection and disclosure. Still, consumers are ultimately responsible for using care and caution when engaging in online behavior, including e-commerce. Consumers have a choice of whether or not to divulge personal information and monitor how their information is being used.

What role should the U.S. government, company self-regulation, and consumer vigilance play in dealing with privacy and security issues in the digital marketspace?

CROSS-CHANNEL SHOPPERS AND MULTICHANNEL MARKETING

LO4

Consumers are more likely to browse than buy online. Consumer marektspace browsing and buying in the traditional marketplace has given rise to the cross-channel shopper and the importance of multichannel marketing.

Who Is the Cross-Channel Shopper?

cross-channel shopper

An online consumer who researches products online and then purchases them at a retail store

A **cross-channel shopper** is an online consumer who researches products online and then purchases them at a retail store.[26] Recent research shows that 51 percent of U.S. online consumers are cross-channel shoppers. These shoppers represent both genders equally and are only slightly younger than online consumers. They tend to have a higher education, earn significantly more money, and are more likely to embrace technology in their lives than online consumers who don't cross-channel shop.

Cross-channel shoppers want the right product, at the best price, and they don't want to wait days for delivery. The top reasons these shoppers research items online before buying in stores are: (1) the desire to compare products among different retailers, (2) the need for more information than is available in stores, and (3) the ease of comparing their options without having to trek to multiple retail locations.

Research shows that sales arising from cross-channel shoppers dwarf exclusive on-line retail sales. Retail sales revenue from cross-channel shoppers in 2012 is estimated to be $1 trillion—about three times greater than online retail sales.[27]

Implementing Multichannel Marketing

The prominence of cross-channel shoppers has focused increased attention on multi-channel marketing. Recall from Chapter 13 that multichannel marketing is the blend-ing of different communication and delivery channels that are mutually reinforcing in attracting, retaining, and building relationships with consumers who shop and buy in the traditional marketplace and online—the cross-channel shopper.

The most common cross-channel shopping and buying path is to browse one or more websites and then purchase an item at a retail store. This shopping path might suggest that company websites for cross-channel shoppers should be similar. But they are not. Websites play a multifaceted role in multichannel marketing because they can serve as either a communication or delivery channel. Two general applications of websites exist based on their intended purpose: (1) transactional websites and (2) promotional websites.

Multichannel Marketing with Transactional Websites

Transactional websites are essentially electronic storefronts. They focus principally on con-verting an online browser into an online, catalog, or in-store buyer using the website design elements described earlier. Transactional websites are most common among store and catalog retailers and direct selling companies, such as Tupperware. Re-tailers and direct selling firms have found that their websites, while cannibalizing sales volume from stores, catalogs, and sales representatives, attract new customers and influence sales. Consider Victoria's Secret, the well-known specialty retailer of intimate apparel for women ages 18 to 45. It reports that almost 60 percent of its website customers are men, most of whom generate new sales volume for the company.[28]

Transactional websites are used less frequently by manufacturers of consumer prod-ucts. A recurring issue for manufacturers is the threat of *channel conflict,* described in Chapter 13, and the potential harm to trade relationships with their retailing inter-mediaries. Still, manufacturers do use transactional websites, often cooperating with retailers. For example, Callaway Golf Company markets its golf merchandise at www.callawaygolf.com but relies on a retailer close to the buyer to fill the order. The retailer ships the order to the buyer within 24 hours and its credited with the sale. The majority of retailers that sell Callaway merchandise participate in this relationship, including retail chains Golf Galaxy and Dick's Sporting Goods. According to Callaway's chief executive officer, "This arrangement allows us to satisfy the consumer but to do so in a way that didn't violate our relationship with our loyal trade partners—those 15,000 outlets that sell Callaway products."[29]

Multichannel Marketing with Promotional Websites

Promotional websites have a very different purpose than transactional sites. They advertise and promote a company's products and services and provide information on how items can be used and where they can be purchased. They often engage the visitor in an interac-tive experience involving games, contests, and quizzes with electronic coupons and other gifts as prizes. Procter & Gamble has separate websites for dozens of its lead-ing brands, including Vidal Sassoon hair products (www.vidalsassoon.com), Scope mouthwash (www.getclose.com), and Pampers diapers (www.pampers.com). Pro-motional sites are effective in generating interest in and trial of a company's products (see Figure 18–5 on the next page).[30] General Motors reports that 80 percent of the people visiting a Saturn store first visited the brand's website (www.saturn.com), and 70 percent of Saturn leads come from its website.

FIGURE 18–5

Implementing multichannel marketing with promotional websites is common today. Two successes are found at Saturn Corporation and the Clinique Division of Estée Lauder, Inc.

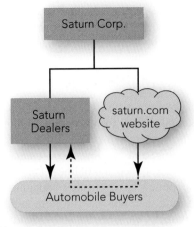

- 70% of Saturn leads come from its website.
- 80% of people visiting a Saturn dealer first visited its website.

- 80% of current Clinique buyers who visit its website later purchase a Clinique product at a store.
- 37% of non-Clinique buyers make a Clinique purchase after visiting its website.

Promotional websites also can be used to support a company's traditional marketing channel and build customer relationships. This is the objective of the Clinique Division of Estée Lauder Inc., which markets cosmetics through department stores. Clinique reports that 80 percent of current customers who visit its website (www.clinique.com) later purchase a Clinique product at a department store; 37 percent of non-Clinique buyers make a Clinique purchase after visiting the company's website.

The popularity of multichannel marketing is apparent in its growing impact on online retail sales.[31] Fully 70 percent of U.S. online retail sales in 2008 were made by companies that practiced multichannel marketing. Multichannel marketers are expected to register about 90 percent of U.S. online retail sales in 2012.

learning review

5. A cross-channel shopper is _____.

6. Channel conflict between manufacturers and retailers is likely to arise when manufacturers use _____ websites.

LEARNING OBJECTIVES REVIEW

LO1 *Describe what interactive marketing is and how it creates customer value, customer relationships, and customer experiences.*

Interactive marketing involves two-way buyer–seller electronic communication in a computer-mediated environment in which the buyer controls the kind and amount of information received from the seller. It creates customer value by providing time, place, form, and possession utility for consumers. Customer relationships are created and sustained through two unique capabilities of Internet technology: interactivity and individuality. From an interactive marketing perspective, customer experience represents the sum total of the interactions that a customer has with a company's website, from the initial look at a homep-

age through the entire purchase decision process. Companies produce a customer experience through seven website design elements. These elements are context, content, community, customization, communication, connection, and commerce.

LO2 *Explain why certain types of products and services are particularly suited for interactive marketing.*

Certain types of products and services seem to be particularly suited for interactive marketing. One category consists of items for which product information is an important part of the purchase decision, but prepurchase trial is not necessarily critical. A second category involves items for which audio or video demonstration is important. A third category contains items that can be digitally delivered. Unique items represent a fourth category. A fifth category includes items that are regularly purchased and where convenience is very important. A final category consists of highly standardized items for which information about price is important.

LO3 *Describe why consumers shop and buy online, and how marketers influence online purchasing behavior.*

There are six reasons consumers shop and buy online. They are convenience, choice, customization, communication, cost, and control. Marketers have capitalized on these reasons through a variety of means. For example, they provide choice assistance using choiceboard and collaborative filtering technology, which also provides opportunities for customization. Company-hosted web communities and viral marketing practices capitalize on the communications dimensions of Internet-enabled technologies. Dynamic pricing provides real-time responses to supply and demand conditions, often resulting in lower prices to consumers. Permission marketing is popular given consumer interest in control.

LO4 *Define cross-channel shoppers and the role of transactional and promotional websites in reaching these shoppers.*

A cross-channel shopper is an online consumer who researches products online and then purchases them at a retail store. These shoppers are reached through multichannel marketing. Websites play a multifaceted role in multichannel marketing because they can serve as either a delivery or communication channel. In this regard, transactional websites are essentially electronic storefronts. They focus principally on converting an online browser into an online, catalog, or in-store buyer using the website design elements described earlier. On the other hand, promotional websites serve to advertise and promote a company's products and services and provide information on how items can be used and where they can be purchased.

FOCUSING ON KEY TERMS

blog p. 416
bots p. 414
choiceboard p. 408
collaborative filtering p. 408
cookies p. 417

cross-channel shopper p. 418
dynamic pricing p. 417
interactive marketing p. 407
permission marketing p. 409
personalization p. 409

spam p. 416
viral marketing p. 416
web communities p. 415

APPLYING MARKETING KNOWLEDGE

1 About 70 percent of Internet users have actually purchased something online. Have you made an online purchase? If so, why do you think so many people who have access to the Internet are not also online buyers? If not, why are you reluctant to do so? Do you think that electronic commerce benefits consumers even if they don't make a purchase?

2 Like the traditional marketplace, marketspace offers marketers opportunities to create greater time, place, form, and possession utility. How do you think Internet-enabled technology rates in terms of creating these values? Take a shopping trip at a virtual retailer of your choice (don't buy anything unless you really want to). Then compare the time, place, form, and possession utility provided by the virtual retailer that you enjoyed during a nonelectronic experience shopping for the same product category.

3 Visit Amazon.com (www.amazon.com) or Barnes & Noble (www.barnesandnoble.com). As you tour the company's website, think about how shopping for books online compares with a trip to your university bookstore to buy books. Specifically, compare and contrast your shopping experiences with respect to convenience, choice, customization, communication, cost, and control.

4 Visit the website for your university or college. Based on your visit, would you conclude that the site is a transactional site or a promotional site? Why? How would you rate the site in terms of the six website design elements that affect customer experience?

building your marketing plan

Does your marketing plan involve a marketspace presence for your product or service? If the answer is no, read no further and do not include this element in your plan. If the answer is yes, then attention must be given to developing a website in your marketing plan. A useful starting point is to:

1 Describe how each website element—context, content, community, customization, communication, connection, and commerce—will be used to create a customer experience.

2 Identify a company's website that best reflects your website conceptualization.

"All my life, I've been underwhelmed by the sports action figures sold in the toy aisles," says Todd McFarlane, founder of McFarlane Toys.

This assessment of the marketplace led McFarlane to create his own toy manufacturing company, an entirely new category of toys called "upscale figures," and an extraordinarily sophisticated marketing strategy based on traditional and interactive approaches. McFarlane Toys is now one of the world's largest toy companies. The company's products include action figures of professional athletes, rock stars, NASCAR drivers, and characters from movies such as *The Terminator*, *The Matrix*, and *Austin Powers*. Its marketing programs have used Internet contests, virtual showrooms, online catalogs, and a variety of other award-winning tools. Overall, McFarlane Toys has transformed a category that used to be just plastic replicas for children into an art collectible for adults. McFarlane explains, "It's about creating a toy that, if you had it on your shelf, somebody wouldn't say, 'Are you collecting toys? How old are you?'"

THE COMPANY

McFarlane started his career as an artist for Marvel/Epic Comics, working on issues of *Incredible Hulk, Amazing Spider-Man, Batman,* and *Coyote.* Eventually he formed Image Comics with six other Marvel artists and began work on his own comic book, *Spawn.* The first issue of *Spawn* sold a record-breaking 1.7 million copies. Since then the series has become a top-selling comic published in 16 languages and sold in more than 120 countries.

The success of *Spawn* soon generated licensing proposals from toy companies, movies studios, and television producers. When McFarlane met with each of the companies, however, he was concerned about his ability to have creative control over the toy production. As a result, he started his own toy company, McFarlane Toys, in order to guarantee his fans high quality, intricately detailed, and reasonably priced action figures. *Spawn* action figures quickly became one of the most successful toys on the market.

Following the introduction of the *Spawn* action figures, McFarlane began producing action figures of pop culture icons in film, music, gaming, and sports. The company also signed license agreements with the four major North American sports leagues—football, baseball, basketball, and hockey. In addition, McFarlane Toys produced toys for licensors such as the Beatles, *Shrek,* KISS, *The Simpsons, Alien,* AC/DC, Jimi Hendrix, and many others. The quality and the collectibility of the figures has given McFarlane Toys a worldwide reputation among retailers and consumers.

When he founded McFarlane Toys, McFarlane said, "I'm just going to do action figures. I'm going to be the king of Aisle 7." Other opportunities soon appeared, however, and he became involved in the production of feature films, music videos, electronic games, and animated television. Some of these projects have included the live-action film *Spawn* which grossed $50 million in just 19 days; the HBO series *Todd McFarlane's Spawn* which won an Emmy award; and the music video for Korn's *Freak on a Leash,* which received a Grammy award. These activities have helped expand the growing number of McFarlane Toy fans.

Today McFarlane Toys is ranked among the top five makers of action figures. McFarlane manages the company as the "creative force" from its headquarters in Tempe, Arizona. The toy designers work in New Jersey and the toys are manufactured in China. Currently, it takes about 12 months for a product idea on paper to make its way through the rigorous process of becoming a toy on the shelf.

THE TOY INDUSTRY

Toys are big business. Worldwide toy sales exceed $60 billion. The United States is the largest toy market and accounts for 35 percent of worldwide industry sales. A child in the United States receives about $242 worth of toys per year on average. By comparison, the average

FIGURE 1

Toy Category Sales in the United States
(Listed alphabetically)

Category	Sales ($ Billions)
Action figures and accessories	$ 1.3
Arts and crafts	2.4
Building sets	0.7
Dolls	2.7
Games/puzzles	2.4
Infant/preschool	3.1
Learning and exploration	0.4
Outdoor and sports toys	2.7
Plush	1.3
Vehicles	1.8
All other toys	2.5
TOTAL	$21.3

annual expenditure per child outside the United States is $26. Dolls represent the largest single category of toys, although action figures account for $1.3 billion in sales. Figure 1 shows the dollar sales of individual toy categories in the United States.

U.S. mass merchants are the principal retailers of toys. General merchandise and discounters like Wal-Mart, Kmart, and Target register 54 percent of retail toy sales. Toy chains account for 20 percent of retail sales. Other retailers, such as catalog, toy, hobby and game stores, department stores, and food and drug stores, record 20 percent of sales. Online sales account for 6 percent of sales. Wal-Mart stores are the number one toy retailer in the United States.

The worldwide toy industry is dominated by two U.S. toy makers: Mattel and Hasbro. Japan's Bandai Company and Sanrio, and Denmark's LEGO Company are also major toy makers.

E-COMMERCE AND INTERACTIVE MARKETING AT MCFARLANE TOYS

Shortly after forming McFarlane Toys, McFarlane set up a booth in the annual industry trade show in New York called Toy Fair. Even though the new company didn't have any toys produced yet, an action figure buyer from a toy chain store saw photos of the proposed toys and agreed to place an order. Other traditional retailing opportunities in large discount stores such as Wal-Mart and small, local comic book stores such as Diamonds soon followed. McFarlane Toys also utilized traditional forms of marketing, including media interviews and public relations events, to reach buyers who represented toy stores. McFarland also recently opened its first retail store in Arizona, which showcases current products and prototypes of future releases of the various lines of action figures. Collectors from around the world have visited the store to purchase products, attend artist autograph sessions, and to meet McFarlane!

Since the target market for McFarlane Toys products is older children and young adults—who make 30 to 40 percent of all action figure purchases—e-commerce and interactive marketing offered another opportunity to reach action figure consumers. The McFarlane Toys website (www.spawn.com) is a good example of the *convenience* online marketing can offer. The site provides a store for purchasing action figures in each of the lines (e.g., movie figures, music figures, baseball figures, comic book figures, etc.). High-quality images allow shoppers to view each figure before adding it to a "basket" and then placing the order. The site also offers visitors a *choice* for the location of their purchase. A "Where to Buy" link lists all retailers and other online "e-tailers" such as www.comicsplusonline.com and www.allstarfigures.com.

The website also provides a variety of opportunities for *communication*. Consumer-to-marketer communication is provided through the "Contact Us" link. In addition, marketer-to-consumer information is provided through the McFarlane newsletter, which is sent to visitors who register to receive the update. Finally, consumers can use the spawn.com message board to participate in discussions about action figures, movies, and comics, or to buy, sell, and trade McFarlane products. There are 54,400 registered users of the message board forums. A unique way that McFarlane provides *customization* of his offerings for his customers is through the Collector's Club, which offers exclusive, limited-edition action figures to members.

Online consumers are also typically concerned about *cost* and *control*. McFarlane tries to keep the cost of most of his toys under $15 by keeping production expenses low. Online shoppers also receive special offers when warehouse inventory is being reduced or eliminated. Of course, sales and discounts can often be found by utilizing the links to the many stores and online retailers that carry McFarlane Toys. Online users control their interaction with McFarlane by providing information only through "opt-in" solicitation for purchases, message board use, and newsletter e-mail delivery.

ISSUES FOR THE FUTURE

Of course, McFarlane's success has attracted attention from consumers, retailers, and competitors. New small firms such as Palisades Toys, Art Asylum, Playmates, and Mezco are now turning out action figures. Larger firms, such as Hasbro, are also trying to compete. As more companies enter the category, obtaining new licensing agreements is also becoming more difficult.

While McFarlane has been heard to comment, "It's just stuff," he is very committed to continuing to develop and grow the category he created. In the future, expect to see additional action figures, movies, music videos, and video games. McFarlane Toys is also working at maintaining the strong relationship with its loyal customers through online contests, customer polls about potential new products, and a new product idea link to company designers.

Questions

1 Describe the channels of distribution McFarlane Toys uses to reach its action figure customers.
2 Why have interactive marketing strategies been successful for McFarlane Toys? What unique elements are part of its online experience?
3 How does McFarlane Toys address each of the six Cs consumers consider when shopping and buying online?

B

PLANNING A CAREER IN MARKETING

GETTING A JOB: THE PROCESS OF MARKETING YOURSELF

Getting a job is usually a lengthy process, and it is exactly that—a *process* that involves careful planning, implementation, and evaluation. You may have everything going for you: a respectable grade point average (GPA), relevant work experience, several extracurricular activities, superior communication skills, and demonstrated leadership qualities. Despite these, you still need to market yourself systematically and aggressively; after all, even the best products lie dormant on the retailer's shelves unless marketed effectively.

The process of getting a job involves the same activities marketing managers use to develop and introduce products and brands into the marketplace.[1] The only difference is that you are marketing yourself, not a product. You need to conduct marketing research by analyzing your personal qualities (performing a self-audit) and by identifying job opportunities. Based on your research results, select a target market—those job opportunities that are compatible with your interests, goals, skills, and abilities—and design a marketing mix around that target market. *You* are the "product";[2] you must decide how to "position" yourself in the job market. The price component of the marketing mix is the salary range and job benefits (such as health and life insurance, vacation time, and retirement benefits) that you hope to receive. Promotion involves communicating with prospective employers through written and electronic correspondence (advertising) and job interviews (personal selling). The place element focuses on how to reach prospective employers—at the career services office or job fairs, for example.

This appendix will assist you in career planning by (1) providing information about careers in marketing and (2) outlining a job search process.

CAREERS IN MARKETING

The diversity of marketing opportunities is reflected in the many types of marketing jobs, including product management, marketing research, and public relations. While many of these jobs are found at traditional employers such as manufacturers, retailers, and advertising agencies, there are also many opportunities in a variety of other types of organizations. Professional services such as law, accounting, and consulting firms, for example, have a growing need for marketing expertise. Similarly, nonprofit organizations such as universities, the performing arts, museums, and government agencies are developing marketing functions. Event organizations such as athletic teams, golf and tennis tournaments, and the Olympics are also new and visible sources of marketing jobs.

Recent studies of career paths and salaries suggest that marketing careers can also provide excellent opportunities for advancement and substantial pay. For example, about one of every five chief executive officers (CEOs) of the nation's 500 most valuable publicly held companies have a career history that is heaviest in marketing.[3] Similarly, reports of average starting salaries of college graduates indicate that salaries in marketing compare favorably with those in many other fields. The average starting salary of new marketing undergraduates in 2008 was $43,318, compared with $35,213 for journalism majors and $35,937 for communications majors.[4] The future is likely to be even better. The U.S. Department of Labor reports that employment of advertising, marketing, promotions, public relations, and sales managers is expected to increase faster than the average for all occupations through 2014, spurred by intense domestic and global competition in products and services offered to consumers.[5]

Figure B–1 describes marketing occupations in seven major categories: product management and physical distribution, advertising and promotion, retailing, sales,

Product Management and Physical Distribution

Product development manager creates a road map for new products by working with customers to determine their needs and with designers to create the product.

Product manager is responsible for integrating all aspects of a product's marketing program including research, sales, sales promotion, advertising, and pricing.

Supply chain manager oversees the part of a company that transports products to consumers and handles customer service.

Operations manager supervises warehousing and other physical distribution functions and often is directly involved in moving goods on the warehouse floor.

Inventory control manager forecasts demand for goods, coordinates production with plant managers, and tracks shipments to keep customers supplied.

Physical distribution specialist is an expert in the transportation and distribution of goods and also evaluates the costs and benefits of different types of transportation.

Sales

Direct or retail salesperson sells directly to consumers in the salesperson's office, the consumer's home, or a retailer's store.

Trade salesperson calls on retailers or wholesalers to sell products for manufacturers.

Industrial or semitechnical salesperson sells supplies and services to businesses.

Complex or professional salesperson sells complicated or custom-designed products to businesses. This requires understanding of the product technology.

Customer service manager maintains good relations with customers by coordinating the sales staff, marketing management, and physical distribution management.

Nonprofit Marketing

Marketing manager develops and directs marketing campaigns, fund-raising, and public relations.

Global Marketing

Global marketing manager is an expert in world-trade agreements, international competition, cross-cultural analysis, and global market-entry strategies.

Advertising and Promotion

Account executive maintains contact with clients while coordinating the creative work among artists and copywriters. Account executives work as partners with the client to develop marketing strategy.

Media buyer deals with media sales representatives in selecting advertising media and analyzes the value of media being purchased.

Copywriter works with art director in conceptualizing advertisements and writes the text of print or radio ads or the storyboards of television ads.

Art director handles the visual component of advertisements.

Sales promotion manager designs promotions for consumer products and works at an ad agency or a sales promotion agency.

Public relations manager develops written or video messages for the public and handles contacts with the press.

Internet marketing manager develops and executes the e-business marketing plan and manages all aspects of the advertising, promotion, and content for the online business.

Retailing

Buyer selects products a store sells, surveys consumer trends, and evaluates the past performance of products and suppliers.

Store manager oversees the staff and services at a store.

Marketing Research

Project manager for the supplier coordinates and oversees the market studies for a client.

Account executive for the supplier serves as a liaison between client and market research firm, like an advertising agency account executive.

In-house project director acts as project manager (see above) for the market studies conducted by the firm for which he or she works.

Competitive intelligence researcher uses new information technologies to monitor the competitive environment.

Data miner compiles and analyzes consumer data to identify behavior patterns, preferences, and user profiles for personalized marketing programs.

Source: Adapted from Lila B. Stair and Leslie Stair, *Careers in Marketing* (New York: McGraw-Hill, 2001), p. 100; and David W. Rosenthal and Michael A. Powell, *Careers in Marketing*, ©1984, pp. 352–54.

FIGURE B–1

Marketing offers a variety of exciting occupations.

marketing research, global marketing and nonprofit marketing. One of these may be right for you. (Additional sources of marketing career information are provided at the end of this appendix.)

Product Management and Physical Distribution

Many organizations assign one manager the responsibility for a particular product. For example, Procter & Gamble (P&G) has separate managers for Tide, Cheer, Gain, and

Bold. Product or brand managers are involved in all aspects of a product's marketing program, such as marketing research, sales, sales promotion, advertising, and pricing, as well as manufacturing. Managers of similar products typically report to a category manager and may be part of a *product management team*.[6]

Several other jobs related to product management (Figure B–1) deal with physical distribution issues such as storing the manufactured product (inventory), moving the product from the firm to the customers (transportation), and engaging in many other aspects of the manufacture and sale of goods. Prospects for these jobs are likely to increase as wholesalers increase their involvement with selling and distribution activities and begin to take advantage of overseas opportunities.[7]

Product or brand managers are involved in all aspects of a product's marketing program.

Advertising and Promotion

Advertising positions are available in three kinds of organizations: advertisers, media companies, and agencies. Advertisers include manufacturers, retail stores, service firms, and many other types of companies. Often they have an advertising department responsible for preparing and placing their own ads. Advertising careers are also possible with the media: television, radio stations, magazines, and newspapers. Finally, advertising agencies offer job opportunities through their use of account management, research, media, and creative services.

Starting positions with advertisers and advertising agencies are often as assistants to employees with several years of experience. An assistant copywriter facilitates the development of the message, or copy, in an advertisement. An assistant art director participates in the design of visual components of advertisements. Entry-level media positions involve buying the media that will carry the ad or selling airtime on radio or television or page space in print media. Advancement to supervisory positions requires planning skills, a broad vision, and an affinity for spotting an effective advertising idea. Students interested in advertising should develop good communication skills and try to gain advertising experience through summer employment opportunities or internships.[8]

Retailing offers careers in merchandise management and store management.

Retailing

There are two separate career paths in retailing: merchandise management and store management. The key position in merchandising is that of a buyer, who is responsible for selecting merchandise, guiding the promotion of the merchandise, setting prices, bargaining with wholesalers, training the salesforce, and monitoring the competitive environment. The buyer must also be able to organize and coordinate many critical activities under severe time constraints. In contrast, store management involves the supervision of personnel in all departments and the general management of all facilities, equipment, and merchandise displays. In addition, store managers are responsible for the financial performance of each department and for the store as a whole. Typical positions beyond the store manager level include district manager, regional manager, and divisional vice president.[9]

Most starting jobs in retailing are trainee positions. A trainee is usually placed in a management training program and then given a position as an assistant buyer or assistant department manager. Advancement and responsibility can be achieved quickly because there is a shortage of qualified personnel in retailing and because superior performance of an individual is quickly reflected in sales and profits—two visible measures of success. In addition, the growth of multichannel retailing has created new opportunities such as website management and online merchandise procurement.[10]

Sales

College graduates from many disciplines are attracted to sales positions because of the increasingly professional nature of selling jobs and the many opportunities they can

Xerox is well-known for its sales career opportunities.

provide. A selling career offers benefits that are hard to match in any other field: (1) the opportunity for rapid advancement (into management or to new territories and accounts); (2) the potential for extremely attractive compensation (the average salary of all sales representatives is $119,637);[11] (3) the development of personal satisfaction, feelings of accomplishment, and increased self-confidence; and (4) independence—salespeople often have almost complete control over their time and activities.

Employment opportunities in sales occupations are found in a wide variety of organizations, including insurance agencies, retailers, and financial service firms. In addition, many salespeople work as manufacturer's representatives for organizations that have selling responsibilities for several manufacturers.[12] Activities in sales jobs include *selling duties,* such as prospecting for customers, demonstrating the product, or quoting prices; *sales-support duties,* such as handling complaints and helping solve technical problems; and *nonselling duties,* such as preparing reports, attending sales meetings, and monitoring competitive activities. Salespeople who can deal with these varying activities and have empathy for customers are critical to a company's success. According to *Business-Week,* "Great salespeople feel for their customers. They understand their needs and pressures; they get the challenges of their business. They see every deal through the customer's eyes."[13]

Marketing Research

Marketing researchers play important roles in many organizations today. They are responsible for obtaining, analyzing, and interpreting data to facilitate making marketing decisions. This means marketing researchers are basically problem solvers. Success in the area requires not only an understanding of statistical analysis, research methods, and programming, but also a broad base of marketing knowledge, writing and verbal presentation skills, and an ability to communicate with colleagues and clients.[14] Individuals who are inquisitive, methodical, analytical, and solution oriented find the field particularly rewarding.

The responsibilities of the men and women currently working in the market research industry include defining the marketing problem, designing the questions, selecting the sample, collecting and analyzing the data, and, finally, reporting the results of the research. These jobs are available in three kinds of organizations. *Marketing research consulting firms* contract with large companies to provide research about their products or services.[15] *Advertising agencies* may provide research services to help clients with questions related to advertising and promotional problems. Finally, some companies have an *in-house research staff* to design and execute their research projects. Online marketing research, which is likely to become the most common form of marketing research in the near future, requires understanding of new tools such as dynamic scripting, response validation, intercept sampling, instant messaging surveys, and online consumer panels.[16]

International Careers

Many of the careers just described can be found in international settings—in large multinational U.S. corporations, small- to medium-size firms with export business, and franchises. The international consulting firm, Accenture, for example, has 38,000 consultants around the world. Similarly, many franchises such as Blockbuster Entertainment, which has 8,000 locations, are rapidly expanding outside of the United States.[17] The changes in the European Union, BRIC (Brazil, Russia, India, China), and other growing markets are likely to provide many opportunities for international careers. In many organizations, international experience has become a necessity for promotion and career advancement. "If you are going to succeed, an expatriate assignment is essential," says Eric Kraus of Gillette Co. in Boston.[18]

THE JOB SEARCH PROCESS

Activities you should consider during your job search process include assessing yourself, identifying job opportunities, preparing your résumé and related correspondence, and going on job interviews.

Assessing Yourself

You must know your product—you—so that you can market yourself effectively to prospective employers. Consequently, a critical first step in your job search is conducting a self-inquiry or self-assessment. This activity involves understanding your interests, abilities, personality, preferences, and individual style. You must be confident that you know what work environment is best for you, what makes you happy, the balance you seek between personal and professional activities, and how you can be most effective at reaching your goals. This process helps ensure that you are matching your profile to the right job, or as business consultant and author Jim Collins explains, "Finding the right seat on the bus."[19]

A self-analysis, in part, entails identifying your strengths and weaknesses. To do so, draw a vertical line down the middle of a sheet of paper and label one side of the paper "strengths" and the other side "weaknesses." Record your strong and weak points in their respective column. Ideally, this cataloging should be done over a few days to give you adequate time to reflect on your attributes. In addition, you might seek input from others who know you well (such as parents, close relatives, friends, professors, or employers) and can offer more objective views. A hypothetical list of strengths and weaknesses is shown in Figure B–2.

Personality and vocational interest tests, provided by many colleges and universities, can give you other ideas about yourself. After tests have been administered and scored, test takers meet with testing service counselors to discuss the results. Test results generally suggest jobs for which students have an inclination. The most common tests at the college level are the Strong Interest Inventory and the Campbell Interest and Skill Survey. Some counseling centers and career coaches also use the Myers-Briggs Type Indicator personality inventory and the Peoplemap assessments to help identify professions you may enjoy.[20] If you have not already done so, you may wish to see whether your school offers such testing services.

Identifying Your Job Opportunities

To identify and analyze the job market, you must conduct some marketing research to determine what industries *and* companies offer promising job opportunities that relate to the results of your self-analysis. Several sources that can help in your search are discussed next.

FIGURE B–2

Hypothetical list of a job candidate's strengths and weaknesses

Strengths	Weaknesses
I have good communication skills.	I have minimal work experience.
I work well independently.	I have a mediocre GPA.
I am honest and dependable.	I will not relocate.
I am willing to travel in the job.	I lack a customer orientation.
I am a good problem solver.	I have poor technical skills.

Your campus career center is an excellent source of job information.

Career Services Office   Your career services office is an excellent source of job information. Personnel in that office can (1) inform you about which companies will be recruiting on campus, (2) alert you to unexpected job openings, (3) advise you about short-term and long-term career prospects, (4) offer advice on résumé construction, (5) assess your interviewing strengths and weaknesses, and (6) help you evaluate a job offer. In addition, the office usually contains a variety of written materials focusing on different industries and companies and tips on job hunting.

Online Career and Employment Services   Many companies no longer make frequent on-campus visits. Instead, they may use the many online services available to advertise an employment opportunity or to search for candidate information. The National Association of Colleges and Employers, for example, maintains a site on the Internet called JobWeb (www.jobweb.org). Similarly, Monster.com and Careerbuilder.com are online databases of employment ads, candidate résumés, and other career-related information. Some of the information resources include career guidance, a cover letter library, occupational profiles, résumé templates, and networking services.[21] Employers may contact students directly when the candidate's qualifications meet their specific job requirements.

Library   The public or college library can provide you with reference material that, among other things, describes successful firms and their operations, defines the content of various jobs, and forecasts job opportunities. For example, *Fortune* publishes a list of the 1,000 largest U.S. and global companies and their respective sales and profits, and Dun & Bradstreet publishes directories of all companies in the United States with a net worth of at least $500,000. A librarian can indicate reference materials that will be most pertinent to *your* job search.

Advertisements   Help-wanted advertisements provide an overview of what is happening in the job market. Local (particularly Sunday editions) and college newspapers, trade press (such as *Marketing News* or *Advertising Age*), and business magazines (such as *Sales & Marketing Management*) contain classified advertisement sections that generally have job opening announcements, often for entry-level positions. Reviewing the want ads can help you identify what kinds of positions are available and their requirements and job titles, which firms offer certain kinds of jobs, and levels of compensation.

Employment Agencies   An employment agency can make you aware of several job opportunities very quickly because of its large number of job listings available through computer databases. Many agencies specialize in a particular field (such as sales and marketing). The advantages of using an agency include that it (1) reduces the cost of a job search by bringing applicants and employers together, (2) often has exclusive job listings available only by working through the agency, (3) performs much of the job search for you, and (4) tries to find a job that is compatible with your qualifications and interests.[22]

Personal Contacts and Networking   An important source of job information that students often overlook is their personal contacts. People you know often may know of job opportunities, so you should advise them that you're looking for a job. Relatives and friends might aid your job search. Instructors you know well and business contacts can provide a wealth of information about potential jobs and even help arrange an interview with a prospective employer. They may also help arrange *informational interviews* with employers that do not have immediate openings. These interviews allow you to collect information about an industry or an employer and give you an advantage if a position does become available. It is a good idea to leave your résumé with all your personal contacts so they can pass it along to those who might be in need of your services.

State Employment Office   State employment offices have listings of job opportunities in their state and counselors to help arrange a job interview for you. Although state employment offices perform functions similar to employment agencies, they differ in listing only job opportunities in their state and providing their services free.

Direct Contact Another means of obtaining job information is direct contact—personally communicating to prospective employers (either by mail, e-mail, or in person) that you would be interested in pursuing job opportunities with them. Often you may not even know whether jobs are available in these firms. If you correspond with the companies in writing, a letter of introduction and an attached résumé should serve as your initial form of communication. Your major goal in direct contact is ultimately to arrange a job interview.

Writing Your Résumé

A résumé is a document that communicates to prospective employers who you are. An employer reading a résumé is looking for a snapshot of your qualifications to decide if you should be invited to a job interview. It is imperative that you design a résumé that presents yourself in a favorable light and allows you to get to that next important step. Personnel in your career services office can provide assistance in designing résumés.

The Résumé Itself A well-constructed résumé generally contains up to nine major sections: (1) identification (name, address, telephone number, and e-mail address), (2) job or career objective, (3) educational background, (4) honors and awards, (5) work experience or history, (6) skills or capabilities (that pertain to a particular kind of job for which you may be interviewing), (7) extracurricular activities, (8) personal interests, and (9) personal references.[23] If possible, you should include quantitative information about your accomplishments and experience, such as "increased sales revenue by 20 percent" for the year you managed a retail clothing store.

Today most career experts suggest that résumés accommodate delivery through mail, e-mail, and fax machines. In addition, résumés must accommodate employers who use scanning technology to enter résumés into their own databases or who search commercial online databases. To fully utilize online opportunities, an electronic résumé with a popular font (e.g., New Times Roman) and relatively large font size (e.g., 10–14 pt.)—and without italic text, graphics, shading, underlining, or vertical lines—must be available. In addition, because online recruiting starts with a keyword search, it is important to include keywords, focus on nouns rather than verbs, and avoid abbreviations. Related to this use of technology, don't forget that many employers may visit social networking sites such as Facebook and MySpace, or may simply "Google" your name, to see what comes up. Review your online profiles before you start your job search to provide a positive image![24]

Letter Accompanying a Résumé The letter accompanying a résumé, or cover letter, serves as the job candidate's introduction. As a result, it must gain the attention and interest of the reader or it will fail to give the incentive to examine the résumé carefully. In designing a letter to accompany your résumé, address the following issues:

- Address the letter to a specific person.
- Identify the position for which you are applying and how you heard of it.
- Indicate why you are applying for the position.
- Summarize your most significant credentials and qualifications.
- Refer the reader to the enclosed résumé.
- Request a personal interview, and advise the reader when and where you can be reached.

As a general rule, nothing works better than an impressive cover letter and good academic credentials.[25]

Interviewing for Your Job

The job interview is a conversation between a prospective employer and a job candidate that focuses on determining whether the employer's needs can be satisfied by the candidate's qualifications. The interview is a "make or break" situation: If the interview goes well, you have increased your chances of receiving a job offer; if it goes poorly, you probably will be eliminated from further consideration.

Preparing for a Job Interview To be successful in a job interview, you must prepare for it so you can exhibit professionalism and indicate to a prospective employer that you are serious about the job. When preparing for the interview, several critical activities need to be performed.

Before the interview, gather facts about the industry, the prospective employer, and the job. Relevant information might include the general description for the occupation; the firm's products or services; the firm's size, number of employees, and financial and competitive position; the requirements of the position; and the name and personality of the interviewer. Obtaining this information will provide you with additional insight into the firm and help you formulate questions to ask the interviewer. This information might be gleaned, for example, from corporate annual reports, *The Wall Street Journal,* Moody's manuals, Standard & Poor's *Register of Corporations, Directors, and Executives, The Directory of Corporate Affiliations,* selected issues of *BusinessWeek,* or trade publications. If information is not readily available, you could call the company and indicate that you wish to obtain some information about the firm before your interview.[26]

Preparation for the job interview should also involve role playing, or pretending that you are in the "hot seat" being interviewed. Before role playing, anticipate questions interviewers may pose and how you might address them (Figure B–3). Do not memorize your answers, though, because you want to appear spontaneous, yet logical and intelligent. Nonetheless, it is helpful to practice how you might respond to the questions. In addition, develop questions you might ask the interviewer that are important and of concern to you (Figure B–4). "It's an opportunity to show the recruiter how smart you are," comments one recruiter.[27]

Before the job interview you should attend to several details. Know the exact time and place of the interview; write them down—do not rely on your memory. Get the full company name straight. Find out what the interviewer's name is and how to pronounce

FIGURE B–3
Anticipate questions frequently asked by interviewers to practice how you might respond.

Interviewer Questions
1. What do you consider to be your greatest strengths and weaknesses?
2. What do you see yourself doing in 5 years? In 10 years?
3. What are three important leadership qualities? How have you demonstrated these qualities?
4. What jobs have you enjoyed the most? The least? Why?
5. Why do you want to work for our company?

FIGURE B–4
Interviewees should develop questions about topics that are important to them.

Interviewee Questions
1. Describe the typical first-year assignment for this job.
2. How is an employee evaluated?
3. What is the company's promotion policy?
4. How much responsibility would I have in this job?
5. Why do you enjoy working for your firm?

it. Bring a notepad and pen along to the interview, in case you need to record anything. Make certain that your appearance is clean, neat, professional, and conservative. And be punctual; arriving tardy to a job interview gives you an appearance of being unreliable.

Succeeding in Your Job Interview   You have done your homework, and at last the moment arrives and it is time for the interview. Although you may experience some apprehension, view the interview as a conversation between the prospective employer and you. Both of you are in the interview to look over the other party, to see whether there might be a good match. When you meet the interviewer, greet him or her by name, be cheerful, smile, and maintain good eye contact. Take your lead from the interviewer at the outset. Sit down after the interviewer has offered you a seat. Sit up straight in your chair, and look alert and interested at all times. Appear relaxed, not tense. Be enthusiastic.

During the interview, be yourself. If you try to behave in a manner that is different from the real you, your attempt may be transparent to the interviewer or you may ultimately get the job but discover that you aren't suited for it. In addition to assessing how well your skills match those of the job, the interviewer will probably try to assess your long-term interest in the firm.

As the interview comes to a close, leave it on a positive note. Thank the interviewer for his or her time and the opportunity to discuss employment opportunities. If you are still interested in the job, express this to the interviewer. The interviewer will normally tell you what the employer's next step is—probably a visit to the company.[28] Rarely will a job offer be made at the end of the initial interview. If it is and you want the job, accept the offer; if there is any doubt in your mind about the job, however, ask for time to consider the offer.

View the interview as a conversation between the prospective employer and you.

Following Up on Your Job Interview   After your interview, send a thank-you note to the interviewer and indicate whether you are still interested in the job. If you want to continue pursuing the job, polite persistence may help you get it. While e-mail is a common form of communication today, it is often viewed as less personal than a letter or telephone call, so be confident that e-mail is preferred before using it to correspond with the interviewer.[29]

As you conduct your follow-up, be persistent but polite. If you are too eager, one of two things could happen to prevent you from getting the job: The employer might feel that you are a nuisance and would exhibit such behavior on the job, or the employer may perceive that you are desperate for the job and thus are not a viable candidate.

Handling Rejection   You have put your best efforts into your job search. You developed a well-designed résumé and prepared carefully for the job interview. Even the interview appears to have gone well. Nevertheless, a prospective employer may send you a rejection letter ("We are sorry that our needs and your superb qualification don't match"). Although you will probably be disappointed, not all interviews lead to a job offer because there normally are more candidates than there are positions available. Try to learn lessons to apply in future interviews. Keep interviewing and gaining interview experience; your persistence will eventually pay off.

SELECTED SOURCES OF MARKETING CAREER INFORMATION

The following is a selected list of marketing information sources that you should find useful during your academic studies and professional career.

BUSINESS AND MARKETING PUBLICATIONS

Scott Dacko, *A Dictionary of Marketing: Concepts, Laws, Theories, Effects* (Oxford University Press, 2007). This dictionary of marketing terms focuses on key concepts, grouped into four categories: concepts, laws, theories, and effects. Containing over 500 entries, ranging in length and depth, the book will be the ideal reference guide for practitioners and students.

Hoover's Handbook of World Business (Austin, TX: Hoover's Business Press, 2007). A detailed source of information about companies outside of the United States, including firms from Canada, Europe, Japan, China, India, and Taiwan.

Barbara Lewis and Dale Littler, eds., *The Blackwell Encyclopedic Dictionary of Marketing* (Cambridge, MA: Blackwell Publishers, 1999). Part of the 10-volume *Blackwell Encyclopedia of Management,* this book provides clear, concise, up-to-the-minute, and highly informative definitions and explanations of the key concepts and terms in marketing management, consumer behavior, segmentation, organizational marketing, pricing, communications, retailing and distribution, product management, market research, and international marketing.

Cynthia L. Shamel, *Introduction to Online Market & Industry Research* (Mason, OH: Thomson Learning, 2004). This comprehensive reference provides search strategies and valuable data source information, including rankings of data sources, for industry researchers.

Linda D. Hall, *Encyclopedia of Business Information Sources,* 21st ed. (Detroit: Gale Group, 2006). A bibliographic guide to over 35,000 citations covering more than 1,100 primary subjects of interest to business personnel.

CAREER PLANNING PUBLICATIONS

Richard N. Bolles, *What Color Is Your Parachute? 2008: A Practical Manual for Job-Hunters and Career-Changers* (Berkeley, CA: Ten Speed Press, 2008). A companion workbook is also available. See www.jobhuntersbible.com.

Dennis V. Damp, *The Book of U.S. Government Jobs: Where They Are, What's Available, and How to Get One,* 10th ed. (Moon Township, PA: Bookhaven Press, 2008).

Margaret Riley Dikel and Frances E. Roehm, *Guide to Internet Job Searching* (New York: McGraw-Hill, 2008).

Princeton Review: Best Entry-Level Jobs, 2009 Edition (Random House Information Group, 2008).

Margery Steinberg, *Opportunities in Marketing Careers* (New York: McGraw-Hill, 2006).

SELECTED PERIODICALS

Advertising Age, Crain Communications, Inc. (weekly). See www.adage.com. (subscription rate: $99)

BusinessWeek, McGraw-Hill Companies (weekly). See www.businessweek.com. (subscription rate: $45.97)

Journal of Marketing, American Marketing Association (quarterly). See www.marketingpower.com. (subscription rates: $90 nonmembers; $53 members)

Marketing Management, American Marketing Association (six times per year). See www.marketingpower.com. (subscription rates: $80 nonmembers; $53 members)

Marketing News, American Marketing Association (biweekly). See www.marketingpower.com. (subscription rates: $100 nonmembers; $39 members)

Marketing Research, American Marketing Association (quarterly). See www.marketingpower.com. (subscription rates: $85 nonmembers; $53 members)

The Wall Street Journal Interactive, Dow Jones & Company, Inc. (weekly). See www.wsj.com. (subscription rates: $198 print; $79 online; $34.95 (15 weeks) for students, both print and online)

PROFESSIONAL AND TRADE ASSOCIATIONS

American Advertising Federation
1101 Vermont Ave. NW., Suite 500
Washington, DC 20005-6306
(202) 898-0089
www.aaf.org

American e-Commerce Association
2346 Camp St.
New Orleans, LA 70130
(504) 495-1748
www.aeaus.com

American Marketing Association
311 S. Wacker Dr., Suite 5800
Chicago, IL 60606
(800) AMA-1150
www.marketingpower.com

Direct Marketing Association
1120 Avenue of the Americas
New York, NY 10036-6700
(212) 768-7277
www.the-dma.org

Marketing Science Institute
1000 Massachusetts Ave.
Cambridge, MA 02138-5396
(617) 491-2060
www.msi.org

Sales and Marketing Executives International
P.O. Box 1390
Sumas, WA 98295-1390
(312) 893-0751
www.smei.org

GLOSSARY

80/20 rule A concept that suggests 80 percent of a firm's sales are obtained from 20 percent of its customers. p. 195

account management policies Specifies whom salespeople should contact, what kinds of selling and customer service activities should be engaged in, and how these activities should be carried out. p. 395

adaptive selling A need-satisfaction presentation format that involves adjusting the presentation to fit the selling situation, such as knowing when to offer solutions and when to ask for more information. p. 391

advertising Any paid form of nonpersonal communication about an organization, good, service, or idea by an identified sponsor. p. 338, 360

attitude A learned predisposition to respond to an object or class of objects in a consistently favorable or unfavorable way. p. 107

baby boomers The generation of children born between 1946 and 1964. p. 62

back translation The practice where a translated word or phrase is retranslated into the original language by a different interpreter to catch errors. p. 148

beliefs A consumer's subjective perception of how a product or brand performs on different attributes based on personal experience, advertising, and discussions with other people. p. 107

blog A web page that serves as a publicly accessible personal journal for an individual or organization. p. 416

bots Electronic shopping agents or robots that comb websites to compare prices and product or service features. p. 414

brand equity The added value a given brand name gives to a product beyond the functional benefits provided. p. 248

brand loyalty A favorable attitude toward and consistent purchase of a single brand over time. p. 107

brand name Any word, device (design, shape, sound, or color), or combination of these used to distinguish a seller's goods or services. p. 247

brand personality A set of human characteristics associated with a brand name. p. 247

branding A marketing decision by an organization to use a name, phrase, design, or symbols, or combination of these to identify its products and distinguish them from those of competitors. p. 247

break-even analysis A technique that analyzes the relationship between total revenue and total cost to determine profitability at various levels of output. p. 275

brokers Independent firms or individuals whose principal function is to bring buyers and sellers together to make sales. p. 330

business The clear, broad, underlying industry or market sector of an organization's offering. p. 24

business products Products that assist directly or indirectly in providing products for resale. Also called *B2B products*, or *industrial products*. p. 213

business marketing The marketing of goods and services to companies, governments, or not-for-profit organizations for use in the creation of goods and services that they can produce and market to others. p. 122

buy classes Consists of three types of organizational buying situations: straight rebuy, new buy, and modified rebuy. p. 130

buying center The group of people in an organization who participate in the buying process and share common goals, risks, and knowledge important to purchase decisions. p. 129

capacity management Integrating the service component of the marketing mix with efforts to influence consumer demand. p. 256

category management An approach to managing the assortment of merchandise in which a manager is assigned the responsibility for selecting all products that consumers in a market segment might view as substitutes for each other, with the objective of maximizing sales and profits in the category. p. 325

cause marketing Occurs when the charitable contributions of a firm are tied directly to the customer revenues produced through the promotion of one of its products. p. 88

channel conflict Arises when one channel member believes another channel member is engaged in behavior that prevents it from achieving its goals. p. 300

choiceboard An interactive, Internet-enabled system that allows individual customers to design their own products and services by answering a few questions and choosing from a menu of product or service attributes (or components), prices, and delivery options. p. 408

code of ethics A formal statement of ethical principles and rules of conduct. p. 84

collaborative filtering A process that automatically groups people with similar buying intentions, preferences, and behaviors and predicts future purchases. p. 408

communication The process of conveying a message to others and requires six elements: a source, a message, a channel of communication, a receiver, and the processes of encoding and decoding. p. 336

competition The alternative firms that could provide a product to satisfy a specific market's needs. p. 69

consultative selling A need-satisfaction presentation format that focuses on problem identification, where the salesperson serves as an expert on problem recognition and resolution. p. 391

consumer behavior The actions a person takes in purchasing and using products and services, including the mental and social processes that come before and after these actions. p. 98

Consumer Bill of Rights (1962) Codified the ethics of exchange between buyers and sellers, including the rights to safety, to be informed, to choose, and to be heard. p. 82

consumer products Products purchased by the ultimate consumer. p. 213

consumerism A grassroots movement started in the 1960s to increase the influence, power, and rights of consumers in dealing with institutions. p. 71

consumer-oriented sales promotions Sales tools used to support a company's advertising and personal selling directed to ultimate consumers. Also called *consumer promotions*. p. 373

cookies Computer files that a marketer can download onto the computer of an online shopper who visits the marketer's website. p. 417

cooperative advertising Advertising programs by which a manufacturer pays a percentage of the retailer's local advertising expense for advertising the manufacturer's products. p. 376

core values The fundamental, passionate, and enduring principles of an organization that guide its conduct over time. p. 22

cross-channel shopper A consumer who researches offerings online and then purchases them at retail stores. p. 418

cross-cultural analysis The study of similarities and differences among consumers in two or more nations or societies. p. 146

cultural symbols Things that represent ideas and concepts. p. 147

culture The set of values, ideas, and attitudes that are learned and shared among the members of a group. p. 65

currency exchange rate The price of one country's currency expressed in terms of another country's currency. p. 150

customer experience management (CEM) The process of managing the entire customer experience within the firm. p. 226

customer service The ability of logistics management to satisfy users in terms of time, dependability, communication, and convenience. p. 307

customer value The unique combination of benefits received by targeted buyers that includes quality, convenience, on-time delivery, and both before-sale and after-sale service at a specific price. p. 11

customs What is considered normal and expected about the way people do things in a specific country. p. 147

data The facts and figures related to the problem, divided into two main parts: secondary data and primary data. p. 168

demand curve A graph relating the quantity sold and price, which shows the maximum number of units that will be sold at a given price. p. 272

demographics Describing a population according to selected characteristics such as age, gender, ethnicity, income, and occupation. p. 60

derived demand The demand for industrial products and services is driven by, or derived from, demand for consumer products and services. p. 124

direct investment A global market-entry strategy that entails a domestic firm actually investing in and owning a foreign subsidiary or division. p. 154

direct marketing A promotion alternative that uses direct communication with consumers to generate a response in the form of an order, a request for further information, or a visit to a retail outlet. p. 341

direct orders The result of direct marketing offers that contain all the information necessary for a prospective buyer to make a decision to purchase and complete the transaction. p. 350

disintermediation Channel conflict that arises when a channel member bypasses another member and sells or buys products directly. p. 300

dual distribution An arrangement whereby a firm reaches different buyers by using two or more different types of channels for the same basic product. p. 295

dumping When a firm sells a product in a foreign country below its domestic price or below its actual cost. p. 157

dynamic pricing The practice of changing prices for products and services in real time in response to supply and demand conditions. p. 417

economy Pertains to the income, expenditures, and resources that affect the cost of running a business and household. p. 65

e-marketplaces Online trading communities that bring together buyers and supplier organizations to make possible the real time exchange of information, money, products, and services. Also called *B2B exchanges* or *e-hubs.* p. 132

environmental forces The uncontrollable social, economic, technological, competitive, and regulatory forces that affect the results of a marketing decision. p. 11

environmental scanning The process of continually acquiring information on events occurring outside the organization to identify and interpret potential trends. p. 60

ethics The moral principles and values that govern the actions and decisions of an individual or group. p. 80

exchange The trade of things of value between buyer and seller so that each is better off after the trade. p. 6

exclusive distribution A level of distribution density whereby only one retail outlet in a specific geographical area carries the firm's products. p. 299

exporting A global market-entry strategy in which a company produces goods in one country and sells them in another country. p. 151

family life cycle The distinct phases that a family progresses through from formation to retirement, each phase bringing with it identifiable purchasing behaviors. p. 112

Foreign Corrupt Practices Act (1977) A law, amended by the *International Anti-Dumping and Fair Competition Act* (1998), that makes it a crime for U.S. corporations to bribe an official of a foreign government or political party to obtain or retain business in a foreign country. p. 147

four I's of services The four unique elements to services: intangibility, inconsistency, inseparability, and inventory. p. 215

Generation X Includes the 15 percent of the population born between 1965 and 1976. Also called *baby bust.* p. 62

Generation Y Includes the 72 million Americans born between 1977 and 1994. Also called *echo-boom* or *baby boomlet.* p. 63

global brand A brand marketed under the same name in multiple countries with similar and centrally coordinated marketing programs. p. 144

global competition Exists when firms originate, produce, and market their products and services worldwide. p. 142

global consumers Consumer groups living in many countries or regions of the world who have similar needs or seek similar features and benefits from products or services. p. 145

global marketing strategy The practice of standardizing marketing activities when there are cultural similarities and adapting them when cultures differ. p. 143

goals Statements of an accomplishment of a task to be achieved, often by a specific time. Also called *objectives.* p. 24

gray market A situation where products are sold through unauthorized channels of distribution. Also called *parallel importing.* p. 157

green marketing Marketing efforts to produce, promote, and reclaim environmentally sensitive products. p. 88

hierarchy of effects The sequence of stages a prospective buyer goes through from initial awareness of a product to eventual action (either trial or adoption of the product). The stages include awareness, interest, evaluation, trial, and adoption. p. 346

idle production capacity Occurs when the service provider is available but there is no demand for the service. p. 216

infomercials Program-length (30-minute) advertisements that take an educational approach to communication with potential customers. p. 367

institutional advertisements Advertisements designed to build goodwill or an image for an organization rather than promote a specific good or service. p. 361

integrated marketing communications (IMC) The concept of designing marketing communications programs that coordinate all promotional activities—advertising, personal selling, sales promotion, public relations, and direct marketing—to provide a consistent message across all audiences. p. 336

intensive distribution A level of distribution density whereby a firm tries to place its products and services in as many outlets as possible. p. 298

interactive marketing Two-way buyer–seller electronic communication in a computer-mediated environment in which the buyer controls the kind and amount of information received from the seller. p. 407

involvement The personal, social, and economic significance of the purchase to the consumer. p. 100

joint venture A global market-entry strategy in which a foreign company and a local firm invest together to create a local business in order to share ownership, control, and profits of the new company. p. 153

laws Society's values and standards that are enforceable in the courts. p. 80

lead generation The result of a direct marketing offer designed to generate interest in a product or service and a request for additional information. p. 351

learning Those behaviors that result from (1) repeated experience and (2) reasoning. p. 106

logistics Those activities that focus on getting the right amount of the right products to the right place at the right time at the lowest possible cost. p. 302

major account management The practice of using team selling to focus on important customers so as to build mutually beneficial, long-term, cooperative relationships; also called *key account management*. p 394

manufacturer's agents Agents who work for several producers and carry noncompetitive, complementary merchandise in an exclusive territory. Also called *manufacturer's representatives*. p. 330

market People with both the desire and the ability to buy a specific offering. p. 9

market orientation Occurs when an organization focuses its efforts on (1) continuously collecting information about customers' needs, (2) sharing this information across departments, and (3) using it to create customer value. p. 14

market segmentation Involves aggregating prospective buyers into groups, or segments, that (1) have common needs and (2) will respond similarly to a marketing action. pp. 34, 190

market segments The relatively homogeneous groups of prospective buyers that result from the market segmentation process. p. 190

market share The ratio of sales revenue of the firm to the total sales revenue of all firms in the industry, including the firm itself. p. 24

marketing The activity for creating, communicating, delivering, and exchanging offerings that benefit the organization, its stakeholders, and society at large. p. 6

marketing channel Individuals and firms involved in the process of making a product or service available for use or consumption by consumers or industrial users. p. 290

marketing concept The idea that an organization should (1) strive to satisfy the needs of consumers (2) while also trying to achieve the organization's goals. p. 14

marketing dashboard The visual display of the essential information related to achieving a marketing objective. p. 25

marketing metric A measure of the quantitative value or trend of a marketing activity or result. p. 25

marketing mix The marketing manager's controllable factors—product, price, promotion, and place—that can be used to solve a marketing problem. p. 10

marketing plan A road map for the marketing activities of an organization for a specified future time period such as one year or five years. p. 26

marketing program A plan that integrates the marketing mix to provide a good, service, or idea to prospective buyers. p. 12

marketing research The process of defining a marketing problem and opportunity, systematically collecting and analyzing information, and recommending actions. p. 164

marketing strategy The means by which a marketing goal is to be achieved, usually characterized by a specified target market and a marketing program to reach it. p. 37

marketing tactics Detailed day-to-day operational decisions essential to the overall success of marketing strategies. p. 37

market–product grid A framework to relate the market segments of potential buyers to products offered or potential marketing actions by an organization. p. 198

marketspace Information- and communication-based electronic exchange environment mostly occupied by sophisticated computer and telecommunication technologies and digitized offerings. p. 68

measures of success Criteria or standards used in evaluating proposed solutions to a problem. p. 166

merchant wholesalers Independently owned firms that take title to the merchandise they handle. p. 329

mission A statement of the organization's function in society, often identifying its customers, markets, products, and technologies. Often used interchangeably with *vision*. p. 23

moral idealism A personal moral philosophy that considers certain individual rights or duties as universal, regardless of the outcome. p. 85

motivation The energizing force that stimulates behavior to satisfy a need. p. 103

multibranding A branding strategy that involves giving each product a distinct name when each brand is intended for a different market segment. p. 251

multichannel marketing The blending of different communication and delivery channels that are mutually reinforcing in attracting, retaining, and building relationships with consumers who shop and buy in traditional intermediaries and online. p. 295

multichannel retailers Retailers that utilize and integrate a combination of traditional store formats and nonstore formats such as catalogs, television, and online retailing. p. 325

multicultural marketing Combinations of the marketing mix that reflects the unique attitudes, ancestry, communication preferences, and lifestyles of different races. p. 64

multidomestic marketing strategy A multinational firm's offering as many different product variations, brand names, and advertising programs as countries in which they do business. p. 143

multiproduct branding A branding strategy in which a company uses one name for all its products in a product class. p. 250

new-product process The seven stages an organization goes through to identify business opportunities and convert them to a salable good or service. p. 224

North American Industry Classification System (NAICS) Provides common industry definitions for Canada, Mexico, and the United States, which makes it easier to measure economic activity in the three member countries of the North American Free Trade Agreement (NAFTA). p. 123

objectives Statements of an accomplishment of a task to be achieved, often by a specific time. Also called *goals*. p. 24

observational data Facts and figures obtained by watching, either mechanically or in person, how people actually behave. p. 170

off-peak pricing Charging different prices during different times of the day or days of the week to reflect variations in demand for the service. p. 257

opinion leaders Individuals who have social influence over others. p. 109

order getter Sells in a conventional sense and identifies prospective customers, provides customers with information, persuades customers to buy, closes sales, and follows up on customers' use of a product or service. p. 386

order taker Processes routine orders or reorders for products that were already sold by the company. p. 386

organizational buyers Those manufacturers, wholesalers, retailers, and government agencies that buy goods and services for their own use or for resale. pp. 16, 122

organizational buying behavior The decision-making process that organizations use to establish the need for products and services and identify, evaluate, and choose among alternative brands and suppliers. p. 128

organizational culture The set of values, ideas, attitudes, and norms of behavior that is learned and shared among the members of an organization. p. 23

packaging A component of a product that refers to any container in which it is offered for sale and on which label information is displayed. p. 253

perceived risk The anxieties felt because the consumer cannot anticipate the outcomes of a purchase but believes that there may be negative consequences. p. 106

perception The process by which an individual selects, organizes, and interprets information to create a meaningful picture of the world. p. 104

perceptual map A means of displaying or graphing in two dimensions the location of products or brands in the minds of consumers to enable a manager to see how consumers perceive competing products or brands and then take marketing actions. p. 204

permission marketing The solicitation of a consumer's consent (called *opt-in*) to receive e-mail and advertising based on personal data supplied by the consumer. p. 409

personal selling The two-way flow of communication between a buyer and seller, often in a face-to-face encounter, designed to influence a person's or group's purchase decision. pp. 339, 384

personal selling process Sales activities occurring before and after the sale itself, consisting of six stages: (1) prospecting, (2) preapproach, (3) approach, (4) presentation, (5) close, and (6) follow-up. p. 388

personality A person's consistent behaviors or responses to recurring situations. p. 104

personalization The consumer-initiated practice of generating content on a marketer's website that is custom tailored to an individual's specific needs and preferences. p. 409

points of difference Those characteristics of a product that make it superior to competitive substitutes. p. 35

posttests Tests conducted after an advertisement has been shown to the target audience to determine whether it accomplished its intended purpose. p. 372

pretests Tests conducted before an advertisement is placed in any medium to determine whether it communicates the intended message or to select among alternative versions of the advertisement. p. 371

price The money or other considerations (including other goods and services) exchanged for the ownership or use of a good or service. p. 264

price elasticity of demand The percentage change in quantity demanded relative to a percentage change in price. p. 273

pricing constraints Factors that limit the range of prices a firm may set. p. 278

pricing objectives Specify the role of price in an organization's marketing and strategic plans. p. 277

primary data Facts and figures that are newly collected for the project. p. 168

product A good, service, or idea consisting of a bundle of tangible and intangible attributes that satisfies consumers' needs and is received in exchange for money or something else of value. p. 212

product advertisements Advertisements that focus on selling a good or service and that take three forms: (1) pioneering (or informational), (2) competitive (or persuasive), and (3) reminder. p. 360

product differentiation A marketing strategy that involves a firm using different marketing mix activities to help consumers perceive the product as being different and better than competing products. p. 190

product item A specific product that has a unique brand, size, or price. p. 214

product life cycle Describes the stages a new product goes through in the marketplace: introduction, growth, maturity, and decline. p. 236

product line A group of product or service items that are closely related because they satisfy a class of needs, are used together, are sold to the same customer group, are distributed through the same outlets, or fall within a given price range. p. 214

product mix All of the of product lines offered by an organization. p. 214

product placement A consumer sales promotion tool that uses a brand-name product in a movie, television show, video, or a commercial for another product. p. 375

product positioning The place an offering occupies in consumers' minds on important attributes relative to competitive products. p. 203

product repositioning Changing the place an offering occupies in consumers' minds relative to competitive products. p. 203

profit The money left after a business firm's total expenses are subtracted from its total revenues or sales and is the reward for the risk it undertakes in marketing its offerings. p. 22

profit equation Profit = Total revenue − Total cost; or Profit = (Unit price × Quantity sold) − (Fixed cost + Variable cost). p. 266

promotional mix The combination of one or more communication tools used to: (1) inform prospective buyers about the benefits of the product, (2) persuade them to try it, and (3) remind them later about the benefits they enjoyed by using the product. p. 336

protectionism The practice of shielding one or more industries within a country's economy from foreign competition through the use of tariffs or quotas. p. 140

public relations A form of communication management that seeks to influence the feelings, opinions, or beliefs held by customers, prospective customers, stockholders, suppliers, employees, and other publics about a company and its products or services. p. 340

publicity A nonpersonal, indirectly paid presentation of an organization, good, or service. p. 340

publicity tools Methods of obtaining nonpersonal presentation of an organization, good, or service without direct cost. Examples include news releases, news conferences, and public service announcements. p. 377

pull strategy Directing the promotional mix at ultimate consumers to encourage them to ask the retailer for a product. p. 345

purchase decision process The five stages a buyer passes through in making choices about which products and services to buy: (1) problem recognition, (2) information search, (3) alternative evaluation, (4) purchase decision, and (5) postpurchase behavior. p. 98

push strategy Directing the promotional mix to channel members to gain their cooperation in ordering and stocking the product. p. 345

questionnaire data Facts and figures obtained by asking people about their attitudes, awareness, intentions, and behaviors. p. 173

quota A restriction placed on the amount of a product allowed to enter or leave a country. p. 140

reference groups People to whom an individual looks as a basis for self-appraisal or as a source of personal standards. p. 110

regulation Restrictions state and federal laws place on business with regard to the conduct of its activities. p. 70

relationship marketing Linking the organization to its individual customers, employees, suppliers, and other partners for their mutual long-term benefits. p. 11

relationship selling The practice of building ties to customers based on a salesperson's attention and commitment to customer needs over time. p. 385

retail life cycle The process of growth and decline that retail outlets, like products, experience. The retail life cycle consists of the early growth, accelerated development, maturity, and decline stages. p. 328

retailing All activities involved in selling, renting, and providing goods and services to ultimate consumers for personal, family, or household use. p. 314

retailing mix The activities related to managing the store and the merchandise in the store, which includes retail pricing, store location, retail communication, and merchandise. p. 323

reverse auction In an e-marketplace, it is an online auction in which a buyer communicates a need for a product or service and would-be suppliers are invited to bid in competition with each other. p. 133

sales forecast The total sales of a product that a firm expects to sell during a specified time period under specified environmental conditions and its own marketing efforts. p. 182

sales management Planning the selling program and implementing and controlling the personal selling effort of the firm. p. 384

sales plan A statement describing what is to be achieved and where and how the selling efforts of salespeople are to be deployed. p. 394

sales promotion A short-term inducement of value offered to arouse interest in buying a good or service. p. 341

sales quota Specific goals assigned to a salesperson, sales team, branch sales office, or sales district for a stated time period. p. 398

salesforce automation The use of computer, information, communication, and Internet technologies to make the sales function more effective and efficient. p. 398

scrambled merchandising Offering several unrelated product lines in a single store. p. 319

secondary data Facts and figures that have already been recorded before the project at hand. p. 168

selective distribution A level of distribution density whereby a firm selects a few retail outlets in a specific geographical area to carry its products. p. 299

self-regulation An alternative to government control where an industry attempts to police itself. p. 73

services Intangible activities or benefits that an organization provides to satisfy consumers' needs in exchange for money or something else of value. p. 212

situation analysis Taking stock of where the firm or product has been recently, where it is now, and where it is headed in terms of the organization's plans and the external factors and trends affecting it. p. 32

social audit A systematic assessment of a firm's objectives, strategies, and performance in terms of social responsibility. p. 88

social forces The demographic characteristics of the population and its values. p. 60

social responsibility The idea that organizations are part of a larger society and are accountable to that society for their actions. p. 86

societal marketing concept The view that organizations should discovers and satisfy the needs of consumers in a way that provides for society's well-being. p. 15

spam Communications that take the form of electronic junk mail or unsolicited e-mail. p. 416

strategic marketing process The approach whereby an organization allocates its marketing mix resources to reach its target markets. p. 32

strategy An organization's long-term course of action designed to deliver a unique customer experience while achieving its goals. p. 22

subcultures Subgroups within the larger, or national, culture with unique values, ideas, and attitudes. p. 114

supply chain A sequence of firms that perform activities required to create and deliver a good or service to consumers or industrial users. p. 303

SWOT analysis An acronym describing an organization's appraisal of its internal **S**trengths and **W**eaknesses and its external **O**pportunities and **T**hreats. p. 33

synergy The increased customer value achieved through performing organizational functions more efficiently. p. 193

target market One or more specific groups of potential consumers toward which an organization directs its marketing program. p. 10

tariffs A government tax on goods or services entering a country, primarily serving to raise prices on imports. p. 140

technology Inventions or innovations from applied science or engineering research. p. 67

telemarketing Using the telephone to interact with and sell directly to consumers. p. 322

total cost (TC) The total expense incurred by a firm in producing and marketing a product. Total cost is the sum of fixed cost and variable cost. p. 275

total logistics cost Expenses associated with transportation, materials handling and warehousing, inventory, stockouts (being out of inventory), order processing, and return goods handling. p. 306

total revenue (TR) The total money received from the sale of a product. p. 274

trade-oriented sales promotions Sales tools used to support a company's advertising and personal selling directed to wholesalers, distributors, or retailers. Also called *trade promotions*. p. 376

traditional auction In an e-marketplace, it is an online auction in which a seller puts an item up for sale and would-be buyers are invited to bid in competition with each other. p. 133

traffic generation The outcome of a direct marketing offer designed to motivate people to visit a business. p. 351

ultimate consumers The people who use the goods and services purchased for a household. Also called *consumers*, *buyers*, or *customers*. p. 16

usage rate The quantity consumed or patronage (store visits) during a specific period. p. 195

utilitarianism A personal moral philosophy that focuses on the "greatest good for the greatest number," by assessing the costs and benefits of the consequences of ethical behavior. p. 86

utility The benefits or customer value received by users of the product. p. 16

value The ratio of perceived benefits to price; or Value = Perceived benefits ÷ Price. p. 265

values A society's personally or socially preferable modes of conduct or states of existence that tend to persist over time. p. 146

vendor-managed inventory An inventory-management system whereby the supplier determines the product amount and assortment a customer (such as a retailer) needs and automatically delivers the appropriate items. p. 308

vertical marketing systems Professionally managed and centrally coordinated marketing channels designed to achieve channel economies and maximum marketing impact. p. 296

viral marketing An Internet-enabled promotional strategy that encourages individuals to forward marketer-initiated messages to others via e-mail. p. 416

web communities Websites that allow people to congregate online and exchange views on topics of common interest. p. 415

wheel of retailing A concept that describes how new forms of retail outlets enter the market. p. 327

word of mouth The influencing of people during conversations. p. 110

World Trade Organization (WTO) A permanent institution that sets rules governing trade between its members through panels of trade experts who decide on trade disputes between members and issue binding decisions. p. 140

LEARNING REVIEW ANSWERS

CHAPTER 1

1. What is marketing?

Answer: Marketing is the activity for creating, communicating, delivering, and exchanging offerings that benefit the organization, its stakeholders, and society at large.

2. Marketing focuses on _____ and _____ consumer needs.

Answer: discovering; satisfying

3. An organization can't satisfy the needs of all consumers, so it must focus on one or more subgroups, which are its _____.

Answer: target markets

4. What are the four marketing mix elements that make up the organization's marketing program?

Answer: product, price, promotion, place

5. What are environmental forces?

Answer: Environmental forces are those that the organization's marketing department can't control. These include social, economic, technological, competitive, and regulatory forces.

6. What are the two key characteristics of the marketing concept?

Answer: An organization should (1) strive to satisfy the needs of consumers (2) while also trying to achieve the organization's goals.

7. What is the difference between ultimate consumers and organizational buyers?

Answer: Ultimate consumers are the people who use the goods and services purchased for a household. Organizational buyers are those manufacturers, retailers, or government agencies that buy goods and services for their own use or for resale.

CHAPTER 2

1. What is the difference between a business firm and a nonprofit organization?

Answer: A business firm is a privately owned organization that serves its customers in order to earn a profit so that it can survive. A nonprofit organization is a nongovernmental organization that serves its customers but does not have profit as an organizational goal. Instead, its goals may be operational efficiency or client satisfaction.

2. What is the meaning of an organization's mission?

Answer: A mission is a statement of the organization's function in society, often identifying its customers, markets, products, and technologies. Often used interchangeably with vision.

3. What are examples of an organization's goals?

Answer: Goals for business firms include profits, sales, market share, quality, customer satisfaction, employee welfare, and social responsibility. Nonprofit organizations often seek to serve consumers as efficiently as possible. Government agencies seek to serve the public good.

4. What is the difference between a marketing dashboard and a marketing metric?

Answer: A marketing dashboard is the visual display of the essential information related to achieving a marketing objective. Each variable in a marketing dashboard is a marketing metric, which is a measure of the quantitative value or trend of a marketing activity or result.

5. Explain what a marketing plan is.

Answer: A marketing plan is a road map for the marketing activities of an organization for a specified future period of time.

6. Describe the three levels in an organization.

Answer: An organization consists of three levels—corporate, business unit, and functional. The corporate level is where top management directs overall strategy for the firm. At the business unit level managers set a more specific strategic direction for their businesses to exploit value-creating opportunities. At the functional level, the firm's strategic direction becomes its most specific and focused.

7. What is business portfolio analysis?

Answer: Business portfolio analysis quantifies performance measures and growth targets to analyze a firm's strategic business units (SBUs) as though they were a collection of separate investments.

8. Explain the four market-product strategies in diversification analysis.

Answer: The four market-product strategies in diversification analysis are market penetration, market development, product development, and diversification. In market penetration, there is no change in either the basic product line or the markets served. Rather, increased sales are generated by selling more of the product or selling the product at a higher price. In market development, existing products are sold to new markets. In product development, new products are sold to existing markets. In diversification, a potentially high-risk strategy, new products are sold in new markets.

9. What is market segmentation?

Answer: Market segmentation involves aggregating prospective buyers into groups, or segments, that (1) have common needs and (2) will respond similarly to a marketing action.

10. What are points of difference, and why are they important?

Answer: Points of difference are those characteristics of a product that make it superior to competitive substitutes. They are the single most important factor in the success or failure of a new product.

11. What is the implementation phase of the strategic marketing process?

Answer: This is the phase that involves carrying out the marketing plan that emerges from the planning phase. The implementation phase consists of: (1) obtaining resources; (2) designing the marketing organization; (3) developing schedules; and (4) executing the marketing program designed in the planning phase.

12. How do the goals set for a marketing program in the planning phase relate to the evaluation phase of the strategic marketing process?

Answer: The planning phase goals are used as the benchmarks with which the actual performance results are compared in the evaluation phase.

CHAPTER 3

1. Describe three generational cohorts.

Answer: (1) Baby boomers are those among the U.S. population born between 1946 and 1964. (2) Generation X are those among the U.S. population born between 1965 and 1976. (3) Generation Y are those among the U.S. population born between 1977 and 1994.

2. Why are many companies developing multicultural marketing programs?

Answer: (1) The racial and ethnic diversity of the United States is changing rapidly due to the increases in the African American, Asian, and Hispanic populations, which increases their economic impact. (2) An accurate understanding of the culture of each group is essential if marketing efforts are to be successful.

3. How are important values such as "health and fitness" reflected in the marketplace today?

Answer: Millions of Americans are trying to live a healthier lifestyle. In response, companies have new foods such as immunity-boosting yogurt to target these consumers.

4. What is the difference between a consumer's disposable and discretionary income?

Answer: Disposable income is the money a consumer has left after paying taxes to use for food, clothing, and shelter. Discretionary income is the money that remains after paying for taxes and necessities.

5. How does technology affect customer value?

Answers: (1) Consumers assess value on the basis of other dimensions, such as quality, service, and relationships, due to the decline in the cost of technology. (2) Technology provides value through the development of new products.

6. In pure competition every company has a _____ product.

Answer: similar

7. The _____ Act forbids monopolies, whereas the _____ Act forbids actions that would lessen competition.

Answers: Sherman Antitrust; Clayton

8. Describe some of the recent changes in trademark law.

Answer: In 2003 the United States agreed to participate in the Madrid Protocol, a treaty that facilitates the protection of U.S. trademark rights throughout the world. Also, the U.S. Supreme Court recently ruled that a company may obtain trademarks for colors associated with its products.

9. How does the Better Business Bureau encourage companies to follow its standards for commerce?

Answer: Companies must agree to follow BBB standards before they are allowed to display the BBB logo.

CHAPTER 4

1. What are ethics?

Answer: Ethics are the moral principles and values that govern the actions and decisions of an individual or group. They serve as guidelines on how to act rightly and justly when faced with moral dilemmas.

2. What are four possible reasons for the present state of ethical conduct in the United States?

Answer: (1) Pressure on businesspeople to make decisions in a society with diverse value systems. (2) Business decisions being judged publicly by groups with different values and interests. (3) The public's expectations of ethical business behavior have increased. (4) Ethical business conduct may have declined.

3. What rights are included in the Consumer Bill of Rights?

Answer: The rights to safety, to be informed, to choose, and to be heard.

4. Economic espionage includes what kinds of activities?

Answer: Economic espionage includes trespassing, theft, fraud, misrepresentation, wiretapping, searching competitors' trash, and violations of written and implicit employment agreements with noncompete clauses.

5. What is meant by moral idealism?

Answer: Moral idealism is a personal moral philosophy that considers certain individual rights or duties as universal, regardless of the outcome.

6. What is meant by social responsibility?

Answer: Social responsibility means that organizations are part of a larger society and are accountable to that society for their actions.

7. Marketing efforts to produce, promote, and reclaim environmentally sensitive products are called _____.

Answer: green marketing

8. What is a social audit?

Answer: A social audit is a systematic assessment of a firm's objectives, strategies, and performance in terms of social responsibility.

CHAPTER 5

1. What is the first stage in the consumer purchase decision process?

Answer: problem recognition

2. The brands a consumer considers buying out of the set of brands in a product class of which the consumer is aware is called the _____.

Answer: consideration set

3. What is the term for postpurchase anxiety?

Answer: cognitive dissonance

4. The problem with the Toro Snow Pup was an example of selective _____.

Answer: comprehension

5. What three attitude-change approaches are most common?

Answer: (1) Change beliefs about the extent to which a brand has certain attributes. (2) Change the perceived importance of the attributes. (3) Add new attributes.

6. What does *lifestyle* mean?

Answer: Lifestyle is a mode of living that is identified by how people spend their time and resources, what they consider important in their environment, and what they think of themselves and the world around them.

7. What are the two primary forms of personal influence?

Answer: opinion leadership; word of mouth

8. Marketers are concerned with which types of reference groups?

Answer: membership groups; aspiration groups; dissociative groups

9. What two challenges must marketers overcome when marketing to Hispanics?

Answer: diversity of this subculture; the language barrier

CHAPTER 6

1. What are the three main types of organizational buyers?

Answer: industrial firms; resellers; government units

2. What is the North American Industry Classification System (NAICS)?

Answer: The NAICS provides common industry definitions for Canada, Mexico, and the United States, which makes it easier to measure economic activity in the three member countries of NAFTA.

3. What one department is almost always represented by a person in the buying center?

Answer: purchasing department

4. What are the three types of buying situations, or buy classes?

Answer: straight rebuy, modified rebuy, and new buy

5. What are e-marketplaces?

Answer: E-marketplaces are online trading communities that bring together buyers and supplier organizations to make possible the real time exchange of information, money, products, and services.

6. In general, which type of online auction creates upward pressure on bid prices and which type creates downward pressure on bid prices?

Answer: traditional auction; reverse auction

CHAPTER 7

1. What is protectionism?

Answer: Protectionism is the practice of shielding one or more industries within a country's economy from foreign competition, usually through the use of tariffs or quotas.

2. The North American Free Trade Agreement was designed to promote free trade among which countries?

Answer: United States, Canada, and Mexico

3. What is the difference between a multidomestic marketing strategy and a global marketing strategy?

Answer: A multidomestic marketing strategy means that firms have as many different product variations, brand names, and advertising programs as countries in which they do business. A global marketing strategy standardizes marketing activities when there are cultural similarities and adapts them when cultures differ.

4. Cross-cultural analysis involves the study of _____.

Answer: similarities and difference among consumers in two or more nations or societies

5. When foreign currencies can buy more U.S. dollars, are U.S. products more or less expensive for a foreign consumer?

Answer: less expensive

6. **What mode of entry could a company follow if it has no previous experience in global marketing?**

Answer: indirect exporting through intermediaries

7. **How does licensing differ from a joint venture?**

Answer: In licensing, the firm offers the right to a trademark, patent, or trade secret in return for a fee or royalty. In a joint venture, a foreign and a local firm invest together to produce some product or service. The two companies share ownership, control, and profits of the new entity.

8. **Products may be sold globally in three ways. What are they?**

Answers: Products can be sold: (1) in the same form as in its home market (product extension); (2) with some adaptations (product adaptation); and (3) as a totally new product (product invention).

9. **What is dumping?**

Answer: Dumping is when a firm sells a product in a foreign country below its domestic price or below its actual cost.

CHAPTER 8

1. **What is marketing research?**

Answer: Marketing research is the process of defining a marketing problem and opportunity, systematically collecting and analyzing information, and recommending actions.

2. **What is the five-step marketing research approach?**

Answer: The five steps are: (1) define the problem, (2) develop the research plan, (3) collect relevant data, (4) develop findings, and (5) take marketing actions.

3. **What are constraints as they apply to developing a research plan?**

Answer: Constraints in a decision are the restrictions placed on potential solutions to a problem, such as time and money.

4. **What is the difference between secondary and primary data?**

Answer: Secondary data are facts and figures that have already been recorded before the project at hand, whereas primary data are facts and figures that are newly collected for the project.

5. **What are some advantages and disadvantages of secondary data?**

Answer: Advantages of secondary data are the time savings and the low cost. Disadvantages of secondary data are that the data may be out of date, unspecific, or have definitions, categories, or age groupings that are wrong for the project at hand.

6. **What is the difference between observational and questionnaire data?**

Answer: Observational data are facts and figures obtained by watching, either mechanically or in person, how people actually behave. Questionnaire data are facts and figures obtained by asking people about their attitudes, awareness, intentions, and behaviors.

7. **Which survey provides the greatest flexibility for asking probing questions: mail, telephone, or personal interview?**

Answer: personal interview survey

8. **What is the difference between a panel and an experiment?**

Answer: A panel is a sample of consumers or stores from which researchers take a series of measurements. An experiment involves changing a variable in a customer purchase and seeing what happens.

9. **How does data mining differ from traditional marketing research?**

Answer: Data mining is the extraction of hidden predictive information from large databases to find statistical links that suggest marketing actions. Marketing research identifies possible drivers and then collects data.

10. **In the marketing research for Tony's Pizza, what is an example of (*a*) a finding and (*b*) a marketing action?**

Answer: (*a*) Figure 8–9A shows a finding that depicts annual sales from 2001 to 2004. (*b*) Figure 8–9D shows a finding (the decline in pizza consumption) that leads to a recommendation to develop an ad targeting children 6 to 12 years old.

11. **What are the three kinds of sales forecasting techniques?**

Answer: They are (1) judgments of the decision maker; (2) surveys of knowledgeable groups; and (3) statistical methods.

12. **How do you make a lost-horse forecast?**

Answer: To make a lost-horse forecast, begin with the last known value of the item being forecast, list the factors that could affect the forecast, assess whether they have a positive or negative impact, and then make the final forecast.

CHAPTER 9

1. **Market segmentation involves aggregating prospective buyers into groups that have two key characteristics. What are they?**

Answer: The groups should (1) have common needs and (2) will respond similarly to a marketing action.

2. **In terms of market segments and products, what are the three market segmentation strategies?**

Answer: The three market segmentation strategies are: (1) one product and multiple market segments, (2) multiple products and multiple market segments, and (3) "segments of one," or mass customization.

3. **The process of segmenting and targeting markets is a bridge between what two marketing activities?**

Answer: identifying market needs and taking marketing actions

4. **What is the difference between the demographic and behavioral bases of market segmentation?**

Answer: Demographic segmentation is based on some objective physical (gender, race), measurable (age, income), or other classification attribute (birth era, occupation) of prospective customers whereas behavioral segmentation is based on some observable actions or attitudes by prospective customers—such as where they buy, what benefits they seek, how frequently they buy, and why they buy.

5. **What are some criteria used to decide which segments to choose for targets?**

Answer: These criteria include market size, expected growth, competitive position, cost of reaching the segment, and compatibility with the organization's objectives and resources.

6. **What factor is estimated or measured for each of the cells in a market-product grid?**

Answer: Each cell in the grid can show the estimated market size of a given product sold to a specific market segment.

7. **How are marketing and product synergies different in a market-product grid?**

Answer: Marketing synergies run horizontally across a market–product grid. Each row represents an opportunity for efficiency in the marketing efforts to reach a market segment. Product synergies run vertically down the market-product grid. Each column represents an opportunity for efficiency in research and development (R&D) and production.

8. **What is the difference between product positioning and product repositioning?**

Answer: Product positioning refers to the place an offering occupies in consumer's minds on important attributes relative to competitive products. Product repositioning refers to changing the place an offering occupies in a consumer's mind relative to competitive products.

9. **Why do marketers use perceptual maps in product positioning decisions?**

Answer: Perceptual maps are a means of displaying or graphing in two dimensions the location of products or brands in the minds of consumers. Managers use perceptual maps to see how consumers perceive competing products or brands and then take marketing actions.

CHAPTER 10

1. **What are the four main types of consumer products?**

Answer: convenience products, shopping products, specialty products, and unsought products.

2. **What is the difference between a product line and a product mix?**

Answer: A product line is a group of product or service items that are closely related because they satisfy a class of needs, are used together, are sold to the same customer group, are distributed through the same type of outlets, or fall within a given price range. The product mix consists of all the product lines offered by an organization.

3. **What are the 4 I's of services?**

Answer: The 4 I's of services—intangibility, inconsistency, inseparability and inventory—are unique elements that distinguish services from goods. Intangibility refers to the tendency of services to be a performance rather than an object. Inconsistency refers to the variability of the quality of the performance of the people who deliver services. Inseparability means that the consumer cannot distinguish the service provider from the service itself. Inventory refers to the need to have serviced production capability when there is service demand.

4. **What kind of innovation would an improved electric toothbrush be?**

Answer: continuous innovation

5. **Why can an "insignificant point of difference" lead to new-product failure?**

Answer: The product must have superior characteristics that deliver unique benefits to the user compared to those of competitors. Without this the product will probably fail.

6. **What step in the new-product process has been added in recent years?**

Answer: New-product strategy development has been added recently by many companies to provide focus for ideas and concepts developed later.

7. **What are the main sources of new-product ideas?**

Answer: Customer and supplier suggestions, employee and co-worker suggestions, R&D laboratories, competitive products, universities, inventors, and small technology firms.

8. **How do internal and external screening and evaluation approaches differ?**

Answer: In internal screening, company employees evaluate the technical feasibility of new product ideas. In external screening, evaluation consists of preliminary testing of the concept (not the actual product) with consumers.

9. **How does the development stage of the new-product process involve testing the product inside and outside the firm?**

Answer: Internally, laboratory tests are done to see if the product achieves the physical, quality, and safety standards; externally, consumer tests are done.

10. **What is a test market?**

Answer: A test market is a city that is viewed as being representative of U.S. consumers in terms of demographics and brand purchase behaviors, is far enough from big markets to allow low-cost advertising, and has tracking systems to measure sales.

11. **What is the commercialization of a new product?**

Answer: Commercialization involves positioning and launching a firms new product in-full-scale production and sales and is the most expensive stage for most new products.

CHAPTER 11

1. **Advertising plays a major role in the _____ stage of the product life cycle, and _____ plays a major role in maturity.**

Answer: introductory; sales promotion

2. **How do high-learning and low-learning products differ?**

Answer: A high-learning product requires significant customer education and there is an extended introductory period. A low-learning product requires little customer education because the benefits of purchase are readily understood, resulting in immediate sales.

3. **What does "creating a new use situation" mean in managing a product's life cycle?**

Answer: Finding new uses for an existing product.

4. **Explain the difference between trading up and trading down in repositioning.**

Answer: Trading up involves adding value to the product (or line) through additional features or higher-quality materials. Trading down involves reducing the number of features, quality, or price, or downsizing—reducing the content of packages without changing package size and maintaining or increasing the package price.

5. **What is the difference between a line extension and a brand extension?**

Answer: A line extension uses a current brand name to enter a new market segment in its product class, whereas a brand extension involves using a current brand name to enter a completely different product class.

6. **Explain the role of packaging in terms of perception.**

Answer: A package's shape, color, and graphics conveys a brand's positioning and builds brand equity.

7. **How do service businesses use off-peak pricing?**

Answer: They charge different prices during different times of day or days of the week to reflect variations in demand for the service.

CHAPTER 12

1. **Value is _____.**

Answer: the ratio of perceived benefits to price.

2. **What are the circumstances in pricing a new product that might support skimming or penetration pricing?**

Answer: Skimming pricing is an effective strategy when (1) enough prospective customers are willing to buy the product immediately at the high initial price to make these sales profitable, (2) the high initial price will not attract competitors, (3) lowering price has only a minor effect on increasing the sales volume and reducing the unit costs, and (4) customers interpret the high price as signifying high quality. These four conditions are most likely to exist when the new product is protected by patents or copyrights or its uniqueness is understood and valued by consumers. The conditions favoring penetration pricing are the reverse of those supporting skimming pricing: (1) many segments of the market are price sensitive, (2) a low initial price discourages competitors from entering the market, and (3) unit production and marketing costs fall dramatically as production volumes increase.

3. **What are the three key factors when estimating consumer demand?**

Answer: consumer tastes, price and availability of similar products, and consumer income

4. **Price elasticity of demand is _____.**

Answer: the percentage change in the quantity demanded relative to a percentage change in price

5. **What is the difference between fixed costs and variable costs?**

Answer: Fixed cost is the sum of the expenses of the firm that are stable and do not change with the quantity of the product that is produced and sold. Variable cost is the sum of the expenses of the firm that vary directly with the quantity of the product that is produced and sold.

6. **What is a break-even point?**

Answer: A break-even point (BEP) is the quantity at which total revenue and total cost are equal.

7. **What is the difference between pricing objectives and pricing constraints?**

Answer: Pricing objectives specify the role of price in an organization's marketing and strategic plans. Pricing constraints are factors that limit the range of prices a firm may set.

8. **Explain what bait and switch is and why it is an example of deceptive pricing.**

Answer: Bait and switch is the practice of offering a very low price on a product (the bait) to attract customers to a store. Once in the store, the customer is persuaded to purchase a higher-priced item (the switch) using a variety of tricks, including (1) degrading the promoted item and (2) not having the promised item in stock or refusing to take orders for it.

9. **What are the three steps in setting a final price?**

Answer: (1) Select an approximate price level, (2) Set the list or quoted price, (3) Make special adjustments to the list or quoted price.

10. **What is the purpose of (a) quantity discounts and (b) promotional allowances?**

Answer: Quantity discounts are used to encourage customers to buy larger quantities of a product. Promotional allowances are used to encourage customers to undertake advertising or selling activities to promote a product.

CHAPTER 13

1. **What is meant by a marketing channel?**

Answer: A marketing channel consists of individuals and firms involved in the process of making a product or service available for use or consumption by consumers or industrial users.

2. **What are the three basic functions performed by intermediaries?**

Answer: Intermediaries perform transactional, logistical, and facilitating functions.

3. **What is the difference between a direct and an indirect channel?**

Answer: A direct channel is one in which a producer of consumer or business goods and services and ultimate consumers or industrial users deal directly with each other whereas an indirect channel has intermediaries that are inserted between the producer and consumers or industrial users and who perform numerous channel functions.

4. **What is the principal distinction between a corporate vertical marketing system and an administered vertical marketing system?**

Answer: A corporate vertical marketing system combines successive stages of production and distribution under a single ownership. An administered vertical marketing system achieves coordination by the size and influence of one channel member rather than through ownership.

5. **What are the three questions marketing executives consider when choosing a marketing channel and intermediaries?**

Answer: (1) Which channel and intermediaries will provide the best coverage of the target market? (2) Which channel and intermediaries will best satisfy the buying requirements of the target market? (3) Which channel and intermediaries will be the most profitable?

6. **What are the three degrees of distribution density?**

Answer: intensive; exclusive; selective.

7. **What is the principal difference between a marketing channel and a supply chain?**

Answer: A supply chain also includes suppliers who provide raw materials to a manufacturer as well as the wholesalers and retailers—the marketing channel—who deliver the finished goods to consumers.

8. **The choice of a supply chain involves what three steps?**

Answer: (1) Understand the customer. (2) Understand the supply chain. (3) Harmonize the supply chain with the marketing strategy.

9. **A manager's key task is to balance which four customer service factors against which five logistics cost factors?**

Answer: A supply chain manager's key task is to balance four customer service factors—time, dependability, communication, and convenience—against the five total logistics cost factors—transportation, materials handling and warehousing, inventory, stockouts, and order processing.

CHAPTER 14

1. **When Polo makes shoes to a customer's exact preferences, what utility is provided?**

Answer: form utility

2. **Two measures of the impact of retailing in the global economy are _____ and _____.**

Answer: total sales; number of employees

3. **Centralized decision making and purchasing are an advantage of _____ ownership.**

Answer: corporate chain

4. **What are some examples of new forms of self-service retailers?**

Answer: US Airways and Hilton self-service kiosks for customer check-in as well as others.

5. **Would a shop for big men's clothes carrying pants in sizes 40 to 60 have a broad or deep product line?**

Answer: deep product line

6. **Successful catalog retailers often send _____ catalogs to _____ markets identified in their databases.**

Answer: specialty; niche

7. **How are retailers increasing consumer interest and involvement in online retailing?**

Answer: Retailers have improved the online retailing experience by adding experiential or interactive activities to their websites. Car manufacturers, for example, encourage website visitors to "build" a customized virtual car.

8. **Where are direct selling retail sales growing?**

Answer: Direct-selling retailers are expanding into global markets such as China.

9. **How does original markup differ from maintained markup?**

Answer: The original markup is the difference between retailer cost and initial selling price whereas maintained markup is the difference between the final selling price and retailer cost.

10. **A huge shopping strip with multiple anchor stores is a _____ center.**

Answer: power

11. **What is a popular approach to managing the assortment of merchandise in a store?**

Answer: Category management. This approach assigns a manager with the responsibility for selecting all products in a category with the objective of maximizing sales and profits.

12. **According to the wheel of retailing, when a new retail form appears, how would you characterize its image?**

Answer: A low-status, low-margin, low-price outlet.

13. **Market share is usually fought out before the _____ stage of the retail life cycle.**

Answer: maturity

14. **What is the difference between merchant wholesalers and agents?**

Answer: Merchant wholesalers are independently owned firms that take title to the merchandise they handle. Agents do not take title to merchandise and typically perform fewer channel functions.

CHAPTER 15

1. **What are the six elements required for communication to occur?**

Answer: They are a source, a message, a channel of communication, a receiver, and the processes of encoding and decoding.

2. **A difficulty for U.S. companies advertising in international markets is that the audience does not share the same _____.**

Answer: field of experience

3. **A misprint in a newspaper ad is an example of _____.**

Answer: noise

4. **Explain the difference between advertising and publicity when both appear on television.**

Answer: Because advertising space on TV is paid for, a firm can control what it wants to say and to whom the message is sent. Because publicity is an indirectly paid presentation of a message about a firm or its goods or services, there is little control over what is said to whom or when.

5. **Which promotional element should be offered only on a short-term basis?**

Answer: sales promotion

6. **Cost per contact is high with the _____ element of the promotional mix.**

   Answer: personal selling

7. **Promotional programs can be directed to _____, to _____, or both.**

   Answer: the ultimate consumer; an intermediary (retailer, wholesaler, or industrial distributor)

8. **Describe the promotional objective for each stage of the product life cycle.**

   Answer: Introduction—to inform; growth—to persuade; maturity—to remind; and decline—none

9. **Explain the differences between a push strategy and a pull strategy.**

   Answer: In a push strategy, a firm directs the promotional mix to channel members to gain their cooperation to carry the product. In a pull strategy, a firm directs the promotional mix at ultimate consumers to encourage them to ask retailers for the product, who then orders it from wholesalers.

10. **What are the stages of the hierarchy of effects?**

    Answer: The five stages of the hierarchy of effects are awareness, interest, evaluation, trial, and adoption.

11. **What are the four approaches to setting the promotion budget?**

    Answer: The four approaches are percentage of sales, competitive parity, all you can afford, and objective and task.

12. **How have advertising agencies changed to facilitate the use of IMC programs?**

    Answer: Some agencies have adopted: (1) a total communications solutions approach, (2) a long-term perspective in which all forms of promotion are integrated, and (3) an IMC audit to analyze the internal communication network of their clients.

13. **The ability to design and use direct marketing programs has increased with the availability of _____ and _____.**

    Answer: customer information databases; new printing technologies

14. **What are the three types of responses generated by direct marketing activities?**

    Answer: They are direct orders, lead generation, and traffic generation.

CHAPTER 16

1. **What is the difference between pioneering and competitive ads?**

   Answer: Pioneering ads tell people what a product is, what it can do, and where it can be found. Competitive ads promote a specific brand's features and benefits to persuade the target market to select the firm's brand rather than that of a competitor.

2. **What is the purpose of an institutional advertisement?**

   Answer: To build goodwill or an image for an organization.

3. **The Federal Communications Commission suggests that advertising program decisions be based on _____.**

   Answer: marketing research about the target audience.

4. **Describe three common forms of advertising appeals.**

   Answer: Fear appeals suggest that a consumer avoid a negative experience; sex appeals suggest a way to increase attractiveness; humorous appeals imply fun and excitement.

5. **You see the same ad in *Time* and *Fortune* magazines and on billboards and TV. Is this an example of reach or frequency?**

   Answer: frequency

6. **Why has the Internet become a popular advertising medium?**

   Answer: The Internet offers a visual message, can use both audio and video, is interactive through rich media, and tends to reach younger consumers.

7. **Describe three approaches to scheduling advertising.**

   Answer: continuous (steady) schedule; flighting (intermittent) schedule; pulse (burst) schedule

8. **Explain the difference between pretesting and posttesting advertising copy.**

Answer: Pretests are conducted before ads are placed in any medium to determine whether the ads communicate the intended message or to select among alternative versions. Posttests are conducted after an advertisement has been shown to the target audience to determine whether it accomplished its intended purpose.

9. **What is the difference between aided and unaided recall posttests?**

   Answer: Aided recall involves showing an ad to respondents who then are asked if their previous exposure to it was through reading, viewing, or listening. Unaided recall involves asking respondents if they remember an ad without any prompting to determine if they saw or heard its message.

10. **Which sales promotional tool is most common for new products?**

    Answer: samples

11. **Which trade promotion is used to encourage local advertising efforts of resellers?**

    Answer: cooperative advertising

12. **What is a news release?**

    Answer: An announcement regarding changes in the company or the product line.

CHAPTER 17

1. **What is personal selling?**

   Answer: Personal selling involves the two-way flow of communication between a buyer and seller, often in a face-to-face encounter, designed to influence a person's or group's purchase decision.

2. **What is involved in sales management?**

   Answer: Sales management involves planning the selling program and implementing and controlling the personal selling effort of the firm.

3. **What is the principal difference between an order taker and an order getter?**

   Answer: An order taker processes routine orders or reorders for products that were already sold by the company. An order getter sells in a conventional sense and identifies prospective customers, provides customers with information, persuades customers to buy, closes sales, and follows up on their use of a product or service.

4. **What percentage of an order-getting salesperson's time is spent selling?**

   Answer: 55 percent

5. **What are the six stages in the personal selling process?**

   Answer: The six stages in the personal selling process are: (1) prospecting, (2) preapproach, (3) approach, (4) presentation, (5) close, and (6) follow-up.

6. **Which presentation format is most consistent with the marketing concept? Why?**

   Answer: The need-satisfaction presentation format of probing and listening by the salesperson to identify needs and interests of prospective buyers and then tailoring the presentation to the prospect and highlighting product benefits, consistent with the marketing concept.

7. **What are the three types of selling objectives?**

   Answer: (1) output-related (dollars or unit sales, new customers, profit); (2) input-related (sales calls, selling expenses); and (3) behavioral-related (product knowledge, customer service, selling and communication skills).

8. **What three factors are used to structure sales organizations?**

   Answer: geography, customer, and product or service

CHAPTER 18

1. **The consumer-initiated practice of generating content on a marketer's website that is custom tailored to an individual's specific needs and preferences is called _____.**

   Answer: personalization

2. **Companies produce a customer experience through what seven website design elements?**

   Answer: context, content, community, customization, communication, connection, and commerce.

3. **What is viral marketing?**

   Answer: An Internet-enabled promotional strategy that encourages individuals to forward marketer-initiated messages to others via e-mail.

4. **What are the six reasons consumers prefer to shop and buy online?**

   Answer: convenience, choice, customization, communication, cost, and control

5. **A cross-channel shopper is _____.**

   Answer: a consumer who researches offerings online and then purchases them at retail stores

6. **Channel conflict between manufacturers and retailers is likely to arise when manufacturers use _____ websites.**

   Answer: transactional

CHAPTER NOTES

CHAPTER 1

1. The 3M Post-it® Flag Highlighter and Post-it® Flag Pen examples are based on a series of interviews and meetings with David Windorski, 3M, from 2004 to 2008.
2. *The Oprah Winfrey Show,* January 15, 2008.
3. John Reinan, "Millionaire Whiz Kid," *Star Tribune,* October 13, 2006, pp. A1, A18; John Cloud, "The YouTube Gurus," *Time,* December 25, 2006–January 1, 2007, pp. 66–74; Lev Grossman, "Invention of the Year 2006," *Time,* November 13, 2006, pp. 64–65; "Two Kings Get Together," *The Economist,* October 14, 2006, pp. 67–68; and Yi-Wyn Yen, "YouTube Looks for the Money Clip," CNNMoney.com, March 25, 2008.
4. To compare the 2004 and 2007 American Marketing Association definitions of "marketing," see Lisa M. Keefe, "Marketing Defined," *Marketing News,* January 15, 2008, pp. 28–29.
5. Richard P. Bagozzi, "Marketing as Exchange," *Journal of Marketing,* October 1975, pp. 32–39; and Gregory T. Gundlach and Patrick E. Murphy, "Ethical and Legal Foundations of Relational Marketing Exchanges," *Journal of Marketing,* October 1993, pp. 35–46.
6. "The Rise of the Creative Consumer," *The Economist,* March 12, 2005, pp. 54–60.
7. Productscan® Online database of new products, from *Marketing Intelligence Service,* December 17, 2003, www.productscan.com.
8. Robert M. McMath and Thom Forbes, "What *Were* They Thinking?" (New York: Times Business, 1998), pp. 3–22.
9. From the New Product Works website, "Favorite Failures," www.newproductworks.com.
10. From the Hot Pockets website, www.chefamerica.com and www.hotpockets.com.
11. From the iRobot website, www.irobot.com; Peter Lewis, "Keep Up With the Jetsons," *Fortune,* February 20, 2006, p. 146.
12. Chad Terhune, "Coca-Cola's Low-Carb Soda Loses Its Fizz," *The Wall Street Journal,* October 20, 2004, pp. B1, B9; "Things Go Worse with Coke," *The Economist,* December 17, 2005, p. 61; and Chad Terhune, "Coke Tries to Pop Back in Vital Japan Market," *The Wall Street Journal,* July 11, 2006, pp. C1, C3.
13. Jonathan Clements, "Dodging the Hazards of Post-College Life: Financial Strategies for New Graduates," *The Wall Street Journal,* December 7, 2005, p. D1; Kara McGuire, "Sweat the Small Stuff," *Star Tribune,* September 9, 2005, p. D6; and Amy Hoak, "Debt 101 for College Kids," *Star Tribune,* September 17, 2006, p. D7.
14. E. Jerome McCarthy, "Basic Marketing: A Managerial Approach" (Homewood, IL: Richard D. Irwin, 1960); and Walter van Waterschool and Christophe Van den Bulte, "The 4P Classification of the Marketing Mix Revisited," *Journal of Marketing,* October 1992, pp. 83–93.
15. Ashish Kothari and Joseph Lackner, "A Value Based Approach to Management," *Journal of Business and Industrial Marketing,* 21, no. 4, pp. 243–49; and James C. Anderson, James A. Narius, and Wouter van Rossum, "Customer Value Propositions in Business Markets," *Harvard Business Review,* March 2006, pp. 91–99.
16. For an examination of both the drivers and outcomes of consumer satisfaction programs, see Leslie M. Fine, "Spotlight on Marketing," *Business Horizons,* 49 (2006), pp. 179–83.
17. V. Kumar, *Managing Customers for Profit,* (Upper Saddle River, NJ: Pearson Education, 2008); and "What's a Loyal Customer Worth?" *Fortune,* December 11, 1995, p. 182.
18. Robert W. Palmatier, Rajiv P. Dant, Dhruv Grewal, and Kenneth R. Evans, "Factors Influencing the Effectiveness of Relationship Marketing: A Meta-Analysis," *Journal of Relationship Marketing,* October 2006, pp. 136–53; and William Boulding, Richard Staelin, Michael Ehret, and Wesley J. Johnson, "A Customer Relationship Management Roadmap: What Is Known, Potential Pitfalls, and Where to Go," *Journal of Marketing,* October 2005, pp. 155–66.
19. See www.oprah.com for January 15, 2008; and "Post-it® Flags Co-Sponsors Oprah's Live Web Event," *3M Stemwinder,* March 4–17, 2008, p. 3.
20. Reservations about and elaborations of these simplified stages appear in D.G. Brian Jones and Eric H. Shaw, "A History of Marketing Thought," Chapter 2 in *Handbook of Marketing,* edited by Barton Weitz and Robin Wensley (London: Sage Publications, 2006), pp. 39–65; Frederic E. Webster, Jr., "The Role of Marketing and the Firm," Chapter 3 in *Handbook of Marketing,* ed. Barton Weitz and Robin Wensley (London: Sage Publications, 2006), pp. 66–82; and Frederick E. Webster, Jr., "Back to the Future: Integrating Marketing as Tactics, Strategy and Organizational Culture," *Journal of Marketing,* October 2005, pp. 4–8.
21. Robert F. Keith, "The Marketing Revolution," *Journal of Marketing,* January 1960, pp. 35–38.
22. *Annual Report* (New York: General Electric Company, 1952), p. 21.
23. John C. Narver, Stanley F. Slater, and Brian Tietje, "Creating a Market Orientation," *Journal of Market Focused Management,* no. 2 (1998), pp. 241–55; Stanley F. Slater and John C. Narver, "Market Orientation and the Learning Organization," *Journal of Marketing,* July 1995, pp. 63–74; and George S. Day, "The Capabilities of Market-Driven Organizations," *Journal of Marketing,* October 1994, pp. 37–52.
24. The definition of customer relationship management is adapted from Rajendra K. Srivastava, Tasadduq A. Shervani, and Liam Fahey, "Marketing, Business Processes, and Shareholder Value: An Embedded View of Marketing Activities and the Discipline of Marketing," *Journal of Marketing,* special issue (1999), pp. 168–79; Gary F. Gebhardt, Gregory S. Carpenter, and John F. Sherry Jr., "Creating a Market Orientation: A Longitudinal, Multifirm, Grounded Analysis of Cultural Transformation," *Journal of Marketing,* October 2006, pp. 37–55; and Christopher Meyer and Andre Schwager, "Understanding Customer Experience," *Harvard Business Review,* February 2007, pp. 117–26.
25. Michael E. Porter and Claas van der Linde, "Green and Competitive Ending the Stalemate," *Harvard Business Review,* September–October 1995, pp. 120–34; Jacquelyn Ottman, "Edison Winners Show Smart Environmental Marketing," *Marketing News,* July 17, 1995, pp. 16, 19; and Jacquelyn Ottman, "Mandate for the '90s: Green Corporate Image," *Marketing News,* September 11, 1995, p. 8.
26. Philip Kotler and Sidney J. Levy, "Broadening the Concept of Marketing," *Journal of Marketing,* January 1969, pp. 10–15; and Jim Rendon, "When Nations Need a Little Marketing," *New York Times,* November 23, 2003, p. BU6.
27. William L. Wilkie and Elizabeth S. Moore, "Marketing's Relationship to Society," Chapter 1 in *Handbook of Marketing,* ed. Barton Weitz and Robin Wensley (London: Sage Publications, 2006), pp. 9–38.

3M's Post-it® Flag Highlighters: This case was written by Michael J. Vessey and William Rudelius and is based on personal interviews with David Windorski and 3M in 2007 and 2008.

CHAPTER 2

1. Information obtained from selected webpages and press releases from the Ben & Jerry's website. See www.benjerry.com.
2. Mark Scott and Cassidy Flanagan, "Ice Cream Wars: Nestlé vs. Unilever," *BusinessWeek,* August 24, 2007. See http://www.

businessweek.com/globalbiz/content/aug2007/gb20070824230078.htm.

3. Roger Kerin and Robert Peterson, *Strategic Marketing Problems: Cases and Comments*, 11th ed. (Upper Saddle River, NJ: Prentice Hall, 2007), p. 141.

4. For a discussion on how industries are defined and offerings are classified, see the following resources: the American Marketing Association website, which provides one definition of an industry (www.marketingpower.com/mg-dictionary-view1509.php); and the Census Bureau's Economic Classification Policy Committee Issues Paper #1 (www.census.gov/epcd/naics/issues1), which aggregates industries in the NAICS (www.census.gov/epcd/www/naicsdev.htm) from a "production-oriented" view (see Chapter 6).

5. Michael E. Porter, "What Is Strategy?" *Harvard Business Review* OnPoint Article, November–December 1996, p. 2.

6. The definition of *strategy* reflects thoughts appearing in Porter, "What Is Strategy?" pp. 4, 8; a condensed definition of strategy is found on the American Marketing Association website (www.marketingpower.com); and Gerry Johnson, Kevan Scholes, and Richard Wittington, *Exploring Corporate Strategy* (Upper Saddle River, NJ: Prentice Hall, 2005), p. 10.

7. Taken in part from Jim Collins and Jerry I. Porras, *Built to Last: Successful Habits of Visionary Companies* (New York: HarperCollins Publishers, 2002), p. 54.

8. Collins and Porras, *Built to Last,* p. 73; Patrick M. Lencioni "Make Your Values Mean Something," *Harvard Business Review,* July 2002, p. 6; and Aubrey Malphurs, *Values-Driven Leadership: Discovering and Developing Your Core Values for Ministry,* 2nd ed. (Grand Rapids, MI: BakerBooks, 2004), p. 31.

9. Collins and Porras, *Built to Last,* p. 73; and Lencioni, "Make Your Values Mean Something," p. 6.

10. Catherine M. Dalton, "When Organizational Values Are Mere Rhetoric," *Business Horizons* 49 (September–October 2006), p. 345.

11. Collins and Porras, *Built to Last,* pp. 94–95; and Tom Krattenmaker, "Write a Mission Statement That Your Company Is Willing to Live," *Harvard Management Communication Letter,* March 2002, pp. 3–4.

12. Nikos Mourkogiannis, "The Realist's Guide to Moral Purpose," *Strategy + Business,* no. 41 (Winter 2005), pp. 42, 45, 47.

13. Kenneth E. Goodpaster and Thomas E. Holloran, "Anatomy of Spiritual and Social Awareness: The Case of Medtronic, Inc.," *Third International Symposium on Catholic Social Thought and Management Education,* Goa, India, 1999, pp. 9–11.

14. Theodore Levitt, "Marketing Myopia," *Harvard Business Review,* July–August 1960, pp. 45–56.

15. The definition is adapted from Stephen Few, *Information Dashboard Design: The Effective Visual Communication of Data* (Sebastopol, CA: O'Reilly Media, Inc., 2006) pp. 2–46.

16. Ibid; Bruce H. Clark, Andrew V. Abela, and Tim Ambler, "Behind the Wheel," *Marketing Management,* May–June 2006, pp. 19–23; Spencer E. Ante, "Giving the Boss the Big Picture," *BusinessWeek,* February 13, 2006, pp. 48–49; and *Dashboard Tutorial* (Cupertino, CA: Apple Computer; 2006).

17. Few, *Information Dashboard Design,* p. 13.

18. Michael Krauss, "Balance Attention to Metrics with Intuition," *Marketing News,* June 1, 2007, pp. 6–8; John Davis, *Measuring Marketing: 103 Key Metrics Every Marketer Needs* (Singapore: John Wiley & Sons (Asia) Pte Ltd., 2007); Paul W. Farris, Neil T. Bendle, Phillip E. Pfeifer, and David J. Reibstein, *Marketing Metrics* (Upper Saddle River, NJ: Wharton School Publishing, 2006); and Marcel Corstjens and Jeffrey Merrihue, "Optimal Marketing," *Harvard Business Review,* October 2003, pp. 114–121.

19. The now-classic reference on effective graphic presentation is Edward R. Tufte. *The Visual Display of Quantitative Information,* 2nd ed. (Chesire, CN: Graphic Press, 2001); see also Few, *Information Dashboard Design,* chs. 3, 4, and 5.

20. Roger A. Kerin, Vijay Mahajan, and P. Rajan Varadarajan, *Contemporary Perspectives on Strategic Marketing Planning* (Boston: Allyn & Bacon, 1990), ch. 1; and Orville C. Walker Jr., Harper W. Boyd Jr., and Jean-Claude Larreche, *Marketing Strategy* (Burr Ridge, IL: Richard D. Irwin, 1992), chs. 1 and 2.

21. George Stalk, Phillip Evans, and Lawrence E. Shulman, "Competing on Capabilities: The New Rules of Corporate Strategy," *Harvard Business Review,* March–April 1992, pp. 57–69; and Darrell K. Rigby, *Management Tools 2007: An Executive's Guide* (Boston: Bain & Company, 2007), p. 22.

22. Michael Arndt, "High-Tech and Handcrafted," *BusinessWeek,* July 5, 2004, pp. 86–87.

23. Kerin and Peterson, *Strategic Marketing Problems,* pp. 2–3; and Derek F. Abell, *Defining the Business* (Englewood Cliffs, NJ: Prentice Hall, 1980), p. 18.

24. Robert D. Hof, "How to Hit a Moving Target," *BusinessWeek,* August 21, 2006, p. 3; and Peter Kim, *Reinventing the Marketing Organization* (Cambridge, MA: Forrester, July 13, 2006), pp. 7, 9, and 17.

25. Adapted from *The Experience Curve Reviewed, IV. The Growth Share Matrix of the Product Portfolio* (Boston: The Boston Consulting Group, 1973).

26. Kerin, Mahajan, and Vardarajan, *Contemporary Perspectives,* p. 52.

27. "Kodak Institutional Investor Meeting," February 7, 2008, p. 27.

28. Stephen Shankland, "Canon Loses SLR Share as Nikon Surges," CNETNews, April 2, 2008, see www.news.cnet.com; Mike Pasini, "IDC on 2007 Sales: Nikon, Sony Gain in dSLRs; Samsung Up, Kodak Holds on in Digicams," *Imaging Resource,* April 7, 2008; Jennifer Nelson, "InfoTrends: 'Digital Ecosystem' Closer Than Ever," DigitalCameraInfo.com, February 1, 2008. See www.digitalcamerainfo.com; Tomohiro Otsuki, "Samsung Techwin Takes Third Place in Digital Camera Market Share," *Tech-On!,* February 20, 2008; Stephen Shankland, "Cameras: Shipments Rising, But Prices Falling," CNETNews, September 19, 2007. See www.news.cnet.com; Stephen Shankland, "Forecast: SLR Growth Rate to Taper Off," CNETNews, January 31, 2008. See www.news.cnet.com; and "Kodak Institutional Investor Meeting," February 7, 2008, p. 59.

29. "New InfoTrends Data Indicates the Ink-Jet Photo-Centric MFPs Present Best Growth Area in Home Photo Printer Market," InfoTrends, August 24, 2007. See www.InfoTrends.com; Karen M. Cheung, "InfoTrends: Online Printing to Double by 2011," DigitalCameraInfo.com, August 13, 2007. See www.digitalcamerainfo.com; Jefferson Graham, "Kodak Plans to Sell Inkjet Printers with Cheaper Ink," *USA Today,* February 6, 2007, p. 51; Simon Burns, "Printer Market Shows Steady Growth," VNUNET.com, September 19, 2007; Greg Scoblete, "PMA: Photo Printer Sales Drop," Photo Marketing Association, March 31, 2008. See www.pma.i.org; and Stephen H. Wildstrom, "Kodak Moments for Less," *BusinessWeek,* May 14, 2007, p. 24.

30. "InfoTrends Projects Digital Photo Frame Shipments to Achieve over 25% Annual Growth through 2012," InfoTrends, January 24, 2008. See www.InfoTrends.com; Karen M. Cheung, "IDC: Digital Photo Frames to Sell 42 Million Units by 2011," DigitalCameraInfo.com, September 13, 2007. See www.digitalcamerainfo.com; "Kodak Institutional Investor Meeting—Presentation," February 7, 2008, p. 4; Jennifer Nelson, "InfoTrends: Online Photo Printing Market Needs Innovation," DigitalCameraInfo.com, February 1, 2008; and "Kodak Institutional Investor Meeting—Transcript," February 7, 2008, p. 4.

31. Strengths and weaknesses of the BCG technique are based on Derek F. Abell and John S. Hammond, *Strategic Market Planning: Prob-*

lem and Analytic Approaches (Englewood Cliffs, NJ: Prentice Hall, 1979); Yoram Wind, Vijay Mahajan, and Donald Swire, "An Empirical Comparison of Standardized Portfolio Models," *Journal of Marketing,* Spring 1983, pp. 89–99; and J. Scott Armstrong and Roderick J. Brodie, "Effects of Portfolio Planning Methods on Decision Making: Experimental Results," *International Journal of Research in Marketing,* Winter 1994, pp. 73–84.

32. H. Igor Ansoff, "Strategies for Diversification," *Harvard Business Review,* September–October 1957, pp. 113–24.

33. Linda Swenson and Kenneth E. Goodpaster, *Medtronic in China (A)* (Minneapolis, MN: University of St. Thomas, 1999), pp. 4–5.

34. William M. Bulkeley, "When Neighbors Become Rivals," *The Wall Street Journal,* February 22, 2007, pp. B1, B8; and "Kodak Institutional Investor Meeting," February 7, 2008, p. 8.

BP Video Case: This case was prepared by Michael J. Vessey based on interviews with Ann Hand and Kathy Seegebrecht.

APPENDIX A

1. Personal interview with Arthur R. Kydd, St. Croix Management Group.

2. Examples of guides to writing marketing plans include William A. Cohen, *The Marketing Plan,* 5th ed. (New York: Wiley, 2006); and Roman G. Hiebing, Jr., and Scott W. Cooper, *The Successful Marketing Plan: A Disciplined and Comprehensive Approach* (New York: McGraw-Hill, 2003).

3. Examples of guides to writing business plans include Rhonda Abrams, *The Successful Business Plan: Secrets & Strategies,* 4th ed. (Grants Pass, OR: Oasis Press/PSI Research, 2003); Joseph A. Covello and Brian J. Hazelgren, *The Complete Book of Business Plans,* 2nd ed. (Naperville, IL: Sourcebooks, 2006); Joseph A. Covello and Brian J. Hazelgren, *Your First Business Plan,* 5th ed. (Naperville, IL: Sourcebooks, 2005); and Mike McKeever, *How to Write a Business Plan,* 8th ed. (Berkeley, CA: Nolo, 2007).

4. Abrams, *The Successful Business Plan,* p. 35.

5. Some of these points are adapted from Abrams, pp. 35–43; others are adapted from William Rudelius, *Guidelines for Technical Report Writing* (Minneapolis: University of Minnesota, undated). See also William Strunk, Jr., and E. B. White, *The Elements of Style,* 4th ed. (Needham Heights, MA: Allyn & Bacon, 2000).

6. Rebecca Zimoch, "The Dawn of the Frozen Age," *Grocery Headquarters,* December 2002; see www.groceryheadquarters.com.

7. ACNielsen Strategic Planner as reported to the National Frozen & Refrigerated Foods Association for the week ending February 24, 2007; see www.nfraweb.org.

8. Chuck Van Hyning, *NPD's National Eating Trends;* see www.npdfoodworld.com.

9. Jeffery M. Humphreys, "The Multicultural Economy 2006," *Georgia Business and Economic Conditions* 66, no. 3, (Third Quarter 2006), pp. 6, 10–11; see www.selig.uga.edu/forecast.

CHAPTER 3

1. Allison Enright, "Get Clued In: Mystery of 'Web 2.0' Concept Solved," *Marketing News,* January 15, 2007, p. 20; Jeff Howe, "Your Web, Your Way," *Time,* December 25, 2006, pp. 60–61; Bob Greenberg, "On Web 2.0's Impact," *Adweek.com,* January 1, 2007; Robert D. Hof, "There's Not Enough 'Me' in Myspace," *BusinessWeek,* December 4, 2006, p. 40; and Sebastian Rupley, "You've Heard of Web 2.0. What About Web 3.0?" *PC Magazine,* December 20, 2006.

2. "A Quarter-Century of Changes," *USA Today,* March 26, 2007, p. 8B; "Social Networking, User-Generated Content and Green Technology Are Top Trends for 2007," *Wireless News,* January 21, 2007; George

Ochoa and Melinda Corey, *The 100 Best Trends 2006* (Avon, MA: Adams Media, 2006), p. 128; "Future Options," *Marketing News,* January 15, 2007, pp. 16–17; "Top 10 Trend in Tech, Media, and Telecom," Canadian Corporate Newswire, January 15, 2007.

3. World Population Prospects: The 2006 Revision (Geneva: United Nations Department of Economic and Social Affairs, 2007), Table I.1, p. 1; and "New Facts on Globalization, Poverty, and Income Distribution," International Chamber of Commerce, January 15, 2003.

4. Lawrence A. Crosby, Sheree L. Johnson, and John Carroll III, "When We're 64," *Marketing Management,* December 2006, p. 14; "U.S. Interim Projections by Age, Sex, Race, and Hispanic Origin," U.S. Census Bureau, Table 1a, Table 2a; and Alison Stein Wellner, "The Next 25 Years," *American Demographics,* April 2003, pp. 24–27.

5. Kimberly Palmer, "Gen X-ers: Stingy or Strapped?" *USNews.com,* February 14, 2007; Paul J. Lim, "Baby Boomers Outpace Gen X-ers," *USNews.com,* March 12, 2007; and Megan Rowe, "Marketing to Gen X," *Financial & Insurance Meetings,* July 1, 2006, p. 19.

6. Sharon Jayson, "The Goal: Wealth and Fame, but 'the Good Life' Could Elude Gen Y," *USA Today,* January 10, 2007, p. 1D; Sharon Jayson, "Gen Y Makes a Mark: Their Imprint is Entrepreneurship," *USA Today,* December 7, 2006, p. 1D; "Millennial Moral," *BusinessWeek,* November 6, 2006, p. 13; Richard H. Levey, "Gen Y Phones It In," *Direct,* September 1, 2006, p. 18; Michael J. Weiss, "To Be about to Be," *American Demographics,* September 2003, pp. 29–36; Peter Francese, "Ahead of the Next Wave," *American Demographics,* September 2003, pp. 42–43; and Don O'Briant, "Millenials: The Next Generation," *Atlanta Journal-Constitution,* August 11, 2003, p. 1D.

7. Pamela Paul, "Global Generation Gap," *American Demographics,* March 2002, pp. 18–19; and Allyson L. Stewart-Allen, "EU's Future Consumers: 3 Groups to Watch," *Marketing News,* June 4, 2001, p. 9.

8. Robert Bernstein, "Louisiana Loses Population, Arizona Edges Nevada as Fastest-Growing State," *U.S. Census Bureau News,* December 22, 2006; Marc J. Perry and Paul J. Mackun, "Population Change and Distribution," Census 2000 Brief: U.S. Bureau of the Census, April 2001; and Paul Campbell, "Population Projection: States, 1995–2025," Current Population Report, U.S. Department of Commerce, May 1997.

9. Joshua Bolten, "Update of Statistical Area Definitions and Additional Guidance on Their Use," Office of Management and Budget, *OMB Bulletin* No. 04–03, February 18, 2004; and "About Metropolitan and Micropolitan Statistical Areas," U.S. Census Bureau, www.census.gov/population/www/estimates/aboutmetro.html.

10. Alison Stein Wellner, "Our True Colors," *American Demographics,* November 2002, pp. S2–S20; Eduardo Porter, "Even 126 Sizes Don't Fit All," *The Wall Street Journal,* March 2, 2001, pp. B1, B4; and William H. Frey, "Micro Melting Pots," *American Demographics,* June 2001, pp. 20–23.

11. Robert Bernstein, "Census Bureau Releases Population Estimates by Race," *U.S. Bureau News,* August 4, 2006; Hikki Hopewell, "U.S. Buying Power by Race," *Marketing News,* July 15, 2006, p. 29; Brian Grow, "Hispanic Nation," *BusinessWeek,* March 15, 2004, pp. 58–70; Wellner, "Our True Colors"; Deborah L. Vence, "You Talkin' to Me?" *Marketing News,* March 1, 2004, pp. 1, 9–11; and Alison Stein Wellner, "The Next 25 Years," *American Demographics,* April 2000, pp. 24–27.

12. John Carey and Michael Arndt, "Hugging the Tree-Huggers: Why So Many Companies Are Suddenly Linking Up with Eco Groups," *BusinessWeek,* March 12, 2007, p. 66; David Kiley, "Toyota: How the Hybrid Race Went to the Swift," *BusinessWeek,* January 29, 2007, p. 58; Stephanie Thompson, "Want That Perfect Body? Have Some More Dannon," *Advertising Age,* September 25, 2006, p. 3; and Edward B. Keller and Thomas A. W. Miller, "Remapping the World of Consumers," *American Demographics,* October 2000, pp. S1–S20.

13. Melissa Ludwig, "College Costs Still Going Up," *San Antonio Express-News,* October 25, 2006, p. 9A; and Jonathan D. Glater,

"Weighing the Costs in Public vs. Private Colleges," *The New York Times,* December 13, 2006, p. 7.

14. James C. Cooper, "The R-Word is 'Rocky,' Not 'Recession,'" *BusinessWeek,* March 19, 2007, p. 31; and Michael J. Mandel, "Inventing the Clinton Recession," *BusinessWeek,* February 23, 2004, p. 48.

15. Carmen DeNavas-Walt, Bernadette D. Proctor, and Jessica Smith, "Income, Poverty and Health Insurance Coverage in the United States: 2006," *Current Population Reports* (Washington, DC: U.S. Census Bureau, August 2007), p. 29.

16. Don Carlson, "The Old Economy in the New Economy," *Business-Week,* November 13, 2000, p. 42H; Owen Ullmann, "Forget Saving, America. Your Job Is to Spend," *BusinessWeek,* December 28, 1998, p. 54; Gene Koretz, "Savings' Death Is Exaggerated," *BusinessWeek,* September 14, 1998, p. 26; and Marcia Mogelonsky, "No More Food, Thanks," *American Demographics,* August 1998, p. 59.

17. "Consumer Expenditure Survey 2006," U.S. Department of Labor, Bureau of Labor Statistics, October 26, 2007, Table 3; "Spending on Necessities," *Monthly Labor Review,* U.S. Department of Labor, Bureau of Labor Statistics, June 24, 2003; and "The Negative Saving Rate," *Monthly Labor Review,* U.S. Department of Labor, Bureau of Labor Statistics, June 2007, p. 25.

18. Tom Giles, "Tech Trends for 2007," *BusinessWeek Online,* January 29, 2007; Aili McConnon, "The Mind-Bending New World of Work," *BusinessWeek,* April 2, 2007, pp. 46–54; and John Carey, "Tiny Smart Bombs vs. Cancer?" *BusinessWeek,* March 1, 2004, p. 115.

19. Michael Krauss, "Young Net Entrepreneurs Leverage Web Anew," *Marketing News,* February 1, 2004, p. 6.

20. Leon Jaroff, "Smart's the Word in Detroit," *Time,* February 6, 1995, pp. 50–52.

21. Clint Willis, "25 Cool Things You Wish You Had and Will," *Forbes ASAP,* June 1, 1998, pp. 49–60.

22. Henry Goldblatt, "The End of the Long Distance Club," *Fortune,* May 26, 1997, p. 30; and "Wheel of Fortune," *The Economist,* November 21, 1998, p. 53.

23. DeAnn Welmer, "Don't Be Shocked by Surges in the Price of Power," *BusinessWeek,* July 27, 1998, p. 33.

24. Jay Greene, "Microsoft: First Europe, Then…?" *BusinessWeek,* March 22, 2004, p. 86.

25. "Small Business Resources for Faculty, Students, and Researchers: Answers to Frequently Asked Questions," Small Business Administration, Office of Advocacy, March 2004.

26. "A New Copyright Law?" *BusinessWeek,* August 3, 1998, p. 45.

27. "Highlights of Food Labeling," *Marketing News,* March 15, 2004, p. 14.

28. Dorothy Cohen, "Trademark Strategy Revisited," *Journal of Marketing,* July 1991, pp. 46–59.

29. Maxine L. Retsky, "Review Int'l Filing Process for Marks," *Marketing News,* September 29, 2003, p. 8.

30. Michael Fielding, "Doppelgangers: Monitor Parodies to Measure Brand Value," *Marketing News,* October 15, 2006, p. 13–15; and Craig J. Thompson, Aric Rindfleisch, and Zeynep Arsel, "Emotional Branding and the Strategic Value of the Doppelganger Brand Image," *Journal of Marketing,* January 2006, pp. 50–64.

31. Paul Barrett, "High Court Sees Color as Basis for Trademarks," *The Wall Street Journal,* March 29, 1995, p. A6; Paul Barrett, "Color in the Court," *The Wall Street Journal,* January 5, 1995, p. A1; and David Kelly, "Rainbow of Ideas to Trademark Color," *Advertising Age,* April 24, 1995, pp. 20, 22.

32. Maxine L. Retsky, "Dilution of Trademarks Hard to Prove," *Marketing News,* May 12, 2003, p. 6.

33. Dick Mercer, "Tempest in a Soup Can," *Advertising Age,* October 17, 1994, pp. 25–29.

34. Maxine L. Retsky, "Stakes Are High for Direct Mail Sweepstakes Promotions," *Marketing News,* July 3, 2000, p. 8; Catherine Arnold, "Picky, Picky, Picky" *Marketing News,* February 15, 2004, p. 17; Catherine Arnold, "No Can Spam," *Marketing News,* January 15, 2004, p. 3; Arundhati Parmar, "Can't Say You Weren't Warned," *Marketing News,* February 15, 2004, p. 4; and James Heckman, "Laws That Take Effect—and Some Likely to Return in 1999 Mean Marketers Must Change Some Policies," *Marketing News,* December 7, 1998, p. 1, 16.

35. Mark McFadden, "The BBB on the WWW," *HP Professional,* September 1997, p. 36.

Geek Squad: This case was written by Steven Hartley. Sources: Mary Ellen Lloyd, "Camp Teaches Power of Geekdom," *The Wall Street Journal,* July 11, 2007; Dean Foust, Michael Mandel, Frederick F. Jespersen and David Henry, "The Business Week 50—The Best Performers," *BusinessWeek,* March 26, 2007, p. 58; Jessica E. Vascellaro, "What's a Cellphone For? Businesses are Finding All Sorts of New Uses for Mobile Devices," *The Wall Street Journal,* March 26, 2007, p. R5; Cade Metz, "Just How Stupid Are You? Geek Squad War Stories," *PC Magazine,* February 1, 2006; Brad Stone, "Lore of the Geek Squad," *Newsweek,* February 20, 2006, p. 44; Michelle Conlin, "Smashing the Clock," *BusinessWeek,* December 11, 2006, p. 60; "Best Buy: How to Break Out of Commodity Hell," *BusinessWeek,* March 27, 2006, p. 76; Pallavi Gogoi, "Meet Jane Geek," *BusinessWeek,* November 28, 2005, p. 94; Desiree J. Hanford, "Geek Squad Is Popular at Best Buy," *The Wall Street Journal,* December 14, 2005, p. 1; Michelle Higgins, "Getting Your Own IT Department," *The Wall Street Journal,* May 20, 2004, p. D1; and information contained on the Geek Squad website (www.geeksquad.com).

CHAPTER 4

1. www.beeresponsible.com, downloaded March 30, 2008; www.beerinstitute.org, downloaded March 30, 2008; "America's Most Admired Companies," *Fortune,* March 17, 2008, p. 79.

2. For a discussion of the definition of ethics, see Eugene R. Lazniak and Patrick E. Murphy, *Ethical Marketing Decision: The Higher Road* (Boston: Allyn & Bacon, 1993), chap. 1.

3. "Honorable?" Business 2.0, February 2000, p. 92.

4. The 2007 National Business Ethics Survey (Washington, DC: Ethics Resource Center 2008); "Poll: Ad Execs Are Icky," *Advertising Age,* January 16, 2006, p. 26; and Ronald W. Clement. "Just How Ethical Is American Business?" *Business Horizons,* July–August 2006, pp. 313–27.

5. See, for example, Lawrence B. Chonko, *Ethical Decision Making in Marketing* (Thousand Oaks, CA: Sage, 1995).

6. Thomas Donaldson, "Values in Tension: Ethics Away from Home," *Harvard Business Review,* September–October 1996, pp. 48–62.

7. "Levi Only Comfortable Dealing with Countries That Fit Its Image," *Dallas Morning News,* January 9, 1995, p. D2.

8. These statistics were obtained from Recording Industry Association of America (www.riaa.com), Motion Picture Association of America (www.mpaa.com), and the Business Software Alliance (www.bsa.org).

9. *Internet Piracy on Campus* (Washington, DC: IPSOS, September 16, 2003).

10. Vern Terpstra and Kenneth David, *The Cultural Environment of International Business,* 3rd ed. (Cincinnati: South-Western Publishing, 1991), p. 12.

11. Hukari Kane, "Recall Shows Battery Limits," *The Wall Street Journal,* August 18, 2006, p. A13; and "Dell Announces Recall of Notebook Computer Batteries Due to Fire Hazard," U.S. Consumer Product Safety Commission Press Release, August 15, 2006.

12. "Three Ad Agencies Settle FTC Charges of Deceptive Car-Leasing Commercials," *The Wall Street Journal,* January 21, 1998, p. B2.

13. Timothy Muris, "Protecting Consumers' Privacy," www.FTC.gov, downloaded January 3, 2007.

14. For an extensive examination on slotting fees, see Paul N. Bloom, Gregory T. Gundlach, and Joseph P. Cannon, "Slotting Allowances and Fees: Schools of Thought and Views of Practicing Managers," *Journal of Marketing,* April 2000, pp. 92–109. Also see, "FTC Pinpoints Slotting Fees," *Advertising Age,* February 26, 2001, p. 52.

15. Hedich Nasheri, *Economic Espionage and Industrial Spying* (Cambridge, UK: Cambridge University Press, 2005).

16. "Coke Employee Faces Charges in Plot to Sell Secrets," *The Wall Street Journal,* July 6, 2006, p. B6; "Do the Right Thing? Not with a Rival's Inside Info," *Advertising Age,* July 17, 2006, p. 4; "You Can't Beat the Real Thing," *Time,* July 17, 2006, pp. 10–11; and "Former Coke Secretary Sentenced to 8 Years," www.msnbc.com, May 23, 2007.

17. These examples are highlighted in Thomas W. Dunfee, N. Craig Smith, and William T. Ross, Jr., "Social Contracts and Marketing Ethics," *Journal of Marketing,* July 1999, pp. 14–32; and Andy Pasztor, *When the Pentagon Was for Sale: Inside America's Biggest Defense Scandal* (New York: Scribner, 1995).

18. www.transparency.org, downloaded April 1, 2008.

19. "U.S. Firms Raise Ethics Focus," *The Wall Street Journal,* November 28, 2005, p. B4; and Thomas Donaldson, "The Corporate Ethics Boom: Significant, or Just for Show?" Knowledge@Wharton, downloaded February 25, 2002.

20. "Coca-Cola Unit Head Resigns After Rigged Test," www.forbes.com, downloaded August 25, 2003.

21. The 2007 National Business Ethics Survey.

22. "Whistleblowers: Tales from the Back Office," *The Economist,* March 25, 2006, p. 67; and C. Fred Alford, *Whistleblowers: Broken Lives and Organizational Power* (Ithaca, NY: Cornell University Press, 2002).

23. For an extensive discussion on these moral philosophies, see R. Eric Reidenbach and Donald P. Robin, *Ethics and Profits* (Englewood Cliffs, NJ: Prentice Hall, 1989); Chonko, *Ethical Decision Making;* and Lazniak and Murphy, *Ethical Marketing Decisions.*

24. "Scotchgard Working Out Recent Stain on Its Business," www.mercurynews.com, downloaded June 22, 2003.

25. James O. Wilson, "Adam Smith on Business Ethics," *California Management Review,* Fall 1989, pp. 57–72.

26. Alix M. Freedman, "Bad Reaction: Nestlé's Bid to Crash Baby-Formula Market in U.S. Stirs a Row," *The Wall Street Journal,* February 16, 1989, pp. Al, A6; and Alix Freedman, "Nestlé to Drop Claim on Label of Its Formula," *The Wall Street Journal,* March 13, 1989, p. B5.

27. Harvey S. James and Farhad Rassekh, "Smith, Friedman, and Self-Interest in Ethical Society," *Business Ethics Quarterly,* July 2000, pp. 659–74.

28. "Cost of Living," *The Economist,* March 1, 2003, p. 60.

29. "Perrier—Overresponding to a Crisis," in Robert F. Hartley, *Marketing Mistakes and Successes,* 10th ed. (New York: John Wiley & Sons, 2006), pp. 119–30.

30. "Ford Explorers with Firestone Tires: Ill Handling of a Killer Scenario," in Hartley, *Marketing Mistakes and Successes,* pp. 105–18.

31. "Pollution Prevention Pays." www.3M.com, downloaded March 28, 2008; www.xerox.com/environment, downloaded March 28, 2008; Elizabeth Royte, "Corn Plastic to the Rescue?" *Smithsonian,* August 2006, pp. 84–88; Jerry Adler, "Going Green," *Newsweek,* July 17, 2006, pp. 42–52; and "Hugging the Tree Huggers," *BusinessWeek,* March 12, 2007, pp. 66–68.

32. For an extended discussion on this topic, see P. Rajan Varadarajan and Anil Menon, "Cause-Related Marketing: A Coalignment of Marketing Strategy and Corporate Philanthropy," *Journal of Marketing,* July 1988, pp. 58–74. The examples are found in Nancy Coltun Webster, "Color Coded Causes," *Advertising Age,* June 13, 2005, pp. 31–35; www.avoncompany.com, downloaded April 3, 2008; and Christine Bittar, "Seeking Cause and Effect," *Brandweek,* September 11, 2002, pp. 19–23.

33. "The Big Picture," *BusinessWeek,* November 6, 2006, p. 13; "Cause and 'Affect,'" *Brandweek,* October 7, 2002, p. 16; and Bittar, "Seeking Cause and Effect." Also see Larry Chiagouris and Ipshita Ray, "Saving the World with Cause-Related Marketing," *Marketing Management,* July–August 2007, pp. 48–51.

34. These steps are adapted from J. J. Carson and G. A. Steiner, *Measuring Business Social Performance: The Corporate Social Audit* (New York: Committee for Economic Development, 1974). See also Sandra Waddock and Neil Smith, "Corporate Responsibility Audits: Doing Well by Doing Good," *Sloan Management Review,* Winter 2000, pp. 75–84.

35. "Marketers Become Own Watchdogs," *Advertising Age,* June 12, 2006, p. 57; and "Sweatshops: Finally, Airing the Dirty Linen," *BusinessWeek,* June 23, 2003, pp. 100–01.

36. "Economics—Creating Environmental Capital," *The Wall Street Journal,* March 24, 2008, Section R; Remi Trudel and June Cotte, "Does Being Ethical Pay?" *The Wall Street Journal,* May 12, 2008, p. R4; and Pete Engardio, "Beyond the Green Corporation," *BusinessWeek,* January 29, 2007, pp. 50–64.

37. This discussion is based on Wayne D. Hoyer and Deborah J. MacInnis, *Consumer Behavior,* 4th ed. (New York: Houghton Mifflin Company, 2007), pp. 535–37; "Factoids," *Research Alert,* December 8, 2005, p. 5; Elizabeth Woyke, "Attention Shoplifters," *BusinessWeek,* September 11, 2006, pp. 46–50; and "Putting Return Policies to the Test," *The Wall Street Journal,* February 22, 2007, p. D3.

38. "A Pirate and His Penance," *Time,* January 26, 2004, p. 60; and Roger D. Crockett, "Hauling in the Hollywood Hackers," *BusinessWeek,* May 15, 2006, pp. 80–82.

39. Mark Dolliver, "Deflating a Myth," *Brandweek,* May 12, 2008, pp. 30–32; and "Schism on the Green," *Brandweek,* February 26, 2001, p. 18.

40. "FTC Stands by Regs for 'Green' Ad Claims," *Advertising Age,* October 7, 1996, p. 61.

Starbucks Corporation: This case is based on information on the company website (www.starbucks.com) and the following sources: "Living Our Values ," *2003 Corporate Social Responsibility Annual Report;* "Starbucks Annual Shareholder meeting," Starbucks press release, March 30, 2004; Ranjay Gulati, Sarah Haffman, and Gary Neilson, "The Barista Principle: Starbucks and the Rise of Relational Capital," *Strategy and Business,* 3rd Quarter 2002, pp. 58–69; and Andy Serwer, "Hot Starbucks to Go," *Fortune,* January 12, 2004, pp. 52ff.

CHAPTER 5

1. "Automakers Getting up to Speed," *BrandWeek,* December 3, 2007, p. S8; Marti Barletta, "Who's Really Buying that Car? Ask Her," *BrandWeek,* September 4, 2006, p. 20; Joan Voight, "The Lady Means Business," *BrandWeek,* April 30, 2006, pp. 28ff; and Jennifer Saranow, "Car Dealers Recruit Saleswomen at the Mall," *The Wall Street Journal,* April 12, 2006, pp. B1, B3.

2. Roger D. Blackwell, Paul W. Miniard, and James F. Engel, *Consumer Behavior,* 10th ed. (Mason, OH: South-Western Publishing, 2006).

3. For in-depth studies on external information search patterns, see Brian T. Ratchford, Myung-Soo Lee, and Debabrata Talukdar, "The Impact of the Internet on Information Search for Automobiles," *Journal of Marketing Research,* May 2003, pp. 193–209; Sridhar Moorthy, Brian T. Ratchford, and Debabrata Talukdar, "Consumer Information

Research Revisited: Theory and Empirical Analysis," *Journal of Consumer Research,* March 1997, pp. 263–77; Joel E. Urbany, Peter R. Dickson, and William L. Wilkie, "Buyer Uncertainty and Information Search," *Journal of Consumer Research,* March 1992, pp. 452–63; and Sharon E. Beatty and Scott M. Smith, "External Search Effort: An Investigation across Several Product Categories," *Journal of Consumer Research,* June 1987, pp. 83–95.

4. *Consumer Reports Buying Guide Best Buys for 2007* (Yonkers, NY: Consumers Union, 2007).

5. For an extended discussion on evaluative criteria, see Del J. Hawkins, David L. Mothersbaugh, and Roger J. Best, *Consumer Behavior: Building Marketing Strategy,* 10th ed. (Burr Ridge, IL: McGraw-Hill/Irwin, 2007).

6. John A. Howard, *Buyer Behavior in Marketing Strategy,* 2nd ed. (Englewood Cliffs, NJ: Prentice Hall, 1994). For an extended discussion on consumer choice sets, see Allan D. Shocker, Moshe Ben-Akiva, Brun Boccara, and Prakesh Nedungadi, "Consideration Set Influences on Consumer Decision Making and Choice: Issues, Models, and Suggestions," *Marketing Letters,* August 1991, pp. 181–98.

7. These estimates given in Jagdish N. Sheth and Banwari Mitral, *Consumer Behavior,* 2nd ed. (Mason, OH: South-Western Publishing, 2003), p. 32.

8. For an overview of research on involvement, see John C. Mowen and Michael Minor, *Consumer Behavior: A Framework,* 5th ed. (Upper Saddle River, NJ: Prentice Hall, 2001); and Wayne D. Hoyer and Deborah J. MacInnis, *Consumer Behavior,* 4th ed. (Boston: Houghton Mifflin Co., 2007).

9. Russell Belk, "Situational Variables and Consumer Behavior," *Journal of Consumer Research,* December 1975, pp. 157–63.

10. A. H. Maslow, *Motivation and Personality* (New York: Harper & Row, 1970). Also see Richard Yalch and Frederic Brunel, "Need Hierarchies in Consumer Judgments of Product Design: Is It Time to Reconsider Maslow's Hierarchy?" in *Advances in Consumer Research,* ed. Kim Corfman and John Lynch (Provo, UT: Association for Consumer Research, 1996), pp. 405–10.

11. Joel B. Cohen, "An Interpersonal Orientation to the Study of Consumer Behavior," *Journal of Marketing Research,* August 1967, pp. 270–78; and Rena Bartos, *Marketing to Women around the World* (Cambridge, MA: Harvard Business School, 1989).

12. Myron Magnet, "Let's Go for Growth," *Fortune,* March 7, 1994, p. 70.

13. This example provided in Michael R. Solomon, *Consumer Behavior,* 4th ed. (Upper Saddle River, NJ: Prentice Hall, 1999), p. 59.

14. For further reading on subliminal perception, see Anthony G. Greenwald, Sean C. Draine, and Richard L. Abrams, "Three Cognitive Markers of Unconscious Semantic Activation," *Science,* September 1996, pp. 1699–701; B. Bahrami, N. Lavie, and G. Rees, "Attentional Load Modulates Responses of Human Primary Visual Cortex to Invisible Stimuli," *Current Biology,* March 2007, pp. 39–47; Dennis L. Rosen and Surendra N. Singh, "An Investigation of Subliminal Embedded Effect on Multiple Measures of Advertising Effectiveness," *Psychology & Marketing,* March–April 1992, pp. 157–73; and Kathryn T. Theus, "Subliminal Advertising and the Psychology of Processing Unconscious Stimuli: A Review of the Research," *Psychology & Marketing,* May–June 1994, pp. 271–90.

15. August Bullock, *The Secret Sales Pitch* (San Jose, CA: Norwich Publishers, 2004); E. Parpis, "Sex, Crackers and Subliminal Ads," *Adweek,* March 31, 2003, p. 18; "GOP Commercial Resurrects Debate on Subliminal Ads," *The Wall Street Journal,* September 13, 2000, p. B10; and "I Will Love This Story," *U.S. News & World Report,* May 12, 1997, p. 12.

16. Martin Fishbein and I. Aizen, *Belief, Attitude, Intention and Behavior: An Introduction to Theory and Research* (Reading, MA: Addison-Wesley, 1975), p. 6.

17. Richard J. Lutz, "Changing Brand Attitudes through Modification of Cognitive Structure," *Journal of Consumer Research,* March 1975, pp. 49–59.

18. "The VALS™ Types," www.sric-bi.com/VALS, downloaded April 1, 2008.

19. This discussion is based on Ed Keller and Jon Berry, *The Influentials* (New York: Simon and Schuster, 2003).

20. "Word of Mouth Is Where It's At," *BrandWeek,* June 2, 2003, p. 26.

21. BzzAgent.com, downloaded April 15, 2008; Matthew Creamer, "BzzAgent Seeks to Turn Word of Mouth into a Saleable Medium," *Advertising Age,* February 13, 2006, p. 12; "Word on the Street," *Time,* April 12, 2007, pp. 34–35; and "Is Talk cheap? How Cheap?," *BrandWeek,* June 30, 2008, p. 6.

22. For extensive review on consumer socialization of children, see Deborah Roedder John, "Consumer Socialization of Children: A Retrospective Look at Twenty-Five Years of Research," *Journal of Consumer Research,* December 1999, pp. 183–213. Also see, Gwen Bachmann Achenreiver and Deborah Roedder John, "The Meaning of Brand Names to Children: A Developmental Investigation," *Journal of Consumer Psychology* 13, no. 3 (2003), pp. 205–19; and Elizabeth S. Moore, William L. Wilkie, and Richard J. Lutz, "Passing the Torch: Intergenerational Influences as a Source of Brand Equity," *Journal of Marketing,* April 2002, pp. 17–37.

23. J. Paul Peter and Jerry C. Olson, *Consumer Behavior and Marketing Strategy,* 8th ed. (Burr Ridge, IL: McGraw-Hill/Irwin, 2008). Also see, Rex Y. Du and Wagner A. Kamakura, "Household Life Cycles and Lifestyles in the United States," *Journal of Marketing Research,* February 2006, pp. 121–32.

24. This discussion is based on Hawkins, Mothersbaugh, and Best, *Consumer Behavior: Building Marketing Strategy;* "How the Male of the Species Shops," *Advertising Age,* March 3, 2008, p. 12; www.teenresearch.com, downloaded April 1, 2008; "Teens Rule," MediaBuyer.com, downloaded April 7, 2008; and "Trillion-Dollar Kids," *The Economist,* December 2, 2006, p. 66.

25. Jeffrey M. Humphreys, "The Multicultural Economy in 2007," Selig Center for Economic Growth, Terry College of Business, The University of Georgia, downloaded February 14, 2008.

26. The remainder of this discussion is based on Hoyer and MacInnis, Consumer Behavior; "American Demographics," *Advertising Age,* January 1, 2007, pp. 45–46; "Hispanic Wanted," *BrandWeek,* April 12, 2004, p. 22; and "Engaging Today's Latino Consumers," *Advertising Age,* March 3, 2008, Special Section.

27. The remainder of this discussion is based on Peter and Olson, *Consumer Behavior and Marketing Strategy;* and "Multicultural Marketing: African Americans," *Marketing News,* October 15, 2006, pp. 19, 22.

28. The remainder of this discussion is based on "Marketing to Asian Americans," *BrandWeek,* May 26, 2008, Special Section.

Best Buy: This case was written by David P. Brennan of the University of St. Thomas and is based on interviews with Joe Brandt and Best Buy employees and customers, and materials supplied by Best Buy.

CHAPTER 6

1. Interview with Kim Nagele, JCPMedia, June 10, 2008.

2. John Paterson, "Evolution, Innovation are Constants," *Purchasing,* September 7, 2006, p. 55.

3. Figures reported in this discussion are found in *Statistical Abstract of the United States:* 2007, 126th ed. (Washington, DC: U.S. Census Bureau, 2007).

4. "Lockheed Wins Major Spacecraft Job," *The Wall Street Journal,* September 1, 2006, p. A3.

5. *2002 NAICS United States Manual* (Washington, DC: Office of Management and Budget, 2002).

6. This listing and portions of the following discussion are based on F. Robert Dwyer and John F. Tanner, Jr., *Business Marketing,* 4th ed. (Burr Ridge IL: McGraw-Hill/Irwin, 2008); Michael D. Hutt and Thomas W. Speh, *Business Marketing Management,* 9th ed. (Mason, OH: South-Western, 2007); and Frank G. Bingham, Jr., Roger Gomes, and Patricia A. Knowles, *Business Marketing,* 3rd ed. (Burr Ridge, IL: McGraw-Hill/Irwin, 2005).

7. "Siemens Awarded $28 Million Contract for JetBlue Airways' Baggage Handling System with Integrated Security," Siemens USA press release, July 12, 2006.

8. Gwen Moran, *The Business Case for Diversity,* 5th ed. (Newark, NJ: Diversity Inc., 2006); "The 2007 DiversityInc Top 10 Companies for Supplier Diversity," www.diversity.com, April 2, 2007; and "Supplier Diversity Pays Off," *Purchasing,* September 7, 2006, p. 28.

9. www.pg.com/supplier_diversity, downloaded January 15, 2007.

10. "Boise Cascade Turns Green," *The Wall Street Journal,* September 3, 2003, p. B6. Also see Minette E. Drumwright, "Socially Responsible Organizational Buying: Environmental Concern as a Noneconomic Buying Criterion," *Journal of Marketing,* July 1994, pp. 1–18.

11. For a study of buying criteria used by industrial firms, see Daniel H. McQuiston and Rockney G. Walters, "The Evaluation Criteria of Industrial Buyers: Implications for Sales Training," *Journal of Business & Industrial Marketing,* Summer–Fall 1989, pp. 65–75.

12. This example is found in Sandy D. Jap and Jakki J. Mohr, "Leveraging Internet Technologies in B2B Relationships," *California Management Review,* Summer 2002, pp. 24–38.

13. "America's Most Admired Companies," *Fortune,* March 8, 2004, pp. 80ff; Brian Milligan, "Medal of Excellence: Harley-Davidson Wins by Getting Suppliers on Board," *Purchasing,* September 2000, pp. 52–65; and "Harley-Davidson Company," *Purchasing Magazine Online,* September 4, 2003.

14. "The Smartest Machines on Earth," *Fortune,* September 18, 2006, pp. 129–36.

15. This discussion is based on www.ibm.com/procurement/html/principles.practices, downloaded January 10, 2007.

16. "EDS Signs $1.7 Billion IT Services Agreement with Kraft Foods," EDS news release, April 28, 2006; and "HP Finalizes $3 Billion Outsourcing Agreement to Manage Procter & Gamble's IT Infrastructure," Hewlett-Packard news release, May 6, 2003.

17. This discussion is based on James C. Anderson and James A. Narus, *Business Market Management,* 2nd ed. (Upper Saddle River, NJ: Prentice Hall, 2004); Jeffrey K. Liker and Thomas Y. Choi, "Building Deep Supplier Relationships," *Harvard Business Review,* December 2004, pp. 104–13; and Joseph P. Cannon and Christian Homburg, "Buyer–Supplier Relationships and Customer Firm Costs," *Journal of Marketing,* January 2001, pp. 29–43.

18. Thomas V. Bonoma, "Major Sales: Who Really Does the Buying?" *Harvard Business Review,* May–June 1982, pp. 11–19. For recent research on buying centers, see Morry Ghingold and David T. Wilson, "Buying Center Research and Business Marketing Practices: Meeting the Challenge of Dynamic Marketing," *Journal of Business & Industrial Marketing* 13, no. 2 (1998), pp. 96–108; Philip L. Dawes, Don Y. Lee, and Grahame R. Dowling, "Information Control and Influence in Emerging Buying Centers," *Journal of Marketing,* July 1998, pp. 55–68; and Thomas Tellefsen, "Antecedents and Consequences of Buying Center Leadership: An Emergent Perspective," *Journal of Business-to-Business Marketing,* 13, no. 1 (2006), pp. 53–59.

19. Allison Enright, "It Takes a Committee to Buy into B-to-B," *Marketing News,* February 15, 2006, pp. 11–13. For academic research on roles in buying centers, see R. Vekatesh, Ajay Kohli, and Gerald Zaltman, "Influence Strategies in Buying Centers," *Journal of Marketing,* October 1995, pp. 61–72; Gary L. Lilien and Anthony Wong, "An Exploratory Investigation of the Structure of the Buying Center in the Metal Working Industry," *Journal of Marketing Research,* February 1984, pp. 1–11; and Wesley J. Johnston and Thomas V. Bonoma, "The Buying Center: Structure and Interaction Patterns," *Journal of Marketing,* Summer 1981, pp. 143–56. Also see Christopher P. Puto, Wesley E. Patton III, and Ronald H. King, "Risk Handling Strategies in Industrial Vendor Selection Decisions" *Journal of Marketing,* Winter 1985, pp. 89–98.

20. These definitions are adapted from Frederick E. Webster, Jr., and Yoram Wind, *Organizational Buying Behavior* (Englewood Cliffs, NJ: Prentice Hall, 1972), p. 6.

21. "Can Corning Find Its Optic Nerve?" *Fortune,* March 19, 2001, pp. 148–50.

22. Representative studies on the buy-class framework that document its usefulness include Erin Anderson, Wujin Chu, and Barton Weitz, "Industrial Purchasing: An Empirical Exploration of the Buy-Class Framework," *Journal of Marketing,* July 1987, pp. 71–86; Morry Ghingold, "Testing the 'Buy-Grid' Buying Process Model," *Journal of Purchasing and Materials Management,* Winter 1986, pp. 30–36; P. Matthyssens and W. Faes, "OEM Buying Process for New Components: Purchasing and Marketing Implications," *Industrial Marketing Management,* August 1985, pp. 145–57; and Thomas W. Leigh and Arno J. Ethans, "A Script-Theoretic Analysis of Industrial Purchasing Behavior," *Journal of Marketing,* Fall 1984, pp. 22–32. Studies not supporting the buy-class framework include Joseph A. Bellizi and Philip McVey, "How Valid Is the Buy-Grid Model?" *Industrial Marketing Management,* February 1983, pp. 57–62; Donald W. Jackson, Janet E. Keith, and Richard K. Burdick, "Purchasing Agents' Perceptions of Industrial Buying Center Influences: A Situational Approach," *Journal of Marketing,* Fall 1984, pp. 75–83.

23. "B2B E-Commerce Headed for Trillions," www.clickz.com, downloaded March 1, 2008.

24. This discussion is based on Jennifer Reinhold, "What We Learned in the New Economy," *Fast Company,* March 4, 2004, pp. 56ff; Mark Roberti, "General Electric's Spin Machine," *The Industry Standard,* January 22–29, 2001, pp. 74–83; "Grainger Lightens Its Digital Load," *Industrial Distribution,* March 2001, pp. 77–79; and www.boeing.com/procurement, downloaded February 6, 2005.

25. "B2B, Take 2," *BusinessWeek Online,* November 25, 2005.

26. "New Study Reveals 724,000 Americans Rely on eBay Sales for Income," eBay press release, July 21, 2005; Robyn Greenspan, "Net Drives Profits to Small-Biz," www.clickz.com, March 25, 2004; and www.ebaybusiness.com.

27. www.agentrics.com, downloaded January 8, 2007.

28. www.ghx.com, downloaded January 8, 2007.

29. This discussion is based on Robert J. Dolan and Youngme Moon, "Pricing and Market Making on the Internet," *Journal of Interactive Marketing,* Spring 2000, pp. 56–73; and Ajit Kambil and Eric van Heck, *Making Markets: How Firms Can Benefit from Online Auctions and Exchanges* (Boston, MA: Harvard Business School Press, 2002).

30. Susan Avery, "Supply Management is Core of Success at UTC," *Purchasing,* September 7, 2006, pp. 36–39.

31. Shawn P. Daley and Prithwiraz Nath, "Reverse Auctions for Relationship Marketers," *Industrial Marketing Management,* February 2005, pp. 157–66; Sandy Jap, "An Exploratory Study of the Introduction of Online Reverse Auctions," *Journal of Marketing,* July 2003, pp. 96–107; and Sandy Jap, "The Impact of Online Reverse Auction Design on Buyer-Supplier Relationships," *Journal of Marketing,* January 2007, pp. 146–59.

Lands' End: This case is based on information available on the company website (www.landsend.com) and the following sources: Robert Berner, "A Hard Bargain at Lands' End?" *BusinessWeek,* May 28, 2001, p. 14; Rebecca Quick, "Getting the Right Fit—Hips and All—Can a Machine Measure You Better than Your Tailor?" *The Wall Street Journal,* October 18, 2000, p. B1; Stephanie Miles, "Apparel E-tailers Spruce Up for Holidays," *The Wall Street Journal,* November 6, 2001, p. B6; and Dana James, "Custom Goods Nice Means for Lands' End," *Marketing News,* August 14, 2000, p. 5.

CHAPTER 7

1. Normandy Madden, "P&G Launches Cover Girl in China," *Advertising Age,* October 31, 2005, p. 22; www.pg.com.cn, downloaded October 11, 2006; and Sheridan Prasso, "Battle for the Face of China," www.cnnmoney.com, December 12, 2005.

2. Dennis R. Appleyard and Alfred J. Field, Jr., *International Economics,* 5th ed. (Burr Ridge, IL: McGraw-Hill/Irwin, 2005), chapter 15; "Banana Growers Find EU Tariff Mitigated by End of Quotas," *The Wall Street Journal,* April 26, 2006, p. B2; and *Economic Report of the President* (Washington, DC: U.S. Government Printing Office, 2007).

3. This discussion is based on information provided by the World Trade Organization, www.wto.org, downloaded August 3, 2008.

4. This discussion on the European Union is based on information provided at www.europa.eu, downloaded July 30, 2008.

5. This discussion is based on *Probable Effect of Certain Modifications to the North American Free Trade Agreement Rules of Origin* (Washington, DC: U.S. International Trade Commission, 2006); and Michael Fielding, "CAFTA-DR to Build Options Over Time," *Marketing News,* February 1, 2006, pp. 13–14.

6. For an overview of different types of global companies and marketing strategies, see, for example, Warren J. Keegan, *Global Marketing,* 4th ed. (Upper Saddle River, NJ: Prentice Hall, 2005); and Michael Czinkota and Ilka A. Ronkainen, *International Marketing,* 8th ed. (Mason, OH: South-Western, 2007).

7. Johnny K. Johansson and Ilkka A. Ronkainen, "The Brand Challenge," *Marketing Management,* March–April 2004, pp. 54–55.

8. Michael Fielding, "Global Brands Need Balance of Identity, Cultural Respect," *Marketing News,* September 1, 2006, pp. 8–10; and Kevin Lane Keller, *Strategic Brand Management,* 3rd ed. (Upper Saddle River, NJ: Prentice Hall, 2008), pp. 602–603.

9. Christopher Leporini, "Are U.S. Companies Losing Their Cool Abroad," *Marketing Matters Newsletter* at www.marketingpower.com, downloaded February 16, 2006; D. Kjeldgaard and S. Askegaard, "The Globalization of Youth Culture: The Global Youth Segment as Structures of Common Difference," *Journal of Consumer Research,* September 2006, pp. 231–47; www.mtv.com/company, downloaded January 10, 2007; Elissa Moses, *The $100 Billion Allowance: Accessing the Global Teen Market* (New York: Wiley, 2000); Bay Fong, "Spending Spree," *U.S. News & World Report,* May 1, 2006, pp. 42–50; and "The Emerging Middle Class," *Business 2.0,* July 2006, p. 96.

10. "B2B Blossoms," www.clickz.com, downloaded February 10, 2007.

11. For comprehensive references on cross-cultural aspects of marketing, see Paul A. Herbig, *Handbook of Cross-Cultural Marketing* (New York: Halworth Press, 1998); Jean Claude Usunier, *Marketing Across Cultures,* 4th ed. (London: Prentice Hall Europe, 2005); and Philip R. Cateora and John L. Graham, *International Marketing,* 13th ed. (Burr Ridge, IL: McGraw-Hill/Irwin, 2007). Unless otherwise indicated, examples found in this section appear in these excellent sources.

12. These examples appear in Del I. Hawkins, David L. Mothersbaugh, and Roger J. Best, *Consumer Behavior,* 10th ed. (Burr Ridge, IL: McGraw-Hill/Irwin, 2007), chapter 2.

13. "Greeks Protest Coke's Use of Parthenon," *Dallas Morning News,* August 17, 1992, p. D4.

14. "If Only Krispy Kreme Meant 'Makes You Smarter,'" *Business 2.0,* August 2005, p. 108.

15. "Navigating the Labyrinth: Sales and Distribution in Today's China," *Knowledge@Wharton,* October 16, 2006; and Cateora and Graham, *International Marketing.*

16. Vijay Mahajan and Kamini Banga, *The 86 Percent Solution: How to Succeed in the Biggest Market Opportunity of the Next 50 Years* (Upper Saddle River, NJ: Pearson Education, 2006).

17. "Mattel Plans to Double Sales Abroad," *The Wall Street Journal,* February 11, 1998, pp. A3, A11.

18. Eric Clark, *The Real Toy Story* (New York: The Free Press, 2007); and Cateora and Graham, *International Marketing.*

19. For an extensive and recent examination of these market-entry options, see for example, Johnny K. Johansson, *Global Marketing: Foreign Entry, Local Marketing, and Global Management,* 3rd ed. (Burr Ridge, IL: McGraw-Hill/Irwin, 2003); A. Coskun Samli, *Entering & Succeeding in Emerging Countries: Marketing to the Forgotten Majority* (Mason, OH: South-Western, 2004); Keegan, *Global Marketing;* and Cateora and Graham, *International Marketing.*

20. Based on an interview with Pamela Viglielmo, director of international marketing, Fran Wilson Creative Cosmetics; and "Foreign Firms Think Their Way into Japan," www.successstories.com/nikkei, downloaded March 24, 2003.

21. *Small and Medium Sized Exporting Companies: A Statistical Handbook* (Washington, DC: International Trade Administration, June 2006).

22. "Overseas is McDonald's Kind of Place," www.forbes.com, February 8, 2008.

23. "FedEx Expands Reach in China with Buyout of Joint Venture," *The Wall Street Journal,* January 25, 2006.

24. This discussion is based on Todd J. Gillman, "Chip Off the Old Block," *Dallas Morning News,* July 30, 2006, pp. 1A, 22A; "Machines for the Masses," *The Wall Street Journal,* December 9, 2003, pp. A19–A20; "The Color of Beauty," *Forbes,* November 22, 2000, pp. 170–76; "It's Goo, Goo, Goo, Goo Vibrations at the Gerber Lab," *The Wall Street Journal,* December 4, 1996, pp. A1, A6; Donald R. Graber, "How to Manage a Global Product Development Process," *Industrial Marketing Management,* November 1996, pp. 483–98; and Herbig, *Handbook of Cross-Cultural Marketing.*

25. Jagdish N. Sheth and Atul Parvatiyar, "The Antecedents and Consequences of Integrated Global Marketing," *International Marketing Review* 18, no. 1 (2001), pp. 16–29. Also see D. Szymanski, S. Bharadwaj, and R. Varadarajan, "Standardization versus Adaptation of International Marketing Strategy: An Empirical Investigation," *Journal of Marketing,* October 1993, pp. 1–17.

26. "With Profits Elusive, Wal-Mart to Exit Germany," *The Wall Street Journal,* July 29, 2006, pp. A1, A6.

27. "Rotten Apples," *Dallas Morning News,* April 7, 1998, p. 14A.

28. For an in-depth discussion on gray markets, see Kersi D. Antia, Mark Bergen, and Shantanu Dutta, "Competing with Gray Markets," *Sloan Management Review,* Fall 2004, pp. 63–69; and Kersi D. Antia, Mark E. Bergen, Shantanu Dutta, and Robert J. Fisher, "How Does Enforcement Deter Gray Market Incidence?" *Journal of Marketing,* January 2006, pp. 92–106.

CNS Breathe Right Strips: This case was prepared by Mary L. Brown based on interviews with Kevin McKenna, vice president, international, and Nick Naumann, senior marketing services manager of CNS Inc., September 2004.

CHAPTER 8

1. See www.boxofficemojo.com for the release schedule of movies for 2008, 2009, and beyond.
2. John Horn, "Studios Play Name Games," *Star Tribune,* August 10, 1997, p. F11; and "Flunking Chemistry," *Star Tribune,* April 11, 2003, p. E13.
3. "2007 U.S. Theatrical Market Statistics—Worldwide Market Research & Analysis," Motion Picture Association of America, p. 6. See www.mpaa.org/2007-Theatrical-Market-Statistics.pdf.
4. Based on a cursory analysis of the data presented in "All Time Box Office: Worldwide Grosses." See Box Office Mojo at www.boxofficemojo.com/alltime/world.
5. Willow Bay, "Test Audiences Have Profound Effect on Movies," *CNN Newsstand & Entertainment Weekly,* September 28, 1998. See www.cnn.com/SHOWBIZ/Movies/9809/28/screen.test.
6. Helene Diamond, "Lights, Camera…Research!" *Marketing News,* September 11, 1989, pp. 10–11; and "Killer!" *Time,* November 16, 1987, pp. 72–79.
7. Carl Diorio, "Tracking Projectings: Box Office Calculations an Inexact Science," *Variety,* May 24, 2001.
8. A lengthier, expanded definition from 2004 is found on the American Marketing Association's website at www.marketingpower.com. For a researcher's comments on this and other definitions of marketing research, see Lawrence D. Gibson, "Quo Vadis, Marketing Research?" *Marketing Research,* Spring 2000, pp. 36–41.
9. Etienne Benson, "Toy Stories," *Observer,* 19, no. 12 (December 2006).
10. Lawrence D. Gibson, "Defining Marketing Problems," *Marketing Research,* Spring 1998, pp. 4–12.
11. "Inside TV Ratings" and "National Audience Sample" from the Nielsen Media Research website, www.nielsenmedia.com; and Richard Siklos, "Made to Measure," *Fortune,* March 3, 2008, p. 72.
12. "Our Measurement Techniques: Meters and Diaries" from "Inside TV Ratings." See www.nielsenmedia.com.
13. "Nielsen Media Research Local Market Universe Estimates" and "Nielsen to Offer Integrated, All-Electronic Television Measurement Across Multiple Media Platforms," Nielsen Media Research press release from June 14, 2006. See http://a2m2.nielsenmedia.com.
14. "Top TV Ratings" from Nielsen Media Research. See www.nielsenmedia.com.
15. Robert Coen, "Insider's Report," *Universal McCann,* December 2007. Data obtained from tables: "The Outlook for 2008 National Advertising" (TV only) and "The Outlook for Total Advertising 2008" (Local TV only), p. 6. See www.mccann.com/news/pdfs/Insiders12_07.pdf.
16. David Kiley, "Counting the Eyeballs," *BusinessWeek,* January 16, 2006, pp. 84–85; and "The Ultimate Marketing Machine," *The Economist,* July 8, 2006, pp. 61–64.
17. Robert Frank, "How to Live Large, and Largely for Free, Jennifer Voitle's Way," *The Wall Street Journal,* June 9, 2003, pp. A1, A8.
18. Sarah Ellison, "P&G Chief's Turnaround Recipe: Find Out What Women Want," *The Wall Street Journal,* June 1, 2005, p. A1; Mark Maremont, "New Toothbrush Is Big-Ticket Item," *The Wall Street Journal,* October 27, 1998, pp. B1, B6; and Emily Nelson, "P&G Checks Out Real Life," *The Wall Street Journal,* May 17, 2001, pp. B1, B4.
19. Kenneth Chang, "Enlisting Science's Lessons to Entice More Shoppers to Spend More," *The New York Times,* September 19, 2006, p. D3; and Janet Adamy, "Cooking Up Changes at Kraft Foods," *The Wall Street Journal,* February 20, 2007, p. B1.
20. For a more complete discussion of questionnaire methods, see David A. Aaker, V. Kumar, and George S. Day, *Marketing Research,* 8th ed. (New York: John Wiley & Sons, 2004), pp. 188–272.
21. Jyoti Thottam, "How Kids Set the (Ring) Tone," *Time,* April 4, 2005, pp. 40–45.
22. Jonathan Eig, "Food Industry Battles for Moms Who Want to Cook—Just a Little," *The Wall Street Journal,* March 7, 2001, pp. A1, A10; and Susan Feyder, "It Took Tinkering by Twin Cities Firms to Saver Some Sure Bets," *Star Tribune,* June 9, 1982, p. 11A.
23. Constance Gustke, "Built to Last," *Sales & Marketing Management,* August 1997, pp. 78–83.
24. "Focus on Consumers," *General Mills Midyear Report,* Minneapolis, January 8, 1998, pp. 2–3.
25. See the TRU/A Research International Company website, which is www.teenresearch.com.
26. Clayton M. Christensen and Michael E. Raynor, *The Innovator's Solution: Creating and Sustaining Successful Growth* (Cambridge, MA: Harvard Business School Press, 2003); Clayton M. Christensen, *The Innovator's Dilemma: When Technologies Cause Great Firms to Fail* (Cambridge, MA: Harvard Business School Press, 1997); Clayton M. Christensen and Michael Overdorf, "Meeting the Challenge of Descriptive Change," *Harvard Business Review,* March–April 2000, pp. 67–76; and Clayton M. Christensen and Michael E. Raynor, "Creating a Killer Product," *Forbes,* October 13, 2003, pp. 82–84.
27. Information obtained from the websites of Information Resources Inc. (www.infores.com) and AC Nielsen (www.acnielsen.com).
28. Dale Buss, "The Race to RFID," *CEO Magazine,* November 2004, pp. 32–36.
29. The step 4 discussion was written by David Ford and Don Rylander of Ford Consulting Group Inc.; the Tony's Pizza example was provided by Teré Carral of Tony's Pizza.

Ford Consulting Group, Inc.: This case was written by David Ford of Ford Consulting Group, Inc.

CHAPTER 9

1. Kimberly Weisal, "A Shine in Their Shoes," *BusinessWeek,* December 5, 2005, p. 84; and information from the "Executive Biographies" section of the Zappos.com website.
2. Duff McDonald, "Zappos.com: Success Through Simplicity," *CIO Insight,* November 10, 2006; and the "About Zappos.com" section of the Zappos.com website.
3. Weisal, "A Shine in Their Shoes," p. 84.
4. McDonald, "Zappos.com."
5. See "The Zappos Story" on www.zappos.com.
6. "The NPD Group Finds Bright Spots in the 2007 U.S. Footwear Market," NPD Group press release, February 14, 2008. See www.npd.com/press/releases/press_080214.html; and Tony Hsieh, Zappos.com Update blog, February 19, 2008, http://blogs.zappos.com/blogs/ceo-and-coo-blog/tags/company.
7. Devin Leonard, "Nightmare on Madison Avenue," *Fortune,* June 28, 2004, pp. 93–108; Anthony Bianco, "The Vanishing Mass Market," *BusinessWeek,* July 12, 2004, pp. 61–65; and Geoff Colvin, "Selling P&G," *Fortune,* September 17, 2007, pp. 163–169.
8. Larry Neumeister, "Rowling to Testify Against Fan in Bid to Block Publication of 'Harry Potter' Encyclopedia," StarTribune.com from an Associated Press article, April 13, 2008; www.startribune.com/entertainment/17761909.html.
9. "Special Report on Mass Communication: A Long March," *The Economist,* July 14, 2001, pp. 63–65.
10. Amy Merrick, "Once a Bellwether, Ann Taylor Fights Its Stodgy Image," *The Wall Street Journal,* July 12, 2005, pp. A1, A8; and "Ann Taylor Launches Strategic Restructuring Program To Enhance Profitability," press release dated January 30, 2008, http://investor.anntaylor.com.

11. The relation of these criteria to implementation is discussed in Jacqueline Dawley, "Making Connections: Enhance the Implementation of Value of Attitude-Based Segmentation," *Marketing Research,* Summer, 2006, pp. 16–22.

12. The discussion of fast-food trends and market share is based on Simmons Market Research Bureau NCS/NHCS Spring 2007 Adult Full-Year Choices System Crosstabulation Report, based on visits within the past 30 days.

13. Jennifer Ordonez, "Taco Bell Chief Has New Tactic: Be Like Wendy's," *The Wall Street Journal,* February 23, 2001, pp. B1, B4; and Jennifer Ordonez, "An Efficiency Drive: Fast-Food Lanes Are Getting Even Faster," *The Wall Street Journal,* May 18, 2000, pp. A1, A10.

14. "Great Expectations: Wendy's Moves Ahead With New Strategic Plan," www.wendys-invest.com/strategic1206/strategicplan.php.

15. Bruce Horovitz, "Fast-Food Rivals Suit Up for Breakfast War," *USA Today,* February 20, 2007, p. 3B; Janet Adamy, "Wendy's Considers Possible Sale," *The Wall Street Journal,* April 26, 2007, p. A2; Janet Adamy, "How Wendy's Faltered, Opening Way to Buyout," *The Wall Street Journal,* August 29, 2007, pp. A1, A11; "Great Expectations: Wendy's Rolls Out Phase 2 of Its Strategic Plan," Wendy's Corporate & Investors website, www.wendys-invest.com/strategic-plan/phase2.pdf; and Monique Curet, "Wendy's Era Ends with Sale to Arby's," *The Columbus Dispatch*, April 24, 2008, www.dispatch.com/live/content/local_news/stories/2008/04/24/wendy.html.

16. Michael Arndt, "McDonald's 24/7: By Focusing on the Hours Between Traditional Meal Times, the Fast-Food Giant is Sizzling," *Business-Week,* February 5, 2007, pp. 64–72.

17. The discussion of Apple's segmentation strategies through the years is based on information from its website, www.apple.com; and www.apple-history.com/history.html.

18. This discussion is based on Roger A. Kerin and Robert A. Peterson, *Strategic Marketing Problems: Cases and Comments,* 11th ed. (Upper Saddle River, NJ: Prentice Hall, 2007), pp. 147–49; John M. Mullins, Orville C. Walker Jr., Harper W. Boyd Jr., and Jean-Claude Larreche, *Marketing Management: A Strategic Decision-Marketing Approach,* 5th ed. (Burr Ridge, IL: McGraw-Hill/Irwin, 2005), p. 216; and Carol Traeger, "What Are Automakers Doing for Women? Part III: Volvo," www.edmund.com, July 26, 2005.

19. Nicholas Zamiska, "How Milk Got a Major Boost by Food Panel," *The Wall Street Journal,* August 30, 2004, pp. B1, B5.

20. Rebecca Winter, "Chocolate Milk," *Time,* April 30, 2001, p. 20.

Rollerblade: This case was written by Michael J. Vessey and William Rudelius and is based on personal interviews with Jeremy Stonier and Nicholas Skally in 2005 and Joe Olivas in 2007.

CHAPTER 10

1. Jena McGregor, "The World's 50 Most Innovative Companies," *BusinessWeek,* April 17, 2008, http://bwnt.businessweek.com/interactive_reports/innovative_companies.

2. Jefferson Graham, "Apple Earnings Only Expected to Grow," *USA Today,* April 27, 2007, p. 3B; and John Markoff, "Ringing in the Future," *Star Tribune,* January 10, 2007, pp. A1, A6.

3. Roger A. Kerin and Robert A. Peterson, *Strategic Marketing Problems: Cases and Comments,* 11th ed. (Upper Saddle River, NJ: Prentice-Hall, 2007), p. 141.

4. Peter C. Honebein and Roy F. Cammarano, "Customers at Work: Self-service Customers Can Reduce Costs and Become Co-creators of Value," *Marketing Management,* January–February 2006, pp. 26–31; and Matthew L. Meuter, Amy L. Ostrom, Robert I. Roundtree, and Mary Jo Bittner, "Self-Service Technologies: Understanding

Customer Satisfaction with Technology-Based Service Encounters," *Journal of Marketing,* July 2000, pp. 50–64.

5. Janet R. McColl-Kennedy and Tina White, "Service Provider Training Programs at Odds with Customer Requirements in Five Star Hotels," *Journal of Services Marketing,* 11, no. 4 (1997), pp. 249–64; Ellyn A. McColgan, "How Fidelity Invests in Service Professionals," *Harvard Business Review,* January–February 1997, pp. 137–43; and Frederick F. Reichheld and W. Earl Sasser Jr., "Zero Defections: Quality Comes to Services," *Harvard Business Review,* September–October 1990, pp. 105–11.

6. Christopher Lovelock and Event Gummesson, "Whither Services Marketing?" *Journal of Services Research*, 7 (August 2004), pp. 20–41; and Christopher H. Lovelock and George S. Yip, "Developing Global Strategies for Service Businesses," *California Management Review*, Winter 1996, pp. 64–86.

7. "HP Positioned to Lead in New Era of Business Technology; New Solutions and Services to Help Enterprises Optimize Business Outcomes," *Business Wire,* April 24, 2007.

8. Interview with Geek Squad founder Robert Stephens on *60 Minutes,* January 28, 2007, www.geeksquad.com; Debora Viana Thompson, Rebecca W. Hamilton, and Roland Rust, "Feature Fatigue: When Product Capabilities Become Too Much of a Good Thing," *Journal of Marketing Research,* November 2005, pp. 431–42; and Roland T. Rust, Debora Viana Thompson, and Rebecca W. Hamilton, "Defeating Feature Fatigue," *Harvard Business Review,* February 2006, pp. 98–107.

9. Youngme Moon, "Break Free from the Product Life Cycle," *Harvard Business Review,* May 2005, pp. 86–94.

10. Interview with Geek Squad founder Robert Stephens on *60 Minutes,* January 28, 2007.

11. Greg A. Stevens and James Burley, "3,000 Raw Ideas = 1 Commercial Success!" *Research-Technology Management,* May–June 1997, pp. 16–27.

12. R. G. Cooper and E. J. Kleinschmidt, "New Products—What Separates Winners from Losers?" *Journal of Product Innovation Management,* September 1987, pp. 169–84: Robert G. Cooper, *Winning at New Products,* 2nd ed. (Reading, MA: Addison-Wesley. 1993), pp. 49–66; and Thomas D. Kuczmarski, "Measuring Your Return on Innovation," *Marketing Management,* Spring 2000, pp. 25–32.

13. Julie Fortser, "The Lucky Charm of Steve Sanger," *BusinessWeek,* March 26, 2001, pp. 75–76.

14. "Cost of Poor Quality," *SixSigma Dictionary*, www.isixsigma.com/dictionary/Cost_of_Poor_Quality_-_COPQ-63.htm; Ben Patterson, "Microsoft Fesses Up to Xbox 360 Glitches," Yahoo! Tech Blog, July 6, 2007, http://tech.yahoo.com; and Matt Richtel, "Xbox 360 Out of Order? For Loyalists, No Worries," *The New York Times,* August 13, 2007, www.nytimes.com/2007/08/13/technology/13halo.html.

15. John Gilbert, "To Sell Cars in Japan, U.S. Needs to Offer More Right-Drive Models," *Star Tribune,* May 27, 1995, p. M1.

16. See Productscan Online at www.productscan.com/index.cfm?nid=5.

17. The Avert Virucidal Tissues and Hey! There's A Monster In My Room spray examples are adapted from Robert M. McMath and Thom Forbes, *What Were They Thinking?* (New York: Random House, 1998).

18. Robert Cooper, *The Accelerate to Market—Small-Medium Enterprise: A Stage-Gate Roadmap from Idea to Launch* (Ontario, Canada: Product Development Institute, 2002); and Pierre Loewe and Jennifer Dominiquini, "Overcoming the Barriers to Effective Innovation," *Strategy & Leadership,* 34, 1 (2006), pp. 24–31.

19. Dan P. Lovallo and Olivier Sibony, "Distortions and Deceptions in Strategic Decisions," *The McKinsey Quarterly,* 1 (2006), pp. 19–29; and Byron G. Augusto, Eric P. Harmon, and Vivek Pandit, "The Right Service Strategies for Product Companies, *The McKinsey Quarterly,* 1 (2006), pp. 41–51.

20. Isabelle Royer, "Why Bad Projects Are So Hard to Kill," *Harvard Business Review,* February 2003, pp. 48–56; John T. Morn, Dan P. Lovallo, and S. Patrick Viguerie, "Beating the Odds in Market Entry," *The McKinsey Quarterly,* 4 (2005), pp. 35–45; Leslie Perlow and Stephanie Williams, "Is Silence Killing Your Company?" *Harvard Business Review,* May 2003, pp. 52–58; Beverly K. Brockman and Robert M. Morgan, "The Moderating Effect of Organizational Cohesiveness in Knowledge Use and New Product Development," *Journal of Marketing Science,* 3 (Summer 2006), pp. 295–306; Eyal Biyalogorsky, William Boulding, and Richard Staelin, "Stuck in the Past: Why Managers Persist with New Product Failures," *Journal of Marketing,* April 2006, pp. 108–21; and Irwin L. Janis, *Groupthink* (New York: Free Press, 1988).

21. Jena McGregor, "How Failure Breeds Success," *BusinessWeek,* July 10, 2006, pp. 42–52.

22. Ken Belson, "Oh, Yeah, There's a Ballgame, Too," *The New York Times,* October 22, 2006, pp. 3–1, 3–7.

23. Kimberly Judson, Denise D. Schoenabachler, Geoffrey L. Gordon, Rick E. Ridnour, and Dan C. Weilbaker, "The New Product Development Process: Let the Voice of the Salesperson Be Heard," *Journal of Product & Brand Management,* 15, no. 3 (2006), pp. 194–202.

24. Morgan L. Swink and Vincent A. Mabert, "Product Development Partnerships: Balancing Needs of OEMs and Suppliers," *Business Horizons,* May–June 2000, pp. 59–68.

25. C. K. Prahalad and Venkat Ramswamy, *The Future of Competition* (Boston: Harvard Business School Press, 2004); and Steve Hamm, "Adding Customers to the Design Team," *BusinessWeek,* March 1, 2004, pp. 22–23.

26. Anthony W. Ulwick, "Turn Customer Input into Innovation" *Harvard Business Review,* January 2002, pp. 91–97.

27. Sarah Ellison, "P & G Chief's Turnaround Recipe: Find Out What Women Want," *The Wall Street Journal,* June 1, 2005, pp. A1, A16.

28. Adam Aston and Gail Edmonson, "This Volvo Is Not a Guy Thing," *BusinessWeek,* March 15, 2004, pp. 84–86.

29. Joseph Weber, Stanley Holmes, and Christopher Palmeri, "Mosh Pits' of Creativity," *BusinessWeek,* November 7, 2005, pp. 98–100.

30. Peter Lewis, "Texas Instruments' Lunatic Fringe," *Fortune,* September 4, 2006, pp. 121–28.

31. Steve Hoeffler, "Measuring Preferences for Really New Products," *Journal of Marketing Research,* November 2003, pp. 406–20.

32. Christopher Lovelock and Jochen Wirtz, *Services Marketing* (Englewood Cliffs, NJ: Prentice Hall, 2007), pp. 260–84.

33. Larry Huston and Nobil Sakkab, "Connect and Develop," *Harvard Business Review,* March 2006, pp. 58–66; and "Pringles Announces First-of-Its-Kind Technology that Prints Directly on Individual Crisps," www.pg.com, accessed April 6, 2004.

34. Vicki Clift, "Everyone Needs Service Flow Charting," *Marketing News,* October 23, 1995, pp. 41, 43; Mary Jo Bitner, Bernard H. Booms, and Mary Stanfield Tetreault, "The Service Encounter: Diagnosing Favorable and Unfavorable Incidents," *Journal of Marketing,* January 1990, pp. 71–84; Eberhard Scheuing, "Conducting Customer Service Audits," *Journal of Consumer Marketing,* Summer 1989, pp. 35–41; and W. Earl Susser, R. Paul Olsen, and D. Daryl Wyckoff, *Management of Service Operations* (Boston: Allyn & Bacon, 1978).

35. Jack Neff, "White Bread, USA," *Advertising Age,* July 9, 2001, pp. 1, 12, 13.

36. Yuhong Wu, Sridhar Balasubramanian, and Vijay Mahajan, "When Is a Pre-announced New Product Likely to Be Delayed?" *Journal of Marketing,* April 2004, pp. 101–13.

37. Mark Leslie and Charles J. Holloway, "The Sales Learning Curve," *Harvard Business Review,* July–August 2006, pp. 115–23.

38. Kim Schatzel and Roger Calantone, "Creating Market Anticipation: An Exploratory Evaluation of the Effect of Preannouncement Behavior on a New Product Launch," *Journal of the Academy of Marketing Sciences,* Summer 2006, pp. 357–66.

39. Jennifer Ordonez, "How Burger King Got Burned in Quest to Make the Perfect Fry," *The Wall Street Journal,* January 16, 2001, pp. A1, A8.

40. Kerry A. Dolan, "Speed: The New X Factor," *Forbes,* December 26, 2005, pp. 74–77.

Warm Delights: This video case was prepared by David Ford based on interviews with Vivian Millroy Callaway, General Mills.

CHAPTER 11

1. "Tiger Woods, Gatorade Team Up on Gatorade Tiger," *Advertising Age,* October 17, 2007, p. 4; Betsy McKay, "Pepsi Launches Low-Calorie Gatorade," *The Wall Street Journal,* September 7, 2007, p. B6; Cheryl Jackson, "Quaker Acquisition a Big Winner for Pepsi," *Chicago Sun-Times,* December 1, 2006, pp. D1, 5; Darren Rovell, *First in Thirst: How Gatorade Turned the Science of Sweat into a Cultural Phenomenon* (New York: AMACOM, 2005); "Cindy Alston: CMO, Gatorade and Propel," *Advertising Age,* November 13, 2006, p. S6; and "Gatorade Works on Endurance," *The Wall Street Journal,* March 21, 2005, p. B6.

2. For an extended discussion of the generalized product life cycle, see Donald R. Lehmann and Russell S. Winer, *Product Management,* 5th ed (Burr Ridge, IL: McGraw-Hill, 2008).

3. Jack Neff, "Six-Blade Blitz," *Advertising Age,* September 19, 2005, pp. 3, 53; and Jack Neff, "Fusion's Nuclear Launch Isn't Good Enough—Yet," *Advertising Age,* July 3, 2006, pp. 3, 23.

4. John W. Mullins, Orville C. Walker, Jr., Harper W. Boyd, Jr., and Jean-Claude Larréché, *Marketing Management: A Strategic Decision-Making Approach,* 5th ed. (Burr Ridge, IL: McGraw-Hill/Irwin, 2005), p. 396.

5. Portions of this discussion on the fax machine product life cycle are based on Karen Prema, "Faxes Are Evolving," *Purchasing Magazine Online,* March 16, 2006; "When Your Time Has Come—and Gone," *EDN.com,* November 27, 2003; and "Atlas Electronics Corporation," in Roger A. Kerin and Robert A. Peterson, *Strategic Marketing Problems: Cases and Comments,* 8th ed. (Upper Saddle River, NJ: Prentice Hall, 1998), pp. 494–506.

6. "How Many Active Email Mailboxes Are There in the World Today?" The Radicate Group Inc., downloaded January 25, 2007; and "If You Think Fax Is Dead, Think Again," dallasnews.com, downloaded February 10, 2007.

7. Kate MacArthur, "Coke Energizes Tab, Neville Isdell's Fave," *Advertising Age,* August 29, 2005, pp. 3, 21.

8. "Gillette Rings in New Era as World's Leading Male Grooming Brand," Procter & Gamble press release, July 11, 2008.

9. "Hosiery Sales Hit Major Snag," *Dallas Morning News,* December 18, 2006, p. 50.

10. "How to Separate Trends from Fads," *BrandWeek,* October 23, 2000, pp. 30, 32.

11. Everett M. Rogers, *Diffusion of Innovations,* 5th ed. (New York: Free Press, 2003).

12. Jagdish N. Sheth and Banwasi Mitral, *Consumer Behavior: A Managerial Perspective,* 2nd ed. (Mason, OH: South-Western College Publishing, 2003).

13. "When Free Samples Become Saviors," *The Wall Street Journal* August 14, 2001, pp. B1, B4.

14. Terry Box, "Biker Chic," *Dallas Morning News,* June 24, 2007, pp. 1D, 6D; and "Dried Plum Print Push Paces Prunes," *BrandWeek,* August 12, 2002, p. 6.

15. "Dockers Adds Diversity to Message," *BrandWeek,* September 11, 2006, p. 18.

16. "New Balance Steps Up Marketing Drive, *The Wall Street Journal,* March 21, 2008, p. B3.

17. Sheth and Mitral, *Consumer Behavior;* and Marsha Cohen, *Marketing to the 50+ Population* (New York: EPM Communications, Inc., 2007).

18. "General Mills Sees Wealth via Health," *The Wall Street Journal,* February 25, 2008, p. A9; and "A Little Less Salt, A Lot More Sales," *Advertising Age,* March 10, 2008, pp. 1, 23.

19. "Shoppers Beware: Products Shrink But Prices Stay the Same," USAtoday.com, down loaded June 27, 2008; "The Shrink Wrap," *Time,* June 2, 2003, p. 81; "Don't Raise the Price, Lower the Water Award," *BrandWeek,* January 8, 2001, p. 19; and "More For Less," *Consumer Reports,* August 2004, p. 63.

20. This discussion is based on Kevin Lane Keller, *Strategic Brand Management,* 3rd ed. (Upper Saddle River, NJ: Prentice Hall, 2008). Also see, Tulin Erdem, Joffre Swait, and Ana Valenzuela, "Brands as Signals: A Cross-Country Validation Study," *Journal of Marketing,* January 2006, pp. 34–49.

21. Keller, *Strategic Brand Management.*

22. This discussion is based on John Deighton, "How Snapple Got Its Juice Back," *Harvard Business Review,* January 2002, pp. 47–53; and "Can Lender's Get Out of Marketing Pickle? *BrandWeek,* March 5, 2007, p. 6. Also see Vithala R. Rao, Manj K. Agarwal, and Denise Dahlhoff, "How Is Manifest Branding Strategy Related to the Value of a Corporation?" *Journal of Marketing,* October 2004, pp. 125–41.

23. "Hummer Markets Shoes for Offroad Set," *Advertising Age,* January 12, 2004, pp. 3, 40; "Judge Pooh-Poohs Lawsuit over Disney Licensing Fees," USAToday.com, March 30, 2004; and Keller, *Strategic Brand Management.*

24. Rob Osler, "The Name Game: Tips on How to Get It Right," *Marketing News,* September 14, 1998, p. 50; "Porn.com Price May Be Shattered by WallStreet.com," bloomberg.com, October 12, 2007; and Keller, *Strategic Brand Management.* Also see Pamela W. Henderson and Joseph A. Cote, "Guidelines for Selecting or Modifying Logos," *Journal of Marketing,* April 1998, pp. 14–30; and Chiranjeev Kohli and Douglas W. LaBahn, "Creating Effective Brand Names: A Study of the Naming Process," *Journal of Advertising Research,* January–February 1997, pp. 67–75.

25. "When Brand Extension Becomes Brand Abuse," *BrandWeek,* October 26, 1998, pp. 20, 22.

26. This discussion is based on David Aaker, *Brand Portfolio Strategy* (New York: Free Press, 2004); and Ramin Setoodeh, "Barbie vs. Bratz: Which Doll Will Win?" MSNBC.com, December 11, 2006.

27. "Claiborne Seeks to Shed 16 Apparel Brands," *The Wall Street Journal,* July 11, 2007, pp. B1, B2.

28. "Private Labels Stock on Growth," *The Wall Street Journal,* July 18, 2007, p. B8.

29. www.pez.com, downloaded February 1, 2008; David Welch, *Collecting Pez* (Murphysboro, IL: Bubba Scrubba Publications, 1995); and "Elements Design Adds Dimension to Perennial Favorite Pez Brand," *Package Design Magazine,* May 2006, pp. 37–38.

30. "Market Statistics," Packaging-Gateway.com, downloaded March 25, 2007.

31. "Green Bean Casserole Turns 50," *Dallas Morning News,* November 19, 2005, p. 10D.

32. "L'eggs Hatches a New Hosiery Package," *BrandWeek,* January 1, 2001, p. 6.

33. Representative recent scholarly research on packaging and labeling perceptions includes: Priya Rgahubir and Eric A. Greenleaf, "Ratios in Proportion: What Should the Shape of the Package Be?" *Journal of Marketing,* April 2006, pp. 95–107; Peter H. Bloch, Frederic F. Brunel, and Todd Arnold, "Individual Differences in the Centrality of Visual Product Aesthetics: Concept and Measurement," *Journal of Consumer Research,* March 2003, pp. 551–65: and Pamela Anderson, Joan Giese, and Joseph A. Cote, "Impression Management Using Typeface Design," *Journal of Marketing,* October 2004, pp. 60–72.

34. Betsy McKay, "Pepsi's New Marketing Dance: Can Can," *The Wall Street Journal,* January 12, 2007, p. B3.

35. "Asian Brands Are Sprouting English Logos in Pursuit of Status, International Image," *The Wall Street Journal,* August 7, 2001, p. B7C.

36. Susanna Hamner, "Packaging that Pays," *Business 2.0,* July 26, 2006, pp. 68–69.

37. "Wal-Mart: Use Less Packaging," *Dallas Morning News,* September 23, 2006, p. 2D. For an overview of Procter & Gamble's environmental efforts, see *Sustainability Report 2007* (Cincinnati, OH: Procter & Gamble Company, 2008).

38. "Packaging," www.hp.com, downloaded January 17, 2008.

39. This discussion is based on Valarie A. Zeithaml, Mary Jo Bitner, and Dwayne D. Gremler, *Services Marketing: Integrating Customer Focus Across the Firm,* 4th ed. (Burr Ridge, IL: McGraw-Hill/Irwin, 2006).

40. Kent B. Monroe, *Pricing: Making Profitable Decisions,* 3rd ed. (Burr Ridge, IL: McGraw-Hill/Irwin, 2003).

Philadelphia Phillies: This case was prepared by William Rudelius based on interviews with David Montgomery, David Buck, Marisol Lezeano, and Scott Brandreth; internal company materials: and the Phillies website (www. phillies.com).

CHAPTER 12

1. Interview with Erin Patton, The Master Mind Group, June 7, 2007; and "Stephon Marbury—Doing the Right Thing," www.sportsbusiness-news.com, December 11, 2006.

2. Sue Zesiger Callaway, "Bachelor Meets Bugatti, *Fortune,* March 19, 2007, pp. 214–15; and www.bugatti.com.

3. Adapted from Kent B. Monroe, *Pricing: Making Profitable Decisions,* 3rd ed. (New York: McGraw-Hill, 2003).

4. Numerous studies have examined the price-quality-value relationship. See, for example, Jacob Jacoby and Jerry C. Olsen, eds., *Perceived Quality* (Lexington, MA: Lexington Books, 1985); F. Volckner and J. Hoffman, "The Price-Perceived Quality Relationship: A Meta-Analytic Review and Assessment of Its Determinants," *Marketing Letters,* September 2007, pp. 181–96. For a thorough review of the price-quality-value relationship, see Valerie A. Ziethami, "Consumer Perceptions of Price, Quality, and Value," *Journal of Marketing,* July 1988, pp. 2–22.

5. Roger A. Kerin and Robert A. Peterson, "Crestfield Furniture Industries, Inc. (A)," *Strategic Marketing Problems: Cases and Comments,* 11th ed. (Upper Saddle River, NJ: Prentice Hall, 2007), pp. 275–86.

6. For the classic description of skimming and penetration pricing, see Joel Dean, "Pricing Policies for New Products," *Harvard Business Review,* November–December 1976, pp. 141–53.

7. Jean-Noel Kapferer, *The New Strategic Brand Management,* 4th ed. (London: Kogan Page Ltd., 2008).

8. "Premium AA Alkaline Batteries," *Consumer Reports,* March 21, 2002, p. 54; Kemp Powers, "Assault and Batteries," *Forbes,* September 4, 2000, pp. 54, 56; and "Razor Burn at Gillette," *BusinessWeek,* June 18, 2001, p. 37.

9. "Why That Deal Is Only $9.99," *BusinessWeek,* January 10, 2000, p. 36. For further reading on odd-even pricing, see Mark Stiving and Russell S. Winer, "An Empirical Analysis of Price Endings with Scanner Data," *Journal of Consumer Research,* June 1997, pp. 57–67; and Robert M. Schindler, "Patterns of Rightmost Digits Used in Advertised Prices: Implications for Nine-Ending Effects," *Journal of Consumer Research,* September 1997, pp. 192–201.

10. For an overview on target pricing, see Stephan A. Butscher and Michael Laker, "Market Driven Product Development," *Marketing Management,* Summer 2000, pp. 48–53.

11. Monroe, *Pricing,* pp. 420–30.

12. Peter M. Noble and Thomas S. Gruca, "Industrial Pricing: Theory and Managerial Practice," *Marketing Science* 18, no. 3 (1999), pp. 435–54.

13. George E. Belch and Michael A. Belch, *Introduction to Advertising and Promotion,* 7th ed. (New York: McGraw-Hill/Irwin, 2007).

14. "Is the Music Store Over?" *Business 2.0,* March 2004, pp. 115–19.

15. Robert J. Dolan and Hermann Simon, *Power Pricing: How Managing Price Transforms the Bottom Line* (New York: Free Press, 1996).

16. "Why Gas Won't Get Cheaper," *Time,* May 9, 2005, pp. 40–41

17. For an overview on motion picture economics, see Charles C. Moul, ed., *A Concise Handbook of Movie Industry Economics* (Cambridge: Cambridge University Press, 2005).

18. Information pertaining to HDTV is based on Pete Engardio, "Flat Panels, Thin Margins," *BusinessWeek,* February 26, 2007, pp. 50–51.

19. "Six Vitamin Firms Agree to Settle Price-Fixing Suit," *The Wall Street Journal,* October 11, 2000, p. B10.

20. "How Dell Fine-Tunes Its PC Pricing to Gain Edge in a Slow Market," *The Wall Street Journal,* June 8, 2001, pp. A1, A8.

21. Michael Levy and Barton A. Weitz, *Retailing Management,* 6th ed. (Burr Ridge, IL: McGraw-Hill/Irwin, 2007).

22. "The Web's Role as Equalizer," *BusinessWeek Online,* May 13, 2002; and "Are Minority Shoppers Treated Unfairly? An Expensive Reason to Care," www.diversityinc.com, downloaded May 18, 2002.

The Starbury Collection: This case was written by Roger A. Kerin based on interviews and materials provided by Erin Patton, The Master Mind Group.

CHAPTER 13

1. Jerry Useem, "Simply Irresistible," *Fortune,* March 19, 2007, pp. 107–12; Nick Wingfield, "How Apple's Store Strategy Beat the Odds," *The Wall Street Journal,* May 17, 2006, pp. B1, B10; Kevin O'Marah, "The Top 25 Supply Chains—2007," *Supply Chain Management Review,* September 2007, pp. 16–22; and www.apple.com/retail, downloaded May 20, 2008.

2. Andrew Raskin, "Who's Minding the Store?" *Business 2.0,* February 2003, pp. 70–74.

3. "Eddie Bauer's Banner Time of Year," *Advertising Age,* October 1, 2001, p. 55.

4. www.generalmills.com, downloaded May 15, 2008; Emily Woon, "Cereal Partners Worldwide Exploits Developing Markets," www.euromonitor.com, November 1, 2007; and Ian Friendly, "Cereal Partners Worldwide: A World of Opportunity," Nestlé Invester Seminar, Vevey, Switzerland, June 8, 2005.

5. For an overview of vertical marketing systems, see Lou Peltson, David Strutton, and James R. Lumpkin, *Marketing Channels,* 2nd ed. (Burr Ridge, IL: McGraw-Hill/Irwin, 2002), chapter 11.

6. For an extended discussion on retail distribution, see Anne T. Couglan, Erin Anderson, Louis W. Stern, and Adel I. El-Ansary, *Marketing Channels,* 7th ed. (Upper Saddle River, NJ: Prentice Hall, 2006).

7. Ethan Smith, "Why a Grand Plan to Cut CD Prices Went Off the Track," *The Wall Street Journal,* June 4, 2004, pp. A1, A6; and "Feud with Seller Hurts Nike Sales, Shares," *Dallas Morning News,* June 28, 2003, p. 30.

8. "Dealer Surplus," *Forbes,* October 16, 2006, pp. 50–52; and Kevin Kelleher, "Giving Dealers a Raw Deal," *Business 2.0,* December 2004, pp. 82–83.

9. Representative studies that explore the dimensions and use of power and influence in marketing channels include the following: Kenneth A. Hunt, John T. Mentzer, and Jeffrey E. Danes, "The Effect of Power Sources on Compliance in a Channel of Distribution: A Causal Model," *Journal of Business Research,* October 1987, pp. 377–98; John F. Gaski, "Interrelations among a Channel Entity's Power Sources: Impact of the Exercise of Reward and Coercion on Expert, Referent, and Legitimate Power Sources," *Journal of Marketing Research,* February 1986, pp. 62–67; Gary Frazier and John O. Summers, "Interfirm Influence Strategies and Their Application within Distribution Channels," *Journal of Marketing,* Summer 1984, pp. 43–55; George H. Lucas and Larry G. Gresham, "Power Conflict, Control, and the Application of Contingency Theory in Channels of Distribution," *Journal of the Academy of Marketing Science,* Summer 1985, pp. 27–37; F. Robert Dwyer and Julie Gassenheimer, "Relational Roles and Triangle Dramas: Effects on Power Play and Sentiments in Industrial Channels," *Marketing Letters* 3 (1992), pp. 187–200; Jean L. Johnson, Tomoaki Sakano, Joseph A. Cote, and Naoto Onzo, "The Exercise of Interfirm Power and its Repercussions in U.S.–Japanese Channel Relationships," *Journal of Marketing,* April 1993, pp. 1–10; and Janice M. Payan and Richard G. McFarland, "Decomposing Influence Strategies: Argument Structure and Dependence as Determinants of the Effectiveness of Influence Strategies in Gaining Channel Member Compliance," *Journal of Marketing,* July 2005, pp. 66–79.

10. David Simchi-Levi, Philip Kaminsky, and Edith Simchi-Levi, *Designing and Managing the Supply Chain,* 3rd ed. (Burr Ridge, IL: McGraw-Hill/Irwin, 2007).

11. Jeffrey McCracken, "Ford Seeks Big Savings by Overhauling Supply System," *The Wall Street Journal,* September 29, 2005, p. All; April Terreri, "Driving Efficiencies in Automotive Logistics," www.inboundlogistics.com, January 2004; and Robyn Meredith, "Harder Than Hype," *Forbes,* April 16, 2001, pp. 188–94.

12. Major portions of this discussion are based on Sunil Chopra and Peter Meindl, *Supply Chain Management: Strategy, Planning, and Operations,* 3rd ed. (Upper Saddle River, NJ: Prentice Hall, 2007), chapters 1–3; and Hau L. Lee, "The Triple-A Supply Chain," *Harvard Business Review,* October 2004, pp. 102–12.

13. David Drickhamer, "Supply-Chain Superstars," *Industry Week,* May 1, 2004, pp. 5–7; "IBM Leans Out Its Supply Chain," *Modern Materials Handling,* November 9, 2005, p. 35; Brian T. Eck and Murry Mitchell, "Transformation at IBM," *Supply Chain Management,* November–December 2003, pp. 56–62; and Thomas A. Foster, "World's Best-Run Supply Chains Stay on Top Regardless of the Competition," *Global Logistics & Supply Chain Strategies,* February 2006, pp. 27–41.

14. This discussion is based on Kathryn Jones, "The Dell Way," *Business 2.0,* February 2003, pp. 61–66; Charles Fishman, "The Wal-Mart You Don't Know," *Fast Company,* December 2003, pp. 68–80; "Michael Dell: Still Betting on the Future of Online Commerce and Supply Chain Efficiencies," Knowledge@Wharton, September 7, 2006; and Chopra and Meindl, *Supply Chain Management.*

15. "Beyond Buying," *The Wall Street Journal,* March 10, 2008, p. R8.

16. "Logistics Are in Vogue with Desiqners," *The wall Street Journal,* June 27, 2008, P. B1.

17. Chopra and Meindl, *Supply Chain Management.*

Golden Valley Microwave foods: This case was written by Thomas J. Belich, Mark T. Spriggs, and Steven W. Hartley based on personal interviews with Jack McKeon and Frank Lynch, company data they provided, and the following sources: "Snagging a Pop Fly," *Snack Food and Wholesale Bakery* (May 2004), p. 48; "Choosing the Right Growth Strategy," *PR Newswire* (November 13, 2003); and "Company Information," from the website (see www.actii.com/company).

CHAPTER 14

1. Paige Wiser, "Dressing Rooms of the Future: All Eyes On You," *Chicago Sun-Times,* April 29, 2007, p. A24; Vanessa O'Connell, "Reinventing the Luxury Department Store," *The Wall Street Journal,*

July 15–16, 2006, p. P1; Teresa Mez, "High-tech Dressing Rooms Become Virtual Reality," *Christian Science Monitor,* April 20, 2007, p. 11; "Magic Mirror Debuts at NRF Convention & Expo," *Display & Design Ideas,* January 16, 2007; and "Neiman Launches Cusp," www.shopdiary.com, July 27, 2006; Joseph Olewitz, "Facebook Meets the Mall," Icon Nicholson Media Release, http://www.iconnicholson.com/news/press_releases/doc/nrf011407.pdf, January 14, 2007.

2. Kate Betts, "So You Want To Be a Designer," *Time,* May 17, 2004, p. 85.

3. "Fortune 500 Ranked Within Industries," *Fortune,* May 5, 2008, pp. F-46–60.

4. International Monetary Fund, *World Economic Outlook Database,* April 2008; *Statistical Abstract of the United States: 2008,* 127th ed. (Washington, DC: U.S. Department of Commerce, Bureau of the Census, 2008), Table 20.

5. "Fortune Global 500," *Fortune,* July 23, 2007, p. 133.

6. "Retail Trade—Establishments, Employees, and Payroll," *Statistical Abstract of the United States: 2007,* 126th ed., (Washington, DC: U.S. Department of Commerce, Bureau of the Census, 2007), pp. 651–52; "County Business Patterns," Bureau of the Census, www.census.gov/epcd/cbp/view/cbpview.html (accessed May 29, 2007).

7. Matthew Boyle, Jenny Mero, and Dana Castillo, "Why Costco Is So Damn Addictive," *Fortune,* October 30, 2006, p. 126; Andrew A. Caffey, "Are You Franchisee Material?" *Entrepreneur,* January 2007; Tanisha A. Sykes, "Prosper With Innovative Business Ideas," *Black Enterprise,* May 2007, p. 132; and Nichole L. Torres, "Turn Up the Crazy," *Entrepreneur,* May 2007.

8. "Franchise 500," *Entrepreneur,* January 2007; and Scott Shane and Chester Spell, "Factors for New Franchise Success," *Sloan Management Review,* Spring 1998, pp. 43–50.

9. "US Airways Enhancing Customer Service With New Self-Service Check-In Kiosks," *Business Wire,* May 30, 2007; Kyla King, "Self-service Evolves with Technology," *The Star-Ledger,* April 29, 2007, p. 3; Michelle Higgins, "Go Directly to Your Room Key! Pass the Desk!" *The New York Times,* August 20, 2006, p. 6; and Peter C. Honebein and Roy F. Cammarano, "Customers at Work," *Marketing Management,* January/February 2006, pp. 26–31.

10. Michael A. Wiles, "The Effect of Customer Service on Retailers' Shareholder Wealth: The Role of Availability and Reputation Cues," *Journal of Retailing,* 2007, pp. 19–31; Cate T. Corcoran, "Nordstrom 'Simplifies' Customer Satisfaction," *Women's Wear Daily,* March 22, 2007, p. 8; Vanessa O'Connell, "Posh Retailers Pile on Perks for Top Customers," *The Wall Street Journal,* April 26, 2007, p. D1; and Robert Berner, "Retail: This Rising Tide Won't Lift All Boats," *BusinessWeek,* January 12, 2004, p. 114.

11. Mathew Boyle, "Best Buy's Giant Gamble," *Fortune,* April 3, 2006, p. 68; and Pallavi Gogoi, "Staples Makes Selling Look Easy," *BusinessWeek Online,* December 7, 2006.

12. Chris Serres, "Your Next-Tech Toy Might Come from a Vending Machine," *Star Tribune,* December 9, 2006, p. 1D; "Zoom Unveils Motorola-Themed Vending Machines," *Airports,* October 31, 2006, p. 2; Elliot Maras, "State of the Vending Industry Report," *Automatic Merchandiser,* August, 2006, pp. 40–56; and "Sony Tests Luxury Vending Machines Nationwide," *Display & Design Ideas,* June 16, 2006.

13. Hisashi Kiyooka Yomiuri Shimbun, "Cell Phones Fast Becoming E-wallets," *Daily Yomiuri,* January 24, 2006, p. 8; "Convenience to the Max," *CSNews Online,* September 7, 2006; "Nation's First Automated Video Rental Store Opens in Reno," *Display & Design Ideas,* January 25, 2007; and Andy Reinhardt, "A Machine-to-Machine Internet of Things," *BusinessWeek,* April 26, 2004, p. 102.

14. "DMA Encourages Catalog & Direct Mail Recycling," *PR Newswire,* May 23, 2007; and "IKEA in the World," www.idkea.com, accessed June 1, 2007.

15. Sandra Guy, "Sears to Light Up Ad Plan, Expands Catalog Concept for New Century," *Chicago Sun-Times,* May 5, 2007, p. 25; Monica Roman, "You Gotta Have a Catalog," *BusinessWeek,* May 14, 2001, p. 56; and Beth Viveiros, "Catalog and Internet Sales Grow More Quickly than Retail," *Direct,* July 2001.

16. "Corporate Facts," from the QVC website, www.qvc.com, accessed June 1, 2007.

17. "QVC, NFL, and GSI Commerce to Create New, Multichannel, Direct-to-Consumer Opportunity," QVC press release, May 23, 2007; Gina Salamone, "Shopping With the Stars. QVC Viewers Take a Shine to Celeb Lines," *Daily News,* October 1, 2006, p. 14; Ron Grover and Deborah Stead, "Adding Some Sparkle to QVC," *BusinessWeek,* September 25, 2006, p. 16; and Stewart Schley, "New Technologies Send Sales Execs Back to School; Reps Bone Up on VOD, Interactive TV, and 'Addressable' Applications," *Multichannel News,* May 7, 2007, p. 5A.

18. "Order Online, Pick Up Items at Local Wal-Mart," *St. Petersburg Times,* May 23, 2007, p. 1D; and Nikki Hopewell, "Marketing Factbook; Online Retail Sales," *Marketing News,* July 15, 2006, p. 37.

19. "Former Cendant Marketing Chief Will Help Company Leverage Core Media Products while Broadening Member Benefit Offerings," *PR Newswire,* February 21, 2001; Tim Mullaney, "And All the Price Trimmings," *BusinessWeek,* December 18, 2000, p. 68; Mary J. Cronin, "Business Secrets of the Billion-Dollar Website," *Fortune,* February 2, 1998, p. 142; Robert D. Hof, Ellen Neuborne, and Heather Green, "Amazon.com: The Wild World of E-Commerce," *BusinessWeek,* December 14, 1998, pp. 106–19; "Future Shop," *Forbes ASAP,* April 6, 1998, pp. 37–52; Chris Taylor, "Cybershop," *Time,* November 23, 1998, p. 142; Stephen H. Wildstrom, "'Bots' Don't Make Great Shoppers," *BusinessWeek,* December 7, 1998, p. 14; and Jeffrey Ressner, "Online Flea Markets," *Time,* October 5, 1998, p. 48.

20. Roger O. Crocket, "Let the Buyer Compare," *BusinessWeek,* September 3, 2001, p. EB10.

21. Thomas L. Zeller and David R. Kublank, "Focused E-Tail Measurement and Resource Management," *Business Horizons,* January–February 2002, pp. 53–60.

22. "Economic Impact: U.S. Direct Marketing Today Executive Summary—2003," Direct Marketing Association, New York; and Kelly Shermach, "Outsourcing Seen as a Way to Cut Costs, Retain Service," *Marketing News,* June 19, 1995, pp. 5, 8.

23. Deborah L. Vence, "Majority Rules," Marketing News, February 15, 2006, p. 4; Catherine Arnold, "Law Gives Industry a Buzz," *Marketing News,* February 1, 2004, p. 11; Scott Reeves, "Back to (Old) School, 'Do-Not-Call' Revives Door-to-Door Sales," *Marketing News,* December 8, 2003, p. 13; and "Direct Marketing," *Marketing News,* January 15, 2004, p. 16.

24. "Direct Selling by the Numbers," Direct Selling Association, www.dsa.org; and "Need Income? Try Direct Selling," *Grand Rapids Press,* March 18, 2007, p. G1.

25. Anya Sostek, "It's Not Your Mother's Tupperware Party," *Pittsburgh Post-Gazette,* July 23, 2006, p. C1; and "Avon, The Net, and Glass Ceilings," *BusinessWeek,* February 6, 2006, p. 104.

26. Francis J. Mulhern and Robert P. Leon, "Implicit Price Bundling of Retail Products: A Multiproduct Approach to Maximizing Store Profitability," *Journal of Marketing,* October 1991, pp. 63–76.

27. Marc Vanhuele and Xavier Dreze, "Measuring the Price Knowledge Shoppers Bring to the Store," *Journal of Marketing,* October 2002, pp. 72–85.

28. Gwen Ortmeyer, John A. Quelch, and Walter Salmon, "Restoring Credibility to Retail Pricing," *Sloan Management Review,* Fall 1991, pp. 55–66.

29. William B. Dodds, "In Search of Value: How Price and Store Name Information Influence Buyers' Product Perceptions," *Journal of Consumer Marketing,* Spring 1991, pp. 15–24.

30. Leonard L. Berry, "Old Pillars of New Retailing," *Harvard Business Review,* April 2001, pp. 131–37.

31. Eric Anderson and Duncan Simester, "Mind Your Pricing Cues," *Harvard Business Review,* September 2003, pp. 96–103.

32. Julie Baker, A. Parasuraman, Dhruv Grewal, and Glenn B. Voss, "The Influence of Multiple Store Environment Cues on Perceived Merchandise Value and Patronage Intentions," *Journal of Marketing,* April 2002, pp. 120–41.

33. Hyeong Min Kim, "Consumer Responses to Price Presentation Formats in Rebate Advertisements," *Journal of Retailing,* no. 4 (2006), pp. 309–17.

34. Rita Koselka, "The Schottenstein Factor," *Forbes,* September 28, 1992, pp. 104, 106.

35. Barry Brown, "Edmonton Makes Size Pay Off in Down Market," *Advertising Age,* January 27, 1992, pp. 4–5.

36. James R. Lowry, "The Life Cycle of Shopping Centers," *Business Horizons,* January–February 1997, pp. 77–86; Eric Peterson, "Power Centers! Now!" *Stores,* March 1989, pp. 61–66; and "Power Centers Flex Their Muscle," *Chain Store Age Executive,* February 1989, pp. 3A, 4A.

37. Robert A. Peterson and Sridhar Balasubramanian, "Retailing in the 21st Century: Reflections and Prologue to Research," *Journal of Retailing,* Spring 2002, pp. 9–16.

38. Jim Carter and Norman Sheehan, "From Competition to Cooperation: E-Tailing's Integration with Retailing," *Business Horizons,* March–April 2004, pp. 71–8.

39. Pierre Martineau, "The Personality of the Retail Store," *Harvard Business Review,* January–February 1958, p. 47.

40. Julie Baker, Dhruv Grewal, and A. Parasuraman, "The Influence of Store Environment on Quality Inferences and Store Image," *Journal of the Academy of Marketing Science,* Fall 1994, pp. 328–39; Howard Barich and Philip Kotler, "A Framework for Marketing Image Management," *Sloan Management Review,* Winter 1991, pp. 94–104; Susan M. Keaveney and Kenneth A. Hunt, "Conceptualization and Operationalization of Retail Store Image: A Case of Rival Middle-Level Theories," *Journal of the Academy of Marketing Science,* Spring 1992, pp. 165–75; James C. Ward, Mary Jo Bitner, and John Barnes, "Measuring the Prototypicality and Meaning of Retail Environments," *Journal of Retailing,* Summer 1992, p. 194; and Dhruv Grewal, R. Krishnan, Julie Baker, and Norm Burin, "The Effect of Store Name, Brand Name and Price Discounts on Consumers' Evaluations and Purchase Intentions," *Journal of Retailing,* Fall 1998, pp. 331–52. For a review of the store image literature, see Mary R. Zimmer and Linda L. Golden, "Impressions of Retail Stores: A Content Analysis of Consumer Images," *Journal of Retailing,* Fall 1988, pp. 265–93.

41. Mary Jo Bitner, "Servicescapes: The Impact of Physical Surroundings on Customers and Employees," *Journal of Marketing,* April 1992, pp. 57–71.

42. Jans-Benedict Steenkamp and Michel Wedel, "Segmenting Retail Markets on Store Image Using a Consumer-Based Methodology," *Journal of Retailing,* Fall 1991, p. 300; and Philip Kotler, "Atmospherics as a Marketing Tool," *Journal of Retailing* 49 (Winter 1973–74), p. 61.

43. Roger A. Kerin, Ambuj Jain and Daniel L. Howard, "Store Shopping Experience and Consumer Price-Quality-Value Perceptions," *Journal of Retailing,* Winter 1992, pp. 376–97.

44. Kusum L. Ailwadi and Bari Harlam, "An Empirical Analysis of the Determinants of Retail Margins: The Role of Store-Brand Share," *Journal of Marketing,* January 2004, pp. 147–65; Joseph Tarnowski, "And the Awards Went to …" *Progressive Grocer,* April 15, 2004; Betsy Spethmann, "Shelf Sets," *Promo,* May 1, 2004, p. 6; and "Study Shows Continued Support for Category Management," *CSNews Online,* March 17, 2004.

45. John Davis, *Measuring Marketing* (Singapore: John Wiley & Sons, 2007), p. 46

46. Paul W. Farris, Neil T. Bendle, Phillip E. Pfeifer, David J. Reibstein, *Marketing Metrics* (Philadelphia: Wharton School Publishing, 2006), p. 106; Jerry Useem, "Simply Irresistible," *Fortune,* March 19, 2007, pp. 107–12; "Apple 2.0," www.blogs.business2.com; Steve Lohr, "Apple, a Success at Stores, Bets Big on Fifth Avenue," *The New York Times,* May 19, 2006; Jim Dalrymple, "Inside the Apple Stores," *MacWorld,* June 2007, pp. 16–17; and Davis, *Measuring Marketing,* pp. 280–81.

47. The wheel of retailing theory was originally proposed by Malcolm P. McNair, "Significant Trends and Development in the Postwar Period," in A. B. Smith, ed., *Competitive Distribution in a Free, High-Level Economy and Its Implications for the University* (Pittsburgh: University of Pittsburgh Press, 1958), pp. 1–25; also see Stephen Brown, "The Wheel of Retailing—Past and Future," *Journal of Retailing,* Summer 1990, pp. 143–49; and Malcolm P. McNair and Eleanor May, "The Next Revolution of the Retailing Wheel," *Harvard Business Review,* September–October 1978, pp. 81–91.

48. Michael Arndt, "McDonald's 24/7," *BusinessWeek,* February 5, 2007, p. 64; "Resolved: No Trans Fats in 2007," *BusinessWeek,* January 15, 2007, p. 27; Kate Macarthur, "McDonald's Coffee," *Advertising Age,* November 13, 2006, p. S-10; and Bill Saporito, "What's for Dinner?" *Fortune,* May 15, 1995, pp. 51–64.

49. William R. Davidson, Albert D. Bates, and Stephen J. Bass, "Retail Life Cycle," *Harvard Business Review,* November–December 1976, pp. 89–96.

Mall of America: This case was written by David P. Brennan and is based on an interview with Maureen Cahill and materials provided by Mall of America.

CHAPTER 15

1. Jennifer Netherby, "High-Def Keeps Growing," *Video Business,* January 8, 2007, p. 23; "Rewind," *Promo,* December 1, 2006, p. 30; Gregory A. Quirk, "Rivalry in Consoles Is No Game," *Electronic Engineering Times,* May 14, 2007, p. H92; Lewis Lazare, "Wii Effort Should Inspire More 'Wow,'" *Chicago Sun-Times,* December 5, 2006, p. 57; "Drinks Brands in Wii Promotion," *In Store Marketing,* June 11, 2007, p. 7; Joanne Payne, "Nintendo Plans Live Wii Stunts for Pirates Release," *Brand Republic News,* May 29, 2007, p. 1; "Sony Computer Entertainment America Announces New Marketing Campaign for PlayStation 3: Inspiring Gamers to 'Play Beyond,'" *PR Newswire,* November 15, 2006; Beth Snyder Bulik, "PS3, Wii Get All the Buzz, but Xbox Could Have the Happiest Holidays," *Advertising Age,* October 30, 2006, p. 3.

2. Shu-pei Tsai, "Integrated Marketing As Management of Holistic Consumer Experience," *Business Horizons* 48 (2005), pp. 431–41; and Mike Reid, Sandra Luxton, and Felix Mavondo, "The Relationship Between Integrated Marketing Communication, Market Orientation, and Brand Orientation," *The Journal of Advertising* 34 (Winter 2005), pp. 11–23.

3. Wilbur Schramm, "How Communication Works," in Wilbur Schramm, ed., *The Process and Effects of Mass Communication* (Urbana, IL: University of Illinois Press, 1955), pp. 3–26.

4. E. Cooper and M. Jahoda, "The Evasion of Propaganda," *Journal of Psychology* 22 (1947), pp. 15–25; H. Hyman and P. Sheatsley, "Some Reasons Why Information Campaigns Fail," *Public Opinion Quarterly* 11 (1947), pp. 412–23; and J. T. Klapper, *The Effects of Mass Communication* (New York: Free Press, 1960), chap. VII.

5. Cynthia L. Kemper, "Biting Wax Tadpole, Other Faux Pas," *Denver Post,* August 3, 1997, p. G4.

6. Rik Pieters and Michel Wedel, "Attention Capture and Transfer in Advertising: Brand Pictorial, and Text-Size Effects," *Journal of Marketing,* April 2004, pp. 36–50.

7. Adapted from *Dictionary of Marketing Terms,* 2nd ed., Peter D. Bennett, ed. (Chicago: American Marketing Association, 1995), p. 231.

8. David Robinson, "Public Relations Comes of Age," *Business Horizons* 49 (2006), pp. 247–56; and Dick Martin, "Gilded and Gelded: Hard-Won Lessons from the PR Wars," *Harvard Business Review,* October 2003, pp. 44–54.

9. "RSS, Blogs, Podcast and Social Media Experts to Share Knowledge at PR Online Convergence Conference," *Business Wire,* April 11, 2007; "Business and the Media Forum Focuses on Social Media," *Business Wire,* July 9, 2007; Sarah Murray, "Public Relations: The Ease of Online Communication Is Undermining Companies' Control of Their Image and Reputation," *Financial Times,* November 8, 2006, p. 14; and Matthew Creamer, "Slowly, Marketers Learn How to Let Go and Let Blog," *Advertising Age,* October 31, 2005, p. 1.

10. Marsha d. Loda and Barbara Carrick Coleman, "Sequence Matters: A More Effective Way to Use Advertising and Publicity," *Journal of Advertising Research* 45 (December 2005), pp. 362–71.

11. Amy Johannes, "Made For Each Other," *Promo,* June 1, 2007, p. 16.

12. Kusum L Ailawadi, Scott A. Neslin, and Karen Gedenk, "Pursuing the Value-Conscious Consumer: Store Brands versus National Brand Promotions," *Journal of Marketing,* January 2001, pp. 71–89.

13. B. C. Cotton and Emerson M. Babb, "Consumer Response to Promotional Deals," *Journal of Marketing* 42 (July 1978), pp. 109–13.

14. Robert George Brown, "Sales Response to Promotions and Advertising," *Journal of Advertising Research* 14 (August 1974), pp. 33–40.

15. Adapted from *Economic Impact: U.S. Direct Marketing Today* (New York: Direct Marketing Association, 1998), p. 25.

16. Siva K. Balasubramanian and V. Kumar, "Analyzing Variations in Advertising and Promotional Expenditures: Key Correlates in Consumer, Industrial, and Service Markets," *Journal of Marketing,* April 1990, pp. 57–68.

17. "Multitasking Sports Viewers Engaged With Advertising," *PR Newswire US,* June 28, 2007; Alice Z. Cuneo, "Yard' Sale? Sprite Talks to Teen with Mobile Promotions, Coca-Cola Launches Interactive Site in Shift from Traditional Media to the 'Critical' Third Screen," *Advertising Age,* June 11, 2007, p. 23; "How Is Multitasking Affecting TV Networks and Online Video Sites?" *Business Wire,* February 6, 2007; Greg Lindsay, "Demanding Boomers, MultiTasking Gen Yers Decide What, How, When," *Advertising Age,* January 2, 2006, p. 22; Don E. Shultz, "Include SIMM in Modern Media Plans," *Marketing News,* January 15, 2004, p. 6; and Christopher Vollmer, John Frelinghuysen, and Randall Rothenberg, "The Future of Advertising Is Now," *Strategy 1 Business* 43 (Summer 2006), pp. 38–51.

18. James M. Olver and Paul W. Farris, "Push and Pull: A One-Two Punch for Packages Products," *Sloan Management Review,* Fall 1989, pp. 53–61.

19. Terry Box, "Pressure's Rising for Ford Dealers," *Dallas Morning News,* February 10, 2007; and Richard Truett, "Ford to Dealers: We'll Support Sales," *Automotive News,* June 18, 2007, p. 3.

20. Fusun F. Gonul, Franklin Carter, Elina Petrova, and Kannan Srinivasan, "Promotion of Prescription Drugs and Its Impact on Physicians' Choice Behavior," *Journal of Marketing,* July 2001, pp. 79–90.

21. Robert J. Lavidge and Gary A. Steiner, "A Model for Predictive Measurement of Advertising Effectiveness," *Journal of Marketing,* October 1961, p. 61.

22. "100 Leading National Advertisers," *Advertising Age,* June 25, 2007, 51–517.

23. Don E. Schultz and Anders Gronstedt, "Making Marcom an Investment," *Marketing Management,* Fall 1997, pp. 41–49; and J. Enrique Bigne, "Advertising Budget Practices: A Review," *Journal of Current Issues and Research in Advertising,* Fall 1995, pp. 17–31.

24. John Philip Jones, "Ad Spending: Maintaining Market Share," *Harvard Business Review,* January–February 1990, pp. 38–42; and Charles H. Patti and Vincent Blanko, "Budgeting Practices of Big Advertisers," *Journal of Advertising Research* 21 (December 1981), pp. 23–30.

25. James A. Schroer, "Ad Spending: Growing Market Share," *Harvard Business Review,* January–February 1990, pp. 44–48.

26. James E. Lynch and Graham J. Hooley, "Increasing Sophistication in Advertising Budget Setting," *Journal of Advertising Research* 30 (February–March 1990), pp. 67–75.

27. Jimmy D. Barnes, Brenda J. Muscove, and Javad Rassouli, "An Objective and Task Media Selection Decision Model and Advertising Cost Formula to Determine International Advertising Budgets," *Journal of Advertising* 11, no. 4 (1982), pp. 68–75.

28. Don E. Schultz, "Olympics Get the Gold Medal in Integrating Marketing Event," *Marketing News,* April 27, 1998, pp. 5, 10.

29. Cornelia Pechman, Guangzhi Zhao, Marvin E. Goldberg, and Ellen Thomas Reibling, "What to Convey in Antismoking Advertisements for Adolescents: The Use of Protection Motivation Theory to Identify Effective Message Themes," *Journal of Marketing,* April 2003, pp. 1–18.

30. "More from Adage.com/Madisonandvine," *Advertising Age,* April 28, 2008, p. 22; T. L. Stanley, "LG, 7-Eleven to Pump Paramount's 'Iron Man,'" Brandweek.com, January 7, 2008; and T. L. Stanley, "Tie-ins: BK, 7-Eleven Adding Bulk to Hulk Redux," Brandweek.com, April 21, 2008.

31. Mike Reid, "Performance Auditing of Integrated Marketing Communication (IMC) Actions and Outcomes," *Journal of Advertising* 34 (Winter 2005), p. 41.

32. Jeremy Jullman, "Retooled Starcom Makes Its Own Rules," *Advertising Age,* February 26, 2007, p. S-12; and www.starcomworldwide.com, July 21, 2007.

33. Tom Duncan, "Is Your Marketing Communications Integrated?" *Advertising Age,* January 24, 1994, p. 26.

34. Don E. Schultz, "IMC Is Do or Die in New Pull Marketplace," *Marketing News,* August 15, 2006, p. 7; and Don E. Schultz, "Integration's New Role Focuses on Customers," *Marketing News,* September 15, 2006, p. 8.

35. *Direct Marketing Key Statistics at a Glance, 2006–2007* (New York: Direct Marketing Association, 2006), pp. 1, 5; and *Statistical Fact Book,* 29th ed. (New York: Direct Marketing Association, 2007), p. 17, 18.

36. Robert Berner, "Going that Extra Inch," *BusinessWeek,* September 18, 2000, p. 84.

37. Adapted from *Economic Impact: U.S. Direct Marketing Today* (New York: Direct Marketing Association, 1998), pp. 25–26.

38. Patricia ODell, "Hello, Old Friend," *Promo,* February 1, 2007, p. 26.

39. Julie Tilsner, "Lillian Vernon: Creating a Host of Spin-offs from Its Core Catalog," *BusinessWeek,* December 19, 1994, p. 85; and Lisa Coleman, "I Went Out and Did It," *Forbes,* August 17, 1992, pp. 102–4.

40. "The Data Dilemma," *Marketing Direct,* February 6, 2007, p. 37; and Marc Nohr, "South Africa—A Worthy Contender," *Marketing Direct,* March 5, 2007, p. 20.

41. Allison Enright, "Direct Mail Challenged," *Marketing News,* April 1, 2007, p. 3; Juliana Koranten, "European Privacy Rules Go into Effect in 15 EU States," *Advertising Age,* October 26, 1998, p. S31; and Rashi Glazer, "The Illusion of Privacy and Competition for Attention," *Journal of Interactive Marketing,* Summer 1998, pp. 2–4.

42. "Spam Is Now 77% of All E-Mail," *The Calgary Herald,* February 1, 2007, p. E1; Randi Schmelzer, "Opt-in E-mail Offers Welcome, Extended Interactions," *PR Week,* June 11, 2007, p. 11; "Opt-in Plans Could Spell Disaster for DM," *Printweek,* June 7, 2007, p. 24; "Japan to Toughen Regulations on Unsolicited E-mails," *Japan Economic Newswire,* July 17, 2007; LaToya Dream Rembert, "Will CAN-SPAM Affect You?" *Marketing Research,* Spring 2004, p. 8; and Douglas Wood and David Brosse, "Mulling E-Mail Options," *Promo,* September 2001, p. 18.

Las Vegas: This case was prepared by Steven Hartley and Roger Kerin. Sources: Bob Garfield, "This Time, Vegas Tourism Gets the Credit It Deserves," *Advertising Age,* August 21, 2006, p. 25; Greg Lindsay, Las Vegas Turns Inward for Next Act," *Advertising Age,* June 5, 2006, p. 10; Hilary Potkewitz, "As Demand Grows, Airlines Say, 'Viva, Las Vegas!'" *Crain's New York Business,* September 27, 2007, p. 30; Marc Graser, "Marketers Have A Lot To Learn About Good Integration," *Advertising Age,* February 20, 2006, p. 4; Corey Hajim and Kate Bonamici, "Insider's Guide to Vegas," *Fortune,* January 23, 2006, p 154; Rich Thomaselli, "Las Vegas Ad Slogan Takes On Life Of Its Own," *Advertising Age,* March 8, 2004, p. 6; Joel Stein and Laura A. Locke, "The Strip Is Back!," *Time,* July 26, 2004, p. 22; Julie Rawe, "Vegas Plays to the World," *Time,* July 26, 2004, p. 34; and information contained on the Las Vegas Convention and Visitors Authority website (www.lvcva.com) and the R&R Partners website (www.rrpartners.com).

CHAPTER 16

1. Brooke Capps, "How to Succeed in Second Life," *Advertising Age,* May 28, 2007, p. 6; Jon Fine, "Ready to Get Weird, Advertisers?" *BusinessWeek,* January 8, 2007, p. 24; Andrew Hampp, "Second Life Losing Lock on Virtual-site Marketing," *Advertising Age,* July 9, 2007, p. 10; Aili McConnon and Reena Jana, "Beyond Second Life," *BusinessWeek,* June, 11, 2007, p. 24; Brian Steinberg, "How to Stop Them From Skipping: TiVo Tells All," *Advertising Age,* July 16, 2007, pp. 1, 33; Nat Ives, "Where Have All the Girls Gone?" *Advertising Age,* July 16, 2007, pp. 1, 37; and Todd Wasserman, "15-Second Ads Getting Their Moment," *Brandweek,* September 11, 2006, p. 20.

2. David A. Aaker and Donald Norris, "Characteristics of TV Commercials Perceived as Informative," *Journal of Advertising Research* 22, no. 2 (April–May 1982), pp. 61–70.

3. Larry D. Compeau and Dhruv Grewal, "Comparative Price Advertising: An Integrative Review," *Journal of Public Policy & Marketing,* Fall 1998, pp. 257–73; and William Wilkie and Paul W. Farris, "Comparison Advertising: Problems and Potentials," *Journal of Marketing,* October 1975, pp. 7–15.

4. Jennifer Lawrence, "P&G Ads Get Competitive," *Advertising Age,* February 1, 1993, p. 14; Jerry Gotlieb and Dan Sorel, "The Influence of Type of Advertisement, Price, and Source Credibility on Perceived Quality," *Journal of the Academy of Marketing Science,* Summer 1992, pp. 253–60; and Cornelia Pechman and David Stewart, "The Effects of Comparative Advertising on Attention, Memory, and Purchase Intentions," *Journal of Consumer Research,* September 1990, pp. 180–92.

5. Bruce Buchanan and Doron Goldman, "Us vs. Them: The Minefield of Comparative Ads," *Harvard Business Review,* May–June 1989, pp. 38–50; Dorothy Cohen, "The FTC's Advertising Substantiation Program," *Journal of Marketing,* Winter 1980, pp. 26–35; and Michael Etger and Stephen A. Goodwin, "Planning for Comparative Advertising Requires Special Attention," *Journal of Advertising* 8, no. 1 (Winter 1979), pp. 26–32.

6. Lewis C. Winters, "Does It Pay to Advertise to Hostile Audiences with Corporate Advertising?" *Journal of Advertising Research,* June–

July 1988, pp. 11–18; and Robert Selwitz, "The Selling of an Image," *Madison Avenue,* February 1985, pp. 61–69.

7. Jeremy Mullman, "No Sugar and Spice Here," *Advertising Age,* June 18, 2007, p. 3.

8. "Claritin Springs into Allergy Season with New Consumer Programs," *PR Newswire,* February 20, 2001.

9. Ira Teinowitz, "Self-regulation Urged to Prevent Bias in Ad Buying," *Advertising Age,* January 18, 1999, p. 4.

10. Bob Donath, "Match Your Media Choice and Ad Copy Objective," *Marketing News,* June 8, 1998, p. 6.

11. Award information available at The Magazine Publishers of America Kelly Award website, www.kellyawardsgallery.org.

12. Kate Maddox, "ARF Forum Examines Internet Research Effectiveness," *Advertising Age,* January 11, 1999, p. 28.

13. Bob Garfield; "Mad Ave. Blows Big Game," *Advertising Age,* February 4, 2008, p. 1; Brain Steinberg, "Super Bowl Spots Hit $3 Million," *Advertising Age,* May 12, 2008, p. 4; Claire Atkinson, "Measuring Bowl ROI? Good Luck," *Advertising Age,* January 29, 2007, p. 9; and Rama Ylkur, Chuck Tomkovick, and Patty Traczyk, "Super Bowl Effectiveness: Hollywood Finds the Games Golden," *Journal of Advertising Research,* March, 2004, pp. 143–59.

14. Michael S. LaTour and Herbert J. Rotfeld, "There Are Threats and (Maybe) Fear-Caused Arousal: Theory and Confusions of Appeals to Fear and Fear Arousal Itself," *Journal of Advertising,* Fall 1997, pp. 45–59.

15. Cornelia Pechmann, Guangzhi Zhao, Marvin E. Goldberg, and Ellen Thomas Reibling, "What to Convey in Antismoking Advertisements for Adolescents: The Use of Protection Motivation Theory to Identify Effective Message Themes," *Journal of Marketing,* April, 2003, pp. 1–18; Jeffrey D. Zbar, "Fear!" *Advertising Age,* November 14, 1994, pp. 18–19; John F. Tanner Jr., James B. Hunt, and David R. Eppright, "The Protection Motivation Model: A Normative Model of Fear Appeals," *Journal of Marketing,* July 1991, pp. 36–45; and Michael S. LaTour and Shaker A. Zahra, "Fear Appeals as Advertising Strategy: Should They Be Used?" *Journal of Consumer Marketing,* Spring 1989, pp. 61–70.

16. Stuart Elliot, "Can Beer Ads Extol Great Taste in Good Taste?" *The New York Times,* April 16, 2004, p. C2; and "Operating Strategy," Bebe website, www.bebe.com.

17. Steve McClellan, "The Caveman: Evolution of a Character," *Adweek,* March 12, 2007, p. 78.

18. Theresa Howard, "Thinking Outside the TV Box Ads Get Creative in Midst of New Media Choices," *USA Today,* June 22, 2004, p. 4B; Anthony Vagnoni, "Best Awards," *Advertising Age,* May 28, 2001, pp. S1–18; Dana L. Alden, Wayne D. Hoyer, and Chol Lee, "Identifying Global and Culture-Specific Dimensions of Humor in Advertising: A Multinational Analysis," *Journal of Marketing,* April 1993, pp. 64–75; and Johny K. Johansson, "The Sense of 'Nonsense': Japanese TV Advertising," *Journal of Advertising,* March 1994, pp. 17–26.

19. *2006 Television Production Cost Survey* (New York, New York: American Association of Advertising Agencies, 2006); and Jean Halliday, "Exotic Ads Get Noticed," *Advertising Age,* April 9, 2001, p. jS4.

20. Campaign information accessed at Berlin Cameron website, www.bc-p.com, July 27, 2007; and Lisa Sanders, "Berlin Cameron Stands on Its Own," *Advertising Age,* January 12, 2004, p. S2.

21. "Ad Spending Totals by Medium," *Advertising Age,* June 23, 2008, p. S-15.

22. Giles D'Souza and Ram C. Rao, "Can Repeating an Advertisement More Frequently Than the Competition Affect Brand Preference in a Mature Market?" *Journal of Marketing,* April 1995, pp. 32–42.

23. Vicki R. Lane, "The Impact of Ad Repetition and Ad Content on Consumer Perceptions of Incongruent Extensions," *Journal of Marketing,* April 2000, pp. 80–91.

24. Katherine Barrett, "Taking a Closer Look," *Madison Avenue,* August 1984, pp. 106–9.

25. "Nielsen and Integrated Media Measurement Launch Out-of-Home Television Ratings Measurement Service," *PR Newswire,* April 12, 2007; and Holly M Sanders, "You Can Run But You Can't Hide From TV Ads," *New York Post,* July 29, 2007.

26. Brian Steinberg, "McPricey ABC Leads Way With 'Grey' This Fall," *Advertising Age,* October 1, 2007, p. 1, 41.

27. Surendra N. Singh, Denise Linville, and Ajay Sukhdial, "Enhancing the Efficacy of Split Thirty-Second Television Commercials: An Encoding Variability Application," *Journal of Advertising,* Fall 1995, pp. 13–23; Scott Ward, Terence A. Oliva, and David J. Reibstein, "Effectiveness of Brand-Related 15-Second Commercials," *Journal of Consumer Marketing,* no. 2 (1994), pp. 38–44; and Surendra N. Singh and Catherine Cole, "The Effects of Length, Content, and Repetition on Television Commercial Effectiveness," *Journal of Marketing Research,* February 1993, pp. 91–104.

28. Cara Beardi, "Radio's Big Bounce," *Advertising Age,* August 27, 2001, p. S2.

29. Larry Dobrow, "Parenting Newbie Cookie Is A Friend To Upscale Moms," *Advertising Age,* October 29, 2007, p. S8-9; *The Magazine Handbook: A Comprehensive Guide 2008/2009,* (New York, New York: Magazine Publishers of America), p. 5; "Number of Magazines by Category," *Editorial Trends and Magazine Handbook* (New York, New York: Magazine Publishers of America). Kate Fitzgerald, "Launches Crowd Already Tough Field," *Advertising Age,* April 5, 2004, p. S2; Jon Fine, "Silicon Valley Spawns New Nascar Lifestyle Magazine," *Advertising Age,* January 12, 2004, p. 8; Jon Fine, "Magazine of the Year: Lucky," *Advertising Age,* October 20, 2003, p. S1; *A Magazine for Everyone* (New York: The Magazine Publishers Association, 2003), p. 6; R. Craig Endicott, "Past Performance Is Not a Guarantee of Future Returns," *Advertising Age,* June 18, 2001, pp. S1, S6; and George R. Milne, "A Magazine Taxonomy Based on Customer Overlap," *Journal of the Academy of Marketing Science,* Spring 1994, pp. 170–79.

30. Julia Collins, "Image and Advertising," *Harvard Business Review,* January–February 1989, pp. 93–97.

31. Abbey Klassen, "Here's a $14 Billion Print Business That's Loving the Digital Revolution," *Advertising Age,* August 28, 2006, p. 3; Lisa Sanders, "Major Marketers Turn to Yellow Pages," *Advertising Age,* March 8, 2004, p. 4; "Yellow Pages Still 'Gold Standard' for Searches," *USA Today,* February 16, 2004, p. 10A; Avery M. Abernethy and David N. Laband, "The Impact of Trademarks and Advertisement Size on Yellow Page Call Rates," *Journal of Advertising Research,* March 2004, pp. 119–25; and "Yellow Pages and the Media Mix," Yellow Pages Publishers Association, Troy, MI.

32. Pierre Berthon and James M. Hulbert, "Marketing In Metamorphosis: Breaking Boundaries," *Business Horizons,* May–June 2003, pp. 31–40.

33. Sandeep Krishnamurthy, "Deciphering the Internet Advertising Puzzle," *Marketing Management,* Fall 2000, pp. 35–39; Judy Strauss and Raymond Frost, *Marketing on the Internet: Principles of Online Marketing* (Englewood Cliffs, NJ: Prentice Hall, 1999), pp. 196–249; and Maricris G. Briones, "Rich Media May Be Too Rich for Your Blood," *Marketing News,* March 29, 1999, p. 4.

34. Brian Grow and Ben Elgin, "Click Fraud," *BusinessWeek,* October 2, 2006, pp. 46–57; Rob Hof, "Is Google Too Powerful?" *BusinessWeek,* April 9, 2007, p. 48; Eric J. Hansen, "Apply Online Market Data for Offline Insights," *Marketing News,* April 1, 2007, p. 30; "Out of Site at AdAge.com," *Advertising Age,* November 6, 2006, p. 12; Michael Fielding, "Click Fraud Settles Down," *Marketing News,* September 1, 2006, p. 4; Brian Grow, "This Mouse for Hire," *BusinessWeek,* October 23, 2006, p. 104.

35. Dana Blankenhorn, "Bigger, Richer Ads Go Online," *Advertising Age,* June 18, 2001, p. T10; Patricia Riedman, "Poor Rich Media," *Advertising Age,* February 5, 2001, p. 26; Heather Green, "Net Advertising: Still the 98-Pound Weakling," *BusinessWeek,* September 1l, 2000, p. 36; and Thom Weidlich, "Online Spots—A New Generation," *Advertising Age,* July 30, 2001, p. S10.

36. Arch G. Woodside, "Outdoor Advertising as Experiments," *Journal of the Academy of Marketing Science* 18 (Summer 1990), pp. 229–37.

37. Andrew Hampp, "Rise of Out-of-Home Video Sparks Metrics Push," *Advertising Age,* November 19, 2007, p. 8; Ed Brown, "Advertisers Skip to the Loo," *Fortune,* October 26, 1998, p. 64; John Cortex, "Growing Pains Can't Stop the New Kid on the Ad Block," *Advertising Age,* October 12, 1992, pp. 5–28; Allen Banks, "How to Assess New Place-Based Media," *Advertising Age,* November 30, 1992, p. 36; and John Cortex, "Media Pioneers Try to Corral On-the-Go Consumers," *Advertising Age,* August 17, 1992, p. 25.

38. "It's An Ad, Ad, Ad, Ad World," *Time,* July 9, 2001, p. 17; "Triton, Secora in Alliance for Advertising on ATMs," *Marketing News,* June 5, 2000, p. 12; and Joan Oleck, "High-Octane Advertising," *BusinessWeek,* November 29, 1999, p. 8.

39. Sehoon Park and Minhi Hahn, "Pulsing in a Discrete Model of Advertising Competition," *Journal of Marketing Research,* November 1991, pp. 397–405.

40. Peggy Masterson, "The Wearout Phenomenon," *Marketing Research,* Fall 1999, pp. 27–31; and Lawrence D. Gibson, "What Can One TV Exposure Do?" *Journal of Advertising Research,* March–April 1996, pp. 9–18.

41. Rob Norton, "How Uninformative Advertising Tells Consumers Quite a Bit," *Fortune,* December 26, 1994, p. 37; and "Professor Claims Corporations Waste Billions on Advertising," *Marketing News,* July 6, 1992, p. 5.

42. The discussion of posttesting is based on William F. Arens, *Contemporary Advertising,* 6th ed. (Burr Ridge, IL: Richard D. Irwin, 1996), pp. 181–82.

43. David A. Aaker and Douglas M. Stayman, "Measuring Audience Perceptions of Commercials and Relating Them to Ad Impact," *Journal of Advertising Research* 30 (August–September 1990), pp. 7–17; and Ernest Dichter, "A Psychological View of Advertising Effectiveness," *Marketing Management* 1, no. 3 (1992), pp. 60–62.

44. David Kruegel, "Television Advertising Effectiveness and Research Innovation," *Journal of Consumer Marketing,* Summer 1988, pp. 43–51; and Laurence N. Gold, "The Evolution of Television Advertising Sales Measurement: Past, Present, and Future," *Journal of Advertising Research,* June–July 1988, pp. 19–24.

45. Kathleen M. Joyce, "Higher Gear," *PROMO 14th Annual Sourcebook,* 2007, p. 5–7.

46. Tom Hansen, "Media Mash," *PROMO,* February 1, 2007, p. 66; Magid M. Abraham and Leonard M. Lodish, "Getting the Most out of Advertising and Promotion," *Harvard Business Review,* May–June 1990, pp. 50–60; Steven W. Hartley and James Cross, "How Sales Promotion Can Work for and against You," *Journal of Consumer Marketing,* Summer 1988, pp. 35–42; Robert D. Buzzell, John A. Quelch, and Walter J. Salmon, "The Costly Bargain of Trade Promotion," *Harvard Business Review,* March–April 1990, pp. 141–49; and Mary L. Nicastro, "Break-Even Analysis Determines Success of Sales Promotions," *Marketing News,* March 5, 1990, p. 11.

47. "We've Been Clipped," *PROMO,* September 2007, p. AR11; Natalie Schwartz, "Clipping Path," *Promo,* April 1, 2004, p. 4; Mathew Kinsman, "The Hard Sell," *Promo's 11th Annual Source Book* (2004), p. 19; Betsy Spethmann, "Going for Broke," *Promo,* August 2001, pp. 27–31; and Mathew Kinsman, "Bad Is Good," *Promo,* April 2001, pp. 71–74.

48. Karen Holt, "Coupon Crimes," *Promo,* April 2004, pp. 23–26, 70.

49. Amy Johannes, "Box Office Buz," *Promo,* October 1, 2006, p. 34; Carrie MacMillan, "Creature Features," *Promo,* October 2001, p.11; and Dan Hanover, "Not Just for Breakfast Anymore," *Promo,* September 2001, p. 10.

50. Amy Johannes, "Do It Yourself," *PROMO,* September 1, 2007, p. AR14; Patricia Odell, "Hooray For Us," *PROMO,* October 1, 2007, p. 44.

51. "Eight Ways to Win," *PROMO,* May 1, 2007, p. 42; "Campaign Index," *PROMO,* November 1, 2007, p. 12; Amy Johannes, "Band Wagon," *PROMO,* August 1, 2007, p. 12.

52. Edward Kabak, "Staking out the States," *Promo,* October 2001, p. 11; Maxine Lans Retsky, "Stakes Are High for Direct Mail Sweepstakes Promotions," *Marketing News,* July 3, 2000, p. 8; Richard Sale, "Sweeping the Courts," *Promo,* May 1998, pp. 42–45; and Fred C. Allvine, Richard D. Teach, and John Connelly, Jr., "The Demise of Promotional Games," *Journal of Advertising Research* 16 (October 1976), pp. 79–84.

53. Larry Jaffee, "Try It," *PROMO,* September 1, 2007, p. AR25. Lorin Cipolla, "Instant Gratification," *Promo,* April 1, 2004, p. 4; "Best Activity Generating Brand Awareness/Trial," *Promo,* September 2001, p. 51; and "Brand Handing," *Promo's 9th Annual Sourcebook* (2002), p. 32.

54. Patricia Odell, "Shopping List," *PROMO,* September 1, 2007, p. AR23.

55. See www.fordcollegegrad.com.

56. Marvin A. Jolson, Joshua L. Wiener, and Richard B. Rosecky, "Correlates of Rebate Proneness," *Journal of Advertising Research,* February–March 1987, pp. 33–43.

57. Patricia Odell, "Star Struck," *PROMO,* April 1, 2007, p. 16; Michael Idato, "A Word From Our Sponsors—Great Moments In Product Placement," *The Age,* October 2, 2003, p. 17; M. Ellen Peebles, "And Now, a Word From Our Sponsors," *Harvard Business Review,* October 2003, pp. 31–42. M. Ellen Peebles, "And Now, a Word from Our Sponsor," *Harvard Business Review,* October 2003, pp. 31–42; Paula Lyon Andruss, "Survivor Packages Make Real-Life Money," *Marketing News,* March 26, 2001, p. 5;

58. Allison Enright, "Apu Buzz, Krusty–Oh My!" *Marketing News,* August 15, 2007, p. 3; Rob Walker, "False Endorsement," *The New York Times,* November 18, 2007, p. 38;

59. This discussion is drawn particularly from John A. Quelch, *Trade Promotions by Grocery Manufacturers: A Management Perspective* (Cambridge, MA: Marketing Science Institute, August 1982).

60. Michael Chevalier and Ronald C. Curhan, "Retail Promotions as a Function of Trade Promotions: A Descriptive Analysis," *Sloan Management Review* 18 (Fall 1976), pp. 19–32.

61. G. A. Marken, "Firms Can Maintain Control over Creative Co-op Programs," *Marketing News,* September 28, 1992, pp. 7, 9.

62. Scott Hue, "Free 'Plugs' Supply Ad Power," *Advertising Age,* January 29, 1990, p. 6.

63. David Welch, "Importer's Worst Nightmare," *BusinessWeek,* July 23, 2007, p. 46; Troy Wolverton, "Apple's Backdating Scandal," *San Jose Mercury News,* January 7, 2007, p. 1.

Fallon Worldwide: This case was written by Mark T. Spriggs, William Rudelius, Linda Rochford, and Steven Hartley based on interviews with Fallon personnel and material on the Citi and Holiday Inn Express promotional campaigns provided by Fallon Worldwide. Sources: Lori McLeod, "Holiday Inn: A Road-Trip Staple Rebranded," *The Globe and Mail,* November 10, 2007, p. B3; Cecil Johnson, "The Ad Pitch: Creativity, Not Saturation, Is Key," *The Boston Globe,* August 6, 2006, p. D2; "New Campaigns—The World," *Campaign,* May 27, 2005, p. 52; Aaron Baar, "Fallon Showers Intelligence on Hotel Guests," *Adweek,* October 7, 2004; and the Holiday Inn Express website (http://www.ihgplc.com).

CHAPTER 17

1. "Executive Biographies—Anne Mulcahy," www.xerox.com, downloaded July 8, 2008; "Back From the Brink," *The Wall Street Journal,* April 24, 2006, pp. B1, B3; "Xerox—Dedicated to Customer Success," www.sspa.com, February 20, 2007; and "Turning the Page," *Business 2.0,* July 2005, pp. 98–100.

2. "Leading CEOs: A Statistical Snapshot of S&P 500 Leaders," www.spencerstuart.com, February 2008.

3. "Surgical Visits," *Business 2.0,* April 2006, p. 94.

4. Mark W. Johnston and Greg W. Marshall, *Relationship Selling,* 2nd ed. (Burr Ridge, IL: McGraw-Hill/Irwin, 2008).

5. Barton A. Weitz, Stephen B. Castleberry, and John F. Tanner, Jr., *Selling: Building Partnerships,* 6th ed. (Burr Ridge, IL: McGraw-Hill/Irwin, 2007), p. 8.

6. "Stop Calling Us," *Time,* April 29, 2003, pp. 56–58.

7. Scott Sterns, "Cold Calls Have Yet to Breathe Their Last Gasp," *The Wall Street Journal,* December 14, 2006, p. D2.

8. Jim Edwards, "Dinner, Interrupted," *Brandweek,* May 26, 2003, pp. 28–32.

9. Christopher Conkey, "Record Fine Levied for Telemarketing," *The Wall Street Journal,* December 14, 2005, pp. D1, D4.

10. This discussion is based on Weitz, Castleberry, and Tanner, *Selling;* and Johnston and Marshall, *Relationship Selling.*

11. Kapil R. Tuli, Ajay K. Kohli, and Sundar G. Bharadwaj, "Rethinking Customer Solutions: From Product Bundles to Relational Processes," *Journal of Marketing,* July 2007, pp. 1–17.

12. For an extensive discussion of objections, see Charles M. Futrell, *Fundamentals of Selling,* 9th ed. (Burr Ridge, IL: McGraw-Hill/Irwin, 2007), chap. 12.

13. Theodore Levitt, *The Marketing Imagination* (New York: Free Press, 1983), p. 111.

14. Weitz, Castleberry, and Tanner, *Selling.*

15. *Management Briefing: Sales and Marketing* (New York: Conference Board, October 1996), pp. 3–4.

16. For an overview of team selling, see Eli Jones, Andrea Dickson, Lawrence B. Chonko, and Joseph P. Cannon, "Key Accounts and Team Selling: A Review, Framework, and Research Agenda," *Journal of Personal Selling & Sales Management,* Spring 2005, pp. 181–98.

17. See Gilbert A. Churchill Jr.; Neil M. Ford; Orville C. Walker Jr.; Mark W. Johnson; and Greg Marshall, *Sales Force Management,* 9th ed. (Burr Ridge, IL: McGraw-Hill/Irwin, 2009), chap. 9.

18. Rosann L. Spiro, Gregory A. Rich, and William J. Stanton, *Management of the Sales Force,* 12th ed. (Burr Ridge, IL: McGraw-Hill/Irwin, 2008), chap. 7.

19. Ibid., chap. 8.

20. This discussion is based on Churchill et al., *Sales Force Management,* chap. 11.

21. Vasanth Srihavan, "Riding Sporty in Pink," *Dallas Morning News,* July 16, 2007, pp. 1D, 5D.

22. This discussion is based on Churchill et al., *Sales Force Management,* chap. 13.

23. Mark Cotteleer, Edward Inderrieden, and Felissa Lee, "Selling the Sales Force on Automation," *Harvard Business Review,* July–August 2006, pp. 18–22.

24. "Corporate America's New Sales Force," *Fortune,* August 11, 2003, special advertising section.

25. www.toshiba.com/technology, downloaded May 15, 2004.

Xerox: This case was written by Steven Hartley and Roger Kerin. Sources: Joseph Kornik, "Table Talk: A Sales Leaders Roundtable," *Sales & Marketing Management,* February, 2007; Philip Chadwick, "Xerox Global Services," *Printweek,* October 11, 2007, p. 32; Kevin Maney, "Mulcahy Traces Steps of Xerox's Comeback," *USA Today,* September 11, 2006,

p. 4B; Sarah Campbell, "What It's Like Working for Xerox," *The Times,* September 14, 2006, p. 9; "Anne Mulcahy: How I Compete," *Business-Week,* August 21, 2006, p 55; Simon Avery, "CEO's HR Skills Turn Xerox Fortunes," *The Globe and Mail,* June 2, 2006, p. B3; Julia Chang, "Ultimate Motivation Guide: Happy Sales Force, Happy Returns," *Sales & Marketing Management,* March 2006; "The World's Most Powerful Women," forbes.com, August 27, 2008; and resources available on the Xerox website (www.xerox.com) including About Xerox, Executive Biographies, the Xerox 2007 Fact Sheet, the Online Fact Book: Historical Highlights, and the Online Fact Book: How Xerox Sells.

CHAPTER 18

1. Interview with Jennifer Miller, director of marketing at Seven Cycles Inc., July 20, 2007; and www.sevencycles.com, January 20, 2008.
2. "Where Are All the Online Shoppers Going?" www.emarketer.com, May 16, 2007; and "U.S. Retail e-Commerce Forecast, 2007–2012," www.foresterresearch.com, March 2008.
3. "Statistics: U.S. Online Shoppers," www.shop.org, downloaded June 26, 2005.
4. "The Sky Will Now Have Some Limits," *Brandweek,* June 18, 2007, pp. S62–63.
5. Rafl A. Mohammed, Robert J. Fisher, Bernard J. Jaworski, and Gordon J. Paddison, *Internet Marketing: Building Advantage in a Networked Economy,* 2nd ed. (Burr Ridge, IL: McGraw-Hill/Irwin, 2004).
6. Ward A. Hanson and Kirthi Kalyanam, *Internet Marketing & Electronic Commerce* (Mason, OH: Thompson Higher Education, 2007).
7. Ibid.
8. Stephen Chen, *Strategic Management of e-Business,* 2nd ed. (New York: John Wiley & Sons, 2005).
9. Judy Strauss, Adel El-Ansary, and Raymond Frost, *E-Marketing,* 4th ed. (Upper Saddle River, NJ: Prentice Hall, 2006).
10. "Gartner: Nearly $2 Billion Lost in E-Sales in 2006 Due to U.S. Consumers' Security Concerns," www.the-dma.org, downloaded January 6, 2007.
11. This discussion is drawn from Jeffrey F. Rayport and Bernard J. Jaworski, *e-Commerce,* 2nd ed. (Burr Ridge, IL: McGraw-Hill/Irwin, 2004); and *The Essential Guide to Best Practices in eCommerce* (Portland, OR: Webtrends, Inc., 2006).
12. "We Can All Get Along," *Marketing News,* May 15, 2007, p. 4.
13. "Now US Is Online, And How!" www.emarketer.com, February 28, 2008.
14. "The 90/20 Rule of E-Commerce: Nearly 90% of Online Sales Accounted for by 20% of Consumers," Cyber Dialogue press release, September 25, 2000.
15. "My Mommy's Online," www.emarketer.com, March 17, 2008; "How Many Moms are Online?" www.emarketer.com, May 6, 2008; "New Study Reveals Internet Is the Medium Moms Rely on Most," Disney Online news release, March 2004; "On a Mission: The New Internet Mom," *FC NOW: The Fast Company Weblog,* May 25, 2004; and "Working Moms Develop Internet Habit," BizReport.com, November 30, 2006.
16. "U.S. Retail e-Commerce Forecast, 2007–2012."
17. Jerry Wind and Arvind Ranaswamy, "Customerization: The Next Wave in Mass Customization," *Journal of Interactive Marketing,* Winter 2001, pp. 13–32.
18. Kenneth Hein, "Shooting Your Mouth Off," *Other Advertising,* December 2005, pp. 20–21. Also see, Kate Fitzgerald, "Blogs Fascinate, Frighten Marketers," *Advertising Age,* March 5, 2007, p. S-4.
19. Quoted in Strauss et al., *E-Marketing,* p. 357.
20. Hanson and Kalyanam, *Internet Marketing & Electronic Commerce.*
21. Stephen Baker, "The Online Ad Surge," *BusinessWeek,* November 22, 2004, pp. 76–81.
22. "Branding on the Net," *BusinessWeek,* November 2, 1998, pp. 78–86.
23. David Kesmodel, "Marketers Seek to Make Cookies More Palatable," *The Wall Street Journal,* June 17, 2005, pp. B1, B2.
24. Mary Lou Roberts, *Internet Marketing: Integrating Online and Offline Strategies,* 2nd ed. (Mason, OH: Thomson, 2008), chap. 12; Jean Chatzky, "Let the EBuyer Beware," *Time,* April 10, 2006, p. 80; Ben Elgin, "The Plot to Hijack Your Computer," *BusinessWeek,* July 17, 2006, pp. 40–48; and "Gartner: Nearly $2 Billion Lost in E-Sales in 2006 Due to Consumers' Security Concerns."
25. Susan Adams et al. "This Time It Is Personal: Employee Online Shopping at Work," *Interactive Marketing,* April 2005, pp. 326–36; and "Shop Around the Clock," *American Demographics,* September 2003, p. 18.
26. This discussion is based on "Shop Online, Spend Offline," www.emarketer.com, July 11, 2007; Tamera Mendelsohn, "Are You Prepared for the Cross-Channel Shopper?" *Self-Service World Magazine,* May/June 2006, p. 94; and Tamera Mendelsohn, "The State of Multichannel Consumers in the U.S. and Europe," www.forresterresearch.com, June 25, 2007.
27. "Multi-Channel Retailing," www.emarketer.com, April 8, 2008.
28. "Retailers' Panty Raid on Victoria's Secret," *The Wall Street Journal,* June 20, 2007, pp. B1, B12.
29. Stephanie Kang, "Callaway Will Use Retailers to Sell Goods Directly to Consumers Online," *The Wall Street Journal,* November 6, 2006, p. B5.
30. *The Next Chapter in Business-to-Consumer E-Commerce: Advantage Incumbent* (Boston: The Boston Consulting Group, 2001); and Timothy J. Mullaney, "E-Biz Strikes Again," *BusinessWeek,* May 10, 2004, pp. 80–90.
31. "The State of Multichannel Consumers in the U.S. and Europe." Also see, "Ring Up E-Commerce Gains with A True Multichannel Strategy," *Advertising Age,* March 10, 2008, p. 15.

McFarlane Toys: This case was written by Steve Hartley and Roger Kerin. Sources: www.spawn.com, downloaded July 30, 2007; Bruce Handy, "Small Is Beautiful," *Vanity Fair,* December 2003, p. 208; Wes Orshoski, "McFarlane Adds Hendrix, Elvis to Action-Figure Series," *Billboard,* December 20, 2003, p. 65; and *U.S. Department of Commerce Industry Outlook: Dolls, Toys, Games, and Children's Vehicles* (Washington, DC: International Trade Association, 2007).

APPENDIX B

1. Diane Brady, "Creating Brand You," *BusinessWeek,* August 22, 2007, pp. 72–73; and Denny E. McCorkle, Joe F. Alexander, and Memo F. Diriker, "Developing Self-Marketing Skills for Student Career Success," Journal of Marketing Education, Spring 1992, pp. 57–67.
2. Marianne E. Green, "Marketing Yourself: From Student to Professional," *Job Choices for Business & Liberal Arts Students,* 50th ed., 2007, pp. 30–31; Joanne Cleaver, "Find a Job Through Self-Promotion," *Marketing News,* January 31, 2000, pp. 12, 16.
3. Deborah L. Vence, "CEO Job Demands Big Picture View, Integration Skills," *Marketing News,* May 1, 2006, p. 14; and Paula Lyon Andruss, "So You Want to Be a CEO?" *Marketing News,* January 29, 2001, pp. 1, 10.
4. "Average Yearly Salary Offers," *Salary Survey* (Bethlehem, PA: National Association of Colleges and Employers, Spring 2008), p. 4.
5. "Advertising, Marketing, Promotions, Public Relations, and Sales Managers," *Occupational Outlook Handbook* (Indianapolis: JIST Works, 2006–2007), www.bls.gov/oco/pdf/ocos020.pdf.
6. Matthew Creamer, "P&G Primes Its Pinpoint Marketing," *Advertising Age,* May 7, 2007; and Linda M. Gorchels, "Traditional Product Management Evolves," *Marketing News,* January 30, 1995, p. 4.
7. Robin T. Peterson, "Wholesaling: A Neglected Job Opportunity of Marketing Majors," *Marketing News,* January 15, 1996.

8. S. William Pattis, *Careers in Advertising* (New York: McGraw-Hill, 2004); and "Advertising," *Career Guide to Americas Top Industries* (Indianapolis, IN: JIST Works, 1994), pp. 142–45.

9. Roslyn Dolber, *Opportunities in Retailing Careers* (New York: McGraw-Hill, 2003); and "The Climb to the Top," *Careers in Retailing,*" January 1995, p. 18.

10. "Playing the Retail Career Game," *Careers in Retailing 2001* (New York: DSN Retailing Today, January 2001), pp. 4, 6.

11. Joseph Kornik, "The 2007 Compensation Survey," *Sales and Marketing Management,* May 2007, pp. 27–35.

12. Rebecca Aronaur, "Shaping the Profession of Sales," *Sales & Marketing Management,* July 1, 2006.

13. Jack and Suzy Welch, "Dear Graduate… To Stand Out Among Your Peers, You Have to Overdeliver," *BusinessWeek,* June 19, 2006, p. 100.

14. Edmund Hershberger and Madhav N. Segal, "Ads for MR Positions Reveal Desired Skills," *Marketing News,* February 1, 2007, p. 28.

15. "Market Research Analyst," in Les Krantz, ed., *Jobs Rated Almanac,* 5th ed. (New York: St. Martin's Press, 2000).

16. Deborah L. Vence, "In an Instant, More Researchers Use IM for Fast, Reliable Results," *Marketing News,* March 1, 2006, p. 53; and Joshua Grossnickle and Oliver Raskin, "What's Ahead on the Internet," *Marketing Research,* Summer 2001, pp. 9–13.

17. International Franchise Association, http://franchise.org/Blockbuster_Inc_franchise.aspx, August 20, 2007.

18. Lisa Bertagnoli, "Marketing Overseas Excellent for Career," *Marketing News,* June 4, 2001, p. 4.

19. Barbara Flood, "Turbo Charge Your Job Search, Job Searching and Career Development Tips," *Information Outlook,* May 1, 2007, p. 40.

20. Ibid.

21. Barbara Kiviat, "The New Rules of Web Hiring," *Time,* November 24, 2003, p. 57; Karen Epper Hoffman, "Recruitment Sites Changing Their Focus," *Internet World,* March 15, 1999; Pamela Mendels, "Now That's Casting a Wide Net," *BusinessWeek,* May 25, 1998: and James C. Gonyea, *The Online Job Search Companion* (New York: McGraw-Hill, 1995).

22. Ronald B. Marks, *Personal Selling: A Relationship Approach,* 6th ed. (New York: Pearson, 1996).

23. Marianne E. Green, "Resume Writing: Sell Your Skills to Get the Interview!" *Job Choices for Business & Liberal Arts Students,* 50th ed., 2007, pp. 39–47.

24. "If I 'Google' You, What Will I Find?" *Job Choices for Business and Liberal Arts Students,* 50th ed., 2007, p. 16; and Joyce Lain Kennedy, "Computer-Friendly Résumé Tips," *Planning Job Choices: 1999,* 42nd ed. (Bethlehem, PA: National Association of Colleges and Employers, 1998), p. 49; and Joyce Lain Kennedy and Thomas J. Morrow, *Electronic Résumé Revolution* (New York: Wiley, 1994).

25. William J. Banis, "The Art of Writing Job-Search Letters," *Job Choices for Business and Liberal Arts Students,* 50th ed., 2007, pp. 32–38; and Arthur G. Sharp, "The Art of the Cover Letter," *Career Futures* 4, no. 1 (1992), pp. 50–51.

26. Alison Damast, "Recruiters' Top 10 Complaints," *BusinessWeek,* April 26, 2007; and Marilyn Moats Kennedy, "Don't List' Offers Important Tips for Job Interviews," *Marketing News,* March 15, 2007, p. 26.

27. Dana James, "A Day in the Life of a Corporate Recruiter," *Marketing News,* April 10, 2000, pp. 1, 11.

28. Robert M. Greenberg, "The Company Visit—Revisited," *NACE Journal,* Winter 2003, pp. 21–27.

29. Mary E. Scott, "High-Touch vs. High-Tech Recruitment," *NACE Journal,* Fall 2002, pp. 33–39.

CREDITS

CHAPTER 11

P. 234, ©Kan Photography 2005. P. 236, ©David Young-Wolff/PhotoEdit. P. 239, Courtesy Rubin Postaer & Associates. P. 239, Courtesy Panasonic Consumer Electronics Company. P. 243, Courtesy Women Riders Now. P. 245, Courtesy of the National Fluid Milk Processor Promotion Board; Agency: Bozell/Chicago. P. 246, *No credit.* P. 247, Courtesy Advanced Research Labs. P. 247, Courtesy Donna Karan International, Inc. P. 249, Courtesy Roper Footwear & Apparel. P. 251, ©M. Hruby. P. 252, Courtesy Marriott International, Inc. P. 253, ©M. Hruby. P. 254, Photo by: Arthur Meyerson. "Coca-Cola, the Contour Bottle design and the Coca-Cola Fridge Pack are trademarks of The Coca-Cola Company. Copyright 1994. All rights reserved. P. 254, ©M. Hruby. P. 255, ©2001 Susan G. Holtz. P. 256, Used with permission from McDonald's Corporation. P. 257, Trademarks and copyrights used herein are properties of the United States Postal Service and are used under license to McGraw-Hill. All Rights Reserved. P. 259, Courtesy Philadelphia Phillies. P. 260, Courtesy Philadelphia Phillies.

CHAPTER 12

P. 262, AP Photo/Mark Lennihan. P. 264, ©Robert Yager. Pg. 267, ©Terry McElroy. P. 268, Courtesy of Rock & Roll Hall of Fame. P. 269, Courtesy of The Caplow Company. P. 272, ©M. Hruby. P. 279, Courtesy Panasonic Consumer Electronics Company. P. 281, Photo by James Leynse/Corbis. P. 282, Courtesy Mardi Larsen Communications. P. 285, Courtesy Steve and Barry's University Sportswear. Pg. 286, Courtesy Steve and Barry's University Sportswear.

CHAPTER 13

P. 288, Photo by Graeme Robertson/Getty Images. P. 296, Courtesy Nestle SA. P. 297, AP Photo/Nick Ut. P. 297, Jill Braaten/The McGraw-Hill Digital Library. P. 299, Courtesy Jiffy Lube International, Inc. P. 299, ©Amy Etra. P. 302, ©Joe & Kathy Heiner. P. 305,

Courtesy IBM Corporation. P. 306, Courtesy Dell, Inc. P. 306, Courtesy Wal-Mart Stores, Inc. P. 310, Courtesy Golden Valley. P. 311, Mark Wilson/Getty Images. P. 311, Photo by Justin Sullivan/Getty Images. P. 311, Photo by Justin Sullivan/Getty Images.

CHAPTER 14

P. 312, Courtesy IconNicholson LLC. P. 315, Courtesy Polo Ralph Lauren Corporation. P. 315, Jochen Luebke/AFP/Getty Images. P. 317, Courtesy Entrepreneur Media, Inc. P. 317, Courtesy Doctor's Associates, Inc. P. 319, Courtesy Staples, Inc. P. 319, Courtesy Get & Go Express. P. 320, Courtesy J.C.Penney. P. 320, Courtesy Lillian Vernon Corporation. P. 320, Courtesy L.L.Bean. P. 321, Photo by Matt Peyton/Getty Images for QVC. P. 321, Courtesy MySimon, Inc. P. 324, Photo by Tim Boyle/Getty Images. P. 324, AP Photo/Paul Sakuma. P. 327, Courtesy Taco Bell. P. 333, *Both* Courtesy Mall of America.

CHAPTER 15

P. 334, Fred Prouser/Reuters/Landov. P. 337, Courtesy Jaguar Cars Limited; Agency: Euro RSCG Worldwide. P. 340, Courtesy The Coca-Cola Company. P. 340, ©2007 Llewellyn/Frommer's Australia From $60 a Day. Reprinted with permission of John Wiley & Sons, Inc. P. 340, Courtesy International Dairy Queen, Inc. P. 342, Courtesy of Lebhar-Friedman, Inc. P. 343, Courtesy Nokia North America. P. 344, Courtesy Purina Incredible Dog Challenge. P. 345, Courtesy Allergan, Inc. P. 347, Imaginechina via AP Images. Pg. 348, ©M. Hruby. P. 351, Courtesy 4 Seasons Hotels & Resorts. P. 355, Gabriel Bouys/AFP/Getty Images. P. 357, Jerry Metellus/Las Vegas Stock/Getty Images.

CHAPTER 16

P. 358, Courtesy There.com. P. 360, Courtesy Verizon Wireless. P. 360, Courtesy Sony Electronics, INC. P. 360, Courtesy Mars, Inc. P. 361,

Courtesy National Fluid Milk Processor Promotion Board; Agency: Lowe Worldwide, Inc. P. 362, *No credit.* P. 363, Courtesy Diesel S.p.A. P. 363, Courtesy Samsung Electronics America. P. 367, Courtesy Speed Channel 2004. P. 368, Courtesy Cosmo Girl. P. 368, ©M. Hruby. P. 370, Courtesy Double Click, Inc. P. 370, Courtesy Nationwide Insurance. P. 370, Courtesy ecast. P. 372, Courtesy GfK Custom Research North America. P. 373, Courtesy of Valpak Direct Marketing Systems, Inc. P. 374, Courtesy CIT Group, Inc. P. 375, *No credit.* P. 375, Ron P. Jaffe/CBS/Landov. P. 375, ©M. Hruby. P. 379, Courtesy CIT Group, Inc. P. 380, *No credit.*

CHAPTER 17

P. 382, Courtesy Xerox Corporation. P. 384, ©John Madere. P. 386, ©Mitch Kezar/Windigo Images. P. 389, Einzig Photography. P. 390, ©Image Source/Corbis. P. 391, Richard Pasley/Stock Boston LLC. P. 392, Frank Herholdt/Stone/Getty Images. P. 395, Courtesy Xerox Corporation. P. 397, ©Rex C. Curry. P. 400, Royalty-Free/Corbis. P. 403, Courtesy Xerox Corporation.

CHAPTER 18

P. 404, *Both* Courtesy Seven Cycles, Inc. P. 408, ©Nike. All Right Reserved. P. 410, *No credit.* P. 410, *No credit.* P. 413, ©Paul Barton/CORBIS. P. 415, ©Tom Grill/Corbis. Pg. 416, Courtesy Diamond Trading Company; Agency: J. Walter Thompson. P. 417, ©Ray Bartkus.

APPENDIX B

P. 426, ©Paul Elledge. P. 426, Courtesy The May Department Stores Company. P. 427, Courtesy Xerox Corporation. P. 429, Reprinted from Job Choices 2002 with permission of the National Association of Colleges and Employers, copyright holder. P. 429, Courtesy Monster Worldwide, Inc. P. 432, Thatch Cartoon by Jeff Shesol; Reprinted with permission of Vintage Books. P. 432, White Packert/The Image Bank/Getty Images.

NAME INDEX

COMPANY/PRODUCT INDEX

SUBJECT INDEX

a mobile resource to revise and test your knowledge of key marketing concepts.

CHAPTER 1: Creating Customer Relationships and Value through Marketing (L04)

The essence of successful marketing is to provide sufficient value to gain loyal, long-term customers. **Customer value** is the unique combination of benefits received by targeted buyers that usually includes quality, convenience, on-time delivery, and both before-sale and after-sale service at a specific price. Successful **relationship marketing** links an organization to its individual customers, employees, suppliers, and other partners for their mutual long-term benefits. In terms of selling a product, relationship marketing involves a personal, ongoing relationship between the organization and its individual customers that begins before and continues after the sale. Information about a product concept is converted into a tangible **marketing program**—a plan that integrates the marketing mix to provide a good, service, or idea to prospective buyers.

CHAPTER 1: Creating Customer Relationships and Value through Marketing (L02)

The first objective in marketing is discovering the needs and wants of prospective customers. A need occurs when a person feels deprived of basic necessities. A want is a need that is shaped by a person's knowledge, culture, and personality. To discover needs and wants, a firm's marketing department must carefully scrutinize potential customers. People with both the desire and the ability to buy a specific offering make up a **market**. The second objective in marketing is satisfying needs and wants. Because the organization can't satisfy all needs and wants, it must concentrate its efforts on certain needs of a specific group. This is the **target market**—one or more specific groups of potential consumers toward which an organization directs its marketing program.

CHAPTER 1: Creating Customer Relationships and Value through Marketing (L01)

Marketing is the activity for creating, communicating, delivering, and exchanging offerings that benefit the organization, its stakeholders, and society at large. To serve both buyers and sellers, marketing seeks (1) to discover the needs and wants of prospective customers and (2) to satisfy them. The key to achieving these two objectives is the idea of **exchange**, which is the trade of things of value between buyer and seller so that each are better off after the trade.

Marketing: The Core / Kerin Hartley Rudelius — Card 5
CHAPTER 2: Developing Successful Marketing and Organizational Strategies (L05)

The implementation phase of the strategic marketing process carries out the marketing plan that emerges from the planning phase. It has four components: (1) obtaining resources, (2) designing the marketing organization, (3) developing planning schedules, and (4) actually executing the marketing program designed in the planning phase. A **marketing strategy** is the means by which a marketing goal is to be achieved, usually characterized by a specific target market and a marketing program to reach it. To implement a marketing program successfully, detailed day-to-day decisions, called **marketing tactics,** are essential.

Marketing: The Core / Kerin Hartley Rudelius — Card 3
CHAPTER 2: Developing Successful Marketing and Organizational Strategies (L03)

To set a strategic direction, an organization needs to answer two difficult questions: (1) where are we now? and (2) where do we want to go? Answering the first question requires an organization to identify its competencies, customers, and competitors. Answering the second question is accomplished with business portfolio analysis and diversification analysis. Managers in an organization use business portfolio analysis to assess its strategic business units (SBUs), product lines, or products as though they were a collection of separate investments (cash cows, stars, question marks, and dogs).

Marketing: The Core / Kerin Hartley Rudelius — Card 1
CHAPTER 2: Developing Successful Marketing and Organizational Strategies (L01)

Core values are the organization's fundamental, passionate, and enduring principles that guide its conduct over time. The organization's **mission** is a statement of its function in society, often identifying its customers, markets, products, and technologies. **Organizational culture** is a set of values, ideas, attitudes, and norms of behavior that is learned and shared among the member of an organization in order to connect with its stakeholders. A **business** describes the clear, broad, underlying industry or market sector of an organization's offering. **Goals or objectives** are statements of a task to be accomplished, often by a specific time.

Marketing: The Core / Kerin Hartley Rudelius — Card 9
CHAPTER 3: Scanning the Marketing Environment (L05)

Competition refers to the alternative firms that could provide a product or satisfy a specific market's needs. Four basic forms of competition form a continuum: in *pure competition,* every company has a similar product; in *monopolistic competition,* many sellers compete with substitutable products; in an *oligopoly,* a few companies control the majority of industry sales; and in a *pure monopoly,* only one firm sells a product. While large companies are often used as examples of marketplace competitors, there are 23 million small businesses in the United States that have a significant impact on the economy.

Marketing: The Core / Kerin Hartley Rudelius — Card 7
CHAPTER 3: Scanning the Marketing Environment (L03)

The **economy** pertains to the income, expenditures, and resources that affect the cost of running a business or household. Economic forces include the strong relationship between consumers' expectations about the economy and their spending. *Gross income* is the total amount of money made in one year by a person, household, or family unit. *Disposable income* is the money a consumer has left after paying taxes to use for food, shelter, clothing, and transportation. *Discretionary income* is the money that remains after paying for taxes and necessities.

Marketing: The Core / Kerin Hartley Rudelius — Card 13
CHAPTER 3: Scanning the Marketing Environment (L01)

Environmental scanning is the process of acquiring information about events outside the organization to identify and interpret potential trends. There are five environmental forces businesses must monitor: social, economic, technological, competitive, and regulatory.

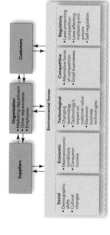

Marketing: The Core / Kerin Hartley Rudelius — Card 17

Marketing: The Core / Kerin Hartley Rudelius — Card 18

Regulation consists of restrictions state and federal laws place on business with regard to the conduct of its activities. Legislation that ensures a competitive marketplace includes the Sherman Antitrust Act. Product-related legislation includes copyright and trademark laws that protect companies and packaging and labeling laws that protect consumers. Pricing- and distribution-related laws are designed to create a competitive marketplace with fair prices and availability. Regulation related to promotion and advertising reduces deceptive practices and provides enforcement through the Federal Trade Commission. Self-regulation, where an industry attempts to police itself through organizations such as the Better Business Bureau, provides an alternative to federal and state regulation.

CHAPTER 1: Creating Customer Relationships and Value through Marketing (L05)

U.S. business history is divided into four periods: the production era, the sales era, the marketing concept era, and the current customer relationship era. In the production era, goods were scarce and buyers were willing to accept virtually any goods that were available. In the sales era, manufacturers found that they could produce more goods than buyers could consume. The **marketing concept** is the idea that an organization should (1) strive to satisfy the needs of consumers, (2) while also trying to achieve the organization's goals. In today's customer relationship era, organizations have a **market orientation** that focuses their efforts on (1) continuously collecting information about customers' needs, (2) sharing this information across departments, and (3) using it to created customer value.

Marketing: The Core / Kerin Hartley Rudelius — Card 6

CHAPTER 2: Developing Successful Marketing and Organizational Strategies (L06)

The evaluation phase of the strategic marketing process seeks to keep the marketing program moving in the direction that was established in the marketing plan. This requires the marketing manager to (1) compare the results from the marketing program with the marketing plan's goals to identify deviations and (2) act on the deviations. Planners call the difference between the goal and the results the planning gap. When performance is different from expectations managers can (1) exploit positive deviations and (2) correct negative deviations.

Marketing: The Core / Kerin Hartley Rudelius — Card 12

CHAPTER 3: Scanning the Marketing Environment (L06)

Technology refers to inventions from applied science or engineering research. Technological innovations can replace existing products and services. Changes in technology can also have an impact on customer value by reducing the cost of products, improving the quality of products, and providing new products that were not previously feasible. An example of the transformative power of technology is the growth of the **marketspace**, an information- and communication-based electronic exchange environment occupied by digitized offerings. Any activity that uses some form of electronic communication in the inventory, exchange, advertisement, distribution, and payment of goods and services is often called electronic commerce.

CHAPTER 1: Creating Customer Relationships and Value through Marketing (L03)

Four elements in a marketing program designed to satisfy customer needs are product, price, promotion, and place. These elements are called the **marketing mix**, the four Ps, or the controllable variables because they are under the general control of the marketing department. **Environmental forces**, also called uncontrollable variables, are largely beyond the organization's control. These include social, economic, technological, competitive, and regulatory forces.

Marketing: The Core / Kerin Hartley Rudelius — Card 4

CHAPTER 2: Developing Successful Marketing and Organizational Strategies (L04)

An organization uses the **strategic marketing process** to allocate its marketing mix resources to reach its target markets. This process is divided into three phases: planning, implementation, and evaluation. The planning phase consists of three steps: (1) situation (SWOT) analysis, (2) market product focus and goal setting, and (3) the marketing program.

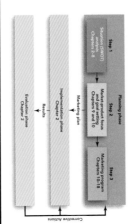

Marketing: The Core / Kerin Hartley Rudelius — Card 10

CHAPTER 3: Scanning the Marketing Environment (L04)

Demographics describes a population according to selected characteristics such as age, gender, ethnicity, income, and occupation. Racial and ethnic diversity of the population has led to multicultural marketing programs. **Culture** is the set of values, ideas, and attitudes that are learned and shared among the members of a group. Cultural factors include the impact of the values such as "health and fitness" on consumer preferences.

CHAPTER 1: Creating Customer Relationships and Value through Marketing (L01)

Factors influencing marketing activities include departments such as marketing, finance, and manufacturing within an organization; relationships with shareholders; suppliers, other organizations, and customers; and **environmental forces** consisting of social, economic, technological, competitive, and regulatory forces.

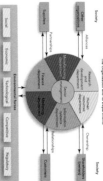

Marketing: The Core / Kerin Hartley Rudelius — Card 2

CHAPTER 2: Developing Successful Marketing and Organizational Strategies (L02)

Marketing managers use **marketing dashboards** to visually display the essential information related to achieving a marketing objective. This information consists of key performance measures of a product category, such as sales or market share, and is known as a **marketing metric**, which is a measure of quantitative value or trend of a marketing activity or result. Most organizations tie their marketing metrics to quantitative objectives established in their **marketing plan**, which is a road map for the marketing activities of an organization for a specified future time period.

Marketing: The Core / Kerin Hartley Rudelius — Card 8

CHAPTER 3: Scanning the Marketing Environment (L02)

CHAPTER 4: Ethical and Social Responsibility in Marketing — LO1

CHAPTER 4: Ethical and Social Responsibility in Marketing — LO3 — Card 21

Social responsibility means that organizations are part of a larger society and are accountable to that society for their actions. Figure 4–4 shows three concepts of social responsibility: *profit responsibility* holds that companies have a simple purpose, to maximize profits for their owners or stockholders; *stakeholder responsibility* focuses on the obligations an organization has to those who can affect achievement of its objectives; *societal responsibility* refers to obligations that organization have to preserve the environment and to the general public.

CHAPTER 5: Understanding Consumer Behavior — LO1 — Card 23

Consumer behavior involves the actions a person takes in purchasing and using products and services, including the mental and social processes that come before and after these actions. The stages a buyer passes through in making choices about which products and services to buy are known as the **purchase decision process**. This process has five stages, as shown in Figure 5–1.

Marketing: The Core / Kerin Hartley Rudelius — Card 19 — CHAPTER 4: Ethical and Social Responsibility in Marketing — LO1

Ethics are the moral principles and values that govern the actions and decisions of an individual or group. **Laws** are society's values and standards that are enforceable in the courts. This distinction is a good starting point for explaining the differences between legal and ethical behavior in marketing. Four reasons for these perceptions are (1) diverse value systems, (2) public judgment of business decisions, (3) increased expectations about ethical behavior, and (4) the decline of ethical business conduct.

Marketing: The Core / Kerin Hartley Rudelius — Card 21 — CHAPTER 5: Understanding Consumer Behavior — LO2

The decision to purchase a product involves important (1) psychological influences such as motivation, perception, learning, values, beliefs, attitudes, and lifestyle; (2) sociocultural influences such as personal influences, reference groups, family, culture, and subculture; (3) marketing mix (the four Ps) influences; and (4) situational influences such as the purchase task, social surroundings, physical surroundings, temporal effects, and antecedent states.

Marketing: The Core / Kerin Hartley Rudelius — Card 23 — CHAPTER 6: Understanding Organizations as Customers — LO2

Major characteristics of organizational buying make it different from consumer buying. These include:

- *Demand characteristics*: demand for industrial products and services is driven by **derived demand.**
- *Size of the order or purchase*: the size of the purchase involved in organizational buying is typically much larger.
- *Number of potential buyers*: firms selling to organizations are often restricted to a small number of buyers.
- *Buying objectives*: objectives may include reducing costs, increasing revenues, and others.
- *Organizational buying criteria*: include price, ability to meet specifications, delivery, technical capability, warranties, past performance, and facilities.
- *Buyer–seller relationships and supply partnerships.*

Marketing: The Core / Kerin Hartley Rudelius — Card 25 — CHAPTER 5: Understanding Consumer Behavior — LO4

Sociocultural influences evolve from a consumer's formal and informal relationships with other people, and include:

- *Personal influence*: includes opinion leaders who exert direct or indirect social influence over others and word of mouth—influencing people during conversation.
- *Reference groups*: people to whom an individual looks as a basis for self-appraisal.
- *Family influence*: results from consumer socialization; the **family life cycle**; and family decision making (spouse-dominant or joint decision).
- *Culture and subculture*: culture refers to the set of values, ideas, and attitudes that are learned and shared among the members of a group; **subcultures** are subgroups within a larger culture that have unique values, ideas, and attitudes.

Marketing: The Core / Kerin Hartley Rudelius — Card 25 — CHAPTER 6: Understanding Organizations as Customers — LO4

Organizations dwarf consumers in terms of online transactions made and purchase volume. Online buying is popular for three reasons: it provides timely information, it reduces buyer order processing costs, and it can reduce marketing costs. Two developments in online buying include: online trading communities that bring together buyer and supplier organizations, called **e-marketplaces**, and auctions. A **traditional auction** occurs when a seller puts an item up for sale and would-be buyers bid in competition with each other. A **reverse auction** occurs when a buyer communicates a need for something and would-be suppliers bid in competition with each other.

Marketing: The Core / Kerin Hartley Rudelius — Card 27 — CHAPTER 7: Understanding and Reaching Global Consumers and Markets — LO2

Three environmental factors shape global marketing efforts:

- *Cultural diversity*: marketers use **cross-cultural analysis**, or the study of similarities and differences among consumers to understand cultural diversity and the values, customs, symbols, and language of other societies.
- *Economic considerations*: include an assessment of the economic infrastructure, consumer income and purchasing power, and the price of one country's currency expressed in terms of another country's currency, or **currency exchange rate.**
- *Political-regulatory climate*: includes political stability factors, such as a government's orientation toward foreign companies, and trade regulations, which are the rules that govern business practices.

Marketing: The Core / Kerin Hartley Rudelius — Card 29 — CHAPTER 7: Understanding and Reaching Global Consumers and Markets — LO4

Companies distinguish between standardization and customization when crafting worldwide marketing programs. Standardization means that all elements of the marketing program are the same across countries and cultures. Customization means that one or more elements of the marketing program are adapted to meet the needs or preferences of consumers in a particular country or culture. Global marketers apply a simple rule when crafting worldwide marketing programs: Standardize marketing programs whenever possible and customize them whenever necessary.

CHAPTER 5: Understanding Consumer Behavior
 LO2

Consumers don't always engage in the five-stage purchase decision process. Instead, they skip or minimize one or more stages depending on the level of **involvement**—the personal, social, and economic significance of the purchase. Figure 5–3 compares three problem solving variations: extended problem solving, limited problem solving, and routine problem solving.

Marketing: The Core / Kerin Hartley Rudelius   Card 20

CHAPTER 4: Ethical and Social Responsibility in Marketing
LO4

Consumers, like marketers, have an obligation to act ethically and responsibly in the exchange process and in the use and disposition of products. Unfortunately, consumer behavior is spotty on both counts. Unethical consumer behavior includes filing warranty claims after the claim period; incorrectly redeeming coupons; pirating music, movies, and software from the Internet; and submitting phony insurance claims, among other behaviors. Unethical behavior is rarely motivated by economic need. Rather, research indicates that this behavior is influenced by (1) a belief that a consumer can get away with the act and it is worth doing and (2) the rationalization that such acts are justified or driven by forces outside the individual—"everybody does it."

Marketing: The Core / Kerin Hartley Rudelius   Card 22

CHAPTER 4: Ethical and Social Responsibility in Marketing
LO2

Four factors influence ethical marketing behavior. First, societal culture and norms serve as socializing forces that dictate what is morally right and just. Second, business culture and industry practices affect ethical conduct both in the exchange relationships between buyers and sellers and the competitive behavior among sellers. Third, corporate culture and expectations are often defined by corporate ethics codes and the ethical behavior of top management and co-workers. Finally, an individual's personal moral philosophy, such as **moral idealism** (individual rights and duties are universal) or **utilitarianism** (greatest good for the greatest number), will dictate ethical choices.

Marketing: The Core / Kerin Hartley Rudelius   Card 24

CHAPTER 5: Understanding Consumer Behavior
LO3

Psychology helps marketers understand why and how consumers behave as they do. Psychological concepts useful for interpreting buying processes and directing marketing efforts include:

- **Motivation**: the energizing force that stimulates behavior to satisfy a need.
- **Personality**: a person's consistent behaviors or responses to recurring situations.
- **Perception**: the process by which an individual selects, organizes, and interprets information.
- **Learning**: behaviors that result from repeated experience or reasoning.
- **Attitude**: the tendency to respond to something in a consistently favorable or unfavorable way.
- **Lifestyle**: a mode of living identified by how people spend their time and resources.

Marketing: The Core / Kerin Hartley Rudelius   Card 20

CHAPTER 6: Understanding Organizations as Customers
LO3

A group of people in an organization who participate in the buying process is called a buying center. Roles in a **buying center** include users, influencers, buyers, deciders, and gatekeepers. Three types of organizational buying situations, called **buy classes**, are straight rebuy, modified rebuy, and new buy. Figure 6–4 summarizes how buy classes affect buying center behavior.

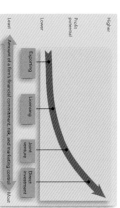

Marketing: The Core / Kerin Hartley Rudelius   Card 24

CHAPTER 6: Understanding Organizations as Customers
LO1

Business marketing is the marketing of goods and services to companies, governments, or not-for-profit organizations for use in the creation of goods and services that they can produce and market to others. **Organizational buyers** are those manufacturers wholesalers, retailers, and government agencies that buy goods and services for their own use or for resale. There are three different organizational markets: industrial firms in some way reprocess a product or service they buy before selling it to the next buyer; resellers—wholesalers and retailers—buy physical products and resell them again without any reprocessing; government agencies buy goods and services for the constituents they serve. The North American Industry Classification System (NAICS) facilitates the measurement of economic activity for these markets.

Marketing: The Core / Kerin Hartley Rudelius   Card 22

CHAPTER 8: Marketing Research: From Customer Insights to Actions
LO1

To be successful, products and marketing programs must meet the wants and needs of potential customers. So marketing research reduces risk by providing the vital information to help marketing managers understand those wants and needs and translate them into marketing actions. **Marketing research** is the process of defining a marketing problem and opportunity, systematically collecting and analyzing information, and recommending actions.

Marketing: The Core / Kerin Hartley Rudelius   Card 36

CHAPTER 7: Understanding and Reaching Global Consumers and Markets
LO3

Companies have four alternative approaches for entering global markets. These are exporting, licensing, joint venture, and direct investment. Figure 7–6 shows the financial risk, marketing control, and profit potential for each type of market entry strategy.

Marketing: The Core / Kerin Hartley Rudelius   Card 34

CHAPTER 7: Understanding and Reaching Global Consumers and Markets
LO1

Four major trends have influenced the landscape of global marketing in the past decade: the decline of economic protectionism, economic integration and free trade, global competition, and the networked global marketplace. **Protectionism** is the practice of shielding one or more industries within a country's economy from foreign competition, usually through the use of tariffs or quotas. Two examples of transnational trade groups are the European Union and the North American Free Trade Agreement (NAFTA). Three types of companies compete in the global marketplace: international firms, multinational firms, and transnational firms. A networked global marketspace enables the exchange of goods, services, and information from companies anywhere to customers anywhere at any time and at a low cost.

Marketing: The Core / Kerin Hartley Rudelius   Card 32

... they are designed to be torn along the perforation into business-card sized units. Use these as a mobile resource to revise and test your knowledge of key marketing concepts.

CHAPTER 8: Marketing Research: From Customer Insights to Actions (LO02) — Card 37

Marketing researchers engage in a five-step decision-making process that improves marketing decisions: (1) define the problem, (2) develop the research plan, (3) collect relevant information, (4) develop findings, and (5) take marketing actions. The approach is shown in Figure 8–1.

Step 1 — Define the problem
- Set research objectives
- Identify possible marketing actions

Step 2 — Develop the research plan
- Specify constraints
- Identify data needed for marketing actions
- Determine how to collect data

Step 3 — Collect relevant information by specifying
- Secondary data
- Primary data

Step 4 — Develop findings
- Analyze data
- Present findings

Step 5 — Take marketing actions
- Make action recommendations
- Implement action recommendations
- Evaluate results

Lessons learned for future research

Marketing: The Core / Kerin Hartley Rudelius

CHAPTER 8: Marketing Research: From Customer Insights to Actions (LO04) — Card 39

Observing people and asking them questions are the two principal ways to collect new or primary data for a marketing study. **Observational data** are the facts and figures obtained by watching, either mechanically or in person, how people behave. **Questionnaire data** are facts and figures obtained by asking people about their attitudes, awareness, intentions, and behaviors. Questionnaires involve asking people questions (1) in person using interviews or *focus groups* or (2) by a questionnaire using a telephone, fax, print, e-mail, or an Internet survey. *Panels* involve a sample of consumers or stores that are repeatedly measured through time to see if their behaviors change. *Experiments*, such as test markets, involve measuring the effect of marketing variables such as price or advertising on sales.

Marketing: The Core / Kerin Hartley Rudelius

CHAPTER 8: Marketing Research: From Customer Insights to Actions (LO06) — Card 41

Sales forecast refers to the total sales of a product that a firm expects to sell during a specified time period under specified environmental conditions and its own marketing efforts. Three main sales forecasting techniques are often used:

- *Judgments of the decision maker:* up to 99 percent of all sales forecasts may be the judgment of the person who must act on the results of the forecast.
- *Surveys of knowledgeable groups:* two common groups that are surveyed to develop sales forecasts are prospective buyers and the firm's salesforce.
- *Statistical methods:* these involve extending a pattern observed in past data into the future.

Marketing: The Core / Kerin Hartley Rudelius

CHAPTER 9: Segmenting Markets and Positioning Offerings (LO02) — Card 43

There are five key steps in segmenting and targeting markets:

- Step 1 is to group potential buyers into segments. Buyers within a segment should have similar characteristics to each other and respond similarly to marketing actions.
- Step 2 involves putting related products to be sold into meaningful groups.
- Step 3 is to develop a market-product grid with estimated size of markets in each of the market-product cells of the resulting table.
- Step 4 involves selecting the target market segments on which the organization should focus.
- Step 5 involves taking marketing mix actions—often in the form of a marketing program—to reach the target market segments.

Marketing: The Core / Kerin Hartley Rudelius

CHAPTER 9: Segmenting Markets and Positioning Offerings (LO04) — Card 45

A market-product grid is a framework to relate the market segments of potential buyers to products offered or potential marketing actions by an organization. Organizations use five key criteria to select target markets:

- Market size.
- Expected growth.
- Competitive position.
- Cost of reaching the segment.
- Compatibility with organization's objectives and resources.

Once the target markets are selected, organizations identify marketing mix actions—often in a marketing program—to reach the target market most efficiently.

Marketing: The Core / Kerin Hartley Rudelius

CHAPTER 10: Developing New Products and Services (LO01) — Card 47

A **product** is a good, service, or idea consisting of tangible and intangible features that satisfies consumers and is received in exchange for money or something else of value. A *good* has tangible attributes that a consumer's senses can perceive, and can be described as durable or nondurable goods. **Services** are intangible activities or benefits that an organization provides to satisfy consumers' needs. An *idea* is a thought that leads to a product or action.

Marketing: The Core / Kerin Hartley Rudelius

CHAPTER 10: Developing New Products and Services (LO03) — Card 49

The four unique elements of services—**the four I's**—are intangibility, inconsistency, inseparability, and inventory. *Intangibility* refers to the tendency of services to be a performance that cannot be held or touched. *Inconsistency* is a characteristic of services because they depend on people to deliver them, and people vary in their capabilities and in their day-to-day performance. *Inseparability* refers to the difficulty of separating the deliverer of the service from the service itself. *Inventory* refers to the need to have service production capability when there is service demand.

Marketing: The Core / Kerin Hartley Rudelius

CHAPTER 10: Developing New Products and Services (LO05) — Card 51

Many factors contribute to the success or failure of a new product. Research results from several studies suggest that some of the reasons for failure are:

1. Insignificant point of difference.
2. Incomplete market and product definition before product development starts.
3. Too little market attractiveness.
4. Poor execution of the marketing mix.
5. Poor product quality.
6. Not satisfying customer needs on critical factors.
7. Bad timing.
8. No economical access to buyers.

Marketing: The Core / Kerin Hartley Rudelius

CHAPTER 11: Managing Products, Services, and Brands (LO01) — Card 53

The concept of the **product life cycle** describes the stages a new product goes through in the marketplace: introduction, growth, maturity, and decline. Product sales growth and profitability differ at each stage and marketing managers have marketing objectives and marketing mix strategies unique to each stage. Some important aspects of product life cycles are (1) their length, (2) the shape of their sales curves, and (3) the rate at which consumers adopt products. The shapes of life cycles vary for four different types of products: high-learning, low-learning, fashion, and fad. A concept called the *diffusion of innovation* describes five profiles of product adopters: innovators, early adopters, early majority, late majority, and laggards.

Marketing: The Core / Kerin Hartley Rudelius

a mobile resource to revise and test your knowledge of key marketing concepts.

CHAPTER 9: Understanding and Reaching Global Consumers and Markets (L01)

Market segmentation involves aggregating prospective buyers into groups that (1) have common needs and (2) will respond similarly to a marketing action. Figure 9-1 shows how market segmentation links needs to actions. Organizations go to the expense of segmenting their markets when it increases their sales, profits, and ability to serve customers better.

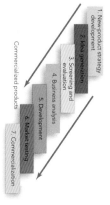

Identify market needs
Benefits in terms of:
• Product features
• Expense
• Quality
• Savings in time and convenience

Link needs to actions
Take steps to segment and target markets

Execute marketing program actions
A marketing mix in terms of:
• Product
• Price
• Promotion
• Place (Distribution)

CHAPTER 8: Marketing Research: From Customer Insights to Actions (L05)

Information technology involves operating computer networks that can store and process data. Traditional marketing research typically involves identifying problems and collecting data. In contrast, *data mining* is the extraction of hidden predictive information from large databases in order to find statistical links between consumer purchasing patterns and marketing actions. Firms such as Information Resources' InfoScan and ACNielsen's ScanTrack collect this information through bar-code scanners at the checkout counters in retail stores.

CHAPTER 8: Marketing Research: From Customer Insights to Actions (L03)

Data are the facts and figures related to a marketing research problem and are divided into two types:

• **Secondary data:** facts and figures that have already been recorded before the project at hand; these data are often easier to obtain and less expensive than primary data.

• **Primary data:** facts and figures that are newly collected for a project. These data are more specific to the problem studied but more costly and time consuming to collect than secondary data.

CHAPTER 10: Developing New Products and Services Offerings (L02)

Consumer products are products purchased by the ultimate consumer. **Business products** are products that assist directly or indirectly in providing products for resale. There are four types of consumer products: convenience, shopping, specialty, and unsought. There are two types of business products: (1) components and support products, which include installations, accessory equipment, supplies, and (2) industrial services. Services can be classified according to whether they are delivered by (1) people or equipment, (2) business firms or nonprofit organizations, and (3) government agencies. Firms can offer a range of products, which involve decisions regarding the product item, product line, and product mix.

CHAPTER 9: Segmenting Markets and Positioning Offerings (L05)

Product positioning refers to the place an offering occupies in consumers' minds on important attributes relative to competitive products. Marketing managers often locate competing products on two-dimensional **perceptual maps** to visualize the products in the minds of consumers. Companies use three types of data to develop a perceptual map:

1. Identification of the important attributes for a product class.
2. Judgments of existing product or brands with respect to these attributes.
3. Ratings of an "ideal" product's or brand's attributes.

Managers then try to position new products or reposition existing products in this space.

CHAPTER 9: Segmenting Markets and Positioning Offerings (L03)

Four general bases of segmentation can be used to segment markets. They are:

• *Geographic segmentation,* which is based on where customers live or work.

• *Demographic segmentation,* which is based on some objective physical, measurable, or classification attribute.

• *Psychographic segmentation,* which is based on subjective mental or emotional attributes.

• *Behavior segmentation,* which is based on observable actions or attitudes.

Organizational markets use the same bases except the psychological ones.

CHAPTER 11: Managing Products, Services, and Brands (L02)

Marketing executives manage a product's life cycle three ways:

• First, they can modify the product itself by altering its characteristics such as product quality, performance, or appearance.

• Second, they can modify the market by finding new customers for the product, increasing a product's use among existing customers, or creating a new use situation for the product.

• Third, they can reposition a product using any one or a combination of marketing mix elements. Four factors trigger a repositioning action: reacting to a competitor's position, reaching a new market, catching a rising trend, and changing the value offered to consumers.

CHAPTER 10: Developing New Products and Services Offerings (L06)

The **new-product process** is the seven stages an organization goes through to identify business opportunities and convert them into salable goods or services. Figure 10-6 illustrates the steps and the sequence of the process:

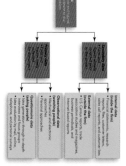

1. New-product strategy development
2. Idea generation
3. Screening and evaluation
4. Business analysis
5. Development
6. Market testing
7. Commercialization

Commercialized products

CHAPTER 10: Developing New Products and Services Offerings (L04)

"Newness" is often seen as the degree of learning that a consumer must engage in to use a product. Figure 10-4 describes three levels of innovation in new products.

BASIS OF COMPARISON	LOW — Degree of New Consumer Learning Needed — HIGH		
	CONTINUOUS INNOVATION	DYNAMICALLY CONTINUOUS INNOVATION	DISCONTINUOUS INNOVATION
Definition	Requires no new learning by consumers	Disrupts consumer's normal routine but does not require totally new learning	Requires new learning and consumption patterns by consumers
Examples	New improved shaver or detergent	Electric toothbrush, compact disk player, and automatic flash unit for cameras	VCR, digital video recorder, electric car
Marketing strategy	Gain consumer awareness and wide distribution	Advertise points of difference and benefits to consumers	Educate consumers through product trial and personal selling

a mobile resource to revise and test your knowledge of key marketing concepts.

CHAPTER 11: Managing Products, Services, and Brands (LO3)

A basic decision in marketing products is branding, in which an organization uses a name, phrase, design, symbols, or combination of these to identify its products and distinguish them from those of competitors. A **brand name** is any word, device (design, sound shape, or color), or combination of these used to distinguish a seller's goods or services. Branding strategies include multiproduct branding, multibranding, private branding, or mixed branding.

Marketing: The Core / Kerin Hartley Rudelius   Card 55

CHAPTER 12: Pricing Products and Services (LO4)

Pricing objectives specify the role of price in a firm's marketing strategy and may include profit, sales, market share, unit volume, survival, or some socially responsible price level. **Pricing constraints** are factors that limit the range of price a firm may set and include demand for the product class, product, and brand; newness of the product; cost of producing the product; competitors' prices; and legal and ethical consideration. Legal and ethical considerations include:

- *Price fixing*: a conspiracy among firms to set prices.
- *Price discrimination*: the practice of charging different prices to different buyers.
- *Deceptive pricing*: price deals that mislead consumers.
- *Predatory pricing*: charging a very low price with the intent of driving competitors out of business.

Marketing: The Core / Kerin Hartley Rudelius   Card 57

CHAPTER 13: Managing Marketing Channels and Supply Chains (LO1)

A **marketing channel** consists of individuals and firms involved in the process of making a product or service available for use or consumption by consumers or industrial users. Intermediaries make possible the flow of products from producers to buyers by performing three basic functions: the transactional function, the logistical function, and the facilitating function. Figure 13–1 describes a variety of intermediaries.

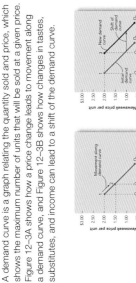

TERM	DESCRIPTION
Middleman	Any intermediary between manufacturer and end-user markets
Agent or broker	Any intermediary with legal authority to act on behalf of the manufacturer
Wholesaler	An intermediary who sells to other intermediaries, usually to retailers; term usually applies to consumer markets
Retailer	An intermediary who sells to consumers
Distributor	An imprecise term, usually used to describe intermediaries who perform a variety of distribution functions, including selling, maintaining inventories, extending credit, and so on; a more common term in business markets but may also be used to refer to wholesalers
Dealer	A more imprecise term than distributor that can mean the same as distributor, retailer, wholesaler, and so forth

Marketing: The Core / Kerin Hartley Rudelius   Card 61

CHAPTER 14: Retailing and Wholesaling (LO1)

Retailing includes all activities involved in selling, renting, and providing goods and services to ultimate customers for personal, family or household use. Retailers provide time, place, form, and possession utilities. *Time utility* is provided by stores with convenient time-of-day (e.g., open 24 hours) or time-of-year (e.g., seasonal sports equipment available all year) availability. *Place utility* is provided by the number and location of the stores. *Possession utility* is provided by making a purchase possible (e.g., financing) or easier (e.g., delivery). *Form utility* is provided by producing or altering a product to meet the customer's specifications (e.g., custom-made shirts).

Marketing: The Core / Kerin Hartley Rudelius   Card 67

CHAPTER 11: Managing Products, Services, and Brands (LO2)

The four Ps framework also applies to services with some adaptations. Three aspects of the product/service element warrant special attention: exclusivity, branding, and capacity. Price plays two roles: (1) to affect consumer perceptions and (2) to be used in capacity management. **Off-peak pricing** is an important marketing tool for services that now often use multiple locations. Electronic distribution through the Internet now provides global coverage for many services. In recent years, service organizations have increased their promotional activities.

Marketing: The Core / Kerin Hartley Rudelius   Card 59

CHAPTER 12: Pricing Products and Services (LO5)

A demand curve is a graph relating the quantity sold and price, which shows the maximum number of units that will be sold at a given price. Figure 12–3A shows how a price change leads to movement along a demand curve, and Figure 12–3B shows how changes in tastes, substitutes, and income can lead to a shift of the demand curve.

Marketing: The Core / Kerin Hartley Rudelius   Card 63

CHAPTER 13: Managing Marketing Channels and Supply Chains (LO3)

Marketing executives consider three questions when selecting and managing a marketing channel. (1) Which channel will provide the best coverage of the target market? There are three levels of coverage: **intensive, selective, or exclusive.** (2) Which channel will best satisfy the buying requirements of the target market? These buying requirements fall into four categories: *information, convenience, variety, and pre- or postsale services.* (3) Which channel will be the most profitable? Here marketers look at the margins earned (revenues minus cost) for each channel member and for the channel as a whole. Disintermediation is channel conflict that arises when a channel member bypasses another member and sells or buys products direct.

Marketing: The Core / Kerin Hartley Rudelius   Card 65

CHAPTER 14: Retailing and Wholesaling (LO3)

Nonstore retailing includes automatic vending, direct mail and catalogs, television home shopping, online retailing, telemarketing, and direct selling. **Telemarketing** involves using the telephone to interact with and sell directly to consumers. The methods of nonstore retailing vary by the level of involvement of the retailer and the level of involvement of the customer. Vending, for example, has low involvement, whereas direct selling involves both the consumer and the retailer have high involvement in direct selling.

Marketing: The Core / Kerin Hartley Rudelius   Card 69

CHAPTER 14: Retailing and Wholesaling (LO5)

The **wheel of retailing** is a concept that describes how new forms of retail outlets enter the market and change over time. Figure 14–4 describes the changes. The retail life cycle is the process of growth and decline that retail outlets experience over time. Figure 14–5 describes the stages.

Marketing: The Core / Kerin Hartley Rudelius   Card 71

a mobile resource to revise and test your knowledge of key marketing concepts.

CHAPTER 12: Pricing Products and Services (L03)

Four cost concepts are important in pricing decisions:

- *Total cost:* the total expense incurred by a firm in producing and marketing a product; it is the sum of fixed cost and variable cost.
- *Fixed cost:* the sum of the expenses of the firm that are stable and do not change with the quantity of a product that is produced.
- *Variable cost:* the sum of the expenses of the firm that vary directly with the quantity of a product that is produced.

Break-even analysis is a technique that analyzes the relationship between total revenue and total cost to determine profitability at various levels of output.

$$BEP_{quantity} = \text{Fixed cost}/(\text{Unit price} - \text{Unit variable cost})$$

Marketing: The Core / Kerin Hartley Rudelius — Card 72

CHAPTER 13: Managing Marketing Channels and Supply Chains — Card 60 (L04)

Logistics involves those activities that focus on getting the right amount of the right products to the right place at the right time at the lowest possible cost. A **supply chain** is a sequence of firms that perform activities required to create and deliver a good or service to consumers or industrial users. The relation among marketing channels, logistics management, and supply chain management is shown in Figure 13–7.

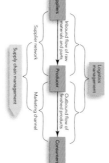

Marketing: The Core / Kerin Hartley Rudelius — Card 70

CHAPTER 14: Retailing and Wholesaling — Card 66 (L06)

There are three types of firms that perform wholesaling functions:

- *Merchant wholesalers:* independently owned firms that take title to the merchandise they handle.
- *Agents and brokers:* manufacturer's agents work for several producers and carry noncompetitive, complementary merchandise in an exclusive territory; brokers are independent firms or individuals whose main function is to bring buyer and sellers together to make sales.
- *Manufacturer's branches and offices:* wholly owned extensions of the producer that perform wholesaling activities.

Marketing: The Core / Kerin Hartley Rudelius — Card 68

CHAPTER 12: Pricing Products and Services (L01)

Price is the money or other consideration (including other goods and services) exchanged for the ownership or use of a good or service. **Value** is the ratio of perceived benefits to price. Four common approaches to setting an approximate price level are (1) demand-oriented, (2) cost-oriented, (3) profit-oriented, and (4) competition-oriented. Figure 12-2 identifies several types of each approach.

CHAPTER 11: Managing Products, Services, and Brands — Card 56 (L04)

The packaging component of a product refers to any container in which it is offered for sale and on which label information is conveyed. A label is an integral part of the package and typically identifies the product or brand, who made it, where and when it was made, how it is to be used, and package contents and ingredients. Manufacturers, retailers, and consumers acknowledge that packaging and labeling provide communication, functional, and perceptual benefits. Contemporary packaging and labeling challenges include (1) the continuing need to connect with customers; (2) environmental concerns; (3) health, safety, and security issues; and (4) cost reduction.

Marketing: The Core / Kerin Hartley Rudelius — Card 56

CHAPTER 13: Managing Marketing Channels and Supply Chains — Card 58 (L02)

Marketing channels can range from a direct channel with no intermediaries to indirect channels where intermediaries are inserted between a producer and consumer. **Electronic marketing channels** employ the Internet to make goods and services available for consumption or use by consumer or business buyers. **Vertical marketing systems (VMSs)** are professionally managed and centrally coordinated marketing channels designed to achieve channel economies and maximum marketing impact. There are three types of vertical marketing systems:

- *Corporate:* combines successive stages of production and distribution under single ownership.
- *Contractual:* exists when independent production and distribution firms integrate their efforts on a contractual basis.
- *Administered:* achieves coordination by the size and influence of one channel member.

Marketing: The Core / Kerin Hartley Rudelius — Card 58

CHAPTER 14: Retailing and Wholesaling — Card 64 (L04)

Retailing mix actions are used to manage a retail store and the merchandise in a store. The mix variables include pricing, store location, communication, and merchandise. Figure 14–3 shows the elements of a retailing strategy. Two common forms of assessment for retailers are "sales per square foot" and "same store growth." **Category management** is an approach to managing the assortment of merchandise, which maximizes sales and profits.

Marketing: The Core / Kerin Hartley Rudelius — Card 64

CHAPTER 12: Pricing Products and Services — Card 62 (L05)

Three common steps to setting a final price are (1) select an approximate price level; (2) set the list or quoted price; and (3) modify the list or quoted price with discounts, allowances, and geographic adjustments.

- *Discounts* include quantity discounts, seasonal discounts, trade (functional) discounts, and cash discounts.
- *Allowances* include trade-in allowances and promotional allowances.
- *Geographic adjustments* include FOB ("free on board") origin pricing and uniform delivered pricing.

Marketing: The Core / Kerin Hartley Rudelius — Card 62

CHAPTER 14: Retailing and Wholesaling (L02)

Retail outlets can be classified by their form of ownership, level of service, and type of merchandise line. The forms of ownership include independent retailers, corporate chains (e.g., Macy's) and contractual systems that include retailer-sponsored cooperatives, wholesaler-sponsored voluntary chains, and franchises. The levels of service include self-service (e.g., Costco), limited-service (e.g., Target), and full-service outlets (e.g., Nordstrom). Stores classified by their merchandise line include stores with breadth, such as sporting good specialty stores, and stores with depth, such as large department stores. Some outlets use **scrambled merchandising** by offering several unrelated product lines in a single store.

Marketing: The Core / Kerin Hartley Rudelius — Card 66

a mobile resource to revise and test your knowledge of key marketing concepts.

CHAPTER 15: Integrated Marketing Communications and Direct Marketing (L01) · Card 73

Integrated marketing communication (IMC) is the concept of designing marketing communications programs that coordinate all promotional activities—advertising, personal selling, sales promotion, public relations, and direct marketing—to provide a consistent message across all audiences. **Communication** is the process of conveying a message to others, as shown in Figure 15–1.

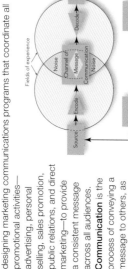

CHAPTER 15: Integrated Marketing Communications and Direct Marketing (L03) · Card 7[?]

The promotional mix depends on the target audience. Programs for consumers, business buyers, and intermediaries might emphasize advertising, personal selling, and sales promotion, respectively. The promotional mix also changes over the product life-cycle stages. During the introduction stage, all promotional mix elements are used. During the growth stage advertising is emphasized, while the maturity stage utilizes sales promotion and direct marketing. Little promotion is used during the decline stage. Finally, the promotional mix can depend on the channel strategy. **Push strategies** require personal selling and sales promotions directed at channel members, while **pull strategies** depend on advertising and sales promotion directed at consumers.

CHAPTER 15: Integrated Marketing Communications and Direct Marketing (L05)

The value of direct marketing for consumers is indicated by its level of use. For example, 43 percent of consumers have made a purchase by phone, mail, Internet, or a television offer. The value of direct marketing for sellers can be measured in terms of three responses:

- **Direct orders:** the result of direct marketing offers that contain all the information necessary for a potential buyer to make a decision to complete the transaction.
- **Lead generation:** the result of direct marketing offers designed to generate interest in a product or a service and a request for additional information.
- **Traffic generation:** outcome of direct marketing offers designed to motivate people to visit a business.

Marketing: The Core / Kerin Hartley Rudelius · Card 75

CHAPTER 16: Advertising, Sales Promotion, and Public Relations (L02)

The promotion decision process can be applied to each of the promotional elements. The steps to develop an advertising program include identifying the target audience, specifying the advertising objectives, setting the advertising budget, designing the advertisement, creating the message, selecting the media, and assessing the program requires posttesting. Executing the program requires pretesting, and assessing the program requires posttesting. Designing the advertisement typically uses one of three common appeals:

- *Fear appeal:* suggests a consumer can avoid a negative experience.
- *Sex appeal:* suggests how a consumer can increase attractiveness.
- *Humorous appeal:* suggests that a product is fun or exciting.

Marketing: The Core / Kerin Hartley Rudelius · Card 7[?]

CHAPTER 16: Advertising, Sales Promotion, and Public Relations (L04)

Coupons encourage consumer trial but are often more expensive than the face value of the coupon. *Deals* increase trial and may be used during a competitor's promotion. *Premiums* offer consumers merchandise free or at a savings over its retail price. *Contests* create involvement but require creative thinking. *Sweepstakes* encourage repeat purchases and require no creative effort. *Samples* are used to encourage purchase of a product. *Loyalty programs* reward repeat purchases. *Displays* provide visibility in high-traffic areas. *Rebates* offer a return of money based on proof of purchase. *Product placement* involves the use of a brand-name product in a movie, TV show, or commercial. Trade-oriented sales promotions include (1) allowances and discounts, (2) cooperative advertising, and (3) salesforce training.

Marketing: The Core / Kerin Hartley Rudelius · Card 77[?]

CHAPTER 17: Personal Selling and Sales Management (L01)

Personal selling is the two-way flow of communication between a buyer and seller, often in a face-to-face encounter, designed to influence a persons or group's purchase decision. **Sales management** involves planning the selling program and implementing and evaluating the personal selling effort of the firm. Personal selling serves three roles: (1) to link the firm and its customers, (2) to represent what a company is or attempts to be, and (3) to participate in the marketing program. **Relationship selling** is the practice of building ties to customers based on a salesperson's attention and commitment to customer needs over time.

Marketing: The Core / Kerin Hartley Rudelius · Card 79

CHAPTER 17: Personal Selling and Sales Management (L03)

The personal selling process consists of six stages:

1. *Prospecting:* search for and qualify prospects.
2. *Preapproach:* gather information and decide how to approach the prospect.
3. *Approach:* gain prospect's attention, stimulate interest, and make transition to the presentation.
4. *Presentation:* begin converting a prospect into a customer by creating a desire for the product or service.
5. *Close:* obtain a purchase commitment from the prospect and create a customer.
6. *Follow-up:* ensure that the customer is satisfied with the product or service.

Marketing: The Core / Kerin Hartley Rudelius · Card 81

CHAPTER 18: Implementing Interactive and Multichannel Marketing (L01)

Interactive marketing involves two-way buyer–seller electronic communication in a computer-mediated environment in which the buyer controls the kind and amount of information received from the seller. Customer relationships are created through two unique capabilities of Internet technology: *interactivity* and *individuality*. From an interactive marketing perspective, customer experience represents the sum total of the interactions that a customer has with a company's website, from the initial look at a homepage through the entire purchase process. Companies produce a customer experience through seven website design elements: *context, content, community, customization, communication, connection, and commerce.*

CHAPTER 18: Implementing Interactive and Multichannel Marketing (L03) · Card 8[?]

There are six reasons consumers shop online:

1. *Convenience.*
2. *Choice.*
3. *Customization.*
4. *Communication.*
5. *Cost.*
6. *Control.*

Marketspace features that address these reasons include: **bots, choiceboards, collaborative filtering,** company-hosted **web communities, blogs, viral marketing** practices, and **dynamic pricing. Permission marketing** is also popular given consumer interest in control.

CHAPTER 16: Advertising, Sales Promotion, and Public Relations

Card 78 (LO1)

Product advertisements focus on selling a good or service and take three forms: *pioneering* advertisements tell people what a product is, what it can do, and where it can be found; *competitive* advertisements persuade the target market to select the firm's brand rather than a competitor's; and *reminder* advertisements reinforce previous knowledge of a product. **Institutional advertisements** are used to build goodwill or an image for an organization. They include advocacy advertisements, which state the position of a company on an issue, and pioneering, competitive, and reminder advertisements, which are similar to the product ads but focused on the institution.

CHAPTER 17: Personal Selling and Sales Management

Card 78 (LO2)

There are two types of personal selling:

- **Order taking:** an order taker processes routine orders or reorders for products that were already sold by the company. An order taker does little selling in a conventional sense and engages in only modest problem solving with customers.
- **Order getting:** an order getter is a salesperson who sells in a conventional sense and identifies prospective customers, provides customers with information, persuades customers to buy, closes sales, and follows up on customers' use of a product or service. Order getting involves a high degree of creativity and customer empathy and is typically required for selling complex or technical products with many options.

CHAPTER 18: Implementing Interactive and Multichannel Marketing

Card 84 (LO4)

A **cross-channel shopper** is an online consumer who researches products online and then purchases them at a retail store. These shoppers are reached through multichannel marketing. Websites play a multifaceted role in multichannel marketing because they can serve as either a delivery or communication channel. In this regard, *transactional websites* are essentially electronic storefronts. They focus principally on converting an online browser into an online, catalog, or in-store buyer. On the other hand, *promotional websites* serve to advertise and promote a company's products and services and provide information on how items can be used and where they can be purchased.

CHAPTER 15: Integrated Marketing Communications and Direct Marketing

Card 76 (LO4)

The promotion decision process consists of three steps: planning, implementation, and evaluation. Figure 15-5 shows elements of each of the three steps.

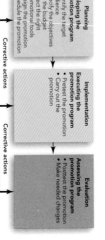

CHAPTER 16: Advertising, Sales Promotion, and Public Relations

Card 76 (LO5)

Public relations is a form of communication management that seeks to influence the image of an organization and its products and services. A frequently used public relations tool is publicity. Publicity tools are methods of obtaining nonpersonal presentation of an organization, good, or service without a direct cost. Common publicity tools are:

- *News releases:* announcements regarding changes in the company or the product line.
- *News conferences:* representatives of the media are all invited to an informational meeting.
- *Public service announcement:* free space or time donated by the media; often used by nonprofit organizations.

CHAPTER 17: Personal Selling and Sales Management

Card 80 (LO4)

The sales management process involves sales plan formulation, sales plan implementation, and evaluation of the salesforce. A sales plan is a statement describing what is to be achieved and where and how the selling effort of salespeople is to be deployed. Figure 17-3 describes the tasks involved in each element of the process.

CHAPTER 15: Integrated Marketing Communications and Direct Marketing

Card 74 (LO2)

There are five promotional alternatives:

- **Advertising:** any paid form of nonpersonal communication about an organization, good, service, or idea by an identified sponsor.
- **Personal selling:** the two-way flow of communication between a buyer and seller.
- **Public relations:** a form of communication management that seeks to influence the feelings, opinions, or beliefs held about a company and its products or services.
- **Sales promotion:** a short-term offer designed to arouse interest in buying a good or service.
- **Direct marketing:** direct communication with consumers to generate a response.

CHAPTER 16: Advertising, Sales Promotion, and Public Relations

Card 74 (LO3)

Television advertising reaches large audiences and uses picture, print, sound, and motion; its disadvantages are that it is expensive and perishable. Radio is inexpensive and can be placed quickly, but it has no visual element and is perishable. Magazine advertising can target specific audiences, but it is relatively expensive. Newspapers provide coverage of local markets and can be changed quickly, but they have a short life span and poor color. Yellow Pages reach almost all households with telephones; however, there is a proliferation of directories and they cannot be updated frequently. Internet advertising can be interactive, but its effectiveness is difficult to measure. Outdoor advertising provides repeat exposures, but its message must be very short and simple. Direct mail can be very targeted, but its cost per contact is high.